Multinational Enterprise Management Strategies in Developing Countries

Mohammad Ayub Khan
Tecnológico de Monterrey, Mexico

A volume in the Advances in Logistics, Operations, and Management Science (ALOMS) Book Series

BUSINESS SCIENCE Reference
An Imprint of IGI Global

Published in the United States of America by
Business Science Reference (an imprint of IGI Global)
701 E. Chocolate Avenue
Hershey PA, USA 17033
Tel: 717-533-8845
Fax: 717-533-8661
E-mail: cust@igi-global.com
Web site: http://www.igi-global.com

Library of Congress Cataloging-in-Publication Data

Names: Khan, Mohammad Ayub, 1966- editor.
Title: Multinational enterprise management strategies in developing countries / Mohammad Ayub Khan, editor.
Description: Hershey : Business Science Reference, 2016. | Includes bibliographical references and index.
Identifiers: LCCN 2016003470| ISBN 9781522502760 (hardcover) | ISBN 9781522502777 (ebook)
Subjects: LCSH: International business enterprises--Developing countries. | Strategic planning--Developing countries.
Classification: LCC HD2932 .M8458 2016 | DDC 658/.049091724--dc23 LC record available at https://lccn.loc.gov/2016003470

This book is published in the IGI Global book series Advances in Logistics, Operations, and Management Science (ALOMS) (ISSN: 2327-350X; eISSN: 2327-3518)

British Cataloguing in Publication Data
A Cataloguing in Publication record for this book is available from the British Library.

Advances in Logistics, Operations, and Management Science (ALOMS) Book Series

John Wang
Montclair State University, USA

ISSN: 2327-350X
EISSN: 2327-3518

Mission

Operations research and management science continue to influence business processes, administration, and management information systems, particularly in covering the application methods for decision-making processes. New case studies and applications on management science, operations management, social sciences, and other behavioral sciences have been incorporated into business and organizations real-world objectives.

The **Advances in Logistics, Operations, and Management Science** (ALOMS) Book Series provides a collection of reference publications on the current trends, applications, theories, and practices in the management science field. Providing relevant and current research, this series and its individual publications would be useful for academics, researchers, scholars, and practitioners interested in improving decision making models and business functions.

Coverage

- Operations Management
- Political Science
- Marketing engineering
- Decision analysis and decision support
- Organizational Behavior
- Networks
- Information Management
- Risk Management
- Services management
- Computing and information technologies

The Advances in Logistics, Operations, and Management Science (ALOMS) Book Series (ISSN 2327-350X) is published by IGI Global, 701 E. Chocolate Avenue, Hershey, PA 17033-1240, USA, www.igi-global.com. This series is composed of titles available for purchase individually; each title is edited to be contextually exclusive from any other title within the series. For pricing and ordering information please visit http://www.igi-global.com/book-series/advances-logistics-operations-management-science/37170. Postmaster: Send all address changes to above address.

Titles in this Series

For a list of additional titles in this series, please visit: www.igi-global.com

Handbook of Research on Global Fashion Management and Merchandising
Alessandra Vecchi (London College of Fashion, U.K.) and Chitra Buckley (London College of Fashion, U.K.)
Business Science Reference • copyright 2016 • 862pp • H/C (ISBN: 9781522501107) • US $335.00 (our price)

Handbook of Research on Managerial Strategies for Achieving Optimal Performance in Industrial Processes
Giner Alor-Hernández (Instituto Tecnológico de Orizaba, Mexico) Cuauhtémoc Sánchez-Ramírez (Instituto Tecnológico de Orizaba, Mexico) and Jorge Luis García-Alcaraz (Universidad Autónoma de Ciudad Juárez, Mexico)
Business Science Reference • copyright 2016 • 674pp • H/C (ISBN: 9781522501305) • US $365.00 (our price)

Supply Chain Strategies and the Engineer-to-Order Approach
Richard Addo-Tenkorang (University of Vaasa, Finland) Jussi Kantola (University of Vaasa, Finland) Petri Helo (University of Vaasa, Finland) and Ahm Shamsuzzoha (Sultan Qaboos University, Oman)
Business Science Reference • copyright 2016 • 283pp • H/C (ISBN: 9781522500216) • US $200.00 (our price)

Optimal Inventory Control and Management Techniques
Mandeep Mittal (Amity School of Engineering and Technology, India) and Nita H. Shah (Gujarat University, India)
Business Science Reference • copyright 2016 • 406pp • H/C (ISBN: 9781466698888) • US $170.00 (our price)

Stochastic Processes and Models in Operations Research
Neelamegam Anbazhagan (Alagappa University, India)
Business Science Reference • copyright 2016 • 338pp • H/C (ISBN: 9781522500445) • US $185.00 (our price)

Sustainable Logistics and Strategic Transportation Planning
Tomaž Kramberger (University of Maribor, Slovenia) Vojko Potočan (University of Maribor, Slovenia) and Vesna Mia Ipavec (University of Maribor, Slovenia)
Business Science Reference • copyright 2016 • 511pp • H/C (ISBN: 9781522500018) • US $225.00 (our price)

Handbook of Research on Strategic Supply Chain Management in the Retail Industry
Narasimha Kamath (JDA Software, India) and Swapnil Saurav (JDA Software, India)
Business Science Reference • copyright 2016 • 429pp • H/C (ISBN: 9781466698949) • US $235.00 (our price)

IGI GLOBAL
DISSEMINATOR OF KNOWLEDGE
www.igi-global.com

701 E. Chocolate Ave., Hershey, PA 17033
Order online at www.igi-global.com or call 717-533-8845 x100
To place a standing order for titles released in this series, contact: cust@igi-global.com
Mon-Fri 8:00 am - 5:00 pm (est) or fax 24 hours a day 717-533-8661

Editorial Advisory Board

Table of Contents

Detailed Table of Contents

Globalization has dramatically changed the competitive landscape in many national markets. Evidence shows that Foreign Direct Investment (FDI) had doubled and even tripled in the last fifteen years in Less-Developed Countries (LDCs), generating a tremendous impact on the economic development and welfare of these countries. Yet, less attention has been given to the role that domestic customers and domestic competitors play in shaping the strategic behaviour and performance of MNEs in the targeted markets and the strategies which need to be adopted to enhance the competitiveness of MNEs. Through grounded theory approach and in depth literature review, the chapter aims to examine the positioning of MNEs to extend existing perspectives and incorporating competitive interactions between the external environments, competitive strategy and in particular, evaluates the strategic positioning and competitive behaviour of MNEs.

Globalization has been a factor that has brought countries closer worldwide, and Multinational Enterprises (MNEs) are eager to look for new market opportunities in developing countries. This chapter analyzes the implementation of MNEs' global ethical principles in business into local moral standards of societies from developing countries. The author will discuss, using current scenarios, how principles of both moral relativism and moral absolutism can provide a profitable or punishable opportunity within developing countries when MNEs operate accordingly, or not, to ethical decision making processes in business. Additionally, the chapter proposes how MNEs' managers can discover the limits of moral free space, to distinguish a moral value in tension with their own from one that is intolerable. At the end, it is expected that MNEs' managers can apply ethical decision making in business by clearly perceiving and understanding their corporate culture in a developing country society.

Measuring the marketing performance of multinational enterprises poses special challenges. Coordination of marketing activities across markets is difficult due to possible differences in customer priorities and the consequent optimal positioning of products or services. The availability of marketing tactics may vary by country due to custom, infrastructure, or regulations. Country markets may be in different stages of the competitive life cycle which affects business performance. The purposes of this chapter are: 1) to examine and define a multi-country marketing strategy, 2) to explore the process of developing a multi-country marketing strategy, 3) to identify metrics for evaluating the performance of a multi-country marketing strategy, 4) to share and comment on the results of surveys of international managers with respect to their multi-country strategies and the metrics they employ to evaluate strategy performance, and 5) to suggest measures for evaluating a multi-country marketing strategy.

Multinational Corporations (MNC) face the challenge of compete in the new interconnected business environment. In particular technology is recognized as a factor that boost productivity and competitiveness and drives the business connectivity which in turn involves cross-borders goods, services and financial flows. MNC is recognized as being possessed of high-tech assets, and also, resources including capital, management skills and R&D capabilities and subsidiaries can get them, from its holding company, and they transfer technology to local businesses. A knowledge transfer, running parallel to the technology transfer take place benefiting to the local economy. Foreign Direct Investment (FDI) is considered as the primary vehicle to facilitate technology transfer (and underlying knowledge flows) toward emerging countries. The ultimate goal of the MNC is related to leverage technology and knowledge transfer in order to maintain a competitive edge and move toward even higher value-added activities.

This chapter analyzes the challenge of organizational setup in developing countries faced by MNEs. In doing so the chapter focuses on different types of structural options available for MNEs and studies factors influencing the decision of how to structure the MNE in developing countries. In essence, the chapter presents a list of structural options for MNEs to choose from according to their needs, contextual situations and strategic direction. The factors influencing the decision to structure the company are general factors, management orientations, corporate culture, information and communication technologies, strategy and learning organizations. Finally, the chapter forwards some essential recommendations for MNEs to follow when deciding about which organizational structure is relatively more suitable than others while operating in developing countries.

The purpose of this chapter is to describe the most important theories that explain the possible motivations of some enterprises to compete in the international arena. Besides describing and summarizing the internationalization theories of an enterprise, the cases of some Mexican firms, which have grown successfully internationally, will be presented and compared with all the elements established in the different theories. This chapter starts by describing the different characteristics of firms competing in international markets. After that, the most important theories of MNEs are explored. The chapter ends with the discussion of the internationalization process followed by CEMEX, GRUMA and TELMEX (America Movil), Mexican enterprises that have successfully grown in the international spectrum.

This chapter examines innovation in socio-institutional environments of three largest and most diverse emerging markets: Russia, India and China over the period 1990-2014. It considers formal (proxied by corruption) and informal (proxied by trust) institutions and non-linear forces. It also examines the role of Foreign Direct Investment (FDI) in (the likelihood of) fostering innovation and of two research and development (R&D) inputs: R&D expenditures and personnel. A significantly positive direct effect of trust and a negative direct effect of corruption are confirmed, whilst there is a significant non-linear decreasing relationship with trust and increasing relationship with corruption. Interestingly, FDI and R&D expenditures are found to decrease innovation, whilst R&D personnel increase innovation output across the sample.

Despite the vast and growing literature on the economic impact of foreign direct investment (FDI), its social significance is somewhat a neglected issue. Focusing on Russia, this chapter examines the effect of FDI and (formal) institutions (proxied, alternatively, by the [1] accumulated stock of small and medium sized firms or SMEs and [2] number of economic crimes per 100,000 population or corruption) on (informal) institutional change (proxied by the change in the number of violent and property crimes per 100,000 population). The empirical findings provide robust support for a significantly positive direct impact of SMEs, whilst observing a significantly negative effect of corruption and either significantly positive impact of FDI or insignificant effect of multinational firms in this context.

This chapter contributes to the theory of a firm's globalization processes reflected in the Uppsala Globalization Process Model (UGPM). The Gotheborg IV (G4) model is introduced, mapping the knowledge zones of the UGPM in a four quadrant axis model. Using language in its meta-capacity as theory and framework of analysis the G4 model makes a distinction between the words 'enterprise' (Hn) and 'subsidiary' (H1), addressing the core features of firm globalization with geographically dispersed foreign subsidiaries and globally coordinated activities of manufacturing, sourcing and R&D capabilities. With the distinction between Hn and H1, the G4 model is able to present eight perspectives of the globalization process from interior and exterior to the enterprise and subsidiary. As method, this chapter will show how using the G4 model results in a richer analysis and findings from qualitative data. In this study Swedish top-level managers working in Asia show how they foster an organization culture of continuous learning and change that supports the MNE's globalization efforts.

The typical feature of emergent economies is a slow, apparent transformation from being predominantly a home base of Foreign Direct Investments (FDI) to becoming more home markets for various firms that expand internationally. In this aspect, China differs from its Asian forerunners. Without question, the most rapid development in recent decades within East Asia and the global economy as a whole is the (re-)emergence of China. While most studies on growth strategies for multinational corporations from emerging economies come from the perspective of economic strategies in international business, this study offers a novel perspective by using visual semiotics as a framework of study and analysis of data. It uses theories of social semiotics borne of the traditions of linguistics to conduct a systematic analysis of the representations of China's desire to go global with their automobile industry. The company in focus is China's Zhejiang Geely Holding Group (Geely) in the years between 2007 to 2011, just prior to an after its acquisition of Volvo Car Corporation (VCC).

Social capital is an abstract concept, yet it is widely believed the core aspects of social capital, the quality and quantity of social relationships, are important factors in organizational and individual success. An examination of the use of bonding and bridging social capital within Thailand was made. It was found, in principle; the managing of social capital in Thailand is similar to managing social capital in other locations, although the specific practices should be aligned with the unique cultural values found in Thailand. It is suggested that creating and using both bridging and bonding social capital are important components of the business environments found in Thailand.

There are a number of national competitive disadvantages multinational firms in Thailand face, but these disadvantages do not create insurmountable barriers. The national competitive disadvantages found in Thailand include a national brand which is not associated with advanced technology and a lack of an innovative national environment. At the strategic level, foreign multinationals can often overcome these disadvantages by using competitive advantages coming from their country of origin while local multinationals can select to operate in more mature industries or through positioning into segments where the national competitive disadvantages do not create significant barriers to success.

This chapter aims to analyze conflict resolution between Multinational Enterprises (MNEs) operating in Latin America and their host countries. The chapter focuses on the importance of establishing a policy for addressing local governments through permanent channels, as a strategy to solve disagreements with the authorities. The analysis includes different scenarios drawn from the experience of foreign firms in Argentina, Brazil, Chile, Colombia, Mexico, Peru and Venezuela. Thus, international managers may get a deeper view about the consequences of relying on formal diplomatic channels when conflict arises. Decision makers at MNEs need to evaluate separately each country outlook in order to assess the level of confidence that may be placed on diplomatic representation from the parent country and, consequently, the convenience of developing additional ties with local authorities through international business diplomacy.

This chapter, which is about institutional leadership and governance, examines leadership from the institutional perspective, but, in the African context. Context is virtually important because it shapes the opportunity structure of any time. The peculiarity of the African continent would require that the chapter examines leadership and governance as most of the economies of Africa are still practically dominated by government activities in so many dimensions where governance is poor. Neglecting governance therefore would mean not doing justice to the leadership context. Since leadership in context is not leadership that emerges solely from the qualities of the human character, but leadership that springs forth from an apprcciation and understanding of one's situation in the world, and the situation, in this respect includes; economic, social and political conditions that change over time, and these changes require distinct leadership styles and approaches for success, the tripod of institution, leadership and governance are therefore critical for success.

The operational structures of Multinational Enterprises (MNEs) in Africa, a developing and emerging economy do not necessarily differ from those of the developed or even Less Developed Economies (LDEs) except in few areas such as size and capital outlay. Meanwhile, both MNEs of African origin and those which originate from outside Africa do have salient attributes: they have many foreign affiliates or subsidiaries in foreign countries; they operate in a wide variety of countries around the globe; the proportion of assets, revenues, or profits is high; their employees, stockholders, owners, and managers are from many different countries; and they are involved in much more than merely establishing sales office, but incorporate a full range of manufacturing, research and development activities. This chapter examined operational structures of MNEs with focus on meaning, attributes, financing, exchange rate risk and international financial investment, strategies for improved financing and outlay of MNEs in selected African countries.

Foreword

For too long organizations doing business in western world resisted the temptation to go global. Not anymore. Many of these organizations in developed countries began to realize that economic prosperity can no longer only depend on domestic markets. Aging workforce coupled with rising of wages, natural economic cycle between expansion and contraction, continuous change in consumers' tastes and preferences are among host of challenges confronting organizations today. On the other hand, new opportunities availed themselves to organizations today where not present in the near past. Communications technologies, the engineering miracles of the past twenty years, paved the way for the rise of the Internet and the acceptance of mobile technologies with high levels of penetration worldwide. Accordingly, collaboration among team members of the same organization halfway around the globe became the norm. The enhancements in computing technologies and cloud computing facilitated the possibility of instantaneous exchange of business documents, training videos, and projects' progress updates. Furthermore, the opening of new markets, the creation of new demand based on localized products and services, and the availability of talented, well-educated workforce overseas are among the positive issues that matters most to organizations when thinking about doing business globally in general, in developing countries in particular.

This book on Multinational Enterprises Management Strategies in Developing Countries represents extensive research efforts to provide organizations and their managers that tackle most issues vital to cross the bridge and become a multinational enterprise. The book is an excellent source that provide in depth discussion on strategic options available to enterprises to develop global operations and what are the challenges multinational enterprises face in terms of ethical, socio-economic, and political environments globally. The book is an invaluable addition to cumulative wealth of knowledge in doing business internationally and especially in developing countries.

Khalid S. Soliman
International Business Information Management Association (IBIMA), USA
January 2, 2016

Khalid S. Soliman, *Ph.D., is President of the International Business Information Management Association (IBIMA), USA.*

Preface

Multinational enterprises (MNEs) are expanding across markets, nations and cultures at an accelerating pace and scope. In particular, MNEs expansion and diversification in developing countries has a lion share in this development. For example, according to Contessi and El-Ghazaly (2010) a decade ago only 20 companies on the list of Fortune Global 500 were located in developing countries or emerging markets but today more than 20 thousand multinationals are doing business in these countries. Similarly, the percentage of foreign direct investments by MNEs in emerging markets has also grown from a minuscule of below 1% foreign direct investment to an estimated 16% and above. There are over 40,000 multinational corporations currently operating in the global economy, in addition to approximately 250,000 overseas affiliates running cross-continental businesses. In 1995, the top 200 multinational corporations had combined sales of $7.1 trillion, which is equivalent to 28.3 percent of the world's gross domestic product. The top multinational corporations are headquartered in the United States, Western Europe, and Japan; they have the capacity to shape global trade, production, and financial transactions. China, Brazil, Russia and India are also expected to house many more home grown coupled with foreign MNEs in the coming years.

Multinational corporations are viewed by many as favoring their home operations when making difficult economic decisions, but this tendency is declining as companies are forced to respond to increasing global competition and local needs. Emerging markets such as China, India, Brazil, Mexico and South Africa for example, have received a jump increase in their international business sector. The growth of MNEs in emerging markets is expected to keep increasing despite the facts and factors that these markets inherit a variety of complex conventional and contemporary problems of lack of innovation, creativity, huge bureaucracy, diminishing physical infrastructure and indigenous financial and banking systems. Lack of availability of reliable and timely business information and local business alliances of suppliers and distributors based on family connections are some of the hindrances causing big business costs and frustrations for MNEs managers. The challenge for MNEs is two dimensional. One is to achieve growth, stability and strength internally as an institution of global business, and two, to influence positively and significantly the external forces including the industry and home-host governments to create a fair and conducive business environment for all the players in the market.

MNEs' RELATIONSHIPS WITH EMERGING MARKETS

National governments in emerging markets are often wary of foreign investors, especially investments coming from big conglomerates whose economic values may be much higher than the economic values of some nation states. In more recent times, multinational corporations have grown in power and visibility, but have come to be viewed more ambivalently by both governments and consumers worldwide. Indeed, multinationals today are viewed with increasing suspicion given their perceived lack of concern for the economic well-being of particular geographic regions and the public impression that multinationals are gaining power in relation to national government agencies, international trade federations and organizations, and local, national, and international labor organizations. Therefore, governments in general, politicians and bureaucrats in particular tend to focus on regularizations, increasing barriers, imposing tax, production and price control mechanisms and other micro issues (Horwitz & Budhwar, 2015).

MNE managers are aware that developing countries lack related and supporting institutions such as financial institutions, insurance agencies, trading companies, consultancy firms, quality education and training institutions, and, other public services. Foreign investors face transactional risks, income risks from operation, income risks from financing, and accounting risks due to fluctuations in the rate of exchange of the local currency. Additionally, MNEs manager also face political risks, inflation risks, bank instability, and legal risks. The issue of human resource management is another area of concerns for MNEs moving into developing countries, where lack of modern education facilities is the main cause of the shortage of local talents and specialized knowledge workforce. Therefore selecting good workers, training them in both social and technical areas is a challenging task for MNEs (Arnold & Quelch, 1998). In fact, developing countries are strategically important for both home-grown as well foreign MNEs since for most of the MNEs originating from developed countries the domestic or home markets do not present growth opportunities. Developed countries have matured markets where growth opportunities are considered minimal.

It is a widely held belief that globalization of business organizations has brought positive outcomes for the host countries and as well as home countries. Such positive outcomes are economic, financial and social development including job creation, human resource development, infrastructure development including physical and technological and institutional reforms (establishing industrial standards, competition law etc.). Especially, such outcomes are even more visible in the context of developing countries or emerging markets where development is at the embryonic stage to a large extent, and given the fact that developing countries still struggle with uncertain and unstable political, economic and legal environment combined with poorly developed institutions, lack of market information and communication system. MNEs are expected to become more responsible socially in the larger interest of the business organization itself and the society at large. All relevant players including companies, social activists, investors, employees, consumers and government should establish long-term bonds in order to make this happen and identify further opportunities of collaborations and joint efforts.

The risk factors associated with developing markets appear to be transitional and short term and MNEs can cope with these problems by considering the following strategic actions when establishing and developing businesses in emerging countries:

1. Balancing their role in economic development with social responsibilities toward the country in which they operate, including investment in local infrastructure development.
2. Adapting to the cultural differences, standards and practices.
3. Designing locally responsive marketing strategies, creating a balance between two opposing business variables: price and quality for the low-end customers.

4. Working and collaborating with the local institutions influencing the business environment, for example the judicial system, political system, educational system as well as local suppliers and distributors.
5. Having a strong legal support system to face off low or no protection for intellectual property rights, huge bureaucracy, local industrial mafia, anti-business rules and regulations, monopoly over local distributors and suppliers.
6. Developing local human capital by appointing host country managers and investing in training and development.
7. Conducting research and development activities in host country in order to avoid not invented here syndrome.

EMERGING MARKETS' RELATIONSHIPS WITH MNEs

MNEs can have quite positive effects on emerging or developing countries. MNEs can stimulate economic growth. In turn, growth creates jobs, promotes investment, and develops skills so that the people residing in the emerging countries benefit. Growth provides mutual benefits for both the business organizations and developing nations. Therefore, the national leaders of emerging countries or markets have responsibilities for proposing and implementing measures that create an environment friendly for investment by both domestic companies as well as foreign MNEs (Sauvant, Maschek & McAllister, 2009):

1. Supplying information and technical support when and wherever needed by the companies.
2. Allowing access to inexpensive, convenient, and timely financial support.
3. Offering fiscal incentives, such as tax holidays, especially in the initial stages of the investment.
4. Providing investment security, investment insurance and guarantees.
5. Developing international trade related alliances and agreements.
6. Permitting inter-organizational alliances such as joint ventures and consortiums to form and grow.
7. Setting up Official Development Assistance (ODA) programs.
8. Creating an overall environment and infrastructure encouraging and supporting business.

MNEs' STRATEGIES IN EMERGING MARKETS

MNEs challenges in emerging countries are to exist and continue in one way or the other in future as long as it takes for these nations to bring about radical reforms and improvements in their existing modus operandi: economic reforms; institutional reforms, infrastructure development; human resource development; political stability and creating an investment friendly environment. Zhang (2008) suggests that more than 2 billion consumers in emerging markets present profitable business opportunities and MNEs should focus on those markets to generate both profit and societal values. Zhang (2008) also finds that while these markets are full of opportunities at the same time these markets are full of troubles and weaknesses such as: security, environment, health, bad or weak public governance and administration, lack of public transparency, high levels of bribery and corruption, poor records on human rights, inadequate environmental, safety and labor standards and high levels of poverty and inequality.

To succeed in emerging markets requires an MNE to have specific skills. Some are the same skills needed to succeed in any market while others, such as those proposed by Birkinshaw, Ghoshal, Markides, Stopford and Yip (2003), are specific to succeed in emerging markets.

Skills Needed in Any Market

1. Establishing ambitious and interesting goals that stimulate, motivate, and develop capabilities and are well understood by all members of the organization.
2. Building an organization culture of confidence and pride where all stakeholders, especially, general employees and managers are provided opportunities to participate actively in the decisions of the company.
3. Being proactive and searching actively for best practices.
4. Encouraging innovation and risk-taking for organizational learning.
5. Managing product and service quality with respect to the needs of the target markets.
6. Building and managing appropriate competencies with respect to competitive factors affecting activities such as production, logistics, marketing, finance, and planning to be both effective and efficient.
7. Collecting business intelligence and instituting information systems to inform and monitor production, finance, marketing and other decisions.

Additional Skills Needed for Emerging Markets

8. Creating a global orientation so planning is globally focused rather than locally focused.
9. Recruiting and rewarding internationally experienced managers.
10. Investing in global research and development.
11. Influencing trade relationships by establishing close relations with the government and trade-oriented associations.
12. Managing trade-offs such as those between cost and quality, centralized and decentralized authority, and global and local cultures.

GOING FORWARD

Multinational corporations have existed since the beginning of overseas trade. They have remained a part of the business scene throughout history, entering their modern form in the 17th and 18th centuries with the creation of large, European-based monopolistic concerns such as the British East India Company during the age of colonization. Multinational concerns were viewed at that time as agents of civilization and played a pivotal role in the commercial and industrial development of Asia, South America, and Africa. By the end of the 19th century, advances in communications had more closely linked world markets, and multinational corporations retained their favorable image as instruments of improved global relations through commercial ties. The existence of close international trading relations did not prevent the outbreak of two world wars in the first half of the twentieth century, but an even more closely bound world economy emerged in the aftermath of the period of conflict.

In more recent times, multinational corporations have grown in power and visibility, but have come to be viewed more ambivalently by both governments and consumers worldwide. Indeed, multinationals today are viewed with increased suspicion given their perceived lack of concern for the economic well-being of particular geographic regions and the public impression that multinationals are gaining power in relation to national government agencies, international trade federations and organizations, and local, national, and international labor organizations.

Despite such concerns, multinational corporations appear poised to expand their power and influence as barriers to international trade continue to be removed. Furthermore, the actual nature and methods of multinationals are in large measure misunderstood by the public, and their long-term influence is likely to be less sinister than imagined. Multinational corporations share many common traits, including the methods they use to penetrate new markets, the manner in which their overseas subsidiaries are tied to their headquarters operations, and their interaction with national governmental agencies and national and international labor organizations.

WHY READ THIS BOOK

The chapters of this book address all the important issues discussed above. The book's contents should be invaluable to managers developing strategies for emerging markets or evaluating their current strategies in emerging markets as well as to researchers seeking understanding of the ongoing relationships between multinational enterprises and emerging markets.

The authors of these chapters represent many different viewpoints – from various disciplines and from a variety of geographical regions. They explore a wide range of issues concerning multinational enterprises operating or planning to operate in developing countries with a special focus on countries in Asia, Africa, Russia, and Latin America. Major issues examined include:

1. Conventional and contemporary environmental challenges.
2. Organizational growth paths to follow.
3. Strategic growth options and alternatives.
4. Institutional leadership and governance.
5. Structuring and design organizations
6. The ethical and social responsibility issues.
7. Measuring the organizational-market performance.
8. Managing national competitive disadvantage.
9. The use of technologies in organizations.
10. International relations and diplomacy.
11. The importance of standards and certifications for exports.

Following are summaries of the chapters.

Chapter 1, "The Environmental Challenges for MNEs", establishes the context for this book by analyzing how multinational enterprises (MNEs) operating in emerging or developing countries face a variety of complex and multifaceted challenges categorized into two broader spheres: conventional and contemporary. Conventional challenges are market forces (i.e., demand, supply, prices), industrial trends (structure, degree of competition, bases of competition) and national environment (i.e., political, economic, cultural and legal). Contemporary challenges include growth paths, strategic direction, new management styles, risk management, corporate social responsibility and new environmental dynamics in the context of the UN Global Compact. The real challenge for MNEs therefore, is to achieve sustainable growth and profitability while respecting and promoting the human and environmental concerns simultaneously.

Chapter 2, "Strategic Options for MNEs Operating in Developing Countries", outlines some of the basic opportunities, conditions, and strategic options for firms operating in emerging markets. Increasing FDI figures show that emerging markets offer many opportunities for foreign investors, but also pose specific challenges for doing business. Some factors are more abundant and less expensive, especially low to medium-skilled labor and natural resources, while sophisticated services are more difficult to obtain. A specific characteristic of emerging markets is the lack of business-enabling intermediaries. Therefore, foreign MNEs frequently need to fulfill tasks that are not within their range of activities in their home countries. Additionally, many governments in emerging economies act slowly and erratically; and laws are often not enforced systematically. In this context, foreign MNEs can choose between acquiring a local company, partnering up, or going it alone. The chapter looks at the pros and cons of these modes of internationalization and presents some concluding comments on the flexibility required by working under such conditions.

Chapter 3, "Strategies for Enhancing the Competitiveness of MNEs", studies how globalization has dramatically changed the competitive landscape in many national markets. There are concrete evidences that foreign direct investment (FDI) had doubled and even tripled in the last fifteen years in less-developed countries (LDCs), generating a tremendous impact on the economic development and welfare of these countries. Yet, less attention has been given to the role that domestic customers and domestic competitors play in shaping the strategic behavior and performance of MNEs in the targeted markets and the strategies which need to be adopted to enhance the competitiveness of MNEs. Through grounded theory approach and in depth literature review, the chapter aims to examine the positioning of MNEs to extend existing perspectives and incorporating competitive interactions between the external environments, competitive strategy and in particular, evaluates the strategic positioning and competitive behavior of MNEs.

Chapter 4, "Ethical and Social Challenges: Ethics Is Profitable, No-ethics Is Punishable", explains that how globalization has been a factor in bringing diverse nations closer worldwide, and how multinational enterprises (MNEs) are eager to look for new market opportunities in developing countries. In essence, this particular chapter analyzes the implementation of MNEs' global ethical principles in business into local moral standards of societies from developing countries. The author will discuss, using current scenarios, how principles of both moral relativism and moral absolutism can provide a profitable or punishable opportunity within developing countries when MNEs operate accordingly, or not, to ethical decision making processes in business. Additionally, the chapter proposes how MNEs' managers can discover the limits of moral free space, to distinguish a moral value in tension with their own from one that is intolerable. At the end, it is expected that MNEs' managers can apply ethical decision making in business by clearly perceiving and understanding their corporate culture in a developing country society.

Chapter 5, "Measuring Multinational Enterprise Marketing Performance", explores the use of performance measures for international marketing strategies. The key components of marketing strategies are explained and the major types of international marketing strategies explored. Metrics specific to different stages of the competitive life cycle are examined and metrics useful for evaluating country market performance are suggested. A framework for measures for multinational enterprise marketing strategies and tactics is explained. Current metrics practices are examined through the review of findings from three recent studies conducted by the author who surveyed managers on their use of metrics in international marketing strategies. The concluding thoughts suggest where multinational enterprises might improve their efforts in utilizing marketing performance metrics.

Chapter 6, "The Use of Technology in Organizations" studies how business corporations face the challenge of compete in the new interconnected business environment? In particular technology is recognized as a factor that boosts productivity and competitiveness and drives the business connectivity which in turn involves cross-borders goods, services and financial flows. An MNE is recognized as being possessed of high-tech assets, and also, resources including capital, management skills and R&D capabilities and subsidiaries can get them, from its holding company, and they transfer technology to local businesses. A knowledge transfer running parallel to the technology transfer takes place benefiting to the local economy. Foreign direct investment (FDI) is considered as the primary vehicle to facilitate technology transfer (and underlying knowledge flows) toward emerging countries. The ultimate goal of the MNE is related to leverage technology and knowledge transfer in order to maintain a competitive edge and move toward even higher value-added activities.

Chapter 7, "Operational Approaches in Organizational Design: a Case for MNEs in Emerging Markets", analyzes the challenge of organizational setup and operational model in emerging countries or markets faced by MNEs. In doing so the chapter focuses on different factors influencing the decision of a company leadership of how to organize and structure the MNE in emerging markets. Those factors are for instance, the national and organizational culture, management system, size of the company, nature of business, ownership whether private or public, the level of economic progress in a particular country, technological advances, and the level and standard of national educational services and system. The chapter searches for the successful organizational structure used by MNEs to operate in emerging markets. Finally, the chapter presents some recommendations for MNEs to follow when deciding about which organizational structure or design is relatively more suitable than others while operating in emerging markets.

Chapter 8, "Emerging MNEs Successfully Operating in International Markets: The cases of some Mexican MNEs" describes the most important theories that explain the possible motivations of some enterprises to compete in the international arena. Besides describing and summarizing the internationalization theories of an enterprise, the cases of some Mexican firms, which have grown successfully internationally, will be presented and compared with all the elements established in the different theories. This chapter starts by describing the different characteristics of firms competing in international markets. After that, the most important theories of MNEs are explored. The chapter ends with the discussion of the internationalization process followed by CEMEX, GRUMA and TELMEX (America Movil), Mexican enterprises that have successfully grown in the international spectrum.

Chapter 9, On the Relationship between Informal and Formal Institutions, Foreign Direct Investment and Innovation in Emerging Markets: The Case of Russia, India and China, 1990-2014", analyses empirically the relationship between informal (proxied by trust) and formal (proxied by corruption) institutions, foreign direct investment (FDI) and innovation in Russia, India and China between 1990 and 2014. Using the sample of these largest emerging markets enables to estimate the potential differences of the institutional effects on innovation across countries of different sizes and over the course of years. A significantly positive effect of trust and a negative effect of corruption and insignificant effect of FDI on innovation are confirmed. Further, there is an evidence for non-linearity of the effect of trust and corruption on innovation outcomes across the countries. The results confirm that, as societies become more trusting and institutional inefficiencies take effect, trust becomes an obstacle but corruption starts to 'help' innovators.

Chapter 10, "Exploring the Social Impact of Foreign Direct Investment on Institutional Change: The Case of Russia", studies that despite the vast and growing literature on the economic impact of foreign direct investment (FDI), its social significance is somewhat a neglected issue. Focusing on Russia, this chapter examines the effect of FDI and (formal) institutions (proxied, alternatively, by the (I) accumulated stock of small and medium sized firms or SMEs and (ii) number of economic crimes per 100,000 population or corruption) on (informal) institutional change (proxied by the change in the number of violent and property crimes per 100,000 population). The empirical findings provide robust support for a significantly positive direct impact of SMEs, whilst observing a significantly negative effect of corruption and either significantly positive impact of FDI or insignificant effect of multinational firms in this context.

Chapter 11, "The Gotheborg IV (G4) Model and the Function of Language in the Globalization Process of the Firm: the Case of Swedish MNEs", contributes to the theory of a firm's globalization processes reflected in the Uppsala Globalization Process Model (UGPM). The Gotheborg IV (G4) model is introduced, mapping the knowledge zones of the UGPM in a four quadrant axis model. Using language in its meta-capacity as theory and framework of analysis the G4 model makes a distinction between the words 'enterprise' (Hn) and 'subsidiary' (H1), addressing the core features of firm globalization with geographically dispersed foreign subsidiaries and globally coordinated activities of manufacturing, sourcing and R&D capabilities. With the distinction between Hn and H1, the G4 model is able to present eight perspectives of the globalization process from interior and exterior to the enterprise and subsidiary. As method, this chapter will show how using the G4 model results in a richer analysis and findings from qualitative data. In this study Swedish top-level managers working in Asia show how they foster an organization culture of continuous learning and change that supports the MNE's globalization efforts.

Chapter 12, "Chinese Wisdom. World Quality: A Visual Semiotic Analysis of China's 'Zou Xiang Shi Jie' (Going Global)", discusses comprehensively the Chines going global strategy in comparison with other regional players. The typical feature of emergent economies is a slow, apparent transformation from being predominantly a home base of foreign direct investments (FDI) to becoming more home markets for various firms that expand internationally. In this aspect, China differs from its Asian forerunners. Without question, the most rapid development in recent decades within East Asia and the global economy as a whole is the (re-)emergence of China. While most studies on growth strategies for multinational corporations from emerging economies come from the perspective of economic strategies in international business, this study offers a novel perspective by using visual semiotics as a framework of study and analysis of data. It uses theories of social semiotics borne of the traditions of linguistics to conduct a systematic analysis of the representations of China's desire to go global with their automobile industry. The company in focus is China's Zhejiang Geely Holding Group (Geely) in the years between 2007 and 2011, just prior to an after its acquisition of Volvo Car Corporation (VCC).

Chapter 13, "Social Capital Management Challenges: Thailand", studies the importance of social capital for organizations. Social capital is an abstract concept, yet it is widely believed the core aspects of social capital, the quality and quantity of social relationships, are important factors in organizational and individual success. An examination of the use of bonding and bridging social capital within Thailand was made. It was found, in principle; the managing of social capital in Thailand is similar to managing social capital in other locations, although the specific practices should be aligned with the unique cultural values found in Thailand. It is suggested that creating and using both bridging and bonding social capital are important components of the business environments found in Thailand.

Chapter 14, "Managing National Competitive Disadvantages: Thailand", looks at a number of national competitive disadvantages faced by multinational firms in Thailand and suggests that these disadvantages do not necessarily create insurmountable barriers for MNEs to do business in Thailand. The national competitive disadvantages found in Thailand include a national brand which is not associated with high technology and a lack of an innovative national environment. At the strategic level, foreign multinationals can often overcome these disadvantages by using competitive advantages coming from their country of origin while local multinationals can select to operate in more mature industries or through positioning into segments where the national competitive disadvantages do not create significant barriers to success.

Chapter 15, "International Business Diplomacy: Lessons from Latin America", analyzes conflict resolution mechanisms and channels between multinational enterprises (MNEs) operating in Latin America and their host countries. The chapter focuses on the importance of establishing a policy for addressing local governments through permanent channels, as a strategy to solve disagreements with the authorities. The analysis includes different scenarios drawn from the experience of foreign firms in Argentina, Brazil, Chile, Colombia, Mexico, Peru and Venezuela. Thus, international managers may get a deeper view about the consequences of relying on formal diplomatic channels when conflict arises. Decision makers at MNEs need to evaluate separately each country outlook in order to assess the level of confidence that may be placed on diplomatic representation from the parent country and, consequently, the convenience of developing additional ties with local authorities through international business diplomacy.

Chapter 16, "Institutional Leadership and Governance: The African Perspective", examines leadership from the institutional perspective, but, in the African context. Context is virtually important because it shapes the opportunity structure of any time. The peculiarity of the African continent would require that we examine not only leadership but governance as most of the economies of Africa are still practically dominated by government activities in so many dimensions where governance is poor. Neglecting governance therefore would mean not doing justice to the leadership context. Since leadership in context is not leadership that emerges solely from the qualities of the human character, but leadership that springs forth from an appreciation and understanding of one's situation in the world, and the situation, in this respect includes; economic, social and political conditions that change over time, and these changes require distinct leadership styles and approaches for success, the tripod of institution, leadership and governance are therefore critical for success.

Chapter 17, "Operational Structure of Multinational Enterprises in Africa", suggests that the operational structures of multinational enterprises (MNEs) in Africa, a developing and emerging economy do not necessarily differ from those of the developed or even Less Developed Economies (LDEs) except in few areas such as size and capital outlay. Meanwhile, both MNEs of African origin and those which originate from outside Africa do have salient attributes: they have many foreign affiliates or subsidiaries in foreign countries; they operate in a wide variety of countries around the globe; the proportion of assets, revenues, or profits is high; their employees, stockholders, owners, and managers are from many different countries; and they are involved in much more than merely establishing sales office, but incorporate a full range of manufacturing, research and development activities. This chapter examined operational structures of MNEs with focus on meaning, attributes, financing, exchange rate risk and international financial investment, strategies for improved financing and outlay of MNEs in selected African countries.

Chapter 18, "Multinational Enterprises and African Economy" studies how the Africa's economy, an emerging economy is gradually being re-positioned in the global economy as a focus of investment.

Multinational enterprises have helped to shape the economy of Africa. An overview of Africa's economy was examined; top 20 Africa's largest economies were highlighted; major sectors perceived as paths to growth of Africa's economy were examined – Agriculture, Banking, Consumer goods, infrastructure, mining, oil and gas, and telecommunications. The chapter also enunciated the concept, 'diversified economy' in relation to oil exporters, the transition economies and the pre-transition economies. It is therefore concluded that Multinational Enterprises will continue to contribute to the growth of Africa's economy, especially as more indigenous enterprises are being launched by African countries. It is therefore recommended that African countries should continue to diversify her economy to take advantage of large labor potential and natural resources endowment.

Chapter 19, "Standards Certifications and Its Influence on Exports Performance: Evidence from the Processed Food Industry in Colombia", emphasizes upon the importance of Standards Certifications for the promotion of exports related business. The integration of the world economy and the internationalization of companies have resulted in consumers' demand for high quality goods. Standards have emerged as a way of reducing the information asymmetries that consumers face when purchasing a product, and have gained importance in the processed food industry as they allow them to assess the quality of goods and may influence the export performance of certified firms. Certifications may act as promoters of international trade, but they can also constitute a barrier when the costs associated with the certification process exceed the potential benefits. The present study aims to compare the export performance of certified vs. non-certified firms in the Colombian processed food industry. A Mann-Whitney Test was used to analyze the difference of exports value for the selected companies, and then, non-structured interviews to the quality managers of these companies were conducted to gain greater understanding about the impact of standards certifications on their export performance.

Chapter 20, "Social Capital Management Challenges in Malaysia", highlights the challenges of social capital management in Malaysia and explores how social capital able affect Malaysian firms to be successful in international business with the global market's environment, there is full of uncertainty impact that may affect the entrepreneur's international performance. At the end of this chapter able to have an idea how to handle social capital and outcome all challenges. Not just so, in the chapter enable manager and student to discover more about Malaysian culture, value and firm behavior. Social capital might not a common term that can be found in business area. In this chapter we will discuss further more in the term of social capital.

Mohammad Ayub Khan
Tecnológico de Monterrey, Mexico

Don Sexton
Columbia University, USA

REFERENCES

Arnold, D. J., & Quelch, J. A. (1998). New Strategies in Emerging Markets. Sloan Management Review. Retrieved from http://sloanreview.mit.edu/article/new-strategies-in-emerging-markets/

Bennett, R. (1995), *International Marketing–Strategy, Planning, Market entry & Implementation.* London: Kogan Page Limited. pp, 18,97, 179-180, 182.

Birkinshaw, J., Ghoshal, S., Markides, C. C., Stopford, J., & Yip, G. (2003). *The Future of the Multinational Company*. John Wiley & Sons, Inc.

Contessi, S., & El-Ghazly, H. (2010). Multinationals from emerging economies growing but ittle understood. *The Regional Economist, retrieved from*research.stlouisfed.org/econ/contessi

Ghoshal, S., & Bartlett, C. (1990). *The multinational corporation as an inter-organizational network*. Academy of Management. *Academy of Management Review*, *15*(4), 603–603.

Gutierrez, B., Spencer, S. M., & Zhu, G. (2012). Thinking globally, leading locally: Chinese, Indian, and Western leadership. *Cross Cultural Management*, *19*(1), 67–86. doi:10.1108/13527601211195637

Horwitz, F., & Budhwar, P. (2015). Strategies and structures of MNCs from emerging economies. In Handbook of Human Resource Management in Emerging Markets.

Prahalad, C. K., & Lieberthal, K. (1998). The End of Corporate Imperialism. *Harvard Business Review*, (July-August): 69–79. PMID:12884671

Sauvant, K. P., Maschek, W. A., & McAllister, G. (2009). Foreign Direct Investment by Emerging Market Multinational Enterprises, the Impact of the Financial Crisis and Recession and Challenges Ahead. OECD Global Forum on International Investment. Retrieved from www.oecd.org/investment/gfi-8/

Zainulbhai, A. S. (2005). *What Executives are Asking about India, McKinsey Quarterly* (Special Edition). Fulfilling India's Promise.

Zhang, F. (2008). *Corporate Social Responsibility in Emerging Markets: The Role of Multinational Corporations*. An Initial Paper for the Launch of the Foreign Policy Centre Project on "Corporate Responsibility in Emerging Markets" in association with Coca-Cola Great Britain.

Acknowledgment

This book on "Multinational Enterprises Management Strategies in Developing Countries" is the product of highly professional efforts and collaborations with sincerity of many researchers, professors and students. I am thankful to all of them for sharing their ideas and experiences in the initial stages of the development of the book and their continued interest in the publication of the book to the end. All the chapter contributors are equally part and parcel of this project and without their contributions it would not have possible to get the book published timely and with quality. My sincere regards for all of them. I remember in particular my colleague Professor Armando Quintanilla visiting my office on regular basis and giving his opinions on which themes and issues to be covered in the book based on his vast experience as a faculty of international business and director of the undergraduate international business program at campus Monterrey, Tecnológico de Monterrey. His interests and involvement in the book project are highly appreciated and valued.

This book, as any other book projects demanded technical, logistical and administrative help in different stages of the publication process, therefore, and especially, I extend many thanks and gratitude to the teaching assistants and postgraduate students at the EGADE Business School, Tecnológico de Monterrey, for providing timely helping hands in searching for articles, cross-checking references and printing materials, to mention a few:

Marinette Bisteni,
María Esther García Mátar,
Víctor Julián De la Torre,
Federico Salazar,
Wilbert Pérez Torres,
Ricardo García.

As always, my sincere appreciations go to the School of Business, Social Sciences and Humanities, campus Monterrey, Tecnológico de Monterrey, for providing me space, time and all the relevant supports whenever needed in order to initiate such an important research project and complete it on time. Last but not the least, all those scholars who have created and built the knowledge body of international business in general, and theories and concepts in the field of managing multinational enterprises in particular, deserve appreciations and thanks.

In life we learn from others. We should share with others in life.

Mohammad Ayub Khan
Tecnológico de Monterrey, Mexico

Chapter 1
MNEs Management Strategies in Developing Countries:
Establishing the Context

Mohammad Ayub Khan
Tecnológico de Monterrey, Mexico

ABSTRACT

Multinational Enterprises (MNEs) operating in emerging or developing countries face a variety of complex and multifaceted challenges categorized into two broader spheres: conventional and contemporary. Conventional challenges are market forces (i.e., demand, supply, prices), industrial trends (structure, degree of competition, bases of competition) and national environment (i.e., political, economic, cultural and legal). Contemporary challenges include growth paths, strategic direction, new management styles, risk management, corporate social responsibility and new environmental dynamics in the context of the emerging global dynamics. The real challenge for MNEs therefore, is to achieve sustainable growth and profitability and facing effectively all these multi-faceted challenges simultaneously.

INTRODUCTION

Globalization as well as regionalization is the driving force behind the expansion of MNEs into foreign markets especially, into the markets of developing countries. Developing countries present enormous opportunities for MNEs, however, these countries are considered highly volatile as a marketplace because of the lack of institutional stability, insufficient infrastructure and weak economic base attributed to them. MNEs require to looking for sustainable approaches to establish and grow business operations in these marketplaces. MNEs need context-specific combination of relationships, resources and capabilities in these markets. Imperfect market conditions combined with fragmented industrial structure found in these markets make them highly investor-unfriendly. With the entry of new investors into these developing marketplaces and the un-ability to establish a conducive and fair market conditions by the national leadership of developing countries, the already downtrodden conditions may further deteriorate. Since early 1990s, most of the developing countries particularly in Asia and Latin America have been

DOI: 10.4018/978-1-5225-0276-0.ch001

the fastest-growing markets in the world for most products and services. Companies can lower costs by setting up manufacturing facilities and service centers in these countries, where skilled labor and trained managers are relatively inexpensive. Moreover, several developing-country transnational corporations especially from China and India have already entered North America and Europe with low-cost cum push-marketing strategies. According to an estimated number more than 20,000 multinationals are operating in emerging countries and many more MNEs from western markets foresee China and India as their future business fields. In order to exploit the huge emerging market and at the same time to face off the troubles ahead for them, MNEs import their domestic models into emerging markets by lowering prices, selling smaller size and using lower cost labor, and materials. Locally fit business models and consumer responsive business strategies will help MNEs to tap the existing as well as the future opportunities in these countries (Eyring, Johnson & Nair, 2011). Moreover, a balanced strategic approach to managing operations in developing or emerging markets, will help MNEs avoid a number of potential strategic errors or management blunders as follows (Breemen, 2014):

1. Committing insufficient resources.
2. Implementing an international strategy.
3. Unwillingness to adapt product to fit local market demand.
4. Targeting a nation like India or China as one big market.

ENVIRONMENTAL CHALLENGES FOR MNEs

The literature review is dedicated to the analysis of diverse both conventional and contemporary challenges facing the MNEs doing business internationally, and especially in the context of developing countries or markets. In this chapter the terms developing countries and emerging markets are interchangeable used even though these terms are interpreted differently by different authors in the existing body of knowledge in the field. Some authors understand that a country or market is considered in the emerging stage because the nation is gradually improving its overall economic and business conditions for businesses and investments in comparison with underdeveloped countries or markets. So to say otherwise, these countries or markets are just emerging from the underdeveloped economic and business conditions on several fronts including economic stability, infrastructure development and good governance. Other authors are of the view that a nation or market is defined as an emerging country or market after the country or market has progressed from underdeveloped conditions into developing conditions before becoming an emerging country or nation. The overall business, economic and governance conditions in an emerging nation are relatively better than a developing country or market. For example, some countries or markets such as China, Mexico, India and Brazil used to be considered as developing countries but in the past several years these nations have achieved tremendous economic and business success and thus are directly competing with the global business and economic powers of Europe, Asia and North America.

What is an Emerging Market?

Fan (2008) suggests that emerging market is a term which refers to a country that has undertaken transition in its political or economic systems and experienced rapid economic development. Although there is no exact list of emerging market or emerging countries, China, India, Indonesia and South Korea in Asia; Poland and Turkey in Europe; Brazil, Mexico and Argentina in South America and South Africa in Africa are considered as developing countries. The BRICS (Brazil, Russia, India, China and South Africa) is another term widely used to describe the five largest emerging countries. Group of Next Eleven is another list of emerging countries which include Pakistan, Bangladesh, Egypt, Indonesia, Iran, South Korea, Mexico, Nigeria, the Philippines, Turkey and Vietnam. All these countries have growing population and relatively stable economy.

Several terms including emerging markets, newly industrializing countries, emerging countries, developing countries, and emerging economies are interchangeably used in the existing literature. Also, emerging markets refers to those countries that are starting to participate globally by implementing reform programs and are undergoing economic improvement. The term emerging market was first used by the International Finance Corporation to describe those nations whose economies were growing continuously and were liberating national markets especially security markets for foreign investors. Later on, the term emerging markets gave coverage to those developing countries with improving gross national income (Zhang, 2008). Emerging countries are those countries which lie between the developed and less developing or Third World countries with cheap raw materials and labor rather than their markets (Arnold & Quelch, 1998). Other terms or names used when referring to emerging countries such as emerging economies, emerging countries, and emerging markets etc. In sum, nations with an undeveloped industrial base and infrastructure on the one hand, but a rapid rate of growth (usually exceeding that of developed nations) on the other hand are considered emerging nations (Guillen & Garcia-Canal, 2013). "Geographically, these markets span the globe and possess vastly differing economic and political conditions. Those economies outside of the developed world- US, Canada, Japan and Europe-are what are commonly referred to as the emerging market (Guarino, 2010)". "Emerging markets are now responsible for nearly 40 percent of global GDP and an even larger share of GDP growth. Many of these markets are dominated by able and ambitious local competitors that often have superior local knowledge, stronger government relationships, and lower cost structures (Guarino, 2010)".

Although there is no commonly accepted definition of the term "emerging market," however, there are three key aspects of a country's economy that often underlie various definitions (Arnold & Quelch, 1998): *First* is the absolute level of economic development, usually indicated by the average GDP per capita, or the relative balance of agrarian and industrial/commercial activity. This overlaps with other categorizations such as "less developed countries" (LDCs) or "Third World countries." *Second* is the relative pace of economic development, usually indicated by the GDP growth rate. *Third* is the system of market governance and, in particular, the extent and stability of a free-market system; if the country is in the process of economic liberalization from a command economy, it is sometimes defined as a "transitional economy (Arnold & Quelch, 1998). Vladimir Kvint, who is the President of the International Academy of Emerging Markets (an organization which educates business, academic and political leaders from industrialized countries on how to combat poverty on the basis of cooperation with multilateral institutions, research organizations, universities and companies from developed countries), define the term "emerging market" as a "society transitioning from a dictatorship to a free market-oriented economy, with increasing economic freedom, gradual integration within the global marketplace, an expanding middle class, improving standards of living and social stability and tolerance, as well as an increase in corporations with multilateral institutions (Kvint, 2015)".

MNEs (multinational enterprises) are companies or business corporations with operations in more than one country. MNEs do not just mean Western or Japanese multinational corporations, but also a growing number of companies from emerging economies in Asia, Africa, and Latin America (Zhang, 2008). Below are some of the definitions of an MNE in the context of this chapter:

1. MNE is a local (home grown) organization which goes beyond the national frontiers to do business in different other markets including developing and developed. For example, a Mexican MNE CEMEX has operations in many countries in the world including developed and developing.
2. MNE is originating from a foreign country (foreign MNE): MNEs operating in other countries (hosts markets) other than their local or parent countries. These MNEs may come from a developed country such as a US MNE moving into the Mexican market or MNEs moving into the Mexico market from another developing country such as a Brazilian MNE doing business in Mexico.

A company or any overseas ventures are not considered MNEs unless they have substantial investment in foreign countries and actively manage those operations and regard those operations as integral parts of the company both strategically and organizationally (Bartlett & Ghoshal, 2002).

Which Growth Path to Follow by MNEs?

The growth path option implies which investment form or forms MNEs pursue or should pursue while internationalizing their operations. For example, if an MNE plans to sell (export) to, or buy (import) from, or produce (manufacture, assemble) in, a foreign market which investment alternatives are available for the MNE. For MNEs to expand and grow from the local or domestic market into foreign markets, a variety of growth paths are available. The challenge, thus, for MNEs is to decide which of these diverse growth options are the most viable and effective options. MNEs have traditionally these growth options available for them (Root; 1994; Buckley & Casson, 1998):

1. Importing/exporting.
2. Licensing.
3. Franchising.
4. Direct investment (wholly owned independent ventures).
5. Consortium.
6. Joint ventures.
7. A combination of two or more options.

Several factors cause the decision to opt for one or the other option. For example, the degree of risk associated with each of these paths; the need for control and coordination of your business; the need for locally responsiveness; the nature of your business; and various other characteristics of the target market/country. Existing literature suggests that MNEs generally expand the national boarders to other markets through mergers, acquisitions, sequential entry and various forms of joint ventures. Of which mergers and acquisitions being the most popular paths to pursue to penetrate new foreign markets since these options are considered risk-proofs. Simply because of merging with or acquiring an already established operation means having acquired the experience and access to suppliers, distributors and customers.

Other relevant factors that might also influence such important decisions of MNEs in their expansion struggle are:

1. What about the historical relationships between the home and host country of the MNE?
2. How many different and complex lines or types of products and services an MNE is planning to expand into the new foreign market?
3. To how many host markets (countries), an MNE is planning to expand its business operation?
4. To what extend the new host market or country is similar or different culturally and socially from the home country or market?
5. If an MNE is going abroad on its own and alone through direct investment; or with the help of a foreign entity (host organization or group) in host market through joint venture or other strategic alliances; or with the support of home (local) entity operating in a foreign or host market through joint investment or any other business collaborations.

A good understanding of all these issues and based on that crafting a comprehensive investment-operational strategy will surely enable an MNE to avoid potential preliminary foreign market entry losses and risks.

Growth Strategies Used by MNEs

Establishing a business operation is one challenge, but keep the business entity of a large scale running and growing at a desirable speed demands selecting adequate growth strategies. Growth strategies include strategies relating to the functional, product and operations of the company. For example, functional strategies include branding strategies, distribution strategies, supplier management strategies, and production and marketing strategies. Product strategies refer to innovating, designing and developing new products, product diversification, and product branding for example. Operational strategies include the geographical location of the operation in terms of closeness to the suppliers, customers, distributors or financial institutions. The decision about which growth strategies to use by MNEs in emerging markets is also a challenging task for the management. For example, in theory the following strategies are available for MNEs to pursue in order to invest and grow (Lasserre, 2007; Collis, 2014).

1. Integration strategies (backward, forward and horizontal integration). Backward integration means buying or integrating your suppliers into your business operations as your own business. Similarly, forward integration means buying or integrating your distributors into your business operation as your own business. The horizontal integration means buying o integrating your direct competitors into your business operations.
2. Diversification strategies (concentric, conglomerate and horizontal diversification). Offering new products to new customers, offering new products to existing customers, offering new but related products to new customers are some of the examples of the diversification strategies that can be used by MNEs as their growth strategies.
3. Aggressive strategies (i.e., product development, market development, market penetration, takeovers, and acquisitions). For aggressive strategies to be successful MNEs must be positioned in the star situation in the industry which means that the company is doing above average in terms of the market shares and at the same time the industrial growth is obviously steady and fast.

4. Defensive strategies (i.e., mergers, divestitures, retrenchment, liquidation). Such strategies are more effective in market conditions where the company´s market shares are not very high in the industry and at the same time the growth of the industry is not very encouraging either.
5. The generic strategic strategies of Michael Porter (cost leadership, focus, and differentiation) are also available for MNEs to consider. Especially, the cost leadership strategy which could be very effective in developing countries or emerging countries where consumers tend to be highly price-sensitive.

In designing and implementing these strategies, MNEs are expected rather required to incorporate a variety of corporate social responsibility dimensions including stakeholder considerations into its existing business management models. Kourdi (2009) suggests five routes companies can take in order to expand on their activities after entering the market(s).

1. Organic growth (expanding through green field investment).
2. Mergers and acquisitions.
3. Integration (strategic alliances and joint ventures with relevant stakeholders).
4. Diversification (based on market, product and customer).
5. Specialization (focusing on certain products and services and serving a special group market segment).

Peng (2006) discussing the growth strategies of businesses focuses solely on diversification and describes organic growth, mergers and acquisition and integration as means to achieve diversification. Therefore, companies have the opportunity to diversify their products or diversify geographically (Peng, 2006). Other writers in the field such as Meyer and Thu Tran (2004) suggest other growth strategies for MNEs as alternatives:

1. Global branding strategy: Global brand with little or no adaptation, positioned as premium brand.
2. Local branding strategy: Portfolio of local brands, positioned to serve mass markets.
3. Multi-tier branding strategy: Portfolio of global local and brands, positioned to serve different segments of the market.

Risk Management Approaches to be Adopted by MNEs

Business organizations face a variety of risks which are tangible and intangible, big or small, simple or complex, economic or political and social or business. Learning about all those real and potential risks regardless of their nature, size and scope is surely helpful for MNEs to avoid business disasters in their global approach and reach. Although, it is difficult to foresee exactly the type of risks an MNE may confront since the global business dynamic is complex and volatile, nonetheless, the purpose is to provide some thinking ground for the organizational decision makers (managers) about the potential risks their organizations may face. In the following some of the critical risks are divided into different classes (Lillie et al, 2002):

1. Market Risk: the potential loss due to market factors in the portfolio.
2. Credit Risk: the potential loss due to changes in counterparty credit.

3. Business Risk: the potential loss due to changes in economic factors.
4. Operational Risk: the potential loss due to system, people, legal and external events.
5. Commodity prices.
6. Counterparty defaults.
7. Economic factors.
8. Technology factors.
9. Market competitiveness.
10. People (e.g. human error).
11. Country risk (e.g. political).
12. Reputation and public image.
13. Weather conditions.
14. Privacy related issues.
15. Legal aspects.
16. Increase in fuel oil prices.
17. Levels of risks (individual employee relations to corporate to corporate to, corporate to government, to industry or to the nation (market).
18. Natural calamities (floods, rains, earthquakes, fire etc.).

Other events, conditions or circumstances that cause risk for business operations include (Edmonton, n/a):

1. External environment: Events originating outside the organization such as decisions made by all levels of government; public reaction or confidence; demographic changes; social factors; environmental damage; economic factors; natural disasters; terrorism/vandalism; legal/compliance (events related to compliance and legal agreements); legislation; regulatory changes; health and safety laws; environmental laws; by-laws; administrative directives; policies; contracts.
2. Culture (intangible events that shape the way business is conducted): Leadership or management philosophy; stewardship, fiduciary or policy responsibilities; tone at the top; governance; level of trust; lines of authority; communications; ethics and values; decision model; integration across organization; change management practices; ability to apply learning and redirect energies; monitoring/performance measures; adaptability to change.
3. Operations (events related to business processes): Assumptions/methodologies; quality of planning; process/service quality; process/service efficiency; business continuity; fraud (employee, customer, vendor); security of assets; policies and procedures; reliance on third party; operational capacity; internal controls; customer needs.
4. Financial resources (events related to the financial health of the organization): Return on investment; asset valuation; protection from loss; sources of revenue; alternate funding mechanisms (new taxes, fees, charges); ability to meet financial obligations; capital funding; operational funding; material price fluctuations; pricing or market positioning; level and type of insurance.
5. Physical assets (events relate to tangible assets): Suitability; breakdown; level of maintenance; misuse; obsolescence; theft.
6. Human resource (events related to staffing): Training and development programs; changing resource needs; authority, accountability and responsibility; staffing levels; staff competencies; recruitment/

retention decisions; performance incentives & compensation; staff turnover; job action; succession planning.

7. Information resources (events related to the storage and use of information): Availability (information/communication/ computer systems); infrastructure (capacity and ability to support business initiatives); freedom of information and privacy legislation (FOIP); security; information quality (relevance, integrity); integration/coordination; performance information.

The following list expands and further elaborates some of the uncontrollable enterprise risks with a potential tangible impact on the financial and operating performance of the company (i.e., Krechowicz & Hiranya, 2009; Dominion CSR, n/a):

1. Regulatory risks: Regulators may introduce new rules and regulations causing additional expenses for the company, for example, quality standards, customer privacy protection laws, environmental laws etc.
2. Weather-related risks: Such risks including hurricanes, winter snow storms and other weather-related incidents can cause damage to the physical infrastructure (roads, buildings) and disrupt energy services (water supply, electricity supply and communication services).
3. Risks of cyber-attacks: Cyber-attacks are another emerging risk area for the big companies. Attackers and hackers disrupt the internet-based operations and activities, hack emails and can get access to the confidential information/database of the company. The risk of losing the business privacy as the core competence of any organization is increasingly high. This requires from business organizations to invest in advanced technologies and human expertise in order to protect themselves from such risks.

The more risk you take the more profit you earn as the slogan goes in the business world. The business environment is dynamic and complex posing even greater risks for business organizations. Emerging markets primarily considered profit centers (i.e.., low product and labor cost) by MNEs have grown tremendously creating new growth frontiers and consumer base. There are risks associated with any foreign investments but the pace of growth and changes in these specific markets have caused some high risks. Therefore, business organizations should approach these markets with carefully crafted risk management strategies (approaches).

Operating successfully in these markets has become a business imperative for most sectors of the global economy. There are risks associated with investing in any new market, but the pace of expansion in these high-growth economies has resulted in rapidly changing and highly complex and diverse risk environments. Despite these challenges, there is tremendous opportunity for organizations approaching these markets with a clearly defined risk strategy. Understanding market specific risk in early stages of the business expansion will help avoid many of these risks. There are all types of risks associated with the business environment in emerging markets such as bribery, corruption, facilitation fees, inappropriate gratuities, and gift giving. Other practices such as commercial bribery, vendor collusion, conflicts of interest, asset misappropriation, and fraudulent financial reporting have been reported in case of emerging markets (Boets, 2008). Guarino (2010) suggests that in the not so distant past, military coups, hyper-inflation and crippling foreign debt were also very common in the emerging markets.

Risks associated with these markets do not only belong to their early growth stages as considered by many as transitional risks. These emerging markets may also present for MNEs several other types of risks as they get matured (Boets, 2008):

1. Contract non-compliance.
2. Intellectual property theft.
3. Non-compliance with laws and regulations.
4. Counterfeiting and gray marketing of high-value or high-margin products.

Moreover, MNEs can face tough competition from the domestic companies who can focus on its homework; adapt more quickly to the changing conditions; and have access to the capital, technology and support from the local industry and government. They can take more risk at home and attract local talents (The Economist, 2013) by improving compensation programs, offering trainings and chanting the slogan of nationalism.

Interestingly, many of the risks faced by MNEs are also found to be based on the general perceptions of various stakeholders in the business. These perceptual risks are (Moffett, Stonehill, & Editeman, 2003):

1. MNEs are bigger than many nation states in terms of their economic and financial values and thus can easily exploit underdeveloped and poor countries in the name of investment.
2. MNEs tend to atomize their business operations by using advanced technologies and thus increasing unemployment in the areas where they do businesses.
3. MNEs are global corporations and helping global rich class and consequently widening the rich-poor gap.
4. MNEs are promoting consumerism since they have the resources and capacity to offer and promote new products and services highly attractive for the current as well as the potential customers. Such consumerism trend has also generated social classes among the consumers population based on the brands and imported vs local goods one can buy and consume. Such tendencies may lead to social problems such as discrimination, thefts, bribery, corruption and bankruptcies so and so forth.
5. MNEs are influencing nation states to open their economies and markets for open business. Therefore, privatization is taking place in developing countries at an increasingly high speed in the name of fair market, competition based business and efficiency etc. This has opened the door for governments to withdraw social welfare programs and projects for their citizens especially in the field of education, health and other poverty alleviation sectors.
6. Small and local companies cannot and may not be able to compete with MNEs having global business experience and with a lot of resources and networking.
7. Cultural homogenization: MNEs promote globalization of everything and globalization may lead to cultural homogenization and thus creating a global culture. Local customs and traditions will be washed away by the forces of globalization in the name of standardization and synergy.

Multinational enterprises are the backbones of the world globalized economy system. Cut-throat competition among the firms based on quality, timeliness, price and other services has led to the work environment where indicators such as organizational productivity and low operational cost surpass the human needs and concerns. MNEs are also perceived to have manipulated the global wealth whereby influencing the global political and regulatory systems. Many MNEs are also considered to be the least environmentally friendly businesses especially, MNEs in the energy, mining, and construction sectors.

In order for an MNE to identify, measure, and manage its political risks, it needs to define and classify these risks (Moffett, Stonehill, & Editeman, 2003):

1. Firm-specific risks are those political risks that affect the MNE at the project or corporate level. Governance risk, due to goal conflict between an MNE and its host government, is the main political firm-specific risk. An MNE also faces business risks and foreign exchange risks.
2. Country-specific risks are those political risks that also affect the MNE at the project or corporate level but originate at the country level. The main political risk categories at the country level are transfer, cultural and institutional risks. Transfer risk concerns mainly the problem of blocked funds, but also peripherally sovereign credit risk. Cultural and institutional risks spring from ownership structure, human resource norms, religious heritage, nepotism and corruption, intellectual property rights, and protectionism.
3. Global-specific risks are terrorism and war, anti-globalization movement, environmental concerns, poverty, cyber-attacks.

Boets (2008) proposes few suggestions for MNEs to follow in order to deal with the various risks:

1. MNEs should develop risk assessment mechanisms as part and parcel of the overall management system.
2. MNEs should understand local laws, regulations, cultures, and ethics.
3. Establishing strategic and operational alliances with local organizations is critically important in avoiding and managing risks.
4. Underestimating the pace of change, or being slow to respond to it, can also hinder success. Organizations must be vigilant, cautious, and flexible.

Other strategies and techniques to manage risks involving bribery and corruptions include (Boets, 2008):

1. Establishing appropriate standards of conduct through global policies and procedures.
2. Implementing the standards through training, communications, and education.
3. Conducting fraud risk assessments specific to the circumstances of operations.
4. Instituting anti-corruption specific internal controls such as unannounced internal audits, management rotation, data-analysis procedures and whistleblower hotlines.
5. Establishing escalation, investigation, remediation, and disciplinary protocols.

These are some of the questions to ask if your company is planning to enter an emerging market (Boets, 2008):

1. Does your organization conduct a formal risk assessment when considering whether to become involved in an emerging market?
2. Does your organization have a documented risk-management strategy that covers the ongoing management of risk in emerging markets?

3. Do you truly understand your risk profile in each emerging market where you operate?
4. What issues are you struggling with most in your emerging markets?
5. Do these issues vary in different parts of the world?
6. What groups within your organization are providing risk coverage for these issues? Are there challenges these groups are having in providing the risk coverage required?
7. Does your internal audit function conduct sufficient testing of risk management systems and processes in emerging markets?

Overall, establishing a risk management culture, properly aligning organizational structure and risk management processes, and improving communications can create a strong foundation for better risk management in any market (Boets, 2008).

Given the fact that emerging economies (or countries or markets) of the world are considered risky, uncertain, unstable and complex, it is imperative to discuss and learn about the various approaches used by MNEs to manage those business conditions (risk, unstable, uncertain and complex). In broader terms MNEs have three strategic options to handle the risk factors in emerging countries. One is being offensive (offensive strategy) and which requires an MNE to be very powerful in many senses (financially, politically, technologically etc.). Second is being on the defensive (defensive strategy) and which means and MNE should respect and adopt the host country and market policies and standards. An MNE should abide by the local government rules and regulations and industrial standards. And the third option is to have a mixed (balanced) strategy and by which it means that an MNE should be defensive (cooperate) in areas where it has weaknesses and in areas where it has strengths to be offensive (compete).

Institutional Leadership and Governance

This particular section discusses the MNE´s overall governance and management strategies while conducting business globally. Generally speaking, MNE´s governance and management is divided into the following main responsibility zones or organizational hierarchies:

1. The board of directors (BoD) which involves the top policy making people. These people come with different background in terms of their experience, relationship with the company, social status and political influence. The board of directors is composed of owners, investors, social activists, government people, and industry experts, for example. The board is responsible for the strategic direction, mission and vision of the company.
2. The management team which involves the chief executive officer, top managers, middle managers and lower managers. This team is mainly held responsible for the execution of the business and organizational policies designed by the board of directors.
3. The operational staff involves employees responsible as supervisors and coordinators for the operation of different functional areas of the organization.
4. The support staff involves employees supporting the operational staff. Both operational staff and support staff are also called the floor-staff.

One of the main concerns for MNEs to establish and run business abroad is how to approach to lead, manage and coordinate the operations in different foreign markets especially, decision making issues or aspects of the organization. Well managed and led firms from the inception are better placed in comparison with firms having organizational problems. Several studies find that the overall strategic approach of MNEs largely influences their strategic choices, power and polices of the local subsidiary. For example, a more centralized approach of the MNE to decision making may make the subsidiaries dependent on the MNE and thus, increasing the possibility of having inter head-office and subsidiary conflict and organizational politics. In contrary to this, if the MNE approach is to give more power to the subsidiaries in decision making involving both strategic and operational issues, subsidiaries may accumulate more power and resources and thus, indirectly threatening the head-office authority in the long run. Researchers in the field are of the view that a balanced approach which is negotiated between the head-office and subsidiary may help create a condition for interdependency between the two offices and thus, avoiding conflicts and increasing organizational harmony. Several factors influencing the decision to give more or less power to the foreign subsidiaries are listed below (Geppert, 2005):

1. The influence of the subsidiary's strategic position and its performance within the MNE on local management and employee representatives' ability to shape the implementation of the MNE´s global strategies.
2. The influence of MNE´s strategies on local management's ability to shape the implementation of the MNE global strategies.
3. The influence of the degree of institutional embeddedness of the subsidiary in the host country environment on the ability of local management to shape the implementation of the MNE´s global strategies.

Additionally, institutional leadership of an MNE in foreign markets encompasses these major areas of management concerns:

- General management.
- Management orientation.
- Management challenges.
- E-management.
- Organizational design.
- Operational issues.
- Corporate governance.
- Network Management.
- Media management.

In general, leading and managing big corporations involve confronting boldly and timely a number of contemporary challenges which makes the job of MNEs managers even more complicated and risk-full. For example (Barttlet & Ghoshall, 2002):

- Globalization of markets.
- Short product and technology life cycle.
- Assertions of national government demands.
- Intensification of global competition.
- Global scale efficiency and competitiveness.
- National responsiveness and flexibility.
- Worldwide innovation and learning capability.

Changes in Operations and Structures

For companies to cope with these changing forces, it is imperative for MNEs to search for, hire, develop and retain managers who are multifunctional and multidisciplinary. Ghoshal & Bartlett (2002) identified three main characteristics of a manager who is considered as a transnational manager:

1. Global business manager**:** These managers are the worldwide business strategists (configure information, planning and control systems country-by-country and global business report); architect of asset and resource configuration (coordinating the distribution of key assets and resources); cross-border coordinator (coordination of sourcing of raw materials, components, and finished goods, transfer policies).
2. Worldwide functional manager: These managers are worldwide intelligence scanner, cross-pollinator of best practices (transfer of technology and innovations from one country to another). These are the champions of transnational innovation.
3. Geographic subsidiary management: These managers are the bicultural interpreter; national defender and advocate (local information use in centrally decision-making system); and, frontline implementer of the corporate strategy.

MNEs are big organizations with huge impacts on the stakeholders they serve. The stakeholders of MNEs include investors, mangers, employees, customers, suppliers, distributors, governments, communities, partners, competitors and other interest groups. Any decision whether it is about market expansion, new product development or any change in the existing organizational setup of the company may impact positively or negatively these stakeholders. MNEs leadership is expected to protect and promote the interest of these stakeholders and not to harm them intentionally. Lucas and Anello (1995) (cited in Komives, Lucas & McMahon, 2013) proposed eight assumptions about ethical leadership which MNEs can incorporate into their global management philosophy and practices:

1. Ethics is the heart of leadership: Good leadership means leadership that is effective, and follows sound and ethical process.
2. All leadership is value driven: leaders bring to the organization their own values and beliefs and how people should be treated and notions of what is right and wrong.
3. Journey to ethical leadership begins with an examination of personal values: as well as ongoing reflection of personal core values and how these values are related to the values of an organization.
4. Ethical leadership can be learned in a variety of ways through a process involving experience, reflection and application.
5. Ethical leadership involves a connection between ethical thought and action. Actions and moral reasoning should match.
6. Character development is an essential ingredient of ethical leadership: a leader's character is defined by his/her actions and behavior not simply by the values. Do not walk your talk.
7. Members at all levels of an organization or community have the opportunity and responsibility to participate in the process of exercising ethical leadership. Ethical leadership is a shared process not just a responsibility of positional leader.
8. Everything we do teach: role modeling is a powerful way to influence the ethical climate in families, organizations and communities.

MNEs leaders should consider the basic principles in becoming a good leader (Komives, Lucas & McMahon, 2013) and these principles are universal and people oriented.

1. Knowing: You must know yourself, how change occurs, and how others view things differently than you do.
2. Being: You must be ethical, principled, open, caring, and inclusive (involving others).
3. Doing: You must act in socially responsible ways, consistently, congruently, as a participant in a community and on your commitments and passions.

Managing and leading an MNE successfully in an emerging market is no easy task. For example, an MNE leadership must understand and address effectively the general management challenges composed of three broad spheres (Bartlett & Ghoshal, 2002; Hofstede, 1993):

1. Management orientations adopted by the MNE: From which country an MNE should build its staff while operating in foreign markets? Should an MNE bring staff from its home country versus host country or other countries? Generally, ethnocentric management orientation encourages organization to hire home country staff whereas polycentric management orientation encourages organization to bring in staff from the host country. Geocentric and region-centric management orientations support the philosophy and practice of hiring staff from other countries other than the home and host countries. Each of these management orientations has its own specific pros and cons.
2. Organizational architecture involving control mechanisms (HQ and subsidiary relationship). MNEs have to make a choice between giving full power, partial power or no power over decision making aspects to the subsidiaries. In making such choices MNEs should consider a variety of factors, for instances, the nature of the business, the role of the subsidiary and its importance for the corporation and certain specific characteristics (i.e., political, economic, industrial) of a geographic market.
3. Corporate culture management: MNE should also make a choice between adopting the management practices, styles and work culture of the home country versus the host country. Of the three potential choices: imposing home country's culture on host country, or adopting local cultures, or bringing a cultural synergy, MNEs can better opt for the cultural synergy between the home and host country management practices and organizational cultures.

In summary, the general management philosophy and practice of MNEs should reflect not only business and transactional centered approach but also and crucially important the general welfare of employees, managers, customers, community and small competitors must be safeguarded in a manner that should in-turn be beneficial for the MNE. Simply, by having an inclusive management system whereby developing local skills and talent is a big step forward towards an integrative business management by MNEs. The negative perception of the MNEs of being rival to the local political and economic system and dangerous for the indigenous industries is removed by adopting integrative management philosophy and models. The Boston Consulting Group finds that MNEs with their entire top management team sitting in the headquarters can be outperformed by their competitors with some of their top managers handling frontline issues.

Organizational Design and Operational Philosophy

The subject of organizational design is as much important as the subject of managing and governing an enterprise. And even more, these two organizational variables must go hand in hand in order to avoid administrative imbalances, deficiency, and resource mismanagement. During the past few decades, MNEs mainly located their foreign subsidiaries in their home region (Rugman, 2005) and, to some extent, in other regions of the Triad (USA, Japan and Europe) (Flores & Aguilera, 2007). Over the last few years, MNEs from mature economies have heavily increased their investments in developing countries (Dunning 2009), mostly in emerging markets. The role of foreign subsidiaries located in emerging countries has thus considerably increased. This evolution is raising new challenges for the relationships of MNEs with their foreign subsidiaries. In fact, subsidiaries of MNEs are embedded in their local environment (Hennart, 2009), establishing relationships with different local actors including governments, suppliers, distributors, and clients, etc. (Asmussen, 2009). Moreover, the environment of emerging economies differs considerably from the environment of mature markets (Ghemawat & Hout, 2008). It thus seems interesting to examine more specifically the role of location in headquarters-subsidiaries relationships. Given the changing geography of the world economy (Buckley & Ghauri, 2004) and the changing rules of international competition this question seems particularly relevant for MNEs (Hutzschenreuter & Gröne, 2009). Lenartowicz and Johnson (2007) find that there is no one size fits all solution for MNEs operating in foreign markets. Therefore, a combination of different strategies can be helpful here. These authors suggest few important steps in this direction:

1. To attract the host nationals who are currently working or studying in the home country of the MNE.
2. To hire people from the host country and give them intensive trainings involving corporate related issues, job related aspects and social issues.
3. To improve the cross-cultural training provided to expatriate managers. And MNEs should invest in training their expatriates in both soft and hard skills.

All organizations have to make provisions for continuing activities directed towards the achievement of aims. Regularities in activities such as task allocation, supervision, and coordination are developed. Such regularities constitute the organization's structure, and the fact that these activities can be arranged various ways and means that organization can have differing structure. The allocation of responsibilities, the grouping of functions, decision-making, coordination, control, reward, all these are fundamental requirements for the continued operation of an organization. The quality of an organization's structure can affect how well these activities are managed or met. MNEs have four possible management options to deal with their subsidiaries (Bartlett & Ghoshal, 2002):

1. Coordinated federation: In this operational system if adopted, MNEs headquarters or head-offices empower to a certain extent their subsidiaries located in different geographic zones of the world. Such empowerment consists in allowing local subsidiaries to make decisions which are about the daily activities and operations of the company independently from the headquarters. Operational decisions may include for example, hiring local staff, redesigning and modifying the product to adjust it to the local needs, and developing marketing and promotion strategies which locally fit etc. However, under the coordinated federation operational system, head-office keeps the power of

decision-making regarding key and strategic aspects of the business management such as developing a new product, key managers, key assets and research & development.

2. Decentralized federation: Under such operational systems, MNEs fully empower their subsidiaries to make decisions both strategic and operational on their own and thus making them independent from the headquarters. In such operational systems the relationship between the head-office and subsidiary is merely based on information sharing, reporting relationship and financial transactions.
3. Centralized hub: This operational system is just the opposite of the decentralized federation where MNEs´ headquarters or head-offices exercise full and strong control over both strategic and operational decision making aspects of the business management. Such organizational-administrative systems make foreign subsidiaries fully dependent on the headquarters for every decision making aspect of the business.
4. Network or strategic business units: Under the network organizational system, headquarters and subsidiaries work together as strategic business units whereby sharing power, resources, experiences and technologies. So, the concept and practice of having a head-office with superpower and subsidiary being a child-partner in business disappear to a greater extent under such an operational system. Each strategic business unit is given a certain specific role to play within the network organizational system depending on the geographic location and other operational capabilities.

In the existing literature on the organizational system, MNEs managers may also find a number of other options of organizational structures which are considered as conventional structure or design alternatives. The details on these organizational structural alternatives are discussed in the posterior Chapter on Organizational Design & Operational System.

1. Product/service based structure.
2. Functional/activity based structure.
3. Area/geographic/market based structure.
4. Process-based structure.
5. Customer-based structure.
6. Mixed structure.
7. Matrix structure.

One of the many challenges, an MNE manager can face is the challenge of how to design and maintain its organizational-operational systems given the dynamic and globalized business world which is characterized by these diverse forces:

1. Global efficiency in every business functions and activity.
2. Global quality standards in every business functions and activity.
3. Globalization vs localization (how much to be globally scaled and how much to be locally responsive).
4. Technological advancements in the field of transportation, communication, production and management.
5. New global business rules and standards.
6. Human rights involving labor rights.
7. Democratization of global political system, freedom of expression, freedom of media and emerging social networks.
8. Need for worldwide learning and global knowledge/talent.

Furthermore, combined together these forces stimulate MNEs leaders to rethink about their strategic orientation and changes in organizational capabilities. After all, an organizational structure is a means for attaining the goals of an organization effectively and efficiently. An organizational structure is also about the extent to which the organizational members are constrained and controlled by the organization, the distribution of activities and responsibilities, and the organizational procedures and regulations are undertaken. Therefore, changes in strategies often require changes in the structure of the organization because structure dictates how objectives and policies will be established and resources allocated.

The Management Culture of MNEs

Management in the organizational context is broadly defined as getting things done through other people. Managers make decisions, allocate resources, and direct the activities of others to attain goals. Corporations are business organizations and management is about the process and people involved in that process (managers) Hofstede (1993). Though certain management practices are universally applicable, however, some other management aspects vary from culture to culture (Culpan & Kucukemiroglu, 1993; Pheng & Yuquan, 2002). Having said that it is important for MNEs operating in foreign markets or entering into alliances with organizations beyond their national boarders to understand and take into account the differences found in management practices across national cultures since business operations are increasingly becoming global (Hofstede & Bond, 1991). MNEs management styles can be influenced by various organizational variables including values, norms, ethical codes, rules and regulations for example, and such variables vary across national cultures. Definitely, cultural variables do influence managerial functions, roles and responsibilities (Laurent, 1983; Mead, 1998). Management style is about how managers behave and function when dealing with employees inside the company. Management style is the set of principles by which managers capitalize on the abilities of their employees (Schleh, 1977). Some management cultures accept and promote the work culture where managers are responsible for organizing, planning, coordinating, decision making and they have the authority and control over organizational resources. Whereas, some other cultures emphasize on the notion that employees should be treated well, managers should delegate authority and resources to their employees and managers are coaches and mentors (McGregor, 1960; Ouchi, 1981; Brozik, 1994). The management culture is composed of variables such as management style, decision making process, staffing procedures, interpersonal trust and confidence, commitment, control, importance of relationship, team work and role of nature (Greer & Stephens, 1996; Johnson & Sholes, 2007). The management culture also includes the power structure, organizational structure, functional policies and management systems (Johnson & Sholes, 2007; Heller & Yukl, 1969; Goodale, 1973). Management cultures are influenced by the external forces associated with the industrial practices and national characteristics (Gordon & Williams, 2001; DeForrest, 1994). The management culture is also about the values, rules, practices and norms through which organizations manage their business operations (Brache, 2002; Schien, 1985; Titieve, 1959). A strong and dynamic management culture is fundamental for the organizational competitive advantage and sustainability. Therefore, MNEs should nourish a work environment where such a management system is learned, developed and shared across the organizational systems and operations.

The Social Responsibility Challenge

The business, society and government must go hand in hand. Businesses develop and supply products and services to people and thus satisfying their needs, demands, and interests. Businesses make people life easier, comfortable and interesting. Corporates provide jobs to people and pay taxes to the governments. Corporations promote quality life, education, health and other life amenities. People working in companies have opportunities to travel around the globe, receive cross cultural understandings and professional trainings. Because of the tangible and intangible benefits and values created by the business operations for the community around them, social problems such as crimes, poverty, corruption, illiteracy and health issues are at marginal levels. The social responsibility of business organizations is about taking into full considerations the social, economic and environmental issues of nation states where they operate. Therefore, business social responsibility is not only about giving out charities, donations or other philanthropy related funds to the community, but it is also about considering fully the whole package of issues and concerns derived from the business operations: the workplace, the marketplace, the supply chain, the community, and the public policy realm (Zhang, 2008). Business social responsibility is defined as the duty of the organizations to respect the rights of individuals and promote human welfare while conducting their businesses (Manakkalathil & Rudolf, 2005). Writers, activists and business leaders alike, encourage companies to develop specific codes of conduct outlining their objectives, duties and obligations while operating in international market (Manakkalathil & Rudolf, 2005). While conducting businesses in emerging countries, MNEs are expected to be socially responsible in many ways (Manakkalathil & Rudolf, 2005):

- Being ethical.
- Law abiding.
- Economic contribution.
- Protecting consumer rights and interests.
- Respecting the natural environmental.
- Avoid all forms of discriminations.
- Promoting worker safety and welfare.
- Protecting shareholders.

The social responsibility for companies is even bigger when doing business in developing countries where lack of opportunities for the people on the bottom of the pyramid is far greater than in developed nations. In developing countries human rights in general and labor rights in particular are equal to non-existence. For employees workplace safety and job security are also growing concerns in these countries. Therefore, MNEs should use their capital, skills and power to play a proactive role in handling worldwide social and economic problems. At least MNEs should be concerned about the host country´s problems and be partner with local government in solving national problems. MNEs can bring about positive impacts on host countries by providing managerial training, investing capital, new technology, creating jobs and improving infrastructure.

There is no doubt that MNEs can do good things for the host country but it is a hard job for MNEs to address a variety of ethical questions (i.e., Michael, 2005):

1. Should managers of MNE´s subsidiaries base their ethical standards on those of the host country or those of the home country or can be reconciled?
2. What is moral responsibility of expatriate regarding ethical behavior? And how do these issues affect business objectives?
3. How do expatriates simultaneously balance their responsibility to various stakeholders and organizational issues?

A challenging task for the management of MNEs is to integrate the general social responsibility philosophy into its daily operational system by (i.e., Tan, 2009):

1. Creating a safe workplace, produce quality products, and exceeding customer expectations.
2. Developing effective communication system through training programs to employees on how to meet the standards.
3. Designing a formal organization system to support the organization's efforts to change. Policies and procedures should be written. Responsibility should be given to someone credible with a support system.
4. Reinforcing the organization's stated agenda with actions not just words Actions must match the stated goals and ideals.
5. Adopting strategic goals that would move it closer to the stated ideal.
6. Placing measure and rewards in support of the agenda.

The general public (community) should believe that an MNE is serious about the issues like safe organization, quality organization and stakeholder orientation. MNEs social challenges also involve answering these critical questions and putting into practice actions in support of the belief that an MNE should not harm the social fabric of a society (geographic area) in which they operate. One of the greatest challenges inherited by an MNE is to have a balanced approach to business objectives of cost efficiency, productivity, profitability, and social objectives. An MNE can follow the following paths to become socially responsible (DeGeorge, 1993):

1. Do no intentional direct harm.
2. Produce more good than harm for the host country.
3. Contribute by their activity to the host country's development.
4. Respect the human rights of their employees.
5. Respect the local culture and work with and not against it.
6. Pay their fair share of taxes.
7. Cooperate with local government in developing ethical institutions.

Similarly, MNEs can learn from the International Codes of Conducts for Multinational Enterprises provided by several supranational institutions as given below. International codes of conducts are any agreements, declarations, guidelines proposed or published by an international organization that make recommendations or rules about the behavior of multinational enterprises.

1. Organization for Economic Cooperation and Development.
2. International Labor Organization (ILO).
3. United Nations Commission on Transnational Corporations (UN/CTC).
4. International Chamber of Commerce (ICC).
5. European Community Code of Conduct for companies with interests in South Africa.
6. US Foreign Corrupt Practices Act-1977, against US companies using bribery in foreign affiliates.

Tan (2009) suggests that both MNEs and host countries should deal with issues like the overall institutional environment including legal framework, ethical culture, industry associations and local firms. Bennet (2002) is of the view that multinational companies operating across borders should bear some responsibility for the well-being of local communities. Bennet (2002) believes that multinational enterprises have both the power and responsibility to foster goodwill among the people of the nations where they operate. MNEs can and should invest, innovate, and create locally. MNEs can hugely impact the overall economic wellbeing of the local-host communities by executing the following concrete actions, for instances (Bennett, 2002):

1. Design an economic support programs in order to reduce poverty at the grass-root level.
2. Create awareness programs to promote small-local entrepreneurship.
3. Fund social development and environmental protection programs on regular basis.
4. Hire and train local employees which consequently improves the local talent and family income.
5. Initiate community development projects to build schools, hospitals and roads in areas where such services are in shortage.

Measuring the MNEs Performance

The performance measurement techniques used by MNEs in general and which measurement technique is the most appropriate for evaluating MNEs performance in emerging markets in particular are also emerging challenges for the MNEs managers. Generally speaking, MNEs performance can be measured by looking at three different levels or areas of the company: overall business performance in terms of market shares, customer size, revenue generation and profitability; organizational performance in terms of the corporate image, goodwill, acceptability by the local community, organizational stability, corporate culture; and management performance in terms of organizational relationships with stakeholders especially with suppliers, distributors and business partners. The performance of an MNE can also be measured by looking into their performance at these different levels:

1. Strategic levels: This includes the company geographic location, strategic partnerships, core business distinctiveness and market positioning.
2. Business levels: This includes amongst others, the different product lines management, product differentiation, cost and quality management, branding, and pricing strategies, etc.).
3. Functional level: This is composed of more operational variables for example, production system, packaging, distribution, human resources, and marketing etc.

In the industrial world, a variety of performance measurement mechanisms are available for MNEs to base on and each of these mechanisms has its own strengths and weaknesses. A balanced and practically viable combination of these different but interrelated variables or indicators can and will provide MNEs a clear picture of their achievements both in the short and long run. Some of the performance measurement mechanisms are short listed below for the MNEs manager to consider:

- Competitive index.
- Ethics and corporate social responsibility (CSR).
- Quality certification.
- Stakeholder analysis.
- Financial statement analysis.
- Innovation index.
- Total quality management.
- Management by objectives (MBO) method.
- Key performance indicators.

Other commonly used performance measurement systems in the industry are Six Sigma Methodology, Balanced Scorecard, Benchmarking, and Customer Relationship Management. For example, the Six Sigma Method is used to eliminate defects associated with production process by defining, measuring, analyzing, improving and controlling the process. Several companies in different industries already use this method for example, GE, IBM, Ford Motor, Whirpool, and Toyota Automotive Industry (Jacobs, & Chase, 2011). The Balanced Scorecard as a strategy management tool (planning, execution and evaluation) is basically aligns organizational activities to the mission and vision of the company. It also improves efficiency in the process, communication, decision making and measures the progress (targets vs achievements) in four different areas such as customer satisfaction, internal process efficiency, learning and growth and financial indicators (Kaplan & Norton 1992). Benchmarking on the other hand provides a reference point for companies to learn from other business organizations and resultantly improve their organizational and business efficiency. Companies such as Xerox, General Electric, Microsoft and Starbucks (Gillen, 2001) use this method for self-performance analysis. The Customer Relationship Management (also known as CRM) is basically based on indicators which demonstrate the company approaches to build, maintain and improve a business relationship with customers. The CRM involves learning about the customer needs, interests and satisfaction, and based on that information designing business strategies to increase value for the customer. Companies in different sectors like Phone, Internet, Financial Services, Retail, Professional Services Industry, and restaurants such as IHOP use CRM for self-evaluation (Rgiby, 2013).

Managing National Competitive Disadvantages

Another challenge for MNEs entering developing countries is to cope with the national disadvantages of these countries ranging from low industrial activities, corporate mafia to lack of individual competencies to natural calamities. Adding to the complexities is the historical background of nations including their foreign relations, internal national conflicts and natural disasters which further deteriorate the competitiveness of nations and as held belief no nation is spared from such phenomenon. Similarly, other national attributes for example, the level of social progress, political stability, economic development and technological advances indicate the competitive advantage or disadvantage of a nation.

In order to main national competitive advantage developing nations have to learn from nations like Germany, Britain, France, USA, and Japan since these nations have been able to build up a highly competitive home market which demands quality, highly educated, skilled, and motivated workforce. Industrial standards are high, transparent and equally applied for all players. Business organizations and national institutions invest in research, human development, and technological development (Weihrich, 1999). In almost all of the indicators used by the following global indexes, the emerging markets show visibly low performance in that crimes, corruption and other risks are high but innovation, growth and competitiveness indicators evidently much lower than their developed counterparts.

- Innovation index.
- Competitive index.
- Higher education index.
- Health index.
- Risk index.
- Growth index.
- Happiness index.
- Crime index.
- Corruption index.

Why are some national environments more conducive to firm growth and prosperity than others? According to Porter (1990) nation states are like business organizations with their own unique resources and capabilities and similarly nation states' competitiveness and competitive advantages depend on how such resources and capabilities are managed and utilized over a long period of time. Nations must be efficient and effective in utilizing their available resources and build on their comparative advantages over other nations. Another key point in national competitive advantage is its image like brand/product image which is hugely responsible for the success and failure of national products and services in the international markets since there is direct link between the national competitive advantage and firm´s level competitive advantage (Porter, 1990). Like corporate images (brand names) as of IBM, Microsoft and Apple, made-in or assembled-in the USA, Germany, UK, France or in China and Russia, make a big difference when products and services from those countries are exchanged in international markets (Kotler et. al., 1997). The national competitive advantage is lost when the following conditions are created (Porter, 1990; Kotler et. al., 1997):

1. When a nation falls behind in creating and upgrading factors leading to national competitive advantage such as natural resources including energy, water, land and electricity etc.
2. Skills of specialized human resources are not updated relative to another nation.
3. Rising factor costs because of mismanagement and mal-utilization.
4. Failing to deregulate an industry that has been deregulated elsewhere.
5. Ebbing domestic rivalry reduce the pressure of innovation and improvement.
6. Technological change is often a trigger for shifts in national advantage since new technology require a shift in factors creating disadvantage in terms of available human resources, knowledge, or infrastructure. New technology change may also create the need for new supporting industry that a does not possess where a nation has leading suppliers of new input may take over the competitive advantage.
7. The rate of investment in R&D, marketing, information, and physical assets is not consistent with goal of the firm.

8. Management practices and form of organization are rigid.
9. Union restriction and local regulations which impede new innovation is expensive.

Human Capital Challenges for MNEs

One of the many challenges described earlier in the chapter is the human capital management challenge facing MNEs while doing business in the developing markets. The human capital challenge include finding qualified and motivated workers, developing motivation strategies which are successful across work conditions and environment, and managing the knowledge workforce across cultures. MNEs require finding out a talent management system in order to cope with the emerging challenges derived from the mass globalization of products, services, technology and people. It is a universally accepted phenomenon that organizational problems are the creation of people and can only be solved by people themselves. "The world's best companies know that their future is in the hands of a small number of highly talented and productive staff. Therefore, over 70 percent of companies in Europe are constantly looking for talented workforce that will enrich their human potential. The importance of attracting and retaining talent in any organization is similar to the importance and need for football clubs to have the best players. Talents are the ones who contribute the most to the development and achievement of goals, and the creation of additional value for the organization (Kjiroski, 2014)". In the existing literature on international human resource management, major concerns facing business managers are listed as below (Hashim & Hameed, 2012):

- Employee productivity
- Job satisfaction
- Turnover
- Absenteeism
- Human relations skills
- Technical skills
- Conceptual and design skills
- Critical thinking
- Emotional intelligence
- EntreprenuershipWorkforce diversity
- Organizational effectiveness
- Change management
- Maintenance & equal employment
- Globalization
- Leadership development
- Electronic Commerce
- Human Resource Functions 21st century
- Human resource planning
- Job Analysis design
- Recruitment and Selection
- Orientation and Induction
- Training and Development
- Promotion/Transfer/Termination

- Compensation and remuneration
- Motivation, welfare, health and safety
- Industrial Relation
- Technology Health and safety
- Learning and development
- Recruitment and skill labor
- Succession planning
  Compensation

The role and importance of human resources have been evolving with the evolution of organizations and business environment. A variety of attributions have been used to describe human resources in the industrial context such as: factory workers; personnel; human resources; human capital, social capital; knowledge force; and talent management (May, 2014). Regardless of the definition and interpretation, employee management is one of the key driving forces in achieving sustainable organizational productivity and growth. Committed, loyal and happy employees can become a powerful force more than any other forces behind the competitive advantages of the company in all situations. "With the increased rate of globalization, a firm's ability to compete in a global environment becomes increasingly contingent on having the right people. Pressures from competitors, shareholders and customers require people that can create new products, services and processes ahead of the competition (Brockbank, 1999; Bala, 2011)".

International Relations and Diplomacy

The role of international relations and diplomacy is fundamental for the initiation and promotion of bilateral and multilateral business and economic relations. MNEs can play a vital role in influencing the policies and programs of their respective governments and political leadership in advancing international relations. Historically, economics and business have played important role in bringing even warring nations together such as the European Economic Union, the Triad nations: Europe; Japan and the USA for example. Political boycotts of products made in a country considered enemy country have also been seen in the history of international business and international business. The boycott of Israeli products or severing business and economic relations by Islamic countries over the Palestine conflict and the boycott of French products by American after the Iraqi-US war are few such examples. The economic and business sanctions imposed on North Korea, Russia, Iran and Cuba are other examples of international relations and diplomacy. Diaconu and Cuza (2008) explain that MNEs operating in the global markets influence and are influenced by the political, economical, social and cultural environment of the host country. Such influences can be positive and negative. The positive influence can be the net contribution to the trade balance of the host developing country by producing goods that used to be imported (import substitution) and which can ever be exported (reversal of the direction of trade). Also because of their international experience and advanced technology, MNEs are likely to be more productive than their local counterparts and that is why they can offer higher salaries or employee benefits to the employees (Lipsey, 2002). Furthermore, MNEs ca have a positive influence not only on the national markets, raising up the average level of the salaries, but also on the other national firms, determining them either to implement modern methods and technologies, or to attract the labor force that previously had been trained in the multinationals (Malchow-Moller & Markusen, 2007). Diplomatic relations include trade relations, commercial relations, socio-cultural relations, and business to business relations, political and strategic relations. Diplomatic relations among nations exist through histories for different purposes and at different levels.

MNEs and the World of Information and Communication Technology

The current world population of over 6 billion is predicted to grow slowly and gradually. In some nations in Europe and North America, the human population is foreseen declining but the global population in general is going to keep increasing. And the growth of information and communication technologies is expected to expand even faster and further. Mobile phones have already become personal electronic companions, combining computer, GPS, telephone, camera, alarm clock, research assistance, projector, music player, flashlight, newspaper, movie theater, translator, TV, thousands of apps, even on-call armed protectors at the touch of an icon. Collaborative systems, social networks, and collective intelligences are self-organizing into new forms of transnational democracies that address issues and opportunities. This will cause the formation of collective intelligence for businesses which lead to the formation of new kinds of organizations with abilities to solve problems and take advantage of opportunities without conventional management (The Millennium Project, 2010). The challenge for MNEs is to play successfully in the world of Internet while adopting advances in technology which will require resource allocation, knowledge workforce and organizational flexibility.

What is Next for MNEs Doing Business in Developing Countries?

The big questions in the mind of every business management thinker and industry practitioner are:

1. What is next for the existing MNEs and the MNEs to emerge in the near future?
2. Are the challenges going to remain the same?
3. If challenges are going to change then what types of new challenges are going to emerge?
4. Are these MNEs remaining the same in their way of doing business, management system, organizational structure, size and location?
5. How much MNEs are going to depend on new technologies?
6. What mode of doing business these MNEs should pursue?
7. Which strategy is the most effective and appropriate for the MNEs to operate successfully in emerging markets or countries?

The one best answer to the above questions in lump-sum is that the new business dynamic is always and will remain unpredictable. Business organizations whether small, medium size or big ought to remain proactive, flexible, innovative and receptive. All big companies will disappear and be replaced by more agile small companies or by completely new genetically engineered species of virtual corporations. Managing business across borders is an ideal way to develop skills required for managing companies of all kinds in the future corporations. Corporations will be local and global, big and small, decentralized with central reporting and control. Integrated network organization with characteristics like environmentally-friendly, strategic, organizational-operational flexibility, and with managers of high caliber are going to emerge. MNEs will have to develop entrepreneurial process driving the opportunity-seeking, externally focused ability of the organization to open new markets and create new business. MNEs will have to have an integration process allowing it to link and leverage its dispersed worldwide resources and capabilities to a successful company. MNEs will have to have renewal process that maintains its ability to challenging its own beliefs and practices and to continuously revitalize itself so as to develop an enduring institution. Motivation for companies expanding abroad will shift from focusing on new markets or low cost productive inputs to a worldwide search for vital intelligence or scarce competencies not available in the home market. MNEs will be named as Entrepreneurial Transnational Corporations built around core entrepreneurial process that will drive everybody and everything the company does. The company workers will be called entrepreneurs, leaders and coaches. Companies will create management approach to start with opportunity and capitalize upon innovation, creativity, and excellence of people to secure the future of the company (Gutierrez, Spencer, & Zhu, 2012).

FINAL THOUGHTS AND FUTURE DIRECTION

Developing countries continue presenting opportunities for MNEs to do business and keep growing in different dimensions. Moreover, developing countries are democratizing, liberalizing, and becoming investment-friendly. Multinational business agreements and regional associations such as SAARC, ASEAN, BRICS, and Next Eleven, are some of the current business building blocks of the developing nations in the world. Free market orientations, removal of trade barriers and industrial policies and standards of many developing countries are attracting new investments and business partnerships. In order to tap the emerging opportunities in developing countries, MNEs should be innovative, entrepreneurial and dynamic. They need to invest more in market research, product development, and human talent development and management. It is no hidden fact that more than 80% of the world population lives in developing countries including India and China which in turn presents a huge market base for any products and services. Investment return can be relatively higher than the matured or developed markets where growth rate is marginal and business cost is much higher (i.e. Noorani, 2001; Van de Kuil, 2008; Fan, 2008).

MNEs can overcome many of the problems facing emerging markets to a greater extent by demonstrating that their presence is beneficial for the host country in many ways: Improve their balance of payments, increase their exports and earn more hard currencies, reduce imports and save more of their hard currencies, reduce unemployment and improve their fiscal position, and improve their access to higher technologies. In addition, MNEs need to improve their capabilities to develop strong local leaders, create localized business models, and establish growth targets and execution plans -- all capabilities where the performance gap exceeds 20 percent (Boston Consulting Group, 2013). MNEs should first establish themselves in their home countries and then successfully expand into global markets (Veliyath & Brouthers, 2010). Partnerships and strategic alliances with local business and collaboration with local institutions are successful strategies: collaborate and win. MNEs are expected to become more responsible socially in the larger interest of the business organization itself and the society at large. All relevant players including companies, social activists, investors, employees, consumers and government should establish long-term bonds in order to make this happen and identify further opportunities of collaborations and joint efforts. MNEs challenges in emerging countries are to exist and continue in one way or the other in future as long as it takes for these nations to bring about radical reforms and improvements in their existing modus operandi: economic reforms; institutional reforms, infrastructure development; human resource development; political stability and creating an investment friendly environment (Zhang; 2008; Khanna, Palepu & Sinha, 2005). MNEs operating in emerging countries have a number of viable options not only to counterattack timely and effectively those challenges but also to translate them into opportunities:

1. Improve product and service quality.
2. Improve information, production and marketing technologies.
3. Improve economic competitive factors (labor costs, interest rates, exchange rates and economies of scale.
4. Influence trade regulations by establishing close relationship with the government and affiliation with associations (business, political or economic).
5. Develop global orientation such as thinking and planning globally vise-vis locally.
6. Hiring internationally experienced managers and emphasizing upon human resource and work policies and attitude.
7. Investment in global research and development.
8. Being socially responsible and environmentally friendly.

It is also incumbent upon the leadership of emerging nations to create an investment friendly environment for the domestic as well as the foreign MNEs seeking investment in their countries. Sauvant, Maschek and McAllister (2009) propose for emerging nations to undertake measures like the following:

1. The provision of information and technical support.
2. Availability of cheap financial support on time.
3. Fiscal incentives including tax holidays and subsidies in in the initial stages of the establishment of a business.
4. Investment insurance and guaranteed.
5. International investment related agreements.
6. Other institutional support programs to expedite the business start-up activities
7. Remove unnecessary bureaucratic hurdles.
8. Availability of all basic facilities and services including energy and raw materials etc.

At the end of the day MNEs and national governments have no other options except to work in a collaborative manner in order meet these challenges and have a win-win outcome for both of them.

REFERENCES

Arnold, D. J., & Quelch, J. A. (1998). New Strategies in Emerging Markets. *Sloan Management Review*. Retrieved from http://sloanreview.mit.edu/article/new-strategies-in-emerging-markets/

Asmussen, C. G. (2009). Local, Regional, or Global? Quantifying MNE Geographic Scope. *Journal of International Business Studies*, *40*(9), 1192–1205. doi:10.1057/jibs.2008.85

Bala, Y. (2011). *The new human resources management in the 21st century: a strategic view*. Annual Conference on Innovations in Business & Management, London, UK. Retrieved from http://www.cibmp.org/Papers/Paper519.pdf

Bartlett, C. A., & Ghoshal, S. (2002). *Managing Across Borders: The Transnational Solution*. Harvard Business Press.

Bennet, J. (2002). Multinational corporations, social responsibility and conflict. *Journal of International Affairs*, 393. Retrieved from http://0proquest.umi.com.millenium.itesm.mx/

Boets, I. (2008). *Managing Risk in Emerging Markets: An overview of common risk factors in emerging markets and lessons learned from organizations that have ventured into this arena*. Retrieved from http://www.cga-canada.org/en-ca/AboutCGACanada/CGAMagazine/2008/Nov-Dec/Pages/ca_2008_11-12_bsin_feature.aspx

Boston Consulting Group. (2013). *Multinational Companies Target High Growth in Emerging Markets Despite Challenges, A BCG Survey Reveals That Execution Holds Back the High Ambitions of Global Companies*. Retrieved from http://www.marketwired.com/press-release/multinational-companies-target-high-growth-in-emerging-markets-despite-challenges-1830340.htm

Brache, A. P. (2002). *How organizations work*. New York, NY: John Wiley & Sons, Inc.

Breemen, D. (2014). *Five reasons why foreign MNC's fail in China*. Retrieved from https://www.linkedin.com/today/post/article/20140415073136-109792243-five-reasons-why-foreign-mnc-s-fail-in-china/

Brockbank, W. (1999). If HR were really strategically proactive: Present and future directions in HR's contribution to competitive advantage. *Human Resource Management*, *38*(4), 337–352. doi:10.1002/(SICI)1099-050X(199924)38:4<337::AID-HRM8>3.0.CO;2-5

Brozik, D. (1994). The second dimensions for successful management. *Manage*, *45*(4), 4–8.

Buckley, P., & Ghauri, P. (2004). Globalisation, Economic Geography and the Strategy of the Multinational Enterprises. *Journal of International Business Studies*, *35*(2), 81–98. doi:10.1057/palgrave.jibs.8400076

Buckley, P. J., & Casson, C. C. (1998). Analyzing Foreign Market Entry Strategies: Extending the Internalization Approach. *Journal of International Business Studies*, *29*(3).

Collis, D. (2014). *International Strategy: Context, Concepts and Implications*. John Wiley & Sons, Inc.

Culpan, R., & Kucukemiroglu, O. (1993). A Comparison of U.S. and Japanese Management Styles and Unit Effectiveness. *Management International Review*, *33*(1), 27–42.

DeForrest, M. E. (1994). Thinking of a Plant in Mexico? *The Academy of Management Executive*, *8*(1), 33–40.

DeGeorge, R. T. (1993). *Competing with Integrity in International Business*. New York: Oxford University Press.

Diaconu, L., & Cuza, A. L. (2008). *The multinational companies and the emerging markets*. Retrieved from http://steconomice.uoradea.ro/anale/volume/2008/v1-international-business-and-european-integration/018.pdf/

Dominion CSR. (n.d.). Retrieved from http://www.dominioncsr.com/business/risk_management.php

Dunning, J. (2009). Location and the Multinational Enterprise: A Neglected Factor? *Journal of International Business Studies*, *40*(1), 5–19. doi:10.1057/jibs.2008.74

Edmonton. (n.d.). Retrieved from http://www.edmonton.ca/city_government/documents/ERM_CBRP_Model_Sept_05.pdf

Eyring, M. J., Johnson, M. W., & Nair, H. (2011). *New Business Models in Emerging Markets*. Retrieved from http://hbr.org/2011/01/new-business-models-in-emerging-markets

Fan, Y. (2008). The rise of emerging market multinationals and its impact on marketing. *Marketing Intelligence & Planning*, *26*(4), 353–358. doi:10.1108/02634500810879269

Flores, R. G., & Aguilera, R. V. (2007). Globalization and location choice: an analysis of US multinational firms in 1980 and 2000. *Journal of International Studies*, 1-2. Retrieved from www.jibs.net

Geppert, M. (2005). Global, National and Local Practices in Multinational Corporations – Towards a Socio-political Framework. *International Journal of Human Resource Management*.

Ghemawat, P., & Hout, T. (2008). Tomorrow's Global Giants. Not the Usual Suspects. *Harvard Business Review*, *86*(11), 80–88.

Gillen, D. (2001). *Benchmarking and performance measurement: the role in quality management. Amsterdam*. Retrieved from School of Business & Economics - Wilfrid Laurier University website: https://www.wlu.ca/documents/4293/Benchmarking.pdf

Goodale, J. (1973). Effects of Personal Background and Training on Work Values of the hard-core unemployed. *The Journal of Applied Psychology*, *57*(1), 1–9. doi:10.1037/h0034190

Gordon, G., & Williams, T. (2001). How do you Spell Success in Mexico? CALICA. *Business Horizons*, *44*(1), 11–18. doi:10.1016/S0007-6813(01)80003-3

Greer, S. K., & Stephens, C. (1996). Employee issues for companies in Mexico. *California Management Review*, *38*(3), 121–145. doi:10.2307/41165846

Guarino, P. (2010). *Emerging Markets: Growth, Opportunities and Challenges*. Retrieved from http://www.elementiconsulting.com/insights/emerging-markets-growth-opportunities-and-challenges/

Guillen, M., & Garcia-Canal, E. (2013). *Emerging Markets Rule: Growth Strategies of the New Global Giants*. McGraw-Hill. Retrieved from http://knowledge.wharton.upenn.edu/article/emerging-market-multinationals-new-giants-on-the-block/

Gutierrez, B., Spencer, S. M., & Zhu, G. (2012). Thinking globally, leading locally:Chinese, Indian, and Western leadership. *Cross Cultural Management*, *19*(1), 67–86. doi:10.1108/13527601211195637

Hashim, M., & Hameed, F. (2012). Human Resource Management in 21st Century: Issues & Challenges & Possible Solutions to Attain Competitiveness. *International Journal of Academic Research in Business and Social Sciences*, *2*(9). Retrieved from http://www.hrmars.com/admin/pics/1090.pdf

Heller, F. A., & Yukl, G. (1969). Participation, managerial decision-making and situational variables. *Organizational Behavior and Human Performance*, *4*(3), 227–241. doi:10.1016/0030-5073(69)90007-5

Hennart, J. F. (2009). Down with MNE-Centric Theories! Market Entry and Expansion as the Bundling of MNE and Local Assets. *Journal of International Business Studies*, *40*(9), 1432–1454. doi:10.1057/jibs.2009.42

Hofstede, G. (1993). Cultural constraints in management theories. *The Executive*, *7*(1), 81–95.

Hofstede, G., & Bond, M. H. (1988). The Confucius connection: From cultural roots to economic Growth. *Organizational Dynamics*, *16*(4), 4–21. doi:10.1016/0090-2616(88)90009-5

Jacobs, F. R., & Chase, R. B. (2011). *Operations and Suply Chain Managemet* (13th ed.). Singapore: McGraw-Hill Education.

Johnson, G., & Scholes, K. (2007). *Exploring Corporate Strategy.* Financial Times/Prentice Hall.

Kaplan, R. S., & Norton, D. (1992). The Balanced Scorecard: Measures that Drive Performance. *Harvard Business Review*, *70*(1), 71–79. PMID:10119714

Kaplan, R. S., & Norton, D. P. (2005). The Balanced Scorecard: Measures That Drive Performance. *Harvard Business Review.* Retrieved from https://hbr.org/2005/07/the-balanced-scorecard-measures-that-drive-performance

Khanna, T., Palepu, K. G., & Sinha, J. (2005). Strategies That Fit Emerging Markets. *Harvard Business Review*. Retrieved from http://hbr.org/2005/06/strategies-that-fit-emerging-markets/ar/1

Kjiroski, I. (2014). *Human resource management –new challenges in the modern era*. Retrieved from http://www.eapm.org/wp-content/uploads/2014/05/Macedonia-HRM-challenges-of-the-modern-era.pdf

Komives, S. R., Lucas, N., & McMahon, T. R. (2013). *Exploring Leadership: For College Students Who Want to Make a Difference* (3rd ed.). Jossey-Bass.

Kotler, P., Jatusripitak, S., & Maesincee, S. (1997). *The marketing of nations*. New York: The Free Press.

Kourdi, J. (2009). *Business Strategy: A Guide to Taking Your Business Forward*. John Wiley & Sons.

Krechowicz, D., & Hiranya, F. (2009). *Emerging Risks: Impacts of Key Environmental Trends in Emerging Asia*. Retrieved from http://www.wri.org/publication/emerging-risks/

Kvint, V. (2015). *Strategy for the Global Market: Theory and Practical Applications*. Academic Press.

Lasserre, P. (2007). Global Strategic Management (2nd ed.). Palgrave Macmillan.

Laurent, A. (1983). The cultural diversity of Western conceptions of management. *International Studies of Management & Organization*, *13*(1-2), 75–96. doi:10.1080/00208825.1983.11656359

Lenartowicz, T., & Johnson, J. P. (2007). Staffing managerial positions in emerging markets: A cultural perspective. *International Journal of Emerging Markets*, *2*(3), 207–214. doi:10.1108/17468800710758369

Lilie, M., Patrick, R., & Lindblom, S. (2012). *International Finance Corporation Risk Taking: A Corporate Governance Perspective*. Retrieved from http://www.ifc.org/wps/wcm/connect/9ff11a804c40464698dddaf12db12449/RiskGovJuly2012.pdf

Lipsey, R. E. (2002). *Home and Host Country Effects of FDI*. NBER Working Paper No. 9293. JEL No. F21, F23, O01, O03, O04.

Malchow-Moller, N., Markusen, J. R., & Schjerning, B. (2007). *An analysis Foreign firms, domestic wages*. Working Paper 13001. Retrieved from http://www.nber.org/papers/w13001

Manakkalathil, J., & Rudolf, E. (2005). Corporate Social Responsibility in International Development: An Overview and critique. *Journal of Advanced Management*. Retrieved from http://0-proquest.umi.com.millenium.itesm.mx/

May, K. E. (2014). *Work in the 21st Century: The Changing Role of Human Resources*. Terranova Consulting Group Society for Industrial and Organizational Psychology. Retrieved from http://www.siop.org/tip/backissues/tipjan98/may.aspx

McGregor, D. (1960). *The human side of enterprise*. New York: McGraw-Hill.

Mead, R. (1998). *International management* (2nd ed.). Cambridge, MA: Blackwell Publishers.

Meyer, K. E., & Thu Tran, Y. T. (2004). *Entry and growth strategies for emerging economies*. Retrieved from http://r4d.dfid.gov.uk/PDF/Outputs/CNEM/dp38.pdf

Michael, B. (2005). *Corporate social responsibility in International Development: an overview and critique*. ABI/INFORM Global.

Moffett, M. H., Stonehill, A. I., & Editeman, D. (2003). *Fundamentals of Multinational Finance*. Pearson Education, Inc.

Noorani, H. (2001). *Foreign Investment in Emerging Economies*. Retrieved from http://www.powerfulmethods.com/FIEE.pdf

OECD Investment Division. (n.d.). Retrieved from www.oecd.org/investment/gfi-8/

Ouchi, W. G. (1981). *Theory Z: How can American business meet the Japanese challenge*. Reading, MA: Addison-Wesley. doi:10.1016/0007-6813(81)90031-8

Peng, M. W. (2006). Making M&A fly in China. *Harvard Business Review*, *84*(3), 26–27.

Pheng, L. S., & Yuquan, S. (2002). An exploratory study of Hofstede's cross-cultural dimensions in construction projects. *Management Decision*, *40*(1), 7–16. doi:10.1108/00251740210423036

Porter, M. (1990). *The Competitive Advantage of Nations*. New York: The Free Press. doi:10.1007/978-1-349-11336-1

Rajaram, V. R., & Lance, B. L. (2010). How Emerging Market Firms Compete in Global Markets. *Journal of Emerging Knowledge on Emerging Markets*, 2. Retrieved from http://digitalcommons.kennesaw.edu/cgi/viewcontent.cgi?article=1017&context=jekem/

Rigby, D. K. (2013). *Management tools 2013 - An executives guide*. Boston: Bain & Company, Inc.

Root, F. (1994). *Entry Strategies for International markets*. Routledge.

Rugman, A. (2005). *The Regional Multinationals*. Cambridge, UK: Cambridge University Press. doi:10.1017/CBO9780511614071

Sauvant, P. K., Maschek, W. A., & McAllister. (2009). *Foreign direct investment by emerging market multinational enterprises, the impact of the financial crisis and recession and challenges ahead*. OECD Global Forum on International Investment.

Schein, E. H. (1985). *Organizational Culture and Leadership*. San Francisco, CA: Jossey-Bass.

Schleh, E. C. (1977). A matter of management style. *Management Review*, *66*(8), 8–14.

Tan, J. (2009). Multinational Corporations and Social Responsibility in Emerging Markets: Opportunities and Challenges for Research and Practice. *Journal of Business Ethics*, *1*(32), 55–75.

The Economist. (2013). *Multinationals in emerging markets, Must try harder. The ambitions of Western firms in emerging markets far exceed their efforts*. Retrieved from http://www.economist.com/news/business/21586320-ambitions-western-firms-emerging-markets-far-exceed-their-efforts-must-try-harder

The Millennium Project. (2010). *Some Elements of the Next Global Economic System: How Might These New Elements Affect the Human Condition over the Next 20 Years?*. Retrieved from http://www.millennium-project.org/millennium/RTD-Econ.html

Titiev, M. (1958). *Introduction to Cultural Anthropology*. New York: Henry Holt and Co.

Van de Kuil, A. (2008). *Strategies of multinational corporations in the emerging markets China and India*. GRIN Publishing GmbH. Retrieved from http://www.grin.com/en/e-book/117743/strategies-of-multinational-corporations-in-the-emerging-markets-china/

Veliyath, R. & Brouthers, L. (2010). How Emerging Market Firms Compete in Global Markets. *Journal of Emerging Knowledge on Emerging Markets*, *2*(3).

Weihrich, H. (1999). Analyzing the competitive advantages and disadvantages of Germany with the tows matrix—an alternative to porter's model. *European Business Review*, *99*(1), 9–22. doi:10.1108/09555349910251822

Zhang, F. (2008). *Corporate Social Responsibility in Emerging Markets: The Role of Multinational Corporations*. An Initial Paper for the Launch of the Foreign Policy Centre Project on "Corporate Responsibility in Emerging Markets" in association with Coca-Cola Great Britain.

KEY TERMS AND DEFINITIONS

Business Performance Measurement: Explains different methods, mechanisms, tools available for an MNE to measure its business and organizational performance in international business. To decide about which of these performance measurement mechanisms for example, financial analysis tools, balanced scorecard, stakeholder analysis or KPIs a challenging task for the company managers.

Ethics and Corporate Social Responsibility: How much an MNE should be held responsible for the benefits and welfare of the general society living arounds it, let alone its direct or primary stakeholders? Which ethical codes of conducts (of the host country, of the home country or of the supranational institutions) an MNE and its managers must abide by while doing business in foreign markets?

Growth Paths: Growth path means the business and investment options, modes and alternatives pursued by a particular company in order to grow internationally. A company can grow through export, licensing, franchising or direct investment.

Growth Strategies: Growth strategies mean that the specific actions and moves undertaken by a company in order to grow and expand internationally. A company can grow through market diversification, product diversification, vertical integration, horizontal integration or conglomerate diversification for example.

Institutional Leadership: This explains the overall governance infrastructure of the company including its management and leadership styles and corporate management culture.

International Diplomacy: Analyzes the importance of the role of diplomacy and relationships between countries for the success of international business.

MNE: Multinational enterprises or business organizations with business operations in several countries or markets with major ownerships and management control of the business.

Organizational Structure and Design: Organizational structure and design demonstrate the overall organizational and operational system of the company operating globally. Simply, it means how organizational activities, functions, resources and other control mechanisms are distributed, allocated, and coordinated inside the company. Especially, how the relationship between the main or core office and its regional offices (or subsidiaries) is defined and maintained.

Chapter 2
Strategic Options for MNEs Operating in Emerging Markets

Andreas M. Hartmann
Tecnológico de Monterrey, Mexico

ABSTRACT

This chapter outlines some of the basic opportunities, conditions, and strategic options for firms operating in emerging markets. Increasing FDI figures show that emerging markets offer many opportunities for foreign investors, but also pose specific challenges for doing business. Some factors are more abundant and less expensive, especially low to medium-skilled labor and natural resources, while sophisticated services are more difficult to obtain. A specific characteristic of emerging markets is the lack of business-enabling intermediaries. Therefore, foreign MNEs frequently need to fulfill tasks that are not within their range of activities in their home countries. Additionally, many governments in emerging economies act slowly and erratically; and laws are often not enforced systematically. In this context, foreign MNEs can choose between acquiring a local company, partnering up, or going it alone. The chapter looks at the pros and cons of these modes of internationalization and presents some concluding comments on the flexibility required by working under such conditions.

INTRODUCTION

Any company with significant operations in more than one country is a multinational enterprise (MNE) by definition. When the general conditions between the two or more countries are relatively similar, going international does not require major departures from the ways of doing business in the company's home base. Expanding operations from a developed country to an emerging economy, however, often demands significant changes. This chapter deals with the conditions and opportunities of such moves.

The traditional literature on multinational enterprises and their options for expanding into new markets has centered on two major themes: location choice and entry mode choice. For the first of these topics, there has been a certain discrepancy between the academic focus and the decision horizon for acting managers: While scholars prefer to look at the obstacles to internationalization that derive from cultural, administrative, geographic, and economic differences (Ghemawat, 2003), often under the label

DOI: 10.4018/978-1-5225-0276-0.ch002

of "liability of foreignness" (cf. Denk, Kaufmann, & Roesch, 2012), practitioners are more concerned with opportunities opened through internationalization: On the supply side, the main motives are the availability of production factors, such as cheap or qualified labor, raw materials, or strategic locations, while on the demand side, growing and increasingly wealthy populations translate into market opportunities for goods and services to be sold to consumers, companies, and authorities. The second choice addressed by the scholarly literature on internationalization concerns the question whether a foreign enterprise should find a partner in the host country or whether it is preferable to establish a wholly owned subsidiary (either as a greenfield investment or through an acquisition), exposing the company to all the risks but also keeping full control and all of the expected benefits. Both research topics are typically framed as either-or decisions, where a company invests either in country A or in country B and then either operates with a partner or goes it alone.

The present chapter tries to deal with these issues a bit more from a practitioners' perspective: In many cases, the options for expanding are rather clear: Small firms need to consider issues of proximity or serendipity to expand into those countries where internationalization does not impose an excessive burden on their scarce financial and managerial resources. Large firms, on the other hand, need to access large markets with growth potential, such as the BRIC countries, or countries with abundant resources in order to keep up with international competitors. Once the location decision has been made, entry mode is often dictated by circumstances: The Chinese government, for example, requires foreign firms in many industries to work with a domestic partner. In other circumstances, finding a suitable partner might prove difficult. A third focus on strategic options for internationalization complements home-country activities with functions located in foreign country, thereby establishing internationally distributed value chains that take advantage of each location's particular strengths (cf. Coe, Dicken, & Hess, 2008).

This chapter is organized as follows: The first part establishes the general importance of emerging markets for MNEs from developed countries. The second part deals with the external conditions that these emerging markets offer to or impose on firms. The third part presents the option space for MNEs in the emerging market context. The concluding section looks at flexibility in investing abroad and at the special challenges of maintaining ethical business practices in countries with weak enforcement of regulations.

CONTEXT: THE INCREASING IMPORTANCE OF EMERGING MARKETS FOR MNES FROM DEVELOPED COUNTRIES

Even if the emerging economies still lag behind the developed countries in almost all socioeconomic indicators, they now have collectively become the target for more than half of the world's foreign direct investment. According to the 2014 World Investment Report, "FDI flows to developing economies reached a new high at $778 billion, accounting for 54 per cent of global inflows, although the growth rate slowed to 7 per cent, compared with an average growth rate over the past 10 years of 17 per cent" (UNCTAD, 2014: xiii). On the other hand, the developing economies accounted only for 32.3% of worldwide FDI outflows, which shows that the most common direction is still from developed to emerging countries.

The attractiveness of emerging economies as markets lies in their demographic and economic growth, which translates into growing markets for products and services. On the other hand, emerging economies often hold a plethora of underexploited resources ranging from raw materials to semi-qualified labor. These structural attractors are further enhanced by national governments inviting foreign firms through special mechanisms such as free-trade zones and tax exemptions, or national development policies like the one that jump-started the Chinese economy under Deng Xiaoping in the late 1970s. International free-trade agreements have also increased the attractiveness of some countries for FDI; for example, Mexico is becoming the prime manufacturing location for cars sold in the NAFTA area, while the Republic of South Africa is increasingly functioning as a platform for exporting industrial goods to many African countries.

The general trend of increasingly globalized markets has also increased competitive pressures. In many industries, MNEs that want to sell products to local customers need to be close to them in order to understand their specific needs and complement their offer through services produced at their foreign subsidiaries or with the help of local partners. From the supply side, there has been an ongoing trend to shifting labor-intensive activities to lower-cost countries. Some industries that used to be strongly concentrated in developed countries have almost completely offshored their production over the past decades (e.g., the garment industry), with a pattern of moving on whenever costs increase in one country, a part of the so-called "flying geese" phenomenon among East Asian nations (cf. Ozawa, 2011). In other industries, value-added activities have been fragmented among low-cost and high-cost countries, benefitting from an increased flexibility in the MNE's global network. The results have led to a partial de-industrialization of developed countries and a simultaneous build-up of manufacturing capacities in emerging economies. These trends are still going on and have included some service industries, too. For example, the US-based computer and software company IBM has now probably more employees in India then in its home country (Thibodeau, 2012). Only few products are not susceptible to global mobility: On one hand, some premium brands are associated with their places of origin, such as Bordeaux wines and Italian shoes. On the other hand, highly sophisticated products requiring complex networks of specialists often cannot be reproduced in other locations, so advanced robots are still being designed, manufactured, and exported from Japan.

Even among small and medium-size enterprises, there is a tendency to go abroad since the early stages, a phenomenon that has been labeled as "international new ventures" (cf. Oviatt & McDougall, 1994) or "born globals" (cf. Knight & Cavusgil, 2004). In contrast to more firmly established, large firms, such small ventures benefit from higher degrees of flexibility that allow them to actively explore and exploit opportunities for selling their goods or services in a foreign market or for finding attractive inputs abroad. One basic option for developing such multinational business models is to arbitrage price differentials between developed and emerging nations. Of course such multinational SMEs are barely noticeable in the statistics; however, they may constitute the first step of international expansion of what may well be tomorrow's large enterprises.

THE EXTERNAL CONDITIONS FOR OPERATING IN EMERGING MARKETS

Although there are complete books available on the topic of "Doing business in emerging markets" (cf. the homonymous book by Cavusgil, Ghauri, & Akcal, 2013), a neat distinction between developed and emerging economies is virtually impossible. What is more, the concept of "emergence" itself indicates that less developed countries are on a path towards a greater resemblance to advanced nations. The most notable examples of such ascendance in economic and societal status are the nations formerly known as "Asian Tigers" (Hong Kong, Singapore, South Korea, and Taiwan), which since the 1960s have worked their way into the club of developed nations. In the light of such ambiguities, the author has chosen to focus on some commonalities in factor conditions, governmental frameworks, and their practical implications for conducting business in emerging economies.

Factor Conditions: Relative Abundance and Scarcity Compared to Developed Countries

One of the factors that emerging markets have in common when compared to the developed economies is the basic structure of their economic systems: For most countries, the development process goes hand in hand with a decreasing proportion of agricultural activities, accompanied first by an increase of manufacturing, and then a dominance of a (sophisticated) service sector. Combined with these stages of development, emerging economies tend to have an abundance of unqualified labor while specialist knowledge needs to be imported from countries that have invested heavily in their human capital over several generations. Simultaneously, developed economies normally offer a sophisticated infrastructure in terms of logistics, health care, etc., while getting the same service level in emerging economies may be cumbersome, expensive, or even impossible. Some of these gaps have been closed thanks to cheaply available communication technologies, as witnessed by the cell phone boom in many African countries, while other disadvantageous factor conditions still exist.

On the positive side, emerging economies allow to produce both goods and services at a significantly lower cost, especially where labor cost is a major factor in the value chain. Additionally, emerging economies represent the most important growth potential in the world economy, while most developing economies are stagnating both in population and in GDP growth. For firms based in a country with an ageing or even shrinking population, such as Japan, going into emerging markets is thus a long-term survival imperative.

A special case within this developed-emerging dichotomy are those countries who have become rich based on the natural resources found in their grounds or territorial waters, such as the Arab Gulf states, whose oil income has allowed them to buy in foreign technology and service systems, which are then operated mostly by foreign workers.

Many emerging markets are perceived as being more risky than developing economies. Political risk factors include sudden changes in governmental politics ranging from cancellation or granting of permits or subsidies for specific businesses, over price controls for both inputs and end products, to expropriation of foreign firms. In some countries, civil unrest or even terrorism or warfare can make it almost impossible to operate business normally. On the other hand, economic risk includes general downturns, exchange rate volatility, and credit defaults. In the age of global capital markets, a financial crisis in one country can affect other economies, as evidenced by the spread of the so-called Tequila crisis that originated in Mexico in 1994-1995, and then triggered the withdrawal of funds from other Latin American and Asian economies. Even in the face of generalized crises such as the one derived from the subprime mortgage meltdown in the USA, the general perception is that emerging economies pose far greater risks than developed ones, in spite of decades of uninterrupted high GDP growth in mainland China, for example. Within the Country Risk Ratings elaborated by credit insurer Euler Hermes (2015), all "AA" ratings for medium-term risk are given to developed nations, echoing the risk premium that emerging-market firms have to pay for raising funds internationally. One wonders if this general discrimination is based more on objective data or constitutes more a case of behavioral finance based on investors' herd mentality that leads to self-fulfilling prophecies. The same Euler Hermes list (2015) for the short term classifies many emerging economies as "low risk", which include countries from Africa (e.g., Botswana, Morocco), Asia (e.g., China, India), and Latin America (e.g., Chile, Panama), while many Southern and Southeastern European countries, which would normally be regarded as developed, vary between medium and high risk scores. The point is that firms would be ill advised to base their location decisions on a developed vs. emerging dichotomy, as both groups of countries contain enormous variations in risks and opportunities.

Global Value Chain Integration

The coexistence of differently priced production factors described in the previous paragraphs, in combination with the prevalence of WTO rules and regional trade agreements sets the stage for all kinds of value chain integration between countries and regions of the world. For example, the world's best known sports goods brands locate design and marketing activities in their home countries, while manufacturing is usually outsourced to countries in Asia or Latin America. Another example of the worldwide distribution of value chains is Business Process Outsourcing, where workers in low cost countries process files, handle customer calls, or write code for clients in developing countries. A third example would be universities located in the UK, the USA, or Australia that use their high academic standings to attract the children of well-to-do people in China and other emerging economies, who study either in their original countries or at newly created campuses located in the emerging economies. The actual ownership and control of these processes is a matter of economic convenience and organizational capabilities.

Lower-Quality Inputs and Institutional Voids

Probably, the firm with the highest degree of vertical integration in industrial history was Ford Motor Co., which owned its own steel mills and until WW2, even attempted to produce its own rubber in Brazil in order to secure a steady supply of raw material for tires. However, it has become evident that such an all-encompassing production system does not stand up to competitive pressures: Today's auto firms only add about 25% of the value in the final assembly process; the rest is bought in from suppliers (Maxton & Wormald, 2004). Typically, sophisticated industrial products can only be manufactured by connecting many links forming distributed value chains. This is the point where transplanting a production system from a developed country to an emerging economy becomes difficult, as many of the product and service suppliers either do not exist or are unable to provide the same level of inputs for their customers. Additionally, market intermediaries such as financial services or logistics companies do not provide the same level of service, a situation that is perceived by developed country firms as "institutional voids" (Khanna & Paleppu, 2010), generally considered to be a major obstacle to further development.

Implications for Practical Operation

In practical terms, there is a series of actions that firms most likely will have to undertake when entering an emerging economy. The first step is required even before the official opening of foreign operations: In most target countries with weak government structures, it is important to establish connections with officials to secure their goodwill for dealing with an often ambiguous or intricate business legislation. This requires either befriending government officials directly or hiring intermediaries. In mainland China, for example, there are individuals that offer their *guanxi* (connections) for sale (cf. Seligman, 1999). Of course, foreign managers should be aware of the thin line between little gifts and favors offered – including so-called facilitation payments for speeding up legal procedures – and active bribery with the intent of obtaining illicit advantages. Governments and regulators in many emerging economies do not see it as a priority to even the path for foreign investor beyond the bringing in of a formal commitment for FDI. There are some official indicators, such as the World Bank's *Doing Business* data sets (cf. www.doingbusiness.org), which show the specific conditions for registering a company, obtaining building permits, etc., of which some are even available at the level of regions or cities within certain countries. These indicators provide a general idea about the time and money required to set up shop in a new country.

Another matter of concern is the skill level of the human resources available, which will very much depend on the quality of the pertaining country's national education system. While some industries, such as tourism, apparel, and food processing can function with a majority of workers with little training and even limited literacy, many middle-tech industries require a combination of lowly and highly skilled workers. These conditions restrict the choices of location for FDI between and within countries and often require foreign firms to invest heavily in training where they could simply hire skilled personnel in their home countries. These training requirements slow down or occasionally even disrupt operations, especially in the early phases, and require a substantial input provided by cost-intensive expatriates. In these training phases, the availability of a common language or bilingual individuals as well as a basic understanding of cultural differences become tantamount.

For securing a steady operation of their subsidiaries in emerging markets, firms also have to provide for some basic services that in other places are either assured by the government or can be paid for by the workers themselves, thanks to higher salary levels. Many foreign firms thus offer subsidized food and/or housing for their workers, install daycare facilities for working mothers, and offer shuttle services between their facilities and the neighborhoods where most of their workers live. Another additional effort might be required concerning in-house security, as many emerging countries do not have very effective police forces.

The Role of Government in Emerging Economies

Compared to its counterparts in developed countries, the governmental institutions in emerging economies are often not as fully developed or effective. This leaves room for unregulated areas in business or unenforced regulations, which are evident by the vast role that the informal economy plays in such countries. This lack of order in many product, service and labor markets is sometimes compensated by abrupt changes in laws or applications, which disrupt existing business schemes. In spite of the politics put into practice, it will be hard to find a national government anywhere in the developing world that does not proclaim its support for economic development. These declarations stand in contrast to the countless anecdotes about governmental failures in emerging economies, ranging from large-scale corruption in many African countries, law suits in India that take so long they are passed on to the plaintiff's heirs, to an unwillingness of Chinese authorities to enforce the protection of intellectual property. Fortunately, there have been several efforts by multinational organizations to present more objective data on the relative functioning of governmental institutions throughout the world: Since 2002, the World Bank Group has been publishing its Ease of Doing Business indicators that include eleven items grouped into "complexity and cost of the regulatory environment" and "strength of legal institutions" (cf. http://www.doingbusiness.org). Among the highest-ranked countries, we find not only Western countries with long-standing institutions and democratic traditions, but also the so-called "Asian tigers", notably Singapore, Hong Kong, and South Korea. At the bottom end of the scale, there are several African countries suffering from internal ethnic strive or the war-torn Afghanistan, but also Venezuela, whose socialist government has nationalized many foreign companies (the even more extreme cases of Cuba and North Korea are not included in the list). Most emerging economies, however, are located somewhere in the middle of the ranking, meaning that difficulties with regulations and government officials are to be expected and do affect business development, but can be managed with patience and by nurturing local contacts.

A more ideologically tinted approach to measuring the quality of institutions for business are the different measures of economic freedom, such as the one published by the US-based Heritage Foundation (cf. http://www.heritage.org/index/ranking). Although the outcome of these ranking are not too different from the more objective *Doing Business* indicator mentioned above, focusing exclusively on economic freedom obviates the enabling conditions of effective government regulations (cf. Kitching, Hart, & Wilson, 2015). Foreign firms that need to protect their intellectual property, for example, are not necessarily favored by a laissez-faire capitalism. In any event, the differences in business conditions between developed and emerging economies lie not so much in the terms of rules and regulations as in the consistency of their enforcement. Unfortunately, the lack of regulatory oversight might attract some foreign investors inclined to commit labor abuses and ecological misdemeanors, while discouraging other firms that care about their internal ethics and external reputation.

A correlated view of the business conditions in emerging markets is offered by Transparency International's *Corruption Perception Index* (CPI), which – according to the NGO itself – "has been widely credited with putting the issue of corruption on the international policy agenda" (Transparency International, 2015). In the 2014 CPI report, it is hardly surprising that, among the 174 countries listed, from position 70 downward, one finds only emerging economies and developing countries. On the other hand, some emerging economies are perceived to be only slightly corrupted; for example, Chile and Uruguay jointly occupy rank 21, right between the USA and Austria.

It is hard to ascertain whether adverse governmental conditions really dissuade potential FDI from developed countries when there are promising market or resource opportunity. Due to the unavailability of data about aborted FDI projects, this question can only be answered indirectly, through the conditions that prompt multinational companies to exit countries where they have invested in wholly owned subsidiaries. One factor that does prompt MNEs to withdraw from a country is exposure to armed conflict (cf. Dai, Eden, & Beamish, 2013). In other cases, an unfavorable business environment may nudge foreign MNEs to prefer working with a local partner.

THE OPTION SPACE FOR MNEs

Under the circumstances outlined above, foreign companies have to make some critical decisions about how to deal with the existing conditions. One of the main questions is whether the entry into an emerging economies is carried out in one bold move or rather stepwise, as a learning trajectory for the firm going abroad. Another issue is how much the original business model can be or should be adapted to local conditions. Based on these preliminary considerations, managers must choose an entry mode between acquisitions, partnering, and greenfield investments.

The Role of Strategic Planning

The rational view of strategic planning presents the decision making process for important issues –such as internationalization– as being based on a set of objective data, where executives weigh the pros and cons of different options within a long-term plan that contributes to the growth and profitability of the company. While this may be true for large companies with deep financial pockets and sufficient managerial capacity, many smaller or younger companies grow opportunistically, responding to a perceived growth potential within their sphere of personal and business contacts. In such a way, they might venture into a new country when they have a previous business partner, or when a foreign client asks them to build a presence in order to serve her or him locally. Such forms of induced internationalization are closer to the classical model of stepwise internationalization (Johanson & Vahlne, 1977), according to which manufacturing companies build their foreign presence little by little in order to reduce the risk of unknown business conditions in foreign countries. What we observe today is the co-existence of several internationalization models: gradual expansion close to the home country, internationalization as part of the original business strategy ("born globals"), and steady network building by major MNEs.

Behind these modes of internationalization lies the idea of learning to do business abroad: A company that has mastered doing business in two foreign countries will probably have developed some kind of "contextual intelligence" (Khanna, 2014) that will enable it to adapt more easily to subsequent locations. These learning effects apply not only to cultural aspects of the pertaining countries, such as religious prescriptions or the role of hierarchy within firms but also to institutional factors (cf. Castañer & Genç, 2011): A developing-country firm that has learnt to deal with a partially dysfunctional government in one part of the world may be able to transfer that knowledge to a new country where similar government failures exist.

Adapting the Business Model to Local Conditions

Probably the most critical element in a firm's internationalization process is establishing fruitful relationships with local suppliers, clients, and authorities. However, businesses differ widely in how much local embeddedness they require. For mentioning two examples from service industries: An airline will not have a lot of difficulties in operating at a new foreign destination, as most aviation-related issues are standardized internationally, while a health care operator has to invest a lot of time and effort to adopt to local regulations and the work rules established by local associations of physicians and other health care professionals. Getting embedded in a foreign country is a job that can be partially outsourced. For example, so-called shelter companies in Mexico not only rent out industrial buildings to small foreign manufacturers but also provide different services such as hiring and payroll, all kinds of legal matters including registration of a newly established company, as well as handling taxes and social security issues. Combined with the expanded supply chain management services offered by integrated logistics companies, the initial operation can concentrate on technical matters, although such a solution is normally more costly and in the long run, foreign companies will prefer to take many matters in their own hands.

A different but related question is whether a company can just transplant its home-country business model to a new destination or whether it needs to introduce major modifications. Wherever possible, most decision makers will opt for a stripped-down replica of home-country operations, which can be supported by the continued transfer of inputs from the headquarters. However, such foreign subsidiaries "on a drip" are costly to run and do not provide an adequate mechanism for adopting to the home country. Ultimately, a foreign firm in a new environment is often forced to engage in learning by doing. In extreme cases, these learning processes can take many years –Khanna (2014) reports that a German-based retailer took fourteen years to turn a profit in China–, which is precisely why small firms tend to avoid such endeavors. The learning cycle can be shortened by acquiring an ongoing local concern or by selecting a local partner. Both modes of internationalization require a lot of flexibility, where only the basic rules and objectives can be determined from the headquarters' drawing board, while the specific means have to be adjusted to the specific context.

A major aspect in planning the internationalization of a firm is how quickly the presence in a new country should be established when going beyond mere exportations. The speed of internalization matters most whenever other competitors may beat the focal firm to a new market. Sometimes, new investment opportunities might open up surprisingly, triggering a quick response, especially when local governments ease up prior restrictions for foreign economic activities. Figure 1 lists the basic options for expanding a company, roughly ordered by decreasing speed.

International Mergers and Acquisitions

The difference between takeovers and acquisitions lies in the attitudes of owners and managers at the target firms: While takeovers are defined as a unilateral process where the target firms' needs for continuity in employment and partner relationships are not taken into consideration, acquisitions usually involve a lengthy process where managers and/or owners of both firms exchange information. A key element of this process is the so-called due diligence, i.e., a detailed review of accounting and other documents in order to establish the real value of the target firm and to detect potential problems. When the pair of firms involved has approximately the same size, the result may be a merger that is co-managed and often jointly owned, which is symbolized through a new firm name that may be a combination of the two original ones. In practice, however, real mergers occur seldom, as in the end, usually one of the firm takes control of the merged entities. In general, mergers and acquisitions constitute the quickest path to gaining a sizable position in a foreign market, offering an operating production and service network, proven relationships with suppliers and government authorities, and often an established brand, all of which could take years to build up in a foreign country. A point in case is the global beer industry, where international brewing giants have been buying up local brands in both developed and emerging economies, often keeping the most successful local brands while adding one or two of their international premium brands to be distributed through the newly acquired logistics network (cf. Gammelgaard & Dörrenbächer, 2013). In many emerging economies, however, this option for expanding abroad might be limited: If the firms are considered to be of strategic importance, the local government may restrict foreign ownership. On the other hand, the dominant organizational form in many emerging economies is family capitalism, and families may be very reluctant to sell businesses which have often been the backbone of their livelihood for generations. Another limitation for pursuing an M&A strategy for entering emerging markets is the mere availability of options: Per definition, emerging markets do not include all kinds of industries at a comparable level of development, so M&As are often limited to low and middle-tech industries. In high tech industries, the only option for foreign firms wishing to establish a presence is to start a new business from scratch. Sometimes, there is an opportunity to upgrade an existing facility through a substantial investment both in personnel training and in the previously existing production and service infrastructure, but such "brownfield entries" (Meyer & Estrin, 2001) are not necessarily much speedier than newly established subsidiaries.

Figure 1. Growth options ordered by relative speed

Partnership Approaches for Entering Emerging Economies

Success in a foreign country largely depends on finding the right partners. At the very minimum, these partners are some local providers and customers (except for pure export-oriented production); at the maximum, a local partner firm manages almost all operations in the name of the investing firm, such as in most franchising arrangements. Essentially, partnering with a local firm transfers the risk inherent in one company's inexperience in dealing with local conditions to a relational risk within the partnership, including issues like unsatisfactory inter-firm cooperation, lack of commitment from one partner, self-interest to the detriment of the other partner, distorting information, hidden agenda, delivering defective products, etc. (Das & Teng, 1999).

The major incentive for finding an adequate partner is the complementarity of resources, which is often given between firms from developing and emerging economies. The classical combination consists of a developed-country firm bringing in its technology with our without branding to be used in the new location, and an emerging-economy firm contributing with its distribution systems, although the increasing technological sophistication of many emerging-economy firms has led to partnerships with a reversed combination of capabilities. In any event, this very difference in capabilities is also a potential source of conflicts deriving from differences in management styles and systems. Corporate cultures might be more or less aligned with general national characteristics, but each firm is different and some knowledge of the partner's internal functioning should precede a definite partnership commitment. Care-

Table 1. Dimensions of international strategic partnerships

Purpose and scope • Products to manufacture • Services to deliver • Technologies to develop Governance • Decision rights of partners • Dependence/Independence of Joint Venture Resources committed • Money • Employees • Key technical specialists • Key managers	Time span • Permanent or temporary • Long term or short term Networking • Government • Suppliers • Customers Legal arrangements • Degree of formalization • Dependence or independence • Jurisdiction Adaptability • Dispute resolution mechanisms • Flexibility over time

ful consideration should therefore be given to the relative sizes of the partners: A junior partner might be easier to dominate, but will it have the sufficient strength to push the development of the intended business? On the other hand, if the partner firm is large in its own right and/or already operates other IJVs, its degree of commitment to the joint undertaking might be insufficient. In any case, establishing a successful partnership requires an intensive planning and negotiation process; Table 1 presents a list of issues to be addressed in such negotiations.

A common legal form of strategic partnering are international joint ventures (IJVs), where a foreign firm and a local entity invest equity in a new legal entity. In some countries, such as mainland China, governments mandate such forms of governance for the most important industries, while restricting foreigners completely from investing in other areas, deemed to be vital for the country's economic or military security. For example, IJVs are still the dominant players in China's auto market, the largest in the world by number of vehicles sold. The German-based Volkswagen group, for example, manages two large IJVs with Chinese partners, as well as several smaller ones. The Chinese auto makers still depend on technology from Western, Japanese, and South Korean manufacturers, which some have tried to overcome through acquisitions abroad and others by copying foreign products. The reaction by technology-rich companies has been to control access to key technologies and/or to offer a limited range of models to their Chinese partners.

Under different circumstances, partnering might be the preferred choice of entry for foreign firms. The classical configuration is a developed-country firm that provides technological and managerial skills working together with an emerging-economy partner that brings in manpower, distribution, and marketing. However, such partnerships are not necessarily stable, as the collaboration allows each of the partner to learn a significant part of the other's skills, rendering the partner's contribution superfluous. As a result, one of the partner often ends up acquiring the other one, if the legal framework allows full foreign ownership.

Another form of cooperation that is frequently found in service industries are licensing and franchising agreements, where the major benefit for the emerging-economy partner is the established brand that attracts the aspiring middle classes. Franchising agreements exist both for individual operations and for country-wide operations. For example, the Mexican Alsea group holds the master franchises for US-based food chains such as Burger King, Domino's Pizza, and Starbucks, among others, which they manage in several Latin American countries, in a combination of direct operation and sub-franchising (Alsea, s.d.). From the franchise owner's point of view, this kind of agreement takes away the complication of dealing with government permits, sanitary regulations, real estate management, and subtle local adaptations while guaranteeing a steady stream of income. On the downside, it introduces a major dependency on the franchisor, which cannot easily been replaced, even in the possible event of a (perceived) breach of contract.

The uncertainty involved when dealing with foreign partners have been experienced by French yoghurt maker Danone in its different locations: In Mexico, Danonc operated alone and after some years, had developed a culturally compatible management style that allowed it to function successfully (d'Iribarne, 2007). In Asia, however, Danone pursued a series of joint ventures with local partners that turned out well in most cases but also included a conspicuous failure in China (Anwar, 2009). The Chinese partner had operated a parallel yoghurt business using Danone's technology, which led to a legal dispute that even prompted the intervention of the French government. After years of bitter feuding, in 2009, Danone sold its stake in the JV to its former partner (Barboza, 2009). In contrast, Danone's French competitor Sodiaal entered most countries in the less risky form of franchising agreements. Its yoghurt brand Yoplait, for example, has been sold by Mexican firm Sigma Alimentos since 1994 without any major incidents (CNNExpansión, 2012). However, it seems that this strategy did not allow Sodiaal to build sufficient financial strength to subsist as a global player on its own; so in 2011, its US-based franchisee General Mills acquired 51% of the Yoplait brand. These contrasting stories illustrate the risks and the rewards of the different forms of international expansion.

Going It Alone: Greenfield Investments in Emerging Economies

When companies from developed countries cannot find suitable acquisition targets nor desirable partners, their only choice for entering a new country is to go alone. In principle, this is the slowest form of internationalization, as everything has to be built from scratch, especially the network of ties to all kinds of local partners and government agencies. Industrial plants, for example, require often several years until reaching their full productive capacity. Often, the start of production in emerging economies is delayed by bureaucratic hold-ups, non-compliance of local partners, or low skills of local employees. On the plus side, a greenfield investment leaves the foreign company in full control of planning and operations. Often, bicultural employees turn into key elements for the success of such investments.

SOME CONCLUSIONS: FLEXIBILITY, ETHICS, AND GROWTH OPPORTUNITIES

With the availability of almost costless, worldwide communication and easy travel and transportation, firms have the opportunity to use their operations in different countries as a flexible network, where they can shift some parts of their activities to more convenient locations whenever conditions change (cf. Kogut & Kulatilaka, 1994). These choices are not only between offshoring (locating an activity in another country) and onshoring or reshoring (bringing back an activity) of a full production process, but also include the possibility of slicing up or integrating larger parts of the corresponding value chains. Both for reducing risk and for giving the organization time to learn and adapt, a first step into a foreign country –and especially an emerging economy with the characteristics outlined above– may include only a portion of the total value-adding activities, to be expanded as the firm acquires experience in the new environment and/or the target country's infrastructure and resource capabilities improve over time. For a firm that operates in several countries, frequent shifts of activities according to relative prices and market opportunities can be part of normal operations. Furthermore, the constant adaptation of the network requires a mentality that looks for differentiation between foreign subsidiaries, instead of assuming them to me symmetric (Bartlett & Beamish, 2011). Especially, subsidiaries in emerging markets will have roles that are very distinct from others in developed countries, tailored to local factor and market conditions. Although such highly differentiated networks offer the opportunity to make the best use of resources in both developed and emerging economies, they impose a burden on the MNE's overall management. The need to manage a national subsidiary according to local conditions often clashes with efforts to streamline management systems on a global scale. In the face of such complexity, many MNEs have opted for specializing on certain products or services while shedding others or for reducing their depth of production in favor of a closer cooperation with both worldwide suppliers and local partner firms.

At the end of this chapter, a word of caution might be in order: There have been and still are too many cases where companies from developed nations have lowered their standards when operating in emerging economies. Often, there is no effective governmental control to prevent child labor, shameless exploitation of workers, or hazardous working conditions. Even if the foreign investors are not committing these abuses themselves, they are morally and sometimes also legally responsible for what goes on at their suppliers and partner firms. The turning point for the sports goods and apparel industry was the Nike case, where public pressure forced the world's leading sports good firm to set up a system of compliance for its suppliers (cf. Morris & Lawrence, 2001). Unfortunately, firms that do not sell end-consumer products are a lot less susceptible to public pressure that would lead to increased monitoring of practices in its supply chains. From cases like the Siemens corruption scandal (cf. Crawford & Esterl, 2007), it should also be obvious that firms from richer countries are not necessarily morally superior to what are perceived to be more corrupted countries.

There is no doubt that most of the future growth opportunities around the world lie in emerging markets. China's growth rates alone are now considered to be an important element of the global business cycle. However, growth potential exists not only in Asia. Several African countries seem to be on a steady growth path (cf. The Economist, 2011, Dec 3), while there is both light and shadow among the Latin American economies. Foreign firms that learn to deal with these places' specific conditions will become or remain as leaders in their fields, turning into the effective winners of the ongoing globalization process.

REFERENCES

Alsea. (n.d.). *Investor Relations.* Accessed 2015, Jun 17: http://www.alsea.net/relacion-con-inversionistas/unidades-alsea/unidades-alsea/en/es/es/es/

Anwar, S. T. (2011). Cultural misunderstanding: The Danone-Wahaha joint venture in China. In H. Deresky (Ed.), *International Management: Managing Across Borders and Cultures* (7th ed.; pp. 157–158). Upper Saddle River, NJ: Pearson.

Barboza, D. (2009). Danone exits China venture after years of legal dispute. *New York Times.* Accessed Jun 15, 2015: http://www.nytimes.com/2009/10/01/business/global/01danone.html?_r=0

Bartlett, C. A., & Beamish, P. W. (2011). *Transnational management: Text, cases and readings in cross border management* (6th ed.). Burr Ridge, IL: McGraw-Hill/Irwin.

Business Wire. (2011, Jul 1). *General Mills completes Yoplait acquisition*. Accessed 2015, Jun 15: http://www.businesswire.com/news/home/20110701005199/en/General-Mills-Completes-Yoplait-Acquisition#.VX80IEYm968

Castañer, X., & Genç, M. E. (2011). Expanding to institutionally different countries. In T. Das (Ed.), *Strategic alliances in a globalizing world* (pp. 1–25). Charlotte, N.C.: Information Age Pub.

Cavusgil, S. T., Ghauri, P. N., & Akcal, A. A. (2013). *Doing business in emerging markets* (2nd ed.). San Francisco, CA: Sage.

CNNExpansión. (2012, Oct 2). *Sigma renueva acuerdo con Yoplait* [Sigma renews agreement with Yoplait]. Accessed 2015, Jun 15: http://www.cnnexpansion.com/negocios/2012/10/02/sigma-renueva-acuerdo-por-yoplait

Coe, N. M., Dicken, P., & Hess, M. (2008). Global production networks: Realizing the potential. *Journal of Economic Geography*, *8*(3), 271–295. doi:10.1093/jeg/lbn002

Crawford, D., & Esterl, M. (2007, Nov 16). Siemens ruling details bribery across the globe. *Wall Street Journal*.

D'Iribarne, P. (2007). Growing together in Mexico. In *Successful companies in the developing world: Managing in synergy with cultures* (pp. 37–64). Paris: Agence Française de Développement.

Dai, L., Eden, L., & Beamish, P. W. (2013). Place, space, and geographical exposure: Foreign subsidiary survival in conflict zones. *Journal of International Business Studies*, *44*(6), 554–578. doi:10.1057/jibs.2013.12

Das, T. K., & Teng, B.-S. (1999). Managing risks in strategic alliances. *The Academy of Management Executive*, *13*(4), 50–62.

Denk, N., Kaufmann, L., & Roesch, J.-F. (2012). Liabilities of foreignness revisited: A review of contemporary studies and recommendations for future research. *Journal of International Management*, *18*(4), 322–334. doi:10.1016/j.intman.2012.07.001

Euler Hermes Group. (2015). *Euler Hermes country risk ratings: June 2015 review*. Accessed 2015, Jul 7: www.eulerhermes.com/mediacenter/Lists/mediacenter-documents/Country-Risk-Ratings-Q2-2015.pdf

Gammelgaard, J., & Dörrenbächer, C. (Eds.). (2013). *The global brewery industry: Markets, strategies, and rivalries*. Cheltenham, UK: Edward Elgar. doi:10.4337/9781781006351

Ghemawat, P. (2001). Distance still matters: The hard reality of global expansion. *Harvard Business Review*, *79*(8), 137–147. PMID:11550630

Johanson, J., & Vahlne, J. E. (1977). The internationalization process of the firm: A model of knowledge development and increasing foreign market commitments. *Journal of International Business Studies*, *8*(1), 23–32. doi:10.1057/palgrave.jibs.8490676

Khanna, T. (2014). Contextual intelligence. *Harvard Business Review*, *92*(9), 58–68. PMID:25509576

Khanna, T., & Palepu, K. G. (2010). *Winning in emerging markets*. Boston, MA: Harvard Business Press.

Kitching, J., Hart, M., & Wilson, N. (2015). Burden or benefit? Regulation as a dynamic influence on small business performance. *International Small Business Journal*, *33*(2), 130–147. doi:10.1177/0266242613493454

Knight, G. A., & Cavusgil, S. T. (2004). Innovation, organizational capabilities, and the born-global firm. *Journal of International Business Studies*, *35*(2), 124–141. doi:10.1057/palgrave.jibs.8400071

Kogut, B., & Kulatilaka, N. (1994). Operating flexibility, global manufacturing, and the option value of a multinational network. *Management Science*, *40*(1), 123–139. doi:10.1287/mnsc.40.1.123

Maxton, G. P., & Wormald, J. (2004). *Time for a model change: Re-engineering the global automotive industry*. Cambridge, UK: Cambridge University Press. doi:10.1017/CBO9780511488535

Meyer, K. E., & Estrin, S. (2001). Brownfield entry in emerging markets. *Journal of International Business Studies*, *32*(3), 575–584. doi:10.1057/palgrave.jibs.8490985

Morris, R. J., & Lawrence, A. T. (2001). Nike's dispute with the University of Oregon. *Case Research Journal*, *21*(3), 129–146.

Oviatt, B. M., & McDougall, P. P. (1994). Toward a theory of international new ventures. *Journal of International Business Studies*, *25*(1), 45–64. doi:10.1057/palgrave.jibs.8490193

Ozawa, T. (2011). The (Japan-born) 'flying-geese' theory of economic development revisited – and reformulated from a structuralist perspective. *Global Policy*, *2*(3), 272–285. doi:10.1111/j.1758-5899.2011.00093.x

Seligman, S. D. (1999). *Chinese business etiquette: A guide to protocol, manners, and culture in the People's Republic of China*. New York: Warner Books.

The Economist. (2011, Dec 3). *The hopeful continent: Africa rising*. Accessed June 8, 2013: http://www.economist.com/node/21541015

Thibodeau, P. (2012, Nov 29). In a symbolic shift, IBM's India workforce likely exceeds U.S. *Computerworld.* Accessed June 4, 2015: http://www.computerworld.com/article/2493565/it-careers/in-a-symbolic-shift--ibm-s-india-workforce-likely-exceeds-u-s-.html

Transparency International. (2015). *Corruption Perceptions Index.* Accessed Jun 8, 2015: http://www.transparency.org/research/cpi

UNCTAD. (2014). *World investment report 2014.* New York: United Nations.

UNCTAD. (2015, May 18). *Global investment trends monitor no. 19.* Accessed June 5, 2015: http://unctad.org/en/pages/publications/Global-Investment-Trends-Monitor-%28Series%29.aspx

KEY TERMS AND DEFINITIONS

Ease of Doing Business: A measure of the institutional conditions that facilitate or inhibit business operations in different countries and regions or cities of the world.

Emerging Economy: A nation that is striving to build institutions that allow for the improvement of economic and social conditions.

Entry Mode: A firm's decision on how to internationalize into a foreign country, either through an acquisition, an agreement with a local partner, or as a greenfield investment.

Factor Conditions: The locally differentiated availability and prices of inputs for producing goods and services.

Global Value Chain: An integrated production system where parts and subassemblies are produced in different parts of the world.

Institutional Void: The (perceived) lack of intermediaries that make certain business transactions more difficult or totally impossible.

Multinational Enterprise: Any firm with significant operations in more than one country.

Chapter 3
Strategies for Enhancing the Competitiveness of MNEs

Neeta Baporikar
HP-GSB, Namibia University of Science and Technology, Namibia

ABSTRACT

Globalization has dramatically changed the competitive landscape in many national markets. Dunning (1993) provided evidence that Foreign Direct Investment (FDI) had doubled and even tripled in the last fifteen years in Less-Developed Countries (LDCs), generating a tremendous impact on the economic development and welfare of these countries. Yet, less attention has been given to the role that domestic customers and domestic competitors play in shaping the strategic behaviour and performance of MNEs in the targeted markets and the strategies which need to be adopted to enhance the competitiveness of MNEs. Through grounded theory approach and in depth literature review, the chapter aims to examine the positioning of MNEs to extend existing perspectives and incorporating competitive interactions between the external environments, competitive strategy and in particular, evaluates the strategic positioning and competitive behaviour of MNEs.

INTRODUCTION

The topic of firms' competitiveness is greatly debated today among managers, politicians as well as academics. Globalization and changes in the world economy over the last years have raised new challenges for firms, industries and countries (Baporikar, 2011). The popularity of the concept of competitiveness is clearly demonstrated by the fact that there is an increasing interest around the issue of competitiveness benchmarking at the country level as well as the policies through which governments can enhance national industrial competitiveness. Although the definition of the competitiveness appears to be straightforward, such construct is often used in different and somewhat ambiguous meanings. Moreover, the competitive possibilities of developing economies in the most dynamic international markets depend on a fan of advantages that are defined at firm and national levels including productive, commercial technological capabilities along with influence of external factors (Baporikar, 2015b). Beyond the pioneering discussions of the concept of competitiveness and its application at the aggregated level (Krugman, 1994);

DOI: 10.4018/978-1-5225-0276-0.ch003

the determinant factors of it are defined by the individual behaviour, mainly by the firms' management and technology abilities in a given country. Nonetheless, the adaptation of the competitiveness concept to the country-level of analysis is also methodologically accepted (Porter et al., 2008; Sala-I-Martin et al., 2008). Thus, through grounded theory approach and in depth literature review, the chapter aims to examine the positioning of MNEs to extend existing perspectives and incorporating competitive interactions between the external environments, competitive strategy and in particular, evaluates the strategic positioning and competitive behavior of MNEs.

BACKGROUND

Competitiveness is a concept very discussed among academics and it has been applied to several levels of analysis; the most pertinent applications of it is at firm level because it refers to a comparative notion of competition or market gains, but it has also been broadly applied at the national level in last decades (Fagerberg, 1996; Nelson, 1993; Porter, 1985; Roessner et al., 1996). A general definition of competitiveness relates to productivity and growth of countries (Krugman, 1994) while the more tractable one focuses on the ability of a country to compete by exporting (Fagerberg, 1996; Lall, 2001). Most of the time, the concept of competitiveness reminds us of competitive advantage. According to the largely consolidated view of competitive process, a firm's performance is affected by its competitive advantages. In its turn, the nature of such advantage results in one or more specific sources of competitive advantage which a firm controls. The concept of competitive advantage is central in strategic management studies (Porter, 1985; Ghemawat, 1986). It recalls that of comparison and rivalry. It can be interpreted as "the asymmetry or differential among firms along any comparable dimension that allows one firm to compete better than its rivals" (Ma, 2000: 53). A competitive advantage refers to the position of superiority within an industry that a firm has developed in comparison to its competitors. Firm level competitiveness indicated a firm's ability to design, produce and market products superior to those offered by competitors, where superiority can be evaluated from several factors, like price, quality, technological advancement, etc.

Competitiveness can be considered at different levels of aggregation: firm, industry, and country. Firm level analysis focuses on behaviour and performance of firms. Competitiveness is frequently analyzed also at industry level or "cluster" level. The competitiveness of an industry can be assessed by a comparison with the same industry in another region or country with which there is open trade. Beyond firm-specific and industry-specific factors, in recent years globalization has emphasized the importance of country-related effects as determinants of performance. The different dimensions of competitiveness are strongly related: for example, a country's competitiveness factors are determinants of its firms' international competitiveness. On the other hand, the most evident aspect of a country's international competitiveness is represented by its firms' competitiveness in comparison to other countries' firms. As it is based on comparison, competitiveness is a relative concept in the sense that criteria and variables used to measure such construct cannot be applied regardless of specific time and spatial conditions. At the firm level, profitability, costs, productivity and market share are all indicators of competitiveness. Generally, competitiveness is considered synonymous with success. In very simple terms, success can be intended as achievement of company objectives. Hence, performance should be measured in terms of how an organization manages its critical success factors (Ferguson and Dickenson, 1982). Today, beyond financial or market-based indicators, measures of competitiveness increasingly include other variables such as innovativeness, quality, and social ones like ethical standing, social responsibility, working conditions of employees, etc. However, resource-based view scholars argue that the sources of a firm's competitive advantages rely on its set of unique and differentiated resources (Wernerfelt, 1984; Barney, 1991; Peteraf, 1993). This chapter explores some "open questions" related to positioning of MNEs, reviews existing perspectives on MNEs, competitive interactions between the external environments. Thus, the core objective of the chapter is to contribute a well-grounded basis for future research about the new paths of international expansion and the strategies to enhance the competitiveness in the global context.

Genesis of MNE

The organization of modern MNEs is more complicated than the old models of international exporter, multidomestic (Porter, 1985), and global (Yip, 1989). As a consequence of the intrinsic limitations of each of the pure structures as an optimal form to compete globally, MNEs evolved from these traditional forms into more sophisticated structures intended to combine the advantages of multidomestic and global structures. Initially these led to the concept of transnational corporation (high localization/high global integration) developed and widely studied by Bartlett, Ghoshal, and other scholars (Bartlett & Ghoshal, 1992, 1988, 1987a,b; Harzing, 2000; Yip, 1994). However, the transnational model is still primarily considered a mind-set, idea, or ideal rather than an organization structure found on many MNEs (Segal-Horn & Faulkner, 1999).

It is important to know that, each of these organizational structures has limitations to compete in a global economy. Briefly, the international exporter (low global integration/low localization) is not well positioned to compete in situations where either economies of scale or local responsiveness are critical. The traditional multidomestic (low global integration/high localization) is not well positioned to exploit competitive interdependencies and global efficiencies, and consequently it is in significant disadvantage in situations where economies of scale and scope are critical. Additionally, their inability to extract value from its centre headquarters significantly limits their competitive advantage in global setting where corporate strategy, global integration, coordination, and knowledge transfer play a significant role. Finally, the global company (low localization/high global integration) is not well positioned to compete in situations requiring critical local adaptation. Perhaps more important is the fact that it does not extract value from subsidiaries to make good strategic and tactical decisions.

Given the limitations of each of the structures in terms of global competitiveness, most MNEs have re-evaluated their corporate and competitive strategies and re–structured in order to simultaneously become more globally integrated and locally responsive. As MNEs attempt to optimize their global integration/local responsiveness trade–off (i.e. adopting a more "glocal" strategy) there is a certain degree of convergence, and the old traditional organizational forms are too "pure" in nature to accurate model most modern MNEs. The inability of the traditional (pure) models of multidomestic and global models to accurately describe modern MNEs has led to the new models of modern multidomestic, modern global, and transnational. These models can be briefly summarized as follows:

1. **Modern Multidomestic:** The modern multidomestic follows the tradition of the old (pure) multidomestic but it gives a more significant role to the corporate headquarters. As such, it is no longer a loose confederation of assets, but a MNE with a strong culture of operational decentralization, local adaptation, product differentiation, and local responsiveness. Contrary to the traditional multidomestic where the centre had very little value added, in the modern multidomestic the centre is critical to enhance the competitive strength of the multidomestic. While the role of the subsidiary

is to be locally responsive, the role at the centre is to enhance the global integration by developing global corporate and competitive strategies, play a significant role in resource allocation, selection of markets, developing strategic analysis, mergers and acquisitions, decisions regarding R&D and technology matters, eliminating duplication of capital intensive assets, and knowledge transfer. A representative example of the modern multidomestic is Nestle (Segal-Horn & Faulkner, 1999; Yip, 1996, 1991a, b, 1989; Yip et al., 2000, 1997, 1988; Yip & Madsen, 1996).

2. **Modern Global:** The modern global company follows the tradition of the old (pure) global form but it gives a more significant role to the country subsidiaries. The central authority is responsible for achieving high global integration by providing: low cost sourcing platforms, efficient factor costs, global scale, product standardization, quality assurance, global technology sharing and IT, brand name, and global corporate strategy. Contrary to the traditional (pure) global model, the modern global MNE makes more effective use of the subsidiaries in order to become more locally responsive. Modern global corporations may disperse R&D, manufacture and production, and marketing around the globe. A representative example of the modern global is Gillette. This helps ensure flexibility in the face of changing factor costs for labour, raw materials, exchange rates, as well as hiring talent worldwide (Segal-Horn & Faulkner, 1999; Yip, 1996, 1991a, b, 1989; Yip et al., 2000, 1997, 1988; Yip & Madsen, 1996).
3. **Transnational:** The transnational form is used to characterize MNEs that attempt to achieve high global integration and high local responsiveness. As already pointed out, the limitations of the multidomestic and global structures led to the concept of transnational corporation (high localization/high global integration) proposed by Bartlett and Ghoshal, and widely accepted by the research community (Bartlett & Ghoshal, 2000, 1992, 1988, 1987a, b; Harzing, 2000; Yip, 1994). This organizational structure followed is the network form rather than the multi-divisional, as the ultimate objective is to have access and make effective and efficient use of all the resources the company has at its disposal globally, including knowledge and tacit localized knowledge. A potential limitation of the transnational company is the fact that it requires management intensive processes (Ohmae, 2006). In any case, the transnational model is still primarily considered a mind-set, idea, or ideal rather than an organization structure found, especially in manufacturing (Segal Horn & Faulkner, 1999).

In addition to the structures discussed above, the "virtual" form seems to be the new model or new type of MNEs emerging in the 21st century as a consequence of the globalization forces. This, virtual form models, ventures focus exclusively on their core competencies and "smartsource" that is outsourcing focused on value to global companies optimally positioned to provide services such as R&D, manufacture, production, industrial design, marketing, localization, distribution, and information brokerage. On a first guess, the virtual model resembles the transnational form but uses external partners, global experts, opinion leaders and collaborators instead of corporate subsidiaries. The virtual form tends to focus more on intangible assets rather than tangible/capital intensive assets. This form can be used to model some modern MNEs that do not fit the multidomestic, global, or transnational framework such as of the many recent US start-ups in professional services, manufacture (e.g. medical device manufactures), and dot-com firms (Porter, 2001). MNE can be seen as a vehicle that provides new technology and potential positive external effects in host economies in a first glance, while developing economies moving towards outflows FDI can be seen as a more direct access to foreign markets. However, at least in theory, the process of cumulative learning and know-how that is needed to get successful MNE operations requires a long time period until a developing country can create the conditions that will nurture the creation of home-based MNE as well. The idea is that companies from some of the so-called emerging economies are changing their international strategies and this could derive into competitive improvements (Brouthers et al., 2005; Gammeloft et al., 2010; Singh, 2007). The study of the dimensions of non-market advantages in developing countries MNE provided by Cuervo-Cazurra and Genc (2011) shows that the advantages and disadvantages of competing with MNE from more advanced countries in host economies depend on the characteristics of the dimension of the country environment.

Accordingly, what determines the outcome would not be the level of development of home countries but the relative distance from the host country in question? This outward perspective provides some implications for the competitiveness of developing economies since large corporations affect the integration of dispersed and functionally separated markets and operating activities, and MNE constitute a highly efficient mechanism for creating firm-specific knowledge assets (Cantwell, 1989, 1995, 2005; Frost, 2001; McCann & Mudambi, 2005; Mudambi, 2008; Piscitello, 2004; Singh, 2007; Yang et al., 2008). The MNE's competitive advantage relies on its capability to innovate, accumulate, exploit and recombine set of firm-specific resources as well as transfer such resources among the different nodes of its extended network. These resources include: parent-company-specific resources; subsidiary-specific resources; easy-to-transfer resources and capabilities that can be ascribed to the MNE as a whole Particularly, intangible and knowledge-based resources are largely acknowledged as the most important determinants of a firm's competitiveness as they fit better such condition of imperfect mobility which resource-based view has identified as a potential source of competitive advantage (Peteraf, 1993). The explanation of a firm's international expansion decision is based on the analysis of firm specific and location-specific advantages (Dunning, 1980). In general, the evolution of the MNEs over the last two decades can be summarized as a shift from a prevalence of parent company firm-specific advantages to a mix of location-bound and non-location-bound firm-specific advantages across the MNE network (Rugman and Verbeke, 2001). Rather, recent theoretical perspectives point out that, far from being a centralized hierarchy, MNE is an inter-organizational network (Ghosal & Barlett, 1990) of loosely coupled nodes, characterized by their own unique resource and capability profile. From the above genesis, we can see that the organization of modern MNEs is more complicated than the traditional organizational models in their pure form. As modern MNEs design and adopt new structures in order to optimize their ability to simultaneously achieve higher levels of global integration and local responsiveness, it becomes critical to design, develop and implement new strategies so as to enhance and sustain the competitiveness.

COMPREHENSIVE PERSPECTIVE OF COMPETITIVENESS

Classical theory explains the success of nations in particular industries based on so-called factors of production such as land, labor, and natural resources. Nations gain factor-based comparative advantage in industries that make intensive use of the factors they possess in abundance. Classical theory, however, has been overshadowed in advanced industries and economies by the globalization of competition and the power of technology. A new theory must recognize that in modern international competition, companies compete with global strategies involving not only trade but also foreign investment. What a new theory must explain is why a nation provides a favorable home base for companies that compete internationally. The home base is the nation in which the essential competitive advantages of the enterprise are created and sustained. It is where a company's strategy is set, where the core product and process technology is created and maintained, and where the most productive jobs and most advanced skills are located. The presence of the home base in a nation has the greatest positive influence on other linked domestic industries and leads to other benefits in the nation's economy. While the ownership of the company is often concentrated at the home base, the nationality of shareholders is secondary. A new theory must move beyond comparative advantage to the competitive advantage of a nation. It must reflect a rich conception of competition that includes segmented markets, differentiated products, technology differences, and economies of scale. A new theory must go beyond cost and explain why companies from some nations are better than others at creating advantages based on quality, features, and new product innovation. A new theory must begin from the premise that competition is dynamic and evolving; it must answer the questions: Why do some companies based in some nations innovate more than others? Why do some nations provide an environment that enables companies to improve and innovate faster than foreign rivals?

The only meaningful concept of competitiveness then at the national level seems to be productivity. Productivity is the value of the output produced by a unit of labor or capital. Productivity is the prime determinant of a nation's long-run standard of living; it is the root cause of national per capita income. The productivity of human resources determines employee wages; the productivity with which capital is employed determines the return it earns for its holders. A nation's standard of living depends on the capacity of its companies to achieve high levels of productivity - and to increase productivity over time. Sustained productivity growth requires that an economy continually upgrade itself. A nation's companies must relentlessly improve productivity in existing industries by raising product quality, adding desirable features, improving product technology, or boosting production efficiency. They must develop the necessary capabilities to compete in more and more sophisticated industry segments, where productivity is generally high. They must finally develop the capability to compete in entirely new, sophisticated industries. Competitiveness also does not mean jobs. It's the type of jobs, not just the ability to employ citizens at low wages that is decisive for economic prosperity. Seeking to explain "competitiveness" at the national level, then, is to answer the wrong question.

International Competitiveness Notion

Which considerations should we add to our reasoning when dealing with *international* competitiveness? The topic of international competitiveness raises new issues and makes it necessary to take into account more variables. In broad terms, international competitiveness can be defined as a firm's capability to achieve higher performance than its competitors in foreign markets and preserve the conditions that sustain its higher performance also in the future. Such definition takes into consideration both the spatial and time dimension of the construct. Especially for those firms that mostly compete against foreign competitors, the basic characteristics of the nation (i.e. national economy) like domestic demand conditions, domestic factor conditions, related and supporting industries within the economy, and domestic rivalry (Porter, 1990) play a significant role in the competitive processes. A firm's international competitiveness may diverge from its competitiveness in the home country. In fact, a firm might be profitable in its country with a large domestic market share but it might show low international competitiveness in case the domestic market is protected by barriers to international trade. In this case the present competitiveness would be compromised if domestic market were opened to trade. In addition, some firms may sacrifice competitiveness in the home market for a greater penetration in foreign markets. Export market share is frequently used as international performance measure at the firm level. However, such measure is not satisfactory in case market share is maintained through significant price cutting and, consequently, profitability decrease (Buckley et al., 1988). As a result, the growth of foreign sales is achieved at the expense of profitability and prospective competitiveness.

In our view, international competitiveness is a broader construct than the degree of internationalization. Buckley et al. (1988) propose a framework for the analysis of international competitiveness based on three groups of variables: competitiveness *performance*, competitiveness *potential* and management *processes*. Performance is the outcome of past or present competitiveness. As Buckley at al. (1988: 184) argue, performance measures "provide a historical perspective, and are all characterized by their inability to provide insights into the sustainability of such performance. Using only these measures leaves too many questions unanswered". Economic and market performance achieved by a firm in its internationalization processes derives from past choices and initiatives but does not allow to make a complete evaluation of the firm's capacity to preserve and regenerate that performance over time. Consequently, it is necessary to focus not only on performance but also on competitive potential, intended as a firm's capability to defend and renovate its sources of competitive advantage. As Buckley et al (1988: 179) point out, "when statistical measures have been used to show, for example, that one firm performs better in the market place than its competitors, and has generated and sustained more competitive potential, the qualitative information derived from researching management processes helps to explain the reasons for success". The model by Buckley et al. (1988) has been substantially validated by a few empirical research works, based on the analysis of the most relevant factors of firm competitiveness in the perception of managers (Buckley et al., 1990a; Buckley et al., 1990b; Coviello et al., 1998). These studies also provide evidence of the contingent nature of the construct of competitiveness: industry factors and variables related to firms' international strategies affect managers' perceptions of competitiveness.

FDI theories also show that a firm exploits its firm-specific advantages by transferring them to host countries. Therefore, internationalization should be evaluated also in financial terms, rather than just real, by looking at the extent to which a company internationalizes its financing or ownership structure by approaching international investors. Hassel et al. (2003) identify three measures of internationalization from a financial point of view:

- Foreign owners as percentage of total ownership, to estimate the extent of foreign shareholders of companies and, as a result, the openness to international capital markets;
- The number of listings in foreign stock exchange, which signal the firm's attempts to attract foreign shareholders;
- The adoption of international accounting standards rather than uniquely accounting rules derived from national legislation; such indicator shows the firm's need to communicate effectively with international investors

Specifically, international business literature has proved that firm-specific advantages such as R&D intensity, product differentiation, size and experience push towards higher equity investment modes (Gatinon & Anderson, 1988; Stopford & Wells, 1972). In addition, FDI theories suggest that firms will invest more in those countries where they benefit from greater location-specific advantages. As Erramilli et al. (1997) point out, "though it has been known that both firm- and location-specific advantages separately and jointly influence the parent firms' ownership preferences for foreign subsidiaries, recent theoretical developments have expanded the role of location-specific advantages by suggesting that firm-specific advantages may be tied to a location" (p. 736). The idea is that home-based MNE in developing economies can also play a relevant role to define their competitive patterns; a salient reason for this is how MNE arbitrage the diversity of location across countries, comparative advantages (national level) and competitive advantages (firm level), generating higher returns than pure domestic or non-specialized companies (Luo et al., 2011; Meyer et al., 2011). For these reasons, an updated look to competitiveness should integrate the role of MNE taking explicitly the argument of the international industry value chain in combination with technology. Differences across developing countries are more notable when the dynamism of the so-called emerging economies and those lagging behind is jointly considered in the analysis, being predicted that influential factors levering competitiveness differ not only between developed and developing economies but also inside the latter group.

In international business research, the traditional explanation of a firm's internationalization relies on the opportunity of an exploitation of firm-specific assets, especially intangible ones (Buckley & Casson, 1976). In recent years learning processes have received greater attention in the analysis of an international firm's competitiveness (Barkema & Vermeulen, 1998). Moreover, host country-specific advantages may increase a firm's overall competitiveness. Typical advantages of going international are economies of scale and scope (Caves, 1971, Hymer, 1976; Teece, 1980) and greater market power and operational flexibility (Kogut, 1985; Rugman, 1981). On the other hand, multinational enterprises are more complex organizations than domestic firms (Caves, 1982) and may suffer of the lack of adequate management capabilities. Governance costs and the difficulties associated to coordinating geographical dispersed activities negatively affect a MNE's performance. A newly established subsidiary has a liability of foreignness which reduces its competitiveness compared to an already established firm in the local market. Other problems come from cultural diversity (Hofstede, 1980) and from the difficulties of transferring intangible assets across countries. Lu and Beamish (2004: 599) argue that conflicting results in the literature between internationalization and performance "could be an outcome of incomplete theorization about the full range of benefits and costs, and about the changes in these benefits and costs over the time it takes to fully implement an internationalization strategy".

The relative presence of developing countries in dynamic high-tech markets depends on the evolution of their industrial structure a process that is influenced by a more complex set of elements tied to the environment or national systems of innovation (Narula & Wakelin, 1995). In developing economies, upgrading is at least in the first stages of development (industrialization) mainly focused on the adaptation and use of the already available technologies (Lall, 1996, 2000); although the efficient use of them can be transformed into sustainable growth in the long run, it depends on the generation of absorption capabilities as well as in the adaptation of firm catch up strategies to the evolution of the environment (Kumaraswamy et al., 2012). Linking the concepts of internationalization, performance and competitiveness at the firm level, we build a conceptual framework for the analysis of the different dimensions of competitiveness as well as the approaches of the studies in this field. For these reasons, our understanding of the competitive position of countries in this chapter is closely linked to firm-level factors such as MNE strategies, technology and the integration level in the high-tech industries' international value chain (Cantwell, 2005; Luo et al., 2011).

The speed of economic internationalization process in last decades affects markets and hierarchies, and although the benefits among countries have not been equally distributed worldwide, we have assisted to the emergence of dynamic economies among the group of countries traditionally considered as developing. Although openness does not necessarily mean growth and development per se (Fagerberg & Srholec, 2008; Rodrik, 1999), the process of building capabilities is often graduated and reinforced by external factors as well. MNE play a crucial role in such a process, not only in the configuration and increase of international investment's flows but also in the definition of competitiveness conditions in both home and host economies. On the other hand, data show not only the raise of FDI inflows into developing economies in last decades (UNCTAD, 2005, 2007) but also the emergence of outward FDI from these countries (Cuervo-Cazurra, 2007; Gammeloft et al., 2010; Meyer, 2004).

Fundamentally there are least two main views of the origin of a firm's competitive advantage. On one side, industrial organization scholars focus on the influence of industry-related determinants of firm performance and particularly emphasize the importance of factors like concentration, entry and exit barriers and economies of scale. Classical industrial organization scholars (Mason, 1939; Bain, 1956) claim that a firm can neither influence industry conditions nor own performance. Therefore, the competitive advantage originates from external sources rather than internal (firm-specific) sources. A modified framework has been advanced by the new industrial organization scholars who recognize that firms have a certain influence on the relationship between industry structure and a firm's performance (Hansen and Wernerfelt, 1989). According to Porter (1980), competition within an industry is defined by five structural parameters: current competition within the industry, bargaining power of suppliers, bargaining power of buyers, threat of new entrants, and threat of substitute products or services. In Porter's (1980) view, the paths of industry evolution depend (among other things) on firms' strategic choices.

Success and International Markets

Around the world, companies that have achieved international leadership employ strategies that differ from each other in every respect. But while every successful company will employ its own particular strategy, the underlying mode of operation - the character and trajectory of all successful companies - is fundamentally the same. Companies achieve competitive advantage through acts of innovation. It often involves ideas that are not even "new"—ideas that have been around, but never vigorously pursued. It always involves investments in skill and knowledge, as well as in physical assets and brand reputations. Some innovations create competitive advantage by perceiving an entirely new market opportunity or by serving a market segment that others have ignored. When competitors are slow to respond, such innovation yields competitive advantage. The other important ingredients for companies to succeed in international markets include:

1. Information plays a large role in the process of innovation and improvement - information that either is not available to competitors or that they do not seek.
2. National environment permits and supports the accumulation of specialized assets and skills - simply because of greater effort and commitment - companies gain a competitive advantage.
3. Factor Conditions. According to standard economic theory, factors of production - labor, land, natural resources, capital, and infrastructure - will determine the flow of trade but in today's scenario nation's ability to create important factors of production is important. E.g. scientific institute specialized in optics, a pool of venture capital to fund software companies.
4. Selective disadvantages in the more basic factors can prod a company to innovate and upgrade -a disadvantage in a static model of competition can become an advantage in a dynamic one. E.g. in India, when there is an ample supply of cheap raw materials or abundant labor; companies simply rest on these advantages and often deploy them inefficiently. But when companies face a selective disadvantage, like high land costs, labor shortages, or the lack of local raw materials, they *must* innovate and upgrade to compete. E.g. Japan's oft-repeated statement, "We are an island nation with no natural resources," is the understanding that these deficiencies have only served to spur

Japan's competitive innovation. Disadvantages can become advantages only under certain conditions. First, they must send companies proper signals about circumstances that will spread to other nations, thereby equipping them to innovate in advance of foreign rivals. The second condition for transforming disadvantages into advantages is favorable circumstances. Another precondition is company goals that lead to sustained commitment to the industry. Without such a commitment and the presence of active rivalry, a company may take an easy way around a disadvantage rather than using it as a spur to innovation.

5. Home-demand conditions help build competitive advantage when a particular industry segment is larger or more visible in the domestic market than in foreign markets. Sophisticated, demanding buyers provide a window into advanced customer needs; they pressure companies to meet high standards; they prod them to improve, to innovate, and to upgrade into more advanced segments.
6. The presence in the nation of related and supporting industries those are internationally competitive. E.g. Italian Footwear Cluster and sometimes suppliers themselves being global competitors.
7. National circumstances and context create strong tendencies in how companies are created, organized, and managed, as well as what the nature of domestic rivalry will be. Competitiveness in a specific industry results from convergence of the management practices and organizational modes favored in the country and the sources of competitive advantage in the industry.
8. Individual motivation to work and expand skills is also important to competitive advantage. Outstanding talent is a scarce resource in any nation.
9. Government's role is as a catalyst and challenger; to encourage - or even push - companies to raise their aspirations and move to higher levels of competitive performance. However, policies that convey static, short-term cost advantages but that unconsciously undermine innovation and dynamism represent the most common and most profound error in government industrial policy. Some specific policy approach which Government needs to adopt to gain competitive advantage include: Focus on specialized factor creation; avoid intervening in factor and currency markets. Enforce strict product, safety, and environmental standards. Sharply limit direct cooperation among industry rivals. Promote goals that lead to sustained investment. Deregulate competition. Enforce strong domestic antitrust policies. Reject managed trade.
10. Ultimately, only companies themselves can achieve and sustain competitive advantage. Competitive advantage arises from leadership that harnesses and amplifies the forces in the diamond to promote innovation and upgrading. Here are few company policies that will support that effort: Create pressures for innovation. Seek out the most capable competitors as motivators. Establish early-warning systems. Welcome domestic rivalry. Globalize to tap selective advantages in other nations. Use alliances only selectively. Locate the home base to support competitive advantage.

Strategies to Enhance MNEs Competitiveness

In a world of increasingly global competition, nations have become more, not less, important. As the basis of competition has shifted more and more to the creation and assimilation of knowledge, the role of the nation has grown (Baporikar, 2014b). Competitive advantage is created and sustained through a highly localized process (Baporikar, 2015a). Differences in national values, culture, economic structures, institutions, and histories all contribute to competitive success. There are striking differences in the patterns of competitiveness in every country; no nation can or will be competitive in each and every, or even most industries (Baporikar, 2015b). Ultimately, nations succeed in particular industries because their home environment is the most forward-looking, dynamic, and challenging. More so, the globalization process has changed the markets functioning and also hierarchies, while technology has reshaped international firms, industries and trade; therefore, it can be assumed that national structural competitiveness is related to the ability to enhance collective techno-economic capacities in the world market-place. Too many companies and top managers misperceive the nature of competition and the task before them by focusing on improving financial performance, soliciting government assistance, seeking stability, and reducing risk through alliances and mergers. Today's competitive realities demand leadership. Leaders believe in change; they energize their organizations to innovate continuously; they recognize the importance of their home country as integral to their competitive success and work to upgrade it. Most important, leaders recognize the need for pressure and challenge. They are prepared to sacrifice the easy life for difficulty and, ultimately, sustained competitive advantage. That must be the goal, for both nations and companies: not just surviving, but achieving international competitiveness. This implies that for MNEs to become more competitive they must:

1. Adopt a relative or comparative notion of performance that is shaped by a diversity of influential factors.
2. Take advantage of those structural and productive changes that permit to increase their competitive position in higher value-added industries
3. Upgrading their world output' shares, employment and trade of technology-intensive products (Aharoni & Hirsch, 1997).
4. Exercise caution and prudence in choice between absorption and adaptation of existing technologies and the creation through the expansion of R&D and innovation are quite unique for each nation and also depend on its initial development level (Gerschenkron, 1962).
5. Adopt short term and long term planning methods to gauge the evolution of trade patterns and the impact of technological advancement for their line of business/firm/industry and understand differences across-countries which are due to unique reasons or the configuration of industrial structure in which coexist labour-intensive traditional industries and technologically complex industrial activities (Uchida & Cook, 2005).
6. Cater for diversity especially for MNEs in the heterogeneous group of developing countries, where one common aspect is the support provided by inward technology transfer (Alvarez & Magaña, 2007; Castellacci, 2008; Durlauf & Johnson, 1995; Mowery and Oxley, 1995).
7. Nurturing technological advanced domestic firms in their industrialization process (Agosin & Machado, 2005; Kim, 1997), or expansion of exports.
8. Adapting technology for local consumption to create local industries and make possible to take advantage of the growing number of skills Kumaraswamy et al. (2012).
9. Bettering arm's length technology (licensing, collaboration, Joint venture) and integrating into the industry global value chain.
10. Ensuring competitiveness by progressing to knowledge creation through internal R&D, including global interactions between the institutional environments, governments and catch up strategies.

Hence the critical issue now is of understanding the future factors that will drive the competitive pillars at a global scale. In a knowledge driven society with information, communication and technology convergence (Baporikar, 2014a), the soft issues of managing talent, engaging employees along with the infrastructure development and technological advancement (hardware) for MNE's competitiveness is not only imperative but inevitable. In a more recent work, Belderson and Sleuwaegen (2005) examine the conditions under which a specific global and regional manufacturing strategy is chosen by Japanese multinational firms. Their study provides evidence that the choice for a specific spatial configuration of plants is not only determined by locational characteristics, but is also affected by firm and industry characteristics. They argue that "the location of foreign direct investments is of major importance not only from an efficiency perspective but also as an integral part of the competitive strategy of multinational firms, with important repercussions on performance" (Belderson & Sleuwaegen 2005: 588).

Localization decisions and their impact on firm competitiveness are related to two aspects: the competitive advantages that a firm can acquire thanks to its localization in a given area and the transferability of such advantages from the operating unit localized in that area to the other operating units within the multinational corporation (Baporikar & Deshpande, 2013). The strategic problem is not so much "in which country to localize", but how to reconfigure the firm's value chain on an international basis. By adopting a glocal approach (Deshpande & Baporikar, 2014) on many occasions, economies have based their development strategies by reworking on imported technologies and their local upgrade. It is also recommended that MNE manage the complexity of interactions across locations and tap into resources and capabilities from different multiple local contexts. MNE are indeed becoming multi-centric firms exploiting the diversity of locations accordingly to the setting of a new geography of value chain activities, i.e. in knowledge-intense industries, the higher fragmentation of production and the decentralization of core activities such as R&D explain how MNE are relocating the more standardized parts of their productive activities in emerging economies (Mudambi, 2008). These strategies emphasize the importance of both R&D and marketing intangible assets in value creation, reasons why MNE are becoming increasingly knowledge driven (Meyer et al., 2011).

As it is pointed out by Luo et al. (2011), the MNE effects in both host and home economies depend on some national level differences such as environmental, capabilities and strategic factors. Thus, the appropriate election of techniques in favour of competitiveness improvement and innovation is not in a vacuum but is a part of a continuous technological effort that would enhance risks' assumption in a context of imperfect information (Lall & Teubal, 1998; Teece, 1977). Moreover, comparative advantages may be linked to the capabilities of technology deepening even in contexts of multiple specialization patterns where the efforts would be concentrated in upgrading the possibilities for the development of technology-intensive activities (Rodrik, 1996). Consequently, competitiveness seems to be determined by the ability to integrate rightly in the global value chain in order to gain access and to use effectively a range of products and services related to the activities of MNE such as modern ICT, managerial and financial services and accounting methods (Aharoni & Hirsch, 1997; Rugman & Doh, 2008).

SOLUTIONS AND RECOMMENDATIONS

The processes of building capabilities entail at least two main levels of action: on the one hand, national investments in scientific and technological skills, information flows, infrastructures and supporting institutions; on the other, the cumulative efforts at the firm level to develop new organizational and technological skills, absorptive capacities and the involvement in networks of differentiated nature — such as the interaction with customers, suppliers and other agents of the local and international environments (Alvarez et al., 2009; Cantwell, 1989; Fagerberg & Srholec, 2007; Lall, 1997; Lundvall et al., 2002). Hence, for MNEs to enhance competitiveness global linkages with specialized clusters can generate opportunities for acceding to resources and knowledge flows that can facilitate upgrading and catch up. Some emerging economies have even been able to develop their own technologies (i.e. Brazil in aircraft, electronics and computers; India in computers; Malaysia in electronics) and this has been the result of a combined action of States, institutions, foreign capital and domestic companies. In this approach the configuration of the MNE moves from an hierarchical perspective, in which all the strategic activities fall into the business domain of the parent company, towards a configuration which recognizes the existence of centres of excellence (Holm & Pedersen, 2000) and specialized knowledge in multiple nodes of the MNE, linked to one another by flexible governance mechanisms.

FUTURE RESEARCH DIRECTIONS

All the above aspects have important implications for competitiveness studies since these organizational changes would permit the creation and enlargement of competitive advantages across borders. Subsidiaries could then adopt a key role in doing the exploitation of competencies from over the firm' network but also trying to create entirely new competencies and taking advantage of assets available in the diverse host locations such as knowledge resources (Rugman & Verbeke, 2001; Singh, 2007; Yang et al., 2008). Then, the management of international networks becomes also a very relevant aspect because of the implications associated with the more internationalized value chain (Kaplinsky, 2000). Particularly, an updated view of globalization and MNE that affirms the importance of local contexts (Meyer et al., 2011) seems to provide the foundations for further study. Country specific MNEs strategies would be an interesting area to take up, apart from comparative analysis which could be based on emerging economies, technological advancements or skilled and knowledge workers. Another interesting area of study would be the study complementarities between internationalization and competitiveness, FDI and trade and MNEs adoption models and growth/success. As discussed above, most variables generally accepted as competitiveness measures are hard to "operationalize". The measures proposed in herein could be a basis for further refinements aimed at defining a set of items which reasonably approximate the theoretical concepts. Such items could be validated (and further integrated) from an empirical point of view, for example, through a survey of managers of multinational firms.

CONCLUSION

Strategies to enhance competitiveness of MNEs as discussed in this chapter covers diverse contemporary and conventional issues facing MNEs. The chapter explores the genesis of MNEs, provides comprehensive perspective of competitiveness and deliberates on the international competitiveness notion and what constitutes success in international markets before providing strategies to enhance MNEs competitiveness. These strategies are to overcome those challenges in a fashion that in return make them highly successful and competitive in the globalized world. The attempt has been to analyze all those diverse issues and challenges facing MNEs and more importantly, how those challenges are addressed by the MNEs through appropriate strategies in order to convert those various challenges into opportunities for growth. To the extent that MNEs maintain fit between strategic contexts and innovation and knowledge created within the organization, there can be significant competitive advantages. In addition, this internally generated knowledge represents an invaluable and non-imitable resource that greatly enhances the global competitiveness of the MNE its network of subsidiaries. This conceptual chapter has several implications for practicing managers of MNEs. First, managers of MNEs should view their organizations as a global network of subunits. Moreover, MNE managers should clearly define and communicate the role of each subsidiary within the network, thus allowing the subunits to better understand how their actions contribute to the overall strategic objectives of the firm. Related to this issue, managers should establish flexible structures and processes at the corporate level in order to differentiate its management practices based on the various subsidiary roles. Finally, managers should execute the firm's global strategic decision making process in a manner that provides bilateral communications, information sharing, consistency, autonomy, and familiarity with local conditions that will maximize the competitiveness and sustainability within each strategic context.

REFERENCES

Agosin, M., & Machado, R. (2005). Foreign investment in developing countries: Does it crowd in domestic investment? *Oxford Development Studies*, *33*(2), 149–162. doi:10.1080/13600810500137749

Aharoni, Y., & Hirsch, S. (1997). Enhancing competitive advantages in technological intensive industries. In J. H. Dunning & K. A. Hamdani (Eds.), *The New Globalism and Developing Countries* (pp. 260–302). Tokyo: United Nations University Press.

Alvarez, I., & Magaña, G. (2007). Technological development in middle income countries. In J. A. Alonso (Ed.), *Cooperation with Middle-income Countries*. Madrid: Ed. Complutense.

Alvarez, I., Marín, R., & Fonfría, A. (2009). The role of networking in the competitiveness of firms. *Technological Forecasting and Social Change*, *76*(3), 410–421. doi:10.1016/j.techfore.2008.10.002

Bain, J. S. (1956). *Barriers to New Competition: Their Character and Consequences in Manufacturing Industries*. Cambridge, MA: Harvard University Press. doi:10.4159/harvard.9780674188037

Baporikar, N. (2014a). Information Strategy as Enabler of Competitive Advantage. *International Journal of Strategic Information Technology and Applications*, *5*(1), 30–41. doi:10.4018/ijsita.2014010103

Baporikar, N. (2014b). Knowledge Management Initiatives in Indian Public Sector. In Y. Al-Bastaki & A. Shajera (Eds.), *Building a Competitive Public Sector with Knowledge Management Strategy* (pp. 53–89). Hershey, PA: Business Science Reference. doi:10.4018/978-1-4666-4434-2.ch002

Baporikar, N. (2015a). Drivers of Innovation. In P. Ordoñez de Pablos, L. Turró, R. Tennyson, & J. Zhao (Eds.), *Knowledge Management for Competitive Advantage During Economic Crisis* (pp. 250–270). Hershey, PA: Business Science Reference.

Baporikar, N. (2015b). Effect of National Culture on Development of International Business in the Sultanate of Oman. In B. Christiansen (Ed.), *Handbook of Research on Global Business Opportunities* (pp. 268–288). Hershey, PA: Business Science Reference.

Baporikar, N., & Deshpande, M. (2013). Excellence Strategies of Pune Auto Component SMEs in the Borderless World. In Strategic Initiatives for Competitive Advantage in the Knowledge Society (pp. 144-154), Bloomsbury Publishing India Pvt Limited.

Barkema, H. G., & Vermeulen, F. (1998). International expansion through start-up or acquisition: A learning perspective. *Academy of Management Journal*, *41*(1), 7–26. doi:10.2307/256894

Barlett, C. A., & Ghosal, S. (1987a). Managing Across Borders: New Organizational Responses. *International Executive*, *29*(3), 10–13.

Barlett, C. A., & Ghosal, S. (1987b). Managing across Borders: New Strategic Requirements. *Sloan Management Review*, *28*(4), 7–17.

Barlett, C. A., & Ghosal, S. (1988). Organizing for Worldwide Effectiveness: The Transnational Solution. *California Management Review*, *31*(1), 54–74. doi:10.2307/41166538

Barlett, C. A., & Ghosal, S. (1992). What Is a Global Manager? *Harvard Business Review*, *70*(5), 124–132.

Barlett, C. A., & Ghosal, S. (2000). Going Global. *Harvard Business Review*, *78*(2), 132–142.

Barney, J. B. (1991). Firm resources and sustained competitive advantage. *Journal of Management*, *17*(1), 99–120. doi:10.1177/014920639101700108

Belderbos, R., & Sleuwaegen, L. (2005). Competitive drivers and international plant configuration strategies: A product-level test. *Strategic Management Journal*, *26*(6), 577–593. doi:10.1002/smj.466

Brouthers, L. E., O'Donnell, E., & Hadjimarcou, J. (2005). Generic product strategies for emerging market exports into triad nation markets: A mimetic isomorphism approach. *Journal of Management Studies*, *42*(1), 207–225. doi:10.1111/j.1467-6486.2005.00495.x

Buckley, P. J., & Casson, M. (1976). *The Future of Multinational Enterprise*. London: Holmes & Meier. doi:10.1007/978-1-349-02899-3

Buckley, P. J., Pass, C. L., & Prescott, K. (1988). Measure of International Competitiveness: A Critical Survey. *Journal of Marketing Management*, *4*(2), 175–200. doi:10.1080/0267257X.1988.9964068

Buckley, P. J., Pass, C. L., & Prescott, K. (1990a). Measure of International Competitiveness: Empirical Findings from British Manufacturing Companies. *Journal of Marketing Management*, *6*(1), 1–13. doi: 10.1080/0267257X.1990.9964112

Buckley, P. J., Pass, C. L., & Prescott, K. (1990b). The Implementation of an International Market Servicing Strategy in UK Manufacturing Firms. *British Journal of Management*, *1*(3), 127–136. doi:10.1111/j.1467-8551.1990.tb00001.x

Cantwell, J. (1989). *Technological Innovation and Multinational Corporations*. Oxford, UK: Basil Blackwell.

Cantwell, J. (1995). The globalization of technology: What remains of the product cycle model? *Cambridge Journal of Economics*, *19*(1), 155–174.

Cantwell, J. (2005). Innovation and competitiveness. In J. Fagerberg, D. Mowery, & R. Nelson (Eds.), *The Oxford Handbook of Innovation*. Oxford, UK: Oxford University Press.

Castellacci, F. (2008). Technology clubs, technology gaps and growth trajectories. *Structural Change and Economic Dynamics*, *19*(4), 301–314. doi:10.1016/j.strueco.2008.07.002

Caves, R. E. (1971). International corporations: The industrial economics of foreign investment. *Economica, 38*(149), 1–27. doi:10.2307/2551748

Coviello, N. E., Ghauri, P. N., & Martin, K. (1998). International Competitiveness: Empirical Findings from SME Service Firms. *Journal of Marketing Management, 6*(2), 8–27.

Cuervo-Cazurra, A. (2007). Sequence of value-added activities in the multinationalization of developing country firms. *Journal of International Management, 13*(3), 258–277. doi:10.1016/j.intman.2007.05.009

Cuervo-Cazurra, A., & Genc, M. E. (2011). Obligating, pressuring, and supporting dimensions of the environment and the non-market advantages of developing country multinational companies. *Journal of Management Studies, 48*(2), 441–455.

Deshpande, M., & Baporikar, N. (2014). Excellence in a Borderless World: Evidence from Pune Auto-Components SMEs. *Journal of Shinawatra University, 1*(2), 182–196.

Dunning, J. H. (1993). *Multinational Enterprises and the Global Economy*. New York: Addison Wesley Pub. Co.

Durlauf, S. N., & Johnson, P. A. (1995). Multiple regimes and cross-country growth behaviour. *Journal of Applied Econometrics, 10*(4), 365–384. doi:10.1002/jae.3950100404

Erramilli, M. K., Agarwal, S., & Kim, S.-S. (1997). Are Firm-Specific Advantages Location-Specific Too? *Journal of International Business Studies, 28*(4), 735–757. doi:10.1057/palgrave.jibs.8490117

Fagerberg, J. (1996). Technology and competitiveness. *Oxford Review of Economic Policy, 12*(3), 39–51. doi:10.1093/oxrep/12.3.39

Fagerberg, J., & Srholec, M. (2007). National innovation systems, capabilities and economic development. *Research Policy, 37*(9), 1417–1435. doi:10.1016/j.respol.2008.06.003

Fagerberg, J., & Srholec, M. (2008). *Technology and development: unpacking the relationship(s)*. TIK Working Papers on Innovation Studies No. 20080623. Centre for Technology, Innovation and Culture, University of Oslo, Oslo.

Ferguson, C. R., & Dickenson, R. (1982). *Critical success factors for directors in the eighties. Business Horizons.*

Frost, T. (2001). The geographic sources of foreign subsidiaries' innovations. *Strategic Management Journal, 22*(2), 101–123. doi:10.1002/1097-0266(200101)22:2<101::AID-SMJ155>3.0.CO;2-G

Gammeloft, P., Barnard, E., & Madhok, A. (2010). Emerging multinationals, emerging theory: Macro and micro-level perspectives. *Journal of International Management, 16*(2), 95–101. doi:10.1016/j.intman.2010.03.001

Gatignon, H., & Anderson, E. (1988). The multinational corporations' degree of control over foreign subsidiaries: An empirical test of a transaction cost explanation. *Journal of Law Economics and Organization, 4*(2), 305–336.

Gerschenkron, A. (1962). *Economic Backwardness in Historical Perspective*. Cambridge, MA: Berlknap Press.

Ghemawat, P. (1986). Sustainable advantage. *Harvard Business Review*, *64*, 53–58.

Ghosal, S., & Barlett, C. A. (1990). The multinational corporation as an interorganizational network. *Academy of Management Review*, *15*(4), 603–625.

Hansen, G. S., & Wernerfelt, B. (1989). Determinants of Firm Performance: The Relative Importance of Economic and Organizational Factors. *Strategic Management Journal*, *10*(05), 399–411. doi:10.1002/smj.4250100502

Harzing, A. W. (2000). 'An Empirical Analysis and Extension of the Bartlett and Ghosal Typology of Multinational Companies.'. *Journal of International Business Studies*, *31*(1), 101–119. doi:10.1057/palgrave.jibs.8490891

Hassel, A., Höpner, M., Kurdelbusch, A., Rehder, B., & Zugehöret, R. (2003). Two Dimensions of the Internationalization of Firms. *Journal of Management Studies*, *40*(3), 705–723. doi:10.1111/1467-6486.00357

Hofstede, G. H. (1980). *Culture Consequences: International Differences in Work-related Values*. Beverly Hills, CA: Sage Publications.

Holm, U., & Pedersen, T. (Eds.). (2000). The Emergence and the Impact of MNC Centres of Excellence. London: MacMillan.

Hymer, S. H. (1976). *The International Operations of National Firms: A Study of Direct Foreign Investment*. Cambridge, MA: MIT Press.

Kaplinsky, R. (2000). Spreading the gains from globalisation: What can be learned from value chain analysis? *The Journal of Development Studies*, *37*(2), 117–146. doi:10.1080/713600071

Kim, L. (1997). *Imitation to Innovation: The Dynamics of Korea's Technological Learning*. Boston: Harvard Business School Press.

Kogut, B. (1985). Designing global strategies: Comparative and competitive value-added chains. *Sloan Management Review*, (Fall): 27–38.

Krugman, P. (1994). Competitiveness: A dangerous obsession. *Foreign Affairs*, *73*(2), 28–44. doi:10.2307/20045917

Kumaraswamy, A., Mudambi, R., Saranga, H., & Tripathy, A. (2012). Catch-up strategies in the Indian auto components industry: Domestic firms' responses to market liberalization. *Journal of International Business Studies*, *43*(4), 368–395. doi:10.1057/jibs.2012.4

Lall, S. (1996). *Learning from the Asian Tigers*. London: Macmillan. doi:10.1057/9780230389892

Lall, S. (1997). Investment, technology and international competitiveness. In J. H. Dunning & K. A. Hamdani (Eds.), *The New Globalism and Developing Countries* (pp. 239–259). Tokyo: United Nations University Press.

Lall, S. (2000). Technological change and industrialization in the Asian newly industrializing economies: achievements and challenges. In L. Kim & R. Nelson (Eds.), *Technology, Learning & Innovation Experiences of Newly Industrializing Economies* (pp. 13–68). Cambridge, UK: Cambridge University Press.

Lall, S. (2001). What competitiveness is and why it is important. In S. Lall (Ed.), *Competitiveness, Technology and Skills* (pp. 1–30). Cheltenham, UK: Edward Elgar. doi:10.4337/9781781950555.00008

Lall, S., & Teubal, M. (1998). Market-stimulating technology policies in developing countries: A framework with examples from East Asia. *World Development*, *26*(8), 1369–1385. doi:10.1016/S0305-750X(98)00071-0

Lu, J. W., & Beamish, P. W. (2004). International diversification and firm performance: The S-Curve Hypothesis. *Academy of Management Journal*, *47*(4), 598–609. doi:10.2307/20159604

Lundvall, B. A., Johnson, B., Andersen, E. S., & Dalum, B. (2002). National systems of production, innovation and competence building. *Research Policy*, *31*(2), 213–231. doi:10.1016/S0048-7333(01)00137-8

Luo, Y., Sun, J., & Wang, S. L. (2011). Comparative strategic management: An emergent field in international management. *Journal of International Management*, *17*(3), 190–200. doi:10.1016/j.intman.2011.05.002

Ma, H. (2000). Of Competitive Advantage: Kinetic and Positional. *Business Horizons*, *43*(1), 53–64. doi:10.1016/S0007-6813(00)87388-7

Mason, E. S. (1939). Price and Production Policies of Large-Scale Enterprises. *The American Economic Review*, *29*(3), 61–74.

McCann, P., Mudambi, R., (2005). Analytical differences in the economics of geography: the case of the multinational firm. *Environment and Planning*, *37*, 1857–1876.

Meyer, K. E. (2004). Perspectives on multinational enterprises in emerging economies. *Journal of International Business Studies*, *35*(4), 259–276. doi:10.1057/palgrave.jibs.8400084

Meyer, K. E., Mudambi, R., & Narula, R. (2011). Multinational enterprises and local contexts: The opportunities and challenges of multiple embeddedness. *Journal of Management Studies*, *48*(2), 235–252.

Mowery, D. C., & Oxley, E. (1995). Inward technology transfer and competitiveness: The role of national innovation systems. *Cambridge Journal of Economics*, *19*(1), 67–93.

Mudambi, R. (2008). Location, control and innovation in knowledge-intensive industries. *Journal of Economic Geography*, *8*(5), 699–725. doi:10.1093/jeg/lbn024

Narula, R., & Wakelin, K. (1995). *Technological competitiveness, trade and foreign direct investment.* Research Memorandum, 2/95—019. MERIT, Maastricht.

Nelson, R. (1993). *National Innovation Systems: A Comparative Analysis.* Oxford, UK: Oxford University Press.

Ohmae, K. (2006). Growing in a Global Garden. *Leadership Excellence*, *23*(9), 14–15.

Peteraf, M. A. (1993). The cornerstones of competitive advantage: A resource-based view. *Strategic Management Journal*, *14*(3), 179–191. doi:10.1002/smj.4250140303

Piscitello, L. (2004). Corporate diversification, coherence and economic performance. *Industrial and Corporate Change*, *13*(5), 757–787. doi:10.1093/icc/dth030

Porter, M. E. (1980). *Competitive Strategy*. New York: Free Press.

Porter, M. E. (1985). *Competitive Advantage: Creating and Sustaining Superior Performance*. New York: The Free Press.

Porter, M. E. (1990). *Competitive Advantage of Nations*. New York: The Free Press. doi:10.1007/978-1-349-11336-1

Porter, M.E. (2001). *Strategy and the Internet*. Academic Press.

Porter, M. E., Delgado, M., Ketels, C., & Stern, S. (2008). Moving to a new global competitiveness index. In *The Global Competitiveness Report 2008–2009*. World Economic Forum.

Rodrik, D. (1996). Coordination failures and government policy: A model with applications to East Asia and Eastern Europe. *Journal of International Economics*, *40*(1-2), 1–22. doi:10.1016/0022-1996(95)01386-5

Rodrik, D. (1999). *The New Global Economy and Developing Countries: Making Openness Work. Policy Essay no. 24*. Washington, DC: Overseas Development Council.

Roessner, J. D., Porter, A. L., Newman, N., & Cauffiel, D. (1996). Anticipating the future high-tech competitiveness of nations: Indicators for twenty-eight countries. *Technological Forecasting and Social Change*, *51*(2), 133–149. doi:10.1016/0040-1625(95)00195-6

Rugman, A. M. (1981). *Inside the Multinationals: The Economics of Internal Markets*. New York: Columbia University Press.

Rugman, A. M., & Doh, J. P. (2008). *Multinationals and Development*. New Haven, CT: Yale University Press. doi:10.12987/yale/9780300115611.001.0001

Rugman, A. M., & Verbeke, A. (2001). Subsidiary-specific advantages in multinational enterprises. *Strategic Management Journal*, *22*(3), 237–250. doi:10.1002/smj.153

Rugman, A. M., & Verbeke, A. (2001). Location, competitiveness and the multinational enterprise. In A. M. Rugman & T. L. Brewer (Eds.), *The Oxford Handbook of International Business* (pp. 150–179). Oxford, UK: Oxford University Press. doi:10.1093/0199241821.003.0006

Sala-I-Martin, X., Blanke, J., Drzeniek, M., Geiger, T., Mia, I., & Paua, F. (2008). The global competitiveness index: prioritizing the economic policy agenda. In *The Global Competitiveness Report 2008–2009*. World Economic Forum.

Segal-Horn & Faulkner. (1999). *The Dynamics of International Strategy*. Thomson.

Singh, J. (2007). Asymmetry of knowledge spillovers between MNCs and host country firms. *Journal of International Business Studies*, *38*(5), 764–786. doi:10.1057/palgrave.jibs.8400289

Stopford, J. M., & Wells, L. T. (1972). *Managing the multinational enterprise: Organization of the firm and ownership of the subsidiaries*. New York: Basic Books.

Teece, D. (1977). Technology transfer by multinational firms: The resource cost of transferring technological know-how. *The Economic Journal*, *87*(346), 242–262. doi:10.2307/2232084

Teece, D. J. (1980). Economies of scope and the scope of the enterprise. *Journal of Economic Behavior & Organization*, *1*(3), 223–247. doi:10.1016/0167-2681(80)90002-5

Uchida, Y., & Cook, P. (2005). The transformation of competitive advantage in East Asia: An analysis of technological and trade specialization. *World Development*, *33*(5), 701–728. doi:10.1016/j.worlddev.2005.01.005

UNCTAD. (2005). *World Investment Report Transnational Corporations and the Internationalization of R&D*. New York: United Nations.

UNCTAD. (2007). *World Investment Report Transnational Corporations, Extractive Industries and Development*. New York: United Nations.

Wernerfelt, B. (1984). A resource-based view of the firm. *Strategic Management Journal*, *5*(2), 171–180. doi:10.1002/smj.4250050207

Yang, Q., Mudambi, R., & Meyer, K. E. (2008). Conventional and reverse knowledge flows in multinational corporations. *Journal of Management*, *34*(5), 882–902. doi:10.1177/0149206308321546

Yip, G. S. (1989). Global Strategy a World of Nations? *Sloan Management Review*, *31*(1), 29–41.

Yip, G. S. (1991a). A Performance Comparison of Continental and National Businesses in Europe. *International Marketing Review*, *8*(2), 31. doi:10.1108/02651339110137774

Yip, G. S. (1991b). Strategies in Global Industries: How U.S. Businesses Compete. *Journal of International Business Studies*, *22*(4), 749–753. doi:10.1057/jibs.1991.56

Yip, G. S. (1994). Industry Drivers of Global Strategy and Organization. *International Executive*, *36*(5), 529–556. doi:10.1002/tie.5060360503

Yip, G. S. (1996). Global Strategy as a Factor in Japanese Success. *International Executive*, *38*(1), 145–167. doi:10.1002/tie.5060380111

Yip, G. S. et al.. (1988). How to Take Your Company to the Global Market. *The Columbia Journal of World Business*, *23*(4), 37–48.

Yip, G. S., Biscarri, J. G., & Monti, J. A. (2000). The Role of the Internationalization Process in the Performance of Newly Internationalizing Firms. *Journal of International Marketing*, *8*(3), 10–35. doi:10.1509/jimk.8.3.10.19635

Yip, G. S., Joansson, J. K., & Johan, R. (1997). Effects of Nationality on Global Strategy.[MIR]. *Management International Review*, *37*(4), 365–385.

Yip, G. S., & Madsen, T. L. (1996). Global account management: The new frontier in relationship marketing. *International Marketing Review*, *13*(3), 24–42. doi:10.1108/02651339610122982

ADDITIONAL READING

Alvarez, I., & Marín, R. (2010). Entry modes and national systems of innovation. *Journal of International Management, 16*(4), 340–353. doi:10.1016/j.intman.2010.09.005

Alvarez, I., Marín, R., & Fonfría, A. (2009). The role of networking in the competitiveness of firms. *Technological Forecasting and Social Change, 76*(3), 410–421. doi:10.1016/j.techfore.2008.10.002

Bain, J. S. (1956). *Barriers to New Competition: Their Character and Consequences in Manufacturing Industries*. Cambridge: Harvard University Press. doi:10.4159/harvard.9780674188037

Baporikar, N. (2011). Global Strategic Management, Himalaya Publishing House, Mumbai, India, 2nd Revised Edition, ISBN: 978-81-8488-050-2

Baporikar, N. (2014). Strategic Management Overview and SME in Globalized World. In K. Todorov & D. Smallbone (Eds.), *Handbook of Research on Strategic Management in Small and Medium Enterprises* (pp. 22–39). Hershey, PA: Business Science Reference.

Baporikar, N. (2014). Innovation Strategies in SME: Global Perspective. In C. Machado & P. Melo (Eds.), *Effective Human Resources Management in Small and Medium Enterprises: Global Perspectives* (pp. 315–341). Hershey, PA: Business Science Reference.

Baporikar, N. (2012). Strategies for Sustainable Development – A Case Study of Carrefour. *JIDNYASA Research Journal, 6*, 38–45.

Barney, J. (1997). *Gaining and Sustaining Competitive Advantage*. Reading: Addison-Wesley.

Bartlett, C. A., & Ghoshal, S. (1998). *Managing Across Borders: The Transnational Solution*. Boston: Harvard Business School Press.

Buckley, P. J., & Casson, M. (1976). *The Future of Multinational Enterprise*. London: Holmes &Meier. doi:10.1007/978-1-349-02899-3

Cantwell, J. (2005). Innovation and competitiveness. In J. Fagerberg, D. Mowery, & R. Nelson (Eds.), *The Oxford Handbook of Innovation*. Oxford: Oxford University Press.

Cantwell, J., & Molero, J. (2003). *Multinational Enterprises, Innovative Strategies and Systems of Innovation*. Cheltenham: Edward Elgar.

Dunning, J. H. (1993). *Multinational Enterprises and the Global Economy*. New York: Addison Wesley Pub. Co.

Markusen, J. R. (2002). *Multinational Firms and the Theory of International Trade*. Cambridge: MIT Press.

Narula, R. (1996). *Multinational Investments and Economic Structure*. London: Routledge.

Nelson, R. (1993). *National Innovation Systems: A Comparative Analysis*. Oxford: Oxford University Press.

Nonaka, I., & Takeuchi, H. (1995). *The Knowledge-Creating Company: How Japanese Companies Create the Dynamics of Innovation*. Oxford: Oxford University Press.

Rugman, A. M. (1981). *Inside the Multinationals: The Economics of Internal Markets*. New York: Columbia University Press.

Rugman, A. M., & Doh, J. P. (2008). *Multinationals and Development*. New Haven, London: Yale University Press. doi:10.12987/yale/9780300115611.001.0001

Stopford, J. M., & Wells, L. T. (1972). *Managing the multinational enterprise: Organization of the firm and ownership of the subsidiaries*. New York: Basic Books.

Vernon, R. (1971). *Sovereignty at Bay: The Multinational Spread of US Enterprises*. New York: Basic Books.

Williamson, O. E. (1975). *Markets and Hierarchies*. New York: Free Press.

Zack, M. H. (1999). Developing a Knowledge Strategy. *California Management Review*, *41*(3), 125–145. doi:10.2307/41166000

KEY TERMS AND DEFINITIONS

Business: Pertains broadly to commercial, financial, and industrial activities.

Developing: Means 'steady progress' and stresses effective assisting in hastening a process or bringing about a desired end, a significant consequence or event, the act or process of growing, progressing, or developing.

Enterprises: The act or process of organizing; a structure through which individuals cooperate systematically to conduct business and/or the administrative personnel of such a structure.

Environment: Important or essential in relation to a plan of action; highly important to an intended objective.

Globalization: Worldwide integration and development, the process enabling financial and investment markets to operate internationally, largely as a result of deregulation and improved communications.

International: Involving two or more nations; of or relating to two or more nations or their citizens; an organization, enterprise, or group, especially a major business concern, having branches, dealings, or members in several countries.

Landscape: overall scenario; is a way of regarding situations or topics or a mental view or the state of one's Ideas; prospective means concerned with or related to the future and judging their relative importance. It includes the proper or accurate point of view or the ability to see with objectivity so as to try to get some perspective on issues for better solutions.

Performance: Economic efficiency in terms of productivity and costs.

Strategies: A method or plan chosen to bring about a desired future, such as achievement of a goal or solution to a problem. Strategy is a result of choices made. It is that set of managerial decisions and actions that determine the long term performance of a business enterprise.

Chapter 4
Ethical and Social Challenges:
Ethics Is Profitable, No-Ethics Is Punishable

Francisco A Espinoza S
Tecnologico de Monterrey, Mexico

ABSTRACT

Globalization has been a factor that has brought countries closer worldwide, and Multinational Enterprises (MNEs) are eager to look for new market opportunities in developing countries. This chapter analyzes the implementation of MNEs' global ethical principles in business into local moral standards of societies from developing countries. The author will discuss, using current scenarios, how principles of both moral relativism and moral absolutism can provide a profitable or punishable opportunity within developing countries when MNEs operate accordingly, or not, to ethical decision making processes in business. Additionally, the chapter proposes how MNEs' managers can discover the limits of moral free space, to distinguish a moral value in tension with their own from one that is intolerable. At the end, it is expected that MNEs' managers can apply ethical decision making in business by clearly perceiving and understanding their corporate culture in a developing country society.

INTRODUCTION

This chapter analyzes the implementation of MNEs' global ethical principles in business into local moral standards of societies from developing countries. The author will discuss, using current scenarios, how principles of both moral relativism and moral absolutism can provide a profitable (beneficial), or punishable (detrimental), opportunity within developing countries when MNEs operate, or not, according to ethical decision making processes in business.

The objectives of this chapter are:

1. To sensitize about the moral dilemma within the migration of MNEs into developing countries.
2. To explain how concepts of morality (moral relativism, moral absolutism) can influence MNEs' business ethics in their integration to a developing country's society.

DOI: 10.4018/978-1-5225-0276-0.ch004

3. To demonstrate different global ethical approaches for the integration of MNEs in developing countries according to the UN Global Compact Principles.
4. To propose a guideline for MNEs to overcome the barriers of dissimilar moral realities within developing countries.

Background

Globalization has become a factor that brought countries closer worldwide, and Multinational Enterprises (MNEs) are eager to look for new market opportunities in developing countries. In other words, this new "California Gold Rush"-like situation has attracted some MNEs to developing countries where cheap labor, competitive advantages in resources, tax shelters and relief, market, lax regulations, and weak competition constitute opportunities to increase profits and reduce costs. Developing countries are defined according to their Gross National Income (GNI) per capita per year, and the International Statistical Institute (ISI) has published the new list of developing countries, effective from January 1st until December 31st 2015: Countries with a GNI of US$ 11,905 and less are defined as developing country (World Bank, 2013). Among this list all Latin American countries belong to this group in which, corrupt situations when doing business plays a questionable-ingrained role. Also, many MNEs have been enrooting in their strategies in an accelerated pace in order to gain a coveted market, sometimes coming across ethical issues that could arise from different cultural perspectives concerning values-principles-norms among MNEs and those developing countries in which they do business.

For example, many textile industries from around the world (Nike, H&M, etc.) have moved to developing countries to take advantage of cheaper labor there. Were these developing country workers exploited because they were paid less than their counterparts in developed countries? We cannot determine if they were exploited simply because the workers were paid less; the charge of exploitation needs more than the existence of a comparative low wage scale. In many situations MNEs pay the same rate as the local employers. If the other employers fail to pay a living wage, they are as guilty as the MNEs. However, MNEs have been criticized by local business for paying more than the living wage. The MNEs are thus caught between contradictory demands. So, when MNEs operate in developing countries, sometimes conflicts in ethical decision-making processes can arise due to incongruities between their own corporate culture and original countries' values and interests, and inconsistent cultural values of the hosting country. In this situation, the rightness or wrongness of actions sometimes is determined regarding the differences along cultural issues, from both relative and absolute perspective of morality.

Precisely, these antagonizing situations are one of the main concerns in business ethics: Should MNEs adjust the way they conduct ethical matters by adapting to foreign values or keeping universal principles? This ethical dilemma possess a great significance when MNEs face how to do business in developing countries, and existing MNEs have already demonstrated alternatives to implement their ethical strategies in developing countries. Nowadays, general ethical principles have been established worldwide such as The United Nations Global Compact Principles (UNGC) (UN Global Compact, 2015), The Caux Round Table Principles for Business (CRT) (Caux Round Table, 2015), The International Chamber of Commerce (ICC) (International Chamber of Commerce, 2015), and The International Labour Organization Principles (ILO) (International Labour Organization, 2015). In order to strive for possible answers, or at least to have a silver lining of these situations, this Chapter is aimed to offer a response beginning by explaining some of the main business ethical approaches, and examining some ethical challenges that

MNEs face worldwide in this context. Hence, *to what extent should MNEs adapt their activities and principles in order to meet foreign values-principles-norms?*

MORALITY IN BUSINESS ETHICS

Globally, business ethics or ethical business approaches are moral judgments concerning correct and incorrect practices in a business-enterprise-corporation. It is of particular importance to properly acknowledge that what is considered as a correct practice in one country, might be considered incorrect in another. This condition of moral judgments nurtures the inquiry whether correct, or acceptable, moral practices should be dependent on local cultures or, whether moral practices are universal and should direct the same conduct all over the world. In everyday reality, MNEs intrinsically face this dilemma, especially when establishing in a developing country where capabilities in social, cultural, economical, legal, transparency and in human rights are so dissimilar. To evaluate the impact of these differences in the establishment of operations of MNEs in developing countries, there are two ethical/moral perspectives which could be use in order to support the theoretical background for this analysis: moral relativism and moral absolutism. The concept of moral relativism is often associated with the normative position regarding how people should act towards those who have morally different viewpoints, while moral absolutism proposes that some forms of human conduct are right or wrong (alternatively, good or evil) in any context (Palmer, 2008). Yet in both, the grounds on each moral perspective do not justify bad actions in any case, even for the purpose of doing good. And these perspectives should not be abused by MNEs in any native or foreign context.

Moral Relativism

In 1947, there was a historic moment for Moral Relativism, with the debate about universal rights at the United Nations, when the American Anthropological Association issued a statement declaring that moral values are relative to cultures and that there is no way of proving that the moral standard and values of one culture are better than those of another, no matter how contrasting these might be (Gowans, 2004). Moral Relativism provides an academic foundation for those who are against what they call the imposition of Western values by multinational corporations on the rest of the world. For instance, two cultures may agree about the basic principles of morality (the right of work for a better family living) but disagree about how to implement those principles in any particular scenario (including or not child labor) (Beauchamp, Bowie, and Arnold, 2008). As a general example, follows the maxim: "When in Rome, do as Romans do". Here, problems arise when MNEs deal with ethical practices that are commonly accepted in developed countries, such as prohibiting child labor, but that are not tolerated or accepted by the social or cultural values of the hosting developing country, children can and should work as "family workers" (See Case1: Nestlé Farms In Ivory Coast).

Case 1: Nestlé

A Nestlé spokesperson told the Guardian: "To date we have identified 3,933 children working on their family farms (around 10% of the children surveyed) who were involved in hazardous tasks classified as child labour. We have included half of them in our Child Labour Monitoring and Remediation System, which includes providing school kits, obtaining birth certificates and developing income generating activities for the families of 312 identified children. Unfortunately, the scale and complexity of the issue is such that no company sourcing cocoa from Ivory Coast can guarantee that it has completely removed the risk of child labour from its supply chain. (The Guardian, 2015)

On one side, moral relativism commonly asks for more tolerance when people have moral disagreements, since it considers that the truth or justification of moral judgment to be relative to the moral standard of a certain person or community and, not to an absolute (Gowans, 2004). Therefore, in Case 1 moral relativism would demand a more inclusive practice of the family values and practices in cocoa farms in Ivory Coast, despite the fact that Nestlé as an MNEs doesn't support child labor, and neither do international business ethical codes. In Case 1, the relativist argument states that we ought to reject Moral Absolutism since there is little prospect of rationally resolving moral disagreements that involve parties that have fundamentally contrasting cultures and viewpoints. Furthermore, Nestlé recognizes the magnitude of the cultural issue and that despite their efforts, no company could ever guarantee that has removed child labor from their supply chain. So, should Nestlé censure these farms by refusing to accept them as suppliers or partners? As seen in Case 1, Nestlé demonstrates as well that despite the major moral principle disagreements, collateral actions and ethically-oriented projects from MNEs can contribute to diminish human rights abuses in their operations at developing countries.

However, those who advocate for Moral Relativism point to the evident multiple forms of moral codes and the diversity of human values to support their arguments. Some of them also contend that variations in moral standards reflect opposing factual beliefs and circumstances instead of fundamental differences in values (Shaw & Barry, 2007). And those who criticize Moral Relativism point to its unpleasant implications: First, it undermines any moral criticism of any practice in any society as long as it abides to the local standards; Second, for those who defend Moral Relativism, ethical progress is unobtainable due to the fact that moralities can't improve or diminish, only change (Shaw & Barry, 2007). A relativist explanation may dissolve any disagreement, but why would it be portrayed as a disagreement in the first place? An absolutist could argue that this is because people will automatically assume that moral truth actually is absolute rather than relative (Gowans, 2004). Finally, some relativists could add that in certain cases people ought to be tolerant with whom they morally disagree, but only absolutists are able to establish any particular objective moral truth.

Moral Absolutism

On the other side, the term Moral Absolutism refers to the view that right or wrong doesn't depend on what any person or culture thinks is right and wrong. From this viewpoint, so-called "moral facts" are like "physical facts" in a sense that what is considered a physical fact does not depend on what any group of people thinks about it (Latus, 2001). Today, two commonly accepted theories follow Moral Absolutism:

Duty Based Theories (Deontological Theories): These theories claim that what determines whether an action is morally right or wrong is the kind of action it essentially is. Many philosophers argue that fundamental ethical duties bind us in a stricter way than the manner in which we are bound by contracts. Following this argument, ethical duties ought to be "categorical" imperatives instead of hypothetical. In the case of hypothetical duties, for instance, an individual would have to comply to a professional code of conduct only if he or she is a member of that certain profession, whereas categorical duties do not have that 'if' clause (Hartman & DesJardins, 2008).

Consequentialist Theories (Teleological Theories): These theories hold that in order to determine the rightness of any action one should solely analyze the amount of good consequence it produces. The term Teleological comes from the Greek word *telos*, which alludes to an end. Naturally, the concept of goodness is the pillar of Teleological Theories alongside the concepts of obligation and rightness, which are defined in terms of goodness. A main strength of these theories is that they align with much of society's ordinary moral reasoning. There's also the inherent strength these theories have due to the fact that they provide a reasonably objective system for moral decision making.

The categorical imperative was a key concept the German philosopher Immanuel Kant stood by. According to Kant, our primary duty is to act only in those ways in which the maxim of our acts could be made a universal law. In this view, everyone should treat people with respect and as equally capable of living an autonomous life (DesJardins, 2009). He also claimed that ethics requires every individual to treat all people as ends and never as means. (See Case 2: Levi's Worker Well-Being)

Case 2: Levi Strauss & CO

We have completed pilots for the Worker Well-being initiative in Bangladesh, Cambodia, Egypt, Haiti and Pakistan (...) What distinguishes this initiative from others is that we survey the workers so we can tailor the program to the topics they care about the most, such as women's health and financial inclusion. (...) Through the Worker Well-being initiative, LS&Co. is setting a new standard for corporate responsibility, one in which we aim to empower workers with the tools they need to lead healthier, more productive lives. Our suppliers have seen a significant return — up to $3 for every $1 invested in the program, so we're expanding the program in 2015 to more vendors. (Levi Strauss & CO., 2015)

In Case 2, Levi applies a deontologist perspective in which some actions are right because of their nature or the rules from which they follow (the well-being of the worker), not because of the consequence or benefit to ourselves or others. One of the strengths Deontologists claim is that these theories make sense on cases in which consequences are considered irrelevant, particularly when there's a need to justify the obligations that arise from relations (contracts and roles). A second strength is that these theories account for the role of reasons or motives in evaluating actions. On the other hand, the main question that arises from Consequentialist Theories is: consequence for whom? Considering the possible answers for this question, there are two important consequentialist theories: Egoism argues that individual self-interest should be the guiding principle, whereas Utilitarianism contends that one ought to take into account every individual affected by the action (Shaw and Barry, 2007). As seen in Case 2, we can see these principles of moral absolutist applied in ethical decision making concerning operations of MNEs in developing countries, and furthermore leading to both beneficial results for both the company and the society.

As it often occurs in real life, trying to follow these concepts is not as simple as it may sound, thus the weaknesses of Teleological Theories arise from the same features that constitute their strengths. One should take into account the fact that some of our ordinary reasoning is non-teleological in nature as well. And that one could argue that these theories fail to provide a realistic account of how one could truly know what moral obligations to follow, and resolve what standards to in any particular case of moral conflict (Boatright, 2003).

Table 1. Concepts of morality applied in business ethics

Moral Relativism	
American Anthropological Association	Moral values depend on cultures. Moral standards and values are relative, and cannot be compared (for better or worse) within cultures.
Descriptive Moral Relativism	Moral values within different cultures are significant because of the diversity they provide, not because they follow their own standards.
Metaethical Moral Relativism	Moral values within different cultures are significant because they follow their own standards, not because of the diversity they provide.
Moral Absolutism	
Latus	Moral values do not depend on cultures. Moral standards and values are universal, and can be compared (for better or worse) within cultures.
Deontological Theories	Moral values are significant because of their nature, or rules they follow, not because of their benefits or consequences.
Teleological Theories (Egoism, Utilitarianism)	Moral values are significant because of the amount of good in their benefits or consequences, not because of their nature.

Confounders in Morality Concepts

It is important to underline that empirical research suggests that both Moral Relativism and Moral Absolutism have some merit since the meta-ethical views of common people are quite complex (see Table 1). A common method used to measure whether people are relativists or absolutists about a certain moral belief is to present them with a disagreement between two parties and ask them if at most only one party is correct. If the response considers that there can be only one party correct, that would indicate a commitment to Moral Absolutism whereas arguing for both parties would indicate the opposite, a commitment to Moral Relativism (Gowans, 2004). Those who indicate a commitment to Moral Absolutism are more likely to attribute theological grounding to morality than those who indicate a commitment to Moral Relativism (Goodwin & Darley, 2008). And those who are considered to be more open to experience are more likely to be relativists than absolutists (Feltz & Cokely, 2008).

There are other studies that have shown different types of complexity. For instance, people are more likely to be absolutist about certain moral issues (like robbery) than they are about other moral issues (like abortion). These differences could be a least partially explained due to the fact that regarding a certain issue as absolute could correlate with the strength of belief and consensus on the issue that exists within a certain community, and not necessarily with the moral concepts (Goodwin and Darley, 2008). Could this mean that Moral Absolutism implies intolerance? Well, absolutists always contend that the fact that some culture may view another culture as morally wrong in certain aspects does not necessarily mean that it should interfere with it (Gowans, 2004). Furthermore, moral absolutism promotes universal ethical principles and seeks the promotion of common values around the world. These and other possible confounders and perspectives of morality should be taking into account in every ethical decision making process of MNEs before, during and after establishing operations in a developing country.

Table 2. UN global compact's ten principles

Human Rights	1. Business should support and respect the protection of internationally proclaimed human rights.
	2. Make sure that they are not complicit in human rights abuses.
Labor	3. Businesses should uphold the freedom of association and the effective recognition of the right to collective bargaining.
	4. The elimination of all forms of forced and compulsory labor.
	5. The effective abolition of child labor.
	6. The elimination of discrimination in respect of employment and occupation.
Environment	7. Businesses should support a precautionary approach to environmental challenges.
	8. Undertake initiatives to promote greater environmental responsibility.
	9. Encourage the development and diffusion of environmentally friendly technologies.
Anti-Corruption	10. Businesses should work against corruption in all its forms, including extortion and bribery.

UNIVERSAL ETHICAL PRINCIPLES IN BUSINESS

There have been several attempts by both multinational corporations and government agencies to establish international codes of business conduct that transcend relativism. Regardless of the many contrasting values societies may have, they often do agree about what many call ultimate moral standards. These universal ethical principles and duties can often be found in a corporate code of ethics. One example of such code that has been recognized worldwide is the United Nations Global Compact´s (UNGC) code. (United Nations Global Compact, 2015). The UNGC supports companies in order to:

1. Do business responsibly by aligning their strategies and operations with the Ten Principles on human rights, labor, environment and anti-corruption (see Table 2).
2. Take strategic actions to advance broader societal goals, such as the forthcoming UN Sustainable Development Goals, with an emphasis on collaboration and innovation.

These Ten Principles of the UNGC are derived from: The Universal Declaration of Human Rights (United Nations, 2015), the International Labor Organization's Declaration on Fundamental Principles and Rights at Work (International Labor Organization, 2015), the Rio Declaration on Environment and Development (United Nations, 1992), and the United Nations Convention against Corruption (United Nations Office of Drugs and Crime, 2004).

As moral relativism could be conflicting with some of the worldwide accepted principles proposed by UN Global Compact, it might also be considered that these *universal ethical principles* in the MNEs ought to be adequately applied in developing countries to minimally disrupt their moral values and identity. However, there is a gap in which MNEs must respect fundamental human rights as well as local customs, and to understand that is important when making ethical decisions. Remember that whatever type of principles MNEs are going to follow in the developing country, will determine the way in which MNEs adjust to their ethical conduct.

The Global Compact

The UN Global Compact (UNGC) is the world's largest global corporate sustainability initiative. It has not only drawn a lot of attention and been joined by an impressive number of companies, but it also carries with it the prestige and influence of the United Nations. The Global Compact moreover, is compatible with other codes (CRT, ILO, etc.) and with self-regulation by individual companies through voluntary codes of conduct. For these reasons and other not mentioned explicitly, MNEs should reinforce the UNGC in their own corporate culture. Despite the fact that MNEs have many sites around the world, with varied employee groups and management forms, a person employed in a MNE in one developing country will share various aspects of his or her working culture with someone working for the same MNE in another part of the world. This doesn't mean that their working environments cannot be wholly different in many regards; the corporate culture, however, lasts the distance and differences.

MNEs can adapt their ethical behavior to the local expectations, benefiting from the existence of the weaker ethical norms prevailing in a developing country - México. Nevertheless, that is not always the trend among MNEs. There are some MNEs which have been committed the UN Global Compact Principles since they have joined it (See Case 3: BASF, and Case 4: KPMG).

Case 3: BASF

BASF, a global company that occupies a leading position in the chemical industry. We offer customers a range of high-performance products, including innovative and high-value-added chemicals, plastics, colorants, automotive and industrial coatings, crop protection agents, pharmaceuticals and fine chemicals as well as crude oil, natural gas and petrochemicals. BASF is convinced that the aims of the United Nations - peace and development - and the goals of business - wealth creation and prosperity - are mutually supportive. We thereby believe that business can best contribute to the attainment of the Compact's principles through the manner in which we conduct our own business. BASF is willing to promote the Compact's principles through the spread of our good corporate practices in an open global economy within our sphere of influence. BASF has over 100 000 employees, who enjoy working conditions which fully comply with the principles set out by the Global Compact. Through our foreign direct investment, BASF's business attitude is setting high standards at production sites in 38 countries. We are convinced that economic strength and prosperity - as one pillar of sustainable development – best enable business to contribute to the aims of the Global Compact (United Nations Global Compact, 2015).

Case 4: KPMG

KPMG is a global network of professional firms providing Audit, Tax and Advisory services. We operate in 144 countries and have 140,000 people working in member firms around the world. The independent member firms of the KPMG network are affiliated with KPMG International Cooperative ("KPMG International"), a Swiss entity. Each KPMG firm is a legally distinct and separate entity and describes itself as such. Commitment to our communities is one of KPMG's core values and a cornerstone of the culture of our member firms. Our culture and values, which are aligned with the Ten UN Compact Global Principles, are integrated into how we conduct business. We encourage our people to take leadership in and for our communities, and use their skills in creative and determined ways to help deliver and support solutions. Considering the global challenges we all face, this commitment strikes me as perhaps even more important than ever before. (UN Global Compact, 2010)

As stated before, MNE´s own corporate culture can be enriched by the Ten UN Global Compact Principles (United Nations Global Compact, 2015) in order to reinforce such corporate identity significantly despite the different and contrasting moral values of each locality of MNEs. These principles underline the need that there are moral imperatives that should be acceptable by MNEs in order to establish an international background of ethical practices worldwide. The UNGC organization recognize regarding valuable - profitable - among MNEs established over 160 countries the following companies (just to mention some) which represent every industry sector and size (see Table 3).

Table 3. MNEs belonging to the UNGC

NAME	COUNTRY	NAME	COUNTRY
Acciona	Spain	A.P. Moller - Maersk	Denmark
Daimler AG	Germany	China Ocean Shipping Group - COSCO	China
Pirelli & C. S.P.A.	Italy	Safaricom Limited	Kenya
BASF SE	Germany	SK Telecom	Korea, Republic of
Bayer AG	Germany	China Petroleum and Chemical Corporation - Sinopec	China
Braskem S.A.	Brazil	ENI	Italy
Sumitomo Chemical Company, Limited	Japan	Oando Plc	Nigeria
The Dow Chemical Company	Unites States of America	Sakhalin Energy Investment Company Ltd.	Russian Federation
Yara International ASA	Norway	Total	France
Lafarge	France	Great River Corporation	China
Enel	Italy	PT. Martina Berto Tbk, Martha Tilaar Group	Indonesia
Eskom	South Africa	Rosy Blue	Belgium
AVIVA plc	United Kingdom	Novartis International AG	Switzerland
China Developmental Bank	China	Novo Nordisk AS	Denmark
KPMG International	United States of America	Novozymes	Denmark
Deutsche Telekom AG	Germany	Takeda Pharmaceutical Company Limited	Japan
Nestle S.A.	Switzerland	Infosys Ltd	India
Unilever	United Kingdom	Symantec Corporation	United States of America
Empresa de Energia de Bogota	Colombia	Accenture	United States of America
China Minmetals Corporation	China	Fuji Xerox Co., Ltd.	Japan
Vale	Brazil	LG Electronics, Inc.	Korea, Republic of
Tata Steel	India	Netafim	Israel
Teck Resources Limited	Canada	ARM Holdings plc	United Kingdom

On the other hand, one of the most common problem that MNEs are facing when going to developing countries is a form of corruption known as bribery. In Mexico for example, where corruption – bribery – is often a business practices camouflaged in form of gift giving, is a key procedural. MNEs should define their stance with respect to "collaborations" of bribes to corporate and government officials, concerning local expectations (see Case 5: Wal-Mart).

Wal-Mart Stores Inc. confronted significant legal risks after it disclosed that it is investigating its operations in Mexico for possible violations of the U.S. law that prohibits bribery in foreign countries, legal experts said. (Bustillo, 2012) On one hand, Michael Bergdahl in his book What I Learned from Sam Walton: How to Compete and Thrive in a Wal-Mart World claims that:

Understanding this total integrity standard is critical to the success of vendors and Wal-Mart associates alike. Situational Integrity or ethics [moral relativism] are not tolerated. I once heard Sam Walton say he would walk a million miles with someone who had a job-performance problem but he wouldn't take the first step with someone with an integrity problem. Good old fashioned integrity, honesty, and business ethics are required if a vendor want to do business with Wal-Mart or if a job applicant wants to work there. Employees are held to the highest ethical standards and anything less is unacceptable. (Bergdahl, 2004)

Additionally, Wal-Mart CEO´s Doug McMillon declares at Wal-Mart´s own Global Statement of Ethics:

Case 5: Wal-Mart

Our unique culture drives our purpose of saving people money so they can live better, and the foundation of our culture is a commitment to operating with integrity. Even as we change to meet the needs of our customers, Walmart will stay true to the values, beliefs and behaviors that have guided us over the last 50 years. Regardless of where each of us works in our global company, this Statement of Ethics is the guide to exemplifying integrity as a Walmart associate. It's a daily resource for making honest, fair and objective decisions while operating in compliance with all laws and our policies. This Statement of Ethics applies to me, the board of directors and all associates at every level of our organization. Through your ethical behavior and willingness to speak up for the highest standards, we earn and keep the trust of our customers, each other and our local communities. We believe in everyday low cost and everyday low prices, but only if accomplished through our everyday integrity. Thank you for your commitment to our Statement of Ethics. It means more than making ethical decisions; it demonstrates you care about Walmart, our reputation and our customers. (Walmart, 2015)

Both statements which seem to be a thoughtful guide of ethics turn into a cost of $439 million USD according to Wal-Mart. Why is this cost so high to pay? The New York Times reported in 2012 that Wal-Mart paid $24 million in alleged bribes in Mexico. The probe expanded to other countries, including China, India and Brazil, the retailer said in 2012. The U.S. is investigating possible violations of the Foreign Corrupt Practices Act, which bans payments by companies or their agents to foreign governments to obtain or retain business. Such probes typically end in settlements, with companies paying fines and admitting wrongdoing. Mexican authorities also are investigating, while Wal-Mart faces shareholder lawsuits and is examining its global anti-corruption compliance programs. In addition to the $24 million in alleged bribes, Wal-Mart made $16 million in "donations" to Mexican local governments as late as

2005 to speed store expansions, the New York Times reported in April 2012. The company also failed to examine fully claims by a company lawyer in 2005 that he funneled bribes to Mexican officials, the newspaper reported. "It's relatively safe to assume that this is one of the highest pre-enforcement-action professional fees and expenses ever reported," said Michael Koehler, a law professor at Southern Illinois University who writes the Foreign Corrupt Practices Act (FCPA) (The United States Department of Justice, 2015) professor blog (Barstow, 2012).

The practice of bribery as the act of giving money, goods or other forms of recompense to a recipient in exchange for an alteration of their behavior (to the benefit/interest of the giver) that the recipient would otherwise not alter, it is a practice that is viewed as acceptable in some developing countries, as distinct from being accepted as an inevitable practice, with a feeling of resignation. In other words, in some developing countries, offering, giving, receiving, or soliciting of any item of value to influence the actions of an official or other person in charge of a public or legal duty is an indispensable courtesy and a normal way of doing business. As such, bribery is not always considered as an offence. Unethical practices and corruption in business predominate in various segments of developing countries.

These acts as walls to development and limit the likely opportunity to offer an acceptable quality of life to the people of those developing countries. Corruption can permit preferential access to trading opportunities, favoritism in the processing of investment proposals and bribes derived from the abuse of international procurement procedures with serious economic repercussions. The UN Global Compact announced on January 2015 (United Nations Global Compact, 2015) that it has expelled 372 companies in the second half of 2014 for failure to communicate progress for at least two consecutive years, bringing the total number of expelled companies in 2014 to 657 since 2000. Look for the list of 84 MNEs expelled - punished regarding honourableness - recently from the UN Global Compact in the last six months (see Table 4).

Table 4. MNEs expelled of the UNGC

NAME	COUNTRY	NAME	COUNTRY
Key Tubing & Electrical Industries Pty Ltd	Australia	Korea Cadastral Survey Corporation	Korea
CEMEX Latvia	Latvia	IEWC	United States
Moser Baer India Limited	India	Cognitis Group	France
Ningbo Yusing Electronics Co., LTD	China	Isotrol	Spain
Suzhou Industrial Park XinKai Precision Fasteners	China	Phone Regie	France
Telecom Italia Media S.p.A.	Italy	Pharmaceutical and Foodstuff Industries	Myanmar
The Consortium for Purchasing and Distribution Ltd.	UK	Qsys eSolutions Pvt Ltd	India
Planaxis Canada	Canada	Gulfsands Petroleum Levant Limited	Syria
P and B Metal Components Ltd.	UK	PantaService Group	Italy
Shenzhen Jianchen Industrial Co., Ltd	China	Adesa	France
Danyang Jingyi Aluminum Industry Co., Ltd.	China	Laglasse - Omhovere	France
Digitex Informatica S.L.U.	Spain	Zhongshan Guoan Torch	China

continued on following page

Table 4. Continued

NAME	COUNTRY	NAME	COUNTRY
Enyca Seguridad S.A.	Spain	USCAL, S.L	Spain
CardLogix Incorporated	United States	Westech Solar Technology Wuxi Co., Ltd.	China
China Ciruit Technology(Shantou) Corp.	China	Micrologix Embedded Controls Pvt Ltd	India
Connectis	Spain	International Metals de Mexico, S.A. de C.V.	Mexico
Gandaki Bee Concern	Nepal	Nuevo Sistema Modular S.L.	Spain
Jason Electronics (Pte) Ltd	Singapore	StoveTec	United States
Heliportugal	Portugal	Total Informatica	Brazil
Kaung Htet Myanmar Group of Companies	Myanmar	Closed Joint Stock Company Pinskdrev	Belarus
Office Depot Spain	Spain	ILSCO Corporation	United States
Chakira Cable	Tunisia	Gritech	France
Lanka Hydraulic Institute	Sri Lanka	Mega Corp	Kenya
Arcan Syria	Syria	CODE Incorporated	Canada
Justice Services International	United States	OJSC HaloPolymer	Russia
Ebert Machine Company, Incorporated	United States	Phasetronics/ Motortronics	United States
Indiana Safety Co., Inc.	United States	ECORYS Nederland B.V.	Netherlands
Viru Keemia Grupp AS	Estonia	Prium Partners	France
ATech elektronika d.o.o.	Slovenia	FocusPoint International, Inc.	United States
Atlantis Energy Systems, Inc.	United States	Hunan Xiangchun Agricultural Technology Co., Ltd.	China
Rose Al Basrah Company	Iraq	Servtec - Servicos Tecnicos Terceirizados Ltda.	Brazil
FABRO Construction and Trade Co. Ltd	Turkey	Archirodon Group N.V.	Netherlands
No.(1) Heavy Industries Enterprise	Myanmar	Orisol Corporacion Energetica, S.A	Spain
Peter le Bas Air Division, Inc.	United States	Royo Group	Spain
No. (2) Heavy Industries Enterprise	Myanmar	FRETTE S.R.L.	Italy
No. (3) Heavy Industries Enterprise	Myanmar	Small Parts Inc.	United States
Volt Workforce Solutions	United States	The Electric Controller and Manufacturing	United States
H & Askham Ltd	UK	Greenlight Planet	India
Industrias Zamarbu, S.A.	Spain	Hotel Giada	Costa Rica
Voltran S.A. de C.V.	Mexico	Maeco Eolica	Spain
M & P Nurst AS	Estonia	OPTOKON, a.s.	Czech Republic
Minera Barrick Misquichilca S.A	Peru	Shanghai Chemtron Biotech Co., Ltd.	China

CLOSING THE MORAL DIVIDE

Learning to identify unethical - intolerable - practices and to apply ethical decision making correctly when ethical dilemmas arise requires practice. Implementing a corporate culture that rewards ethical conduct is essential, implying that MNEs must help managers differentiate between practices merely distinct and those that are shady. For moral relativist, nothing is pure and nothing is wrong. For moral absolutist, many issues that are different are wrong. Neither extremes enlighten the real world of ethical-decision-making. The answer lies somewhere in between. When it comes to molding ethical conduct, MNEs' managers must be guide besides any situations by the following principles: a) Respect for core human values, which determine the absolute moral threshold for all business activities. b) Respect for local traditions. c) The belief that context matters when deciding what is right and what is wrong. Considering this, the following guidelines (see Table 5) for developing a global ethical perspective among MNE´s managers when confronting moral relativism or moral absolutism could be useful (Donaldson, Werhane & Cording, 2002).

In addition, a novel business ethics perspective proposed by Andrew Stark can also be seen in the actions taken by Nestlé and Levi. Stark proposes a managerial approach to solve conflicts of cultural and economic norms that can be applied to MNEs and their hosting developing country. By inverting Donaldson's framework around, the conflicts of culture are seen as different stages of cultural development and, the conflicts of economy as economies that contemporaneously interact with each other (Stark, 2015). This is applied in Case 1 and Case 2 by how the MNEs are being aware of the cultural and economic differences of their developing country, and pursue ethically responsible projects that include health and education, to reduce the cultural development gap and the economical disadvantages of the foreign society.

Table 5. Guidelines for ethical leadership

Treat corporate values and formal standards of conduct as absolutes	Whatever ethical standards an MNE chooses, it cannot waver on its principles either at home or abroad.
Design and implement conditions of engagement for suppliers and customers	Will your MNE do business with any customer or supplier? What if a customer or supplier uses child labor? What if it has strong links with organized crime? What if it pressures your MNE to break a host country's laws? Such issues are best not left for spur-of-the-moment decisions. Some MNEs have realized that.
Allow foreign business units to help formulate ethical standards and interpret ethical issues	Create global ethics committee which is made of of managers from countries in which the MNE operates. With the overarching intent to create a "global ethics strategy, locally deployed," the committee mandate is to provide ethics education and create local processes that will help managers in the MNE´s foreign country resolve ethical conflicts.
In host countries, support efforts to decrease institutional corruption	Individual managers will not be able to wipe out corruption in a host developing country no matter how many bribes they turn down. When a host country's tax system, import and export procedures, and procurement practices favor unethical players, MNE must take actions. Many MNEs have begun to participate in reforming host-country institutions.
Exercise moral imagination	Using moral imagination means resolving tensions responsibly and creatively.

CONCLUSION

MNEs and developing countries are likely to present dissimilarities in business ethical standards due to their cultural, geographical, political and economic matters. Hence, MNEs will encounter ethical predicaments derived from the decision-making process of what moral values should they apply: those from their own corporate culture or those from the developing country; that is a decision-making between moral relativism and moral absolutism, respectively.

The mere fact that a developing country´s culture considers a practice correct (moral relativism) does not mean that it is correct (moral absolutism). In fact, some developing country´s culture have practiced slavery and discrimination. Yet each of these practices can be independently criticized on ethical grounds, thus are inconsistent with the use of moral language. On the other side, as the economist Kenneth Boulding argues that without an integrative framework, exchange itself cannot develop; because of exchange, even in it most primitive forms, trust and credibility can be built (Boulding, 1967). Philosophers would distinguish an implicit Kantianism in Boulding's remarks. Kant tried to show that a contemplated action would be immoral if a world in which the contemplated act was universally practiced was self-defeating. Hence, if the moral norms of a developing country permitted practices such the cases mentioned before where human rights are undermined, MNEs should not follow them. Business practices based on such norms could not pass Kant's test. That´s why MNEs need to focus their strategy concerning some of the most common ethical issues that are present in international business such as: hiring-employment practices, human rights, environmental regulations, corruption and social responsibility (Hill, 2013).

Those challenges will take distinct corporate´s approach from MNEs towards the hosting developing countries. In the case of MNEs' native country, the acceptance and observance of universal principles such as the UNGC, CRT, or ILO principles are generally accepted in a worldwide business environment. These are principles that could be taken for granted in developed countries, where child labour is not a tolerable practice, minimum wage is reasonable, or having good working conditions. However, the observance of some principles regarding corruption or environment within developing countries are generally weaker, such as lobbying, tax evasion, discrimination, or failure to protect the environment. There is evidence that right-moral practices are beneficial and should be perceived as the option for MNEs' strategy decision making process when doing business in developing countries.

On the other hand, developing countries have their own ethical codes, which can be in conflict with those followed by the UNGC, CRT, or ILO principles. Implementing the latter and deciding whether to adjust to them or not, constitutes a moral dilemma that MNEs face when shaping their corporate culture in developing countries. An irrefutable fact is that universal ethical principles should lead the guidelines of ethical leadership in doing business. The simple truth is that these are beneficial for business and most MNEs recognize this. There is still a long way to go until developing countries fully embrace the acceptance and observance of universal principles. Hence MNEs must continue striving for understanding the ethical practices in developing countries, and demonstrate in a harmonic interaction between contrasting perceptions of morality, that in the long run: "Ethics is profitable, and no-ethics is punishable".

REFERENCES

Barstow, D. (2012). Vast Mexico Bribery Case Hushed Up by Wal-Mart After Top-Level Struggle. *The New York Times*. Retrieved from http://www.nytimes.com/2012/04/22/business/at-wal-mart-in-mexico-a-bribe-inquiry-silenced.html?pagewanted=all&_r=0

Beauchamp, T., Bowie, N., & Arnold, D. (2008). *Ethical Theory and Business* (8th ed.). Upper Saddle River, NJ: Prentice Hall.

Bergdahl, M. (2004). *What I Learned from Sam Walton: How to Compete and Thrive in a Wal-Mart World*. John Wiley & Sons Inc.

Boatright, J. (2003). *Ethics and the Conduct of Business* (4th ed.). Upper Saddle River, NJ: Prentice Hall.

Boulding, K. (1967). *Human values and Economic Policy*. New York: New York University Press.

Bustillo, M. (2012). Wal-Mart Faces Risk in Mexican Bribe Probe. *The Wall Street Journal*. Retrieved from http://www.wsj.com/articles/SB10001424052702303978104577360283629622556

Caux Round Table. (2015). Retrieved from http://www.cauxroundtable.org/

DesJardins, J. (2009). *An Introduction to Business Ethics* (3rd ed.). New York, NY: McGraw-Hill Higher Education.

Donaldson, T., Werhane, P., & Cording, M. (2002). *Ethical issues in business: a philosophical approach*. Upper Saddle River, NJ: Prentice Hall.

Feltz, A., & Cokely, E. T. (2008). The Fragmented Folk: More Evidence of Stable Individual Differences in Moral Judgments and Folk Intuitions, In B.C. Love, K. McRae, & V.M. Sloutsky (Eds.), *Proceedings of the 30th Annual Conference of the Cognitive Science Society*. Austin, TX: Cognitive Science Society, 1771–76.

Goodwin, G. P., & Darley, J. M. (2008). The Psychology of Meta-ethics: Exploring Objectivism. *Cognition*, *106*(3), 1339–1366. doi:10.1016/j.cognition.2007.06.007 PMID:17692306

Gowans, C. (2004). *Moral Relativism*. Stanford Encyclopedia of Philosophy. Retrieved from http://plato.stanford.edu/entries/moral-relativism/

Hartman, L., & DesJardins, J. (2008). *Business Ethics: Decision-making for Personal Integrity and Social Responsibility* (2nd ed.). Boston: McGraw-Hill/Irwin.

International Chamber of Commerce. (2015). Retrieved from http://www.iccwbo.org/

International Labour Organization. (2015a). *ILO Declaration on Fundamental Principles and Rights at Work*. Retrieved from http://www.ilo.org/declaration/lang--en/index.htm

International Labour Organization. (2015b). Retrieved from http://www.ilo.org/global/lang--en/index.htm

Latus, A. (2001). Moral relativism and objectivism. *Introduction to Philosophy*. Retrieved from http://www.ucs.mun.ca/~alatus/phil1200/RelativismObjectivism.html

Levi Strauss & Co. (2015). *People - Levi Strauss*. Retrieved from http://www.levistrauss.com/sustainability/people/#employee-community-involvement

Palmer, D. (2008). *Does the Center Hold?* Boston: McGraw-Hill.

Shaw, W., & Barry, V. (2007). *Moral Issues in Business* (10th ed.). Belmont: Thomson Wadsworth.

Stark. (n.d.). Inverting Donaldson's Framework: A Managerial Approach To International Conflicts Of Cultural And Economic Norms. *Business Ethics Quarterly*. doi:.10.1017/beq.2015.30

The Guardian. (2015). *Child labour on Nestlé farms: Chocolate giant's problems continue*. Retrieved from http://www.theguardian.com/global-development-professionals-network/2015/sep/02/child-labour-on-nestle-farms-chocolate-giants-problems-continue

The United States Department of Justice. (2015). *Foreign Corrupt Practices Act*. Retrieved from http://www.justice.gov/criminal/fraud/fcpa/

United Nations. (2015). *Report of the United Nations Conference on Environment and Development*. Retrieved from http://www.un.org/documents/ga/conf151/aconf15126-1annex1.htm

United Nations Global Compact. (2010). Communication on Progress. Retrieved from https://www.unglobalcompact.org/system/commitment_letters/5943/original/UN_Global_Compact_2010.pdf?1281012742

United Nations Global Compact. (2015a). *BASF SE*. Retrieved from https://www.unglobalcompact.org/what-is-gc/participants/1194-BASF-SE

United Nations Global Compact. (2015b). *Our Participants*. Retrieved from https://www.unglobalcompact.org/what-is-gc/participants/search?utf8=%E2%9C%93&search[keywords]=&search[initiatives][]=19&search[per_page]=50&search[sort_field]=sector&search[sort_direction]=asc

United Nations Global Compact. (2015c). Retrieved from https://www.unglobalcompact.org/

United Nations Global Compact. (2015d). *UN Global Compact Expels 657 Companies in 2014*. Retrieved from https://www.unglobalcompact.org/news/1621-01-14-2015

United Nations Global Compact. (2015e). *The Universal Declaration of Human Rights*. Retrieved from http://www.un.org/en/documents/udhr/

United Nations Office of Drugs and Crime. (2004). *United Nations Convention Against Corruption*. Retrieved from https://www.unodc.org/documents/treaties/UNCAC/Publications/Convention/08-50026_E.pdf

Wal-Mart. (2015). *Global Statement of Ethics*. Retrieved from https://walmartethics.com/uploadedFiles/Content/U.S.%20-%20English.pdf

KEY TERMS AND DEFINITIONS

Absolutism (Moral): There are facts about which actions are right and wrong, and these facts do not depend on the perspective, opinion, or anything about the person who happens to be describing those facts.

Corruption: Wrongdoing on the part of an authority or powerful party through means that are illegitimate, immoral, or incompatible with ethical standards. Corruption often results from patronage and is associated with bribery.

Ethics: The field of ethics (or moral philosophy) involves systematizing, defending, and recommending concepts of right and wrong behavior. Normative ethics takes on a more practical task, which is to arrive at moral standards that regulate right and wrong conduct. This may involve articulating the good habits that we should acquire, the duties that we should follow, or the consequences of our behavior on others.

Global Compact (UN): It is a United Nations initiative to encourage businesses worldwide to adopt sustainable and socially responsible policies, and to report on their implementation. The UN Global Compact is a principle-based framework for businesses, stating ten principles in the areas of human rights, labor, the environment and anti-corruption. Under the Global Compact, companies are brought together with UN agencies, labor groups and civil society.

MNEs: Enterprises operating in several countries but managed from one (home) country. Generally, any company or group that derives a quarter of its revenue from operations outside of its home country is considered a multinational corporation.

Moral: It refers to plays a crucial, although often unacknowledged, role in formulating ethical theories. To take "moral" to refer to an actually existing code of conduct put forward by a society results in a denial that there is a universal morality, one that applies to all human beings. This descriptive use of "moral" is the one used by anthropologists when they report on the morality of the societies that they study.

Principle: Fundamental norms, rules, or values that represent what is desirable and positive for a person, group, organization, or community, and help it in determining the rightfulness or wrongfulness of its actions. Principles are more basic than policy and objectives, and are meant to govern both.

Relativism (Moral): Actions are not right or wrong "in themselves", but only relative to a person or group. An action is right relative to a person or group if and only if the action is right according to the standards adopted by that person or group.

Chapter 5
Measuring Multinational Enterprise Marketing Performance

Donald E. Sexton
Columbia University, USA

ABSTRACT

Measuring the marketing performance of multinational enterprises poses special challenges. Coordination of marketing activities across markets is difficult due to possible differences in customer priorities and the consequent optimal positioning of products or services. The availability of marketing tactics may vary by country due to custom, infrastructure, or regulations. Country markets may be in different stages of the competitive life cycle which affects business performance. The purposes of this chapter are: 1) to examine and define a multi-country marketing strategy, 2) to explore the process of developing a multi-country marketing strategy, 3) to identify metrics for evaluating the performance of a multi-country marketing strategy, 4) to share and comment on the results of surveys of international managers with respect to their multi-country strategies and the metrics they employ to evaluate strategy performance, and 5) to suggest measures for evaluating a multi-country marketing strategy.

INTRODUCTION

Measuring performance in one country market is challenging. Measuring performance in many country markets across the globe, especially when those markets include emerging markets, is much more challenging. Managing an international marketing strategy requires country market information that is timely and that can be compared across markets. Metrics used should be both leading indicators – where the company is going – and lagging indicators – where it has been. Such information needs to be diagnostic so that strategies and tactics can be optimized.

International marketing strategies require a global perspective. Whether the international marketing strategy can be described as global or as multi-domestic, reviewing measures across markets and over time is crucial for success. Evaluation of measures includes consideration of marketing strategy decisions

DOI: 10.4018/978-1-5225-0276-0.ch005

such as target markets and positioning as well as specific marketing program decisions in areas such as product or service design, communications, pricing, and distribution.

Explained are the key components of marketing strategies including target markets and positioning and programs designed to implement the strategies. Generally, marketing strategies are evaluated by three types of metrics: input metrics, intermediate metrics, and output metrics. Each type of metric has a different role. Input metrics such as expenditures indicate the effort involved in the marketing activity. Intermediate metrics such as awareness and liking are those metrics used primarily by marketers to guide their actions. Output metrics such as revenue and profit are mainly measures of business objectives. Frequently, marketing managers face barriers in linking intermediate metrics to output metrics. The chapter examines how intermediate and output measures can be used to evaluate performance.

International marketing strategies include special concerns. They range from purely multi-domestic to purely global depending on the coordination imposed on the components of the country marketing strategies. Both multi-domestic and global strategies are described and conditions favoring one strategy versus the other are explained. Metrics for international marketing strategies must include metrics that assist in coordinating country marketing strategies. These metrics include both measures of perceived value and measures of cost across country markets.

Performance metrics may need to vary throughout the stages of the competitive life cycle – due to differences in strategic objectives and differences in competitive conditions. Competitive life cycle stages in emerging markets often differ from those in more mature markets. The impact of the competitive life cycle on developing marketing performance metrics is explored.

While many, if not most, of the performance measures used should be common across country markets, some measures should be tailored to the specific competitive circumstances of each country market. Emerging markets, in particular, are often distinguished by particular competitive conditions with respect to customers, competitors, and regulations and those conditions must be kept in mind. In addition, the strategies and tactics employed in emerging markets often are different from those used in more mature markets so may require different evaluation.

Criteria in selecting marketing performance measures are reviewed with special attention to developing metrics for evaluating performance in emerging markets around the world. A systematic approach to evaluating marketing performance in country markets including emerging markets is suggested and explained.

Current practices in the use of metrics to monitor international marketing strategies are explored based on three surveys of marketing managers. The survey respondents were managers responsible for or knowledgeable of international strategies. Their replies indicate that the marketing performance metrics that managers would like to have are in general not the metrics that companies collect. In particular, some key leading indicator measures such as perceived value are not widely collected.

The chapter concludes by suggesting what managers and companies need to do to improve their evaluations of the performance of country markets, especially in emerging economies.

BACKGROUND: MARKETING STRATEGY AND PERFORMANCE METRICS

Performance measures should provide a perspective on all the components of a marketing strategy. There are four main components of any marketing strategy (Sexton, 2007b; Sexton, 2009b):

1. Target market.
2. Business objectives.
3. Positioning.
4. Programs.

The *target market* consists of those customers on which the organization will focus its efforts. Target markets are determined by identifying possible market segments – groups of customers seeking similar benefits – and selecting those market segments which seem to be the most attractive in financial terms where the organization has the highest chance of winning.

Market segments are not necessarily specific to a country market. The same market segment may be found in many countries – in effect, a global market segment (Sexton, 1999; Sexton, 2008).

Business objectives include those financial goals an organization wishes to achieve for the business to be successful. Such goals include revenue, market share, contribution, profit, and cash flow. Generally, these objectives can be expected to vary by country market – because of the differing characteristics of country markets with respect to regulations and logistics and also because they may be in different stages of the competitive life cycle – which means different types of customer and competitor behavior.

Positioning consists of two or three benefits that customers in the target segment want and which the organization can provide at a level superior to that of any other organization. Positioning is sometimes referred to as "the value proposition." Positioning may be based on economic, functional, or emotional benefits. Positioning involves not only the design of the product or service, positioning also involves communications since the customer must perceive the differences in the product or service that make it more appealing than the products or services of provided by competitors.

Programs comprise all the marketing activities focused on the customers in the target market so that they will purchase and continue to purchase the organization's product or service. Programs include activities such as pricing, traditional advertising, non-traditional advertising, personal selling, distribution, and customer service, among others. The actions comprising each program are described by the strategy for that program. For example, the sales force strategy includes the sales objectives and the allocation of the time of the sales representatives.

Target markets must be well selected, positioning must be well defined, and programs must be well executed to achieve the business objectives. Measures of the impact of those strategy components fall into three main categories: input measures, intermediate measures, and output measures (Table 1).

Marketing input measures show the amount of effort being placed in a specific marketing activity and are often spending measures such as how much money is spent on social media or how much money is being spent on the field sales force. Input measures may also include non-monetary measures such as distribution coverage or the amount of training provided to customer service representatives.

Marketing intermediate measures are usually measures specific to marketing programs. These metrics describe the success or failure of particular marketing activities such as advertising, branding, and personal selling. Many of these measures are based on the "purchase funnel" (Colley, 1961; Lavidge & Steiner, 1961), a very well-known model in marketing which suggests that there is a sequence of stages through which a customer may progress before making a purchase: awareness, knowledge, liking, preference, conviction, and purchase. While such a sequence has face validity, research has shown that the sequence of these stages may vary with the product category (Vakratsas & Ambler, 1999; Vaughn, 1980). For certain categories, such as many consumer packaged goods, customers do not conduct substantial research to build their knowledge prior to buying so the sequence may actually start with a purchase.

Table 1. Examples of common marketing metrics

Input Metrics	Intermediate Metrics	Output Metrics
Media spend	Reach	Sales
Advertising creative spend	Frequency	Market share
Packaging spend	Website visits	Market share of target market
Sales force size	Awareness	Life-time customer value
Sales force training	Knowledge	Contribution
Distribution coverage	Liking	Gross margin
End-user pricing	Preference	Profit
Discounts	Conviction	Return on sales
	Trial	Return on investment
	Usage	Cash flow
	Repurchase	
	Recommend	

In contrast, most business organization purchases likely follow the standard purchase funnel since most business purchases begin with a search for alternatives.

The purchase funnel is used by many companies in either its simplest form – one sequence of stages fits all – or in the more complex form where the sequence of stages varies according to how the customer actually purchases the product or service. Whichever sequence is used, each stage of the purchase funnel suggests intermediate measures, such as unaided brand awareness or intention to purchase, that can be used to evaluate the performance of a specific marketing activity such as social media or personal selling.

Marketing *output measures* are primarily financial measures such as revenue, profit, and cash flow. These measures directly measure the performance of marketing efforts with respect to the economic health of the business.

Unfortunately, in many organizations marketers do not utilize such output metrics. In a recent study by the author involving approximately 240 marketing managers, more than 20% declared that the only metric they used to make their decisions was brand awareness (author citation). More generally, several studies over time have shown that many companies use primarily market share and brand awareness as their output measures of marketing performance (ANA, 2004; ANA, 2005; ANA, 2006, ANA, 2007a; ANA, 2007b; ANA, 2007c; ANA, 2008; ANA, 2009; Beaman, Guy, & Sexton, 2008; Sexton & Rogers, 2012; See, 2008Sexton & Charney, 2015a; Sexton, 2015b). Lack of linkages to financial measures is a major weakness of many intermediate measures used by marketing managers in evaluating performance.

In this chapter, the focus is primarily on intermediate and output measures since they directly concern performance – the outcomes from the measures of inputs.

International Marketing Strategies and Performance Metrics

Moving from a one-country, one-market-segment strategy to an international strategy involving many countries increases the number of markets for which overall performance measures are needed and exponentially increases the number of metrics that are needed to evaluate and coordinate marketing activities across all country markets (Bartlett & Ghoshal, 1989; Czinkota & Ronkainen, 2010; Davidson & de la Torre, 1989; Douglas & Craig, 1989; Hamel & Prahalad, 1985; Kogut, 1985; Rudolph, 1985). With a one-country strategy, metrics can focus on performance, both overall and for each marketing program. With

Figure 1. Global vs. multi-domestic marketing strategies

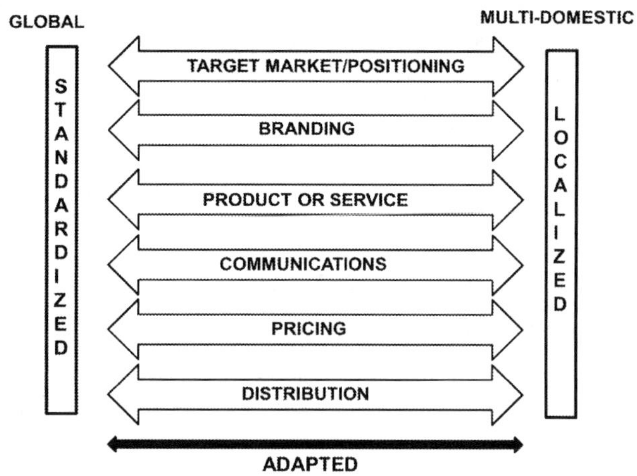

a multi-country strategy, it is necessary not only to employ metrics to evaluate the performance in each country but also to evaluate the coordination of the components of marketing strategies across countries.

There are two extreme forms of international strategies (Sexton, 1997; Sexton, 1999; Craig & Douglas, 2000; Czinkota & Ronkainen, 2010).

At one extreme is a global strategy (Figure 1). In a global strategy, the strategies and tactics for all country markets are identical. The strategy and all its elements are standardized (Buzzell, 1968; Rau & Preble, 1987; Jain, 1989; Laroche, Kirplani, Poris, & Zhou, 2001). At the other extreme is a multi-domestic strategy. In a multi-domestic strategy, each country manager is free to determine marketing strategy and tactics for their own country market on all dimensions – target market, positioning, and programs such as advertising and pricing (Kashani, 1989; Chan, 1990). The strategy and all its elements are localized.

A pure global strategy rarely occurs because country markets differ. Customer needs differ, competitors differ, distribution channels differ, regulations differ. Conditions such as terrain and climate also may differ which can influence operations and logistics as well as product or service usage.

A pure multi-domestic strategy rarely occurs because it ignores all possible cross-border economies such as similar products or similar marketing communications. In addition, a country market may simply not be sufficiently large to support its own distinct strategy.

Whether international strategies tend more to be global or more to be multi-domestic depends on the conditions in country markets, including costs and customers (Sexton, 1999; Czinkota & Ronkainen, 2010). Some industry circumstances favor global strategies and some industry circumstances favor multi-domestic strategies (Levitt, 1983).

A *global industry* consists of country markets which are very similar with respect to costs, customer needs, competitors, regulations, and other characteristics. A multi-domestic industry consists of country markets which are very dissimilar with respect to costs, customer needs, competitors, regulations, and other characteristics. Again, these are descriptions of the extremes of country market conditions. Typically, industries are somewhere between those extremes.

Most international strategies are hybrids – combinations of components such as products and communications which are, to varying degrees, standardized or localized – adapted (Quelch & Hoff, 1986; Sexton, 1999). For example, an international strategy could consist of an adapted product and localized communications, pricing, and distribution. For example, a fast food company may have different menu items in different country markets or an automobile company may utilize cars with different features around the world.

Coordination of marketing programs across country markets depends on finding the appropriate mix of standardization and localization of the various components of the country marketing strategy – the mix that will lead to the most attractive financial returns over time (Hewett, Roth, & Roth, 2003; Sexton, 2007a; Sexton, 2006; Sexton, 2004b).

KEY COUNTRY METRICS: PERCEIVED VALUE AND CUSTOMER VALUE ADDED

How does one determine the appropriate mix of standardization and localization? The concepts of perceived value and customer value added provide insights into those decisions (Sen, 2015; Sexton, 2005; Sexton, 2006b; Sexton, 2009c; Gaber, Sexton, Sen, & Lin, 2009).

Perceived value is the maximum that a customer is willing to pay for a product or service (Figure 2). It is not price but the ceiling on price and depends on the benefits the customer feels the product or service provides and the importance of those benefits to the customer. Sometimes perceived value is called "willingness to pay." If the price of a product is above the product's perceived value to a customer, they will not make the purchase. If the price of a product is below the product's perceived value to a customer, then the probability that they will purchase depends on the difference between the perceived value and the price – the "incentive" for the customer to purchase. The larger the distance, the larger the incentive to buy.

The likelihood of the purchase also depends on the incentives the customer has to purchase competing products or services under consideration. The customer can be expected to purchase the product or service with the highest incentive, other things equal. For example, if the incentive – perceived value less price – for one television set is $200 and for another television set is $100 and if the customer's choice is only between those two television sets, then the customer is more likely to purchase the television set with the $200 incentive. Assuming both alternatives are available and there are no special concerns, usually one can expect the customer to purchase that product or service that has the larger incentive.

Figure 2. Perceived value and customer value added

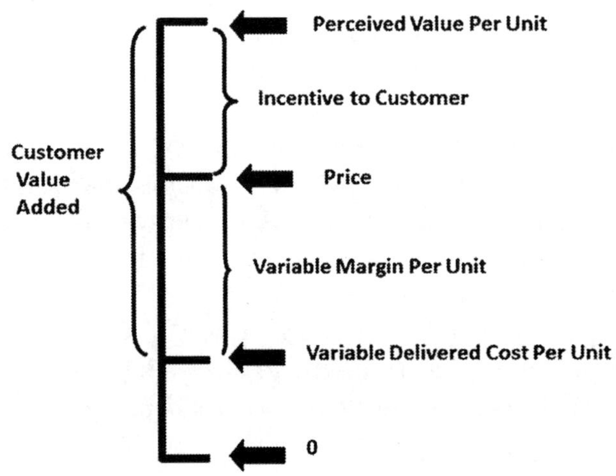

Perceived value has been found in many studies to be strongly associated with a number of financial metrics such as revenue, contribution, profit, cash flow, and shareholder value (Sexton, 2010; Gregory, 2005; Gregory, 2003; Keller 2002; Buzzell & Gale, 1987; Barth, Clement, & Kaznik, 1998; Aaker & Jacobson, 2001; Aaker & Jacobson, 1994; Mizik & Jacobson, 2008; Aksoy 2008). It has also been found to be the most preferred metric among a survey of brand managers asked to evaluate 30 possible measures of marketing performance (Sexton, 2005).

Perceived value can be estimated many ways, including value-in-use models, constrained choice models, and judgment (Sexton, 2009c; Sexton, 2006b).

Value-in-use models are typically based on engineering cost models. Companies compare the costs of a customer using their product or service with the costs of using competing products or services. Then they find that price that makes their product or service and that of the competitor's product or service equal in terms of total cost to the customer. That monetary figure would be perceived value, since the customer would be indifferent to the alternatives at that price. Value-in-use models usually do not include the impact of a positive brand reputation, so the perceived value might be higher than what the value-in-use process finds.

Constrained choice models include both conjoint analysis and discrete choice models. These statistical techniques are often used with consumer packaged goods but they can also be used with business-to-business products or services. With this approach, respondents are presented with a list of possible alternatives (or choices) such as carpets that differ in appearance, ability for stain removal, and price. The respondent is then asked for their first choice among these alternatives. Then that choice is removed from the list and they are asked for their second choice, then their third choice, and so on. This process forces the respondent to make trade-offs. For example, if the ability for stain removal is important to them, then, as the choices become fewer, they may find they need to select an option at a higher price level if they are to keep the ability for stain removal. Such techniques allow an estimate of perceived value in monetary terms. (For the mathematical details, please consult most text books on marketing research.)

Judgment is what a sales representative does when negotiating with a customer. An effective sales person would have some idea of the maximum any customer might pay. That is based on experience with that customer and with other customers. A judgment-based estimate of perceived value is used when there is no time to do a more formal analysis or if the organization has limited funds for marketing research.

Not recommended is asking customers directly how much they are willing to pay for a product or service. Probably all customers understand that that question will be used to set a price for the product or service so they naturally will select the lowest price offered to them. That answer will obviously not be an accurate estimate of perceived value.

Perceived value is whatever the customer thinks it is. Actual value is what the customer would think if he or she had perfect information regarding the product or service. Usually perceived value is below the actual value of the product or service. The challenge for design is to design the product or service – the actual value - to be as close to customer expectations as possible. Then the task of marketing communications is to close the gap between the actual value and the perceived value.

Perceived value consists of both benefits associated with the product or service and the attributes associated with the brand. It differs among customers – customers with different perceived value for a product or service would typically comprise different segments. Perceived value varies with the purchase circumstances. Perceived value also changes over time because perceived value depends on competing products or services (the substitutes) and so, as competition changes over time, perceived value changes over time.

Given its forward linkage to financial outcomes, perceived value is a key metric for understanding the performance of a country market. However, surveys over time have shown that companies do not collect or review perceived value when managing their businesses (ANA, 2004; ANA, 2005; ANA, 2006, ANA, 2007a; ANA, 2007b; ANA, 2007c; ANA, 2009; Beaman, Guy, & Sexton, 2008; Marshall, 2008; Sexton & Rogers, 2012; See, 2008; Sexton, 2012; Sexton, 2013; Sexton, 2015a; Sexton, 2015b).

Customer value added (CVA®) is the difference between perceived value per unit and the variable cost of the product or service (Sexton, 2010; Sexton, 2014). As shown in Figure 2, when a price is set, the price divides customer value added between the variable margin per unit to the company and the incentive to the customer. Higher customer value added leads to higher units sold, higher margin per unit, or both.

The larger perceived value and the larger customer value added, the stronger the financial performance of the company. Companies with high customer value added often can either be the high perceived value producer or the low price producer and succeed with either approach. Conversely, if perceived value per unit for a product or service falls so low that it is below the variable cost per unit, then customer value added becomes negative. Unless that product or service is subsidized in some way, it will go out of business. In effect, the company is spending more to produce the product or service than customers are willing to pay, so the company is destroying the resources of society and in an open economic system it will fail.

Perceived value and customer value added provide a basis for making the trade-off between standardization and localization in an international marketing strategy (Sexton, 2007a). Especially important, both perceived value and customer value added are leading indicators of financial performance so they provide managers with steering control – the ability to forecast outcomes of marketing actions in a country market before those actions are implemented.

Standardization can be expected to lower variable cost per unit through economies of scale. Therefore, companies can decrease their unit costs by standardizing their products or services or their communications or any other part of their business strategy across country markets. Lowering costs is the usual argument to move towards a fully global strategy.

Localization can be expected to increase perceived value per unit since the needs of local customers will be met more closely through communications, distribution, or pricing. Companies can increase perceived value to their customers by supporting country managers in positioning their products or services locally and designing communications that are effective with local customers.

Developing an international strategy then depends on the trade-offs that are made between the costs saved from standardization and the value added from localization (Sexton, 2004b; Subramaniam & Hewett, 2004; Szymanski, Bharadwai, & Varadarajan, 1993). To make those trade-offs requires information on perceived value and costs which needs to be part of any system of measuring performance in country markets.

Perceived Value Predicts Revenue

Higher perceived value allows a higher price or leads to a higher number of units sold or both so higher perceived value is associated with higher revenue. In particular, the author has found that perceived value predicts revenue with R-squared values in excess of 0.90 (Sexton, 2009c).

The relationship between changes in perceived value and changes in revenue is described by Sexton's Revenue Law (Sexton, 2009c). Namely, that the effect of changes in perceived value on revenue is exponential. If perceived value increases, then revenue can be expected to increase with the square of that change. If perceived value decreases, then revenue can be expected to decrease with the square of that change.

Customer Value Added Predicts Contribution

The relationship between changes in customer value added and changes in contribution is similar to the relationship between changes in perceived value and changes in revenue. The relationship is described by Sexton's Contribution Law (Sexton, 2009c), namely that changes in customer value added have an exponential effect on contribution. If customer value added increases, then contribution can be expected to increase with the square of that change. If customer value added decreases, then contribution can be expected to decrease with the square of that change.

Monitoring both perceived value and customer value added allows a manager to understand how the revenue and contribution position in a country market can be expected to evolve over time (Jain, Gorti, Sen, & Sexton, 2015). Perceived value and customer value added are direct measures of the overall marketing performance of a company in a country.

Competitive Life Cycle and Performance Metrics

At any given time, perceived value and customer value added may vary across country markets. In addition, both perceived value per unit and variable cost per unit can be expected to change over time within a given country market. How these metrics change is described by the competitive life cycle (Sexton, 2004a).

The competitive life cycle consists of five stages: Introduction, Rapid Growth, Competitive Turbulence, Maturity, and Decline (Figure 3). There are four curves that describe the competitive conditions in each stage: Unit sales, margin per unit, costs per unit, and perceived value per unit.

During the Introduction Stage, there is but one producer in the market. Competition consists of older technologies. Unit sales of the new product are low. Costs per unit are high due to initial launch costs

Figure 3. Competitive life cycle

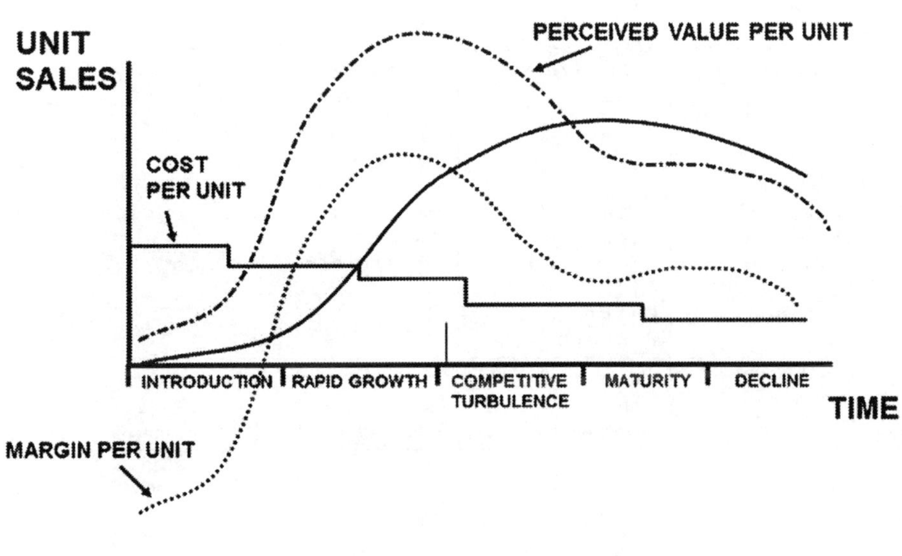

while perceived value is low due to the need to explain the value of the product or service to the customer. Margin per unit may be negative but in any case will likely be low.

During the Rapid Growth Stage, there are a few producers in the market. Unit cost decreases while perceived value rises if the marketing activities such as advertising and personal selling are effective. Usually there is sufficient total demand in the market so that a price war does not begin. Margin per unit is often at a maximum during this stage.

During the Competitive Turbulence Stage, there are many producers in the market. Many of the competitors are imitators that compete on price so perceived value per unit and margin per unit both decline. If the unit cost of a product or service does not decrease faster than the perceived value decreases, then a company's margin is squeezed and it may go out of business. Often this stage is known as "shake-out" since many of the imitators do not survive.

During the Maturity Stage, there are relatively few producers remaining in the market. Perceived value is often constant because most major differences have been incorporated into the products or services and most customers are knowledgeable regarding those differences. Usually competition is stable with regard to price and so margins are relatively stable, increasing mainly due to reductions in costs per unit.

During the Decline Stage, a new technology emerges that supplants the existing technology. If the producers currently in the market do not have the capability to utilize that new technology, they exit the market since their old technology no longer can meet the customers' needs. Perceived value per unit of the old products or services decline, sometimes abruptly, margins shrink, and products or services fail financially.

The competitive life cycle helps one to understand the behavior of metrics in an emerging country market. If a company enters an emerging market during the Introduction Stage, then the metrics of most importance would be those that track a product or service launch (Table 2). Intermediate measures for tracking a product or service launch include perceived value but also metrics from the purchase funnel such as brand awareness and brand knowledge, trial, and repeat purchase. (Repeat purchase signals whether or not the customer liked the product.)

The intermediate measures in the Rapid Growth Stage are similar to those in the Introduction Stage but include brand shift – shifting from a competitor – since there are direct competitors in the Rapid

Table 2. Metrics and competitive life cycle

Metrics	Introduction	Rapid Growth	Competitive Turbulence	Maturity	Decline
Intermediate	Perceived value per unit Cost per unit Margin per unit Brand awareness Brand knowledge Trial Repeat purchase	Perceived value per unit Cost per unit Margin per unit Brand awareness Brand knowledge Trial Repeat purchase Brand shift	Perceived value per unit Cost per unit Margin per unit Brand shift Repeat purchase	Perceived value per unit Cost per unit Margin per unit Repeat purchase Usage rate	Perceived value per unit Cost per unit Margin per unit Usage rate
Output	Market share	Market share Profit Marketing ROI	Market share Profit Marketing ROI	Profit Cash flow Marketing ROI	Cash flow Marketing ROI

Growth Stage and not in the Introduction Stage. Competitive Turbulence Stage intermediate metrics are similar to those in the Rapid Growth stage while Maturity Stage intermediate metrics focus in addition on usage rate, also important in the Decline Stage.

Output measures differ by life cycle stage as well. During the Introduction Stage, the company should be trying to build market share while monitoring margin per unit. During Rapid Growth, the company can expect contribution from the product or service but during Competitive Turbulence, often unit margin will decline and contribution will be squeezed due to the price competition of the imitators. During the Maturity Stage, successful companies can expect profit and cash flow. During the final stage of Decline, focus should be primarily on cash flow in preparation for closing down the product or service in favor of products or services based on the new technology.

Throughout each stage of the competitive life cycle, it is important to monitor perceived value per unit and cost per unit (and therefore customer value added). These metrics furnish insights into how well the product or service is positioned for the next stage in the life cycle.

A company may enter an emerging market during any of these stages and, depending on the stage of that country market, a company may encounter quite different competitive dynamics.

Perceived value per unit and customer value added can provide information quickly as to how the company should develop its marketing strategy.

With respect to emerging markets, the key metrics would likely be those that indicate the costs of launching the product or service and progress in building the brand position within the emerging country market. As a company is present in an emerging market, the metrics most useful would be those that indicate success in the mature stages of the life cycle.

Criteria for Metrics

When selecting measures to evaluate international marketing strategies, the following criteria should be considered:

- **Understandable:** The measure should be easy for all to understand and not require a complicated explanation.
- **Measurable:** There needs to be data available and an unambiguous process for determining the measure.
- **Actionable:** If a metric does not provide a manager with insights into which actions they may take, the metric may be "nice to know" but not directly helpful.
- **Related to Financial Returns:** Marketing must be accountable so it should be possible to link the measures to financial performance such as revenue or profits.
- **Proven in Practice:** The measures must be practical, not just theoretical.
- **Leading or Lagging Indicators:** Some of the measures should be leading indicators and provide steering control. Others should provide insights by showing past performance.
- **Provides Insights into Trade-Off's between Standardization and Localization:** The marketing decisions that most affect cost concern the product or the service. The components that most affect branding and communications concern perceived value. Such trade-offs could be expected to lower costs and raise perceived value.

The metrics suggested below meet these criteria.

Metrics for Evaluating Mature and Emerging Markets

For all country markets, both intermediate and output marketing metrics are required. Table 3 shows the list of basic metrics needed for mature markets and for emerging markets. Note that all metrics selected for the mature markets should also be employed in the emerging markets.

However, there likely should be additional metrics for emerging markets for two reasons:

- Managers may wish to track emerging markets in more detail – at least at the start of country market entry – so that they can more quickly alter strategic choices such as target market or positioning or program choices such as communications and distribution as necessary.
- There may be special circumstances in the emerging markets – such as local competitors or local regulations that must be understood for long-term success in the emerging country market.

There are differences in in the competitive conditions of emerging markets and those in more mature markets. That suggests that for emerging markets, there may be additional metrics to consider so that the standards used for evaluating the performances in emerging markets can be adjusted to those conditions. For example, for some products or services, there may need to be measures of the evolution of the market (Hill & Still, 1984). If the air passenger market in India is growing rapidly but the number of those flying is relatively low due to the income distribution, then one metric that would be useful in evaluating performance would be the number of people who have been persuaded to fly. In turn, such a metric would place in perspective any purchase funnel metrics concerned with preference or conviction.

Metrics specific to the conditions in an emerging market can be developed during the situation analysis of the country market. Before a strategy is developed, typically a situation analysis is conducted. A situation analysis focuses on what are often referred to as "the three C's and the E": Customers, Competitors, Company, and Environment. Measures for characteristics of customers, competitors, company, and environment allow a more precise determination of performance in emerging markets. For example, descriptions of the age and income levels of consumers in a B-to-C market or the distribution by size of the companies in a B-to-B market would provide a frame for evaluating performance levels in those markets.

Table 3. Suggested metrics to evaluate country markets

Metrics	Mature Markets	Emerging Markets	
Intermediate	Perceived value per unit Cost per unit Margin per unit Brand awareness Brand knowledge Trial Repeat purchase Brand shift	Perceived value per unit Cost per unit Margin per unit Brand awareness Brand knowledge Trial Brand shift	Target market penetration Buyer behavior Communications Pricing Distribution Environment (competitors Repeat purchase regulations, etc.)
Output	Market share Profit Marketing ROI Cash flow	Market share Profit Marketing ROI Cash flow	Profit by target market Return on sales Customer value

In addition, the standards to be met for each metric – such as growth in perceived value per unit or return on sales - might be different when focusing on emerging markets rather than mature markets due to the possibly different competitive circumstances.

The metrics in Table 3 comprise a dashboard. Measures can be more detailed than those shown in Table 3. For example, one might also include input measures such as advertising message, more intermediate measures such as attitude change, and more outcome measures such as turnover.

International Marketing Strategy Metrics: What Managers Do

Over the past few years, the author was involved in conducting and analyzing the results of three major surveys of international marketing managers:

- **"International Survey":** A survey of 520 managers from companies in the United States, Australia, Asia, and Europe, conducted from 1982 through 2011. (Sexton, 2015b)
- **"ANA Branding Survey":** Conducted with the Association of National Advertisers, a survey of 53 marketing managers from companies doing business in multiple countries. (Sexton & ANA, 2013)
- **"Emerging Market Survey":** Conducted with Craig Charney, a survey of 313 marketing executives from both client-side companies and agencies. (Sexton & Charney, 2015a)

The results were remarkably consistent across all three studies.

Priority of objectives: With respect to desired objectives, next year's profits and next year's sales received the highest priorities from managers in all three studies (Table 4). Interestingly, market share was generally considered less important than profits, sales, or Return on Investment. Stock price received the lowest average priority score in all three surveys.

Table 4. Priorities of business objectives

Business Objective	International Survey[1]	ANA Branding Survey[2]	Emerging Market Survey[1]
Next year's profit	2.2	84%	2.2
Next year's sales	2.3	82%	2.0
Next year's ROI	2.5	71%	2.4
Next year's market share	2.9	68%	2.6
Long-term profit	2.4	68%	2.4
Long-term sales	2.3	61%	2.2
Long-term ROI	2.4	52%	2.5
Long-term market share	2.9	57%	2.5
Stock price	3.5	20%	4.1

[1]Scale: 1 – Very important, 7 – Not important.

[2]Top two boxes (1 or 2).

Sources: Sexton 2015b; Sexton, 2013; Sexton, 2015a.

- **Importance of Measure in Evaluating Country Market Performance:** Not surprisingly, profitability was rated the most important metric for evaluating a country market (Table 5). However, market share was the second most important metric in the ANA Branding Survey (and a strong third in the Emerging Market Study). Consistent with prior studies by the ANA and others, brand awareness was a high priority performance metric in both the ANA Branding Study and the Emerging Market Study.
- **Measures Collected:** No measure of market performance was found to be collected by all companies in all country markets. The most common measure collected – profitability – was collected in all or most countries by 73% of the companies in the ANA Branding Survey (Table 5). The only other metric collected by more than half of the companies in all or most countries in the ANA Branding Survey was market share. The percentage of companies that considered a measure important was always higher than the percentage of companies that actually collected that measure in all or most country markets. For some metrics, the distance between percentage giving a metric high priority and percentage collecting the metric in all or most countries was very large. For example, in the ANA study, 50% of the respondents claimed that perceived value was a quite important metric but only 20% stated that perceived value was collected in all or most countries. The results from the Emerging Market Study were basically the same.
- **Coordination of Marketing Activities:** Given the apparent importance of the brand in achieving business objectives, it is not surprising that in general brand activities, including expression of the brand, tended to be more standardized than localized (Table 6). Product design was on the average more standardized than other marketing activities such as advertising, packaging, sales force, distribution, and pricing. That result is consistent with the prior discussion that standardization lowers cost and that savings on products due to standardization may be substantial. On the other hand, localization of activities such as communications and distribution may be expected to have more potential for raising perceived value locally.

Table 5. Importance and collection of measures

Measure	Importance of Measure in Performance Evaluation[1]	Extent of Collection of Measure[2]
Profitability	2.0	2.6
Market share	2.5	3.1
Customer satisfaction	2.2	3.0
Brand awareness	2.4	3.5
Brand knowledge	2.6	3.5
Brand attitudes	2.5	3.5
Brand value	2.8	3.7
Recommendation	2.5	3.5
Perceived value	2.4	3.4
Change in brand value	3.1	3.8
Customer lifetime value	2.6	3.5
MROI	2.9	3.6

[1]Scale: 1 – Very important, 7 – Not important.

[2]Scale: 1 – Collected in all countries, 7 – Collected in few countries.

Source: Sexton, 2015a.

Table 6. Coordination of marketing activities

Marketing Activity	International Survey	ANA Survey	Emerging Markets Survey
Brand logo		1.4	2.3
Brand name	2.1	1.6	2.3
Brand position		2.3	2.9
Brand expression		2.8	2.7
Product design	2.9	2.7	3.1
Advertising creative	4.4	3.6	3.5
Advertising content	4.3	3.7	3.5
Traditional media efforts	5.0	4.5	3.7
Digital media efforts		4.4	3.8
Packaging	3.5		
Sales force role	5.1	4.0	
Sales force management	5.0		
Sales promotion	4.6		
Distributor role	5.0		
Distributor type	5.1		
Pricing	5.2		
Customer service	4.8		
Target customers		3.9	3.6
Business objectives		3.9	3.3

Scale: 1 – Standardized, 7 – Localized. Sources: Sexton, 2015b; Sexton, 2013; Sexton, 2015a.

FINAL THOUGHTS

Many of the metrics one might use to evaluate marketing performance in mature markets are also relevant to evaluate performance in emerging markets. However, in emerging markets one might pursue more detail than in the metrics applied in mature markets and there are other metrics that might be included such as measures of the competitive environment.

In general, international managers do not seem to have at hand all the metrics they would like or should like to have – for either mature markets or emerging markets. Three recent surveys found large gaps between the measures needed for international marketing decision-making and the degree to which the measures were being collected in country markets. Those gaps need to be filled to improve the effectiveness of international marketing.

In particular, even though some managers considered perceived value an important metric for their decision-making, very few companies collected perceived value in many of the countries in which they were operating. Given that perceived value (and customer value added) have been shown to be leading indicators of financial performance, it is unfortunate that not many companies are collecting and monitoring those metrics. Perceived value and customer value added could provide them with steering control over their marketing actions, insights for making their marketing strategy and marketing program decisions, and an overall framework for coordinating their international marketing activities.

REFERENCES

Aaker, D. A., & Jacobson, R. (1994). The financial information content of perceived quality. *JMR, Journal of Marketing Research*, *31*(May), 191–201. doi:10.2307/3152193

Aaker, D. A., & Jacobson, R. (2001). The value relevance of brand attitudes in high-technology markets. *JMR, Journal of Marketing Research*, *38*(November), 485–493. doi:10.1509/jmkr.38.4.485.18905

Aksoy, L., Cooil, B., Groening, C., Keiningham, T. L., & Yalçın, A. (2008). The long-term stock market valuation of customer satisfaction. *Journal of Marketing*, *72*(July), 105–122. doi:10.1509/jmkg.72.4.105

Association of National Advertisers (2004). *The state of marketing accountability study*. New York: ANA.

Association of National Advertisers. (2005). *The path to marketing accountability study*. New York: ANA.

Association of National Advertisers. (2006). *The path to marketing accountability study*. New York: ANA.

Association of National Advertisers. (2007a). *Brand deterioration: how to identify, measure, and respond*. New York: ANA.

Association of National Advertisers. (2007b). *Marketing accountability study*. New York: ANA.

Association of National Advertisers. (2007c). *Survey of finance managers*. New York: ANA.

Association of National Advertisers. (2008). *Marketing accountability study*. New York: ANA.

Association of National Advertisers. (2009). *Marketing accountability study*. New York: ANA.

Barth, M. E., Clement, M. B., & Kaznik, R. (1998, March). Brand value and capital market valuation. *Journal of Accounting Studies*, 41-68.

Bartlett, C., & Ghoshal, S. (1989). *Managing across borders*. Cambridge, MA: Harvard Business School Press.

Beaman, K., Guy, G. R., & Sexton, D. E. (2008). *Managing and measuring return on marketing investment, Research Report 1435-08-RR*. New York: The Conference Board.

Buzzell, R. D. (1968). Can you standardize multinational marketing? *Harvard Business Review*, *46*(November/December), 102–113.

Buzzell, R. D., & Gale, B. T. (1987). *The PIMS* principles*. New York: Free Press.

Chan, A. K. (1990). Localization in international branding. *International Journal of Advertising*, *9*(1), 81–91.

Colley, R. (1961). *Defined advertising goals for measured advertising results*. New York: Association of National Advertisers.

Craig, C. S., & Douglas, S. P. (2000). Configural advantage in global markets. *Journal of International Marketing*, *8*(1), 6–25. doi:10.1509/jimk.8.1.6.19564

Czinkota, M. R., & Ronkainen, I. A. (2010). *International marketing*. Mason, OH: South-Western.

Davidson, W., & de la Torre. (1989). *Managing the global corporation.* New York: McGraw-Hill.

Douglas, S. P., & Craig, C. S. (1989). Evolution of global marketing strategy: Scale, scope, and synergy. *The Columbia Journal of World Business*, *24*(3), 47–58.

Gaber, Sexton, Sen, & Lin (2009, October). Customer input: incorporate perceived value into marketing strategy. *Business Digest*, 3-9.

Gregory, J. R. (2003). *The best of branding*. New York: McGraw-Hill.

Gregory, J. R. (2005). *Driving brand equity*. New York: ANA. Hamel, Gary & Prahalad, C. K.(1985), Do you really have a global strategy? *Harvard Business Review*, *63*(July/August), 139–148.

Hewett, K., Roth, M. S., & Roth, K. (2003). Conditions influencing headquarters and foreign subsidiary roles in marketing activities and their effects on performance. *Journal of International Business Studies*, *34*(6), 567–585. doi:10.1057/palgrave.jibs.8400054

Hill, J. S., & Still, R. R. (1984). Adapting products to ldc tastes. *Harvard Business Review*, *62*(March/April), 92–101.

Jain, R., Gorti, V., Sen, K., & Sexton, D. E. (2015). *Brand equity & optimal pricing*. Paper presented at ReThink Conference, ARF, New York, NY.

Jain, S. C. (1989). Standardization of international marketing strategy: Some research hypotheses. *Journal of Marketing*, *53*(January), 70–79. doi:10.2307/1251525

Kashani, K. (1989). Beware the pitfalls of global marketing. *Harvard Business Review*, *67*(September/October), 91–98.

Keller, K. (2002). *Branding and Brand Equity*. Cambridge: Marketing Science Institute. doi:10.4135/9781848608283.n8

Kogut, B. (1985). Designing global strategies: Comparative and competitive value-added chains. *Sloan Management Review*, (Summer): 15–27.

Laroche, M., Kirpalani, V. H., Pons, F., & Zhou, L. (2001). A model of advertising standardization in multinational corporations. *Journal of International Business Studies*, *32*(2), 249–266. doi:10.1057/palgrave.jibs.8490951

Lavidge, R., & Steiner, G. (1961). A model for predictive measurements of advertising effectiveness. *Journal of Marketing*, *25*(October), 137–169.

Levitt, T. (1983). The globalization of markets. *Harvard Business Review*, *61*(May/June), 92–102.

Marshall, J. (2008). *Finance: friend or foe?* Paper presented at the 2008 ANA Marketing Conference.

Mizik, N., & Jacobson, R. (2008). The financial value impact of perceptual brand attributes. *JMR, Journal of Marketing Research*, *45*(February), 15–32. doi:10.1509/jmkr.45.1.15

Quelch, J. A., & Hoff, E. J. (1986). Customizing global marketing. *Harvard Business Review*, *64*(May/June), 59–68.

Rau, P. R., & Preble, J. F. (1987). Standardization of marketing strategy by multinationals. *International Marketing Review*, *4*(3), 18–28. doi:10.1108/eb008333

Rudolph, Alice (1985). Standardization not standard for global marketers. *Marketing News*, 3-4.

See, E. (2008). *What marketing thinks*. Association of National Advertisers.

Sen, K. (2015). *Why pv models are necessary for complete understanding*. Working paper.

Sexton, D. E. (1997). Building global brands. *The Advertiser*.

Sexton, D. E. (1999). Global marketing: balancing global thoughts and local actions. *The Advertiser*, 12-18.

Sexton, D. E. (2004a). Managing brand equity over time. *Quarterly Review of Canada China Business Council*, 9-11.

Sexton, D. E. (2004b). Should your brand be global*? Chazen Web Journal of International Business*, 1-13.

Sexton, D. E. (2005). Building the brand scorecard. *The Advertiser*, 54-58.

Sexton, D. E. (2006a). Implementing your global strategy in country markets. *Effective Executive,* 16-20.

Sexton, D. E. (2006b). Pricing, perceived value, and communications. *The Advertiser*, 56-58.

Sexton, D. E. (2007a). Coordinating brands globally. *Global CEO*, 9-13.

Sexton, D. E. (2007b). The keys to strategic success. *Effective Executive*, 32-34.

Sexton, D. E. (2008). Think markets not countries. *Effective Executive,* 28-30.

Sexton, D. E. (2009a). Achieving marketing nirvana. *Advertiser*, 18.

Sexton, D. E. (2009b). *Marketing 101* (2nd ed.). Hoboken, NJ: John Wiley & Sons, Inc.

Sexton, D. E. (2009c). *Value Above Cost: How CVA® Drives Financial Performance, the Most Important Metric You've Never Used.* Upper Saddle River, NJ: FT Press (Wharton School Publishing).

Sexton, D. E. (2010). Competing with customer value added. *Effective Executive*, 44-47.

Sexton, D. E., & Association of National Advertisers. (2013). *Global brand equity survey results.* New York: ANA.

Sexton, D. E. (2014a). Implementing marketing metrics in organizations: opportunities and challenges. In The Handbook of Customer Equity (pp. 431-447). Northampton, MA: Elgar Publishing.

Sexton, D. E. (2014b). Using metrics to achieve 'steering control' of your marketing actions. *Effective Executive*, *17*(1), 7–19.

Sexton, D. E. (2015b). International marketing strategy – does country nationality matter? *Journal of Marketing Trends*, 47-54.

Sexton, D. E., & Charney, C. (2015a). *Emerging markets attractiveness study*. New York: AMA.

Sexton, D. E., & Rogers, D. (2012). *Marketing roi in the era of big data.* New York: BRITE.

Subramaniam, M., & Hewett, K. (2004). Balancing standardization and adaptation for product performance in international markets: testing the influence of headquarters-subsidiary contact and cooperation. *Management International Review*, *44*, 171-194.

Szymanski, D. M., Bharadwaj, S. G., & Varadarajan, P. R. (1993). Standardization versus adaptation of international marketing strategy: An empirical investigation. *Journal of Marketing*, *57*(October), 1–17.

Vakratsas, D., & Ambler, T. (1999). Advertising effects. *Journal of Marketing*, *63*(January), 26–43. doi:10.2307/1251999

Vaughn, R. (1980). How advertising works. *Journal of Advertising Research*, *30*(1), 57–66.

KEY TERMS AND DEFINITIONS

Competitive Life Cycle: Five stages of competitive conditions – Introduction, Rapid Growth, Competitive Turbulence, Maturity, and Decline – defined by customer and competitor behavior.

Customer Value Added (CVA®): Perceived value (see below) per unit less cost per unit.

Global Industry: Customers are similar across country markets and there are no barriers to country entry.

Global Strategy: Components of country marketing strategy are standardized and are determined by global manager.

Input Metrics: Measures of effort expended in marketing activities.

Intermediate Metrics: Measures of marketing outcomes from marketing activities.

Marketing Strategy: Plans for achieving business objectives through strategic choices and program choices.

Multi-Domestic Industry: Customers vary across country markets and there are barriers to country entry.

Multi-Domestic Strategy: Components of country marketing strategy are localized and are determined by country manager.

Output Metrics: Business objectives achieved by marketing strategies and programs.

Perceived Value: Maximum a customer will pay for a product or service, also known as "willingness to pay."

Chapter 6
The Use of Technology in Organizations

Jorge Ramirez
Tecnológico de Monterrey, EGADE Business School, Mexico

ABSTRACT

Multinational Corporations (MNC) face the challenge of compete in the new interconnected business environment. In particular technology is recognized as a factor that boost productivity and competitiveness and drives the business connectivity which in turn involves cross-borders goods, services and financial flows. MNC is recognized as being possessed of high-tech assets, and also, resources including capital, management skills and R&D capabilities and subsidiaries can get them, from its holding company, and they transfer technology to local businesses. A knowledge transfer, running parallel to the technology transfer take place benefiting to the local economy. Foreign Direct Investment (FDI) is considered as the primary vehicle to facilitate technology transfer (and underlying knowledge flows) toward emerging countries. The ultimate goal of the MNC is related to leverage technology and knowledge transfer in order to maintain a competitive edge and move toward even higher value-added activities.

INTRODUCTION

Cemex, the world's third largest cement company, reached their size thanks to the use of a technique called "The Cemex Way", a corporate philosophy that allows the Mexican company to transfer and obtain the knowledge from an acquired foreign company. Originally designed as a computer system that allows Cemex CEO, Lorenzo Zambrano, to know in real time how the cement plants were performing, "The Cemex Way" today is one of the best examples of how a Multi National Corporation (MNC) can transfer technology using the Direct Foreign Investment (FDI) to create a competitive advantage based in knowledge to their subsidiaries along the world. Zambrano, as many others Multi National CEO's, learned the value of information in an interconnected world. A world in which the difference between a company based on a developed nation and a global leader based in a country like India, Mexico or Brazil is not as clear as before. Technology has been part of the success, because thank to it, these organizations have been able to take advantage of the knowledge and innovation regardless of where they are located. (Stewart, 2015)

DOI: 10.4018/978-1-5225-0276-0.ch006

The knowledge can flow from the parent company to the subsidiary and from the subsidiary to the local companies or vice versa, leveraged by through Direct Foreign Investment (FDI) and technology, the mix will determine different scenarios that describe the way in which organizations create or absorb knowledge. The challenge for the MNCs will be decide which of these scenarios will has the potential to increase their productivity and innovation in line to find their own "Cemex Way".

In this chapter the use of technology in the Multinational Corporation (MNC) is addressed. An interconnected world is emerging and that circumstance implies an increase in worldwide goods, services and financial flows. Technology is well recognized as an enabler of these flows and the MNC faces the challenge to diffuse knowledge across borders taking advantage of the transfer of technology that takes place among headquarters and its subsidiaries. Governments of emerging economies recognize MNC as having superior technology so in recent years have changed their public policies to open the doors to foreign investment. FDI plays the principal role as the technology transfer facilitator. In this chapter the 3M case is presented in order to understand how the following factors; FDI, the factors driving productivity and competitiveness within a country and the country's particular stage of economic development are enablers of technology and knowledge transfer. Also this case helps to understand how using the matrix *Knowledge transfer based on technology and FDI*, helps to select what technology transfer strategy is appropriate to compete. A final section clarifies that MNC must not just use technology to compete, but to diffuse knowledge associated to those technology transfers in emerging countries.

AN INTERCONNECTED WORLD

The rapid advances in technology and infrastructure (nowadays mainly cloud-based), coupled with the pervasiveness of the Internet have brought unexpected growth in ICT access and connectivity to the enterprises around the world, causing major changes in global business scenario. According to the Telecommunication Development Bureau, a business division belonging to International Telecommunication Union (2015), between 2000-2015 global Internet penetration grew 7 fold from 6.5% to 43%, meaning that globally 3.2 billion people are using the Internet and from those about 2 billion come from developing countries. Even though the rate of Internet penetration in emerging countries is increasing quickly (25% per year over 5% in developed countries), this is due to the still low Internet penetration in emerging countries (35% in most of the emerging countries against 70% on average in developed countries) (Nottebohm, et al., 2012).

The Mobile broadband is certainly the most dynamic market segment, reaching an overall 47% mobile penetration in 2015 (a value that increased 12 times since 2007). By end 2015, there are more than 7 billion mobile cellular subscriptions, corresponding to a penetration rate of 97%, up from 738 million in 2000, Mobile-broadband penetration levels for developing countries are around 39 active subscriptions per 100 inhabitants, however in the Americas it is one of the highest (77.6), ranking second globally (ITU, 2015), In developing countries global subscriptions increased from 53% in 2005 up to 73% by 2010, such that the development path taken by emerging countries is partly a result of the high levels of mobile phone adoption(Nottebohm, et al., 2012). Bock et al (2015), emphasized that this new business environment is deeply impacted by a whole new universe of connectivity "that's local (it's always where you are), personal (tailored to your needs and preferences), social (all your friends are there as well)—and it's always on (Continuous access to information)" bringing about a shift towards an increasing mobile, flexible and interconnected business environment (Cisco, 2014). Multinational Corporations

(MNC) – an entity evolved from its national origins to the state of having business activities in more than one country (Porter, 1980) (Kogut & Zander, 2003) – have been affected by this new interconnected business environment, due to the inherent nature of its operations requiring constant communication and information exchange among subsidiaries and parent (Aghina, De Smet, & Heywood, 2014). MNC compete using technologies exploiting this new interconnected business environment, enabling the rise of a new type of MNC that emerge not only in developed countries but have recently emerged from developing countries such as Brazil, India, China, South Africa and Mexico (Santiso, 2007). In some sectors these companies are global leaders beating corporations from developed countries. Examples include: Mittal (India), which in 2006 took control of its competitor Arcelor – headquartered in Europe – and due to this action, Mittal became the leader in the steel sector. Similar examples include: Cemex (Mexico) competing against Lafarge (France) and Holcim (Switzerland), Companhia Vale Do Rio Doce (Brazil) spearheading international rankings, along with the Anglo-Australian company BHP Billiton and the British-Australian company Rio Tinto Group. (de la Torre, Didier, & Pinat, 2014). Underlying the success of these companies is their ability to generate and utilize effectively technological resources (Manolopoulos, Dimitratos, Young, & Lioukas, 2009). The old-fashioned focus where the MNC only seeks profit maximization with different pricing strategies (Magee, 1981) has been evolving to include the dissemination of knowledge across borders where the company develops their activities, using its technology and organizational efficiency. With this productive knowledge, the company is seeking a competitive advantage (Kogut & Zander, 2003). Research pointed out that creation and exploitation of technology is one of the main reasons explaining the success and growth of MNC (Manolopoulos, Dimitratos, Young, & Lioukas, 2009) within a newly interconnected environment that forms a digital ecosystem (Dreischmeier, Close, & Trichet, 2015). Digital ecosystems is a network of companies, individual contributors, institutions, and customers that are interconnected and collaborate (Bock, Field, Zwillenberg, & Rogers, 2015) in the processes of the organization and encompasses different value-chains in different industries and countries in order to increase efficiency and innovation (Dreischmeier, Close, & Trichet, 2015), (World Economic Forum, 2015). Waterman, Peters, & Phillips (1980), established such ecosystems as a framework where structure, people (skills, staff, style and shared values) and processes (systems) perform work to produce specific products/services (Alter, 2013). In these so-called ecosystems, companies are no longer functional silos, they share information throughout the chain, integrating processes, people and technology among different businesses, industries and even countries. In this new interconnected world, emerging countries face a great challenge and several opportunities since the economies of developed countries are more connected than their counterparts in the emerging countries (McKinsey Global Institute, 2014).

Given both the growing business connectivity in emerging markets and the growing impact of mobile technologies, an increasing share of global economic activity involves cross-border flows. Today, 35% of cross-borders goods, up to 20% more than in 1990. In 2012, the combined value of trade in goods and services plus financial flows reached $ 26 trillion, equivalent to 36% of global GDP, compared to $ 5 billion, 23% of the world GDP in 1990 as shown in Figure 1. More than a third of all financial investments in the world are international transactions, and one fifth of Internet traffic is trans-boundary (McKinsey Global Institute, 2014).

Unquestionably, we live in an interconnected world where economies of developed countries remain more connected to these cross-border flows than emerging economies do, Germany tops the list while Hong Kong ranked second and the United States in third place; nevertheless, this situation is rapidly changing. By 1990, developed economies had 54% of all trade in goods, but in 2012 the flows fell to 28%

Figure 1. Worldwide goods, services and financial flows as percentage of the GDP, 1980-2012
Source: McKinsey Global Institute analysis, World Trade Organization.

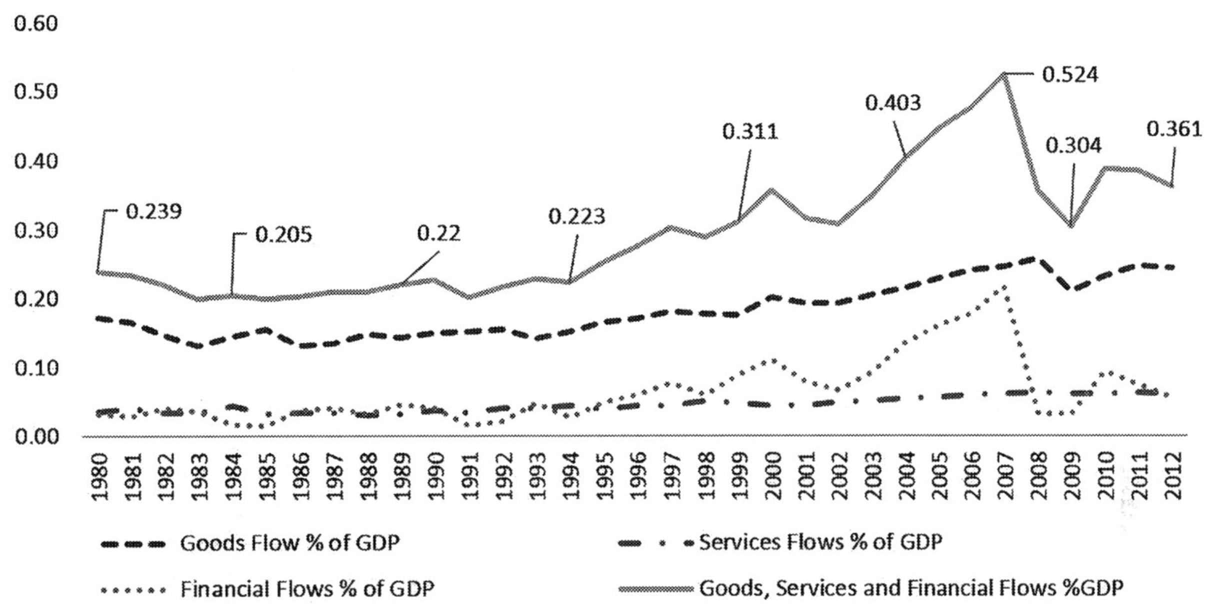

due to the increased participation of emerging economies in world trade. Among the emerging economies increasingly connected to these flows of economic transactions are Brazil, China, India, Morocco and Saudi Arabia. As of 2014, emerging economies account for 40% of the goods flows. (McKinsey Global Institute, 2014)

MULTINATIONAL COMPANIES AND TECHNOLOGY

Before 1980s, governments from developing countries considered that the MNC invested in their countries just to take advantage from laxer local environmental regulations, cheap labor force and to exploit the offer of relatively cheap natural resources. Regarding the technology that MNC was bringing to the host country, it was considered mostly obsolete and/or harmful for the environment (they could even be prohibited in their home country); thus, local governments imposed strict controls or even severe legal restrictions restricting the MNC activity. Nowadays, this situation has changed in many emerging countries, because it is now well recognized that MNC (especially in the most dynamic and knowledge-intensive sectors) have technological assets and knowledge that can help emerging countries to close the technological gap (Chudnovsky & Lopez, 2003). This point of view is extremely important because technology is an enduring good, which is used by modern organizations to compete; its importance is such that current views consider that the corporate resources must be dedicated to its creation, going after the final purpose of generating future benefits, i.e., the enterprise must become a *Technology Producing Company* (TPC) (Magee, 1981). In this point of view, technology is also regarded as a public good, which once created, can be used by other companies (or the same subsidiaries of the MNC). Some authors (Kogut & Zander, 2003), (Teece, 1977) argue that technology is not a public good because the estimated

Table 1. Benefits arisen from MNC's R&D activities

1	Innovation and knowledge creation.
2	Improve Local subsidiaries' technology absorption capacities.

Source: Prepared by the author based on; (Driffield, Love, & Menghinello, The Multinational Enterprise as a Source of International Knowledge Flows: Direct Evidence from Italy, 2010).

technology transfer cost, - i.e. the cost of sharing technology with other companies or subsidiaries of the MNC-, can vary from 2% up to 59% of total costs. These costs are derived from the coding and teaching of complex knowledge to the recipients; reason why these costs are reduced with each technology transfer and with the experience of the technology receptor. However while this situation does not involve reducing performance of the TPC, technology can be considered as a public good (Magee, 1981).

MNC are recognized as specialists in the generation of sophisticated technologies since yields are higher for these technologies than for simpler technologies; as a result, they require highly skilled labor in the creation and ownership of such sophisticated technology work. The abundance of this highly skilled labor in developed countries gives them a comparative advantage in the creation and exportation of new technologies. On the other hand, emerging countries need simple production processes and simple products. Moreover, the MNC can hardly provide the technology that is most useful to these countries, as simpler technologies are easier to copy than sophisticated technologies (Magee, 1981).

The presence of a dominant firm in the industry promotes R&D activities and investment in innovation because the appropriability costs are lower for these structures in the industry. Driffield, Love, & Yong (2014) report two direct effects of MNC's R&D activities, as shown in Table 1; (1) it contributes directly to innovation and knowledge creation; and (2) it forms the basis for the absorption capacity of technology from their subsidiaries.

Thus, the MNC is more efficient in the technology transfer through its own subsidiaries than through cross-border markets, this has been named "the appropriability problem" and is studied in detail within the appropriability theory of the Multinational Corporation that talks about creation and appropriation from the yields of the private inversions in the information market. Chudnovsky and Lopez (2003) consider that as a result of this appropriability problem, the subsidiaries of MNCs in emerging countries often have more advanced technologies and management practices than local businesses usually have; however, MNC occasionally makes the mistake of importing technologies and procedures without any kind of adaptation to the local conditions (Jaguli, Malek, & Palil, 2014); as a result, the local companies take the responsibility of fitting the standards, technologies and management problems of the country (Magee, 1981) with the risk of underestimating the time and resources needed to compete with these technologies globally (Baumgartner, Hatami, & Vander Ark, 2012). MNC should be able to understand the context of the emerging market in which it is located, find the best partners – the company gets greater benefits if it is integrated with key members of their local supply chains (Sanders, 2008)– and develop talent. Khanna (2014) refers to this as contextual intelligence: the ability to understand the limits of our knowledge and adapt that knowledge to a different environment from which it was developed. The degree to which emerging economies benefit from these tangible and intangible assets owned by multinationals, has become a key issue in the research and policy for social and economic development agenda (Chudnovsky & Lopez, 2003). Literature mentions three specific benefits; Firstly, MNC activities in emerging countries have the potential impact of increased competition in domestic markets, forcing local companies to improve their productivity through the optimization in the use of existing technolo-

Table 2. Benefits that a MNC gives to a country in which it operates

1	*Increase competition.* Local companies uses (or adopt) technology to increase competitiveness in order to beat MNCs and local competitors.
2	*Use of superior technology and processes.* Local companies copy superior technologies coming from MNC through imitation or hiring MNC's workers.
3	*Improved human capital.* Local workers acquire the knowledge generated by MNC's innovation activities.
4	*General resources.* Capital, management skills and R&D capabilities

Source: Prepared by the author based on; Diffusion of environmentally friendly technologies by multinational corporations in developing countries, Chudnovsky & Lopez, 2003. Knowledge of the Firm and the Evolutionary Theory of the Multinational Corporation, Kogut & Zander, 2003 . and Do MNCS' high quality and standard requirements matter? A channel for vertical spillovers., Kogut & Zander, 2003.

gies or by adopting new technologies. Secondly, local companies can make use of superior technologies and management practices belonging to multinational companies through imitation or by hiring workers trained by multinational companies. Third, if the subsidiaries of the MNC develop innovation activities in emerging countries, they can generate improved human capital (Chudnovsky & Lopez, 2003), (Kogut & Zander, 2003). Technology transfer lies in the heart of the growth of MNC (Kogut & Zander, 2003), and this perspective is well-known by the governments of emerging countries, which is why according to the new perspective discussed at the beginning of this section, encourage multinationals to establish themselves locally and expect to generate technology transfer to the local businesses (Glass & Kamal, 1999). In general, the MNC brings these emerging countries not only technology, but also, its resources including capital, management skills and R&D capabilities (Jaguli, Malek, & Palil, 2014), as shown below in Table 2.

However, this model assumes that subsidiaries can get technology from its holding company, and they transfer technology – whether by accident or strategy – to local businesses. In practice, there is no guarantee that these conditions are fulfilled, as not all MNC employ cutting edge technology, nor all subsidiaries automatically have access to the technology from its parent (Driffield, Love, & Menghinello, 2010), or just that the parent is not willing to share this technology in order to prevent it from being transferred to third parties or imitated through reverse engineering. The latter is a real threat for MNC, so much that Glass & Kamal (1999) consider putting limitations to imitations is a valid strategy in order to protect the development of innovative products or process innovation. Despite these inherent risks and costs, transfer of technology represents a strategy used by MNC to gain local market share (Saldanha, Mello, Knemeyer, & Vijayaraghavan, 2015).

Local businesses can obtain technology from MNC generally through four forms:

1. Purchase of technology in contractual forms (patents, licenses, turnkey contracts, etc.)
2. Joint ventures between local firms and multinationals (including what has been termed 'strategic partnerships'). Different studies (Luo & Wang, 2012), (Jaguli, Malek, & Palil, 2014) have shown that this relationship between MNC and local businesses is considered an appropriate channel for the technology transfer.
3. Reverse engineering, by imitation, copy, etc. (without the consent of MNC).
4. Foreign direct investment (FDI). Considered one of the most important. Modern theory of Technology Transfer in MNC, measures the growth of the apparent productivity in the host economy, associated with foreign direct investment (Driffield, Love, & Menghinello, 2010), (Jaguli, Malek, & Palil, 2014).

Table 3. Technology transfer flows

		Transfer from subsidiary to parent	
		Yes	**No**
Transfer from parent to subsidiary	**Yes**	(1) Double way transfer	(2) Transfer with knowledge exploitation
	No	(3) Transfer and knowledge acquisition	(4) No knowledge transfer

Adapted from (Driffield, Love, & Menghinello, The Multinational Enterprise as a Source of International Knowledge Flows: Direct Evidence from Italy, 2010)

The choice between these four forms of technology transfer depends mainly on:

- The overall strategy of the MNC
- Factors driving productivity and competitiveness in a country in combination with
- The country particular stage of economic development

This combination of factors determines whether there are local companies with endogenous innovation capacity (Chudnovsky & Lopez, 2003). Recent studies (Driffield, Love, & Yong, 2014) suggest that the technology transfer from the MNC is most effective when the subsidiaries are located in the same regional block as the headquarters. A very high proportion of the flow of goods in the world is made within one of the three main regional blocks: Europe, North America and Asia. Although as noted above, the growth of commodity flows in emerging blocks such as Asia and South America, has been increasing. It is estimated that in 2025, the annual revenue only for the concept of trans-border e-commerce could reach $250 billion and up to 350 billion dollars, against the current $80 million dollars. Asia will account for 40% of the trans-border income, while in North America will account for 20% and South America for 10%. (van Heel, Lukic, & Leeuwis, 2014). So far, the empirical work enables to infer the existence of a knowledge transfer running parallel to the technology transfer from a MNC with advanced technology to a subsidiary in a developing country (Driffield, Love, & Menghinello, 2010). The flow of technology transfer between the parent and the subsidiary where the four possible types of knowledge flow that can occur in an MNC are shown in the Table 3.

It may be observed from the Figure 2 that Quadrant 2 represents the standard situation where a multinational company operates its superior knowledge in an emerging country by transferring knowledge to their subsidiary(ies). Quadrant 3 represents the situation in which knowledge flows from the subsidiary(ies) to the parent company. In the latter situation, the subsidiary is not limited to the adaptation of technology, but it becomes an active technology developer, either because MNC has developed a local research center or merely due to their business strategy, the MNC has developed a "listening post" designed to source knowledge from the host country. Driffield, Love, & Menghinello (2010) describes it as " Placing the R&D near the principal research and innovation clusters enables the absorption of learning due to the geographical proximity to such sites. The research center gathers information about emerging country technology, in order to be transferred to the headquarters". It is a real challenge for the MNC go for a flow of knowledge different that the one presented in quadrant 2 because the company rarely commits resources for R&D outside their home country and little evidence has been found that the use of Information Technology (IT) contributes to decentralize the R&D activities in MNC; on the

Figure 2. R&D expenditures vs. High technology exports
Source: The World Bank IBRD-IDA

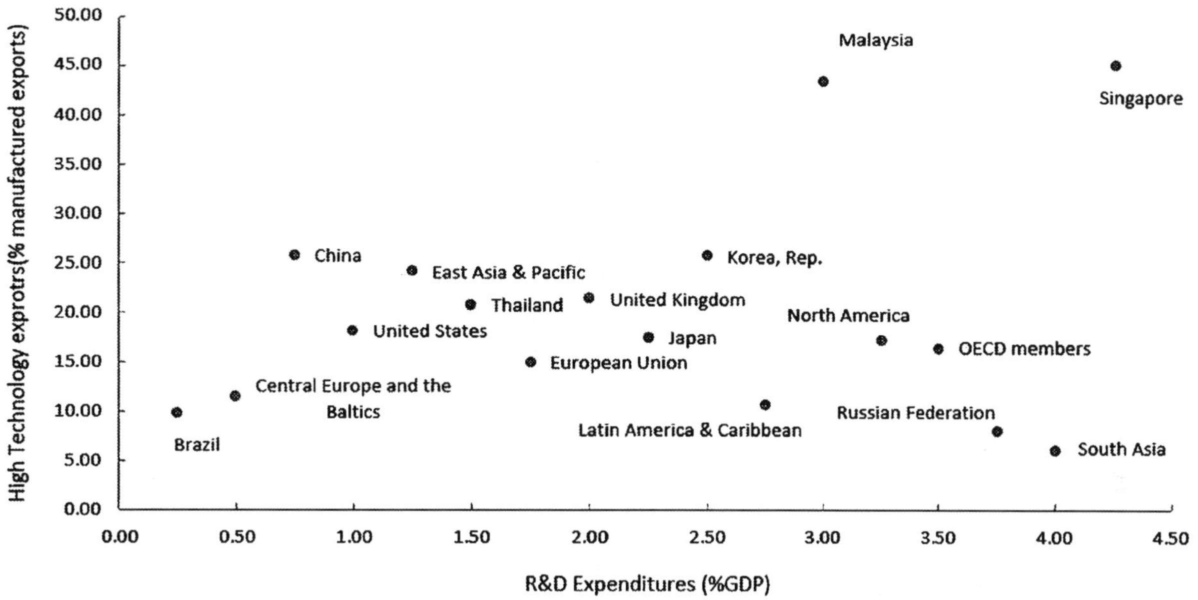

other hand, there seems to be tendency to centralize R&D using IT, just in their own home country or just in subsidiaries within developed countries, discouraging innovative activities from local firms and subsidiaries (Kumar, 1996).

The way in which knowledge flows in the matrix depends equally on the three reasons mentioned above (1) the overall strategy of MNC, (2) the factors driving productivity and competitiveness in a country in combination with (3) a country's particular stage of development. Particularly, technological readiness, workforce preparation and that the country finds itself in the innovation-driven stage (the final stage of economic development of a country) play an important role in the R&D of the local company to generate knowledge directly. Although being in quadrants 1 and 3 of the matrix may be an indicative of the country's technological development; one must be careful with this affirmation since this is also an indicative of privately owned knowledge which usually cannot flow to local businesses (Driffield, Love, & Menghinello, 2010).

Generally, MNC are recognized to have specific advantages with technology that enable them to overcome a potentially unfavorable position relative to domestic firms in foreign markets. Such benefits typically include the possession of information technology or knowledge of a process in which technology is involved, the management capacity, skilled labor in the use of technology, and their ability to perform R&D. However, MNC can also take from the host country's national companies their superior knowledge of local markets as well as consumer preferences and business practices because they possess superior intangible productive assets, a reputation, or even a greater technological knowledge than the MNC (Jaguli, Malek, & Palil, 2014). Moreover, although it is traditionally recognized that the multinational corporations have superior technology, literature (Driffield, Love, & Yong, 2014) reports models that are not based on the assumption that knowledge and/or technology flow only from the parent company to the subsidiary and subsequently to the domestic industry as a 'secondary' effect, but conversely the knowledge or technology flows to the MNC from the national companies, which is known as "reverse spillovers".

The reverse flow occurs when a host country has a significant presence of Multinational Enterprises who have chosen the country for its superior knowledge in technology. In these conditions it is reasonable to expect that the "reverse spillovers" arise either among local companies and national subsidiaries of the MNC or between domestic and foreign MNC subsidiaries (Driffield, Love, & Yong, 2014). Nevertheless, evidence of such "reverse spillovers" in emerging countries remains inconclusive although there have been documented cases of technology transfer and learning between MNCs and their suppliers and subcontractors in emerging countries, these studies rarely reveal that multinational was able to extract all the benefits from new technology generated among their suppliers. Additionally, there is no clear evidence of side effects, such as the use of MNC's employee skills at local companies (Chudnovsky & Lopez, 2003). However, it would be rash to consider that these inverse flows occur only among developed countries. Research on "reverse spillovers" in emerging countries is still a research subject currently in development; for instance, (Luo & Wang, 2012) report the presence of these "reverse spillovers" in regions of China where no sophisticated technology or R&D centers are found.

ACCESS TO TECHNOLOGY THROUGH DIRECT FOREIGN INVESTMENT

If the technology was developed in the emerging country is an irrelevant issue, because the real issue is that companies operating within the country should have access to this technology and the ability to absorb and use it. In this sense, it is widely recognized that foreign direct investment (FDI) is considered as the main vehicle to facilitate technology flows toward emerging countries (Glass & Kamal, 1999), (Jaguli, Malek, & Palil, 2014). Foreign direct investment is the transfer of an intermediate good, which accounts the competitive advantage of a company that may well be either the knowledge that underlies the technology or superior management activities (Kogut & Zander, 2003). Nowadays, most emerging countries look favorably foreign direct investment as a part of a more open and favorable government policy towards international market businesses (Chudnovsky & Lopez, 2003). This policy change is reflected in the growing number of bilateral trade agreements that have been recently negotiated. Certainly, there are many elements that may help explain why a developing country can be interested in attracting foreign direct investment – it is recognized that FDI is multifactorial; therefore, the implications for the local industry can be equally diverse (Driffield, Love, & Yong, 2014)–; nonetheless, technology/knowledge transfer is one of the dominant factors, among several others (Glass & Kamal, 1999), due to the belief that the main advantage of a business takes to foreign markets is its possession of superior knowledge (Kogut & Zander, 2003). The first theory that examined the effects of FDI was the theory of industrial organization (Hymer, 1976). This theory analyzes how FDI affects local businesses in a country. Theoretically, the arguments suggest that FDI can generate positive *spillovers* to local firms through knowledge and technologies. *Spillovers* are defined as the indirect effects in the productivity that occur in domestic firms as a result of transfer intangible assets to the affiliate (Sinani & Meyer, 2004). It is noteworthy that FDI is an important external source for the dissemination of knowledge and thereby promotes competition in the local industry because usually when the MNC invests in a foreign country, it often takes leading and patented technology as well as advanced production skills to successfully compete with local businesses, and these are the comparative advantages that can be transferred to local businesses (Jaguli, Malek, & Palil, 2014).

Case Study[1]: High Technology Markets and Emerging Economies

Minnesota Mining and Manufacturing Co. was founded in 1902 pursuing the goal to extract the mineral corundum from a mine called Crystal Bay at Minnesota. Swiftly the company turned to other materials and other products and nowadays 3M employs 88,000 people worldwide and produces more than 60,000 products. By 2013 3M topped $31.8 billion in sales around the world (international sales $20.1 billion accounts 63% company's total sales), 86 national subsidiaries and 70 international affiliates (3M company information, 2015). Due to 3M Company's policies, several of these affiliates are based on countries classified as emerging economies. Different criteria as those from International Monetary Fund, BRICs+, N-11 (Next eleven), FTSE Group and Russell Investments list China as a country that has some characteristics of a developed market, but does not meet standards to be a developed market. Notwithstanding that, due to its high growing rates, China may be classified as a developed country in the near future.

Since 1984 3M started to set up operations in China and has grown to a $3 billion business, (about 10% of 3M's global business just below $9.5 billion from USA). The company's China R&D center is already the largest one 3M has outside the US and since September 2013 is as a separate business-region; *the greater China region* (China, Hong Kong, Taiwan and Mongolia form the new area known as the Greater China region). 3M subsidiaries are basically local organizations and *greater China region* has 33 or 35 big business units from a division standpoint. All are managed on a local basis, because as Francis Hu, COO of 3M China says "With only a couple of exceptions, virtually all in the management team are local. Localization doesn't only mean people", in product development subsidiary is leveraged by technology/knowledge transferred by headquarters, "but the aim is always local products. From a strategy standpoint, we want to be very local". Business environment is changing rapidly in China, Hu saw the need to reallocate resources to the fast growing water purification business, growing it from RMB 6 million to RMB 25 million in two years. Another fast growing business areas in China, are; automotive (Great Wall Motors, a Chinese auto company is doing well in this sector), security and medicine. 3M China faces serious threats from competition, Hu argue at this point "the improvement of the local companies was surprising to us. So you think about having two groups: the foreign company trying to be local; the local company is trying to be high-tech or move up in the portfolio. I think the (local) group is doing better than the (foreign) group".

The concept of competitiveness has been commonly applied to two levels of analysis, the enterprise level and the national level. The general definition of competitiveness refers to the advantage (or the disadvantage) of the products or services of an organization or a country in the international markets (Hult, 2012). It is considered that competitiveness in high technology markets is closely related to the absorption and creation of technology capabilities of the company as well as various factors such as level of infrastructure of the company/industry and skilled labor, among others. From this perspective, *how 3M in China compete in the high-tech market*? *What technology transfer strategy is appropriate to select in order to make the company competitive in high-technology markets*?

How companies in emerging countries compete in the high-tech market? Empirical evidence shows illustrative cases such as South Korea and Taiwan where companies received strong government support to transfer technology to their national companies during their industrialization process, as well as cases like Malaysia and Thailand who chose to become exporters of high-tech components based on their cheap and highly skilled labor force. A more illustrative example is found in India where technology was adapted for local consumption and in turn generated an industry in the area of computer software. Some countries have developed their own technologies such as Brazil (aviation, electronics and computers), India (software) and Malaysia (electronics). In some cases, the strategy should evolve as the environment changes. An example of this is the case of the automotive components industry in India, which at first started with foreign companies either working collaboratively or as joint ventures and later evolved to integrate themselves into the global industry value chain with the ultimate goal of succeeding in the creation of their own knowledge.

The chance for emerging countries to compete in high-tech markets depends on the factors driving productivity and competitiveness within a country and are in turn influenced by the country's particular stage of economic development (mentioned earlier). Particularly relevant are; the absorptive capacity of technology and FDI as enablers of technology and knowledge transfer, and that the country is in the innovation-driven stage (or as a minimum the MNC has a R&D center in the host country). It is noteworthy that a positive correlation was found between investment in R&D and high-tech exports of a country (Alvarez & Marin, 2013) as shown in Figure 2.

This begs the question *what technology transfer strategy is appropriate select in order to make the company competitive in high-tech markets*?

To answer this question an adjustment was made to the array *of knowledge flow resulting from the technology transfer* involving internal and external factors in technology transfer. Two factors should be considered:

- The technological capacity of the company that involves at least two levels; creation and absorption technology. This factor represents the innovation level at the company and accounts for internal factor.
- The FDI as an external factor to exploit a competitive advantage. Similarly it involves two levels; inward and outward flows. It represents the role of MNC.

The combination of these two positions of internal and external factors define selection strategies of knowledge transfer based on technology and FDI as shown in the following Table 4:

In the matrix there are two quadrants of interest for emerging economies namely CI and AO. Quadrant CI encompasses those countries with sufficient innovation capability to create technology and have inward FDI to the country. The relationship between MNC and innovation in the company usually

Table 4. Knowledge transfer based on technology and FDI

Innovation	**Technology creation** **C**	CI Local Learning (Emerging economies)	CO Knowledge-based update (Developed economies)
	Technology absorption **A**	AI Adaptation (Non-developed economies)	AO Foreign learning (Emerging economies)
		FDI Inward **I**	**FDI Outward** **O**
		MNC	

Adapted from (FDI and Technology as Levering Factors of Competitiveness in Developing Countries, Alvarez & Marin, 2013)

generates involuntary *spillovers* by transferring technology to other local companies. In this situation local businesses may have a learning experience as a result of the *spillover* effect.

Additionally, quadrant AO represents those economies that break into international markets through outward FDI, despite these economies usually have a delay in developing technology compared with developed countries. Learning abroad would be the most relevant process in this quadrant.

The central idea for emerging economies lies in the determination of the transit possibilities to the more dynamic quadrants, moving from AO to CI and to CI to CO; for example, it is remarkable how during 1960-1990 period, the so-called Asian Tigers, Singapore, Hong Kong, Taiwan and Korea were able to leap from quadrant AI to quadrant CO, going through significant increases in FDI flows and achieving high rates of growth and industrialization.

According to Hu, 3M China plans to face threats in the high-tech market using the so called location management strategy, which consists of (1) taking advantage from government drive-innovation policies; as far as China in in the innovation-driven stage (2) being local, (3) putting more resources into technology and R&D; 3M china is updating from quadrant AO to quadrant CO "(We) have to start to think of the alignment with many local companies: customers and suppliers; trying to become part of them … from a manufacturing standpoint, we're going to move over to the west, reason is not cost because 3M is not a low-cost manufacturer … the government is promoting investment, promoting (the) industrialization of those regions so we follow our customers" pointed Hu.

There is substantial evidence to say that technology transfer flows (and underlying knowledge) are a motive for FDI in a country (Guillén & García-Canal, 2011). In MNC, the knowledge transfer usually moves from the headquarters based in a developed country toward a subsidiary based in an emerging country. However, it can also occur as a trans-boundary flow from a developed country with low R&D capacity or like a reverse flow from subsidiaries in the host country to developed countries or else as reverse spillovers.

KNOWLEDGE: THE FINAL QUEST

MNCs have left the old approach based on the market scavenging and the hunt for resources, moving toward a modern vision of efficiency and pursuit of knowledge (Dunning, 2006) where FDI is done not only to exploit the technology in the emerging country where it is taken, but to achieve a technology transfer that implies a transfer of knowledge that is used as a competitive advantage in the local economy or even at their home country (Driffield, Love, & Yong, 2014). Thus, MNC is proven to be an efficient (and effective) way to create and transfer knowledge across borders and the FDI is performed to achieve the transfer of an intermediate good called knowledge, which embodies the advantages of a company, either as knowledge underlying technology, production processes or other management activities in the company, (Kogut & Zander, 2003). Caves (1971) was the first one to establish this relationship when he pointed out that "the company producing a differentiated product controls knowledge about serving the market that can be transferred to other national markets for this product at little or no cost." Alvarez and Marin (2013) further added the condition that "this market is imperfect." However, the cost of the flow condition should be analyzed carefully. As noted in the previous section, technology is a public good and the underlying knowledge has the property of being likewise a public good (Buckley & Casson, 1976), i.e. that can be transferred to a marginal cost zero, so that is easily transferred and difficult to protect. Glass and Kamal (1999) point out that MNC's workers can disseminate their knowledge to local businesses when they change employers, so the MNC should pay a premium wage to avoid leakage of its workers to local businesses. This policy usually does not favor local workers who do not earn this bonus. However, Teece (1977) argues, that the transfer cost is not close to zero (or zero) in all cases; actually, in his research he states that the characteristics of knowledge itself determine the costs and the transfer mode. These characteristics, understood as tacit knowledge and implicit knowledge, are extremely relevant in the context of technology transfer. The information is often delivered through documents that describe the necessary procedures for the use of technology. This information is structured and can be stored (explicit knowledge), but in many cases technology involves factors that are not possible to structure; for example, the knowledge that the engineers and workers who work in the foreign subsidiary of MNC possess (tacit knowledge). Companies create knowledge (tacit and implicit) and use it to produce technologies and successful products (Ichii, Hattori, & Michael, 2012).The main determinants of transfer costs are the degree of previous experience with technology transfer, the country's particular stage of economic development, and the number of companies using similar technologies. These variables capture the direct experience with the transfer of technology, the understanding of its use over time, and the common knowledge of its properties (Dhanaraj, Lyles, Steensma, & Tihanyi, 2004); thus, they represent approximate measures of tacit knowledge transfer. Kogut and Zander (2003) indicate that somehow, the MNC specializes in internal transfer of tacit knowledge. Seen from an "absolutist about coding position," this tacit knowledge can be codified, but the costs of doing so are higher (Ancori, Bureth, & Cohendet, 2000) than the oldest technologies or simple technologies that are often better coded, so they are less costly to transfer. The less easily to be codified and more difficult it turns out to teach the technology, the more likely the transfer is going to be more expensive. This result implies that the choice of transfer mode is determined by the efficiency of the multinational firm in transferring knowledge in relation with other companies, and not to relative to an abstract transaction market (Kogut & Zander, 2003). The activities of FDI and the creation/assimilation of technology enable the MNC to specialize in the transfer and recombination of knowledge. One effect reported by Sjöholm (1999) derived from these transfers is that knowledge, unintentionally overflows (*Spillover*) horizontally or vertically to local businesses. Furthermore, there is empirical evidence that shows examples of these spillovers in emerging countries such as shown by Schoors & Bartoldus (2001) in Hungary; Lopez-Cordova (2003) in Mexico; and Javorcik (2008)in Lithuania. Javorcik himself notes that these *spillovers* are more likely to occur vertically as EMC can benefit from the improved performance of its suppliers. This improvement of local companies supplying EMC leads to the production of a greater variety of intermediate goods, which enables the emerging economy gain a comparative advantage in producing more sophisticated end products (Jaguli, Malek,

Table 5. Technology Transfer flows Parent/Subsidiaries/Local companies

		Transference from subsidiary to local companies	
		Yes	**No**
Transference from parent to Subsidiary	**Yes**	(1) Harnessing knowledge with spillovers	(2) Harnessing knowledge without Spillovers
	No	(3) Only Spillovers from subsidiary	(4) No knowledge transfer or Spillovers

Adapted from (Driffield, Love, & Menghinello, The Multinational Enterprise as a Source of International Knowledge Flows: Direct Evidence from Italy, 2010)

& Palil, 2014). This situation is illustrated in the modified matrix of knowledge flow resulting from the technology transfer between the parent, and the subsidiaries with the inclusion of spillovers and local businesses as shown below in Table 5.

The top row describes knowledge flows from the headquarters of the MNC to its foreign subsidiary. This flow can generate spillovers to local firms (quadrant 1) or not (quadrant 2). In both cases there is utilization of the knowledge, but in the second case, this does not represent an advantage for the emerging economy. Quadrant 3 represents a special situation, where despite the absence of knowledge transfer from the parent to the subsidiary, the latter is able to provide knowledge generated internally (in an intentional or accidental way) to local businesses. Quadrant 4 is the situation where there is no flow of knowledge in any way. This last situation can happen when a government policy, to avoid losing a competitive advantage, or other factors limit the cross-border knowledge flow.

A MNC in an emerging country must compete based on its superior technology and knowledge. This implies that the company has the ability to generate and transfer tacit knowledge that is difficult to imitate. Thus, the MNC must take care not only of the competitiveness of other companies and market demand, but the degree to which its advantage cannot be replicated by competitors or at least it cannot be replicated more quickly through imitation by its competitors.

Evidence from literature demonstrates the importance of technology, or expressed in a better way, knowledge flows (flows underlying technology) represent for the MNC. There are many activities derived from the ideas displayed in this chapter that MNC can be implement in its relations between parent, subsidiary and local companies (including, but not limited to improving the quality of local product suppliers, supporting local suppliers to meet international quality standards) that are not covered here, but it is left to the reader go deepen their study.

THE CHALLENGES FOR MNC

Technology has been the basis of many productivity increases in the enterprise. Emerging countries can improve their productivity not merely by adapting exogenous technologies transferred from parent MNC but taking advantage from underlying knowledge at the technology transfer in cross-borders flows. Knowledge is particularly important for emerging economies as they approach the innovation-stage. In the long run, MNC competitiveness can be largely enhanced by technological innovation. Innovation is therefore the ultimate goal of a MNC. In the end, it is not the objective to adapt or even create technology, and certainly, it is not about being provided by the parent or home country knowledge. In the broadest sense, the real challenge for MNC is related to apply knowledge to maintain a competitive edge and move toward even higher value-added activities.

As mentioned earlier, through the location of subsidiaries in technologically advanced regions, MNCs can gain access to knowledge embedded in the region. These subsidiaries gain access to knowledge from two distinct contexts; (1) the MNC headquarters and the other subsidiaries; and (2) an external environment of regional or host country firms (Almeida & Phene, 2004). A research carried out by Phene & Almeida (2008) suggests that subsidiaries absorb significant knowledge from home country firms and from firms in other countries, with a more limited access to the production of knowledge. Nevertheless, host country knowledge is critical to the scale and quality of innovation while the knowledge absorbed from other subsidiaries and the parent company within the MNC does not lead to increased innovation. However, recent literature (Cowden & Alhorr, 2013), (Mahajan, 2014) offers strong evidence to consider that more disruptive innovation will be discovered through the firm's internal network rather than through an open networks. Specifically, research indicates that the most disruptive innovations will be discovered in subsidiaries that pursue local market initiatives in emerging markets than in the headquarters at their home country.

While MNCs traditionally dominate high-end markets in many industry segments, there is a strong competition at the lower-end and middle markets, and an increasing number of companies are becoming innovative and can often compete fairly aggressively at high-end markets; thus, innovation has become absolutely critical to the long term success of MNCs. Since MNC subsidiaries play a limited role in MNC innovation, emerging economies (especially those that are not in the innovation-stage) face the challenge to harvest the power of innovation Min Zhou & Patrick Berbon (2012) refer three best practices to meet this challenge; (1) Create an ecosystem that encourages ingenious innovation, which consists of supportive government policies, foreign-educated returnees and a vibrant venture capital system, (2) Product/Service customization; consumers are increasingly more demanding of products that are tailored to their unique tastes and habits, and (3) Developing new technologies and business models rooted in very practical approaches to the market. As far as the key role of innovation as a driver of economic growth and well-being is widely recognized, MNC needs educated and strongly motivated people in order to build an innovation-driven enterprise. Workers with advanced degrees are an essential resource for innovation. MNC should not only consider the importance of FDI, knowledge transfer and an innovation-driven approach, but going beyond and setting up the right environment in place that will nurture, promote, and enable the human factor (Dutta, Lanvin, & Wunsch-Vincent, 2014). The need to understand the role that the human factor along with technology/FDI and FDI plays a critical role in innovation, so the MNC is able to compete in the interconnected world.

REFERENCES

3M. (. 2015). *Company information*. Retrieved from: http://solutions.3m.com/wps/portal/3M/en_US/3MCompany/Information/AboutUs/WhoWeAre/

Aghina, W., De Smet, A., & Heywood, S. (2014, September). *The past and future of global organizations*. Retrieved from: http://www.mckinsey.com/insights/organization/the_past_and_future_of_global_organizations

Almeida, P., & Phene, A. (2004). Subsidiaries and Knowledge creation: The influence of the MNC and host country on innovation. *Strategic Management Journal*, *25*(89), 847–864. doi:10.1002/smj.388

Alter, S. (2013, February). Work System Theory: Overview of Core Concepts, Extensions, and Challenges for the Future. *Journal of the Association for Information Systems*, *14*(2), 72-121. Retrieved from: http://www.stevenalter.com/work-system-basics-2/

Alvarez, I., & Marin, R. (2013, March). FDI and Technology as Levering Factors of Competitiveness in Developing Countries. *Journal of International Management*, *19*(3), 232–246. doi:10.1016/j.intman.2013.02.005

Ancori, B., Bureth, A., & Cohendet, P. (2000). The Economics of Knowledge: The Debate about Codification and Tacit Knowledge. *Industrial and Corporate Change*, *9*(2), 255–287. doi:10.1093/icc/9.2.255

Baumgartner, T., Hatami, H., & Vander Ark, J. (2012). *Sales Growth: Five proven strategies from the world's sales Leaders*. Hoboken, NJ: Wiley & Sons Inc.

Berkeley University. (2005). *The Theory of economic growth*. Retrieved from http://eml.berkeley.edu/~webfac/trehan/e100b_sp05/chap4.pdf

Blomkvist, K., Kappen, P., & Zander, I. (2014). Win, Place, or Show? How Foreign Investment Strategies Contribute to the Technological Growth of the Multinational Corporation. *Long Range Planning*, *47*(1-2), 16–31. doi:10.1016/j.lrp.2013.10.001

Blomström, M., & Kokko, A. (1997). *How Foreign Investment Affects Host Countries*. Policy Research Working Paper Series, 2-44.

Bock, W., Field, D., Zwilenberg, P., & Rogers, K. (2015, February). *The Growth of the Global Mobile Internet Economy*. Retrieve from https://www.bcgperspectives.com/content/articles/telecommunications_connected_world_growth_global_mobile_internet_economy/

Buckley, P. J., & Casson, M. (1976). *The future of the multinational enterprise* (Vol. 1). London: Macmillan. doi:10.1007/978-1-349-02899-3

Caves, R. E. (1971). International corporations: The industrial economics of foreign investment. *Economica*, *38*(149), 1–27. doi:10.2307/2551748

Chandler, A. D. (2003). *Strategy and Structure: Chapters in the History of the American Industrial Enterprise*. Washington, DC: Beard Books.

Chudnovsky, D., & Lopez, A. (2003). Diffusion of environmentally friendly technologies by multinational corporations in developing countries. *Journal of Technology Management & Sustainable Development*, *2*(1), 5–18. doi:10.1386/ijtm.2.1.5/0

Cisco. (2014). *2014 Connected world Technology final report*. Retrieved from http://www.cisco.com/c/dam/en/us/solutions/collateral/enterprise/connected-world-technology-report/cisco-2014-connected-world-technology-report.pdf

Cowden, B. J., & Alhorr, H. S. (2013). Disruptive innovation in multinational enterprises. *The Multinational Business Review*, *21*(4), 358–371. doi:10.1108/MBR-05-2013-0027

Czarnitzki, D., & Kraft, K. (2011). Spillovers of Innovation Activities and Their Profitability. *Oxford Economic Papers*, gpr020.

De la Torre, A., Didier, T., & Pinat, M. (2014). *Can Latin America Tap the Globalization Upside?* Policy Research Working Paper Series.

Dhanaraj, C., Lyles, M. A., Steensma, H. K., & Tihanyi, L. (2004). Managing tacit and explicit knowledge transfer in IJVs: The role of relational embeddedness and the impact on performance. *Journal of International Business Studies*, *35*(5), 428–442. doi:10.1057/palgrave.jibs.8400098

Dreischmeier, R., Close, K., & Trichet, P. (2015, March). *bcg perspectives*. Retrieve from https://www.bcgperspectives.com/content/articles/digital_economy_technology_strategy_digital_imperative/

Driffield, N., Love, J., & Yong, Y. (2014, January). Technology Sourcing and Reverse Productivity Spillovers in the Multinational Enterprise: Global or Regional Phenomenon? *British Journal of Management, 25*, 24–41. doi:10.1111/1467-8551.12009

Driffield, N., Love, J. H., & Menghinello, S. (2010). The Multinational Enterprise as a Source of International Knowledge Flows: Direct Evidence from Italy. *Journal of International Business Studies, 41*(2), 350–359. doi:10.1057/jibs.2009.57

Duce, M. (2003). *Definitions of Foreign Direct Investment (FDI): a methodological note*. Banco de España.

Dunning, J. H. (2006). Towards a new paradigm of development: implications for the determinants of international business. *Transnational Corporations, 5*(1), 173-227.

Dutta, S., Lanvin, B., & Wunsch-Vincent, S. (2014). *The Global Innovation Index 2014. The Human Factor in Innovation*. Cornell University, INSEAD, and WIPO.

Financial Times. (2016, December). *FT Lexicon*. Retrieved from http://lexicon.ft.com/Term?term=foreign-direct-investment

Gehani, R. (2013). Innovative Strategic Leader Transforming From a Low-Cost Strategy to Product Differentiation Strategy. *Journal of Technology Management & Innovation*, *8*(2), 144–155.

Glass, A., & Kamal, S. (1999). Multinational Firms and Technology Transfer. *The Scandinavian Journal of Economics*, 495–513.

Guillén, M., & García-Canal, E. (2011). The Rise of Emerging Market Multinationals. *IESE Insight,* (10), 13-19.

Hallin, C., & Holmström Lind, C. (2012). Revisiting the external impact of MNCs: An empirical study of the mechanisms behind knowledge spillovers from MNC. *International Business Review*, *21*(2), 167–179. doi:10.1016/j.ibusrev.2010.12.003

Hoskisson, R. E., Eden, L., Ming Lau, C., & Wright, M. (2000). Strategy in Emerging economies. *Academy of Management Journal*, *43*(3), 249–267. doi:10.2307/1556394

Hult, T. G. (2012). A focus on international competitiveness. *Academy of Marketing Science. Journal*, *40*(2), 195-201.

Hymer, S. H. (1976). *The international operations of national firms: A study of direct foreign investment* (Vol. 14). Cambridge, MA: MIT Press.

Ichii, S., Hattori, S., & Michael, D. (2012). How to Win in Emerging Markets: Lessons from Japan. *Harvard Business Review*, 126-130.

International Telecommunication Union. (2015). *The world in 2015 ICT Facts and Figures*. Retrieved from: https://www.itu.int/en/ITU-D/Statistics/facts/ICTFactsFigures2015.pdf

Jaguli, A. R., Malek, M. M., & Palil, M. R. (2014). Do MNCS' high quality and standard requirements matter? A channel for vertical spillovers. *International Journal of Business & Society*, *15*(1), 127-150.

Javorcik, B. S. (2008). Can survey evidence shed light on spillovers from foreign direct investment? *The World Bank Research Observer*, *23*(2), 139–159. doi:10.1093/wbro/lkn006

Khanna, T. (2014, September). Contextual Intelligence. *Harvard Business Review*, *92*(9), 58–68. PMID:25509576

Kogut, B., & Zander, U. (2003, November). Knowledge of the Firm and the Evolutionary Theory of the Multinational Corporation. *Journal of International Business Studies*, *34*(6), 516–529. doi:10.1057/palgrave.jibs.8400058

Kumar, N. (1996). Foreign direct investments and technology transfers in development: a perspective on recent literature. United Nations University, Institute of Technologies.

Leszczyńska, D., & Pruchnicki, E. (2003). The evolution of knowledge transfer and the location of a multinational corporation: Theory and mathematical model. *Multinational Business Review*, *23*(2), 111–129. doi:10.1108/MBR-06-2014-0031

Lopez-Cordova, E. (2003). NAFTA and Manufacturing Productivity in Mexico. *Journal of the Latin American and Caribbean Economic Association*, *3*, 55.

Luo, Y., & Wang, S. L. (2012). Foreign direct investment strategies by developing country multinationals: A diagnostic model for home country effects. *Global Strategy Journal*, *2*(3), 244–261. doi:10.1111/j.2042-5805.2012.01036.x

Magee, S. P. (1981, November). The Appropriability Theory of the Multinational Corporation. *The Annals of the American Academy of Political and Social Science*, *458*(1), 123–135. doi:10.1177/000271628145800110

Mahajan, N. (2014, February 11). *CKGSB Knowledge*. Retrieved from http://knowledge.ckgsb.edu.cn/2014/02/11/china-business-strategy/venkatesh-shankar-interview-new-lands-innovation/

Manolopoulos, D., Dimitratos, P., Young, S., & Lioukas, S. (2009). Technology Sourcing and Performance of Foreign Subsidiaries in Greece: The Impact of MNE and Local Environmental Contexts. *Management International Review*, *49*(1), 43–60. doi:10.1007/s11575-008-0124-7

McKinsey Global Institute. (2014). *Global flows in a digital age: How trade, finance, people, and data connect the world economy*. McKinsey Global Institute.

Nonaka, I. (1994). A dynamic theory of organizational knowledge creation. *Organization Science*, *5*(1), 14–37. doi:10.1287/orsc.5.1.14

Nottebohm, O., Manyika, J., Bughin, J., Chui, M., Syed, A.-R., & Ledezma, O. (2012). *En linea y en crecimiento: el impacto de internet en los países aspirantes*. McKinsey & Company.

OECD. (2011). *OECD Science, Technology and Industry Scoreboard 2011*. Retrieved from OECD iLibrary: http://www.oecd-ilibrary.org/sites/sti_scoreboard-2011-en/03/10/index.html?contentType=&itemId=%2Fcontent%2Fchapter%2Fsti_scoreboard-2011-31-en&mimeType=text%2Fhtml&containerItemId=%2Fcontent%2Fserial%2F20725345&accessItemIds=

OECD. (2013). *OECD Factbook 2013: Economic, Environmental and Social Statistics*. Retrieved from OECD iLibrary: http://www.oecd-ilibrary.org/sites/factbook-2013-en/04/02/01/index.html?itemId=/content/chapter/factbook-2013-34-en

Peters, T. (1979, September). *Beyond the matrix organization*. McKinsey & Company. Retrieved from http://www.mckinsey.com/insights/organization/beyond_the_matrix_organization

Peters, T. (2014). Tom Peters on leading the 21st-century organization. *McKinsey Quarterly*. Retrieved from http://www.mckinsey.com/insights/organization/tom_peters_on_leading_the_21st_century_organization

Phene, A., & Almeida, P. (2008). Innovation in multinational subsidiaries: The role of knowledge assimilation and subsidiary capabilities. *Journal of International Business Studies*, *39*(5), 901–919. doi:10.1057/palgrave.jibs.8400383

Porter, M. E. (1980). *Competitive Strategy: Techniques for Analyzing Industries and Competitors*. New York: Free Press.

Rostow, W. W. (1960). *The Stages of Economic Growth: A Non-Communist Manifesto*. Cambridge, UK: Cambridge University Press.

Saldanha, J. P., Mello, J. E., Knemeyer, M. A., & Vijayaraghavan, T. (2015, January). Implementing Supply Chain technologies in Emerging markets: An institutional theory Perspective. *Journal of Supply Chain Management*, *51*(1), 5–26. doi:10.1111/jscm.12065

Sanders, N. R. (2008, May). Pattern of information technology use: The impact on buyer–suppler coordination and performance. *Journal of Operations Management*, *26*(3), 349–367. doi:10.1016/j.jom.2007.07.003

Santiso, J. (2007). *The emergence of Latin multinationals*. OECD Emerging Markets Network Working Paper. Retrieved from: http://www.oecd.org/dev/40512615.pdf

Schoors, K., & Bartoldus, V. (2001). *The productivity effect of foreign ownership on domestic firms in Hungary*. In *EAE Conference, Philadelphia*, PA.

Sinani, E., & Meyer, K. E. (2004). Spillovers of technology transfer from FDI: The case of Estonia. *Journal of Comparative Economics*, *32*(3), 445–466. doi:10.1016/j.jce.2004.03.002

Sjöholm, F. (1999). Technology gap, competition and spillovers from direct foreign investment: Evidence from establishment data. *The Journal of Development Studies*, *36*(1), 53–73. doi:10.1080/00220389908422611

Smith, A. (1812). *An Inquiry into the nature and causes of the wealth of nations* (Vol. 3). London: J.M-Dent & Sond LTD.

Teece, D. J. (1977). Technology transfer by multinational firms: The resource cost of transferring technological know-how. *The Economic Journal*, *87*(346), 242–261. doi:10.2307/2232084

Tsai-Ju, L. (2015). Clusters, technological knowledge spillovers, and performance: The moderating roles of local ownership ties and a local market orientation. *Management Decision*, *53*(2), 469–490. doi:10.1108/MD-09-2014-0560

Van Heel, B., Lukic, V., & Leeuwis, E. (2014, September). *Cross-Border E-Commerce Makes the World Flatter*. Retrieved from https://www.bcgperspectives.com/content/articles/transportation_travel_tourism_retail_cross_border_ecommerce_makes_world_flatter/

Waterman, R. H. Jr, Peters, T. J., & Phillips, J. R. (1980, June). Structure is not organization. *Business Horizons*, *23*(3), 14–26. doi:10.1016/0007-6813(80)90027-0

Wikipedia Contributors. (2015). *Spillover effect*. Retrieved from Wikipedia: https://en.wikipedia.org/w/index.php?title=Spillover_effect&oldid=691313422

Winston, M. (2011). Multinational Corporations. In D. K. Chatterjee (Ed.), Encyclopedia of Global Justice (pp. 730-733). Springer Netherlands. doi:10.1007/978-1-4020-9160-5_544

World Economic Forum. (2015). *The Global Competitiveness Report 2014-2015*. Retrieved from http://www.weforum.org/reports/global-competitiveness-report-2014-2015

Zhou, M., & Patrick, B. (2012). *Innovation Management Se*. Retrieved from http://www.innovationmanagement.se/2012/05/17/7-key-steps-to-successful-open-innovation-in-china/

KEY TERMS AND DEFINITIONS

Emerging Countries: Are low-income, rapid growth countries using economic liberalization as their primary engine of growth. They satisfy two criteria; a rapid pace of economic development, and government policies favoring economic liberalization and the adoption of a free-market system (Hoskisson, Eden, Ming Lau, & Wright, 2000).

Foreign Direct Investment (FDI): Is an investment made by a multinational corporation MNC or entity based in one country, into a company or entity based in another country for which the foreign investor has control (owning 10% or more of the business) over the company purchased. (Duce, 2003). FDI comes in three types: Horizontal: where the company carries out the same activities abroad as at home, Vertical: when different stages of activities are added abroad and Conglomerate: where an unrelated business is added abroad. This is the most unusual form of FDI as it involves attempting to overcome two barriers simultaneously - entering a foreign country and a new industry. FDI can take the form of greenfield entry that implies assembling all the elements from scratch or takeover that is often covered by the term 'mergers and acquisitions' (M&As) but internationally, mergers are vanishingly small, accounting for less than 1 per cent of all foreign acquisitions. (Financial Times, 2016). Literature (OECD, 2013)shows that FDI creates direct, stable and long-lasting links between economies. Inward foreign direct investment (FDI) will serve as a channel for knowledge and technology transfer to the host country (Hallin & Holmström Lind, 2012).

Innovation: For this chapter, the author takes the Innovation definition from Czarnitzki and Kraft (2011): Innovation is the efficient use of the scarce resource knowledge. Knowledge in turn is the result of a firm's own R&D or information spillovers from outside. Information spillover possibly result i.e. from research activities conducted by research institutions, suppliers or customers but the most important source is perhaps information from competing companies.

Knowledge Transfer: Knowledge is composed of know-how and skills that reflect a firm's capacity to deploy resources to bring into effect a desired end (Leszczyńska & Pruchnicki, 2003), and exist two dimensions of knowledge in organizations: explicit and tacit. (Nonaka, 1994). Knowledge transfer includes mostly transfer of tacit knowledge such as knowhow, management, and technical skills so they ensure learning of new information, technical and organizational skills and it is quite different from technology transfer which involves rather the transfer of capital goods such as machinery and equipment. In a new perspective Kogurt and Zander (2003) indicated Firms are social communities that specialize in the creation and internal transfer of knowledge, which helps to achieve firm's superior productivity (Driffield, Love and Menghinello, 2010).

Multinational Corporation MNC: The multinational corporation is defined in some sense arbitrarily by where frontiers are drawn, however a generally accepted definition is " a business enterprise comprising entities in two or more countries linked by ownership or significant control which enables decision making permitting coherent policies and a common strategy across national boundaries" (Winston, 2011). A firm becomes a multinational "when the same knowledge is exploited at several different locations, involving several different countries", thus, an MNC may be viewed as a complex pattern of interdependent activities, linked by knowledge flows and intermediate products. (Hoskisson, Eden, Ming Lau, & Wright, 2000).

Spillovers: Traditionally, the multinational corporation (MNC) is ascribed superior technologies and management skills that allow it to compete successfully against local firms however when MNC introduce superior technology, that will "spill over" to local firms. This unintentional transfer of knowledge, are widely believed to benefit firms in the host country, resulting in, e.g., productivity growth among domestic firms (Hallin & Holmström Lind, 2012), moreover there is a positive relationship between intentional knowledge diffusion and unintentional knowledge spillovers. In econometric literature Spillovers effects are events in one context that occur because of something else in a seemingly unrelated context (Wikipedia contributors, 2015). Technological knowledge spillover is the phenomenon by which a group of geographically proximate MNC' inventory of self-generated technological knowledge leaks out to MNC subsidiaries or other member firms within a cluster (Tsai-Ju, 2015) and are defined as the indirect effects in the productivity that occur in domestic firms as a result of transfer intangible assets to the affiliate (Sinani & Meyer, 2004).

Technology Flows: As Manyika et al (2014) stated: "Global flows have been a common thread extending through the mercantilist and colonial eras, from trade routes of old such as the renowned Silk Road through the industrial revolutions that swept across Europe and North America in the 18th and 19th centuries to the more recent rise of emerging economies." But today the web of cross-border Goods, services and financial exchanges has exploded in scope and complexity. Goods and services and financial flows are the sum of imports and exports of goods and services for each country; and financial flows are the inflows and outflows of foreign direct investment, equity and bond flows, and cross-border lending and deposits. Underlying these are technology supporting the mentioned flows and a cross-border technology flow is undertaken in parallel to the Goods and Services flows. Technology flows refer to the average of technological payments and receipts. Trade in technology comprises four main categories: transfer of techniques (through patents and licenses, disclosure of know-how); transfer (sale, licensing, franchising) of designs, trademarks and patterns; services with a technical content, -including technical and engineering studies as well as technical assistance; industrial R&D. (OECD, 2011).

ENDNOTE

[1] Data in this case were taken from CKGSB online article, *3M Company: In China for China* (Mahajan, 2014)

Chapter 7
Operational Approaches in Organizational Structure:
A Case for MNEs in Developing Countries

Mohammad Ayub Khan
Tecnológico de Monterrey, Mexico

ABSTRACT

This chapter analyzes the challenge of organizational setup in developing countries faced by MNEs. In doing so the chapter focuses on different types of structural options available for MNEs and studies factors influencing the decision of how to structure the MNE in developing countries. In essence, the chapter presents a list of structural options for MNEs to choose from according to their needs, contextual situations and strategic direction. The factors influencing the decision to structure the company are general factors, management orientations, corporate culture, information and communication technologies, strategy and learning organizations. Finally, the chapter forwards some essential recommendations for MNEs to follow when deciding about which organizational structure is relatively more suitable than others while operating in developing countries.

INTRODUCTION

The organizational set up used by business firms is called by different names such as organizational design, organizational structure, organizational architecture, organization operational system and organizational infrastructure. In this chapter these names and terms are used interchangeably. For any company the organizational structure is like the foundation stone for a tall and multistorey building. Organizations regardless of the activities and functions they undertake have objectives to obtain within a given period of timetable, have activities and functions to perform on hourly basis, and possess resources (e.g., money, people, technology, and information) to administer effectively and efficiently. Achieving the organizational objectives as desired requires the adequate and appropriate utilization of the existing limited resources and for this to happen successfully it would demand from managers the right configuration and distribution of those resources in order to execute the right functions or activities in the right

DOI: 10.4018/978-1-5225-0276-0.ch007

place and at an appropriate time. Therefore, building both the social and physical infrastructure inside an organization is essential for establishing an environment to maintain and promote communication, cooperation and coordination among different organizational actors and units.

In the MNEs context, the organizational structure involves the type and degree of relationship that exists between the headquarters and its subsidiaries located in foreign regions. Rugman (2005) is of the view that "During the past few decades, MNEs mainly located their foreign subsidiaries in their home regions" and, to some extent, in other regions of the Triad (Flores & Aguilera 2007). Over the last few years, MNEs from mature economies have heavily increased their investments in developing countries (Dunning 2009), mostly in emerging markets. The role of foreign subsidiaries located in developing countries has thus considerably increased. This evolution is raising new challenges for the relationships of MNEs with their foreign subsidiaries. In fact, subsidiaries of MNEs are embedded in their local environment (Hennart 2009), establishing relationships with different local actors including governments, suppliers, distributors, clients, etc. (Asmussen et. al., 2009). Moreover, the environment of developing economies differs considerably from the environment of matured markets (Ghemawat & Hout 2008). It thus seems interesting to examine more specifically the relationship between headquarters and subsidiaries in the context of developing countries. Given the changing geography of the world economy (Buckley & Ghauri 2004) and the changing rules of international business competition this question seems particularly relevant for MNEs (Hutzschenreuter & Gröne 2009) operating in developing countries. Therefore, this chapter is dedicated to the theoretical analysis of different organizational structural options available for MNEs to choose from in the process of market expansion, especially moving into the developing markets.

ORGANIZATIONAL STRUCTURE

The literature review is dedicated to the analysis of diverse both conventional and contemporary challenges facing the MNEs doing business internationally, and especially in the context of developing countries or markets. In this chapter the terms developing countries and emerging markets are interchangeable used even though these terms are interpreted differently by different authors in the existing body of knowledge in the field. Some authors understand that a country or market is considered in the emerging stage because the nation is gradually improving its overall economic and business conditions for businesses and investments in comparison with underdeveloped countries or markets. So to say otherwise, these countries or markets are just emerging from the underdeveloped economic and business conditions on several fronts including economic stability, infrastructure development and good governance. Other authors are of the view that a nation or market is defined as an emerging country or market after the country or market has progressed from underdeveloped conditions into developing conditions before becoming an emerging country or nation. The overall business, economic and governance conditions in an emerging nation are relatively better than a developing country or market. For example, some countries or markets such as China, Mexico, India and Brazil used to be considered as developing countries but in the past several years these nations have achieved tremendous economic and business success and thus are directly competing with the global business and economic powers of Europe, Asia and North America.

Generally, the term of structure and design are interchangeably used in the existing literature on management and organizational theories. However, some scholars look at these terms as they are interdependent but different. An organizational structure is the system and design is the process. For example, organizational structure is about the separation of power, authority, roles, responsibilities and functions inside the organization and how information and decisions flow inside the company. Design is about the grouping, assigning and assessing of these roles, responsibilities and functions in a manner which helps achieving the organizational goals effectively and efficiently. An organizational design is actually a formal process of integrating people, information and technology together in the right mix to achieve objectives of the company. Organizational structure is the formal lines of authority and power, as well as the roles employees assume (Hartzell, 2003).

An organizational structure is basically about identifying, categorizing and arranging of duties and responsibilities necessary to carry out specific tasks and achieve a certain specific organizational objective. The structure is also about the overall architecture of business competence, leadership, talent, functional relationships and arrangement (Tran & Tian, 2013). An organizational structure is the basis for organizing the different functional dynamics happening inside the company, identifying hierarchical levels and spans of responsibility, distributing roles and positions, and putting in place proper mechanisms to integrate organizational events and solving organizational problems (Walton [14]. For an organization to operate properly, power, work procedures and resources are to be allocated among the members of the organization including employees and managers for example (Lilly, 2005; Ghoshal & Noria, 1993). The organizational structure establishes the basic guidelines for carrying out organizational activities where control mechanism, social infrastructure and other hard resources such as money, people and information are managed effectively and efficiently (Hartzell, 2003).

Forces behind the Organizational System Renovation

Organizational behavior theorists view organizations as open systems in that organizations are influenced by forces that are external and at the same time organizations can influence the environment which surrounds them. Such an interaction effects between the organization and its surrounding demands organizations to be receptive and flexible in accepting to changes. A variety of forces that can cause the company leadership to rethink about their existing organizational structures and operational systems are listed below (i.e., Tran & Tian, 2013; Bartlett & Ghoshal, 1998). The objective is to make organizations more responsive to the demands and needs of the emerging business environment.

1. Achieving global efficiency in every business functions whether it is marketing, sales, production or distribution is imperative for business organizations to compete and succeed.
2. Promoting and maintaining global quality standard in every business functions and activities undertaken by the company. It should also be combined with quality service for the customers and competitive prices.
3. Globalization vs localization has led to the slogan of the so-called glocalization which means, business organizations must perform globally, have global efficiency in product and distribution and at the same time should address the peculiar local needs, preferences and interests of the customers.
4. Technological advancements--transportation, communication, production and management. Companies must be on the forefront in adopting the newest technology to support their organizational activities and systems. Internet based marketing such as digital marketing, interactive marketing and overall mobile business and virtual organizations are getting grounds quickly.

5. Global business rules are changing and improving, and therefore, business organizations must be able to learn about those changing rules of the business game and act accordingly. Rules are about work safety, labor rights, environment, customer rights, and overall human rights, for examples.
6. Democratization of global political and economic systems which empower the common customers, small businesses, and promote transparency and equality and thus leading to perfect market conditions for the business.
7. Need for worldwide learning. Since no business is local now, learning from markets is essential to be successful locally and internationally.

The above forces all together create an environment where business organizations need to be more proactive and competitive while remaining flexible and dynamic internally as a business management system and structure.

What Is an Operational System?

In line with the design of an organizational structure, it is imperative for the company managers to understand and adjust the organizational operational system. The operational system including the operational control mechanisms is simply about regulating, monitoring and controlling the routines, hourly and daily bases activities and functions of the company (Rugman, 2005).

1. How organizational activities or functions like research and development, marketing, financing, human resources, and production should be managed?
2. Regulating organizational activities so that actual performance conforms to expected organizational standards and goals.
3. Levels of control: Levels of control are about how and who manage and control strategic and operational aspects of the company? Strategic level control means controlling issues associated with the structure, strategy and long term planning. While operational control is about managing and controlling everyday activities including office-hours, meetings, lunch-breaks, supply procedures, packaging and production area activities, for example (Bartlett & Ghoshal, 1998)
4. Means of control: Which methods and mechanisms to control the business operation are available for companies while operating internationally? There are a variety of controls mechanisms available for companies to use: direct control; indirect control; and, behavioral control. Direct control mechanisms include controlling the structural aspects of the business management aspects like for example, decision making, reporting relationship, information sharing and staffing like top position held by expatriate personnel. Indirect control includes establishing standards for example, sales quotas, budget, feedback and sales performance report on regular basis. The behavioral control method consists of regular visits by HQ staff to subsidiaries, regular HQ meeting in which subsidiaries management staffs are invited, and collection of subsidiary performance data. In the contemporary world of business, most of these controls methods and procedures are facilitated by the use of information and communication technologies in that sharing information, meetings, feedbacks, performance surveys are conducted virtually or/and online (Rugman, 2005; Hartzell, 2003).

The Importance of Organizational Structure

Business organizations are systems, cultures and thus are institutions. Organizations without proper structure and design are vulnerable to any threats that exist within or without the organization. Business organizations are social buildings and therefore, such buildings need and demand proper architectural work (organizational architecture). The role of an organizational structure is like the backbone for building and maintaining a sustainable organizational system with features such as efficiency, effectiveness, quality, competitiveness and flexibility. An organizational structure influences many other aspects of the company such as (Robbins & Judge, 2007):

1. Organizational behavior.
2. Organizational politics.
3. Organizational history.
4. Leadership and management culture.
5. The work environment.
6. Company image and goodwill.
7. Relationship with the stakeholders.

Additionally, all business organizations regardless of their sizes and nature of business need to rethink about their strategic orientations, to identify needs for change in organizational capabilities and create an organizational system which is strong and dynamic at the same time (Asmussen, 2009; Hartzell, 2003; Stopford & Wells, 19972).

1. Structure is a means for attaining the objectives and goals of an organization within the capacity and capabilities of the organization. The organizational capacity is reflected in the availability of required resources (i.e., time, financial, human, technology and information) for the company. And the capability of the organization is based on the experience and skills it possesses in order to use the available resources efficiently and effectively in achieving the organizational goals.
2. Organizational structure is also about how much and how the organizational members are constrained and controlled by the organization.
3. Organizational structure concerns about the distribution of activities, division of responsibilities, establishing organizational procedures, and implementing the organizational rules and regulations.
4. In fact any change in the business strategy of the company often requires corresponding changes in the structure of the organization because structure dictates how objectives and policies are established and also resources allocated.

THE ELEMENTS OF ORGANIZATIONAL STRUCTURE

While working on the organizational structure, companies can focus on two basic elements of which any organizational structure is made (Wheelen & Hunger, 2002): The basic structure; and, the operating mechanism. *The basic structure* is concerned with how the work of the organization is divided and assigned to group of individuals and departments and how coordination and cooperation are achieved systematically, naturally and timely. It involves the allocation of tasks and responsibilities to individuals.

Moreover, the basic structure formulates formal reporting systems, communication channels, feedback mechanisms, performance appraisal mechanisms and levels of hierarchy. For instances, having an organizational chart, job description, advisory boards, committees, project teams and working parties are parts of the basic structure of the organizational structure. On the other hand, the *operating mechanism* is basically concerned about how to operate actually by specifying the expected behavior of the employees, having a motivation strategy and empowering employees to carry out their corresponding responsibilities. It furthermore, involves authority delegation and mechanisms of on the job supervision, monitoring and checks and balances. Generally, budgeting, establishing targets, performance reviews and feedbacks are some of the examples of the operating mechanisms used by the company

Types of Organizational Structure

There are a variety of alternatives available for the companies to choose from as their organizational structures. Hartzell (2003) suggests that "an organization should choose a structure that is appropriate for its individual needs and allows for the company to react and adapt to uncertainties and changes in the internal and external environments. Having a suitable organizational structure in place allows a company to implement proper operating procedures and decision-making processes that will aid the organization in accomplishing its goals". Burns and Stalker (n/a) propose two types of organizational structures: mechanistic and organic structures. According to these authors the mechanistic organizational structure is based on a formal and centralized network and thus considered a beaurucratic structure. Such organizational structures are suitable where the business environment is relatively stable and the industrial structure is monopolistic. The following are some of the characteristics of such organizational structures (Burns & Stalker; Hartzell, 2003):

1. *A mechanistic structure is easy to maintain and rarely needs to be changed when an organization operates in a stable environment.*
2. Authority reflects a well-defined hierarchy where top-level managers make the majority of the decisions.
3. Subordinates are expected to follow the directions of management and not question their rationale.
4. Communication, much like decisions, also flows through hierarchical routes, or from the top to the down levels.
5. Individualized job specialization is used to place employees into designated areas. In mechanistic organizations, it is typical for each person to be assigned one task that is relatively stable and easy to control.
6. Information is communicated based on chain of command, tasks are highly specialized, departments stand alone and operate as their own entity, and change is, for the most part, uncommon. Public sector organizations tend to use such type of structure.

On the other hand, the organic structures are used by business organizations doing business in environments which are changing and dynamic and for that reason, companies need to adjust and adopt as quickly as possible. Organizations are open systems in that organizations largely depend on the events and changes pertaining to the external environment. Globalization, competition and technological development have created such a dynamic environment in which companies must be able to adopt, change, response both proactively and reactively. Therefore, the role of an organizational system which is supportive and conducive under such conditions is critically important for the success of companies locally as well globally. Some of the features of organic organizational structures are (Burns & Stalker, n/a):

1. Communication is lateral and rapid in these complex environments.
2. Integrate functional areas and departments together so that information can flow seamlessly between them.
3. This fast distribution of knowledge results in an increased ability to respond to changes in the internal and external environments.
4. Dynamic, flexible and innovative.

In the existing literature on the organizational structures, a number of types and forms of organizational structures are found. The six most common types or forms found are briefly described below (Lilly, 2005).

- **Simple Structure:** Simple structure for small organizations. Small size business organizations do not need complex and hierarchical structures. Low formalization and low departmentalization and wide span of controls work well in small companies. Authority is centralized.
- **Functional Structure:** The structuring of the organization or organizing the organizational activities, roles, responsibilities and resources around the main functions of the company (marketing, financing, human resource management, production, supplies, distribution, for example).
- **Product/Service Structure:** The structuring of the organization or organizing the organizational activities, roles, responsibilities and resources around the main products/services of the company (product A, product B or Business class, Economy class, First Class, for example).
- **Area/Geographic Structure:** The structuring of the organization or organizing the organizational activities, roles, responsibilities, authority and resources around the area or geographic zones in which the company is operating (Latin America; North America, Asia and Europe for example).
- **Team Structure:** Under this structuring method, the structuring of the organization is done around teams or project teams. Teams work towards a common goal and are expected to perform well and are held responsible for their performance. Team work and team evaluation are important components of this organizational structure.
- **Matrix Structure:** Is a combination of functional, product and area structures. A company may be structured using a combination of function and product (functional/product structure) or combination of function and area (functional/area structure) or combination of function, product and area (functional/product/area structures). Such structures are useful when a company grows in different dimensions in terms of lines, diversity and complexity of products offered by the company, the number of geographical areas or zones in which the company operates and the types and importance organizational functions. In this structure authority is duplicated and decision making is complex and time consuming. Goals and responsibilities should be clearly identified, well distributed and coordinated in order to avoid management confusion and organizational conflicts under this work system. Constant communication and regular meetings are keys for the success of such structures.

Contemporary-Emerging Structures

A number of new structural options have surfaced with the emergence of new business management models and theories. Some of those new structural options are explained below (Lilly, 2005; Hartzell, 2003).

- **Project Structure:** A company can identify projects (i.e. innovation, product design, planning) and assign teams to those projects. Employees work around those projects and once a project is completed, the project members move on to the next projects. Project assignments are based on the experience, skills and expertise of the employees.
- **Autonomous Internal Units:** In this structure there is no centralized control or authority or resource allocation since different units are created and given specific business units to operate independently from others. Each unit produces its own projects, manages its own resources and clients etc.
- **Boundary-Less Organization:** There is no boundary, so there is no structure, no hierarchies or centralized authority etc. A boundary-less organization are like virtual organizations where managers may use virtual, modular, or network organizational structures. Though there are a small number of permanent employees, however, virtual organizations outsource most of its workers and resources.

A number of strategic gurus in the field of international strategic management (i.e, Bartlett & Ghoshal, 1989, 1991; Ghoshal & Nohria, 1993; Prahalad & Doz, 1987; Stopford & Wells, 1972) have studied and proposed different types and forms of organizational structures for MNEs. Of which four organizational management philosophies, which in turns to be considered as structural options for MNEs, are briefly discussed below:

1. **Structural Uniformity:** It happens when there is a uniformed and strong management system in place for the whole company. One way is the global way, and thus structure is standardized across the company.
2. **Differentiated Fit:** It happens when companies use different management systems for different subsidiaries located in different places in order to fit each subsidiary´s context and local conditions.
3. **Integrated Variety:** This is a type of a differentiated approach but within the umbrella of an overall integrated approach. Companies allow their subsidiaries to focus on local-contextual needs but at the same time remaining within the overall governance system of the company, for strategic direction.
4. **Ad Hoc Variation:** Changing the governance system according to changes on the ground whereby it means that there is neither a dominant or permanent integrative-management system nor a permanent differentiated approach.

According to the strategic management gurus MNEs should opt for the structure model which combines the need for global integration and local differentiation and that matches the needs of the environment in order to achieve global competitiveness. MNEs seek global scale efficiency, local acceptance, economies of scale and economies of scope, therefore, the organizational structure they adopt should be dynamic enough to accomplish this.

FACTORS INFLUENCING THE DECISION TO STRUCTURE

The decision of how to structure a company, let alone, an MNE is no any easy task since the overall organizational performance (productivity, quality, and cost-time efficiency) depends on the organizational effectiveness. Company leadership therefore, must take its time and careful considerations of all factors and variables when making a decision about a particular structure to pursue in international business. Those factors and variables influencing the management decisions to choose a structure are briefly explained below.

General Factors

In structuring or designing an organization, managers need to consider all impacting variables. Such variables may associate with the internal and external environments of the organization. Organizations are formed around individuals and groups of individuals (investors, managers, and employees, for examples), in order to achieve certain objectives (profitability, efficiency in managing resources, and growth etc.). Organizations have goals, activities and resources. Organization is a process, system and culture. Structure is about developing activities and allocating resources to each group of individuals inside the organization in order to achieve the established goals efficiently and effectively. Managers should consider these factors in designing and redesigning the company structure:

1. Organizational goals: Profit, quality, growth, customer satisfaction, competitiveness, presence, and image.
2. Organizational activities: planning, procurements, production, distribution, marketing, sales, packaging, branding, pricing, inventory, human resource management, financing, and performance evaluation.
3. Organizational resources: money, people, technology, information, physical spaces, experience, networks and relationships.
4. Organizational environment: Internal which is relatively more uncontrollable and predictable for the company management and external which is relatively less controllable and less predictable for the managers.
5. Country culture, management philosophies and business strategies.
6. Foreign product diversity vs foreign sales as a percentage of total company's sales.
7. Nature and number of products and services provided.
8. Emergence of communication, information, and transportation technologies.
9. Changes in either host or parent country´s attitudes towards international business and investment.
10. Local performance evaluation variables, government regulations and cultural aspects.
11. Geographical and time differences.

Various studies find that organizational structures are the reflections of the environment surround them. Organizational structures that are hierarchical, centralized, tall, bureaucratic, controlled, traditional are less effective in addressing the complex and rapidly changing environment. Organizational structures that are flat, flexible, dynamic, and decisions are decentralized, employees are generally empowered, tend to be more competitive in a changing business environment.

There are several other factors that affect the relationship between organizational design and structure:

1. **Organization Size:** The size of the company is an influential factor in the decision of which structure to adopt. Generally speaking, a small size organization is easy to manage and control and therefore, tend to be centralized.
2. **Organization Life Cycle:** As a product life cycle and industry life cycle, organizations have also their own life cycles. A newly established organization, for example, may need close attention and supervision, and therefore, would require a more centralized and hierarchical structure. Organizations in the growth and matured stages require more flexibility and decentralized approach in order to meet the changing competitive forces. Matured organizations gain experience, accumulate expertise and possess information.
3. **Environment:** The business environment surrounding the company is an important defining factor in structuring the company. If the environment is stable, less complex with few business competitors, national environment which is familiar, the company structures are usually more centralized and rigid. Whereas the business environment global and where complexity of doing business is high while competing with different competitors, facing new industrial rules and regulations, and changing demands and supply conditions may influence companies to be responsive and flexible in the their approaches to do business.
4. **Knowledge Workforce:** The growth of knowledge workforce around the globe has created a work environment where new management practices such as empowerment, delegation of authorities and resources and interdependency, team-work, co-decision making are gaining grounds. This trend has led companies to decentralize power, authority and resources to the managers.
5. **Strategic Alliances:** Another emerging business tendency is strategic alliance between business players in order to share experience, technology, and market to remain competitive. For this to happen and develop, companies need to be flexible and adaptive in their approaches to do business.
6. **Information and Communication Technologies:** Information and communication technologies have also brought dramatic changes in the existing setup of business operations by providing information to employees and making communication between employees and managers much easier and thus, giving power to the employees. Similarly, the relationship between the headquarters and subsidiaries has strengthened because of constant and on time communication and information sharing. This has made subsidiaries to a greater extend free from being dependent on the main office, for every piece of information.
7. **Innovation:** Innovate and create in order to succeed and remain in business. MNEs require local innovation to remain competitive and therefore, should delegate a greater deal of autonomous decision-making to its subsidiaries and companies. New ideas, innovation and knowledge should be developed and shared company-wise.

Strategy and Structure Match

When organizational structure and business strategies do not match, the potential for administrative deficiency delays in decisions, increasing operational cost and organizational conflicts is increasingly high. Therefore, any change in the business of the company should be followed by necessary and adequate adjustments in the existing organizational operational system and structure. An MNE has four possible structural options to choose from depending on its strategic needs and moves. In each of these structural options the type and degree of relationship between the headquarters and its subsidiaries are discussed below (Bartlett & Ghoshal, 1998; Prahalad & Doz, 1987):

1. Multi-domestic structure is recommendable when a company faces low pressure for integration and high pressure for differentiation. This strategy calls for local responsiveness and local self-sufficiency. In this structure, local subsidiaries are given full-fledged power to run the business locally as they feel fit and necessary. Both strategic and operational decisions are handled directly and independently by the subsidiaries.
2. International structure is suitable when a company faces low pressure for integration and low pressure for differentiation (low needs for local responsiveness). In this structure, operational decision making powers such as marketing and distribution are given to the subsidiaries. The rest of the strategic issues such as research and development, technological development, and key assets management are kept in the headquarters.
3. Global structure is more appropriate when the company faces high pressure for integration and low pressure for differentiation. In this structure the head office people runs the overall affairs of the business. The strategy of the company is to achieve scale economies in its operation and making standardized products. Subsidiaries are considered extension agents (assembly centers, distributor centers etc.) for the parent company. Most of the strategic as well as the operations aspects of the business management come under the jurisdiction of the head office.
4. Transnational structure is effective when the company is facing high pressure for integration and high pressure for differentiation. This structure is also called strategic business unit and network structure. In order to support and match the strategy of achieving global efficiency and local responsiveness in all its business activities, the company structure itself as strategic business units. In this structure, unlike the conventional approach to divide the company into headquarters and subsidiaries, the company is divided into several strategic business units. So the traditional practice of having a headquarters (the big partner) and subsidiaries (the small partner) disappears to a large extent. Headquarters and subsidiaries become equally important partners in the business management aspects of the company and each partner (strategic business unit) is given certain roles, resources and targets. Sharing of information, experience and technology within the company becomes fundamental for such an organizational structure to function properly and effectively.

Structure and Managerial Variables

Managers should consider the following key elements or variables when making a decision on how to structure an MNE (Lilly, 2005):

1. **Work Specialization:** Describes the degree to which tasks in an organization are divided into separate jobs.
2. **Departmentalization:** It is the basis by which jobs are grouped together. Different organizations have different ways of classifying and grouping work activities.
3. **Chain of Command:** It is defined as a continuous line of authority that extends from upper organizational levels to the lowest levels and clarifies who reports to whom for example. Three factors: authority, responsibility and unity of command are important here.

4. **Span of Control:** It determines the number of levels and managers an organization has. Also, it determines the number of employees a manager can efficiently and effectively manage at the same time under his or her supervision.

Other important components of organizational structure include (Zhang, 2008; Tran & Tian, 2013):

1. **Formalization:** Formalization measures the extent to which an organization uses rules and procedures to prescribe employee behavior.
2. **Centralization:** Centralization refers to the hierarchical level that has the authority to make decisions.
3. **Control:** Organizational control is a cycle that includes the three stages of target setting, measuring or monitoring and feedback. Control in the bureaucracy can consist of rules, standards, and internal procedures.

Other managerial theories such as theories of X and Y (McGregor, 1960) and theory Z (Ouchi, 1981) are also valuable bases for defining a proper organizational structure for the company. For example, management theory X, assumes that employees generally do not like work and tend to avoid taking responsibility and therefore, must be coerced to work, and it needs strict direction, control and even threatening of punishment if goals are not achieved. And therefore, managers with similar assumptions like to exercise chain of command, close supervision of employees´ behavior and using rewarding and punishing as motivation strategies. In contrary to theory X, managers who follow theory Y, assume that workers are generally committed to work and prefer to work and are able to find solutions to the problems they face on daily basis. These managers tend to empower their subordinates within their areas of responsibilities, and allow them to identify problems and solve them on their own. Also, managers with such mentality create an environment where individual employee goals coincide with the goals of the company and thus, promoting productivity and creativity. Later in early 1981s, the theory of Z developed by William Ouchi (1981, cited in Barney, 2004) emerged bringing a sort of revolution in the management practices of companies. In early 1981s, the emergence of globalization, the need for qualified workforce serving in service industries and customer relationships were coincided with this theory which deals with the way in which workers are perceived by managers, as well as how managers are perceived by workers. Theory Z, speaks of an organizational culture which mirrors the Japanese culture in which workers are more participative, and capable of performing many and varied tasks. Theory Z emphasizes upon things such as job rotation, broadening of skills, generalization versus specialization, and the need for continuous training of workers. One of the most important principles of this theory is that the management must have a high degree of confidence in its workers. In essence, the mutual management-worker confidence is the basis for a participative management system to work (Aydin, 2012).

Structure and Market Entry Modes

The potential and actual risks involved in a certain industry and market and the need for control and coordination of the business are other important variables to be considered while structuring the company. These are the general entry modes used by companies in the conventional business environment:

1. **Exporting:** Companies start internationalization by exporting to other markets. It is considered the initial stage of internationalization. Company controls its products and production and therefore, avoids risk associated with foreign markets and international business (such as political and cultural, for example). Company´s export or international division generally handles the export operation for the company. Companies export to foreign distributors or agents or middleman. Theoretically, because of the low risk and the low need for coordination and integration, companies tend to use lose control over their overseas export operations.
2. **Licensing:** In licensing a company offer or give license to other distributors or producers to use its trademark or brand name or business formula or system and for which the parent company gains license fee. So the licensee business does not directly belong to the licensor company. Therefore, it involves low investment risk and practically no need for coordination and integration.
3. **Franchising:** Franchising is more or less the same as of licensing, but in franchising the franchisor gets involved in the business management aspects of the business of the franchisee. This increases the level of business risks and needs for administrative integration which would then require close supervision and coordination.
4. **Direct Investment:** The direct investment is the real internationalization stage for the company where the company invests in foreign markets by establishing operational offices (production and distribution, for example.), on its own. It increases the level of business risks for the company and therefore, the need for integration and coordination increases to a greater extent as well. This in turn demands from the parent company to closely supervise and coordinate the overall business operation.

Structure and Management Orientation

The following four management orientations proposed by Perlmutter (1969), are also considered important variables in designing the organizational structure of the company. Obviously, managers are the ones who design the structure, need the structure, manage the structure and manage within the structure. That is why the management mindset, style and experience are influential factors in designing and redesigning the organizational structure.

1. **Ethnocentric:** Under ethnocentric management system, the company´s home-country managers are appointed everywhere in the world. Ethnocentric managers consider that the home country culture and management system are better than foreign cultures and management systems. Ethnocentric managers tend to promote hierarchical organizational structure and top-down corporate governance.
2. **Polycentric:** Polycentric managers consider that foreign managers are better than the home country managers. Host country management culture is given preference and corporate structure is designed around area divisions and preferentially local managers are appointed for holding major management positions. Host country´s management system and policies are replicated at home country of the company.
3. **Regio-Centric:** Under this management orientation managers belonging to certain regions are given preferences. Like for example, managers from Latin America are better than the managers from Asia, so and so forth. The type of corporate governance is mutually agreed, accepted and matrix structure is generally used by managers with such management orientation. The corporate culture is more regional and employee performance evaluation criteria are more regional as well.

4. **Geocentric:** Managers with this mentality look for staff from the global labor market in general. Such management orientation promotes global integration and local responsiveness, and therefore, organizational structure is more like of network organizations and therefore, strong collaboration between HQ and subsidiaries are considered must to run the business.

Structure and Organizational Culture Match

The organizational structure and culture must match and managers must realize the importance of this match and relationship. The organizational culture refers to the managerial and organizational variables such as management style, approaches to decision making, staffing procedures, communication protocol, employee relationships, team work, motivation, reward and control mechanisms and time concept, for instances (Sweeney & Hardaker, 1991). The organizational culture is composed of variables such as management style, decision making process, staffing procedures, interpersonal trust and confidence, commitment, control, importance of relationship, team work and role of nature (Greer & Stephens, 1996; Johnson & Sholes, 2007). Organization culture is about the values, rules, practices and norms through which organizations manage their business operations (Brache, 2002; Schien, 1985; Schien, 1992). Inside a company, managers make decisions, allocate resources, and direct the activities of others to attain goals. Though certain management practices are universally applicable, however, some other management aspects vary from culture to culture (Pheng & Yuquan, 2002). Corporate management styles are influenced by various organizational variables such as values, norms, ethical codes, rules and regulations for example, and such variables vary across national cultures. Definitely, cultural variables do influence managerial functions, roles and responsibilities (Laurent, 1983; Mead, 1998). Some management cultures accept and promote the work culture where managers are responsible for organizing, planning, coordinating, decision making and they have the authority and control over organizational resources. Whereas, some other cultures emphasize on the notion that employees should be treated well, managers should delegate authority and resources to their employees and managers are coaches and mentors (McGregor, 1960; Ouchi, 1981; Brozik, 1994). Organizational culture also includes the power structure, organizational structure, functional policies and management systems (Johnson & Sholes, 2007; Heller & Yulk, 1969; Goodale, 1973). Organizational culture, according to Horwath & Morrison (2000), has played prominent roles in adapting to external and internal changes, maximizing the value of employees through organizational learning, knowledge management and creativity, and also the willingness to share knowledge and undertake risks (Sweeney & Hardaker, 1994; Schein, 1985).

Organizational cultures are influenced by the external culture such as industry and nation (Gordon & DeForrest, 1994). A strong and dynamic organizational cultural system is fundamental for the organizational competitive advantage, if such cultural system is learned, developed and shared across the global organizational system (Titieve, 1959). Sweeny and McFarlin (2002) added that a strong culture is a means to the actualization of the strategic intent, mission and vision statement of the organization. It is evident that the culture of the organization influences the style of management and the performance of the employees in the workplace. Schein (1985, 1992) suggests that organizational culture is even more important today than it was in the past. Increased competition, globalization, mergers, acquisitions, alliances, and various workforce developments have created a greater need for (Baker, 2002):

1. Coordination and integration across organizational units in order to improve efficiency, quality, and speed of designing, manufacturing, and delivering products and services.
2. Effective management of dispersed work units and increasing workforce diversity.
3. Cross-cultural management of global enterprises and/or multi-national partnerships.
4. Construction of meta- or hybrid- cultures that merge aspects of cultures from what were distinct organizations prior to an acquisition or merger.
5. Management of workforce diversity.
6. Facilitation and support of teamwork.

Differences in national cultures have been found to have profound effects on leadership style, communication, motivation, organizational design, people expectations of work design and rewards in organizations (Bloom et al., 1999). National and organizational cultures are different in the sense that national cultural differences reside mostly in values, less in practices whereas organizational cultural differences reside in practices, less in value (Hofstede, 1997). But as suggested earlier though organizational and national cultures are different, however, they are interdependent and by that it means that national cultures influence directly or indirectly organizational cultures and vice versa. National cultures promoting high power distance, low risk taking behavior and high masculine tendencies and for example, create a social-work environment where managers tend to be authoritarian and organizations hierarchical. In contrary, national cultures promoting low power distance, high risk taking behavior and more feminine tendencies develop a social-work environment where managers tend to delegate authority and resources to their subordinates and organizations are going to be less hierarchical and more flat (Hofstede, 1997). Organizations of all forms and sizes interact with the society in which they operate and therefore, it is important to analyze the relationship between the national and organizational cultures and the impact of the same on the management styles and orientation within the organization (Pothukuchi, Damanpour, Choi, Chen, & Seung, 2002). When companies´ management practices are compatible with the national cultural values and systems, employees working within those companies are found to perform better (Newman & Nollen, 1996).

LEARNING ORGANIZATION

A learning organization is defined as an organization that has developed the capacity to continuously learn, adapt, and change. In order to have a learning organization a company must have very knowledgeable employees who are able to share their knowledge with others and be able to apply it in a work environment. The learning organization must also have a strong organizational culture where all employees have a common goal and are willing to work together through sharing knowledge and information. A learning organization must have a team design and great leadership. Learning organizations that are innovative and knowledgeable create leverage over competitors. An MNE with such characteristics or intended to have such characteristics need to have a dynamic, flexible and adaptive organizational structure (Senge, 1997).

Information and Communication Technologies

The information and communication technologies have brought revolution in the whole business world (Peyman et. al, 2011). Information sharing, promotion, distribution, payment and negotiation take place virtually and online as and when needed and wherever it needed (Dibrell & Miller, 2002). The ICT has made it very easy and cheap to have access to the valuable and timely information and sharing the same information worldwide with business partners whether they are employees, suppliers or distributors (Behan & Holms, 1999; Bidgoli, 1999). Knowledge is powerful. In an organizational setting, employees have not access to information about the company and its activities, and information about the activities of competing organizations well. So, employees feel more self-confident, more prepared and independent in the workplace. The effects of the emergence of computers on the management aspects of the company have been recorded earlier for example, the elimination of middle management (Leavitt & Whisler, 1958); greater centralization (Stone, 1978) and greater decentralization (Anshen, 1960; Burlingame, 1961) are few to mention. Daft (2004) describes the influence of ICT on organizations and their design and suggests five main such influences: decrease of staff in the organization, increasing decentralization, improving internal coordination, improving inter-organizational cooperation, and better outsourcing. One of the most important determinants of organization is distribution of power and ICT has definitely power dynamics in organizations by distributing the power and influence inside the company. The dispersion of formal authority down through the chain of command, as vertical decentralization; dispersion of formal authority at the same hierarchical level in organization, where decision power is given to staff outside line chain of command, such as specialists and analysts, as horizontal decentralization; physical dispersion of the company, where company allocates its organizational units closer to customers (Whisler, 1970b; Mintzberg, 1984, 1990). The adoption of ICT is correlated to the flattening of hierarchical levels which immensely leads to vertical decentralization (Cudanov, Jasko & Jevtic, 2009; Ziadi & Kufie, 2006). Applying ICT in organizations results in changes which have influence on various aspects of organization including organizational structures (Duval, 2004).

As we can see, organizations develop, modify and change their structures so that they align themselves with their strategies (Ramienski, 2008). A special form of boundary less organization is virtual organization and it works in a network of external alliances, using IT and Internet. This means that while the core of the organization can be small, the company still can operate globally and be a market leader in its niche (Anderson, 2007).

Applying IT results in changes in organizational structures so that they change from hierarchical and vertical into horizontal. All tasks of organization are designed according to information networks and technologies, and the employees perform their duties at home and there is no need for their physical presence (Ghafurian, 2003). Since the ability of a company to compete is based on its ability of learning, the issue of proper organizational structure will gain increasing importance in terms of how it is influenced by IT the organization compositions are empowered (Ghafurian, 2003). Moreover, since the electronic communications can prove effective in particular affairs, especially in relation to administrative issues, compared to communication by phone or in person, the domain of control for managers has increased (Reif, 1968; Edward, 1999). Technology has made it possible to enhance the domain of control and to eliminate the layers in organization (Henry, 1992). Saadatmandi (2004) conducted a research titled the relationship between IT and organizational structure and the barriers to its establishment it in the Iran Steel national company and showed "That with increasing application of IT and the other aspects of IT new terms, new ideas, and new forms of organization and organizational structures at international level emerged".

FINAL THOUGHTS AND FUTURE DIRECTION

All organizations need structures to function as an organization. Organizations exist with objectives to achieve. Organizations have activities and functions to carry out over years and years. Organizations need resources and generate resources and resources need careful and effective management and uses. Organizations need systems, processes, procedures, and work methods and these demands coordination, cooperation and communication among different organizational units and agents. have to make provisions for continuing activities directed towards the achievement of aims. Organizations need rules, regulations and standards to follow. All these elements make up the overall organizational system when combined and integrated. The allocation of responsibilities, the grouping of functions, decision-making, coordination, control, reward, all these are fundamental requirements for the continued operation of an organization (Hall & Hall, 1987). The way these diverse but interrelated activities and elements are combined and integrated together may vary from company to a company. The organizational structure as a "Complex medium of control that is produced and continuously recreated by the interaction, but that determines at the same time that interaction: structures are constituted and constitutive, (Hall & Hall 1987)". Hall and Hall (1987) suggest that there are three elemental function associated with the organizational structure:

1. The structures must produce organizational results and achieve organizational objectives.
2. The structures are designed to minimize or reduce individual differences, meaning that they own a homogenized sense.
3. The structures are formal media to execute power.

The role and importance of the organizational structure in the development and success of any company is imminent. Managers should do their best to consider all relevant factors and variables when designing and redesigning the organizational structure. Changing the organizational structure is not inevitable. Structures should be changed when there is a strong need for it. We should change the structure when we need it really, not necessarily when we want it to change. Organizational philosophy and history are intermingled with the structure and thus, creating the corporate behavior, image and goodwill. Therefore, the management and leadership of MNEs are recommended to consider the following variables and factors when designing and redesigning the organizational structure:

1. The macro-economic environment.
2. The technological environment.
3. The industry life cycle.
4. The social and cultural environment.
5. The demographic environment.
6. The political and legal environment.
7. The globalization and industry structure.
8. New business models and ventures.

There is no size fits all situations and therefore, MNEs must be flexible in combining different structural options, doing benchmarking, and creating a proactive organizational management environment. Organizations are institutions and remain forever, and people working in the company come and go. Changing people inside the company should not necessarily provoke changes in the organizational

Box 1. Main business imperatives

Organizational Effectiveness Highest Quality Product/Service To Most Profitable Worldwide Market At Lowest Costs Under Changing Market and Competitive Conditions Through Global Sourcing Of Raw Materials Technology Capital Facilities Human Resources

structure. Alternatively, changes in the existing organizational setup may demand changes in the people, by changing their roles, responsibilities, and positions etc. Lastly, an organizational structure that is used by a company in any given environment or context, it must guarantee the execution and delivery of the main business imperatives shown in Box 1.

Organizational structures are the backbone for the stability, growth and competitiveness of the company. The managers of MNEs should not forget that their motivation (learning or market share expansion) to grow globally as a business and the importance of all the key stakeholders (i.e., investors, managers, employees, suppliers, distributors and customers) are not the least ingredients in designing and redesigning the company structure.

REFERENCES

Anderson, C. (2007). *The Long Tail*. Random House Business Books.

Anshen, M. (1960). The Manager and the Black Box. *Harvard Business Review*.

Asmussen, C. G. (2009). Local, Regional, or Global? Quantifying MNE Geographic Scope. *Journal of International Business Studies*, *40*(9), 1192–1205. doi:10.1057/jibs.2008.85

Aydın, T. O. (2012).. . *International Review of Management and Marketing*, *2*(2), 106–111. Available at www.managementjournal.info/

Baker, K. A. (2002). *Organizational Culture* [Online]. Retrieved from www.au.af.mil/au/awc/awcgate/doe/benchmark/ch11.pdf/

Barney, J. (2004). Introduction: William Ouchi's Theory Z: How American business can meet the Japanese Challenge. *The Academy of Management Executive*, *18*(4), 106–107. doi:10.5465/AME.2004.15268703

Bartlett, C., & Ghoshal, S. (1991). *Managing Across Borders: The Transnational Solution*. Harvard Business School Press.

Bartlett, C., & Ghoshal, S. (1998). *Managing across Borders: The Transnational Solution* (2nd ed.). London: Random House.

Bartlett, C. A., & Ghoshal, S. (1989). *Managing Across Borders: The Transnational Solution*. Harvard Business School Press.

Behan, K., & Holms, D. (1999). *Introducing to information technology* (1st ed.). (M. Azaraksh & J. Mehrdad, Trans.). Tehran: Samt Pub.

Bidgoli, H. (1999). *Handbook for Management Information System*. Harcourt Brace & Company.

Bloom, N., Garicano, L., Sadun, R., & Reenen, J. V. (2010). *The Distinct Effects of Information Technology and Communication Technology on Firm Organization*. Harvard Business School Working Paper Series, 11-023.

Bloomfield, B., & Coombs, R. (1992). Information technology, control and power: The centralization and decentralization debate revisited. *Journal of Management Studies*, *29*(4), 459–484. doi:10.1111/j.1467-6486.1992.tb00674.x

Brache, A. P. (2002). *How organizations work*. New York, NY: John Wiley & Sons, Inc.

Brozik, D. (1994). The second dimensions for successful management. *Manage*, *45*(4), 4–8.

Buckley, P., & Ghauri, P. (2004). Globalisation, Economic Geography and the Strategy of the Multinational Enterprises. *Journal of International Business Studies*, *35*(2), 81–98. doi:10.1057/palgrave.jibs.8400076

Burke, E. (2002). *Digital Government; the next step to reengineering the Federal government* [Online]. Retrieved from http://pionline.org

Burlingame, J. F. (1961). Information Technology and decentralization. *Harvard Business Review*. Retrieved from http://study.com/academy/lesson/bureaucratic-organizations-mechanic-organic-bureacracies.html

Čudanov, M., Jaško, O., & Jevtić, M. (2009). Influence of Information and Communication Technologies on Decentralization of Organizational Structure. *ComSIS*, *6*(1), 93–109. doi:10.2298/CSIS0901093C

Daft, R. (2004). *Administración*. Editorial Trillas.

DeForrest, M. E. (1994). Thinking of a Plant in Mexico? *The Academy of Management Executive*, *8*(1), 33–40.

Dibrell, C. C., & Miller, T. (2002). Organization Design: The continuing influence of information technology. *Management Design Journal*, *40*(6). doi:10.1108/00251740210434016

Dunning, J. (2009). Location and the Multinational Enterprise: A Neglected Factor? *Journal of International Business Studies*, *40*(1), 5–19. doi:10.1057/jibs.2008.74

Duval, E. (2004). Learning Technology Standardization: Making Sense of it All. *ComSIS*, *1*(1), 33–43. doi:10.2298/CSIS0401033D

Edward, J. (1999). *Electronic commerce change organizational structure*. Department of Management Science, School of Business Public Management.

Flores, R. G., & Aguilera, R. V. (2007). Globalization and location choice: an analysis of US multinational firms in 1980 and 2000. *Journal of International Studies,* 1-2. Retrieved from www.jibs.net

Ghafurian, A. (2003). The effects from applying IT in organizations. *Economy of World Journal.*

Ghemawat, P., & Hout, T. (2008). Tomorrow's Global Giants. Not the Usual Suspects. *Harvard Business Review*, *86*(11), 80–88.

Ghoshal, S., & Nohria, N. (1993). Horses for Courses: Organizational Forms for Multinational Corporations. *MIT Sloan Management Review*, *34*(2), 23–35.

Goodale, J. (1973). Effects of Personal Background and Training on Work Values of the hard-core unemployed. *The Journal of Applied Psychology*, *57*(1), 1–9. doi:10.1037/h0034190

Gordon, G., & Williams, T. (2001). How do you Spell Success in Mexico? CALICA. *Business Horizons*, *44*(1), 11–18. doi:10.1016/S0007-6813(01)80003-3

Greer, S. K., & Stephens, C. (1996). Employee issues for companies in Mexico. *California Management Review*, *38*(3), 121–145. doi:10.2307/41165846

Hall, E. T., & Hall, R. M. (1987). *Hidden Differences. Doing Business with the Japanese*. New York: Anchor Press Doubleday.

Hartzell, S. (2003). *Types of Contemporary Organizational Designs: Matrix, Team & Network Designs*. Retrieved from http://study.com/academy/lesson/types-of-contemporary-organizational-designs-matrix-team-network-designs.html

Heller, F. A., & Yukl, G. (1969). Participation, managerial decision-making and situational variables. *Organizational Behavior and Human Performance*, *4*(3), 227–241. doi:10.1016/0030-5073(69)90007-5

Hennart, J. F. (2009). Down with MNE-Centric Theories! Market Entry and Expansion as the Bundling of MNE and Local Assets. *Journal of International Business Studies*, *40*(9), 1432–1454. doi:10.1057/jibs.2009.42

Henry, L. C. (1992). *IT for Management* (6th ed.). Mcgraw Hill.

Hofstede, G. (1997). *Cultures and organizations: software of the mind*. London: Mc Graw Hill.

Horwath, J., & Morrison, T. (2000). Identifying and implementing pathways for organizational change-using The Framework for the Assessment of Children in Need and their Families as a case example'. *Child & Family Social Work*, *5*(3), 245–255. doi:10.1046/j.1365-2206.2000.00171.x

Hutzschenreuter, T., & Grone, F. (2009). Changing Vertical Integration Strategies under Pressure from Foreign Competition: The Case of US and German Multinationals. *Journal of Management Studies*, *46*(2), 269–307. doi:10.1111/j.1467-6486.2008.00811.x

Johnson, G., & Scholes, K. (2007). *Exploring Corporate Strategy* (8th ed.). Financial Times/Prentice Hall.

Lauden, C. K. (2000). Management Information Systems. *Higher Education Studies, 1*(1).

Laurent, A. (1983). The cultural diversity of Western conceptions of management. *International Studies of Management & Organization*, *13*(1-2), 75–96. doi:10.1080/00208825.1983.11656359

Leavitt, H. J., & Whisler, T. L. (1958). Management in the 1980's. Carnegie Instit Ute Of Technology.

Leavitt, H. J., & Whisler, T. L. (1958). Management in the 1980's. *Harvard Business Review*, (November-December): 1858.

Lenartowicz, T., & Johnson, J. P. (2007). Staffing managerial positions in emerging markets: A cultural perspective. *International Journal of Emerging Markets*, *2*(3), 207–214. doi:10.1108/17468800710758369

Lilly, M. (2005). *Organizational Structure and Designs with Case Study: QUALCOMM*. Retrieved from http://www.emaytrix.com/mgmt307/section3.php/

Mcclure, D. I. (2001). *Electronic government: Challenges must be addressed with effective leadership and management*. Available: http://www.govgovnow.ir/em/do 1959.pdt/

McGregor, D. (1960). *The Human Side of Enterprise*. New York: McGraw-Hill.

Mead, R. (1998). *International management* (2nd ed.). Cambridge, MA: Blackwell Publishers.

Mehri, N. S. (2004). Applying IT in organizations. *Political Economical Information Journal*, 181-182.

Mintzberg, H. (1984). Power and Organization Life Cycles. *Academy of Management Review*, *9*(2), 207–224.

Mintzberg, H. (1990). The Design School: Reconsidering The Basic Premises Of Strategic Management. *Strategic Management Journal*, *11*(3), 171–195. doi:10.1002/smj.4250110302

Newman, L. K., & Nollen, D. S. (1996). Culture and Congruence: The Fit Between Management Practice and National Culture. *Journal of International Business Studies. Fourth Quarter*, *27*(4), 753–779. doi:10.1057/palgrave.jibs.8490152

Ouchi, W. G. (1981). *Theory Z: How can American business meet the Japanese challenge*. Reading, MA: Addison-Wesley.

Perlmutter, H. V. (1969). The Tourtous Evolution of the Multinational Corporation. Columbia Journal of World Business, 4(1), 9-18.

Peyman, Y., Mohsen, A. S., Hassan, G., Aboulghassim, F., & Zaman, A. (2011). The Analysis of the Relationship between Organizational Structure and Information Technology (IT): And the Barriers to Its Establishment at the University of Isfahan from the Faculty Member's Viewpoints. *Higher Education Studies, 1*(1). Retrieved from www.ccsenet.org/hes/

Pheng, L. S., & Yuquan, S. (2002). An exploratory study of Hofstede's cross-cultural dimensions in construction projects. *Management Decision*, *40*(1), 7–16. doi:10.1108/00251740210423036

Pothukuchi, V., Damanpour, F., Choi, J., Chao, C., & Seung, H. P. (2002). National and organizational culture differences and international joint venture performance. *Journal of International Business Studies*, *33*(2), 243–266. doi:10.1057/palgrave.jibs.8491015

Prahalad, C. K., & Doz, Y. (1987). *The Multinational Mission: Balancing Local Demands and Global Vision*. New York: The Free Press.

Ramienski, D. (2008). *Looking For a Holistic Approach*. Available: http://www.federalnewsradio.com/?nid=169&sid=1377323

Reif, W. E. (1968). Computer technology and management organization. Bureau of Business and Economic Research, College of Business Administration, University of Iowa.

Robbins, S. F., & Judge, T. A. (2007). *Organizational Behaviour* (12th ed.). Pearson Education Inc.

Rugman, A. (2005). *The Regional Multinationals*. Cambridge, UK: Cambridge University Press. doi:10.1017/CBO9780511614071

Saadatmandi, H. (2004). *Studying the relation between the IT and organization structure and the barroirs against launching it in Iran national steel company*. (Ms Thesis). Teharan University, Management School.

Schein, E. H. (1985). *Organizational Culture and Leadership*. San Francisco, CA: Jossey-Bass.

Schein, E. H. (1992). *Organizational Culture and Leadership* (2nd ed.). San Francisco, CA: Jossey-Bass.

Senge, P. (1997). The Fifth Discipline: The Art and Practice of The Learning Organization. London: Random House.

Stopford, J. M., & Wells, L. T. (1972). *Managing the Multinational Enterprise: Organization of the Firm and Ownership of the Subsidiary* (French ed.). Basic Books.

Sweeney, E. P. & Hardaker, G. (1994). The importance of organizational and national culture. *European Business Review, 94*(5),3.

Sweeney, P. D., & McFarlin, D. B. (2002). *Organizational Behavior: Solutions for Management*. New York, NY: McGraw-Hill.

Titiev, M. (1958). *Introduction to Cultural Anthropology*. New York: Henry Holt and Co.

Tran, Q., & Tian, Y. (2013). Organizational Structure: Influencing Factors and Impact on a Firm. *American Journal of Industrial and Business Management*, *3*(02), 229–236. doi:10.4236/ajibm.2013.32028

Walton, R. E. (1982). Social Choice in the Development of Advanced Information Technology. *Technology in Society.*, *4*(1), 41–49. doi:10.1016/0160-791X(82)90013-6

Wheelen, T. L., & Hunger, D. J. (2002). *Strategic Management & Business Policy*. Pearson Education Inc.

Whisler, T. L. (1970b). *Information Technology and Organizational Change*. Wadsworth.

Zhang, F. (2008). *Corporate Social Responsibility in Emerging Markets: The Role of Multinational Corporations*. An Initial Paper for the Launch of the Foreign Policy Centre Project on "Corporate Responsibility in Emerging Markets" in association with Coca-Cola Great Britain.

Ziadi, J., & Kuofie, M. (2006). Impact of ICT on organizations in Tunisia. *The Electronic Journal on Information Systems in Developing Countries*, *28*(4), 1–8.

KEY TERMS AND DEFINITIONS

Factors Influencing Organizational Structure: Both internal and external factors to the company influencing its decision to structure and organize.

Organizational Structure: How the objectives, resources, activities and responsibilities are distributed among the employees inside the company in order to achieve coordination and cooperation among different organizational units.

Structure and Culture: When structuring and re-structuring the company especially in foreign markets, managers must learn about the local cultures and consider the cultural variables in decision making. In order for a structure to function properly an organization needs a supportive and friendly socio-cultural environment.

Structure and ICT: The role of information and communication technologies in designing and redesigning the organizational structure.

Structure and Strategy: Any change in the structure should be followed by corresponding changes in the organizational strategies and policies. Structures and strategies must match in order for the organization to function smoothly and without administrative problems.

Types of Organizational Structure: Options, alternatives and forms of organizational structures available for the company to structure itself.

Chapter 8
Emerging MNEs Successfully Operating in International Markets:
The Cases of Some Mexican MNEs

Osmar Hazael Zavaleta-Vazquez
Tecnológico de Monterrey, EGADE Business School, Mexico

Jorge Alberto Wise-Lozano
CETYS, Mexico

ABSTRACT

The purpose of this chapter is to describe the most important theories that explain the possible motivations of some enterprises to compete in the international arena. Besides describing and summarizing the internationalization theories of an enterprise, the cases of some Mexican firms, which have grown successfully internationally, will be presented and compared with all the elements established in the different theories. This chapter starts by describing the different characteristics of firms competing in international markets. After that, the most important theories of MNEs are explored. The chapter ends with the discussion of the internationalization process followed by CEMEX, GRUMA and TELMEX (America Movil), Mexican enterprises that have successfully grown in the international spectrum.

INTRODUCTION

The purpose of this chapter is to explain the internationalization process with a particular focus on emerging MNEs. Here, the need for new theories that explain the factors which make it possible for these Emerging MNEs to extend their operations to international markets is accepted. Therefore, this chapter briefly describes how a firm's internationalization process has been explained. This is done by analyzing the circumstances that allowed some Mexican MNEs to compete internationally for decades, many of which became global benchmarks in their industries.

DOI: 10.4018/978-1-5225-0276-0.ch008

The first part of this chapter describes the evolution of theories, explaining the motivations for companies to internationalize and then compares those drivers with several Mexican Multinational Enterprises (MNEs) that successfully operate in the international arena. Three Mexican MNEs are analyzed in the second part of this chapter. The MNEs analyzed guide and provide a theoretical basis for practitioners and decision makers to understand the most relevant motives for companies from emerging markets to internationalize.

The relevant aspect of this chapter is its focus on emerging markets since the dominant theory on internationalization explains that process considering mainly firms from developed countries.

The chapter is organized as follows: the background section includes a broad description of the most important theories that explain the internationalization process of an enterprise; the main focus of the chapter emphasizes the analysis of three Mexican MNEs that operate successfully in international markets. The closing section comprises relevant findings resulting from comparing classical theories and models of the internationalization process and elements that motivated some Mexican MNEs to go international.

BACKGROUND AND LITERATURE REVIEW

The increasing participation of companies from emerging markets in the international arena poses new questions and dilemmas for academic and scholars (Wells 2009). This is relevant given that most of the theories that explain the internationalization process have been developed considering mainly firms from developed countries. Thus, the understanding of the motives for MNEs from underdeveloped countries creates an opportunity to enlarge and develop new theories.

Since the 1960s, scholars have tried to explain the internationalization of firms. Hymer (1960) and Johanson & Vahlne (1977) are among the most notorious researchers seeking to explain the internationalization process. Their first theories are about the multinational enterprise and provide elements to understand a particular reality faced by companies mainly from the USA and Western Europe which had operations in international markets. In this context, the international expansion pattern of those companies is mainly explained as a result of the differences in the quality of the institutional environment and markets between the firms' country of origin and their international destination. Frequently, the countries of destination of such initiatives were developed economies. It was not until the early 1980s that some authors (c.f. Wells 1983) noted the international expansion experienced by a number of companies from developing economies. In that direction, Wells (1983) and Yeung (1994) propose theories explaining how firms born in underdeveloped environments are also able to compete in developed markets. Among the drawbacks they considered for MNEs from developing countries are the problems their own countries face, such as weak regulatory systems, limited rule of law and judicial issues. Other pondered problems faced by those MNEs are credit restrictions, high levels of corruption, and limited technology. Despite all that, MNEs from underdeveloped countries compete in international markets similar to those from developed ones.

Theories including MNEs from underdeveloped economies are divided into three categories. The first one is based on the so called country-specific advantages (CSAs). These theories were proposed by scholars such as Dunning (1989), Porter (1990), and Buckley & Casson (1998), among others. According to this perspective, the existence of Emerging MNEs is a consequence of the privileged access that these companies have to internationally scarce natural resources or the abundance of generic production resources (usually a cheap labor force) in their domestic markets. Privileged access to scarce natural resources would allow these companies to succeed abroad, given the limited availability of alternative providers. On the other hand, the availability of a cheap labor force in the domestic market would allow productive input substitution strategies. The intensive use of cheap supplies would allow these companies to offset the competitive barriers found in international markets. More recently, Del Sol & Kogan (2007) proposed another type of CSA derived from the institutional reforms implemented by the emerging country. According to these authors, once their institutions have been reformed, companies whose countries are pioneering in liberalizing their labor, capital and product markets have several competitive advantages over domestic companies from emerging economies.

The second group of explanations, according to Dunning (1989), was based on sources of competitive advantage developed at the level of the firm-specific advantages (FSAs). In some cases, the FSAs were a consequence of the way in which some companies responded to specific problems in their local market. For instance, Wells (1983) mentions the cases of some Emerging MNEs that were extremely efficient operating at very small levels of scale. Similarly, Meyer (2004) states that another noteworthy source of FSAs for emerging MNEs derives from competing or collaborating with subsidiaries from developed MNEs operating in an emerging economy. The argument in this case is that the presence of companies from developed countries provided a series of technological, institutional, competitive and managerial benefits that support the performance and development of emerging MNEs. As companies from emerging economies improve their management capacities, their likelihood to compete abroad also increases.

The third group of explanations offered to justify the existence of Emerging MNEs is more generic. Among the most important concepts are opportunities generated by the internationalization of domestic customers or the necessity of providing value-added services in the destination markets of national exports. Although the literature on Emerging MNEs generated during the 1980s is extensive, the interest in this phenomenon diminished significantly over the next decade (Lucea & Lessard 2010). However, in the early 2000s, a significant increase in the levels of foreign direct investment (FDI) flows from emerging to developed countries and a series of highly successful cases of internationalization by Emerging MNEs rekindled the interest of academics and businessmen in these companies. In keeping with this renewed interest, it was essential to understand how these Emerging MNEs were able not only to operate in other emerging economies, but also compete with developed multinational companies in their own countries. For the moment, a consensus on this issue has not been reached. Some authors argue that the new situation can be perfectly explained through any of the theories described above. Others, however, argue that the Emerging MNEs of today and those of the 1980s are qualitatively different and, consequently, it is necessary to develop new theories that help to understand the phenomenon.

On the other hand, Coulter (2005) states that organizational growth is often viewed as a desirable direction for an organization. The pursuit of growth appeals to businesses and not-for-profit organizations alike. Typical growth objectives include sales increases, profits, employees, market shares, risk and resource diversification, and/or other assets. These ideas imply that corporate growth strategy involves the attainment of specific growth objectives by increasing the level of the operations in an organization.

Going further with the previous ideas, Greiner (1998) describes five phases of growth and how the firm evolves in terms of the age of each organization. The five phases are (1) the management focus, (2) the organizational structure, (3) the top-management style, (4) the control system, and (5) the management reward system. Table 1 describes the main characteristics of each of these in terms of the age of the organization. The younger the organization, the lower the phase it faces.

Table 1. The five phases of growth

CATEGORY	PHASE 1 (Young Organizations)	PHASE 2	PHASE 3	PHASE 4	PHASE 5 (Mature Organizations)
Management Focus	Make and sell	Efficiency of operations	Expansion of market	Consolidation of organization	Problem solving and innovation
Organizational Structure	Informal	Centralized and functional	Decentralized and geographical	Line staff and product groups	Matrix of teams
Top-Management Style	Individualistic and entrepreneurial	Directive	Delegative	Watchdog	Participative
Control System	Market results	Standards and cost centers	Reports and profit centers	Plans and investment centers	Mutual goal setting
Management Reward System	Ownership	Salary and merit increases	Individual bonus	Profit sharing and stock options	Team bonus

Source: Adapted from Greiner (1998).

There have been different definitions of the multinational enterprise which was long described as an enterprise that owns and controls income, and generates assets in more than one country (c.f. Dunning 1973, Buckley & Casson 1976, Hood & Young, 1979). More recently, Bartlett, Ghoshal & Beamish (2008) provide important concepts to better understand the scope of an organization that operates in an international market in terms of its "mentality to grow". Table 2 shows the most important characteristics of growth mentalities of a firm that operates in an international scenario.

Table 2. Growth mentalities of a firm that operates in an international market

1. International Mentality •Distributing domestic products in foreign market. •Providing raw materials or parts to the domestic operations. •Internationalization is derived from International Product Life Cycle. •Transfer of technology and knowledge to overseas operations. •Decisions are made at home on an ad hoc basis (opportunistically).
2. Multinational Mentality •Emphasis on the differences among national markets and environment. •Very flexible approach to the company's international operations. •Development of management practices and product country by country. •Sensitivity to local needs and cultures. •Local managers independent from headquarters. •Local knowledge for local growth.
3. Global Mentality •Creating products for one worldwide market •Standardized product with adequate cost and quality •National preferences or tastes are more similar than different •Same products delivered the same way everywhere. •More centralized coordination and direct control over subsidiaries by HQ. •Research and development and strategic issues are retained at HQ.
4. Transnational Mentality •Locally responsive with global scale efficiency •National preferences with adequate cost and quality •Resources and activities are dispersed but specialized •Efficiency and flexibility •Linking and coordinating operations to retain effectiveness and efficiency

Source: Adapted from Bartlett, Ghoshal & Beamish (2008)

With the previous background about some of the most central theories of the internationalization process of an enterprise and the general description of the growth path of a company, the next section focuses on the potential reasons that support the international expansion of several successful Mexican MNEs operating abroad.

RESEARCH ON THE INTERNATIONALIZATION CONCEPT

Internationalization is a concept that is related to the aspect of being international, i.e. concerning two or more nations. In businesses, the concept relates to the constitution of a group or association having members in two or more countries. A firm doing business only within a single country is not international. On the other hand, a firm doing business in two or more countries is international. A firm doing business crossing its country borders is considered international (Welch & Luostarinen, 1988).

Much of the academic research on internationalization is due to the MNE, also referred to as the multinational corporation (MNC), companies operating in more than one country (Rugman, 1982; Roth, Schweiger, & Morrison, 1992). Nevertheless, most of that research has been developed considering the foreign market entry (Ellis, 2000). In a similar vein, Welch and Luostarinen (1988) state that the term internationalization "tends to be used roughly to describe the outward movement in an individual firm's or larger grouping's international operations" (p. 36). Indeed, the phenomenon is the most studied (cf. Johanson & Vahle, 1977; Dunning, 1979; Dunning, 1988; Andersen, 1993; among others). However, there are many other situations firms face in an international evolvement, such as exchange of information (Bowersox & Calantone, 1998) or foreign buying (e.g. components, parts, technology, and similar).

The internationalization of the firm occurs when a company enters a second country. Most of this research has been done considering a firm operating in more than one country. The next section analyzes different perspectives on how firms internationalize, considering aspects of evolutionary and incremental overseas involvement.

Views of Internationalization

The internationalization of the firm through exports has chiefly been studied considering two ways of describing such a process: The Uppsala Internationalization Model (UM) and the Innovation-Related Internationalization Model (IM). While the UM concentrates on a firm's directed internationalization efforts, the IM focuses on internationalization as an innovation for the firm. The UM was developed by Jan Johanson and his associates from Uppsala University in Sweden (i.e. Johanson & Vahle, 1977; Johanson & Wiedersheim-Paul, 1975), while several authors have worked on the IM (i.e. Bilkey & Tesar, 1977; Reid, 1981; Czinkota, 1982).

The Uppsala internationalization model mainly explains the internationalization process of an individual firm considering its export behavior and its foreign investment behavior. This process is carried out through the firm's incremental involvement in the international arena, an endeavor that places the firm within the foreign market perspective. Considering this internationalization process of an individual firm, Johanson and Wiedersheim-Paul (1975) distinguish four different modes of entering an international market, where there are successive stages representing higher degrees of international involvement. A firm in the first stage has no regular export activities, while in the second stage the firm exports via independent representatives or agents. When the firm is in the third stage, it has established an overseas sales subsidiary. In the fourth and final stage the firm has overseas production of manufactured units. Although the model proposed by Johanson and Wiedersheim-Paul was restricted to their research on a specific country market (i.e. Sweden), the model seems to be applicable to many other markets. This internationalization model assumes that firms enter a foreign market by crossing its country borders and their degree of internationalization depends on the step in which the firm is found. However, this is a static model where it was hypothesized that firms would enter new markets with a successively greater psychic distance, which is considered an important variable in understanding the internationalization process (O'Grady and Lane, 1996). Early studies of Nordic multinationals generally are taken as the starting point in discussions and research on the concept of psychic distance (Johanson & Vahle, 1977; Johanson & Wiedersheim-Paul, 1975) and the internationalization process of the firm (Andersen, 1993).

Johanson and Wiedersheim-Paul's work has been further developed and refined by Johanson and Vahle (1977). They describe a dynamic model in which the outcome of one cycle of events constitutes the input of the next. That model explains the incremental character of internationalization and the main structure of the model is given by the distinction between state and change aspects of internationalization variables. Johanson and Vahle (1977) consider the state aspects as "the resource commitment to the foreign markets – market commitment – and knowledge about foreign markets and operations" (p. 26). On the other hand, the change aspects are "decisions to commit resources and the performance of current business activities" (p. 26). The mechanism is shown in Figure 1. A basic assumption here is that market knowledge and market commitment affect both commitment decisions and current activities, which in turn influence market knowledge and market commitment. It is assumed in the model that while the firm strives to increase its long-term profit, it is also striving to maintain risk-taking at a low level. The model assumes that the state of internationalization affects perceived opportunities and risks, which in turn influence commitment decisions and current activities.

Figure 1. The internationalization process of the firm
Adapted from: Johanson and Vahle (1977 p. 26)

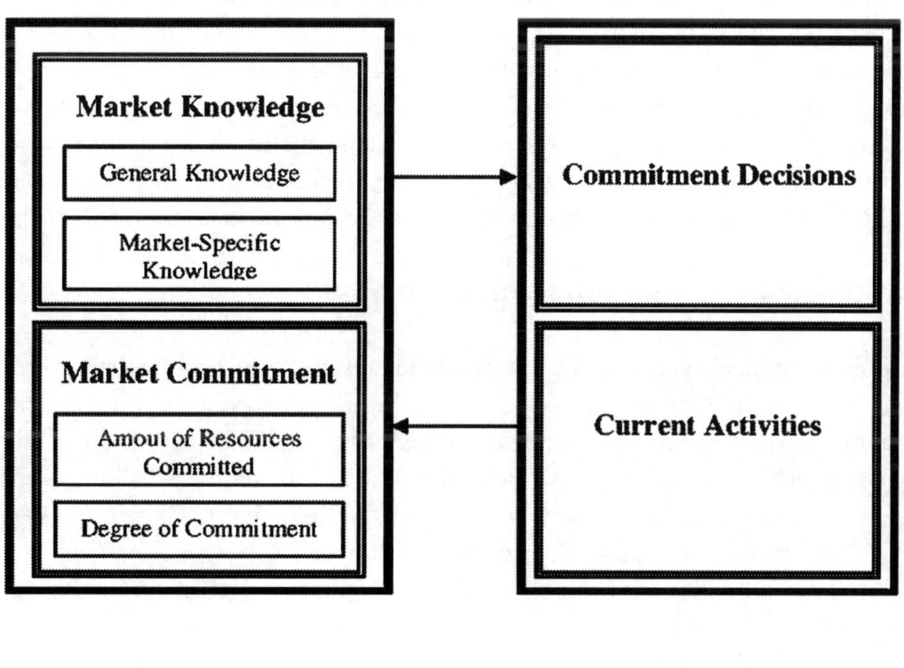

Johanson and Vahle (1977) assume that the market commitment concept is composed of two factors, the amount of resources committed and the degree of commitment. The amount of resources committed could be operationalized as resources located in a particular market area (e.g. marketing, organization, and personal), and the degree of commitment as the difficulty of finding an alternative use for the resources and transferring them to the alternative use. Andersen (1993) considers that "the latter concept seems to be close to the concept of sunk cost" (p. 211).

Market knowledge is a concept required within the firm's international activities. It is possible to distinguish between general knowledge and market-specific knowledge. General knowledge concerns marketing methods and common characteristics of certain types of customers. In foreign operations, market-specific knowledge (i.e. business climate, cultural patterns, structure of the market system, individual customers' characteristics) is assumed to be gained through experience in the country, whereas knowledge of the operations could be transferred from one market to another. This may result in the establishment of technically similar activities in dissimilar business environments facilitating growth of the firm in new markets. Moreover, a direct relationship between market knowledge and market commitment can be postulated: Knowledge can be considered a resource, for example a dimension of human resources; thus, the better the knowledge about the market, the more valued the resources and the stronger the commitment to the market.

Current business activities are also the prime source of experience (Johanson & Vahle, 1977). Marketing activities, under which business activities could be performed, are examples of such experience. Indeed, marketing activities need to be repeated for some time to obtain palpable results, such as sales. Those activities require firm experience and market experience. On the other hand, the committed decisions are concerned with decisions to allocate current resources to foreign operations. In general, it can be assumed that these decisions are made in response to perceived problems and/or opportunities in the international market. In fact, the committed decisions will rely on experience and will be related to the operations currently performed in the international market.

With three exceptions, the Johanson and Vahle (1977) model (Figure 1) implies that additional market commitment will be made in small incremental steps. The exceptions are: (a) firms with large resources experience small consequences of their commitments and can take larger internationalization steps; (b) when market conditions are stable and homogeneous, relevant market knowledge can be gained in other ways than experience; and (c) when the firm has considerable experience from markets with similar conditions, it may be able to generalize this experience to any specific market. Rather, market experience will lead to a step-wise increase in the scale of the firm's operations and of the firm's integration with its market environment, where decisions will be taken to correct imbalance with respect to the risk situation in the international market. Furthermore, such market growth accelerates this process.

The Innovation-Related Internationalization Model

The most well-known models explaining the internationalization process of the firm from an innovation-related perspective are derived from Rogers' stages of the adoption process (Rogers, 1962), which are presented in Figure 2. The three models focus on the learning sequence in connection with adopting an innovation. In other words, the internationalization decision is considered as an innovation for the firm.

The models considered here (i.e. Bilkey & Tesar, 1977; Reid, 1981; Czinkota, 1982) share many features. All of them share a similar gradual pattern of the firm's internationalization process. Their differences are mainly in the description at each stage and in the number of stages: the Bilkey and Tesar

Figure 2. The innovation-related internationalization models of the firm

Bilkey and Tesar(1977)	Czinkota (1982)	Reid (1981)
Stage 1 Management is not interested in exporting	***Stage 1*** The completely uninterested firm	***Stage 1*** Export awareness: Problem of opportunity recognition, arousal of need
Stage 2 Management is willing to fill unsolicited orders, but makes no effort to explore the feasibility of active exporting	***Stage 2*** The partially interested firm	***Stage 2*** Export intention: Motivation, attitude, beliefs, and expectancy about export
Stage 3 Management actively explores the feasibility of active exporting	***Stage 3*** The exploring firm	***Stage 3*** Export trial: Personal experience from limited exporting
Stage 4 The firm export on an experimental basis to some psychologically close country	***Stage 4*** The experimental firm	***Stage 4*** Export evaluation: Results from engaging in exporting
Stage 5 The firm is an experienced exporter	***Stage 5*** The experienced small firm	***Stage 5*** Export acceptance: Adoption of exporting/rejection of exporting
Stage 6 Management explores the feasibility of exporting to other more psychologically distant countries	***Stage 6*** The experienced large firm	

(1977) and Czinkota (1982) models have six stages, while Reid's (1981) has five. The incentives to start exporting, for example, seem to be interpreted differently in the former models versus the latter one. Stage one of the Bilkey and Tesar (1977) and Czinkota (1982) models say, correspondingly, that management and firm are not interested or completely uninterested in exporting. In this context, Step 1 in Reid's (1981) model states that there is an export awareness where the firm has an opportunity recognition problem. At Stage 2, similarly, the firm's management is willing to fill unsolicited orders (Bilkey & Tesar, 1977), being partially interested in exporting (Czinkota, 1982). So, here it is possible to think that there is some kind of "push" mechanism or external change agent that initiates the export decision. On the other hand, at Stage 2 of Reid's (1981) model, the firm is described as a unit that is more interested and active during the early stage due to a firm's export intention shown though its motivation, attitude, beliefs, and expectancy about exports. So, a "pull" mechanism or internal change agent seems to be a more relevant explanation as to why the firm moves to the next stage. After those initial two stages, all three models seem to reflect only semantic differences (e.g. exploring vs. trial, experienced exporter vs. adoption/rejection of exporting) rather than real differences about the nature of the internationalization process of the firm.

While the IM model sees the firm's internationalization decision as an innovation, the UM proposes the firm's incremental involvement in the international arena as its internationalization. Both models seem to benefit from a general acceptance in the prevailing literature and are still being used as a theoretical basis for empirical analyses. However, Andersen (1993) considers the models present some inherent deficiencies. In his evaluation of the two models, Andersen discusses five aspects through a "falsifiability perspective" (p. 226); but, he analyses the weaknesses of the models considering only the outward or export perspective defined in them. The inward or import path is not mentioned either by Andersen or the other two models previously examined (i.e. the Uppsala internationalization model and the innovation-related internationalization model) as a part of the internationalization process of the firm, something that is missing and has been studied inadequately.

An Inward Perspective of the Internationalization of the Firm

The internationalization process of the firm though imports has been studied sparsely. Similarly to the more notorious outward perspective, the literature includes two models that consider the inward perspective, which are specifically related to the internationalization of the firm when importing. One model is related to the buyer (Reichel, 1988) and the other to procurement (Monczka & Trent, 1991). Both models consider that the internationalization of the firm occurs through an incremental and evolutionary involvement of the firm in the international arena, obtaining products or goods from the same. Next, both models are presented.

The Buyer Internationalization Model

The model explains the internationalization process of the firm considering only its buying behavior as an "incremental strategy" (Reichel, 1988: 33). To explain the model, Reichel (1988) uses the physical distance paradox (O'Grady & Lane, 1996) and the buyer psychological compatibility with different countries or cultures. Indeed, using both dimensions the model looks at two forms of internationalization, the incremental strategy and the evolutionary strategy, which, although related, are somehow different. In both cases the model considers that the firm's marketplace is the whole world. However, it recognizes that importers buy their products from a limited geographical region. Here the buying behavior is displayed as an inward perspective where the firm internationalizes. What follows explains the incremental strategy and the evolutionary strategy using the model proposed by Reichel (1988), sketched in Figure 3.

The incremental strategy: In an import company the responsibility for importing products which belong to the same category is usually given to a single person. Thus, a single buyer is responsible for the importation of the same category of products needed by the firm. This kind of assignment demands a widespread network of contacts. If the suppliers are located throughout the world, then the buyer needs to plan the amount of days needed to contact and to travel, particularly to maintain such a network of contacts. The more suppliers a buyer works with, the more important it is for him or her to have the suppliers situated within a limited geographical area. It is easier and more efficient and economical to keep the network of suppliers within a specific geographical region. Only for a very powerful reason will the buyer travel elsewhere in the world while there is a similar product on offer near the normal source of supply. However, having a small number of suppliers gives the importer the freedom to choose new sources of supply within a greater area. Raichel (1988) concludes here "this implicitly means that the more suppliers an importer has, the greater the demands are for him or her to use the incremental

Figure 3. The buyer internationalization model
Adapted from Reichel (1988 p. 35)

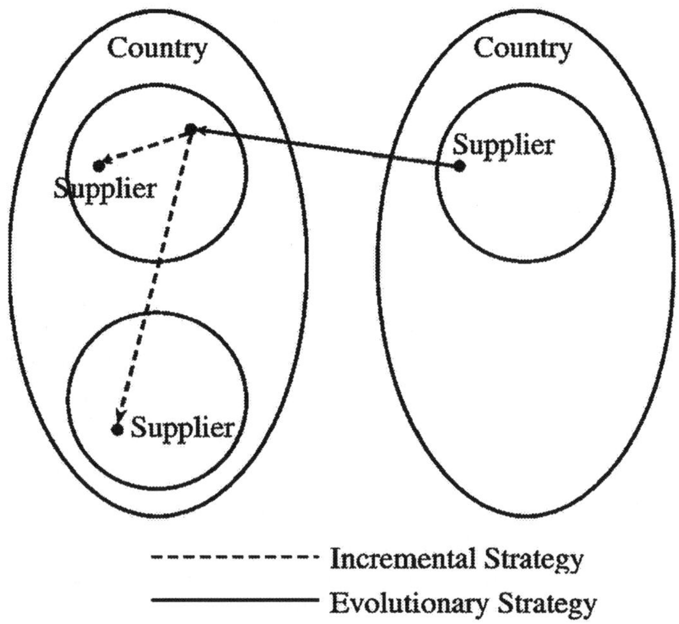

internationalization [sic] strategy" (p. 36). This strategy means that any particular buyer first looks for the product needed by the firm within the same geographical and cultural region in which he or she has previously worked. This method of searching involves physical distance and lower psychological barriers, all of which are well known by the importer.

The evolutionary strategy: When prices rise and no new sources of supply with low prices can be found close at hand, importers are constrained to rethink their buyer strategies. Volume importers start to reduce their number of suppliers, trying to concentrate on only few of them, mainly in their main suppliers. Concentrating on only a few suppliers may give importers the opportunity to use the quantity discounts offered by their suppliers, a condition that in turn will help firms to remain competitive and thus maintain a presence in the region. This allows firms to continue buying from their main suppliers, where co-operation and mutual trust have been established, which is reflected by the fact that the business relationship between buyers (importers) and suppliers works well. All of this is in addition to the importers' investments in educating their suppliers regarding business routines and the dissemination of know-how. Additionally, the demand of time needed to keep the buyer commitments with the suppliers will be greater, reducing the opportunity (i.e. time left) to travel looking for other suppliers located in a different geographical area. Moreover, the ties between the buyer and the exporter somehow contribute to the buyer's reluctance to abandon the exporter for a new supplier. This means that importers of large volumes of goods are less flexible when it comes to choosing the supplying region.

Importers who do not deal in large quantities cannot reduce the number of buying sources and negotiate competitive prices. They will be forced to look at another already known area and try other countries with favorable prices. Raichel (1988) states that such importers limit themselves to one or sometimes two or three suppliers. Faced with this situation, such importers choose to implement an evolutionary internationalization strategy. That is to say, they look for a new supplier in a country which lies outside the region the importers have previously dealt with. Their buying routines undergo a significant change as a result of the new procedures needed for a country that is situated at a greater distance, both physically and psychologically. These importers have taken the necessary steps to find a new country of supply which lies outside the geographical and cultural region where they have normally done their buying and, therefore, they have to overcome the problems of dealing with greater physical distances and greater psychological incompatibility.

The Procurement Internationalization Model

The procurement model explains the internationalization process of the firm considering the internationalization of the procurement process. Correspondingly, Monczka and Trent (1991) developed a four-stage model of the sourcing strategy. The model's vision is rooted in the import side. The four stages are domestic sourcing, foreign sourcing based on competitive needs, foreign sourcing as part of the sourcing strategy (Arnold, 1989), and global sourcing as the integration of the global procurement strategy. Firms in the last stage make strategic sourcing decisions to integrate and coordinate procurement requirements across worldwide business units by looking at common items, processes, technologies, and suppliers. The model proposed by Monczka and Trent (1991) for international sourcing is also a series of incremental decisions where the firm internationalizes through that process.

The Monczka and Trent (1991) model is based on how reactive or proactive the firm is. Domestic sourcing and foreign buying based on needs are reactive, while foreign buying as part of the procurement strategy and integration of a global procurement strategy are proactive, as shown in Figure 4. As each firm is motivated to source globally, for reasons that satisfy unique operational objectives, international sourcing is a way used by the firm to remain as a competitor in the marketplace. If the buyers were forced to source in world markets to prevent further erosion of market share, then foreign buying is often a defensive reaction measure. On the other hand, once firms gain enough international procurement experience, the motivation for foreign sourcing may no longer be survival, but rather to secure cost, quality, technological and other competitive advantages. As such, firms become proactive, developing international sourcing strategies due to an intended response to counter increased global competition.

Figure 4. The procurement internationalization process
Adapted from: Monczka and Trent (1991, p. 3)

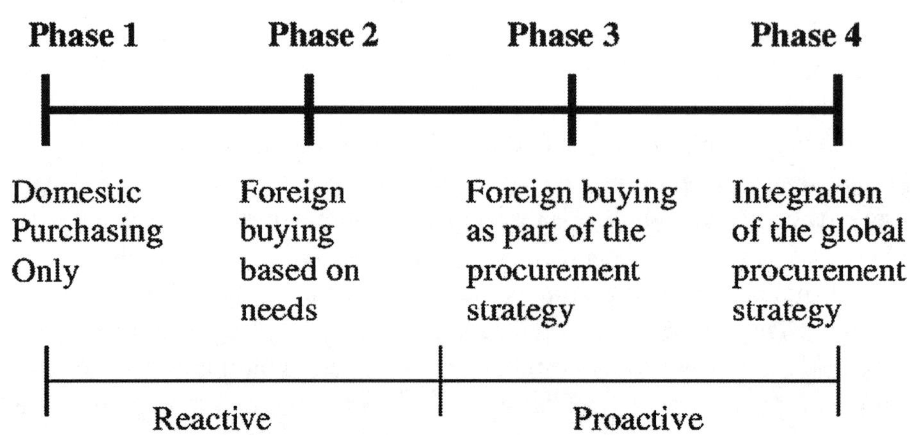

The Internationalization Path of Some Mexican MNEs

Country-specific advantages (CSAs) are derived from the way in which emerging countries reform their institutions (Del Sol & Kogan 2007). In that regard, since the mid-1980s, during the tenure of President Miguel de la Madrid, Mexico was transformed from a closed and protected economy with a highly interventionist state to one of the most open and least interventionist economies in Latin America. The reforms in the Mexican financial sector were an important component of the whole structural reform program (Aspe-Armella 1993). By the end of President Carlos Salinas' tenure in 1994, the Mexican economic reform program was considered one of the most impressive in Latin America. Some of the reasons for that lie in the country's implementation of a very successful macroeconomic stabilization program while establishing an unprecedented free trade agreement (FTA) with the USA and Canada. In addition, the country engaged in an unparalleled privatization and deregulation program, liberalizing the financial sector and emphasizing the government's endorsement for both the health and the education sectors. These crucial transformations are recognized as the key factors that fostered the internationalization process of many Mexican enterprises.

As mentioned above, the international expansion of companies from emerging economies is likely the result of a particular circumstance, either the firm has access to scarce production inputs or the firm can exploit cheap, generic production. In any case, the resulting inputs allow the firm to obtain significant economies of scale (i.e., savings) in its production. Nevertheless, none of that seems to apply to the Mexican companies which are analyzed later. Still, the relevant literature on the topic is provoking and still needs to focus more on the successful determinants of MNEs from developing countries. To advance in that direction, next, three successful Mexican MNEs are analyzed.

THE CASE OF CEMEX

The Origins

CEMEX was founded in 1906 with the opening of the *Cementos Hidalgo* plant in northern Mexico (CEMEX 2015). By 1909, the company had doubled its annual production capacity to 66,000 tons. The Mexican Revolution halted production due to lack of available energy, communication channels, and human resources. The plant resumed operations in 1919 when the conflict diminished and the demand for cement increased.

In 1931, *Cementos Mexicanos*, or CEMEX, resulted from the merger of *Cementos Portland Monterrey* and *Cementos Hidalgo*. *Cementos Portland Monterrey* started operations by 1921 with an annual capacity of 20,000 tons. The plant marketed *Cemento Portland Monterrey* to satisfy customer demand in northeastern Mexico. By the end of 1948, CEMEX's annual production capacity reached 124,000 tons, a nearly fourfold increase from 1906. Between 1950 and 1960, CEMEX continued its expansion. By the end of 1960, its plant located in Monterrey increased its annual production capacity to 180,000 tons. Next, in 1966, CEMEX acquired *Cementos Maya* in Mérida to satisfy demand in southern Mexico through the brand *Cemento Portland Maya*. The same year, CEMEX began production in Valles, serving the Huasteca region in central Mexico through the brand *Cemento Portland Monterrey*. By 1967 CEMEX initiated production in Torreon satisfying a growing demand in northeastern Mexico with two brands: *Cemento Puzolana Monterrey* and *Cemento Portland Monterrey*.

The aggressive growth of CEMEX continued, acquiring in 1973 *Cementos Portland del Bajío* in central Mexico. By 1976, CEMEX was listed on the Mexican Stock Exchange and 70 years after its foundation, it became Mexico's leader with the acquisition of *Cementos Guadalajara.* During its first 70 years of operations, CEMEX has always pioneered in the use of the most modern technology. For instance, at the end of 1970s, the CEMEX Monterrey and Mérida units were producing with their ninth and second kilns (cement furnaces) respectively. These kilns are four-phased pre-heaters reducing installation costs and collecting dust in their filters. With a production capacity of 1,300 tons per day, the kilns helped to meet the growing cement demand of southern and northeastern Mexico. Similarly, in 1982 CEMEX's Monterrey and Torreon plants initiated production with their tenth and fourth kilns, respectively. The kilns' four-stage pre-heaters with pre-calcinators represented an important technological advance. By enabling the de-carbonation of up to 90% of the plants' raw materials and reducing the size of kilns, CEMEX attains cost savings in installation and spare parts. Each plant increased its capacity by 2,200 tons per day. By the end of 1985 CEMEX's annual sales exceeded 6.7 million tons; the annual sales of each of its plants in Monterrey, Guadalajara and Torreon surpassed 1 million metric tons.

The Internationalization Process of CEMEX

The presence of CEMEX in international markets began through exportations. In 1985, CEMEX exports reached 574,000 tons a year. Later, in 1986, through co-investments with North American cement companies, CEMEX consolidated its export program. With the acquisition of *Cementos Tolteca* (Mexico's second-largest cement producer) in 1986, CEMEX became one of the ten largest cement companies in the world. Some years later, in 1992, the company initiated an international expansion into the European market acquiring *Valenciana* and *Sanson*, Spain's largest cement companies. Strategically, these acquisitions were important for two reasons; first, they made CEMEX less dependent on the Mexican market and provided a dominant position in one of the most important markets for its main rivals. Secondly, owning assets in Spain allowed CEMEX access to more convenient financial markets of developed economies.

After the acquisitions, CEMEX conducted a review of each operational and organizational process to capture any source of savings, quickly integrating it into its process (Lessard & Reavis 2009). Those international acquisitions make clear the relevance of post-merger integration (PMI) in subsequent acquirements. As a result, CEMEX began to codify and standardize the steps required in identifying sources of savings in new acquisitions, establishing its own operations and management practices. Those practices helped with the detection of areas of excellence that have become the best practices for the whole company.

CEMEX initiated operations in South America and Central America in 1994 with the acquisition of *Vencemos* (Venezuela's largest cement company) and *Cemento Bayano* in Panama. The same year, the company expanded its operations acquiring Balcones, a cement plant in the USA. The following year, CEMEX established operations in the Caribbean, acquiring the Dominican Republic's leading cement company, *Cementos Nacionales*. By 1996, CEMEX became the world´s third largest cement company with the acquisition of Colombia's *Cementos Diamante* and Samper. The operations in Asia began in 1997 with the acquisition of Rizal Cement in the Philippines and in 1999 acquired APO cement in the same country. CEMEX consolidated its presence in Central America and the Caribbean in 1999 acquiring *Cementos del Pacifico*, Costa Rica's largest cement producer. In order to increase its sources of financing CEMEX was listed in 1999 in the New York Stock Exchange. By 2000, this Mexican MNE had become North America's largest cement producer with the acquisition of the US-based Southdown.

THE CASE OF GRUMA

The Origins

GRUMA was founded in Cerralvo, Mexico by Roberto González Barrera and his father, Mr. Roberto M. González Gutiérrez in 1949 (GRUMA 2015). Cerralvo is a small town in the northern Mexican state of Nuevo León. The company's incorporation solved thc problem of preserving the *nixtamal* dough for the preparation of tortillas, Mexicans' staple food. This innovative product could be preserved for extended periods to be used on demand. Furthermore, it facilitated tortilla manufacturing, simplifying the process since the flour just had to be mixed with water to prepare the dough. In short, it meant significant savings in time and labor which benefited consumers.

Molinos Azteca was the first *nixtamal* corn flour production plant of what is nowadays known as GRUMA. It began with 45 employees working over three shifts to manufacture about 150 tons of product per month. During the 1950s, GRUMA improved the quality of the "nixtamalized" corn flour as well as its manufacturing process, achieving a better final product: a quality tortilla for daily consumption. During that time, the flagship trademark MASECA was born. The name of this product was invented by Mr. González Barrera and derives from the concepts of "Masa and Seca" (dough and dry, i.e. dehydrated corn flour).

The 1950s was a decade of experimentation and was crucial in achieving an acceptable product for the customers who wanted to have a tortilla with optimal color, texture and flavor. During that time, GRUMA built its second facility in Acaponeta, Mexico (in the western state of Nayarit). The operation of the plant faced two challenges: achieving an efficient and uniform industrial production and customers' and dealers' acceptance of a different product for the preparation of tortillas which are consumed daily in the country.

GRUMA expanded its presence in Mexico in the 1960s. It built seven new corn flour mills. The use of corn flour in Mexico became a reality; MASECA positioned itself as a synonym for quality, but also as a staple food in the Mexican diet. A group of researchers and an aggressive program was created to improve equipment and processes to increase profitability. At the same time, next-generation technology was developed and evaluated, thus consolidating the following years.

The Internationalization Process of GRUMA

GRUMA began operations in Costa Rica with the production and marketing of packaged tortillas. The Costa Rica operations provided great lessons to the company, such as the development of high-speed machines; soy protein enrichment of tortillas; proving that tortillas could be manufactured, packaged, preserved and distributed without losing their properties; and developing mass distribution channels with a large quantity of routes. Actually, many of GRUMA's most successful products are first tested in Costa Rica considered as the firm's learning laboratory.

GRUMA arrived in the USA with the purchase of Mission Foods in California in 1975. The learnings the company acquired from this country fostered GRUMA's maturation as an international firm, accelerating at the same time its technology developments. The firm reveals that the result of that learning process is its subsequent success in the world's most developed market.

Due to an increasing investment in technology, a new business growth with proprietary technology, TECNOMAIZ, represented a revolutionary development for GRUMA. The new venture developed, manufactured and marketed corn tortilla production lines with varying capacities. These machines can produce just 50 tortillas per minute for small Mexican neighborhood tortilla shops as well as big production lines with a capacity of 600 tortillas per minute. Those machines were marketed first in Costa Rica and in the USA. The tortilla machines positioned GRUMA in the market as one of the most recognized and best quality brands for its products.

As part of the expansion strategy into international markets, during the 1980s, through its subsidiary MASECA, GRUMA acquired ten plants in the USA. The first corn flour mill was built in Edinburg, Texas, creating Azteca Milling. This subsidiary quickly produced profits representing a significant growth in flour sales for the tortilla industry in that country. Later, the company acquired "Guerrero", a brand with strong roots in southern California which nowadays is well recognized by Mexicans in that country. MASECA became a well-respected international firm accomplishing the highest performance standards, similar to its counterparts in the USA and their MNEs and transnational companies.

GRUMA built a tortilla mega-plant in Los Angeles, California by 1990. It is still the world's largest plant with a capacity of 14 million tortillas per day. The production level the company achieved strengthened its presence in Central America by expanding its operations into Guatemala, El Salvador, Honduras and Nicaragua. During that time, GRUMA entered the South American market establishing operations in Venezuela through the acquisition of Molinos Nacionales (MONACA), the number two manufacturer of corn and wheat flour in that country. With that acquisition, GRUMA consolidated itself as a leading food company.

The company entered into the Mexican Stock Exchange market with an initial public offering in 1994. That event fostered its further expansion and consolidation. The following year, a new plant was built also in Los Angeles by merging the production of two plants. That plant surpassed the Olympic plant's production when it achieved a record production of 25 million tortillas per day. Three years later, its extensive operations in the USA market allowed GRUMA to participate on the New York Stock Exchange under the ticker symbol GMK.

After maintaining a key trade relationship with England since 1997 selling tortillas from the USA, in 2000 a facility in Coventry was inaugurated; GRUMA's first tortilla plant in the United Kingdom. With this decision, the Mexican firm became a local producer instead of an importer, a relevant factor for MNEs. The UK was the beachhead to enter the European market. In addition, a great business opportunity with flatbreads as well as wraps conquered not only English, but also continental European palates. Due to the UK success, in 2004, GRUMA acquired a wheat tortilla factory in Holland and a corn flour mill in Ceggia, near Venice, Italy. Later, GRUMA purchased Pride Valley Foods located in Seaham, England continuing the conquest of the flatbreads market category, which included pita and naan (a kind of Asian bread) as products.

After an exhaustive analysis, GRUMA entered the Asian market in 2006 building a wheat flour tortilla plant in Shanghai, China. With that action, GRUMA recognized the great market potential in the world's most populated country with a growing middle class which is receptive to trying and adopting customs from Western countries. GRUMA is one of the first Mexican companies with presence in that country.

GRUMA expansions continued in Oceania acquiring Rositas Investments Company in Australia. Its manufacturing lines included wheat flour tortillas and corn chips supplied to the local market. In 2007, GRUMA built a new plant in Melbourne, manufacturing wheat flour tortillas and corn taco shells. In that year, the company strengthened its presence in Asia purchasing a Malayan plant specialized in flatbreads (pita, pizza dough, naan and wheat flour tortillas).

In 2008, resources were allocated to build the next generation of plants equipped with cutting-edge technology to diversify their product portfolio while protecting the environment. In addition, GRUMA's plants in Melbourne and California were modified, as well as many of its facilities in Mexico. GRUMA strengthened its share of value-added products, in both local and global markets with products that suited a wide range of tastes and preferences, thus attracting a broad base of consumers seeking healthier foods.

The following year, the company consolidated its operations in Oceania by inaugurating in Melbourne a modern, innovative "model plant" with next-generation proprietary technology. With that facility, GRUMA had an attractive portfolio of products appealing to the Australian consumer. Among other products, the portfolio included corn and wheat flour tortillas, totopos, taco shells and flatbreads, all under the Mission brand. That year, despite the difficult environment due to the global economic crisis, GRUMA achieved the best worldwide sales in its history. In September, GRUMA received the valuable "World Finance 100" award granted by the prestigious London-based magazine World Finance. The award recognized the Company as one of the 100 leading companies in its line of business.

In the USA, GRUMA opened a plant designed to meet the highest specifications in terms of sustainability and environmental care; its construction was certified "Leed gold" (Leadership in Energy and Environmental Design) by the U.S. Government in 2010. With this plant, the firm ensured an efficient use of energy, water and waste, as well as a reduction in pollutant emissions, both in the industrial and administrative areas of the new facilities where there are water and energy saving systems and solar panels. This plant has become the benchmark to improve GRUMA's facilities throughout the world. Also, that year, GRUMA purchased a grits and corn flour manufacturing plant with an installed capacity of 65,000 tons of product per year in Cherkassy, Ukraine. This action provided the company with the opportunity to increase its business in the entire eastern European region and some countries in North Africa.

GRUMA increased and strengthened its global presence through a clear expansion strategy with the acquisition of four plants "Albuquerque Tortilla Company" and "Casa de Oro Foods" (USA), "Solntse Mexico" (Russia), and Semolina (Turkey). These four plants strengthened its presence in each market with tortilla and other products. The mill in Turkey is equipped with the most advanced technology. The acquisition in Turkey complemented GRUMA's operation in Europe. Also in 2011, with great success, GRUMA launched the "Mission" brand in the self-service channel in Singapore and Malaysia opening a door to a mass market in Asia's southern region. Lately, in 2014, GRUMA purchased "Mexifoods" in Spain, the leading company in the production and marketing of corn and wheat tortilla, fried food and salsas. With this acquisition, the company enlarged its presence in Europe, particularly in the Iberian Peninsula, the south of France, Italy, Portugal and Malta.

THE CASE OF AMERICA MOVIL

The Origins

The history of America Movil is a complex one because its origins date a long way back in Mexico's telephone industry. America Movil is the result of a business split from Telmex. It was born in 2000 inside Telmex (*Telefonos de México*) as the result of the separation of its mobile-phone business and most of its international capital investments. As the history of one company is partly the history of the other, both are presented.

The Parent Company: Telmex

Telmex was created in 1947 as a Mexican company in order to acquire the telephone companies providing services in Mexico. At that time, the telephone service in Mexico was provided mainly by L.M. Ericsson from Sweden and Western Electric Telephone Company from the USA. Both companies had pioneered the telephone industry in the country, Western since 1882 and Ericsson since 1905. In both cases, these companies provided their services mainly in larger cities. Western Electric Telephone Company was known as *Telefonica Mexicana*, or MEXTELCO, while Ericsson local firm was *Teleindustria* Ericsson. Even though several smaller companies were established across Mexico during the first half of the 20th Century, MEXTELCO and Ericsson consistently endeavored to monopolize the service. Telmex was the result of the merger of MEXTELCO and Ericsson, an additional effort to dominate the phone industry (Medina Nuñez 1995).

Although Telmex was created under Mexican laws, most of its owners and capitals were foreign. During the end of 1940s and 1950s, the Mexican Government made singular efforts to pass the control of Telmex to Mexican hands. Meanwhile, International Telegraph Corporation (ITT) from the USA acquired a relevant amount of stock in Telmex. Finally, the efforts for its domestic control culminated in 1958 when Mexicans, with the help of the government, gained full control of the company. Even though Telmex has been the dominant telephone service provider in the country for many decades, several local companies have continued providing the service in small and remote areas (Universe 2015).

Telmex established the largest and most developed telephone network in Mexico. During the 1950s and mainly the 1960s, the government drove a continuous upgrade of telephony by installing microwave and satellite technology all over the country for long distance calls and all the necessary infrastructure for local services. As a result, all kinds of cables and networks are settled. At the end of the decade, Telmex connected most of the country with more than one million landlines. Notwithstanding the company's good results and coverage, the Mexican government obtained 51% of the company by 1972. This acquisition represented a conversion of the company into a state-owned-enterprise (SOE), giving the government control in a sensitive, strategic area. Indeed, from that point forward, Telmex in effect operated as a government-owned utility (Universe 2015). Trying to show that the firm needed a new drive, Telmex grew more than ever and at the same time acquired most of the remaining small local companies. As a result of that concentration, Telmex faced a huge problem when the earthquake of 1985 destroyed the main central telecommunication facility in Mexico City. Next, the company moved forward by digitalizing all the services, installing state-of-the-art technology, such as satellite services, digital phones, mobile phones, and optical fibers across the country.

The waves of worldwide privatization reached Mexico and by 1989 President Salinas was eager to participate. Later, by September 1990, Telmex control shares in government hands, about 20.4% of the stock capital, were sold for approximately US$1.76 billion to *Grupo Carso* (Mexico), France Cable and Radio (France Telecomm) and Southwestern Bell (USA). The Mexican government still kept 4.4% of the capital. This was the first part of a selling process that lasted until 1994 when the privatization process ended. *Grupo Carso* put up half of the initial $1.76 billion and received a leading 10 percent equity stock in Telmex, while its partners financed the other half and shared the other 10 percent interest. The group of three agreed that *Grupo Carso* would have operating control of the company, Southwestern Bell would be responsible for improving operations and developing paging and cellular divisions, and France Telecom would concentrate on line expansion and modernization.

At the time of its privatization, Telmex was generating net profits of about US$1.1 billion from sales of roughly $3.8 billion. Despite those impressive numbers, the government-supported monopoly was in serious need of repair. There were only 6 lines per 100 inhabitants when more than 50 were needed. The purchasing agreement included an unparalleled aggressive expansion program. In the following couple of decades, Telmex deployed more than 148,000 kilometers of optical fiber installed throughout the country (Slim Helú 2015).

Since privatization, Telmex made significant progress toward its goals during the early 1990s. In fact, by late 1994, Telmex had replaced most of its obsolete lines and continued converting old switching systems to 75 percent digital switching, one of the highest levels in the world. Furthermore, between 1992 and 1994 the company managed to increase the number of phone lines on its network at an average annual rate of 12.6 percent, bringing the number of phone lines to ten per 100 inhabitants. As a result, Telmex's sales rose to about $6.6 billion in 1992 before jumping to $7.9 billion in 1993 and declining to about $6 billion in 1994 due to the severe economic crisis Mexico suffered that year. At that time, nearly 45 percent of Telmex's revenues came from local services and the rest from domestic long-distance and international calls. Furthermore, Telmex invested more than $2.3 billion as part of an ongoing program to improve services, preparing itself for the upcoming competition in the long-distance market scheduled to start by 1997 (Universe 2015).

The fierce competition in the Mexican market had a big impact on Telmex's revenue and operations. Its revenues declined persistently during the first years of the 1990s due to the government opening of the local and long distance services. New companies entered the market and Telmex's monopolistic position became a heavy burden. As the company owning almost all the interconnections, Telmex accepted an imposed interconnection fee, affecting its income in several ways. The competition uses Telmex's infrastructure offering mainly domestic and international long-distance services, paying less for that than was previously charged. The interconnection fee declined from an average 5.32 cents a minute in 1997 to a mere 3.15 cents by 2001. As of January 1, 1997, Telmex lost its monopoly over Mexico's long-distance phone market with the presence of eight competitors.

Telmex's plan for continuous innovations was permanent since its privatization. So, by 1995, the firm introduced the first cellular public telephone in Mexico City through the company's cellular company, TELCEL. The cellular service was in great demand and by 1998 it expanded its customer base by over one million (Universe 2015). At this time, Telmex was a player with international partners and in the following years that experience was used to enlarge its portfolio of partners and services in Mexico and abroad.

The Internationalization Process of Telmex

Telmex can be seen as an international company since its creation in the 1940s. With partners such as Ericsson and ITT, the firm has dealt recurrently with foreign companies. Moreover, the relevant and key telephone technology used over the years is developed mainly in Sweden and other developed countries, such as the USA. Thus, viewing Telmex as an international player is natural. In 1996, Carso Global Telecom was created with the aim of separating the ownership of Telmex shares from those of the other entities within the company operating in the telecommunications industry. At the same time, Grupo Carso transferred its shares in Telmex to Carso Global Telecom. Carso Global Telecom's assets are represented by the investment in shares of Telmex and subsidiaries and other enterprises of Grupo

Carso involved in the telecommunications industry, mainly in South America (Emis 2015). Telmex as a brand has been internationalized by Grupo Carso.

Grupo Carso is the internationalizing arm of Telmex. Since 1995, Grupo Carso has established diverse enterprises, mainly in Latin America, using Telmex as a flagship brand. The interests of Carso are mainly in telecommunications and cable-TV. Telmex as a brand is recognized in countries such as Argentina, Brazil, Chile, Peru, and the USA. Diverse telecommunications, mobile-phone, and internet services are offered under the Telmex brand.

The Internationalization Process of America Movil

In September 2000, Telmex split both its mobile-phone business and most of its international capital investments in order to create a new enterprise named America Movil. That movement envisaged several gains and such a decision weighed up the benefits of having independent and competing firms with a business approach and financial flexibility in order to face the different strategies of both Telmex and America Movil. Among the companies that were transferred to America Movil are Telcel (Mexico), Teluga (Guatemala), Conecel (Ecuador), and Tracfone (USA). Indeed, Grupo Carso's move generated a combined business that was presented as the largest telecommunications company in Latin America and one of the largest players in that field in the world.

America Movil shares have been listed since 2001 on the Mexico, New York and Madrid stock exchange markets. Next, a new flagship brand, Claro, was created in 2003 in Brazil after the fusion of several firms owned by America Movil. The brand was quickly accepted and introduced into many other markets such as Argentina, Chile, Colombia, Costa Rica, Ecuador, El Salvador, Guatemala, Honduras, Nicaragua, Paraguay, Peru, Puerto Rico, Spain, Uruguay, the USA, and Venezuela. In most cases, Claro replaced local brands in which either Telmex or America Movil had participated directly or through local telecommunications companies. Claro offers mobile- and land-phone, internet, cable-TV, video, and music services, among others. The different services offered with the Claro brand resulted in the generation of related brands, such as Claro TV, Claro Video, Claro Musica, and Claro Play. In Mexico, the brand used is Telcel for mobile-phone and Claro for other services, while in the USA it is Tracfone Wireless.

At the end of 2005, just four years after its creation, America Movil is a company with more than 93 million cellular-phone clients. The company's enormous development is the result of both organic growth and many acquisitions of firms. Its operations encompass 14 countries in the Americas. In addition, the company has more than two million land-line subscribers. Just during 2005, the firm reported one third of its current subscribers. Of the total number of clients, 62% are outside Mexico. America Movil is recognized as the main telecommunications service provider in Latin America and the number one in pre-paid services in the USA. With a coverage of over 100 thousand cities, towns and communities, about 90% of the territory enjoys the services. State-of-the-art technology is frequently updated and revised, totaling at the beginning of 2006 more than US$16 billion (AMX 2005).

Looking to become a fully integrated telecommunications company, America Movil acquired, in June 2010, 99.9% of Carso Global Telecom, 94.6% of Telmex International and 59.4% of Telmex. The second represented the international operations of Telmex. As a consequence of that move, Carso Global Telecom was delisted from Mexico's Stock Exchange (Emis 2015). In addition, America Movil had access to vast networks of optical fiber and cable in all its participating markets, integrating its offerings of land and mobile telephony, fixed and mobile broad band, and video. The firm has more than 259.3 million customers, 211.3 million mobile phone subscribers, 27.4 land phone lines, 12 million broadband accesses and 8.6 million TV subscribers. The America Movil portfolio is divided with the Mexican market representing 29%, Brazil 22%, South America 34%, Central America and the Caribbean 8% and the USA 8%. Mexico represents the most profitable market for the company (36%), followed by Brazil (20%), South America (25%), Central America and the Caribbean (11%) and the USA (8%). In total, America Movil is present in 18 countries from the Americas. Brands like Telmex and Claro are still used in most of those markets along with others, such as Tracfone (USA), Embratel and Net (Brazil), depending on the type of local concession and recognition (AMX 2010).

The expansion of America Movil continued during the following years and by 2014 it offered 368 million accesses in 27 countries. Although the telecommunications area is particularly subject to governmental control, the firm has managed to increase its presence in the Americas while entering the European market. Since 2012, America Movil has investments in KPN which provides its telecommunication services in the Netherlands and Belgium (Alper & Sassard 2013); however, the stake is still below a full control of the company. This, among others, is one of the efforts carried out to enter into additional markets. On the other hand, America Movil acquired about 50.8% of Telekom Austria shares (Reuters 2014). Telekom Austria successfully operates in Austria and several Central and Eastern European countries such as Belarus, Bulgaria, Croatia, Liechtenstein, Macedonia, Slovenia, and Serbia with a base of more than 23 million customers (Telekom 2015), which were added to America Movil's tally.

CONCLUSION

Two of the internationalization perspectives presented above (inward and outward) share some similarities. A firm's accumulated international experience is a common premise, as occurs with an MNE. That premise transforms the focus of international trade from a reactive to a proactive position as the firm reaches the final stage of internationalization and global sourcing (Rexha & Miyamoto, 2000). The two perspectives are based on market knowledge, market commitment, commitment decisions, and current and proposed business activities. These perspectives consider that a firm internationalizes when it crosses its national border, regardless of the conditions, which is what Mexican MNEs are doing. Similarly, both perspectives consider "a sequence of independent one-off events, rather than a continuous systematic process" (Buckley & Casson, 1998: 22). The examples included here share that series of events. However, each perspective considers internationalization in a different fashion, such as entering a market, setting up operations in a second country, and importing from different markets. Moreover, Oviatt and McDougall (1994), taking into account only the Johanson and Vahle (1977) model, state that "this staged development of firm internationalization is described as an incremental, risk-adverse and reluctant adjustment to changes in a firm or its environment" (p. 50). This makes it possible to think that the outsourcing strategy has similar objectives. International outsourcing seeks similar purposes due to comparable causes beyond the purposes of this paper.

While the inward perspective is rooted in the import side, the outward perspective considers that a firm internationalizes through a series of steps when its international involvement increases: start exporting, establish export channels, start a selling subsidiary, establish a production subsidiary, and so on, becoming a real MNE. The outward perspective is rooted in the export side. The outward models do not consider the international sourcing notions. However, they leave the model open and, in that way, it is possible to add other aspects of the internationalization of a firm, such as international outsourcing, among others.

The internationalization of the firm occurs when the firm crosses its country borders, either inward or outward, eventually becoming an MNE. Research on the internationalization of the firm has mainly considered the outward direction, but the inward direction is also a way to internationalize, as is shown with the Mexican MNEs analyzed above. The different perspectives on how firms become MNEs consider aspects of evolutionary and incremental overseas involvement.

On the other hand, the description of the evolution of CEMEX, GRUMA and America Movil shows a growth strategy based on the acquisition and integration of national competitors. While it is true that the protection given by the Mexican government's economic policy of closed borders, limiting international trade, contributed to the domestic growth of these companies, it is also likely that the same restriction deprived it of the benefits usually associated with the presence of multinational companies operating in emerging economies. Finally, it deserves to be mentioned that in order to have a broader scope and a better understanding of the internationalization process of Emerging Multinational Enterprises, companies from other countries and other economic sectors should be included in this analysis. The cases presented in this chapter correspond only to some specific cases of Mexican Multinational Enterprises that have successfully established operations in international markets.

REFERENCES

Alper, A., & Sassard, S. (2013, August). America Movil makes $9.6 billion bid for rest of KPN. *Reuters*. Retrieved from http://www.reuters.com/article/2013/08/09/us-mexico-americamovil-idUSBRE97807T20130809?feedType=RSS&feedName=businessNews&rpc=408

AMX. (2005). *Informe Anual 2005: Una Gran Historia. América Móvil. ....(2010) Informe Anual 2010: Entrando a una Nueva Dimensión*. América Móvil.

Andersen, O. (1993). On the Internationalization Process of Firms: A Critical Analysis. *Journal of International Business Studies*, *24*(2), 209–231. doi:10.1057/palgrave.jibs.8490230

Arnold, U. (1989). Global Sourcing: An Indispensable Element Worldwide Competition. *International Management Review*, *29*(4), 14–28.

Aspe-Armella, P. (1993). *Economic Transformation, The Mexican Way*. The MIT Press.

Austin, J. E. (1990). *Managing in Developing Countries: Strategic Analysis and Operating Techniques*. New York: The Free Press.

Bartlett, C. A., Ghoshal, S., & Beamish, P. W. (2008). *Expanding abroad: Motivations, means, and mentalities in Transnational Management: Text, Cases, and Readings in Cross-Border Management* (5th ed.). New York: McGraw-Hill/Irwin.

Bilkey, W., & Tesar, G. (1977). The Export Behavior of Smaller Wisconsin Manufacturinf Firms. *Journal of International Business Studies*, *9*(1), 93–98. doi:10.1057/palgrave.jibs.8490783

Bowersox, D. J., & Calantone, R. J. (1998). Executive Insights: Global Logistics. *Journal of International Marketing*, *6*(4), 83–93.

Buckley, P. J., & Casson, M. C. (1976). *The Future of Multinational Enterprise*. London: The Macmillan Press. doi:10.1007/978-1-349-02899-3

Buckley, P. J., & Casson, M. C. (1998). Analyzing foreign market entry strategies: Extending the internalization approach. *Journal of International Business Studies*, *29*(3), 539–561. doi:10.1057/palgrave.jibs.8490006

CEMEX. (2015). *CEMEX Group*. Retrieved from http://www.cemex.com/AboutUs/History.aspx, on June 11, 2015.

Coulter, M. (2005). *Strategic Management in Action* (3rd ed.). Prentice Hall.

Czinkota, M. R. (1982). *Export Development Strategies: US Promotion Policies*. New York: Praeger Publishers.

Del Sol, P., & Kogan, J. (2007). Regional competitive advantage based on pioneering economic reforms: The case of Chilean FDI. *Journal of International Business Studies*, *38*(6), 901–927. doi:10.1057/palgrave.jibs.8400299

Dubrow, A. (2011, June). *A decade of discover*. The University of Texas at Austin. Retrieved from http://www.utexas.edu/know/2011/06/21/tacc_anniversary/

Dunning, J. (1973). The determinants of international production. *Oxford Economic Papers*, *25*, 289–335.

Dunning, J. (1989). The Study of International Business: A Plea for a More Interdisciplinary Approach. *Journal of International Business Studies*, *20*(3), 411–436. doi:10.1057/palgrave.jibs.8490371

Dunning, J. H. (1979). Explaining Changing Patterns of the International Production: In Defence of the Eclectic Theory. *Oxford Bulletin of Economics and Statistics*, *41*(4), 269–295. doi:10.1111/j.1468-0084.1979.mp41004003.x

Dunning, J. H. (1988). The Eclectic Paradigm of International Production: A Restatement and Some Possible Extensions. *Journal of International Business Studies*, *19*(1), 1–31. doi:10.1057/palgrave.jibs.8490372

Ellis, P. (2000). Social Ties and Foreign Market Entry. *Journal of International Business Studies*, *31*(3), 443–469. doi:10.1057/palgrave.jibs.8490916

Emis. (2015, July 27). *Companies*. EMIS Professional Database. Retrieved from http://ebiblio.cetys.mx:2083/php/companies?pc=MX&cmpy=2408922

Greiner, L. E. (1998). Evolution and revolution as organizations grow. *Harvard Business Review*, *76*(3), 55–68. PMID:10179654

GRUMA. (2015). *GRUMA Group*. Retrieved from http://www.gruma-en.com/ on July 3, 2015.

Hood, N., & Young, S. (1979). *The Economics of Multinational Enterprise*. London: Longman.

Johanson, J., & Vahle, J.-E. (1977). The Internationalization of the Firm - A Model of Knowledge Development and Increasing Foreign Market Comments. *Journal of International Business Studies*, *8*(1), 23–32. doi:10.1057/palgrave.jibs.8490676

Johanson, J., & Wiedersheim-Paul, F. (1975). The Interantionalization of the Firm: Four Swedish Cases. *Journal of Management Studies*, *12*(3), 305–322. doi:10.1111/j.1467-6486.1975.tb00514.x

Lessard, D. R., & Reavis, C. (2009). *CEMEX: Globalization "The CEMEX Way". A Study Case*. The MIT Sloan School of Management.

Medina Nuñez, I. (1995). Telefonos de Mexico: Modernizacion, Privatizacion y Nuevas Relaciones Laborales. Espiral: *Estudios sobre Estado y Sociedad*, *3*(May-Aug), 133-153.

Monczka, R. M., & Trent, R. J. (1991). Global Sourcing: A Development Approach. *International Journal of Purchasing and Materials Management*, *27*(2), 2–8.

O'Grady, S., & Lane, H. W. (1996). The Psychic Distance Paradox. *Journal of International Business Studies*, *27*(2), 309–333. doi:10.1057/palgrave.jibs.8490137

Porter, M. (1990). The Competitive Advantage of Firms in Global Industries. In *The Competitive Advantage of Nations*. New York, NY: Free Press. doi:10.1007/978-1-349-11336-1_2

Reichel, J. (1988). The Internationalization of Importing Companies. *European Journal of Marketing*, *22*(10), 31–40. doi:10.1108/EUM0000000005302

Reid, S. D. (1981). The Decision-Maker and Export Entry and Expansion. *Journal of International Business Studies*, *12*(2), 101–102. doi:10.1057/palgrave.jibs.8490581

Reuters. (2014, July). America Movil to Own Just Over Half of Telekom Austria. *New York Times*. Retrieved from http://www.nytimes.com/reuters/2014/07/14/business/14reuters-mexico-americamovil.html

Rexha, N., & Miyamoto, T. (2000). International Sourcing: An Australian Perspective. *Journal of Supply Chain Management*, *31*(1), 27–34. doi:10.1111/j.1745-493X.2000.tb00067.x

Rogers, E. M. (1962). *Diffusion of Innovation*. New York: Free Press.

Roth, K., Schweiger, D. M., & Morrison, A. J. (1992). Global Strategy Implementation at the Business Unit Level: Operational Capabilities and Administrative Mechanisms. *Journal of International Business Studies*, *22*(3), 369–402. doi:10.1057/palgrave.jibs.8490307

Rugman, A. M. (1982). Internationalization and Non-equity Forms of International Involvement. In A. M. Rugman (Ed.), *New Theories of the Multinational Enterprise* (pp. 9–23). London: Croom Helm.

Slim Helú, C. (2015, July 27) *Business Activity*. Retrieved from: http://www.carlosslim.com/act_empresarial_ing.html

Sullivan, D. (1994). Measuring the Degree of Internationalization of a Firm. *Journal of International Business Studies*, *25*(2), 325–342. doi:10.1057/palgrave.jibs.8490203

Telekom. (2015, July) Home Page. *Telekom Austria Group*. Retrieved from: http://www.telekomaustria.com

Universe. (2015, July) *Telefonos de Mexico S.A. de C.V.* Retrieved from: http://www.fundinguniverse.com/company-histories/telefonos-de-mexico-s-a-de-c-v-history/

Welch, L., & Luostarinen, R. (1988). Internationalization: Evolution of a Concept. *Journal of General Management*, *14*(2), 34–55.

Wells, L. (1983). *Third World Multinationals*. The MIT Press.

Wells, L. (2009). *Third World Multinationals: A look back*. Cambridge University Press.

Yeung, H. W. C. (1994). Third world multinationals revisited: A research critique and future agenda. *Third World Quarterly*, *15*(2), 297–317. doi:10.1080/01436599408420381

KEY TERMS AND DEFINITIONS

Emerging Multinational Enterprises: Emerging Multinational Enterprises (EMNEs) are companies that began its activities in an emerging economy and operate not only in their country of origin, but they also do in other countries. These companies operate with a global strategy to obtain maximum benefits: buy their raw materials where is cheapest; install their factories in places where they find the biggest comparative and competitive advantage; and sell their products in several markets of the world. Often, multinational enterprises are based and define their strategy in their country of origin, without any influence from their affiliates, although in different cases a strategy of multinational enterprises is to adopt the best practices of the markets where they establish their abroad operations.

International Competitive Advantage: The International or Global Competitive Advantage refers to the process of decision making and strategies execution that allow to a company outperform its competitors throughout the low costs of production, the appropriate logistic system of distribution, the skilled employees, the value added to the final product or service, among many others. The international competitive advantage is relevant to understand the process of internationalization of a company.

International Growth: The international growth refers to the process followed by a local company to operate in an international market. This process is explained in terms of the different theories of internationalization, which allow to understand why a company has decided to operate in an international market and, as a consequence, to experience international growth. The international growth contributes to increase the Gross National Product of a country.

Mexican MNEs: Mexican Multinational Enterprises (Mexican MNEs) are companies that began their operations in Mexico and currently have operations in international markets, as described for the EMNEs.

Theories of Internationalization: Theories about the internationalization of enterprises focus on the understanding of the determinants (reasons) for which a company has decided to operate in an international market. It is important to highlight that the theories of internationalization allow the understanding of what causes international trade between countries.

Chapter 9
On the Relationship between Informal and Formal Institutions, Foreign Direct Investment, and Innovation in Emerging Markets:
The Case of Russia, India, and China, 1990–2014

Natalya Smith
Heelstone Consulting Ltd., UK

Ekaterina Thomas
Staffordshire University, UK

ABSTRACT

This chapter examines innovation in socio-institutional environments of three largest and most diverse emerging markets: Russia, India and China over the period 1990-2014. It considers formal (proxied by corruption) and informal (proxied by trust) institutions and non-linear forces. It also examines the role of Foreign Direct Investment (FDI) in (the likelihood of) fostering innovation and of two research and development (R&D) inputs: R&D expenditures and personnel. A significantly positive direct effect of trust and a negative direct effect of corruption are confirmed, whilst there is a significant non-linear decreasing relationship with trust and increasing relationship with corruption. Interestingly, FDI and R&D expenditures are found to decrease innovation, whilst R&D personnel increase innovation output across the sample.

DOI: 10.4018/978-1-5225-0276-0.ch009

INTRODUCTION

Institutions matter for innovation: they help removing obstacles and provide incentives to direct self-interested individuals towards more economically productive activities (Smith & Thomas, 2014a). Consequently, strong institutions help attracting foreign direct investment (FDI) that, in turn, may determine the flow of innovation by facilitating formation, development and diffusion of new knowledge (Lipsey & Sjöholm, 2005; Smith & Thomas, 2014a,b).

Despite innovation remains the key basis of competitive advantage of nations only a few countries have been able to achieve sustainable progress, however (Smith & Thomas, 2015b). Innovation is a lengthy collaborative process, thus it requires 'innovation-prone environment' (Smith & Thomas, 2015b). What plays a significant role in this process is the social capital.

Indeed, countries abundant with more social capital have been more innovative (Florida, 2002; Fukuyama, 2003; Smith & Thomas, 2015b). Studying social capital is, therefore, important as it can reflect strength and cohesion of a society. For example, when societies are well connected (through cooperation) and highly trusting, the benefits may spillover into the whole economy.

Equally vital is studying corruption, which can deter innovation, putting innovative firms at a disadvantage (Anokhin & Schulze, 2009; Starosta de Waldemar, 2012). For example, innovators can be particularly vulnerable to extortions from government officials, because of high and inelastic demand for government-supplied goods (such as permits and licenses) (Murphy, Shleifer, & Vishny, 1993).

Corruption undermines the foundations of institutional trust (Anderson & Tverdova, 2003; Cleary & Stokes, 2006; Chang & Chu, 2006) required for the development of innovative activities. It reduces the incentives to invest in innovative ideas by negatively affecting the magnitude of rewards that can be earned from innovation.

The current research, however, has largely ignored the role of institutional environment in unlocking entrepreneurial phenomena (Chiles, Bluedorn, & Gupta, 2007). When attempts were made to examine the impact of institutions on innovation in countries outside the United States, either a case-based approach was adopted or research focused only on regulatory (or formal) environment (Manolova, Eunni, & Gyoshev, 2008).

Despite it is hardly possible to understand entrepreneurial behaviour without locating it in the social context (Friedland & Alford, 1991; Smith & Thomas, 2015b), limited research has investigated the implications of a society's institutional context for promoting innovation. This gap in extant research has led scholars to admit that institutions have been ignored (Williamson, 2000).

In particular, the complex effect of the institutional environment on innovation is understudied (Welter & Smallbone, 2003). Largely, a lack of appropriate constructs and measures (able to adequately capture the various informal and formal aspects of institutions) has impeded scholarly understanding of the institutions for promoting entrepreneurship (Meyer & Peng, 2005).

This is exactly what this study contributes to the debate. More specifically, it examines innovation in socio-institutional environments of the three largest and most diverse emerging markets: Russia, India and China (further, RICs). It does so by estimating empirically the impact of informal (proxied by trust) and formal institutions (proxied by corruption) on innovation across the countries.

Considering RICs is important for a number of reasons. These countries have been seeking global competitiveness through deployment of fiscal incentives and by leveraging human resources development in the areas of emerging opportunity in high-tech, industries driven by information and communication technology and intellectual capital.

Among RICs, innovation in China has recently grown faster than in Russia and India, suggesting that innovation determinants across these countries might differ at least in the intensity of their impact. For example, the role of institutions across RICs might be heterogeneous. Indeed, there is vast ethnic, linguistic and cultural diversity. There is also a great deal of variation in the ethnic composition, religious orientation, languages, natural resources, economic and social performances.

Moreover, there is a profound effect of the long pre-market experience on the formation of social capital that may have adopted 'a negative form' (or in a form of corruption) (Rose, 2000; Hjøllund, Paldam & Svendsen, 2001). Indeed, the 'negative form of social capital' in RICs may have resulted from poor institutions and inability of the states and public institutions to meet people's basic necessities (Fidrmuc & Gërxhani, 2008).

Firstly, the study examines the innovation-institutions nexus by considering both (i) formal (corruption) and informal (trust) institutions and (ii) linear and non-linear forces. Secondly, it examines the role of foreign direct investment (FDI) in (the likelihood of) fostering innovation, given the differences in institutions amongst RICs and non-linearity of trust and corruption.

This chapter proceeds as follows. After a brief introduction to the study's context, the key literature on innovation, institutions, social capital and corruption is discussed. Next, chapter proceeds by describing data, model and methodology used. The results are summarised afterwards. The final section concludes, outlining the key policy implications, limitations of the study and refers to potential areas for further research.

Study's Background

During the last decade, the economic performance of RICs has been significantly strong. Russia and India have grown rapidly, whilst China has been the fastest growing economy worldwide (UNCTAD, 2015). Growth in these countries, however, has been due to significant changes in the productive structure that reflected dissimilar development strategies.

Russia's economic development, for example, is heavily dependent on energy and raw material resources. Products based on natural resources and commodities have a relatively greater share of national gross domestic product (GDP) than in China and India (UNCTAD, 2015). India's economic development is characterised by a substantial growth of GDP but is mainly service-led with the share of services (in GDP) of 55 per cent in 2009, for example (UNCTAD, 2015). The competitiveness of China's industrial sector is the main source of the economic growth.

In 2009, the share of industry in the composition of GDP reached 48 per cent, with services accounting for 41 per cent. The share of technologically intensive sectors in industrial output was 42 per cent of the total value added by the manufacturing sector (UNCTAD, 2015). In the last decades, RICs have been the recipients of significant amounts of FDI. In 2008, for example (at the peak of FDI inflows) China recorded about US$108 billion, Russia US$75 billion and India US$42 billion (UNCTAD, 2015). However, again, RICs have followed different approaches to FDI.

China devised a broad strategy to expand its technological knowledge and to strengthen its domestic industries. It imposed conditions on multinational enterprises (MNEs) to carry out research and development (R&D) locally and establish joint ventures with domestic firms to enable technology transfer. Russia has liberalised its economy with few restrictions and, as a result, received more portfolio investment. Most of the investment received by the manufacturing sector has been used to acquire domestic firms. FDI policies in India focused on the role of FDI as a major source of scarce capital, employment, technology and managerial skills. From the mid-1990s, policy makers focused on attracting higher quality (rather than quantity) of FDI in R&D, design, technical support, education and training.

Russia is a former technology and military superpower and its economy has undergone a major contraction during transition towards a market economy. Russia has an exceptionally large science base and spends more on inputs into knowledge-creation processes than other countries at similar levels of GDP per capita, including other emerging economies (Smith & Thomas, 2015a). However, despite scientific potential, Russia has a relatively poor record when it comes to turning knowledge into economic or social benefits (McCarthy, Puffer, Graham, & Satinsky, 2014). Modern Russian economy has some important structural problems and relatively few high-tech industries (except for aerospace and defence).

The collapse of the Soviet Union and the transition to a market economy have dramatically affected the R&D system Russia inherited from the Soviet Union (which was unsuitable for a market, due to its specific characteristics: it was large, centralised and government-financed). In the 1990s, R&D sector in Russia was transformed in the following ways. Government finding grew by 43 per cent in 1998-2004 and by 54 per cent in 2004-07 with about 39 per cent spent on basic research (Science and Technology Indicators, 2008). The number of researchers was around 48 per cent of R&D personnel in 2006 (Science and Technology Indicators, 2008).

At the same time, since beginning of the 2000s, innovation activity in Russia remained at 9-10 per cent as compared to 21 per cent in Hungary and 73 per cent in Germany (Indicators of Innovation, 2008). Demand for R&D came mostly from the government, with the federal budget remaining the key source for R&D finding, growing by almost three-fold in 1998-2007 (Rosstat). The supply of R&D and innovation in Russia is insufficient and based towards R&D.

Russia's technology exports amount to US$ 0.63 billion, as compared to US$ 1.6 billion in Hungary, US$3.3 billion in Finland and US$ 75.4 billion in the United States (Gokhberg, 2007). The relatively high patenting activity (about 23,000 applications per year, ranking Russia 6th highest in the world) and a low share of registered patent licenses compared with the number of annually registered patents of 5-6 per cent (Gokhberg, 2007) is explained by the lack of competitiveness of Russian technologies.

In the era of the planned economy, the business sector in China (in terms of innovation) was weak, with hardly any R&D performed at times. Firms were output-based, with few (if any) incentives for efficiency and profit. Similar to Russia, the research institutions were funded by the government. Since 1978, China went through a transition towards a market-based Science and Technology (S&T) system and several major changes were made, including great efforts to make firms to become the main players in the national innovation system.

S&T and innovation have been a strong force in Chinese economic growth that is strongly dependent on foreign technology and FDI: since the beginning of the 2000s, foreign-invested firms accounted for more than 85 per cent of all high-tech exports (National Bureau of Statistics, 2006). China made substantial investments in basic education. It has the highest literacy rate and the highest average educational levels compare to India and Brazil (UNCTAD, 2015). By 2005, its enrolment rate reached 19 per cent and it now employs the largest number of human resources in R&D in the world, with more than 35 million people involved in S&T system (UNCTAD, 2015)

As shown by the 1958 Science Policy Resolution, India was among the pioneering developing countries to recognise the role of S&T in bringing about the socio-economic change. Various policy measures to help building S&T infrastructure, fiscal policies (including incentives to promote R&D) and various other policies (industry, trade and investment-related) were formulated to promote domestic generation of technology.

Starting in the 1950s, India made some progress in setting up a number of Institutes of Technology and several Institutes of Management, which produced a critical mass of well-educated English speaking professionals who are instrumental in India's emergence in software industry. Despite this, literacy rates in India still remains low with literacy rates among woman being 52 per cent and 27 per cent among men (UNCTAD, 2015).

LITERATURE REVIEW

If entrepreneurship is truly a purposeful activity that facilitates economic prosperity and growth, institutions that provide an enabling environment to support innovation need to be better understood. Indeed, supporting institutions is one of the key determinants of a success in the innovation process (Nelson & Nelson, 2002) and the rate and shape of entrepreneurial activities in a society is strongly influenced by its institutional environment (Chiles et al., 2007; Smith & Thomas, 2015b).

Institutions determine 'the rules of the game' in a country and act as constraints and opportunities shaping human interaction (North, 1990). In developing economies, where the state is a major actor in facilitating the appropriate environment for achieving a strong economy, institutions can have a particularly strong influence (Dahles, 2008).

Institutions vary between countries. For example, in 'innovation-averse' economies, institutions may deter innovation process (Smith & Thomas, 2015b). Corrupt institutions erode trust in institutions and among individuals (Tabellini, 2008) and weak formal institutions suppress cultural transmission of pro-social norms and civic virtues (Tabellini, 2008), while entrenching social practices of adjustment to 'bad institutions' (Smith & Thomas, 2015b).

THE ROLE OF SOCIAL CAPITAL AND TRUST

A great deal of attention is paid to the role of social capital in innovation process (Putnam, Leonardi & Nanetti, 1994; Zak & Knack 2001; Akçomak & Ter Weel, 2009; Dixit, 2009). As a multifaceted concept, social capital captures different aspects (Bjørnskov, 2006) and the selection of indicators to proxy it, therefore, has been heavily conditioned by the availability of data.

In a broad sense, social capital is understood as a set of informal institutions (based on social relationships, networks and associations) that create shared knowledge, mutual trust, social norms and unwritten rules (Durlauf & Aghion, 2005). Social capital can facilitate coordination and cooperation for mutual benefit and it helps to solve problems of collective action by reducing monitoring costs and duplication (Putnam et al., 1994). This, in turn, translates into a reduction of transaction costs in economic operations (Maskell, 2001; Akçomak & Ter Weel, 2009).

Social capital can facilitate complex agreements by mitigating information asymmetries between negotiating parties (Dearmon & Grier, 2009) and can ease the knowledge diffusion and innovation processes (Akçomak & Ter Weel, 2009). As it lowers the costs of working together, it can facilitate cooperation. For example, people might have more confidence to invest in collective activities when they know that others will also do so. People are also less likely to engage in unproductive private actions that result in negative impacts (such as resource degradation).

Trust is one of the central aspects of social capital. The environment of mutual trust, participation and cooperation, where social capital is abundant, can stimulate creativity and entrepreneurship, leading to a higher growth (Putnam et al., 1994; Zak & Knack, 2001; Akçomak & Ter Weel, 2009).

Trust helps cooperation. It reduces transaction costs between people liberating resources as a result. For example, instead of having to invest in monitoring others, individuals may be able to trust them to act as expected. This can save money and time and can help creating a social obligation. Trusting someone engenders reciprocal trust (or trust in individuals whom people know and trust in 'strangers') that arises because of people's confidence in a known social structure. Trust takes time to build and is easily broken (Fukuyama, 2003), and when a society is pervaded by distrust, cooperative arrangements are unlikely to emerge.

Innovation is not generated in isolation: it depends on successful sharing of tacit and codified knowledge (Maskell, 2001; Fukuyama, 2003; Dakhli & De Clercq, 2004; Doh & Acs, 2010; De Dominicis, Florax, & De Groot, 2013; Smith & Thomas, 2015b). However, information exchange within a network (or across networks) requires a high degree of trust between partners and common cultural, institutional and entrepreneurial activities (Doloreux & Parto, 2005).

Wider social setting (such as beliefs, norms and attitudes of the citizens towards each other) is also vital for innovation (Lundvall, 2007). Empirical studies find evidence of the positive impact of social capital on innovation (Murphy, 2002; Cainelli, Mancinelli, & Mazzanti, 2007; Carmona-Lavado, Cuevas-Rodríguez, & Cabello-Medina, 2010; Hsieh & Tsai, 2007).

Trusting relations either are formed through personal contacts through time or may result indirectly from institutions built in the past (Beugelsdijk, 2006; Akçomak & Ter Weel, 2009; Tabellini, 2008). In both cases, highly trustful environments are characterised by sharing of knowledge and higher degree of involvement in innovative activities.

In some instances, informal institutions (or trusted social networks) can replace formal structures (Williamson, 2009; Steer & Sen, 2010; Bjørnskov, 2011). As a regulating mechanism, informal institutions can provide stability and meaning in social behaviour (Scott, 2008).

Formal institutions can have an effect on partner collaborations (Oxley, 1999; Luo, Zhou, & Liu, 2005) by infusing trust into firms and markets and assisting in building local innovation capabilities (Nelson & Nelson, 2002; Mathews & Hu, 2007). In turn, informal institutions can have an impact on innovation through affecting behaviour and attitudes (Shane, Venkataraman, & McMillan, 1995).

Social Capital in RICs

Russia's earlier accounts of social capital points at the lack of trust, capacity for self-organisation, low and 'anti-modern' social capital (characterised by rejecting modern organisations and procedures) that were used to insulate one from the state institutions (Rose, 2000), resulting in discord between the state and its citizens. The radius of trust was very short, including only close friends (Fukuyama, 2003), because its Soviet legacy has left the society with low levels of generalised trust (Misztal, 1996), making cooperation with strangers (for example, business deals) difficult.

Although new market opportunities require the emerging economies to shift from redistributive bureaucracy to open markets (Nee, 1996), current policies in Russia hold significant potential for 'top-down restoration of public trust and social cohesion' (Twigg & Schecter, 2002). Lack of trust, short-termism, profit maximisation and opportunistic behaviour of business owners is a common problem deterring innovation (Bek, Bek, Sheresheva, & Johnston, 2013).

Colton (1995, p. 748) points at the fact that it is the 'history' that 'predisposes Russians toward mutual mistrust and stoic acceptance of what the government does rather than self-confident influence over it'. Saying that, 'political interests will emerge as economic transformation spawns property rights and a civil society, in which members have pecuniary and psychic stakes in what the government does' (Colton, 1995, p. 749).

Gaddy & Ickes (1999, p. 80) argue that much of the Russian modern economy is beset by 'negative' social capital. In particular, regional and national elites have a mutual interest in preserving 'value destroying' Soviet era enterprises. To preserve their own influence, these elites make use personal connections with government officials and oligarchs to maintain their personal influence. In this destructive cycle, ownership of firms nominally changes hands but no real economic reform takes place.

Interestingly, Ledeneva's (1998) research on personal networks (or 'connections') and informal exchange in Russia provides strong evidence that mutual trust is a key component in the functioning of such networks. In line, the Petro's (1995) analysis demonstrates that Russia has democratic traditions, which may facilitate its contemporary democratic development. Marsh (2000) finds that social capital exists in many regions of Russia and confirms that higher levels of social capital associate with higher levels of democracy. Therefore, it appears that social capital can actually facilitate the democratic development of post-Communist societies (Marsh, 2000, p. 198).

India, on the contrary, lacks social capital and social networks are mainly centred on family and identity. A culture of serial entrepreneurship and mobility of entrepreneurial talent across business sectors remains absent: its social structure tends to promote business activity between people of the same community and social class, resulting in a lack of trust and collaboration. Castes are found to be a significant factor in Indian social stratification system (Gupta, 1991; Srinivas, 1996; Sinha, 2005). These castes are endogamous with clear boundaries and permeate Indian social life in many ways.

Traditionally, ritual distance between castes defined, for example, who one may or may not eat with. While this stylised distance is declining in modern India (at least between the upper castes), endogamous marriage and close-knit kinship patterns preserve the distance between various castes. Residential segregation in village life makes inter-group relationships difficult to build. Even in urban areas many residential cooperative societies are set up by people from the same community resulting in continuation of traditional distance. Caste and language cluster at the level of the streets (Sharma, 2000).

China, on another hand, is a traditionally network-oriented economy, where social capital appears to be more important (Zhang & Fung, 2006). The relations among different social capital dimensions (such as social interaction, trust, exchange of information) in China are consistent with Guanxi-based relationships (social or personal connections with appropriate authorities or individuals, see Park & Luo, 2001).

Guanxi is closely related to social capital, which is, indeed, important in developing business relationships in Chinese culture (Theingi & Phungphol, 2008; Li, Ye, & Sheu, 2014). Guanxi is also conducive to nurturing trust between business partners (Luo, Shenkar, & Nyaw 2002). In practice, business deals in China often require a lengthy and elaborate courtship. Firms typically take time to engage in social interaction to establish Guanxi and mutual trust before allowing for meaningful information sharing. This evolving process may explain the indirect rather than direct effect of social interactions. Moreover, there is evidence suggesting the effect of Guanxi on developing common business interests and presenting a possible reciprocal causal relationship between trust and shared vision (Hitt, Lee, & Yucel, 2002).

Social network ties can help firms respond to changes in the business environment and to reduce opportunistic behaviour and moral hazard behaviour, due to the lack of formal legal framework and, hence, improve information sharing among supply chain partners (Li et al., 2014). However, foreign investors in China should develop and nurture mutual trust with local partners in order to foster a shared mindset (Buckley, Clegg, & Tan, 2006).

CORRUPTION

Corruption affects innovation (Smith et al., 2014b; Smith & Thomas, 2015a) but received only limited attention in the innovation literature. Theoretical arguments and some empirical findings point at both negative and positive effects of corruption (Smith, Thomas, & Antoniou, 2014b; Smith & Thomas, 2015a). On the one hand, corruption can discourage innovation (Jain, 2001; Aidt, 2003): it can increase the cost of investments in innovation, leading to greater inefficiencies and lower profitability (Mauro, 1995; Rose-Ackerman, 1999).

Higher bribes can reduce the barriers to entry, thus firms entering corrupt markets may compromise on the quality of their products (Rose-Ackerman, 1999). Corruption can weaken property rights protection, technology transfer and, thus, innovation (Fosu, Bates, & Hoeffler, 2006). Rent-seeking bureaucrats may create a private market for public goods (such as protection of property rights), limiting the number of firms entering the market through 'facilitation payments' (Levin & Satarov, 2000; Hellman, Jones, & Kaufmann, 2003; Smith & Thomas, 2015a).

Murphy et al. (1993) note that corrupt firms often report developed advanced technologies even when this is not the case. As a result, the amount of innovative activity in corrupt environments might seem larger not due to innovation but corruption. Bureaucrats may also reject promising projects (until a threshold level of bribe, which could be extracted, is reached), often waiting until the maximum offer is made (Qian & Xu, 1998; Smith & Thomas, 2015a).

That said, corruption can facilitate innovation: it may help remove obstacles to investment (Leff, 1964; Smith & Thomas, 2015a) by allocating investment by the most efficient and innovative firms, given that they may be able to pay the highest bribes (Smith & Thomas, 2014a; Smith & Thomas, 2015a). Corruption can improve time efficiency of introducing innovation, allowing firms to deal with bureaucracy (or red tape).

By encouraging rent-seeking behaviour, officials can allow firms to win the innovation race (Smith & Thomas, 2015a). Thus, corruption may act as an incentive for bureaucrats to help to fasten the innovation process. That is, in the governance systems that do not allow much scope for innovation, corruption might facilitate entrepreneurial activities (Anokhin & Schulze, 2009: Heckelman & Powell, 2010).

Corruption in RICs

While corruption is a common problem across emerging markets, RICs appear to have a particularly bad reputation. According to the Global Financial Integrity (2013), for example, RICs are the most corrupt amongst other emerging countries. Accordingly, China is the most corrupt of the three, contributing just under US$ 250 billion in illegal financial flows in 2012, followed by Russia whose illegal financial flows were estimated at US$ 125 billion, and India that contributed just over US$ 100 billion to the world's growing pool of illegal money.

Corruption prevalence in Russia is often blamed on behavioural norms inherited from the Soviet period (Roaf, 2000) and the way Russia pursued its political and economic transition in the 1990s (Larsson, 2006). As in many other countries, corruption in Russia results from a combination of opportunities and incentives, which may have arisen over time (Roaf, 2000). For example, Russia's complex tax and customs systems, financial market regulation, and wide-ranging regulations on businesses (including legal rights) provide ample opportunities for abuse of power (Roaf, 2000).

Similar to India, incentives to engage in corrupt behaviour include low government salaries, bureaucracy, weak legal enforcement, and the poor example of standards of public conduct set by the political and business elite. Larsson (2006), for example, explains that corruption in Russia is more damaging than in China due to differences in comparative advantage and the way the two countries persuaded the economic reforms.

When China launched reforms, its comparative advantage was in low-tech, labour- intensive production, so it competed for investment and export markets with other low-wage economies, many of which were also highly corrupt. When Russia launched economic reforms, it had comparative advantages in natural resource extraction and capital- and knowledge-intensive production.

The relatively large gap between comparative advantage and institutional development in Russia, and the high degree of 'fit'' between these attributes in the case of China can help explaining why Russia has been less successful than China in attracting FDI (Larsson, 2006).

Corruption in reform-era China has taken two main forms (He, 2000). It served as a means for non-state actors to develop alongside the planned economy, dominated by large state-owned actors. It also became a means by which local governments competed for favours from the central government (such as preferential financial treatment and special 'flexibility' initially accorded only to special economic zones).

Political corruption has, thus, contributed to the establishment and spread of competitive and growth-enhancing markets and institutions. Local governments in China are also frequently engaged in predatory activities (such as illegal taxation, see Wedeman, 2004). Corruption has become a major social and political issue in China since 1978 when Chinese authorities began to implement the policy of "reform and opening". During the 1990s, the severity of corruption (as reflected in the percentage of major corrupt cases filed) continued to increase (Wedeman, 2008). High-level corruption has increased more rapidly than "ordinary" corruption and other forms of official malfeasance.

Corruption remains to be a serious problem in India. According to the Global Corruption Barometer Survey 2013, more than half of the 1,025 Indian respondents reported having paid a bribe in 2012. The biggest cause of corruption in India is due to the fact that the officials dealing with corruption are inefficient and there is a lack of laws and enforcement (the corrupt are rarely caught and, if caught, it is rarely punished) (Sondhi, 2000).

Corruption in India has become an acceptance in a social behaviour of Indian citizens who often show respect for the corrupt. It involves not just the government actors but also the private sector. Price regulation, reservations for small scale industry, import and export controls, the licensing and permit system, labour legislation and other various interferences in financial markets are some of the many examples of interactions between the government and the corporate sector (Hestona & Kumar, 2008). It is common amongst businesses to manipulate accounts and conduct transactions off the books to evade taxes.

METHODOLOGY

The data used in this study are from the following sources. Data on innovation inputs/outputs are from the World Bank (the Global Indicators). Data on informal institutions (trust) are from the World Value Survey. Data on formal institutions (corruption) are from the Transparency International (the Corruption Perception Index). Due to data availability, the time line of this study is limited to 1990-2014.

To examine the impact of institutions as an innovation predictor across Russia, India and China, the study uses a (modified) knowledge production function inspired by the 'traditional' framework of

Griliches (1979). In this production function, innovation is proxied by the patent intensity and explained by institutions along with key R&D inputs.

The model takes the following form:

$$PATRESit = \beta 0 + \beta 1TRUSTit + \beta 2TRUSTSQit + \beta 3CORRit + \beta 4CORRSQit + \beta 5FDIit + \beta Xit + \varepsilon it \quad (1)$$

where *PATRES* is the innovation output (measured by the patents filed by residents) in a country *i* at time *t*; *TRUST* controls for the impact of informal institutions and is measured by the percentage of people from the World Value Survey that gave a positive answer to the question whether most people in their country can be trusted; *CORR* controls for the impact of formal institutions and is measured by the Transparency International Corruption Perception Index; *FDI* controls for FDI-related spillovers and is measured by the net inflow of FDI in GDP.

Should trust and corruption affect innovation non-linearly, their true effects can be misinterpreted. Analogously, if both effects are heterogenous across countries, adopting the usual estimation methods may lead to underestimation (or overestimation) of the effects. To check the proposition that institutions may affect innovation non-linearly, two quadratic terms (*TRUSTSQ* and *CORRSQ*) were added to Equation (1).

Xit in Equation (1) is the vector of explanatory variables and includes *RDE* (measured by monetary expenditures on R&D) that accounts for the 'allocation of resources to research and other information-generating activities in response to perceived profit opportunities' (Grossman & Helpman, 1991, p. 6); *RDP* (measured by the number of R&D personnel per capita) accounts for human capital and the fact that innovation is a knowledge intensive activity. The error term is modelled as $\varepsilon it = \eta i + mt + \lambda it$, where η and m are time- and regional-invariant effects, respectively, and λ is a random disturbance.

The dependent variable is the patent intensity. However used widely in the empirical studies, this measure is not without controversy. Firstly, not all industries tend to patent with the same intensity and, in an emerging country context, the number of firms or organisations in a position to file patents is rather limited. Secondly, patents measure inventions and tend to be biased towards particular sectors of the economy where inventions are protected via patenting (rather than via trademarks or secrecy) (OECD, 2009).

Since minor innovations/adaptations in emerging countries are patentable, most innovative activity may not be counted (Fagerberg & Srholec, 2009). This is an important issue in the case of China and India, although as both countries rapidly approach the technological frontier in a number of sectors, this objection may be becoming less pertinent.

Other caveats remain. Patent counts that include both domestic and foreign firms may not fully capture domestic innovation capacity (Li & Pai, 2010). In the case of MNEs, patents may be filed in any office around the world, regardless of where the invention takes place, making it hard to assign patents to specific locations. In a study of Chinese patents, Duan & Kong (2008), for example, observe that most 'Chinese' applications during 1988-2007 were owned by MNEs.

In India, the picture is more complex. Albuquerque (2003), for example, finds that between 1981 and 2001, a third of Indian patent applications had foreign assignees, higher than Brazil, South Africa, or Mexico. However, when Mani (2004) examined the Indian-based inventors during the 1990s, 85 per cent of the patents granted were reported to be awarded to public research institutes, as well as to local firms and individuals-as opposed to 'foreign affiliates located in India'.

Table 1. Description of variables and sources

PATRES: The number of patents filed by residents per 1 mln. population (Source: the World Bank)
RDE: Expenditures on R&D (Source: the World Bank)
RDP: The number of people involved in R&D (per 1 mln. population) (Source: the World Bank)
TRUST: Percentage of people said 'most people in their country can be trusted' (%; Source: the World Value Survey)
CORR: Corruption Perception Index (index; Source: the Transparency International)
FDI: Share of net inflow of Foreign Direct Investment in GDP (%; Source: the World Bank)

To deal with these issues, the study opts for the patents filed by residents (only) as a measure of innovation. All three countries in the sample are very heterogenous. To check if this is an econometric issue, the Breusch-Pagan/Cook-Weisberg test was used. As large chi-squares were found, which indicates heteroscedasticity in the sample, the study opted for the instrumental variables (GMM) regression with fixed effects to control for country-specific characteristics not included in the model that is preferred in this case (Baum, Schaffer & Stillman, 2003).

Description of the variables used in the study is in Table 1. Descriptive statistics is in Table 2. Correlation matrix is in Table 3. The results are in Table 4.

DISCUSSION OF RESULTS

The theory of social capital argues that in places with high levels of social capital people are more willing to work together and take chances on risky ideas. It follows, therefore, that high social capital fuels innovation. This study confirms that innovation outputs are enhanced by higher trust, whilst the effect of corruption has a significantly adverse effect on innovation output.

The study reveals a non-linear relationship between trust, corruption and innovation. The quadratic term between trust and innovation shows a negative sign. This means that innovation across countries is fostered by more trust up to a point and after this (given) threshold is reached, an increase in trust decreases innovation, at the margin. With corruption, the relationship is opposite: the square term of corruption exhibits a positive impact on innovation.

That means that innovation outcomes are minimised by corruption but, again, up to a point: the negative effect of corruption start to decrease after a given threshold is exceeded. Above this threshold,

Table 2. Descriptive statistics

Variable	Obs.	Mean	Standard Deviation	Minimum	Maximum
PATRES	68	0.0001	0.0001	1.31E-06	0.0004
RDE	50	0.009	0.005	0.002	0.031
RDP	22	3027.386	1564.677	197.6288	4441.388
TRUST	75	36.94	12.96705	20.7	60.3
CORR	59	0.658661	0.1710472	0.4	0.976
FDI	70	2.316608	1.678091	0.0267563	6.246294

Note: For a description of variables' abbreviations, see Table 1.

Table 3. Correlation matrix

	PATRES	*RDE*	*RDP*	*TRUST*	*CORR*	*FDI*
PATRES	1					
RDE	-0.2381	1				
RDP	0.8836	0.2196	1			
TRUST	-0.5275	-0.2897	-0.4014	1		
CORR	0.2857	0.4323	0.4497	-0.1044	1	
FDI	-0.3925	-0.5790	-0.4021	0.4056	-0.4717	1

Note: For a description of variables' abbreviations, see Table 1.

Table 4. The impact of informal institutions (trust) and formal institutions (corruption) on innovation across Russia, China and India (1990-2014)

Variables	Model 1	Model 2	Model 3	Model 4	Model 5	Model 6	Model 7	Model 8	Model 9
TRUST	1.991**	4.010***	2.603***				3.007***	1.314**	1.832***
	(1.172)	(0.922)	(0.937)				(1.022)	(0.666)	(0.640)
TRUSTSQ	-0.038*	-0.076***	-0.050***				-0.057***	-0.025**	-0.035***
	(0.022)	(0.017)	(0.018)				(0.019)	(0.012)	(0.012)
CORR				-22.13***	-16.70***	-18.33***	-13.09***	-12.68***	-12.21***
				(3.205)	(3.146)	(2.571)	(3.795)	(3.184)	(2.545)
CORRSQ				14.59***	10.40***	11.67***	8.513***	7.714***	7.641***
				(2.186)	(2.080)	(1.705)	(2.550)	(2.095)	(1.658)
RDE	-0.372***	-0.226***	-0.354***	-0.428***	-0.342***	-0.379***	-0.230***	-0.260***	-0.293***
	(0.070)	(0.073)	(0.054)	(0.092)	(0.068)	(0.0642)	(0.066)	(0.093)	(0.0559)
RDP	1.379	1.533**	1.788**	0.240	0.032	0.431	0.478**	0.081	0.650**
	(1.094)	(0.627)	(0.824)	(0.573)	(0.568)	(0.484)	(0.233)	(0.447)	(0.256)
FDI	-0.228**	-0.217**	-0.212***	-0.067*	-0.119*	-0.079*	-0.165*	-0.164*	-0.156**
	(0.100)	(0.094)	(0.076)	(0.106)	(0.087)	(0.076)	(0.092)	(0.085)	(0.066)
Constant	-47.47***	-75.39***	-58.37***	-5.371	-3.465	-6.643	-48.81***	-22.55**	-34.05***
	(17.19)	(12.70)	(13.91)	(5.866)	(5.824)	(5.002)	(15.48)	(9.487)	(9.474)
Observations	22	22	22	22	22	22	22	22	22
R-squared	0.990	0.969	0.988	0.964	0.996	0.992	0.982	0.997	0.996

Note: Robust standard errors in parentheses; all variables are used in natural logarithms. For a description of variables' abbreviations, see Table 1. *** $p<0.01$, ** $p<0.05$, * $p<0.1$.

a decrease in corruption decreases innovation, at the margin. This happens possibly due to the opposite effects that institutional complexity has on the innovation process: before the effect of institutions (formal and informal) begins to increase, countries need to reach a certain (minimum of) institutional level at which institutions can benefit innovation.

The significance of the quadratic term of corruption implies that innovation is deterred in the countries that are more corrupt but when a given threshold of corruption is reached/exceeded, as countries become more corrupt, corruption starts to benefit innovation (as in Smith et al., 2014b). This potentially indicates that as corruption gets widespread (and there are more actors involved in corrupt activities) across the countries, the innovation clusters (the areas with higher innovation) may become more corrupt with more firms involved in corrupt practices.

Finally, FDI exerts a significantly negative effect on innovation. This finding is interesting: if more innovative countries had attracted comparably significant levels but from other corrupt nations, this could have resulted in lower rates of domestic innovation (as in Anokhin & Schulze, 2009). More corrupt places are usually the locations with weak institutions. MNEs may be tempted to go to these locations due to a higher likelihood of obtaining some preferential treatments (Smith & Thomas, 2015a), resulting in more corruption.

CONCLUSION

This study examined the relationship between informal (trust) and formal institutions (corruption), FDI and innovation across Russia, India and China. The main assumption was that individuals that belong to networks with a higher level of social capital are likely to innovate more and that innovation is likely to be higher in the societies with lower corruption. That is, it was expected that innovation output would be higher in countries with higher level of social capital and lower level of corruption. Using a panel data covering the period 1990-2014, the study confirmed these assumptions.

What the study also finds is that the positive effect of trust and negative effect of corruption on innovation is to decline and increase (respectively) after a given threshold of trust/corruption is reached. This might imply that as the relationships between individuals and firms involved in innovation become more 'trustful', these actors might become more 'insulated' from outside information and challenges necessary for innovation to be successful. As the relationships become more trusting in corrupt environments, the actors involved in R&D process might also become more corrupt or become more to involve themselves in corrupt practices.

To deal with a high level of uncertainty (caused by institutional weakness), people might organise themselves in small groups of close friends, which may not foster trust. Instead, tightly controlled relationships may reinforce social obligations and expectations that may limit the freedom of economic agents to recognise and exploit new opportunity (Uzzi, 1997; Light & Izralowitz, 1997). This implies that, as relationships across the countries become more trusting, the areas in which innovation happens may become complacent and 'insulated' from outside information and challenges (necessary for innovation to be successful).

Moreover, creative people (that is, entrepreneurs) may choose not to live in places with high social capital. Instead, they might be found in the environments with low social capital (cities, college towns and 'akadem-gorodki or 'science-cities' as, for example, in Russia) where they can fit in quickly but still find their ideas challenged by other people. This finding has implications for nurturing innovation within firms: firms that foster diversity and openness internally (even at the cost of some cohesiveness) may do better in attracting talented and creative employees and encouraging innovative collaboration.

SOLUTIONS AND RECOMMENDATIONS

The findings presented in this study are critical for policy-makers. More innovative countries are expected to develop better and more rapidly. That is, their prosperity is determined by innovation. Innovation is now seen as a collaborative process between creative people, transforming the ideas into finished product (for example, patents) in which the role of institutions is important. Indeed, for this process to be beneficial strong institutions are vital.

Importantly, trusting can promote the sort of conformity that undermines innovation in the long run: as the maximum level of trust is reached, strong ties will not allow (perhaps, a basic level of) information sharing and collaboration. Therefore, when ties become too strong (if this point is possible to judge), it is important to permit firms and individuals/newcomers with different ideas to be accepted into the social networks.

In that regard, immigration can be a useful tool in fostering innovation, by accepting the entry of a workforce capable of making a real impact on innovation outcomes. That is, immigration reforms promoting greater diversity might help to increase the innovation rates. Empirical evidence shows that Russia, for example, could benefit from a more diverse set of firms and openness to migration (Smith & Thomas, 2015b): diversity was to provide an additional source of an advantage.

Corruption can be caused by uncertainty in the environment or in economic activities (caused by the institutional weakness). To reduce uncertainty experienced by firms-innovators, building an environment that increases information flow among the actors is important. For policy-makers this implies the need to improve the business operations and regulations by improving the existing or introducing the new institutions. That is, more powerful institutions have to be placed to help entrepreneurs to channel their efforts in the right direction, that is, into productive rather than unproductive market activities (for example, legal and political such as lobbying and lawsuits).

The role of governments is critical in fighting corruption. There is a strong incentive for bureaucrats to behave opportunistically and to maximise their budgets at the expense of executing public policies efficiently and effectively. The absence of competition among government agencies can result in output that is significantly larger than that which would have been produced in a competitive environment under similar circumstances (Niskanen, 1975; Lowenberg, 1992).

Society as a whole would benefit if individuals cooperated. However, unless the government's intervention in private exchange is sufficiently constrained by the constitution, a society may deteriorate into a state whose regulatory powers are used by special interest groups to effect inefficient wealth redistribution in their favour (Wiseman, 1990).

RICs can create social capital to prosper in the modern world. At the macro level, market competition can facilitate the creation of social capital and trust. Meaningful economic reforms, rewarding productivity gains and encouraging competition are imperative and should be opted for and economic structures that promote productivity should be put in place.

At the micro level, the best way to create social capital may be by pursuing the dreams and ambitions of innovators, even if it seems difficult or impossible at first. Indeed, getting out of the 'comfort zone' and trying new things, forming groups and organisations where none exist, and bringing together like-minded people whose values and ideas are aligned, though seemingly innocuous, might be deeply transformational.

LIMITATIONS AND FUTURE RESEARCH DIRECTIONS

One of the main limitations of this study is the FDI data available for the analysis. Firstly, the effect of FDI through home institutions may be related to differences among industries. Therefore, examining the effects of institutional changes along with FDI from different industries can be a potential area for further research. It is important, for example, to test further how exactly informal institutions interact with the formal institutions when impacting FDI.

Further testing the insignificance of FDI for innovation in the context of Russia, China and India is vital. For example, due to data availability it was not possible to differentiate between FDI sources. To test whether insignificant association between FDI and innovation is due to the fact that corruption in the countries sampled had caused them to attract low quality FDI (FDI from corrupt countries) better/ disaggregated FDI data level are needed.

Finally, economists have studied the impact of immigration on a variety of host country outcomes. However, the impact of immigration on innovation has received less attention (one exception is the study of Smith & Thomas, 2015b) and needs to be addressed in the further studies. Another understudied area when it comes to innovation is the role of governments. Despite their involvement in R&D process, without a doubt, is critical, the exact effect of such an involvement (also studying the link between rent-seeking and innovation) worth research attention.

REFERENCES

Aidt, T. S. (2003). Economic analysis of corruption: A survey. *The Economic Journal*, *113*(491), 632–652. doi:10.1046/j.0013-0133.2003.00171.x

Akçomak, I. S., & Ter Weel, B. (2009). Social capital, innovation and growth: Evidence from Europe. *European Economic Review*, *53*(5), 544–567. doi:10.1016/j.euroecorev.2008.10.001

Albuquerque, E. (2003). *Immature systems of innovation: Introductory notes about a comparison between South Africa, India, Mexico and Brazil based on science and technology statistics*. Available at: http://www.cedeplar.ufmg.br/pesquisas/td/TD%20221.pdf

Anderson, C. J., & Tverdova, Y. V. (2003). Corruption, political allegiances, and attitudes toward government in contemporary democracies. *American Journal of Political Science*, *47*(1), 91–109. doi:10.1111/1540-5907.00007

Anokhin, S., & Schulze, W. S. (2009). Entrepreneurship, innovation, and corruption. *Journal of Business Venturing*, *24*(5), 465–476. doi:10.1016/j.jbusvent.2008.06.001

Baum, C. F., Schaffer, M. E., & Stillman, S. (2003). Instrumental variables and GMM: Estimation and testing. *The Stata Journal*, *3*(1), 1–31.

Bek, M. A., Bek, N. N., Sheresheva, M. Y., & Johnston, W. J. (2013). Perspectives of SME innovation clusters development in Russia. *Journal of Business and Industrial Marketing*, *28*(3), 240–259. doi:10.1108/08858621311302895

Beugelsdijk, S. (2006). A note on the theory and measurement of trust in explaining differences in economic growth. *Cambridge Journal of Economics*, *30*(3), 371–387. doi:10.1093/cje/bei064

Bjørnskov, C. (2006). The multiple facets of social capital. *European Journal of Political Economy*, *22*(1), 22–40. doi:10.1016/j.ejpoleco.2005.05.006

Bjørnskov, C. (2011). Combating corruption: On the interplay between institutional quality and social trust. *The Journal of Law & Economics*, *54*(1), 135–159. doi:10.1086/652421

Buckley, P. J., Clegg, J., & Tan, H. (2006). Cultural awareness in knowledge transfer to China-the role of guanxi and mianzi. *Journal of World Business*, *41*(3), 275–288. doi:10.1016/j.jwb.2006.01.008

Cainelli, G., Mancinelli, S., & Mazzanti, M. (2007). Social capital and innovation dynamics in district-based local systems. *Journal of Socio-Economics*, *36*(6), 932–948. doi:10.1016/j.socec.2007.01.023

Carmona-Lavado, A., Cuevas-Rodríguez, G., & Cabello-Medina, C. (2010). Social and organisational capital: Building the context for innovation. *Industrial Marketing Management*, *39*(4), 681–690. doi:10.1016/j.indmarman.2009.09.003

Chang, E. C., & Chu, Y. (2006). Corruption and trust: Exceptionalism in Asian democracies? *The Journal of Politics*, *68*(02), 259–271. doi:10.1111/j.1468-2508.2006.00404.x

Chiles, T. H., Bluedorn, A. C., & Gupta, V. K. (2007). Beyond creating distraction and entrepreneurial discover: A radical Austrian approach to entrepreneurship. *Organization Studies*, *28*(4), 467–493. doi:10.1177/0170840606067996

Cleary, M. R., & Stokes, S. C. (2006). *Democracy and the culture of skepticism: Political trust in Argentina and Mexico*. New York, NY: Russell Sage.

Colton, T. (1995). *Moscow: Governing the socialist metropolis*. Cambridge: Belknap Press. doi:10.4159/harvard.9780674283725

Dahles, H. (2008). Entrepreneurship and the legacies of a development state: Singapore enterprises venturing across boarders. *Journal of Developmental Entrepreneurship*, *13*(4), 485–508. doi:10.1142/S1084946708001095

Dakhli, M., & De Clercq, D. (2004). Human capital, social capital, and innovation: A multi-country study. *Entrepreneurship and Regional Development*, *16*(2), 107–128. doi:10.1080/08985620410001677835

De Dominicis, L., Florax, R. J., & De Groot, H. L. (2013). Regional clusters of innovative activity in Europe: Are social capital and geographical proximity key determinants? *Applied Economics*, *45*(17), 2325–2335. doi:10.1080/00036846.2012.663474

Dearmon, J., & Grier, K. (2009). Trust and development. *Journal of Economic Behavior & Organization*, *71*(2), 210–220. doi:10.1016/j.jebo.2009.02.011

Dixit, A. (2009). Governance institutions and economic activity. *The American Economic Review*, 3–24.

Doh, S., & Acs, Z. J. (2010). Innovation and social capital: A cross-country investigation. *Industry and Innovation*, *17*(3), 241–262. doi:10.1080/13662711003790569

Doloreux, D., & Parto, S. (2005). Regional innovation systems: Current discourse and unresolved issues. *Technology in Society*, *27*(2), 133–153. doi:10.1016/j.techsoc.2005.01.002

Duan, Y., & Kong, Y. (2008). *The role of R&D offshoring in explaining the patent growth of China and India at USPTO*. Management of Innovation and Technology, 2008. ICMIT 2008. 4th IEEE International Conference on 2008.

Durlauf, S., & Aghion, P. (2005). *Handbook of economic growth*. Elsevier.

Fagerberg, J., & Srholec, M. (2009). Innovation systems, technology and development: Unpacking the relationships. In B. A. Lundvall, K. J. Joseph, C. Chaminade, & J. Vang (Eds.), *Handbook of Innovation Systems and Developing Countries: Building Domestic Capabilities in a Global Setting* (pp. 83–115). Cheltenham, UK: Edward Elgar Publishing. doi:10.4337/9781849803427.00010

Fidrmuc, J., & Gërxhani, K. (2008). Mind the gap! Social capital, East and West. *Journal of Comparative Economics*, *36*(2), 264–286. doi:10.1016/j.jce.2008.03.002

Florida, R. (2002). The rise of the creative class. *The Washington Monthly*, *34*(5), 15–25.

Fosu, A., Bates, R., & Hoeffler, A. (2006). Institutions, governance and economic development in Africa: An overview. *Journal of African Economies*, *15*(1Supplement 1), 1–9. doi:10.1093/jae/ejk004

Friedland, R., & Alford, R. R. (1991). Bringing society back in: Symbols, practices and institutional contradictions. In W. W. Powel & P. J. DiMaggio (Eds.), *The New Institutionalism in Organisational Analysis* (pp. 232–267). Chicago: University of Chicago Press.

Fukuyama, F. (2003). *Social capital and civil society. Foundations of social capital*. Cheltenham, UK: Edward Elgar Publishing.

Gaddy, C., & Ickes, B. W. (1999). An accounting model of the virtual economy. *Post-Soviet Geography and Economics*, *40*(2), 79–97.

Global Financial Integrity. (2013). *Report*. Available at: http://www.gfintegrity.org/wp-content/uploads/2014/12/Illicit-Financial-Flows-from-Developing-Countries-2003-2012.pdf

Gokhberg, L. (Ed.). (2007). *Science, technology and innovation in Russia and OECD countries*. Moscow: State University, High School of Economics.

Griliches, Z. (1979). Issues in assessing the contribution of research and development to productivity growth. *The Bell Journal of Economics*, *10*(1), 92–116. doi:10.2307/3003321

Gupta, D. (Ed.). (1991). *Social stratification*. New Delhi: Oxford University Press.

He, Z. (2000). Corruption and anti-corruption in reform China. *Communist and Post-Communist Studies*, *33*(2), 243–270. doi:10.1016/S0967-067X(00)00006-4

Heckelman, J. C., & Powell, B. (2010). Corruption and the institutional environment for growth. *Comparative Economic Studies*, *52*(3), 351–378. doi:10.1057/ces.2010.14

Hellman, J. S., Jones, G., & Kaufmann, D. (2003). Seize the state, seize the day: State capture and influence in transition economies. *Journal of Comparative Economics*, *31*(4), 751–773. doi:10.1016/j.jce.2003.09.006

Heston, A., & Kumar, V. (2008). Institutional flaws and corruption incentives in India. *The Journal of Development Studies*, *44*(9), 1243–1261. doi:10.1080/00220380802264960

Hitt, M. A., Lee, H.-U., & Yucel, E. (2002). The importance of social capital to the management of multinational enterprises: Relational networks among Asian and western firms. *Asia Pacific Journal of Management*, *19*(2-3), 353–372. doi:10.1023/A:1016247920461

Hjøllund, L., Paldam, M., & Svendsen, G. T. (2001). Social capital in Russia and Denmark: A comparative study. Department of Economics, Faculty of Business Administration, Aarhus School of Business.

Hsieh, M., & Tsai, K. (2007). Technological capability, social capital and the launch strategy for innovative products. *Industrial Marketing Management*, *36*(4), 493–502. doi:10.1016/j.indmarman.2006.01.002

Indicators of Innovation. (2008). *Data book*. Moscow: State University, High School of Economics.

Jain, A. K. (2001). Corruption: A review. *Journal of Economic Surveys*, *15*(1), 71–121. doi:10.1111/1467-6419.00133

Larsson, T. (2006). Reform, corruption, and growth: Why corruption is more devastating in Russia than in China. *Communist and Post-Communist Studies*, *39*(2), 265–281. doi:10.1016/j.postcomstud.2006.03.005

Ledeneva, A. (1998). *Russia's economy of favours: Blat, networking, and informal exchange*. Cambridge, UK: Cambridge University Press.

Leff, N. H. (1964). Economic development through bureaucratic corruption. *The American Behavioral Scientist*, *8*(3), 8–14. doi:10.1177/000276426400800303

Levin, M., & Satarov, G. (2000). Corruption and institutions in Russia. *European Journal of Political Economy*, *16*(1), 113–132. doi:10.1016/S0176 2680(99)00050-6

Li, X., & Pai, Y. (2010). The changing geography of innovation activities: What do patent indicators imply? In X. Fu & L. Soete (Eds.), *The Rise of Technological Power in the South*. Basingstoke, UK: Palgrave MacMillan.

Li, Y., Ye, F., & Sheu, C. (2014). Social capital, information sharing and performance. *International Journal of Operations & Production Management*, *34*(11), 1440–1462. doi:10.1108/IJOPM-03-2013-0132

Light, I., & Isralowitz, R. E. (1997). *Immigrant entrepreneurs and immigrant absorption in the United States and Israel*. Aldershot, UK: Ashgate England.

Lipsey, R. E., & Sjöholm, F. (2005). Host country impacts of inward FDI: Why such different answers? In M. Blomström, E. Graham, & T. Moran (Eds.), *The Impact of Foreign Direct Investment on Development: New Measurements, New Outcomes, New Policy Approaches* (pp. 23–43). Washington, DC: Institute for International Economics.

Lowenberg, A. D. (1992). A post-apartheid constitution for South Africa: Lessons from public choice. *The Cato Journal*, *12*(2), 297–319.

Lundvall, B. (2007). National innovation systems-analytical concept and development tool. *Industry and Innovation*, *14*(1), 95–119. doi:10.1080/13662710601130863

Luo, X., Zhou, L., & Liu, S. S. (2005). Entrepreneurial firms in the context of China's transition economy: An integrative framework and empirical examination. *Journal of Business Research*, *58*(3), 277–284. doi:10.1016/S0148-2963(03)00159-0

Luo, Y., Shenkar, O., & Nyaw, M. (2002). Mitigating liabilities of foreignness: Defensive versus offensive approaches. *Journal of International Management*, *8*(3), 283–300. doi:10.1016/S1075-4253(02)00073-X

Mani, S. (2004). Institutional support for investment in domestic technologies: An analysis of the role of government in India. *Technological Forecasting and Social Change*, *71*(8), 855–863. doi:10.1016/j.techfore.2004.01.011

Manolova, T. S., Eunni, R. V., & Gyoshev, B. S. (2008). Intuitional environments for entrepreneurship: Evidence from emerging economies in Eastern Europe. *Entrepreneurship Theory and Practice*, *32*(1), 203–218. doi:10.1111/j.1540-6520.2007.00222.x

Marsh, C. (2000). Social capital and democracy in Russia. *Communist and Post-Communist Studies*, *33*(2), 183–199. doi:10.1016/S0967-067X(00)00003-9

Maskell, P. (2001). Towards a knowledge-based theory of the geographical cluster. *Industrial and Corporate Change*, *10*(4), 921–943. doi:10.1093/icc/10.4.921

Mathews, J. A., & Hu, M. (2007). Enhancing the role of universities in building national innovative capacity in Asia: The case of Taiwan. *World Development*, *35*(6), 1005–1020. doi:10.1016/j.worlddev.2006.05.012

Mauro, P. (1995). Corruption and growth. *The Quarterly Journal of Economics*, *110*(3), 681–712. doi:10.2307/2946696

McCarthy, D. J., Puffer, S. M., Graham, L. R., & Satinsky, D. M. (2014). Emerging innovation in emerging economies: Can institutional reforms help Russia break through its historical barriers? *Thunderbird International Business Review*, *56*(3), 243–260. doi:10.1002/tie.21619

Meyer, K. E., & Peng, M. W. (2005). Probing theoretically into Central and Eastern Europe: Transactions, resources, institutions. *Journal of International Business Studies*, *36*(6), 600–621. doi:10.1057/palgrave.jibs.8400167

Misztal, B. (1996). *Trust in modern societies*. Cambridge, MA: Polity Press.

Murphy, J. T. (2002). Networks, trust, and innovation in Tanzania's manufacturing sector. *World Development*, *30*(4), 91–619. doi:10.1016/S0305-750X(01)00131-0

Murphy, K. M., Shleifer, A., & Vishny, R. W. (1993). Why is rent-seeking so costly to growth? *The American Economic Review*, 409–414.

National Bureau of Statistics. (2006). *China statistics yearbook on high-tech technology industry*. Beijing: Chinese Statistical Press.

Nee, V. (1996). The emergence of a market society: Changing mechanisms of stratification in China, *101*(4). *American Journal of Sociology*, *101*(4), 908–949. doi:10.1086/230784

Nelson, R. R., & Nelson, K. (2002). Technology, institutions and innovation systems. *Research Policy*, *31*(2), 265–272. doi:10.1016/S0048-7333(01)00140-8

Niskanen, W. A. (1975). Bureaucrats and politicians. *The Journal of Law & Economics*, *18*(3), 617–643. doi:10.1086/466829

North, D. C. (1990). *Institutions, institutional change and economic performance*. Cambridge University Press. doi:10.1017/CBO9780511808678

OECD. (2009). *OECD patent statistics manual*. Available at: http://browse.oecdbookshop.org/oecd/pdfs/free/9209021E.PDF

Oxley, J. E. (1999). Institutional environment and the mechanisms of governance: The impact of intellectual property protection on the structure of inter-firm alliances. *Journal of Economic Behavior & Organization*, *38*(3), 283–309. doi:10.1016/S0167-2681(99)00011-6

Park, S. H., & Luo, Y. (2001). Guanxi and organisational dynamics: Organisational networking in Chinese firms. *Strategic Management Journal*, *22*(5), 455–477. doi:10.1002/smj.167

Petro, N. (1995). *The rebirth of Russian democracy: An interpretation of political culture*. Cambridge, MA: Harvard University Press.

Putnam, R. D., Leonardi, R., & Nanetti, R. Y. (1994). *Making democracy work: Civic traditions in modern Italy*. Princeton University Press.

Qian, Y., & Xu, C. (1998). Innovation and bureaucracy under soft and hard budget constraints. *The Review of Economic Studies*, *65*(1), 151–164. doi:10.1111/1467-937X.00039

Roaf, J. (2000). *Corruption in Russia*. IMF Conference on Post-Election Strategy.

Rose, R. (2000). How much does social capital add to individual health? *Social Science & Medicine*, *51*(9), 1421–1435. doi:10.1016/S0277-9536(00)00106-4 PMID:11037227

Rose-Ackerman, S. (1999). *Corruption and government: Causes, consequences, and reform*. Cambridge University Press. doi:10.1017/CBO9781139175098

Science & Technology Indicators. (2008). *Data book*. Moscow: State University, High School of Economics.

Scott, W. R. (2008). Institutions and organisations: Ideas and interests. *Sage (Atlanta, Ga.)*.

Shane, S., Venkataraman, S., & Macmillan, I. (1995). Cultural differences in innovation championing strategies. *Journal of Management*, *21*(5), 931–952. doi:10.1177/014920639502100507

Sharma, K. (2000). *Rediscovering dharavi: Stories from Asia's largest slum*. New Delhi: Penguin Books.

Sinha, A. (2005). *The regional roots of development politics in India: A divided Leviathan*. Bloomington, IN: Indian University Press.

Smith, N., & Thomas, E. (2014a). Innovation in emerging economies: The spillover effects of foreign direct investment and institutions in Russia. In S. Marinova (Ed.), Institutional Impacts on Firm Internalisation. Palgrave McMillan.

Smith, N., & Thomas, E. (2015a). The role of foreign direct investment and state capture in shaping innovation outcome in Russia. *Europe-Asia Studies*, *67*(5), 777–808. doi:10.1080/09668136.2015.1042430

Smith, N., & Thomas, E. (2015b). Socio-institutional environment and innovation in Russia. *Journal of East-West Business*, *21*(3), 182–204. doi:10.1080/10669868.2015.1021066

Smith, N., Thomas, E., & Antoniou, C. (2014b). Multi-national firms, corruption and innovation in Russia. In A. Verbeke, R.V. Tulder, & S. Lundan (Eds.), Multinational Enterprises, Markets and Institutional Diversity. Emerald Group Publishing Limited.

Sondhi, S. (2000). Combating corruption in India.*Paper for the XVIII World Congress of International Political Science Association*, Quebec City, Canada.

Srinivas, M. N. (Ed.). (1996). *Caste: Its twentieth century avatar*. New Delhi: Penguin Books.

Starosta de Waldemar, F. (2012). New products and corruption: Evidence from Indian firms. *The Developing Economies*, *50*(3), 268–285. doi:10.1111/j.1746-1049.2012.00171.x

Steer, L., & Sen, K. (2010). Formal and informal institutions in a transition economy: The case of Vietnam. *World Development*, *38*(11), 1603–1615. doi:10.1016/j.worlddev.2010.03.006

Tabellini, G. (2008). Presidential address institutions and culture. *Journal of the European Economic Association*, *6*(2-3), 55–294.

Theingi, P. S., & Phungphol, Y. (2008). Social capital in Southeast Asian business relationships. *Industrial Marketing Management*, *37*(5), 523–530. doi:10.1016/j.indmarman.2007.09.014

Twigg, J. L., & Schecter, K. (2003). Social capital and social cohesion in post-soviet Russia. Armong: ME Sharpe, United States.

UNCTAD. (2015). *OECD patent statistics manual*, available at: http://browse.oecdbookshop.org/oecd/pdfs/free/9209021E.PDF

Uzzi, B. (1997). Social structure and competition in inter-firm networks: The paradox of embeddedness. *Administrative Science Quarterly*, *42*(1), 35–67. doi:10.2307/2393808

Wedeman, A. (2004). The intensification of corruption in China. *The China Quarterly*, *180*, 895–921. doi:10.1017/S0305741004000670

Welter, F., & Smallbone, D. (2003). Entrepreneurship and enterprise strategies in transition economies: An institutional perspective. In D. Kirby & A. Watson (Eds.), *Small Firms and Economic Development in Developed and Transition Economies*. Burlington, VA: Ashgate Publishing.

Williamson, C. R. (2009). Informal institutions rule: Institutional arrangements and economic performance. *Public Choice*, *139*(3/4), 371–387. doi:10.1007/s11127-009-9399-x

Williamson, O. (2000). The new institutional economics: Taking stock, looking ahead. *Journal of Economic Literature*, *38*(3), 595–613. doi:10.1257/jel.38.3.595

Wiseman, J. (1990). Principles of political economy: An outline proposal, illustrated by application to fiscal federalism. *Constitutional Political Economy*, *1*(1), 101–124. doi:10.1007/BF02393035

Zak, P. J., & Knack, S. (2001). Trust and growth. *The Economic Journal*, *111*(470), 295–321. doi:10.1111/1468-0297.00609

Zhang, Q., & Fung, H.-G. (2006). China's social capital and financial performance of private enterprises. *Journal of Small Business and Enterprise Development*, *13*(2), 198–207. doi:10.1108/14626000610665908

KEY TERMS AND DEFINITIONS

Corruption: Dishonest or fraudulent conduct by officials in power.

Foreign Direct Investment (FDI): Controlling ownership in a business enterprise in one country by an entity based in another country.

Formal Institutions: Contracts, incentives, authority, laws and regulations.

Informal Institutions: Norms, routines, political processes and restrictions that economic agents put on their own behaviour.

Innovation: The process of translating an idea or invention into a good or service that creates value or for which customers will pay.

Institutions: Formal and informal rules and norms that organize social, political and economic relations.

Multinational Enterprise: A firm that has its facilities and other assets in at least one country other than its home country.

Social Capital: Informal values or norms.

Chapter 10

Exploring the Social Impact of Foreign Direct Investment on Institutional Change:
The Case of Russia

Natalya Smith
Heelstone Consulting Ltd., UK

Ekaterina Thomas
Staffordshire University, UK

ABSTRACT

Despite the vast and growing literature on the economic impact of foreign direct investment (FDI), its social significance is somewhat a neglected issue. Focusing on Russia, this chapter examines the effect of FDI and (formal) institutions (proxied, alternatively, by the [1] accumulated stock of small and medium sized firms or SMEs and [2] number of economic crimes per 100,000 population or corruption) on (informal) institutional change (proxied by the change in the number of violent and property crimes per 100,000 population). The empirical findings provide robust support for a significantly positive direct impact of SMEs, whilst observing a significantly negative effect of corruption and either significantly positive impact of FDI or insignificant effect of multinational firms in this context.

INTRODUCTION

Evidenced by the research that has addressed locational choices of multinational enterprises (MNEs), foreign direct investment (FDI) has become a popular subject in the literature. This research has recently paid some specific attention to institutions as one of the key FDI determinants. Well-functioning institutions are critical to economic performance (North, 1989; 2005): they instil trust into firms and markets, helping firms to build innovation capabilities (Busenitz, Gomez, & Spencer 2000; Licht & Siegel, 2006; Lam & Lundvall, 2007; Mathews & Hu, 2007; Smith & Thomas, 2015a).

DOI: 10.4018/978-1-5225-0276-0.ch010

Empirical evidence confirm that MNEs tend to invest in countries with strong institutions, or in places with (among others) lower degree of government intervention in business operations, lower level of corruption, better contract enforcement and property rights protection (Du, Lu, & Tao, 2008). Although FDI can benefit host economies, countries seeking to attract foreign investment can have undesirable outcomes (Alexeev & Pyle, 2003; Robertson & Watson, 2004; Kwok & Tadesse, 2006; Halmos, 2011; Petrović & Ranđelović, 2012).

Indeed, the recent literature stresses the importance of bi-directional influence between firm's decisions and institutions and addresses how firms shape institutional framework (Carney, Gedajlovic, & Yang, 2009). In particular, MNEs can act as "institutional entrepreneurs", in that they may initiate change unintentionally by sharing business practices or by internalising their norms and professional standards (Kwok & Tadesse, 2006; Hardy & Maguire, 2008).

Whilst positive change in local institutions caused by MNEs is possible, MNEs can increase social inequality (Halmos, 2011; Petrović & Ranđelović, 2012) and damage institutional quality (Alexeev & Pyle, 2003). For example, competition by MNEs for natural resources can increase the total supply of money (bribery potential), resulting in higher level of corruption and crime in a host country (Robertson & Watson, 2004; Kwok & Tadesse, 2006).

This chapter makes a very first attempt to investigate these issues by contributing to the debate on the social impact of FDI. More specifically, its objective is to empirically examine the effect of FDI and (formal) institutions (measured by the (i) accumulated stock of small and medium sized firms (SMEs) and (ii) number of economic crimes registered per 100,000 population) on (informal) institutional change (measured by the change (to account for dynamism in the social environment) in the number of violent and property crimes) within a country.

Russia provides an interesting context to achieve this purpose, with evolving institutions, slow growth in entrepreneurship and an increasingly recognised importance of FDI in technological catch up of the local firms (Smith & Thomas, 2015a). It is a suitable environment for a cross-regional approach. Russia is the largest country by land, with regions comparable in size to entire countries. This makes this research similar to a cross-national study. The number of regions across Russia is large enough to ensure considerable variations among them, while providing reliable statistical findings.

Russia's regions are diverse (in terms of language, ethnicity, culture and economic performance), while retaining comparable status within the country. Russia is heterogeneous both ethnically and religiously. It displays large and persistent regional disparities in social and economic characteristics, in spite of common policies, institutions and laws. Therefore, changes in these factors are not responsible for socioeconomic differences across the country, and this, in turn, substantially reduce the omitted-variable problems affecting many cross-country studies.

This investigation is novel, thus the results should be viewed as preliminary. The study finds a significant effect of formal institutions on change in informal institutions across the country. Namely, the positive change is observed in the regions with stronger formal institutions (with a higher number of SMEs and a lower number of economic crimes registered), or in the regions with higher entrepreneurship activities and lower corruption. The findings support the premise that the local entrepreneurs along with foreign investors had a positively changing impact on the social environment within the country.

The chapter is structured as follows. The next section briefly discusses the relevant literature. It then describes the empirical specification and data, the model and methodology used. The following section presents results, pointing at policy and managerial implications and potential directions for further research.

LITERATURE REVIEW

Institutions

Appropriate formal institutions (laws and regulations) and informal structures (restrictions to structure human interactions) are the key determinants of a well-functioning society (North, 1989). The cost of information is fundamental for the existence of transaction costs (costs of negotiation, information, search, surveillance and enforcement) (Smith & Thomas, 2015b). Important parts of transaction costs are the costs for acquiring information about true characteristics of exchanging goods.

Institutions play a crucial role in reducing transaction costs (North, 1989): they put constraints on economic agents' behaviour and reduce the risk of opportunistic behaviour (North, 1989; 2005). Institutions that limit governments from 'praying on the market' (by restraining the discretion and authority of individual actors within a government) is a necessary condition for markets to function well (North, 2005). The vital role of institutions lies in defining and enforcing property rights and in providing incentives for firms to engage in productive activity (North 1989; 2005). By defining and enforcing laws, institutions reduce uncertainty of human interaction and, therefore, the costs of cooperation.

Formal institutions (government defined and enforced) play the key role in an economy, so do the informal institutions and social capital embedded in them (Williamson, 2009; Dixit, 2009). Formal rules interact with their informal surrounding shaped by the history of formal institutions (Tabellini, 2008). The relation between informal and formal institutions is dynamic: formal institutions (or rules) can shape the informal institutions, but formal institutions are also the long-run reflections of past values, beliefs and norms (Williamson, 2009).

For example, Johnson, Mcmillan, & Woodruff (2002) find that firms in European post-communist countries resorted to bilateral relationships due to courts' inefficiency. Lambert-Mogiliansky, Majumdar & Radner (2007) point to the fact that across Russia the variation in the outcome of enactment of the bankruptcy law depended on the popularity of governors and the quality of the relationship with the federal center. Steer & Sen (2010) provide evidence that, to compensate for the deficiency of the formal legal system, Vietnamese firms used relational contracts.

What has not been given sufficient attention in the literature is the ways in which MNEs strategy might shape the institutional framework (Carney, Gedajlovic & Yang, 2009). This is rather surprising, as MNEs coordinate their actions through associations of which they are a part and, as a result, can exert some strong influence over the environment, since the relational framework allows them to increase their powers (Smith & Thomas, 2015b) to become "institutional entrepreneurs" (Battilana, Leca & Boxenbaum, 2009).

The Social Impact of MNEs

The literature on the impact of MNEs is vast. In the case of transition economies along, there are over 450 studies that examine the effect of FDI on macroeconomic growth (Iwasaki & Tokunaga, 2014). Most of the studies that examine the economic impact of FDI focus on FDI-related technological spillovers (see Acemoglu, Johnson & Robinson, 2002; Aizenman & Marion, 2004, Driffield & Love, 2007).

However, there does not appear to be much of cumulative benefits, stemming from the presence of MNEs and there is a need for examining the broader impacts of FDI on host countries (Dunning, 2002; Meyer, 2004). As the intangible wealth, among other means, includes the provision of social services and reduction of crimes (which is a much broader definition than that contained in gross domestic product, see Dunning, 2002), considering the social role of FDI on the host economy is vital.

FDI can contribute to achieving the host country social goals (Lall, 2004; Petrović-Ranđelović, 2012; Lehnert, Benmamoun, & Zhao, 2013), by improving social welfare (health, education and standard of living, see Lehnert et al., 2013) or by generating employment, (see Lall, 2004). However, a negative relationship between FDI and income inequality is also found (as in Paus & Robinson, 1999; Goldberg & Pavcnik, 2007; Halmos, 2011; Rafsanjani, Zeinolabedini, Mir, & Far, 2014).

Literature argues that skill-based nature of technology (embodied in FDI) can amplify the inequality effect of FDI (Wang & Blomström, 1992) that also entails social dumping that may reduce socio-economic capabilities of a country and can affect its absorptive capability in terms of political institutions, social cohesion and technological opportunities (Lee & Vivarelli, 2006).

Empirical evidence points at the degree of relative deprivation in a society, the degree of cohesiveness in social relations among citizens and the level of crimes (Kawachi, Kennedy & Wilkinson, 1998; Kennedy, Kawachi, Prothrow-Stit, Lochner, & Gupta, 1999). In this context, social capital can be a precondition for efficient and successful economic activities (Putnam, 1995; Fukuyama, 2003). Indeed, economic and social development of countries may depend on the available stock of social capital (Knack & Keefer, 1997; Rose, 2000; Kaasa, 2009).

Furthermore, economic growth and social prosperity through FDI can be determined by the interaction between governments and MNEs (Spar, 1999). For example, MNEs can influence governments and provide for the social welfare of host-country citizens, by offering foreign aid to developing countries, by expanding international trade and investment and by influencing public policy (Rondinelli, 2002).

On the one hand, MNEs can hamper the economic integrity and sovereignty of the developing world (Hippert, 2002). On the other hand, MNEs can act as institutional entrepreneurs, by initiating and actively participating in the implementation of changes that diverge from existing institutions, 'independent of whether the initial intent was to change the institutional environment and whether the changes were successfully implemented' (Battilana, Leca, & Boxenbaum, 2009).

That said, the nexus between institutions and MNEs' agency (with the latter being purposeful action by MNEs to intentionally pursue their interests and exert some effect on their social environment, see Scott, 1995), remains rather underdeveloped. The current research is yet to answer some important questions regarding the conditions for change (Child, Rodrigues, & Tse, 2012), especially in a context of emerging economies (Smith & Thomas, 2015a,b).

Social Capital and Crime

The concept of social capital (see Putnam, 1995 among many others) is related to institutions: in a similar to institutions way, social capital reduces transaction costs and (in a form of trust and social norms) makes cooperation easier. The existence (or absence) of social capital in a country tends to be self-reinforcing: trust and networks, on the one hand, and distrust and isolation, on the other, seem to self-reinforce.

Higher levels of social capital help to coordinate and implement changes in formal institutions (Platteau, 1994). Countries with higher stock of social capital achieve higher levels of growth (Putnam, Leonardi & Nanetti, 1994; Knack & Keefer, 1997; Rose, 2000): social capital can increase economic efficiency through supporting cooperation and by lowering transaction costs (Knack & Keefer, 1997; Akçomak & Ter Weel, 2009).

People in networks (or communities) with a higher level of social capital can work together more effectively and take chances on risky ideas, fuelling innovation as a result (Florida, 2002; Smith & Thomas, 2015b). In this process, social capital can promote business networking and information flows (Coleman & Coleman, 1994, Putnam et al., 1994; Fukuyama, 2001).

Individual choices of crime participation may be significantly affected by the presence of civic norms and networks. For example, there is an established link between civic engagements, social capital and social outcomes (the level of crimes) (see Rosenfeld, Baumer, & Messner, 2001). Whilst countries with higher levels of social capital may have lower crime rates (due to higher civic engagement), countries with higher crime rates may have weaker social capital (Taylor, Gottfredson & Brower, 1984, Rosenfeld et al., 2001).

That is, strong attachments among citizens may help to deal with crime, as exchange of information on criminal behaviour between them may facilitate responsive action to prevent such behaviour in the first place (Sampson, Morenoff, & Earls, 1999). Strong attachments and involvement in matters within a country leads to strong social bonds and can, as a result, reduce the cost of conflict resolution, since conflicts are resolved in peaceful ways (Hirschi, 2002).

Criminal behaviour not only depends on the individual incentives but also on the incentives of people surrounding the individual: an individual is less likely to commit a crime if peers and the community can punish their criminal behaviour. Informal social control (a response to unusual behaviour, that is not the same as formal regulation designed to prevent and punish crime) helps to achieve social order and increase the level of well being in a community and increase the level of trust among citizens and political involvement (such as voting) (Nie, Powell, & Prewitt, 1969).

According to Sampson & Groves (1988), communities are empowered by the trust in each other to take action against crime and to join with formal control (such as the police). Consistent with this theory, significantly lower crime levels and self-reports of victimisation in neighbourhoods, characterised by social or collective efficacy, are reported (Sampson, Raudenbush, & Earls, 1997).

Bursik & Grasmick (1993) argue that effectiveness of law enforcement and public control is higher in communities with extensive civic engagement (see also Rosenfeld, Messner, & Baumer, 2001; Lederman, Loayza, & Menendez, 2002; Messner, Baumer, & Rosenfeld, 2004). Hence, the cost of conflict resolution decreases and more conflicts can be solved.

Similarly, by being caught, an individual risks to loose the utility generating social capital (loss of reputation and job, divorce) (Williams & Sickles, 2002). This means that the more social capital an individual possesses the higher the expected cost of committing crime, which reduces the probability to engage in criminal activities. Therefore, given the probability of being caught and formal control, higher levels of social capital seem to reduce crime (Williams & Sickles, 2002).

Social capital is closely related to corruption, perceived as a failure of institutions and a lack of capacity to manage society, by means of a framework of social, judicial, political and economic checks and balances. Indeed, there is a strong association between higher levels of social capital and corruption (La Porta, Lopez-de-Silanes, Shleifer & Vishny, 1997).

Social capital can lead to low corruption (Uslaner, 2004) and the level of corruption might decrease because of generalised trust and monitoring (Bjørnskov, 2003). Environments with weak institutions can be the most corrupt and least entrepreneurial, since institutions are essential for business start-ups (Baumol, 1996). Legal quality can reduce corruption in high-trust countries, but might have no significant effect in low-trust countries (Bjørnskov, 2011).

Table 1. Definitions of the variables used

INF_INST: Change in the number of violent and property crimes registered (per 100,000 population)
SMEST: Accumulated stock of SMEs
CORR: The number of economic crimes registered (per 100,000 population)
FDI: Inflow of FDI
FDIST: Stock of FDI
MNE: Number of MNEs
MNEST: Accumulated stock of MNEs

Source: Rosstat

METHODOLOGY

The study is based on the regional panel data collected from Rosstat (Russia's Federal State Bureau of Statistics). The data are available for 83 regions in 1997-2011. To construct dependent variable (*INF_INST*), the change in the number of violent and property crimes registered is used (with the rational that the crime is a mirror of the quality of the social environment, see Kawachi et al., 1999).

This variable is, therefore, binary: change above zero indicates the change is 'positive' and there is either no change or a negative change, otherwise. The model takes the following simple form:

$$INF\_INSTit= \beta 0+ \beta 1FORM\_INSTit+ \beta 2FDIit + \varepsilon it$$

where *INF_INST* is informal institutions in a region *i* at time *t*. Formal institutions (*FORM_INST*) are proxied by two variables. *SMEST* (or entrepreneurship) is the accumulated number of SMEs. The rational here is that stronger institutional environments should be more conductive to the process of new business start-up, see Popov, 2001; Smith, Thomas & Antoniou, 2014; Smith & Thomas, 2015b). *CORR* (or corruption) is measured by the number of economic crimes registered per 100, 000 population (as in Smith et al., 2014).

FDI controls for FDI-related (social) spillovers (number of MNEs and the stock of MNEs are used to check robustness of the results); the error term is modelled as $\varepsilon it = \eta i + mt + \lambda it$, where η and m are time- and regional-invariant effects, respectively, and λ is a random disturbance. Variables' definitions are in Table 1. Descriptive statistics is in Table 2. Table 3 presents a correlation matrix.

Table 2. Summary statistics

Variable	Observations	Mean	Standard Deviation	Minimum	Maximum
INF_INST	1328	0.5	0.5	0	1
FDI	1231	377574.7	6276190	0	2.14E+08
FDIST	1317	688749.7	1.13E+07	0	3.96E+08
MNE	1135	85.7	316.4	0	3361
MNEST	1135	602.1	2731.4	0	35952
SMEST	1391	103833.3	253459.4	100	3444500
CORR	1245	192.8	270.2	14.0	3272.5

Note: See Table 1 for abbreviations' definition.

Table 3. Correlation matrix

	INF_INST	*FDI*	*FDIST*	*MNE*	*MNEST*	*SMEST*	*CORR*
INF_INST	1						
FDI	0.0859	1					
FDIST	0.0864	0.9999	1				
MNE	0.014	0.3609	0.3608	1			
MNEST	0.0579	0.4401	0.4401	0.7821	1		
SMEST	0.1255	0.438	0.4379	0.3928	0.3393	1	
CORR	-0.0613	-0.0683	-0.0681	0.028	-0.0013	-0.0705	1

Note: See Table 1 for abbreviations' definition.

Regions in Russia are very heterogeneous: they are diverse in historic and economic conditions, land mass, ethnic and religious composition and language. For example, in 2004 Vologda had the highest share of ethnic Russians (97 per cent), whilst Ingushetiya - the lowest (1.2 per cent). Many of Russia's ethnic republics (for example, Ingushetiya) have been relatively poor; they are located on the periphery of the country having to bear higher transportation costs in reaching country's main markets – Moscow city and Moscow region.

There is an uneven distribution of population across the country. Russia's average population density is 8.4 people per square kilometre, making it one of the most sparsely populated countries in the world. The population is most dense in the European part of the country, around Moscow city and St. Petersburg.

Just over 11 per cent of the population reside in East-Siberian and Far Eastern territories (combined, these represent over 60 per cent of Russia's landmass). By contrast, 20 per cent of the population reside in Central Russia (2.8 per cent of the area of the country). In 2004, for example, Evensk had a population of 20 people per square kilometre, whilst the population in Moscow city of 9,461 people (Rosstat).

Although (on average) 74 per cent of the population in Russia is urban, its regions differ in industrial development and natural resource endowment, which accounts for the variations in gross regional product (GRP) per capita. In 1995, for example, the difference between the highest GRP (in Moscow city) and the lowest (in Ingushetiya that has one of the largest deposits of oil and gas) was 247 fold; this difference almost doubled by 2009 (to 471 fold).

Taken per capita, the difference between the highest 1995's GRP (in Nenetsk) and the lowest (in Ingushetiya) was 77 fold (this diversity being reduced to 21 fold by 2009). The great majority of regions in Russia have been handicapped by low population density, barriers to labour mobility and poor infrastructure (OECD, 2013).

Therefore, to account for this heterogeneity in the analysis, the study begins by testing the sample for heteroschedasticity by using the Breusch-Pagan/Cook-Weisberg test with null hypothesis that the error variances are all equal versus the alternative that the error variances are a multiplicative function of one or more variables.

Heteroscedasticity is confirmed by the large chi-squares found and the Generalised Method of Moments (GMM) estimation is used as a result, as most efficient in this case (Baum, Schaffer, & Stillman, 2003). Since the basic model is limited to FDI and institutional determinants of social environment only, it may suffer from misspecification.

To deal with the omitted variable bias, the GMM regression with fixed effects (to control for regional-specific characteristics not included in the model) is opted for. As it can be argued that individuals living in more corrupt locations have 'looser' standards for judging corrupt practices, regional-fixed effects that help to control for these (among others) differences are added to the model.

DISCUSSION OF RESULTS

The main results of GMM regression are presented in Table 4. To check the results for robustness, the basic model is re-estimated, using alternative FDI data. The results in Table 5 are with MNEs and their accumulated stocks. Models 1, 3, 5 and 7 are with FDI/MNEs and Models 2, 4, 6 and 8 are with their interactions (that essentially tests if regions with lower corruption can benefit more in terms of social change caused by FDI/MNEs). If this is the case indeed, the impact of these interactions should be positive.

Overall, just with a limited number of selected variables, the explanatory power of the model is satisfactory: the models explain (on average) over 50 per cent of the variance in the change of informal institutions across Russia. The results support the argument regarding the association between FDI and formal institutions, on the one hand, and the informal institutions, on the other. More specifically, the stock of SMEs (at 1 per cent significance) and corruption (at 5 per cent significance) are significant in all eight models.

Table 4. The impact of formal institutions (stock of SMEs and corruption) and FDI on informal institutions (change in the number of violent and property crimes) across Russian regions (1997-2011)

Variables	Model 1	Model 2	Model 3	Model 4
Log SMEST	0.110***	0.112***	0.116***	0.117***
	(0.027)	(0.027)	(0.026)	(0.026)
Log CORR	-0.096**	-0.098**	-0.098***	-0.099***
	(0.042)	(0.042)	(0.038)	(0.038)
Log FDI	0.033***	0.032***		
	(0.007)	(0.007)		
FDIxCORR		9.19e-12***		
		(2.95e-12)		
Log FDIST			0.031***	0.030***
			(0.006)	(0.007)
FDISTxCORR				5.18e-12***
				(1.58e-12)
Regional dummies	yes	yes	yes	(0.428) yes
Time dummies	yes	yes	yes	yes
Constant	-0.441 (0.454)	-0.444 (0.454)	-0.494 (0.428)	-0.445 (0.345)
Observations	1085	1085	1163	1163
R-squared	0.502	0.502	0.501	0.502

Note: See Table 1 for abbreviations' definition. Robust standard errors in parentheses; *** p<0.01, ** p<0.05, * p<0.1; all variables are used in natural logarithms.

Table 5. The impact of formal institutions (stock of SMEs and corruption) and MNEs on informal institutions (change in the number of violent and property crimes) across Russian regions (1997-2011)

Variables	Model 5	Model 6	Model 7	Model 8
LogSMEST	0.268***	0.268***	0.055**	0.078**
	(0.035)	(0.035)	(0.022)	(0.034)
LogCORR	-0.076*	-0.076*	-0.100***	-0.106***
	(0.042)	(0.042)	(0.039)	(0.038)
LogMNE	-0.023	-0.023		
	(0.031)	(0.032)		
MNExCORR		1.50e-08		
		(4.26e-07)		
LogMNEST			0.135***	0.065**
			(0.0250)	(0.0314)
MNESTxCORR				8.83e-08**
				(4.01e-08)
Regional dummies	yes	yes	yes	yes
Time dummies	yes	yes	yes	yes
Constant	-1.954***	-1.952***	-0.392*	-0.531***
	(0.494)	(0.494)	(0.201)	(0.148)
Observations	1010	1010	1054	1054
R-squared	0.545	0.545	0.531	0.529

Note: See Table 1 for abbreviations' definition. Robust standard errors in parentheses; *** p<0.01, ** p<0.05, * p<0.1; all variables are used in natural logarithms.

Hence, the higher stock of SMEs leads to a positive change in informal institutions (or lower crime rates) across the country, whilst such change is either zero or negative in the regions that register higher number of economic crimes (or corruption). That is, between 1997 and 2011 corruption has a damaging effect on the social environment across Russia. The results show regions with higher inflows and stocks of FDI (at 1 per cent significance) changed socially. Although the effect of MNEs per se is insignificant, their stocks have a significantly positive effect on the social change (at 1 per cent significance).

The interaction term between FDI/MNEs and corruption is significantly positive (at 5 per cent significance), confirming that foreign investors across Russia led to a positive change in the informal institutions through their impact on corruption (possibly by minimising its level by not accepting bribes). This confirms that MNEs acted as institutional entrepreneurs, possible due to the uncoupling between them and the unsuitable institutions in the country.

Indeed, early institutional theorists have emphasised that, to gain legitimacy within their organisational field, MNEs conform to institutional pressures (DiMaggio & Powell, 1983). However, a more recent institutional perspective states that MNEs may become institutional entrepreneurs as they can mobilise resources to change the institutions for their own interest (Battilana et al., 2009). On the base of this, the study finds some preliminary but robust empirical arguments in support.

CONCLUSION

Using regional panel data for 1997-2011, the chapter estimated the direct and indirect effects of FDI and formal institutions on the change in informal institutions across Russia's regions. The main assumption of the study was that MNEs would have a significantly positive effect across the country. In other words, it was expected that MNEs would act as institutional entrepreneurs, leading to a positive (as in as in Kwok & Tadesse, 2006) social change across the country, by changing or improving the existing institutions (law and order). A significant link between social institutional environment and SME sector development was also assumed.

In line with the arguments in the literature, the preliminary evidence confirms that, during the period under investigation, both MNEs and domestic SMEs led to a positive change in the social environment in Russia. More specifically, a higher number of MNEs and SMEs are found in regions with positive social change (as characterised by a reduction in violent and property crimes).

That said, the effect of corruption on social change was adverse: regions that registered more economic crimes reported showed the least change (or improvement) in their social environments. The results suggestive of the fact that foreign investors in Russia led to a positive change through the change in institutions, possibly by minimising the levels of corruption, perhaps by not involving in corrupt deals with local business agents.

Policy Implications

The implications of this study for policy makers are straightforward. Firstly, the preliminary empirical evidence confirms that the development of social capital by attracting FDI and promoting the development of SME sector in Russia (as well as elsewhere in emerging world) is paramount, given the obsolete social capital, low capacity for self-organisation and low trust in institutions (Rose, 2000; Tabellini, 2008; Aghion, Cahuc, & Shleifer, 2010).

Indeed, in the context of emerging economies undergoing rapid and profound institutional change, it is vital that resources to finance investments are locally generated (Ghura & Goodwin, 2000). Thus, local policies directed at establishing the environment conducive to development of domestic private sector are necessary. Business environment with a sound domestic institutional framework is also a necessary condition for attracting FDI/MNEs (Smith & Thomas, 2015a).

Although SMEs make up around a quarter of Russia's economy, the proportion of SMEs in Russia remains comparatively small (the European Investment Bank). This study shows, however, the role of SMEs is important not only in driving economic growth (for example, through job generation) but also in building the social infrastructure, as employment is a major determinant of reduced conflict and social empowerment (the World Bank).

As MNEs may exert some strong economic and political influence on the environment in which operate, they should not be considered as 'passive players, submissively seeking legitimacy in their interactions with institutions' (Riaz, 2009, p. 28). Instead, they should be seen as institutional agents of change.

The change actions can be exerted by MNEs either in isolation or through combining efforts with SMEs (that face the same institutions in the host environment). Indeed, institutional change is usually the result of the collective and collaborative actions of many actors (Wright & Zammuto, 2013). Therefore, to help MNEs and SMEs to act as institutional entrepreneurs, policy makers should view them as resources to solve the coordination problems, or develop specific capacities (Jackson & Deeg, 2008).

For example, one way forward may be for managers of MNEs and SMEs to work together, by increasing their participation in the collaborative activities aiming at reducing the risks associated with weak institutions (for example, by targeting corruption and corruptors). By providing incentives (by policy makers) to positively influence the environment, MNEs should make marginal or relevant internal adjustments that take the form of new in-house institutions to which SMEs would also adjust.

In cases of uncertain business environments (when there is an urgent need for changing unsuitable institutions), the pioneering (in the institutional change) role of MNEs (due to their powers) and the role of their followers, or SMEs, should be diffused. On the one hand, MNEs and SMEs may jointly pilot new suitable institutions, for example. On the other hand, it is likely that the introduction and diffusion of new institutions will face some strong resistant forces (Child et al., 2012). Specifically, the attempts from MNEs can probably be in competition with the responses of embedded institutional actors (such as governments) and, as a result, fail. These failed attempts, therefore, should be taken into a consideration.

Managerial Implications

Managerial implications of this study are important. MNEs start interacting with host-country institutions as soon as they enter a country and institutions, indeed, have a significant effect on their continuous operations. For example, an MNE that contemplates FDI has to take into account the characteristics the institutional environment, including the degree of corruption.

Managers of MNEs often impose pressure for subsidiaries to adopt practices used in the home country operations elsewhere (Kostova & Roth, 2002). That is, MNEs' degree of legitimacy in their home environment can affect the degree of legitimacy in a host (Kostova & Roth, 2002). However, in the host corrupt countries MNEs may encounter significant pressure to engage in corruption (Smith & Thomas, 2015).

Possibly, the more MNEs engage in corruption, the greater will be the pressure to offer 'facilitation payments' in the course of their business operations (Smith & Thomas, 2015). Finally, when managers of MNEs recognise that corrupt practices are institutionalised in a host environment, they will be more likely to engage in corrupt practices, even if they personally view them negatively at home (Doh, Rodrigue, Uhlenbruck, Collins, & Eden, 2003).

In the last decade, governments, activists and media have become adept at holding firms accountable for the social consequences of their actions/activities (Porter & Kramer, 2006). Corporate success has, indeed, been largely dependent on corporate ethics practices. From this, therefore, it follows that MNEs should pay more attention to social issues and identify their effects have on host societies.

LIMITATIONS AND FUTURE RESEARCH DIRECTIONS

The study is not without limitations. For example, what type of FDI is accounted for in the data on aggregated FDI inflows published by Rosstat is unknown. As a result, it was not possible to assess exactly why the effect of FDI varied between its aggregated (FDI inflows and stocks) and disaggregated (MNEs) levels. The reason for this could be, for example, a high proportion of FDI (reflected in the data by Rosstat) being the Russian capital returning to the country instead of 'foreign' in origin.

If that holds, one of the most important agendas for policy makers should be the facilitation of the return of this capital, given its positive impact on the social environment. Accelerating capital flight that Russia has suffered in recent years has negative consequences for the economy, as lack of capital may delay the development of the enterprise (or SME) sector. Therefore, strengthening policies and institutions to assist with SME start-ups should remain the precondition for enhancing the quantity and quality of domestic capital formation required for the development of SMEs.

It is important to point out that the study presented in this chapter is exploratory and its results are preliminary. However, it can be a good starting point for further research that should, indeed, consider the role of change agents in emerging economies. It is believed that the following proposed research areas will have some important policy implications, given the promotional efforts made by the governments in emerging economies to attract FDI.

Future research efforts may, for example, focus on examining the conditions under which the interaction effects of corruption and FDI are most prominent. Further papers should also examine the role of SMEs in institutional change. Finally, spatial correlation becomes a crucial issue when evaluating determinants of social change (as various forms of localised social interaction may give rise to a spatial multiplier, by which crime rates in a given region also depend on crime rates in neighbouring regions, see Anselin, Cohen, Cook, Gorr, & Tita, 2000). Therefore, further studies should make an effort to control for spatially lagged crime rates.

REFERENCES

Acemoglu, D., Johnson, S., & Robinson, J. A. (2002). Reversal of fortune: Geography and institutions in the making of the modern world income distribution. *The Quarterly Journal of Economics*, *117*(4), 1231–1294.

Aghion, P., Algan, Y., Cahuc, P., & Shleifer, A. (2010). Regulation and Distrust. *The Quarterly Journal of Economics, MIT Press*, *125*(3), 1015–1049. doi:10.1162/qjec.2010.125.3.1015

Aitken, B. J., & Harrison, A. E. (1999). Do domestic firms benefit from direct foreign investment? Evidence from Venezuela. *The American Economic Review*, *89*(3), 605–618.

Aizenman, J., & Marion, N. (2004). The merits of horizontal versus vertical FDI in the presence of uncertainty. *Journal of International Economics*, *62*(1), 125–148. doi:10.1016/j.jinteco.2003.08.003

Akçomak, I. S., & Ter Weel, B. (2009). Social capital, innovation and growth: Evidence from Europe. *European Economic Review*, *53*(5), 544–567. doi:10.1016/j.euroecorev.2008.10.001

Alexeev, M., & Pyle, W. (2003). A note on measuring the unofficial economy in the former Soviet Republics. *Economics of Transition*, *11*(1), 153–175. doi:10.1111/1468-0351.00143

Anselin, L., Cohen, J., Cook, D., Gorr, W., & Tita, G. (2000). Spatial analyses of crime. Measurement and analysis of crime and justice. In D. Duffee (Ed.), *Criminal Justice* (pp. 213–262). Washington, DC: National Institute of Justice.

Battilana, J., Leca, B., & Boxenbaum, E. (2009). How actors change institutions: Towards a theory of institutional entrepreneurship. *The Academy of Management Annals*, *3*(1), 65–107. doi:10.1080/19416520903053598

Baum, C. F., Schaffer, M. E., & Stillman, S. (2003). Instrumental variables and GMM: Estimation and testing. *The Stata Journal*, *3*(1), 1–31.

Baumol, W. J. (1996). Entrepreneurship: Productive, unproductive, and destructive. *Journal of Business Venturing*, *11*(1), 3–22. doi:10.1016/0883-9026(94)00014-X

Bjørnskov, C. (2003). *Corruption and social capital*. Aarhus School of Business, Department of Economics.

Bjørnskov, C. (2011). Combating corruption: On the interplay between institutional quality and social trust. *The Journal of Law & Economics*, *54*(1), 135–159. doi:10.1086/652421

Blomström, M., & Kokko, A. (1998). Multinational corporations and spillovers. *Journal of Economic Surveys*, *12*(3), 247–277. doi:10.1111/1467-6419.00056

Bursik, R. J., & Grasmick, H. G. (1993). *Neighborhoods and crime: The dimensions of effective community control*. Lexington Books.

Busenitz, L. W., Gomez, C., & Spencer, J. W. (2000). Country institutional profiles: Unlocking entrepreneurial phenomena. *Academy of Management Journal*, *43*(5), 994–1003. doi:10.2307/1556423

Carney, M., Gedajlovic, E., & Yang, X. (2009). Varieties of Asian capitalism: Toward an institutional theory of Asian enterprise. *Asia Pacific Journal of Management*, *26*(3), 361–380. doi:10.1007/s10490-009-9139-2

Child, J., Rodrigues, S. B., & Tse, K. K.-T. (2012). The Dynamics of influence in corporate co-evolution. *Journal of Management Studies*, *49*(7), 1246–1273. doi:10.1111/j.1467-6486.2012.01057.x

Coleman, J. S., & Coleman, J. S. (1994). *Foundations of social theory*. Harvard University Press.

DiMaggio, P. J., & Powell, W. W. (1983). The iron cage revisited: Institutional isomorphism and collective rationality in organisational fields. *American Sociological Review*, *48*(2), 147–160. doi:10.2307/2095101

Dixit, A. (2009). Governance institutions and economic activity. *The American Economic Review*, 3–24.

Doh, P. J., Rodriguez, P., Uhlenbruck, K., Collins, J., & Eden, L. (2003). Coping with corruption in foreign markets. *The Academy of Management Executive*, *17*(3), 114–127. doi:10.5465/AME.2003.10954775

Driffield, N., & Love, J. H. (2007). Linking FDI motivation and host economy productivity effects: Conceptual and empirical analysis. *Journal of International Business Studies*, *38*(3), 460–473. doi:10.1057/palgrave.jibs.8400268

Du, J., Lu, Y., & Tao, Z. (2008). Economic institutions and FDI location choice: Evidence from US multinationals in China. *Journal of Comparative Economics*, *36*(3), 412–429. doi:10.1016/j.jce.2008.04.004

Dunning, J. H. (2002). *Global capitalism, FDI and competitiveness*. Edward Elgar Publishing. doi:10.4337/9781843767060

Florida, R. (2002). The rise of the creative class. *The Washington Monthly*, *34*(5), 15–25.

Fukuyama, F. (2001). Social capital, civil society and development. *Third World Quarterly*, *22*(1), 7–20. doi:10.1080/713701144

Fukuyama, F. (2003). *Social capital and civil society. Foundations of social capital*. Cheltenham: Edward Elgar.

Ghura, D., & Goodwin, B. (2000). Determinants of private investment: A cross-regional empirical investigation. *Applied Economics*, *32*(14), 1819–1829. doi:10.1080/000368400425044

Goldberg, P. K., & Pavcnik, N. (2007). Distributional effects of globalisation in developing countries. *Journal of Economic Literature*, *45*(1), 39–82. doi:10.1257/jel.45.1.39

Halmos, K. (2011). The Effect of FDI, exports and GDP on income inequality in 15 Eastern European Countries. *Acta Polytechnica Hungarica*, *8*(1), 123–136.

Hardy, C., & Maguire, S. (2008). Institutional entrepreneurship. In R. Greenwood, C. Oliver, R. Suddaby, & K. Sahlin-Andersson (Eds.), The Handbook of Organisational Institutionalism. Sage.

Hippert, C. (2002). Multinational corporations, the politics of the world economy, and their effects on women's health in the developing world: A review. *Health Care for Women International*, *23*(8), 861–869. doi:10.1080/07399330290107476 PMID:12487701

Hirschi, T. (2002). *Causes of delinquency*. Transaction Publishers.

Iwasaki, I., & Tokunaga, M. (2014). Macroeconomic impacts of FDI in transition economies: A meta-analysis. *World Development*, *61*, 53–69. doi:10.1016/j.worlddev.2014.03.022

Jackson, G., & Deeg, R. (2008). Comparing capitalism: Understanding institutional diversity and its implications for international business. *Journal of International Business Studies*, *39*(4), 540–561. doi:10.1057/palgrave.jibs.8400375

Johnson, S., Mcmillan, J., & Woodruff, C. (2002). Courts and relational contracts. *Journal of Law Economics and Organization*, *18*(1), 221–277. doi:10.1093/jleo/18.1.221

Kaasa, A. (2009). Effects of different dimensions of social capital on innovative activity: Evidence from Europe at the regional level. *Technovation*, *29*(3), 218–233. doi:10.1016/j.technovation.2008.01.003

Kawachi, I., Kennedy, B. P., & Wilkinson, R. G. (1999). Crime: Social disorganisation and relative deprivation. *Social Science & Medicine*, *48*(6), 719–731. doi:10.1016/S0277-9536(98)00400-6 PMID:10190635

Kennedy, B. P., Kawachi, I., Prothrow-Stith, D., Lochner, K., & Gupta, V. (1998). Social capital, income inequality and firearm violent crime. *Social Science & Medicine*, *47*(1), 7–17. doi:10.1016/S0277-9536(98)00097-5 PMID:9683374

Knack, S., & Keefer, P. (1997). Does social capital have an economic payoff? A cross-country investigation. *The Quarterly Journal of Economics*, *112*(4), 1251–1288. doi:10.1162/003355300555475

Kostova, T., & Zaheer, S. (1999). Organisational legitimacy under conditions of complexity: The case of the multinational enterprise. *Academy of Management Review*, *24*, 64–81.

Kwok, C. Y., & Tadesse, S. (2006). The MNC as an agent of change for host-country institutions: FDI and corruption. *Journal of International Business Studies*, *37*(6), 767–785. doi:10.1057/palgrave.jibs.8400228

La Porta, R., Lopez-de-Silanes, F., Shleifer, A., & Vishny, R. W. (1997). Legal determinants of external finance. *The Journal of Finance*, *52*(3), 1131–1150. doi:10.1111/j.1540-6261.1997.tb02727.x

Lall, S. (2004). The employment impact of globalisation in developing countries. In E. Lee & M. Vivarelli (Eds.), *Understanding Globalisation, Employment and Poverty Reduction* (pp. 73–101). New York: Palgrave Macmillan.

Lam, A., & Lundvall, B. (2007). *The learning organisation and national systems of competence building and innovation.* MPRA Paper No. 12320, 1-28. Available at: http://mpra.ub.uni-muenchen.de/12320/

Lambert-Mogiliansky, A., Majumdar, M., & Radner, R. (2007). Strategic analysis of petty corruption: Entrepreneurs and bureaucrats. *Journal of Development Economics*, *83*(2), 351–367. doi:10.1016/j.jdeveco.2006.06.002

Lederman, D., Loayza, N., & Menendez, A. M. (2002). Violent crime: Does social capital matter? *Economic Development and Cultural Change*, *50*(3), 509–539. doi:10.1086/342422

Lee, E., & Vivarelli, M. (2006). The social impact of globaliSation in the developing countries. *International Labour Review*, *145*(3), 167–184. doi:10.1111/j.1564-913X.2006.tb00016.x

Lehnert, K., Benmamoun, M., & Zhao, H. (2013). FDI inflow and human development: Analysis of FDI's impact on host countries' social welfare and infrastructure. *Thunderbird International Business Review*, *55*(3), 285–298. doi:10.1002/tie.21544

Licht, A. N., & Siegel, J. I. (2006). The social dimensions of entrepreneurship. In M. Casson & B. Yeung (Eds.), *Oxford Handbook of Entrepreneurhip*. Oxford University Press.

Mathews, J. A., & Hu, M. (2007). Enhancing the role of universities in building national innovative capacity in Asia: The case of Taiwan. *World Development*, *35*(6), 1005–1020. doi:10.1016/j.worlddev.2006.05.012

Messner, S. F., Baumer, E. P., & Rosenfeld, R. (2004). Dimensions of social capital and rates of criminal homicide. *American Sociological Review*, *69*(12), 882–903. doi:10.1177/000312240406900607

Meyer, K. (2004). Perspectives on multinational enterprises in emerging economies. *Journal of International Business Studies*, *35*(4), 259–276. doi:10.1057/palgrave.jibs.8400084

Nie, N. H., Powell, G. B., & Prewitt, K. (1969). Social structure and political participation: Developmental relationships, Part I. *The American Political Science Review*, *63*(2), 361–378. doi:10.2307/1954694

North, D. C. (1989). Institutions and economic growth: A historical introduction. *World Development*, *17*(9), 1319–1332. doi:10.1016/0305-750X(89)90075-2

North, D. C. (2005). Institutions and the process of economic change. *Management International*, *9*(3), 1–7.

OECD. (2013). *Russia. Modernising the economy.* Available at: http://www.oecd.org/russia/Russia-Modernising-the-Economy-EN.pdf

Paus, E., & Robinson, M. D. (1999). Real wage performance under greater trade openness: Lessons from Latin America and Asia. *Journal of Developing Areas*, *33*(2), 269–288.

Petrović-Ranđelović, M. (2012). Foreign direct investment as a mechanism for achieving social progress in the host country. *New Challenges in Changing Labour Markets,* 337.

Platteau, J. (1994). Behind the market stage where real societies exist: The role of public and private order institutions. *The Journal of Development Studies*, *30*(3), 533–577. doi:10.1080/00220389408422328

Popov, V. (2001). Reform strategies and economic performance of Russia's regions. *World Development*, *29*(5), 865–886. doi:10.1016/S0305-750X(01)00006-7

Porter, M. E., & Kramer, M. R. (2006). The link between competitive advantage and corporate social responsibility. *Harvard Business Review*, *84*(12), 78–92. PMID:17183795

Putnam, R. D. (1995). Bowling alone: America's declining social capital. *Journal of Democracy*, *6*(1), 65–78. doi:10.1353/jod.1995.0002

Putnam, R. D., Leonardi, R., & Nanetti, R. Y. (1994). *Making democracy work: Civic traditions in modern Italy*. Princeton University Press.

Rafsanjani, H. K., Zeinolabedini, M., Mir, M., & Far, I. M. (2014). Studying the effect of education, trade, and FDI on income inequality in Iran. *Management and Administrative Sciences Review*, *3*(4), 733–745.

Riaz, S. (2009). The global financial crisis: An institutional theory. *Critical Perspectives on International Business*, *5*(1), 26–35.

Robertson, C. J., & Watson, A. (2004). Corruption and change: The impact of foreign direct investment. *Strategic Management Journal*, *25*(4), 385–396. doi:10.1002/smj.382

Rondinelli, D. (2002). Transnational corporations: International citizens or new soveriegns? *Business and Society Review*, *107*(4), 391–413. doi:10.1111/1467-8594.00143

Rose, R. (2000). How much does social capital add to individual health? *Social Science & Medicine*, *51*(9), 1421–1435. doi:10.1016/S0277-9536(00)00106-4 PMID:11037227

Rosenfeld, R., Baumer, E. P., & Messner, S. F. (2001). Social capital and homicide. *Social Forces*, *80*(1), 283–310. doi:10.1353/sof.2001.0086

Sampson, R. J., Morenoff, J. D., & Earls, F. (1999). Beyond social capital: Spatial dynamics of collective efficacy for children. *American Sociological Review*, *64*(5), 633–660. doi:10.2307/2657367

Scott, W. R. (1995). *Institutions and organisations*. Sage.

Smith, N., & Thomas, E. (2015a). The role of foreign direct investment and state capture in shaping innovation outcome in Russia. *Europe-Asia Studies*, *67*(5), 777–808. doi:10.1080/09668136.2015.1042430

Smith, N., & Thomas, E. (2015b). Socio-institutional environment and innovation in Russia. *Journal of East-West Business*, *21*(3), 182–204. doi:10.1080/10669868.2015.1021066

Smith, N., Thomas, E., & Antoniou, C. (2014). Multi-national firms, corruption and innovation in Russia. In A. Verbeke, R.V. Tulder, & S. Lundan (Eds.), Multinational Enterprises, Markets and Institutional Diversity. Emerald Group Publishing Limited.

Spar, D. (1999). Foreign investment and human rights international. *Challenge*, 1–2.

Steer, L., & Sen, K. (2010). Formal and informal institutions in a transition economy: The case of Vietnam. *World Development*, *38*(11), 1603–1615. doi:10.1016/j.worlddev.2010.03.006

Tabellini, G. (2008). Presidential address institutions and culture. *Journal of the European Economic Association*, *6*(2/3), 255–294. doi:10.1162/JEEA.2008.6.2-3.255

Taylor, R. B., Gottfredson, S. D., & Brower, S. (1984). Block crime and fear: Defensible space, local social ties, and territorial functioning. *Journal of Research in Crime and Delinquency*, *21*(4), 303–331. doi:10.1177/0022427884021004003

Uslaner, E.M. (2004). Trust and corruption. *The New Institutional Economics of Corruption,* 76.

Wang, J., & Blomström, M. (1992). Foreign investment and technology transfer: A simple model. *European Economic Review*, *36*(1), 137–155. doi:10.1016/0014-2921(92)90021-N

Williams, J., & Sickles, R. C. (2002). An analysis of the crime as work model: Evidence from the 1958 Philadelphia birth cohort study. *The Journal of Human Resources*, *37*(3), 479–509. doi:10.2307/3069679

Williamson, C. R. (2009). Informal institutions rule: Institutional arrangements and economic performance. *Public Choice*, *139*(3-4), 371–387. doi:10.1007/s11127-009-9399-x

Wright, A. L., & Zammuto, R. F. (2013). Creating opportunities for institutional entrepreneurship. *Journal of Business Venturing*, *28*(1), 51–68. doi:10.1016/j.jbusvent.2011.11.005

KEY TERMS AND DEFINITIONS

Corruption: Dishonest or fraudulent conduct by officials in power.

Foreign Direct Investment (FDI): Controlling ownership in a business enterprise in one country by an entity based in another country.

Formal institutions: Contracts, incentives, authority, laws and regulations.

Informal Institutions: Norms, routines, political processes and restrictions that economic agents put on their own behaviour.

Institutions: Formal and informal rules and norms that organise social, political and economic relations.

Multinational Enterprise: A firm that has its facilities and other assets in at least one country other than its home country.

Social Capital: Informal values or norms.

Chapter 11
The Gotheborg IV (G4) Model and the Function of Language in the Globalization Process of the Firm:
The Case of Swedish MNEs

Cheryl Marie Cordeiro
University of Gothenburg, Sweden

ABSTRACT

This chapter contributes to the theory of a firm's globalization processes reflected in the Uppsala Globalization Process Model (UGPM). The Gotheborg IV (G4) model is introduced, mapping the knowledge zones of the UGPM in a four quadrant axis model. Using language in its meta-capacity as theory and framework of analysis the G4 model makes a distinction between the words 'enterprise' (Hn) and 'subsidiary' (H1), addressing the core features of firm globalization with geographically dispersed foreign subsidiaries and globally coordinated activities of manufacturing, sourcing and R&D capabilities. With the distinction between Hn and H1, the G4 model is able to present eight perspectives of the globalization process from interior and exterior to the enterprise and subsidiary. As method, this chapter will show how using the G4 model results in a richer analysis and findings from qualitative data. In this study Swedish top-level managers working in Asia show how they foster an organization culture of continuous learning and change that supports the MNE's globalization efforts.

1. INTRODUCTION

Despite an increasingly interconnected world, many in the intellectual circles of international business (IB) research seem to relegate to the canon of mythology, true globalization of multinational enterprises (MNEs). Globalization of MNEs simply do not exist in full extent. The reason cited is that MNEs are believed to operate mainly on a regional level, with few achieving coordinated operations at a global

DOI: 10.4018/978-1-5225-0276-0.ch011

level (Dunning, Fujita & Yakova 2007, Flores & Aguilera 2007, Rugman & Verbeke 2004, Ghemawat 2003, Rugman 2003). Yet the long history of Swedish MNEs, notably such MNEs as Volvo AB, IKEA, AstraZeneca, ABB and SKF, present a different perspective to their organizational narrative on MNE globalisation. In an endeavour to theoretically understand and explain the globalization of Swedish MNEs, models of the internationalization of firms have been put forth.

The most prominently cited of internationalization models is the Uppsala Model (UM) by Johanson & Vahlne (1977). Developed on the assumption that knowledge was lacking on the internationalisation operations of the firm, the UM has been widely applied and likewise (Carneiro, Rocha & Silva 2008, Langhoff 1977, Oviatt & McDougall 1994, Andersen 1993). The knowledge of the internationalization process was considered a necessary acquisition if one were to understand the two directions of internationalization, which included "the increasing involvement of the firm in the individual foreign country, and [the] successive establishment of operations in new countries" (Johanson & Vahlne 1977:23). A review of the original UM was put forth by Vahlne & Ivarsson (2014) and called the Uppsala Globalisation Process Model (UGPM). Globalization was defined by Vahlne, Ivarsson and Johansson (2011:1) as "...an effort to optimize a business in terms of its configuration and coordination systems globally and globalization, like the internationalization process, is characterized by the management of complexities and uncertainties requiring learning and commitment building". This meant that the firm encompassed not just a widely dispersed engagement in foreign markets (defined as 'internationalization'), but that it had a network of differentiated units that could exploit advantages of specialization on location that defined the 'globalization' process (Bartlett & Ghoshal 1990). Both the UM and the UGPM were based on empirical studies of Swedish MNEs.

Due to that the founding authors of the model, Vahlne, Ivarsson and Johanson (2014, 2011) believe that the mechanisms of the UGPM encompass those of the UM, and are sufficiently general to allow for its application for most managerial processes characterised by uncertainty, ambiguity and complexity, in this chapter, the word 'globalization' is seen to encompass the processes of 'internationalization', though perhaps not vice versa. Likewise, UGPM is seen as encompassing UM but not vice versa.

In a combination of efforts of the studies that rendered the UM, the UGPM, and studies on Swedish management (Cordeiro-Nilsson 2010, Cordeiro-Nilsson 2009, Cäker, Andersson, Wickelgren 2011, Birkinshaw 2002, Källström 1997, Lindell & Arvonen 1996, Jönsson 1995), the conceptualisations in this chapter serve to bridge the knowledge gap in the globalization process by focusing on the role language can play in the context of Swedish MNEs in the field IB studies. The Gotheborg IV or G4 model is introduced as a richer means of visualising knowledge of the firm's globalization process as reflected in the UGPM.

The G4 model illustrates how language can be used as theory and framework to render a deeper analysis of qualitative data that help uncover knowledge zones in the study of the globalization process of an enterprise as originally set out by the UGPM. In particular, it illustrates how language can be used in its meta-capacity to uncover the agency behind how the firm might take advantage of the local environment for its sustained development, mainly through strategic management, and the management styles of top level managers of Swedish managed firms.

Most studies that apply the UGPM in explaining the processes of globalisation in an enterprise have been quantitative in nature, focusing on geographical configuration and coordination capacities of the firm applied to different industries from fashion retailing to information communication technology (Childs & Jin 2014, Vahlne & Johanson 2013, Figueira-de-Lemos, Johanson & Vahlne 2011, Johanson

& Vahlne 2009, Forsgren & Hagström 2007). The conceived G4 model presented in the following sections, illustrates how the less explicitly analysed knowledge zones in the UGPM pertaining to management in uncertainty, knowledge of foreign market culture and trust-building (Vahlne & Ivarsson 2014) can be complemented by applying qualitative methodology. The qualitative methodology applied here offers a novel perspective to the UGPM in that it situates the function of language in the globalization process, uncovering as it were, a four-quadrant Gotheborg IV (G4) visualisation of a richer landscape of enterprise knowledge zones.

The structure of this chapter is as follows: section 2 maps the zones of knowledge expressed by the UGPM by first disambiguating the word 'firm' into what was initially meant by the authors of the UGPM to mean 'enterprise' and its 'subsidiaries'. With the knowledge zones illustrating the gaps of knowledge to be filled, section 3 outlines how language within the field of IB studies has gained interest and importance in the study of the processes of internationalization and globalization. It also outlines how language can be used in its meta-capacity as both theory and framework of analysis to data in globalization processes. Section 4 gives a text sample of the data analysis using SFL. Section 5 discusses the G4 model and the findings to the data, and section 6 concludes with a summary of the main points of this chapter, touching upon the practical applications of the G4 model, future research possibilities and chapter limitations.

2. KNOWLEDGE ZONES EXPRESSED IN THE UPPSALA GLOBALIZATION PROCESS MODEL (UGPM)

2.1 Distinguishing 'Firm' as 'Enterprise' and its 'Subsidiaries'

Common concepts addressed at the core of the Uppsala Model (see Figure 1) is management under uncertainty, in which MNEs gradually build aptitude by experiential learning and by fostering long standing relationships within a trusted network in the environment. Developed for the purpose of explaining the internationalization process of the firm, the authors of the UM conceived the internationalization process to include the two directions of (i) increasing involvement of the firm in the individual foreign country, and (ii) successive establishment of operations in new countries (Johanson & Vahlne 1977:23). In the later globalization model developed by Vahlne & Ivarsson (2014), the multinational enterprise (MNE) is also referred to as 'the firm as a whole', "in order to grow and improve on their effectiveness, multinational enterprises (MNEs) reconfigure their widely dispersed value chains and develop their coordination systems to make the different units specialize, integrate and operate towards the overall best for the firm as a whole." (Vahlne & Ivarsson 2014:227). Yet it is exactly this duo-directions of internationalization described by the authors, that indicates a need for a non-ambiguous use of the word 'firm', giving rise to the Gotheborg IV or G4 model based on a four-quadrant axis that in turn renders a more dynamic understanding of the globalization process.

For the purpose of clarity, the word 'enterprise', as referred to by the UGPM model will be denoted by the capital letter, H. Because an enterprise can contain an unknown number of subsidiary units, denoted by n, the denotation Hn refers to the enterprise in its entirety. The singular example of a subsidiary within Hn, is denoted by H1.

Figure 1. The Uppsala globalization process model (UGPM)
Source: Vahlne & Ivarsson (2014:242)

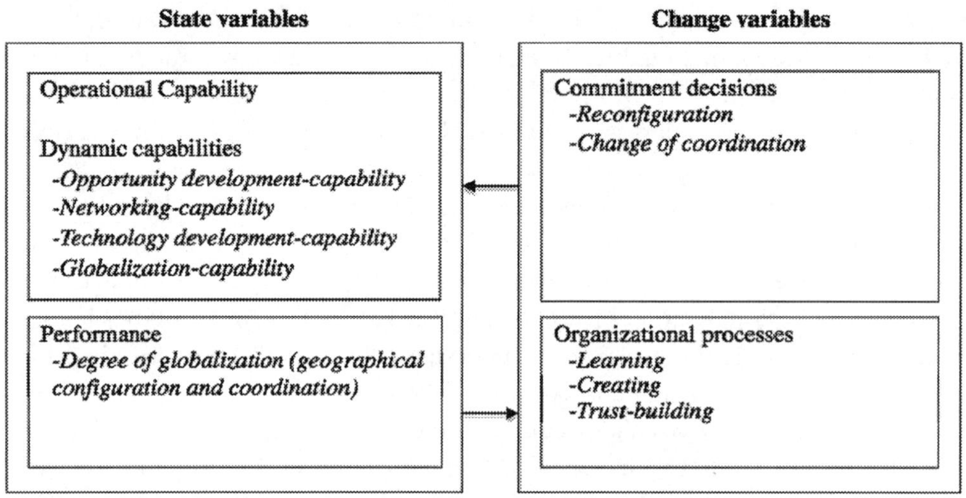

2.2 The Gotheborg IV (G4) Model: Reflecting a Deeper Understanding of the UGPM Knowledge Zones

The UGPM gives attention to four different knowledge zones when theoretically explaining the dialogic relations of the different units of the enterprise (intra-firm trade) and of the enterprise in relation to its larger social collective context (inter-regional coordination). In this sense, H*n* and H1 can be described as holons (i.e. "whole/part") where each unit is a whole that is part of other wholes that form an integral network of entities (Wilber 2006). A study of the processes of internationalization and globalization, would thus encompass a study of the interior and exterior perspectives of how these holons operate in a continuous dialogic, part-orchestrated, synchrony towards the sustained development of H*n* in relation to its larger collective social context. The dialogic nature of interaction between H1 to H*n,* and H*n* to its larger social environment of other networks of H*n*s renders the differentiation between 'state variables' and 'change variables' weak. All relations could be described over time as evolving, so that 'state variables' also change through time. Time is thus not a zone of knowledge to be studied, but rather, time exists in the background fabric of globalization processes. Without time, there will be no globalization process.

Taking the enterprise and its subsidiary as singular holons, labelled H*n* for enterprise, and H1 for subsidiary, a resulting eight Gotheborg IV or G4 model perspectives is rendered using inputs from the UGPM placed in a four quadrant axis diagram shown in Figure 2.

Represented in the G4 model, the Upper Left (UL, *subjective*) quadrant is the zone of H*n* and H1 knowledge pertaining to the consciousness and ideology of the individual interiors of the enterprise and its subsidiary. From the UGPM, this is where the 'Commitment' behind the 'Commitment decisions' is represented. The Lower Left (LL, *intersubjective*) quadrant is the zone of knowledge of H1 and H*n* pertaining to the collective interiors of the subsidiary culture and the enterprise culture. These interior knowledge zones are then expressed in the exterior quadrants, the actions of which can be observed

Figure 2. The Gotheborg IV (G4) model illustrating the four different knowledge zones and eight perspectives of the globalization process

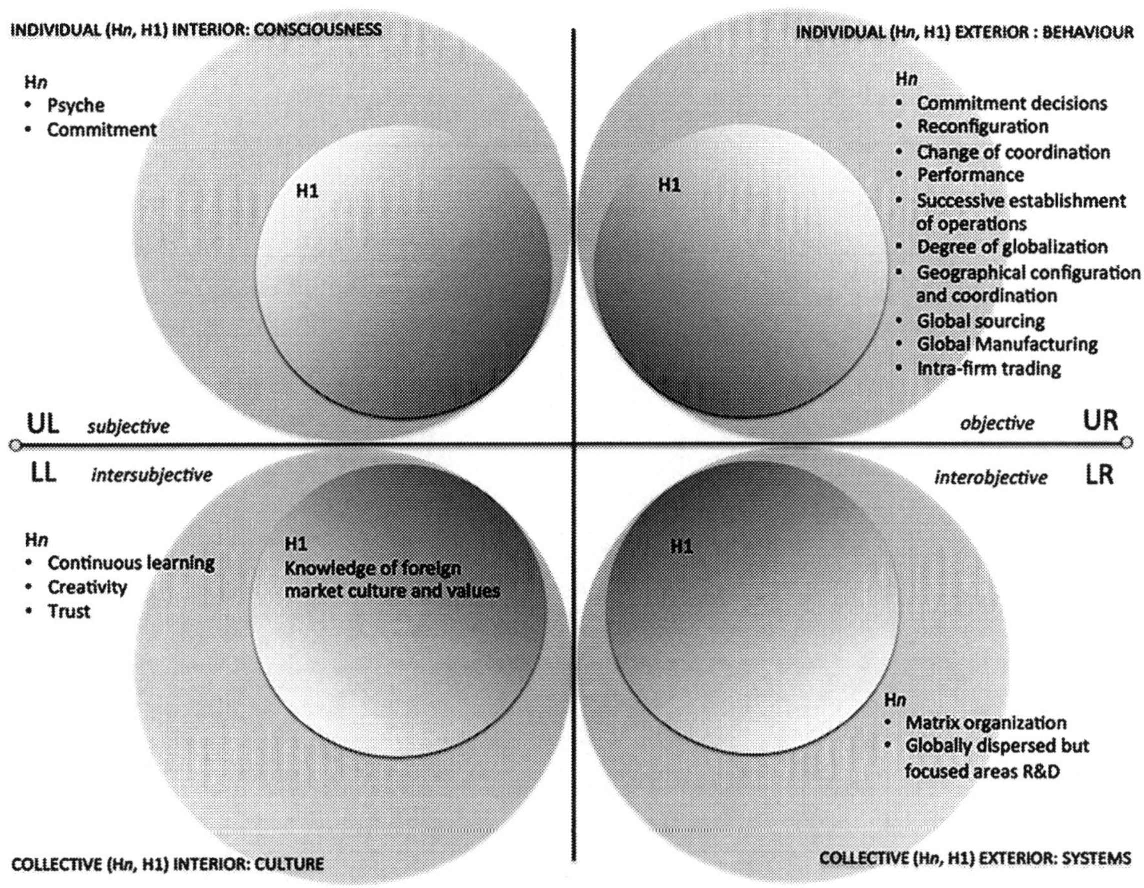

exteriorly. The Upper Right (UR, *objective*) quadrant is the zone of H1 and H*n* knowledge pertaining to individual exteriors of subsidiary and enterprise behaviours, and the Lower Right (LR, *interobjective*) quadrant is the zone of H1 and H*n* knowledge pertaining to collective exteriors of subsidiary and enterprise structures and systems.

Once the knowledge zones are mapped, the G4 model in Figure 2 also reveals that the focus of empirical knowledge of globalization processes from the UGPM lie mainly in the UR quadrant pertaining mainly to the behaviour of H*n*. In almost all quadrants of knowledge, H1 is referred to but never specifically detailed in the understanding of the processes in the UGPM study (Vahlne & Ivarsson 2014). The lack of detailing in H1 reveals a knowledge gap, as acknowledged by Vahlne & Ivarsson (2014:245), "A main impediment to globalization is a lack of knowledge concerning the conditions on foreign markets, such as institutions and business networks that requires experiential learning to acquire". The knowledge gaps shown in Figure 2 point towards areas of future research. Figure 3 shows the focus of this chapter's interest in bridging the gap in knowledge zone in the LL quadrant and its dialogic relationship between H*n* and H1 pertaining to culture and values.

Figure 3. The Gotheborg IV (G4) model: The LL quadrant and its dialogic relations, illustrating the knowledge zone gap in the UGPM and the focus of research interest in this chapter

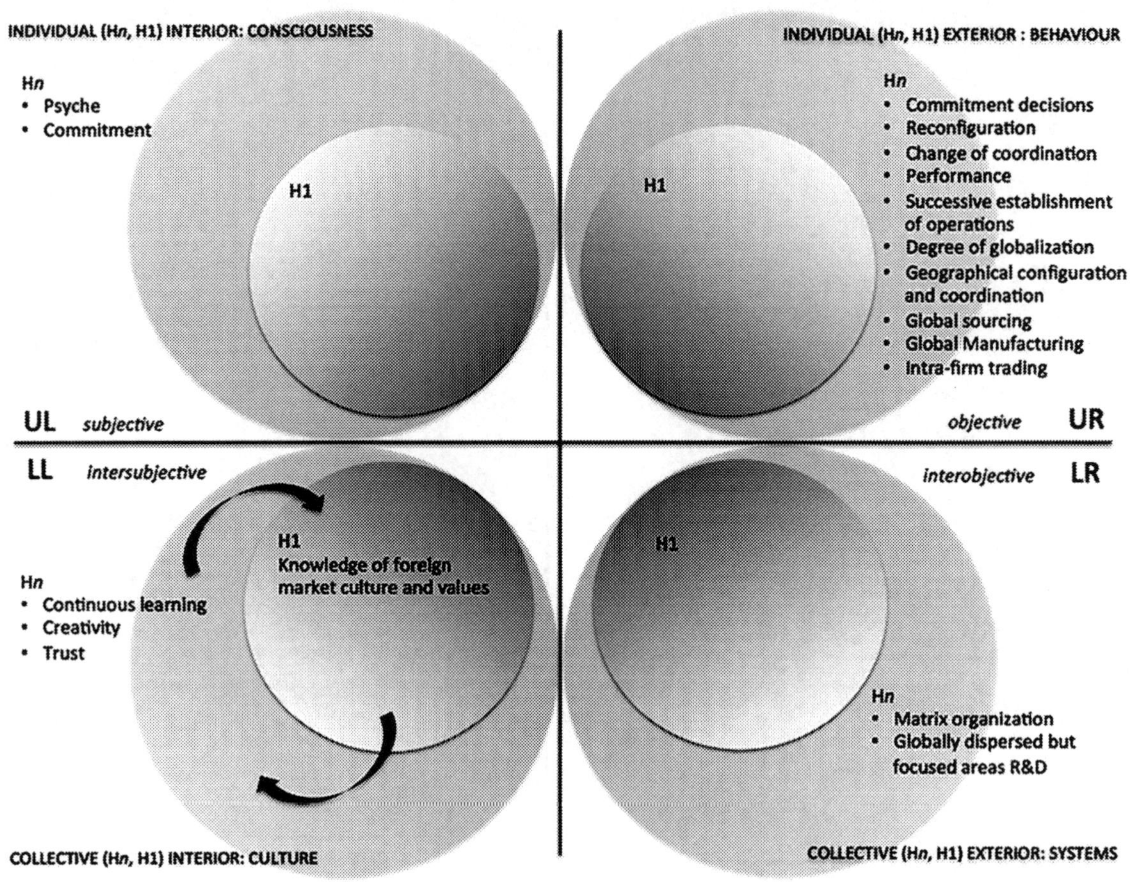

Where the UGPM does not detail knowledge in the LL quadrant, the G4 model contributes in bridging the gap in the LL quadrant of knowledge, by using language as theory and framework of analysis in understanding H*n* and H1 globalization processes, pertaining to the culture and values of the enterprise and the subsidiary.

3. THE GOTHEBORG IV (G4) MODEL: SITUATING THE ROLE OF LANGUAGE IN THE FIRM'S GLOBALIZATION PROCESS

Language is involved in almost every aspect of human interaction. It is the medium in which thoughts are organized and communication proceeds (Hodge & Kress 1993). But even as it is acknowledged, "language lies at the heart of international business (IB) activities", where in the context of globalization and international management, organizations find themselves increasingly having to navigate the different language environments (Brannen, Piekkari & Tietze 2014:495). Few studies outside the field of applied linguistics, specifically that of discourse analysis, have used language as an instrumental tool in understanding the workings of organizations (Leitch and Palmer 2009, Cordeiro-Nilsson 2009, Fairclough 2005, Alvesson & Karreman 2000b, 2000a). The G4 model situates the use of language as theory and framework in the study of organizational processes within the UGPM (Vahlne & Ivarsson 2014).

But where does the role and function of language stand in terms of the IB literature? Currently, IB studies tend to view language as an object / phenomenon. This includes that an overwhelming percentage (more than 90%) of language in IB is being published in English language journals (Terjesen et al. 2014) and that initial language in IB research began in with scholars in Scandinavia (Marschan-Piekkari, et al. 1999b, 1999a, Marschan et al. 1997). Language has been studied as a barrier (object) in firm internalization (Lohmann 2011, Welch, Welch & Piekkari 2005). As an object / phenomenon, language contains properties that enable it to be transferred from one context to another or its use can be moulded by corporate language policies and guidelines (Brannen & Doz 2012, Brannen 2004). Language has desirable properties of being a 'cultural resource' (Duranti 1997, SanAntonio 1987), and a person's career capital (Piekkari 2008). Like an object, language can be labelled "a corporate language", it can be acquired as a second language, or co-exist alongside other languages (Kozlowski et al. 2013, Steyaert et al. 2011, Fredriksson et al. 2006, Vaara et al. 2005). It can also be categorised, belonging to an internal 'hierarchy of languages', an entity shifting between in-house corporate groups to being the official corporate language across nations (Marschan-Piekkari et al. 1999a). Language is also seen as an individual or team level property (Boxenbaum 2006), the diversity of which can be quantified and measured (Tenzer et al. 2014).

Less common in the field of IB at the moment is the study of language in its functional or meta aspect, specifically, studies reflecting the metafunctions of language defined by type iia studies (Cordeiro-Nilsson 2009).

The term 'functional' applied to language is derived from the systemic functional theory/linguistics (SFL). It is a coherent theory and framework of language development and use based on the work of Michael Halliday (1985, 1975), whose work was influenced by the Prague School of the 1920s. The underlying assumption to a 'functional' view of language is that the form of language responds to its functions. It recognizes that we use language as a system to construct meanings in different contexts for different purposes. In this chapter, systemic functional theory is used as instrumental linguistics, which is "the chapter of language for understanding something else" (Fowler 1991:481).

Language in IB studies that focus on the functional aspects of language defined as type iib (non-metafunctional studies) include aspects of social cohesion and as a lingua franca (Wu 2013, Mäkelä et al 2007, Luo & Shankar 2006), language as facilitative in trade (Ly et al. 2013, Beyene et al. 2009, Brannen & Salk 2000, Crick 1999,), language as facilitative in knowledge sharing (Cordeiro-Nilsson & Hawamdeh 2011, Welch & Welch 2008, Holden 2002), language as function of cognition, context (culture) and situation (Cutler 2012, Brannen & Doz 2012, House et al. 2004, Hofstede 2001, Du-Babcock 2006), and language as ideology (Boussebaa et al. 2014, Tietze & Dick 2013, Hofstede 1984).

This chapter addresses the gap in IB literature and research studies of type iia, and uses the four quadrant zones of knowledge of the UGPM, focusing on the LL quadrant to illustrate how the case of globalizing Swedish MNEs might be studied from the perspective of language. The framework of data analysis is set within the broader context of discourse analysis studies in the field of IB, it uses systemic functional linguistics (SFL) and the study of language metafunctions in order to uncover H1 and H*n* collective interior knowledge on subsidiary and enterprise culture dialogic.

The case of illustration here is that of top Swedish managers working in Swedish owned / managed Singapore offices, putting into effect an organizational change. This chapter illustrates how SFL metafunctions can be used in identifying agency and actorship in organization management and change related to the globalization processes of an enterprise.

3.1 The Use of Discourse Analysis in Uncovering the G4 Model LL Quadrant of Knowledge

Discourse analysis refers to all studies within the field of applied linguistics that focus on the units of language beyond the sentence level. It highlights language as text (written and spoken), situated in a context. It is used in order to comprehend the production, dissemination and interpretation of texts in the process of communication.

Developed first within the field of linguistics, anthropology and philosophy, interest in discourse analysis as a framework of analysis in the chapter of organization and management has increased markedly in the last two decades. As such, scholars from a wide variety of disciplines from anthropology to artificial intelligence, have expressed interest in studies framed in a discursive perspective (Schiffrin et al. 2001, Jaworski & Coupland 1999). It is also due to this breadth of scholarly interest that has given rise to a variety of definitions to the terms 'discourse' and what constitutes 'discourse analysis'. For the purposes of this chapter, discourse is defined in its broadest sense as any written or spoken text and discourse analysis is the analysis of language in use where language is viewed as a functional type of social practice (Halliday 1994, Fairclough 1992).

While not without criticism of being both poorly defined and trying to encompass too many aspects at the same time (Reed 2000) and being myopically focused on just language at the expense of context (Deetz 2003), the past few decades has nonetheless seen discourse analysis emerge as a prominent tool used in the field of organization and management studies (Alvesson & Karreman 2000b, 2000a).

There are many tools for discourse analysis, the choice of which will depend on the researcher / practitioner perspective and the type of study conducted. For example, critical discourse analysis (CDA) can be used to investigate organisational power and social hegemonic structures (Grünberg 2014, van Dijk 2001, Wodak et al. 1999, Chouliaraki 1998, Richardson 1998, Fairclough & Wodak 1997, Mumby & Clair 1997), speech acts in argumentation and politeness (Jacobs 1989, Searle 1969, Austin 1962), conversation analysis for group dynamics and identify formation (Wooffitt 2001, Wight 1976, Schegloff 1997, Potter 1997, Watson 1997, Fairclough 1992, Potter & Wetherell 1987, Atkinson and Heritage 1984), register and genre analysis for negotiation (van Leeuwen 1993, Fairclough 1993, 1995, Bahktin 1986, Fowler et al. 1979), and systemic functional linguistics (SFL) in mapping the landscape of human experience and thoughts as expressed in language use (Halliday & Matthiessen 2004, Bloor & Bloor 1995, Halliday 1994, 1985, 1975).

3.2 Systemic Functional Linguistic (SFL) as Theory and Tool of Analysis in the G4 Model of Globalization Processes

3.2.1 Choice of SFL

Traditionally, language has been thought of as a medium for expressing thoughts or reality. SFL reconceptualises language as a semiotic tool connected in the construction, organization and translation of human experiences. It illustrates how linguistic choices systematically contribute to the moulding of social contexts and events. Viewed in this manner language is more than a plane of expression, it actively creates reality. It is simultaneously "a part of reality, a shaper of reality, and a metaphor of reality" (Halliday 1993:8). SLF offers a meticulous and systematic way to analyse language in use.

4. DATA COLLECTION AND METHOD OF ANALYSIS

4.1 Swedish Managers in Singapore

This study combines the primary data collected from Swedish managers working in top level management positions in Swedish managed organizations in Singapore, with the empirical findings that gave rise to the UGPM on Swedish MNEs. The qualitative approach used in the G4 model in semi-structured interviews and language analysis lends complementary insight into the different zones of knowledge represented in the UGPM. The data reflected in this chapter comes from a larger chapter on Swedish managers in Singapore (Cordeiro-Nilsson 2010, Cordeiro-Nilsson 2009).

It was the inherently cosmopolitan fabric of Singapore and the fact that it was home to many important MNE headquarters that made it a country of choice in this study of the G4 model. The targeted group of respondents for the interviews were persons predominantly in leading or managerial positions, such Managing Directors, Chief Executive Officers and Regional Directors etc. The respondents were randomly selected, where no headhunting was conducted for any particular respondent. No single type of organization was targeted, and no one particular industry was targeted either in order to give a broad cross-referential respondent representation.

As such, this study prioritised the selection of participants based on the fact that they were leaders in Swedish managed organizations working in a cross-cultural environment regardless of their age, sex, socio-cultural background and the industry field in which they worked. The assumption was persons in top-level positions were individuals of influence that have the mandate to reconfigure internal organizational structures and practices, especially in the broader context of many Asian cultures that tend to have authoritarian structures of organization. It would also be these individuals in top-level management positions who are key to keeping open, the dialogic relations between the enterprise and the subsidiaries, forming an important aspect of the processes of globalization in both the G4 model and the UGPM.

4.2 Data Collection

The data to this study was collected over a period of ten years, from 2004 to 2014. In the initial 2004 round, a synopsis of the study was emailed to a total of about 147 respondents from Swedish managed organizations in Singapore. There was about a 20% response rate and a total of 23 Swedish respondents were interviewed. This was followed up by a meeting with nine Swedish respondents in Singapore in 2014, with similar questions in semi-structured interviews. All interviews were designed in conversational style, with questions pegged on widening levels of interest that ranged from those regarding the individual at the core, as expatriate managers in Singapore, to what they thought about national / regional policies between Asia and Europe. The main questions of relevance to the purpose of this chapter revolved around organizational structure, transformation, and describing the consequences of such changes. The interviews were of an average time of 1 hour 39 minutes per interview and rendered a total corporate of about 240,000 words after transcription of all interviews. The interviews were transcribed according to the Göteborg Transcription Standard (GTS) version 6.4 (Nivre et al. 2004).

4.3 Framework of Analysis

This section will look at the three types of SFL metafunctions in language that comes through with discourse:

1. The *ideational* metafunction uses language to represent experience, and how experiences are connected with each other.
2. The *interpersonal* uses language to encode interaction. It shows how valid we find our propositions, encoding ideas about obligation and inclination in expression of attitudes.
3. The *textual* metafunction uses language to organise the ideational and interpersonal meanings into a coherent text.

These three types of meaning are not separate but rather, occur simultaneously represented in the text by six processes, where Agency is represented in language via those participants who do (Actors), think (Sensers), say (Sayers), behave (Behaver) and / or exist (Existent). Language is also used to relate participant to an identity or description, in which case, Agency is identified as Carrier and Attribute.

All interviews were analysed for metafunctions. Text Example 1 appears as transcribed in the GTS version 6.4 format. It is used to illustrate Agency found in the various metafunctions. The respondent appears as $M.

4.4 Text Example and Analysis

This section gives an example of how language can be used as a meta-theory, providing a rigorous and systematic framework of data analysis in its various metafunctions. Language reveals itself as a system of meaning codes in terms of revealing underlying ideologies, values and culture. A close analysis of language and how it is used, will reveal how individuals view / interact with each other, construct their organizational practices, and learn from each other. As textual analysis is lengthy, Text Example 1 is given here as an example of data analysis.

Text Example 1: Excerpt from an interview with a Managing Director of a Swedish multinational finance company in Singapore showing the text analysis of metafunctions (most often realized by certain verbs), are square bracketed and italicised. Agency is indicated in **bold.**

1. $M: the values are swedish [*ideational*] /
2. that's one of the most important tasks that **we** have [*ideational, interpersonal*] that when **we** come to singapore from sweden [*interpersonal, textual*] / is to carry the culture [*ideational, interpersonal*] /
3. **we** are called / **we** are sometimes called culture carriers [*ideational, interpersonal*] / and therefore it's important [*ideational*] for **us** to have **swedes or nordic people** [*interpersonal, textual*] /
4. you can say **it's finland denmark norway sweden** [*interpersonal, textual*] / can all serve [*interpersonal*] as cultural carriers because **we** have business in all those countries [*interpersonal, textual*] /
5. so in addition to the business tasks or business responsibilities [*interpersonal, textual*] / **we** also have the responsibility to transfer or carry over [*ideational, interpersonal*] the culture
6. one example maybe um / can describe this /

7. when **i** took over [*interpersonal, textual*] as general manager in 1998 / so **i** came over [*interpersonal, textual*] in another position than general manager position /
8. 1998 **i** was appointed [*interpersonal, textual*] g m for asia /
9. and at that point in time / there were [*interpersonal* more or less nine hierarchic title levels in the bank / **i** mean everything from junior clerk / clerk / senior clerk / junior officer / officer / senior officer / so nine sort of title levels and nine [*interpersonal, textual*] /
10. all levels also had a number of value of annual leave days / as an officer you had one more day than a junior officer [*interpersonal, textual*] /
11. despite the fact that other swedes have / been gms here / **i** don't know why [ideational] **they** didn't find interest to do something about it [*interpersonal*] / but in the bank back home / we have three / so **i** changed that to three [*interpersonal, textual*] /
12. which mean **i** couldn't take away titles [*interpersonal, textual*] / because that would be very sensitive /
13. but **i** tacked them in three main levels and **i** took away all links to annual leave days [*interpersonal, textual*] / it doesn't come from your title / it comes from the number of years in the bank / which is the same in sweden [*ideational, textual*] /
14. everybody starts [*interpersonal*] from the same level and then you add on [*interpersonal*] due to age and due to position /
15. meaning the responsibility you have [*interpersonal*] / not your title / if you have a big responsibility [*interpersonal*] / you're entitled [*interpersonal*] to two more days [*interpersonal*] /
16. so that **i** changed [*interpersonal*] / **i** redid [*interpersonal*] the entire employment hand book because it was quite singaporean style [*interpersonal, ideational*] /
17. it said more or less in every page that everything was uhm / at the discretion [*ideational*] of the general manager [*ideational*] / which is not the case [*ideational*]
18. in the rest of the bank that **staff** should / the **staff** have [*interpersonal*] rights and obligations [*ideational*]/
19. and these are explained and informed [*interpersonal, textual*] in the bank's employment handbook /
20. so **i** took [*interpersonal, textual*] that away / but what can be applied [*interpersonal, ideational*] here / **i** took it over here [*interpersonal*] /
21. everything cannot be applied [*interpersonal, textual*] because the business here is [*interpersonal, textual*] more limited than back home / so a lot of those changes on the soft side [*interpersonal, textual*] /
22. and then **i** also changed [*interpersonal, textual*] the organization so that instead of having [*interpersonal*] one boss here and many people underneath /
23. and **he** was sort of giving instructions [*interpersonal*] to all of them /
24. **i** took away [*interpersonal*] the boss and opened up so that the responsibility [*interpersonal, textual*] was on more people and everybody had more to say / more to decide over / more influence [*ideational, interpersonal, textual*] /
25. but **they** also exposed more [*interpersonal, textual*] / so **customers** if they called in directly you have to be able to answer [*interpersonal, textual*] /
26. **you** cannot go to [*interpersonal, textual*] the boss because he's [*interpersonal, textual*] not there anymore [*ideational*] /
27. so that higher exposure was abit painful [*ideational, intertextual*] for **them** / because **they** were not trained [*interpersonal*] before /
28. so of course that **you** can only do [*interpersonal, textual*] if **you** add on education / training

29. and **you** give [*interpersonal, textual*] responsibility without taking it back / that **you** give [*interpersonal, textual*] a service they can take care and **i** will still have [*interpersonal, textual*] the responsibility if they make a big mistake / **it's still mine** [*interpersonal, textual*]
30. but **i** cannot say okay / you take care of this / but **i** also check [*ideational*] what you do / **you** cannot do that [*interpersonal, textual*]/
31. so **you** have to decide [*ideational*] if **you** can decentralise [*interpersonal, textual*] responsibility and then stay [*interpersonal, textual*] / that took also some time /
32. but now **they** can / **they** can [*interpersonal, textual*]

The following section discusses in general, the findings of the data analysis, thereafter filling in the gaps of knowledge found for the LL quadrant.

5. FINDINGS AND DISCUSSION

5.1 Swedes as Agents of Change

The text analysis showed that Swedish top managers who head foreign units of operations outside of Sweden are agents of change, many of whom have as their portfolio to manage the uncertainties of being in a foreign market with a different local culture. These individuals are part of the subsidiary's essential internationalizing and globalizing processes agents when it comes to fostering a sustainable organizational culture towards the acceptance of uncertainty and continuous learning.

Agency in organisation change is expressed mostly in the *ideational* and *interpersonal* metafunctions. Data from the interviews indicated that at both *ideational* and *interpersonal* levels of meaning, the Swedes in Singapore found themselves to have main Agency (also illustrated in Text Example 1 with $M). The Swedish managers saw themselves as having a responsibility for bringing over and grounding what they considered to be Swedish values in the Singapore subsidiary. Most attribute themselves as personally responsible for the carrying over of culture by the use of the constructs (Text Example 1, lines 1-5), "we also have the responsibility to transfer or carry over the culture".

As managing directors, the Swedes tended to view themselves as the key individuals to make changes. This idea is reflected in Text Example 1 when respondent $M talks about how it was she who had taken on the initiative to flatten the hierarchy of the organization, and create something of a semblance to what she recognized as 'Swedish' with less tiers (in lines 9, 10, 13, 15, 20, 22, 24).

However more than being simply implementers of change or change catalysts by action, top Swedish managers see themselves as bringing ideology from Sweden to Singapore, as a way of seeing / visioning and thus doing / being. For example, the ideology of egalitarianism, and the value of individual empowerment is implemented slowly, by first creating a flatter organizational structure and decentralising decision making (in lines 22 to 26, 29, 30 and 31).

Supported by *ideational* metafunctions, the processes of Thinking reflected in the mental schemas of individuals (line 2, the idea of 'culture carrying'), organizational change is most often marked by the *interpersonal* metafunctions such as tearing down the existing organizational structure and erecting a different one in its place (line 9 and in line 11, the *ideational* metafunction reflects a certain mental focus of intent on making this happen). The material act of re-writing the organization handbook (lines 16 and 17) and of taking the decision as top manager to not interfere (lines 24 to 27) and let mistakes happen, deciding too, to take full responsibility when mistakes do happen (lines 29). Incorporating 'education' and 'training' are also concrete Actions reflected in the *interpersonal* and *textual* metafunctions (line 28) that characterise organizational change.

There seems to be two types of organisational change reflected in the metafunctions of language found in the data in general. The first is the new administrative processes, are usually initiated by the top manager of the organization. This consisted of decentralisation, consensus seeking and a flattening of the organization structure. The second is when employees begin to transition into this new routine with new behaviour and attitudes. The 'opening up' and taking on greater responsibility and even consulting with each other more, as there was no longer an intermediate 'boss' to turn to (lines 22 to 27) marks the beginning of a new type of organization environment and a new way of doing things (line 32).

5.2 Swedish Management Style

Swedish top-level managers interviewed generally preferred to have a facilitative and transpersonal leadership style (Cordeiro-Nilsson 2009, Jönsson 1995). This was characterised by a preference for lateral organizational hierarchies, aligned with the matrix organizational structure of the enterprise. Within the Asian context, they encouraged employees to voice opinions during group meetings, as one Swedish respondent (not shown in Text Example 1) said, "in the management team for example, I said I want to have discussions. I want people to discuss and they have never done that before. I want to have a discussion before we take a decision, because in the beginning, I said this is the problem we have, and I said, what are we going to do with it? And there was absolute silence! "You're the boss you should decide" – No! We have to talk about it we have to decide *together*, because we're going to jump together."

From Text Example 1, the matrix organization style that encourages continuous learning due to the encouraged interaction between subsidiaries in intra-subsidiary trade also percolates down into individual subsidiary practices set in motion by Swedish top-level managers. When the vertical hierarchies prominent in Asian organizations and centralized decision making is flattened and de centralised, $M said that the learning journey was difficult initially because people were forced out of their comfort zones to take on greater responsibility, without being able to go to a 'boss' for a decision. Employees had to accustom themselves to this empowerment which at first they saw as a threat to their own positions within the company because most Asian cultures are unforgiving towards mistakes. In Swedish establishments in foreign markets, part of the open Swedish culture towards learning is to be able to learn from your mistakes. This transfer of ideology and culture is not immediately apparent in the foreign located unit and as $M mentioned, the process of change took time. Employees need time to mature and develop as individuals, which Swedish facilitative leadership encouraged.

Learning was also a two-way process. This is apparent when $M tells of the joy she has had in learning more about the capacities and potentials of her own employees as a result of decentralisation and the flattening of organizational hierarchy. When people were forced to speak with each other across departments and to go to each other for advise or consensus decision making, this opening of network, of sharing information and knowledge, gave her learning insight as a leader, into the talent capacities and knowledge reservoir of the unit.

5.3 Filling in the UGPM Knowledge Gap in the LL Quadrant of the G4 Model

With language as theory and framework of analysis, the results and findings can then be filled into the LL quadrant of the G4 model, giving a richer perspective to the UGPM pertaining to how Swedish top-level managers are agents of change that bring values from H*n* to H1. The new knowledge found from a combination of empirical efforts both quantitative and qualitative, is shown in Figure 4. As the figure illustrates, a language analysis can reveal underlying organizational ideologies, to which fills out the knowledge gap in the UL quadrant of knowledge.

What a language analysis and the G4 model has illustrated is that Swedish top-level managers working in foreign located units of the enterprise are professionals at managing uncertainty and encouraging continuous learning, thereby being key human elements in the dialogic processes of subsidiary and enterprise globalization. Most respondents interviewed reveal themselves to also have many years of experience of living and working in the foreign market context, so that they have acquired some tacit knowledge of the region, its market opportunities and its local culture.

Figure 4. The Gotheborg IV (G4) globalization model expressed in an 8 perspective, four-quadrant axis diagram, for the case of globalized Swedish MNEs
Source: (Vahlne & Ivarsson 2014, Cordeiro-Nilsson 2009, Wilber 2006)

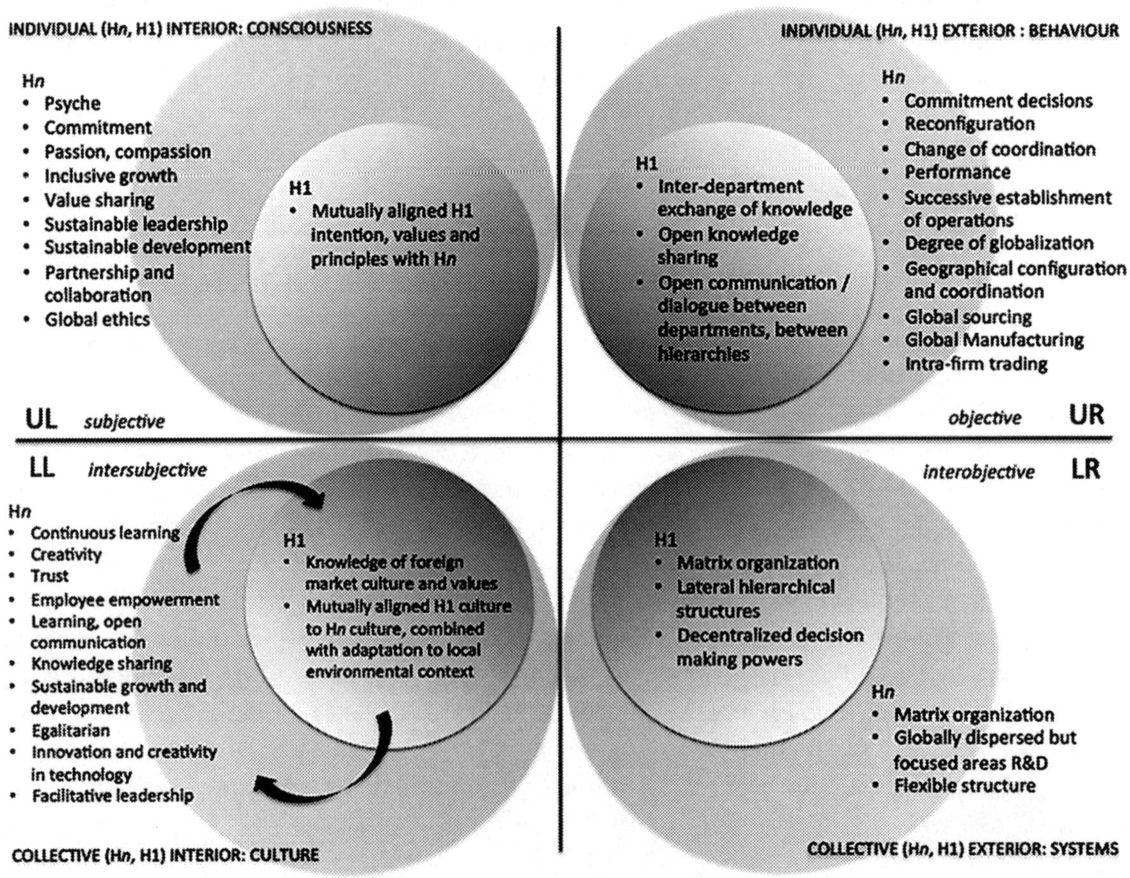

6. CONCLUDING DISCUSSION AND SOME PRACTICAL APPLICATIONS OF THE GOTHEBORG IV (G4) MODEL

In addressing the upcoming interest of the multifaceted role of language in IB, this chapter introduced the Gotheborg IV or G4 model that maps the knowledge zones of the internationalization and globalization processes reflected in the UM, and the later UGPM in a four quadrant axis that renders a more dynamic eight knowledge perspectives to the globalization process.

In the G4 model the use of the words 'enterprise' (H*n*) and 'subsidiary' (H1) is disambiguated. This disambiguation of terms had been implied but not detailed in the UM and UGPM. This distinction in word use is important due to the very nature of the characteristics of both the processes of internationalization and globalization, of the increasing setting up of geographically dispersed foreign subsidiaries and globally coordinated activities of manufacturing, sourcing and R&D capabilities. With the distinction between H*n* and H1 that the G4 model makes, eight interior and exterior perspectives result in the four quadrants of knowledge is reflected, that gives a complementary dynamism to the perspectives of the UGPM. These quadrants of knowledge then allowed for a systematic analysis of the empirical and theoretical efforts towards understanding the processes of globalization, in particular, also showing where knowledge gaps existed. In this case, the key elements to a successful globalization process such as the management of uncertainty, and fostering a culture of continuous learning and creativity that was referred to in the UGPM, but not explicitly detailed in terms of qualitative data analysis was addressed. This knowledge laid in the LL quadrant, where it is in this area that the use of language as theory and framework of analysis could prove useful in uncovering empirical evidence towards the dialogic relations between H*n* and H1.

The gaps in knowledge were then filled into the quadrants of the G4 model where data primarily indicated that Swedish top-level managers were indispensable agents of change management. Swedish managers saw themselves as responsible for bringing H*n* culture to H1, as well as understanding and bridging local and foreign gaps in culture. Many Swedish top-level managers have themselves, lived and worked in Asia, so that the knowledge of foreign markets, and culture resides in them as repositories of tacit knowledge in experience of working across cultures.

The conceiving of the Gotheborg IV (G4) model presented in this chapter was based on the combined efforts of numerous studies on the globalizing processes of Swedish MNEs that also rendered the Upsala Model. This four quadrant, eight perspectives model can be applied both as a theoretical framework and framework of analysis in future research in IB, providing a richer, more dynamic perspective of an MNE's globalization process, where it is acknowledged that the process of globalization is one that is ever evolving, sometimes seen as "a tortuous process" (Vahlne & Ivarsson 2014:245).

REFERENCES

Alvesson, M., & Karreman, D. (2000a). Varieties of discourse: On the chapter of organizations through discourse analysis. *Human Relations*, *53*(9), 1125–1149. doi:10.1177/0018726700539002

Alvesson, M., & Karreman, D. (2000b). Taking the linguistic turn in organizational research: Challenges, responses, consequences. *The Journal of Applied Behavioral Science*, *36*(2), 136–158. doi:10.1177/0021886300362002

Andersen, O. (1993). On the internationalization process of firms: A critical analysis. *Journal of International Business Studies*, *24*(2), 209–231. doi:10.1057/palgrave.jibs.8490230

Atkinson, J., & Heritage, J. (Eds.). (1984). *Structures of Social Action: Studies in Conversation Analysis*. Cambridge, UK: Cambridge University Press.

Austin, J. L. (1962). *How to Do Things with Words*. Oxford, UK: Oxford University Press.

Bahktin, M. (1986). *Speech Gnres and Other Late Essays* (C. Emerson & M. Holquist, Eds.). Austin, TX: University of Texas Press.

Beyene, T., Hinds, P. J., & Crampton, C. D. (2009). *Walking through jelly: language proficiency, emotions and disrupted collborationin global work*. Harvard Business School Working Paper 09-13. Retrieved from http://bit.ly/1zFix3r

Birkinshaw, J. (2002). The art of Swedish management. *Business Strategy Review*, *13*(2), 11–19. doi:10.1111/1467-8616.00205

Bloor, T., & Bloor, M. (1995). *The Functional Analysis of English: A Hallidayan Approach*. London: Arnold.

Boussebaa, M., Sinha, S., & Gabriel, Y. (2014). Englishization in offshore call centers: A postcolonial perspective. *Journal of International Business Studies*, *45*(9), 1152–1169. doi:10.1057/jibs.2014.25

Brannen, M. Y. (2004). When Mickey loses face: Recontextualization, semantic fit and the semiotics of foreignness. *Academy of Management Review*, *29*(4), 593–616.

Brannen, M. Y., & Doz, Y. L. (2012). Corporate languages and strategic agility: Trapped in your jargon or lost in translation? *California Management Review*, *54*(3), 77–97. doi:10.1525/cmr.2012.54.3.77

Brannen, M. Y., Piekkari, R., & Tietze, S. (2014). The multifaceted role of language in international business: Unpacking the forms, functions and features of a critical challenge to MNC theory and performance. *Journal of International Business Studies*, *45*(5), 495–507. doi:10.1057/jibs.2014.24

Brannen, M. Y., & Salk, J. E. (2000). Partnering across borders: Negotiating organizational culture in a German-Japanese joint venture. *Human Relations*, *53*(4), 451–487. doi:10.1177/0018726700534001

Cäker, M., Andersson, T., & Wickelgren, M. (2011). Formal incentive systems in organizations with a swedish management style: Conflict or interaction? *Conference: The Actor-Reality Perspective*. Retrieved from http://bit.ly/1xjBUi7

Carneiro, J., Rocha, A., & Silva, J. F. (2008). Challenging the uppsala internationalization model: A contingent approach to the internationalization of services. *BAR. Brazilian Administration Review*, *5*(2), 85–103. doi:10.1590/S1807-76922008000200002

Childs, M. L., & Jin, B. (2014). Is Uppsala Model valid to fashion retailers?: An analysis from internationalisation patterns of fast fashion retailers. *Journal of Fashion Marketing and Management*, *18*(1), 36–51. doi:10.1108/JFMM-10-2012-0061

Chouliaraki, L. (1998). Regulation in "progressivist" pedagogic discourse: Individualized teacher–pupil talk. *Discourse & Society*, *9*(1), 5–32. doi:10.1177/0957926598009001001

Cordeiro-Nilsson, C. M. (2009). *Swedish Management in Singapore: A Discourse Analysis Chapter.* (Doctoral Dissertation). Department of Philosophy, Linguistics and Theory of Science, University of Gothenburg, Gothenburg, Sweden.

Cordeiro-Nilsson, C. M. (2010). A discourse analysis chapter of assimilation and integration of management style: The case of Swedish managers in Singapore. *The New English Teacher*, *4*(1), 13–53.

Cordeiro-Nilsson, C. M., & Hawamdeh, S. (2011). Leveraging socio-culturally situated tacit knowledge. *Journal of Knowledge Management*, *15*(1), 88–103. doi:10.1108/13673271111108710

Crick, D. (1999). An investigation into SMEs' use of languages in their export operations. *International Journal of Entrepreneurial Behaviour and Research*, *5*(1), 19–31. doi:10.1108/13552559910259810

Cutler, A. (2012). *Native Listening: Language Experience and the Recognition of Spoken Words*. Cambridge, MA: MIT Press.

Deetz, S. (2003). Reclaiming the legacy of the linguistic turn. *Organization*, *10*(3), 421–429. doi:10.1177/13505084030103002

Du-Babcock, B. (2006). An analysis of top management strategies and the turn-taking behaviour in the Hong Kong bilingual environment: The impact of cultural and language use. *Journal of Business Communication*, *43*(1), 21–42. doi:10.1177/0021943605282373

Dunning, J. H., Fujita, M., & Yakova, N. (2007). Some macro-data on the regionalisation/globalisation debate: A comment on the Rugman/Verbeke analysis. *Journal of International Business Studies*, *38*(1), 177–199. doi:10.1057/palgrave.jibs.8400241

Duranti, A. (1997). *Linguistic anthropology*. Cambridge, UK: Cambridge University Press. doi:10.1017/CBO9780511810190

Fairclough, N. (1992). *Discourse and Social Change*. Cambridge, MA: Polity Press.

Fairclough, N. (1993). Critical discourse analysis and the marketization of public discourse: The universities. *Discourse & Society*, *4*(2), 133–168. doi:10.1177/0957926593004002002

Fairclough, N. (1995). *Media Discourse*. London: Edward Arnold.

Fairclough, N. (2005). Discourse analysis in organization studies: The case for critical realism. *Peripheral Vision*, *26*(6), 915–939.

Fairclough, N., & Wodak, R. (1997). Critical discourse analysis. In T. van Dijk (Ed.), *Discourse as Social Interaction: Discourse Studies: A Multidisciplinary Introduction* (Vol. 2). London: Sage.

Figueira-de-Lemos, F., Johanson, J., & Vahlne, J. (2011). Risk management in the internationalization process of the firm: A note on the Uppsala model. *Journal of World Business*, *46*(2), 143–153. doi:10.1016/j.jwb.2010.05.008

Flores, R. G., & Aguilera, R. V. (2007). Globalization and locational choice: An analysis of US multinational firms in 1980 and 2000. *Journal of International Business Studies*, *38*(7), 1187–1210. doi:10.1057/palgrave.jibs.8400307

Forsgren, M., & Hagström, P. (2007). Ignorant and impatient internationalization?: The Uppsala Model and internationalization patterns for internet-related firms. *Critical Perspectives on International Business, 3*(4), 291–305. doi:10.1108/17422040710832559

Fowler, R., Hodge, B., Kress, G., & Trew, T. (1979). *Language and Control*. London: Routledge & Kegan Paul.

Fredriksson, R., Barner-Rasmussen, W., & Piekkari, R. (2006). The multinational corporation as a multilingual organization: The notion of a common corporate language. *Corporate Communications: An International Journal, 11*(4), 406–423. doi:10.1108/13563280610713879

Ghemawat, P. (2003). Semiglobalization and international business strategy. *Journal of International Business Strategy, 34*(2), 138–152. doi:10.1057/palgrave.jibs.8400013

Grünberg, A. (2014). Saying and doing: Speech actions, speech acts and related events. *European Journal of Philosophy, 22*(2), 173–199. doi:10.1111/j.1468-0378.2011.00481.x

Halliday, M. A. K. (1975). *Learning How to Mean: Explorations in the Development of Language*. London: Edward Arnold. doi:10.1016/B978-0-12-443701-2.50025-1

Halliday, M. A. K. (1985). *An Introduction to Functional Grammar*. London: Edward Arnold.

Halliday, M. A. K. (1993). Quantitative studies and probabilities in grammar. In M. Hoey (Ed.), Data, Description, Discourse: Papers on the English Language in Honour of John McH Sinclair. London: HarperCollins.

Halliday, M. A. K. (1994). *An Introduction to Functional Grammar* (2nd ed.). London: Edward Arnold.

Halliday, M. A. K., & Matthiessen, C. (2004). *An Introduction to Functional Grammar*. NY: Routledge.

Hodge, R., & Kress, G. R. (1993). *Language as ideology* (2nd ed.). London: Routledge.

Hofstede, G. (1984). *Culture's consequences: International differences in work-related values*. London: Sage.

Hofstede, G. (2001). *Culture's consequences, comparing values, behaviours, institutions and organizations across nations*. Thousand Oaks, CA: Sage.

House, R. J., Hanges, P. J., Havidan, M., Dorfman, P. W., & Gupta, V. (2004). Culture, leadership and organizations: the GLOBE chapter of 62 societies. Thousand Oaks, CA: Sage.

Introduction. (1997). Invan Dijk, T. (Ed.), *Discourse as Structure and Process: A Multidisciplinary Introduction* (Vol. 1). London: Sage.

Jacobs, S. (1989). Speech acts and arguments. *Argumentation, 3*(4), 345–365. doi:10.1007/BF00182603

Jaworski, A., & Coupland, N. (Eds.). (1999). The Discourse Reader. London: Routledge.

Johanson, J., & Vahlne, J. (1977). The internationalization process of the firm--A model of knowledge development and increasing foreign market commitments. *Journal of International Business Studies, 8*(1), 23.

Johanson, J., & Vahlne, J. (2009). The Uppsala internationalization process model revisited: From liability of foreignness to liability of outsidership. *Journal of International Business Studies*, *40*(9), 1411–1431. doi:10.1057/jibs.2009.24

Jönsson, S. (1995). *Goda Utsikter: Svenskt Management*. Gothenburg: BAS.

Källström, A. (1997). The Swedish leadership style. *Ledelse Og Erhvervsøkonomi*, *61*(1), 67–73.

Kozlowski, S. W. J., Chao, G. T., Grand, J. A., Baun, M. T., & Kuljanin, G. (2013). Advancing multi-level research design: Capturing the dynamics of emergence. *Organizational Research Methods*, *16*(4), 581–615. doi:10.1177/1094428113493119

Langhoff, T. (1997). The influence of culture differences on internationalisation processes of firms: an introduction to a semiotic and intercultural perspective. In I. Bjorkman & M. Forsgren (Eds.), *The nature of the international firm*. Copenhagen: Handelshojskolens Forlag.

Leitch, S., & Palmer, I. (2009). Analysing texts in contexts: Current practices and new protocols for Critical Discourse Analysis in Organization Studies. *Journal of Management Studies*, *47*(6), 1194–1212. doi:10.1111/j.1467-6486.2009.00884.x

Lindell, M., & Arvonen, J. (1996). The Nordic management style – an investigation. In S. Jönsson (Ed.), *Perspectives of Scandinavian Management* (pp. 11–36). Gothenburg Research Institute.

Lohmann, J. (2011). Do language barriers affect trade? *Economics Letters*, *110*(2), 159–162. doi:10.1016/j.econlet.2010.10.023

Luo, Y., & Shenkar, O. (2006). The multinational corporation as a multilingual community: Language and organization in a global context. *Journal of International Business Studies*, *37*(3), 321–339. doi:10.1057/palgrave.jibs.8400197

Ly, A., Esperanca, J. P., Pereira, I. N., & Amaral-Baptista, M. A. (2013). The ten most influential global languages: exploring their effect on international trade. *Academy of Management Proceedings 2013*. Retrieved from http://bit.ly/1I3I1vC

Makela, K., Kalla, H. K., & Piekkari, R. (2007). Interpersonal similarity as a driver for knowledge sharing within multinational corporations. *International Business Review*, *16*(1), 1–22. doi:10.1016/j.ibusrev.2006.11.002

Marschan, R., Welch, D., & Welch, L. (1997). Language: The forgotten factor in multinational management. *European Management Journal*, *15*(5), 591–598. doi:10.1016/S0263-2373(97)00038-8

Marschan-Piekkari, R., Welch, D. E., & Welch, L. S. (1999a). In the shadow: The impact of language on structure, power and communication in the multinational. *International Business Review*, *8*(4), 421–440. doi:10.1016/S0969-5931(99)00015-3

Marschan-Piekkari, R., Welch, D. E., & Welch, L. S. (1999b). Adopting a common corporate language: IHRM implications. *International Journal of Human Resource Management*, *10*(3), 377–390. doi:10.1080/095851999340387

Mumby, D., & Clair, R. (1997). Organisational discourse. In T. van Dijk (Ed.), *Discourse as Social Interaction. Discourse Studies. A Multidisciplinary Introduction* (Vol. 2). London: Sage.

Nivre, J., Allwood, J., Grönqvit, L., Gunnarsson, M., Ahlsén, E., Vappula, H., & Ottesjö, C. et al. (2004). *Gothenburg Transcription Standard 6.4*. Department of Linguistics. Gothenburg University.

Oviatt, B., & McDougall, P. (1994). Toward a theory of international new ventures. *Journal of International Business Studies*, *25*(1), 45–64. doi:10.1057/palgrave.jibs.8490193

Piekkari, R. (2008). Languages and careers in multinational corporations. In S. Tietze (Ed.), *International management and language* (pp. 128–137). London: Routledge.

Potter, J. (1997). Discourse analysis as a way of analysing naturally occurring talk. In D. Silverman (Ed.), *Qualitative Research: Theory, Methods and Practice*. London: Sage.

Potter, J., & Wetherell, M. (1987). *Discourse and Social Psychology*. London: Sage.

Reed, M. (2000). The limits of discourse analysis. *Organization*, *7*(3), 524–530. doi:10.1177/135050840073011

Richardson, K. (1998). Signs and wonders: interpreting the economy through television. In A. Bell & P. Garrett (Eds.), *Approaches to Media Discourse*. Oxford, UK: Blackwell.

Rugman, A. M. (2003). Regional strategy and the demise of globalization. *Journal of International Management*, *9*(4), 409–417. doi:10.1016/j.intman.2003.08.004

Rugman, A. M., & Verbeke, A. (2004). A perspective on regional and global strategies of multinational enterprises. *Journal of International Business Studies*, *35*(1), 3–18. doi:10.1057/palgrave.jibs.8400073

SanAntonio, P. M. (1987). Social mobility and language use in an American company in Japan. *Journal of Language and Social Psychology*, *6*(3–4), 191–200. doi:10.1177/0261927X8763003

Schegloff, E. (1997). Whose text? Whose context? *Discourse & Society*, *8*(2), 165–183. doi:10.1177/0957926597008002002

Schiffrin, D., Tannen, D., & Hamilton, H. E. (2001). *The Handbook of Discourse Analysis*. Oxford, UK: Blackwell.

Searle, J. R. (1969). *Speech Acts: An Essay in the Philosophy of Language*. Cambridge, UK: Cambridge University Press. doi:10.1017/CBO9781139173438

Steyaert, C., Ostendorp, A., & Gaibrois, C. (2011). Multilingual organizations as "linguascapes": Negotiating the position of English through discursive practices. *Journal of World Business*, *46*(3), 270–278. doi:10.1016/j.jwb.2010.07.003

Tenzer, H., Pudelko, M., & Harzing, A. W. (2014). The impact of language barriers on trust formation in multinational teams. *Journal of International Business Studies*, *45*(5), 508–535. doi:10.1057/jibs.2013.64

Terjesen, S., Tenzer, H., Hinger, J., & Harzing, A. W. (2014). *Language in international business: a review and agenda for future research*. Paper presented at the 40th Annual Conference of the European International Business Academy (EIBA), Uppsala, Sweden.

Tietze, S., & Dick, P. (2013). The victorious English language: Hegemonic practices in the management academy. *Journal of Management Inquiry*, *22*(1), 122–134. doi:10.1177/1056492612444316

Vaara, E., Tienari, J., Piekkari, R., & Säntti, R. (2005). Language and the circuits of power in a merging multinational corporation. *Journal of Management Studies*, *42*(3), 595–623. doi:10.1111/j.1467-6486.2005.00510.x

Vahlne, J., & Ivarsson, I. (2014). The globalization of swedish MNEs: Empirical evidence and theoretical explanations. *Journal of International Business Studies*, *45*(3), 227–247. doi:10.1057/jibs.2013.60

Vahlne, J., & Johanson, J. (2013). The Uppsala Model on evolution of the multinational business enterprise: From internalization to coordination of networks. *International Marketing Review*, *30*(3), 189–210. doi:10.1108/02651331311321963

Vahlne, J.-E., Ivarsson, I., & Johanson, J. (2011). The tortuous road to globalization of Volvo's heavy truck business - Extending the scope of the Uppsala model. *International Business Review*, *20*(1), 1–14. doi:10.1016/j.ibusrev.2010.05.003

van Dijk, T. A. (2001). Discourse, ideology and context. *Folia Linguistica*, *35*(1-2), 11–40. doi:10.1515/flin.2001.35.1-2.11

van Leeuwen, T. (1993). Genre and field in critical discourse analysis: A synopsis. *Discourse & Society*, *4*(2), 193–223. doi:10.1177/0957926593004002004

Watson, R. (1997). Ethnomethodology and textual analysis. In D. Silverman (Ed.), *Qualitative Research: Theory, Method and Practice*. London: Sage.

Welch, D. E., & Welch, L. S. (2008). The importance of language in international knowledge transfer. *Management International Review*, *48*(3), 339–360. doi:10.1007/s11575-008-0019-7

Welch, D. E., Welch, L. S., & Piekkari, R. (2005). Speaking in tongues: The importance of language in international management processes. *International Studies of Management & Organization*, *35*(1), 10–27.

Wight, J. (1976). Speech acts: Thought acts. *Educational Review*, *28*(3), 168–179. doi:10.1080/0013191760280302

Wilber, K. (2006). *Integral Spirituality: A startling new role for religion in the modern and postmodern world*. Boston: Integral Books.

Wodak, R., de Cillia, R., Reisigl, M., & Liebhart, K. (1999). *The Discursive Construction of National Identity*. Edinburgh, UK: Edinburgh University Press.

Wooffitt, R. (2001). Researching psychic practitioners: conversation analysis. In M. Wetherell, S. Taylor, & S. Yates (Eds.), *Discourse as Data: A Guide for analysis*. London: Sage Publications.

Wu, Y. (2013). Business English as a lingua franca (BELF). *International Education Studies*, *6*(10), 130–138. doi:10.5539/ies.v6n10p130

KEY TERMS AND DEFINITIONS

Globalization: Definition found on page 1 of chapter contribution, "Globalization was defined by Vahlne, Ivarsson and Johansson (2011:1) as "...an effort to optimize a business in terms of its configuration and coordination systems globally and globalization, like the internationalization process, is characterized by the management of complexities and uncertainties requiring learning and commitment building".

Gotheborg IV / G4 Model: Definition found on page 2 of the chapter contribution, "The Gotheborg IV or G4 model is introduced as a richer means of visualising knowledge of the firm's globalization process as reflected in the UGPM."

Swedish Management: Is both (i) a management style of Swedish leaders in organizations both in Sweden and in Swedish managed subsidiaries abroad, and (ii) a field of study within the discipline of international business studies.

Swedish Management / Swedish MNEs and Language: Reference and context found on page 2 of chapter contribution, "In a combination of efforts of the studies that rendered the UM, the UGPM, and studies on Swedish management (Cordeiro-Nilsson 2010, Cordeiro-Nilsson 2009, Cäker, Andersson, Wickelgren 2011, Birkinshaw 2002, Källström 1997, Lindell & Arvonen 1996, Jönsson 1995), the conceptualisations in this chapter serve to bridge the knowledge gap in the globalization process by focusing on the role language can play in the context of Swedish MNEs in the field IB studies. The Gotheborg IV or G4 model is introduced as a richer means of visualising knowledge of the firm's globalization process as reflected in the UGPM."

Swedish MNEs: Refers to Swedish founded multinational enterprises that include Volvo AB, SKF, Atlast Copco etc.

Uppsala Model: Definition found on page 1 of chapter contribution, "The most prominently cited of internationalization models is the Uppsala Model (UM) by Johanson & Vahlne (1977)."

Chapter 12
Chinese Wisdom, World Quality: A Visual Semiotic Analysis of China's "Zou Xiang Shi Jie" (Going Global)

Cheryl Marie Cordeiro
University of Gothenburg, Sweden

ABSTRACT

The typical feature of emergent economies is a slow, apparent transformation from being predominantly a home base of Foreign Direct Investments (FDI) to becoming more home markets for various firms that expand internationally. In this aspect, China differs from its Asian forerunners. Without question, the most rapid development in recent decades within East Asia and the global economy as a whole is the (re-)emergence of China. While most studies on growth strategies for multinational corporations from emerging economies come from the perspective of economic strategies in international business, this study offers a novel perspective by using visual semiotics as a framework of study and analysis of data. It uses theories of social semiotics borne of the traditions of linguistics to conduct a systematic analysis of the representations of China's desire to go global with their automobile industry. The company in focus is China's Zhejiang Geely Holding Group (Geely) in the years between 2007 to 2011, just prior to an after its acquisition of Volvo Car Corporation (VCC).

1. INTRODUCTION

The typical feature of emergent economies, particularly those in Asia, from Singapore, South Korean, Taiwan and also Thailand is a slow, apparent transformation from being predominantly a home base of foreign direct investments (FDI) to becoming more home markets for various firms that expand internationally (Alvstam & Ivarsson 2014). In this aspect, China differs from its forerunners. Without question, the most rapid development in recent decades within East Asia and the global economy as a whole is the (re-)emergence of China. China recorded the highest growth rate in the world between 1980 and 2003 with annual average rates of more than 10 percent. The IMF World Economic Outlook Database from 2005 has also ranked China's economy as highest in GDP accumulated growth (in percent at constant prices) at above 320% compared to the next highest economies at about 150% (Ireland and Singapore).

DOI: 10.4018/978-1-5225-0276-0.ch012

Two significant characteristics of China's renaissance is its populous, cost-efficient labour force and its openness to global trade (Dicken 2015). It began with its *"yin jin lai"* ('coming-in') strategy (Tang et al. 2008:37) after the relaunch of the 'Four Modernizations' in 1978, where its economic global influences could be seen to increase with the launch of the *"zou xiang shi jie"* (going global) and *"yu lang gong wu"* ('dances with wolves') strategies (Alvstam & Ivarsson 2014, Tang et a. 2008). As a result of its going global efforts, China's influence today stretches deeper than its exports of cost efficient goods, exhibited in its foreign policy and global diplomacy in the aftermath of the global financial crisis that began in 2007/8 (Deng 2014). Many voices seem to regard China's rise with weariness and caution, where those who consider themselves a global power are caught in the web of deciphering a value and meaning system set in a language that is not quite understood (Dicken 2015, Deng 2014).

In this process of the globalization and reconfiguration of China, language plays a focal role, being involved with almost every aspect of human interaction and human cognition (Ng, Ye & Lee 2011, Fairclough 2006). The capacity for language is innate in the human species with a distinct social function. It is the medium in which thoughts are organized and communication proceeds (Hodge & Kress 1993). In the context of globalization and international management, where organizations find themselves having to navigate the different language environments and their meanings, language is increasingly acknowledged as being at the heart of international business (IB) activities (Brannen, Piekkari & Tietze 2014). Yet, few studies outside the field of sociolinguistics have studied language as used in a globalizing context, and in understanding of the workings of organizations (Cordeiro-Nilsson 2009, Leitch & Palmer 2009, Fairclough & Thomas 2004, Alvesson & Karreman 2000).

Language is a semiotic system of symbolic representation of meaning, used to both describe and circumscribe meaning in a certain reality. Being an effective tool of transaction (i.e. taking material action with words), it continues to contribute to the evolving nature of human development and civilization (Cook-Greuter 1995). Because meanings belong to culture, rather than to specific semiotic modes, studying both linguistic and visual structures point towards particular interpretations of experience and forms of organizational interaction (Kress & Van Leeuwen 2006). As such, language in this chapter takes on a more comprehensive definition, encompassing not just the grammar of linguistic structures, but also that of visual structures.

The specific example taken in this chapter as an example of an Asian-founded emerging market firm is the acquisition in 2010 of the originally Swedish company Volvo Car Corporation (VCC) by Chinese Zhejiang Geely Holding Group (Geely). This chapter consists of a visual semiotic analysis of the globalization efforts of Geely. It traces the semiotic developments of China's global ambitions in the automobile industry, analysing the years prior to and after, Geely's acquisition of VCC from between 2007 and 2011, with the years of the negotiation for VCC falling between mainly 2009 and 2010, offering insights to the study of emerging global organizations from emerging economies (Alvstam & Ivarsson 2014). It illustrates how theories of social semiotics borne of the traditions of systemic functional linguistics (SFL) and critical discourse analysis (CDA) can be applied in conducting a systematic analysis of the representations of China's desire to go global with their automobile industry, tracing Geely's organization ideological developments in global corporate visioning and ambition as reflected even in their annual reports between 2007 and 2011.

This chapter is organized in the following manner: the following section will give an overview of the Chinese automobile industry from a Swedish perspective, followed by background information to China's Geely. The background information of Geely serves as the focal points of contributing information to the narrative of Geely, a narrative that is then reproduced in a discourse of text and visuals in secondary data on the company such as appears in print media. Geely's narrative and generated discourse leads to section 2, which gives a current outline of the status of language in the field of IB studies. It situates visual semiotics as both theory and method of analysis for the corporate communication efforts in the study of an Asian-founded company going global. Section 3 describes the framework of analysis, followed by section 4 which illustrates visual semiotics analysis in conjunction with a discussion of the findings. Section 5 is the concluding discussion that illustrates how visual semiotics might be applied for future studies of corporate ideology and as insight into the trajectory of corporate ambitions.

1.1 The Chinese Automobile Industry: A Swedish Perspective

2008 to 2010 were tense and interesting years for those with an interest in the global automobile industry. When the financial crisis of 2008 threatened the US automakers, Ford automobile, facing economic downturns, sold Jaguar Land Rover to Tata Motors of India, thereafter announcing in December of the same year that they were looking at the possibility of selling VCC, a purchase acquired from Sweden Volvo AB in 1999. The rumoured candidates and interested investors to the purchase of VCC were global players who resided in Germany, Sweden, China and Russia. It was soon indicated that the Chinese company Geely Holding Group (Geely) emerged as the most interested party to acquire VCC, although in true Chinese politeness and culture of communication, their intent of purchase was often laid in ambiguity in the press. This characteristic of ambiguity concerning commercial relations between the two entities it seemed would continue with the developments of their relations even after 2011 (Alvstam & Ivarsson 2014).

Even after its brief acquisition by American Ford Motor Company, VCC continues to hold Swedish heritage and values (Jönsson & Wickelgren 2011). Latin for meaning "I roll", it was the Swedish ball bearing manufacturing company Sales Manager, Assar Gabrielsson and Managing Director Björn Prytz that founded Volvo AB in 1926, building its very first cars in the hinterlands of Gothenburg. The long standing brand philosophy of VCC, rooted in driver safety that has today been transformed beyond the individual to safety and responsibility of the environment, resonates to every design detail of each Volvo car and vehicle manufactured since the early 1900s. Their branding is the soul of Swedish design, their care for the environment, a social responsibility shared by each and every individual Swede in the country. With such an entrenched sense of national branding, Swedes both professional and ordinary continue to have personal opinions and points of view on the subject of the ownership of VCC that now belongs to China. Sweden today is both spectator and participant in the growth of China's automobile industry, where the two countries currently work in close collaboration on knowledge sharing and knowledge transfer in maintaining and continuing to build a strong global brand for VCC.

In the past decade alone, numerous studies have focused their research efforts on the various aspects of VCC from its history and heritage (Jönsson & Wickelgren 2011), its outsourcing strategies (Bosnjak & Lewandowski 2010), human resource reward systems (Axelsson & Bokedal 2009), logistics management (Bruks 2008), Ford's acquisition of VCC (Schweizer & Lagerström 2014, Lundbäck & Hörte 2005) and Geely's acquisition of VCC (Alvstam & Ivarsson 2014). The knowledge and know-how that contributed to the large extent to the research literature on VCC in just the last decade, resides in the human capital that VCC has managed to train, develop and retain in their workforce. And in acquiring VCC, Geely has strategically added to both their technological knowledge base and human capital base, even if the effective transfer of knowledge in general from Sweden to China will prove more challenging in practice for both VCC and Geely. This empirical study contributes to this body of research knowledge as a comparative study of VCC and Geely, both at organization level and in the products they market.

1.2 The Geely Narrative and Discourse

The narrative of Geely begins with the humble background of its founder Li Shu Fu, who needed to borrow money to start a company that manufactured refrigerators (Milne 2014, Waldemeir & Reed 2010, The Economist 2010). Founded in 1986 in Taizhou in Zhejiang, China, Geely soon moved into the production of motorcycle parts and by 1997, the company had progressed into automotive manufacturing producing small vans. This was the beginning of the Zhejiang Geely Holding Group, which received State approval to make automobiles in 2001, the same year in which China joined the World Trade Organization (WTO). Today, with Li as its Chairman, Geely has become China's top automobile exporter, in active pursuit of the European and US markets, capitalizing on opportunities to capture market segments in these regions (Li 2013).

To survive the rapidly growing Chinese market, and to cope with their planned rapid volume expansion of global production from about 370 000 units annually in 2010 to 800 000 units in 2020, Geely had in the past years invested heavily in themselves as an organization in its entirety, in what was entitled their "strategic transformation" strategies that saw them amplifying manufacturing capacity, technological research, product development and first-class dealer networks (Gao 2015). Geely's subsequent Strategic Transformation Technology System Innovation Project then saw improvements in the system structure, operation mechanism, strategic product planning as well as human resources engineering. Their Innovation Project won second prize in 2009 in China's "National Prize for Progress in Science and Technology" (Geely 2015a). Their careful monitoring of safety and quality standards saw that they met international standards. For China, this meant a breakthrough in safety, energy efficiency and the very rare perspective at the time in the early 2000s on environmental protection with more than 1,200 patents, thirty of which were international, including two unique technologies known as the "blow-out monitoring and breaking system," and the "energy efficient building system." (Chinese Champions 2015).

Geely's aggressive overseas investments first occurred in 2006. It acquired a 23% stake in Manganese Bronze Holdings, London's leading taxi company, and later established a production joint venture with them to manufacture its renowned London taxis and other limousine and transportation services. In 2009, it purchased Australian auto-parts maker Drivetrain Systems International. The company's transformation efforts saw a steady rate of returns where in 2009, it reported an increase in sales of sedans by 60% compared to 2008, and Geely Auto's total net profit increased 52% to RMB 1.32 billion ($194.2 million) (Geely Annual Report 2009). Prior to 2010 Geely had made several visits to Sweden in an exchange of peer-to-peer information within the automobile industry. In 2010, Geely acquired 100% of Volvo and its assets for $1.8 billion from Ford Motor Company.

The headquarters for Geely today lies in Hangzhou, Zhejiang, and it has nine manufacturing plants in China located in Chengdu, Cixi, Jinan, Lanzhou, Linhai, Luqiao, Ningbo, Shanghai and Xiangtan. As of the last quarter of 2015, these facilities formed an annual production capacity of 630,000 units of vehicles per shift, up from 600,000 engines and 600,000 transmissions in 2012 with US$4.4 billion in total market capitalization (Geely 2015b, 2012). In terms of human resource and capital, Geely today has more than 18,000 employees that includes their own engineering team and R&D team (Geely 2015b, Xia 2011). Considering its growth potential, ambitious production capacity and its strategy for continuous improvements in human resource capacity through in-house training, Geely's listing in 2005 in the Hong Kong Stock Exchange was but its beginner-step towards its global ambitions. Another surprising and unprecedented move for Chinese organizations known traditionally for their stricter hierarchy and control as a method of administrative management, Geely made a strategic top management decision to have VCC and Geely Automobile managed as autonomously as possible, where 'Geely is Geely' and 'Volvo is Volvo' (Bradsher 2010).

2. CORPORATE LANGUAGE AND VISUAL COMMUNICATION IN INTERNATIONAL BUSINESS

In the early 1990s, IB scholars began to note how language in IB had been deemed as one of the most neglected fields of study in the management literature. This gap in knowledge was labelled as "the forgotten factor" (Marschan, Welch & Welch 1997:591) even if language is one of the most pervasive factors in the conduct of international trade. Since then, there has been greater momentum and focus in research on the role of language in organization behaviour and management literature (Tietze, Cohen & Musson 2003) from how narratives and storytelling can be used as a method to study organizations (Czarniawska 2007, Gertsen & Søderberg 2011) to the various perspectives of organization and management from a discourse perspective (Grant 2004). As such, the Geely narrative and its current discourse makes an interesting case to follow in its development because it comes at a time when scholars in the field of IB are beginning to note how the role language plays an important role in IB.

Most studies about language in IB have tended to focus their efforts within or across multinationals. Studies have for example, focused on the various aspects of cross-cultural and multilingual communication in the context of cross-border mergers (Louhiala-Salminen 2002), language diversity and how it affects control and coordination of headquarters-subsidiary have also been studied (Piekkari et al. 2005). Luo and Shenkar (2006) saw language and language design as a key ingredient in the flow of applied global strategies for the multinational corporation in a multilingual community, as the functions of language help shape organizational change process, facilitate information exchange, global coordination and create intra-corporate values. It is through language, deployed and represented in corporate visuals and images through time that constitute its discursive practice, that executives develop their strategies in a process of corporate visioning, defined as how a combination of mission, strategy and corporate culture are developed and formulated (O'Brien & Meadows 2000). Just as how the ancient Greek philosopher Plato argued that societies are invariably formed for a particular purpose, gathering into communities for mutual achievement of our goals, discursive practices in organizations can likewise be seen as the tool for facilitating group functions where organizational discourses "do not just describe things; they do things" (Potter & Wetherell 1987:6) and that "discourse is the principle means by which organization members create a coherent social reality that frames their sense of who they are" (Mumby & Clair 1997:181)

2.1 Language as Both Subject of Study and Method of Analysis

Language has also been studied from the perspective of culture in IB (Janssens, Lambert, & Steyaert 2004), where beyond the study of language diversity in management and leadership teams (Welch, Welch & Piekkari 2005) is the application of the analysis of language in semantics and semiotics as a method (Brannen 2004) of study, arguably situated in alignment with the field of applied CDA (Fairclough & Wodak 1997, Alvesson & Kärreman 2000, Heracleous 2004) that could potentially open the field to further aspects of research at the intersections of these disciplines. Such an approach would enrich the contextual, theoretical and empirical methodologies with regards to the cross-disciplinary approach to the study of language in international business, encompassing a meta-level perspective and analysis of how language is not only a phenomenon to be studied but that it can also be a tool to help study other international business phenomena. Brannen's (2004) study on how firm assets might be transferred across borders in the process of internationalization of the multinational enterprise (MNEs) drew upon the theoretical underpinnings from the field of semiotic analysis and CDA and applied those frameworks to the study of cross-cultural, transnational transfer of firm assets in organizations, demonstrating the effects of the social semiotic context on foreignness and strategic fit. The study incorporated language as both subject of study, "…by showing how language as an important dimension of the cultural context affects success in the transfer of products, processes and practices" (Brannen 2004:612), and language as framework of analysis, "the conceptual model of recontextualization contributes to method by providing an analytical framework for applying semiotic analysis to interpretive research on internationalization, organizational transfer, and the general body of cross-cultural organizational research." (Brannen 2004:613).

As Broadfoot, Deetz and Anderson (2004) argued in their multi-levelled, multi-method approach in the study of organizational discourse, likewise in this study, I am not postulating methodological or theoretical laxity, but would rather like to encourage and continue this dialogical effort on both fronts in terms of intersecting the critical disciplines with international business studies, here using discourse analysis and visual semiotics as a framework of analysis in studying organization ideology. Contextually, one could perhaps situate the contributions of this study in organizational discourse studies, defined as the structured collection of texts embodied in the practices of interaction, text production that includes visual representations that bring organization related objects into existence, their production, dissemination and further interpretation (Hill & Brown 2007, Grant 2004, Parker 1992), as a means of investigating and understanding corporate communication and ideology as part of corporate visioning and strategy.

In line with much of the efforts of scholars who have previously studied the effects of language in organization studies, I view language in use, as manifest in corporate discourse and visual communication, as both the subject of study and as a tool and means to study the ideological dispositions of organizations.

2.2 Visual Semiotics as Theoretical Framework and Tool of Analysis

The advancement in information and communication technology in the past two decades facilitated the fading of geographical boundaries. As such, people from different cultures and countries, with different languages can now communicate across time zones in virtual spaces, if not meeting face-to-face. With the advent of the Internet, we are at an age where social media platforms are no longer activities that we engage in only during our spare time, but rather, activities that have been integrated into all aspects of our lives. Much of this has contributed to a fundamental shift in paradigm regarding how language is used in today's post-modern, partially globalized societies. Norman Fairclough had already in the early 1990s, addressed the issue of the technologisation of discourse in a post-Fordist society that saw the beginnings of mass production and assembly workers working in production lines, away from the customers (Fairclough 2013). Technology advancement in communication means that today, such isolated groups of workers in manufacturing assembly lines have been largely replaced by international teams of workers that network together on different tasks, representing different companies from different parts of the world. This shift in the manner in which people worked and communicated in new media from email and desktop publishing to socializing over internet sites have had a focal and pragmatic effect on the role language now plays in our everyday lives both in the private and public domains. Language studied as discourse opens up new areas for the critical investigation of the various aspects of socio-cultural and political domains society from the composition of cultural groups to the management of organizations and the constitution of political institutions both at state and regional levels (Jaworski & Coupland 1999).

Definitions of discourse range in span from language being "above the sentence or above the clause" to the study of *any* aspect of language use (Stubbs 1983:1). What has been consistent in the literature in most definitions of the study of discourse is the functional aspect of language in use (Schiffrin 1994). However, there has also been a large body of opinion that stresses that discourse is more than just "language in use", so that whether written, spoken or visually represented, these canons of interactions can be seen as a type of social practice, that is shaped by such social dimensions as knowledge, culture, social identities and relations of power, invested with ideologies (Fairclough 2013) set in the context of social and institutional practices that creates, shapes and perpetuates more macro movements in the over-arching social formation (Candlin & Maley 1997). It is this nature of intertextuality / interdiscursivity (Bhatia 2010), the constant interaction of texts, from its production, to its socio-political context of situation, that discourse analysis as a method helps map systematically, analyses of written and spoken texts onto social contexts. It is through this perspective that the critical or socially engaged manner of analysing discourse goes well beyond discourse as "language in use". CDA is a forensic activity that offers a means of uncovering or deconstructing social and organizational practices.

Although the main body of works on CDA, a research tradition that is both modernist and social constructionist, that was developed during the late 1980s onwards by scholars in Europe mainly challenged the paradigms of hegemonic power structures and dominance with the underlying agenda of emancipation from oppression (Van Dijk 2008, Wodak 1997, Caldas-Coulthard & Coulthard 1996), later works have begun to focus on bringing this critical perspective to organizations and globalisation (Alvesson & Kärreman 2000, Fairclough & Thomas 2004) focusing on how organizations created meaning in a global context. To that extent, CDA for the purposes of this study, helps uncover how corporate ideology functions as an organizational practice in which corporate realities are created, sustained, resisted and transformed. The word ideology here is used in similar context to Van Dijk's (1998, 2008) definition of ideology with the assumptions that ideologies are gradually acquired belief systems that are socially shared by a collective of individuals that help organize other socio-cultural and political beliefs and attitudes. Various ideologies in different social groups for example, can provide a coherent foundation for general cultural values that are relevant in the group and to the larger society and ideologies can over time, also disintegrate as was the case with the Arab Nationalist Movement that emerged in the late 1940s and declined towards the end of the 1960s. In the corporate world, the concept of Corporate Social Responsibility (CSR), which is currently in vogue for many multinational corporations today could mean different things to different people, where corporations across the world adopt different business practices in reflection of their CSR ideologies and why they are doing so against a larger capitalist background (Bessire & Onnée 2010, Lazonick & O'Sullivan 2000). To that extent, corporate ideology can act as an "internal compass" with which organizations can navigate and steer their vision, mission and strategy.

As with linguistic structures and language in use, images and visual structures communicate particular interpretations of experience. Semiotics is generally described as the study of signs and for a sign to exist, there needs to be meaning or content (what is 'signified') to be manifested through an expression or representation (the 'sign'). Because every community is different, the semiotic system employed by each community and its culture, will differ across communities. The colour red for example, is used for mourning in the Ivory Coast, whilst it signifies good luck and happiness for the people of China and signifies procreation and life for those in India (Sebeok 2001, Boltz 1994). As such, signs and their meanings exist in dialogic interrelation to a people and their culture, both creating and perpetuating a certain point of view of reality through the form of social interaction. Meanings advocated stem from a people's culture who have at their disposal a range of semiotic modes to convey them. The manner in which meanings are mapped across different semiotic modes, in how some things can be portrayed either visually or verbally, while others only visually, and again some others only verbally, is also culturally and historically specific (Kress & Van Leeuwen 2006). Chinese characters in the Chinese language for example are derivatives of different types of logograms, from pictograms, ideograms to phono-semantic compounds (Boltz 1994). Both (1983) and Brannen (2004) give good theoretical background descriptions to how social semiotics might complement knowledge in the field of international management.

In Europe, the past 75 years saw three schools of semiotics applied to linguistics and non-linguistic domains. The first was the Prague School of the 1930s and 1940s that developed the work of Russian Formalists based on a linguistics foundation, applied to art (Mukarovsky 1972), theatre (Honzl 1976), cinema (Jakobson & Sokol 1976) and costume (Bogatyrev 1976). The second was the Paris School of the 1960s and 1970s (Matejka & Titunik 1976) that applied ideas from Ferdinand de Saussure and other linguists to painting (Schefer), photography (Barthes, Lindekens), fashion (Barthes), cinema (Metz), music (Nattiez) and visual design (Kress & van Leeuwen). American logician and philosopher Charles Sanders Peirce defined semiosis as action or influence that involved the sign, the object and its interpretant, and introduced the terms 'icons', 'indexes' and 'symbols' to the study of semiology, where his conception of representations and interpretations were grounded more in philosophical logic rather than social studies like De Saussure. The third school of semiotics is a most recent movement with theoretical influence from linguistics applied to other modes of representation, growing out of the "critical linguistics" perspective of Michael Halliday during the 1970s at the University of East Anglia. This school of thought led to encompass other semiotic modes in the works of Hodge and Kress (1998) who focused on the uses of semiotic systems in social practice, building on Halliday's critical perspective on ideology and society that sees discourse as a flow of texts in a dynamic process of interaction and interpretation. They also refer to the Peirce's triadic model of semiosis that depicts the "action" of a sign as a limitless process of infinite semiosis, where one "interpretant" generates another. During the 1980s, a further development of the Hallidayan SFL field was carried out by scholars in Asutralia to include semiotically oriented studies of literature (Threadgold, Thibault), visual semiotics (O'Toole, Kress & Van Leeuwen) and music (Van Leeuwen).

The past decade has seen social semiotics extending its general framework beyond linguistics to account for the growing importance of visual images and sound in a multimodal context, where both traditional and digital media intersect at social networking sights for example (Kress & Van Leeuwen 1996) and the semiotics of culture (Randviir 2007). Kress and Van Leeuwen (1992) have built upon Halliday's framework of SFL to encompass grammars related to other semiotic modes that view the production of visual representations as being drawn from a set of available resources for meaning making, shaped by the semiotic metafunctions originally identified by Halliday.

3. THEORETICAL FRAMEWORK, METHOD, AND DATA

This study is corpus driven and qualitative in purpose and design. Data to this study consisted of mainly secondary sources in print and online media that traces Geely's development in the past years beginning from 2007, including the company's annual reports from between 2007 to 2011:

- Geely's official corporate communications in the form of printed annual reports from 2007 to 2011. This rendered a total of 629 of pages for analysis from the annual reports alone, the average number of pages per annual report between these years being approximately 126 pages each.
- Selected online and print news articles based on topic relevancy on Geely and VCC between 2006/7 and 2014.

The visual semiotics framework of analysis is derived from (ii) CDA using Halliday's (2004, 1973) SFL and Kress and (iii) van Leeuwen's (2006) visual semiotics framework. The latter tools from SFL and visual semiotics will be applied to the collected data and they focus on the following metafunctional dimensions of language and visuals in use:

1. **Interpersonal:** Discourse analysis at this metafunction focuses on social distance and relative social status, and how the text represents both external and internal 'reality'. This aspect focuses on appraisal, positive or negative attitudes that help uncover and deconstruct for example, Geely's social relations as an organization. It helps uncover how Geely evaluates its relationships with other organizations or groups that are important for Geely in managing their own brand, tracking their evolving attitudes in their relations with their acquisitions as expressed in their use of language, in particular, VCC. The interpersonal metafunction in visual analysis on the interpersonal metafunction is about the participants involved in producing and interpreting the image, also indicating what 'reality' might be perpetuated or deciphered by viewing the images used. It also uncovers the perspective of how the picture engages the viewer. The choice of pictures used in Geely's annual reports for example has the capacity to immediately engage the viewer, while at the same time, convey an attitude towards its viewers, carrying with it a message from the organization / producer of the message towards its target audience. Social distance, gaze, angles of objects whether horizontal or vertical are features in an image that act to engage the viewer in the process of viewing and interpreting an image.
2. **Ideational / Representational:** This metafunction in discourse analysis systematically uncovers the actors and processes involved in a contextual transaction, helping uncover 'who' does 'what' to 'whom'. In terms of visual images, how objects are represented, whether in terms of vector spaces by distance measurements based on salience and prominence of an object represented, to how it is depicted conceptually or symbolically, all help transmit a certain organization ideology. Geely as an organization for example, is known in China to take active concern for its employees, where human capital, technological and innovation management for example are often highlighted in their organization discourse and likewise, can be expected to be reflected in images used in their corporate brochures, where participants are portrayed as actively contributing to the organization's success.
3. **Textual / Compositional:** In discourse analysis, this dimension focuses on how the text is put together, relying on grammatical rules, syntax and lexis for information to flow coherently. In visual analysis, compositional representations means to look at how the visuals are put together in layout in print or on the webpage, to form a consistent visual image. This aspect of analysis helps uncover consistent themes and strategies in for example, Geely's use of images in their corporate communication, and how both discoursal and visual meanings are organized and emphasized so that both readers and employees in the organization can process or interpret the information.

With the framework presented above, the following sections will illustrate how visual semiotics might be used as theory and framework of analysis in the study of the globalising efforts of a company, in this case, China's Geely Automobile. Using pictures retrieved from the data sources, it illustrates how visual semiotics analysis can help reveal a deeper understanding of corporate ideology, corporate beliefs and values, and create the necessary supporting mechanisms for corporate global ambitions from infrastructure, to human resource support.

4. ANALYSIS, FINDINGS, AND DISCUSSION

As the corpus of data collected is extensive, running over 600 pages of texts that includes visual images, what follows in this section is but a presentation selected examples that are representative of the texts and visuals found in the data set in its entirety.

4.1 Geely's Aspiration, Vision, and a Strategic Direction

China's efforts in catching up with current technology and knowledge platforms was once deemed as 'copying' or 'reverse engineering'. Yet Chinese patenting trends today indicate a very different picture fuelled by the country's desire to go global (Wu, Hu & Matthews 2014, Li & Wei 2012). This desire to go global could be seen in Geely's ambition even before its official acquisition of VCC in 2010 in their corporate communication. Geely's aspirations for global presence and its desire to collaborate with international brands began already in 2006 with Geely's global aspirations illustrated in its reflected alignment and use of VCC corporate colours of steel grey and deep blues. The two circles, with both inner and outer circles being double rimmed in Geely's logo reflect a similar depiction to that of the logo of VCC. The triangular 'arrowhead', used by VCC as a symbol of Mars and its main element of iron, which in turn reflects VCC' commitment to the quality of their products. This 'arrowhead' is likewise a feature used and referred to in Geely's logo, encompassed within the double circle. While the encompassing of the 'arrowhead' renders a conservative outlook for Geely, as compared to the more forward looking, frontier pushing VCC logo (signalled by the symbol of Mars on the outer rim of the logo, with vectors pointing upwards and forwards to the 'future'), still viewers can infer and interpret Geely's corporate visioning and ideology as 'quality oriented', where similar threads of meaning alluding to the organization's commitment to quality products is situated at the 'core' of the company. As Geely automobile had its beginnings producing for lower end markets with affordably priced vehicles that is far from the luxury segment, one could argue that Geely has had its sight for market improvement early on in their corporate visioning and strategy, even if, as my data collected indicated, little was discussed outside of the organization and made known to the press. The design of Geely's 'arrowhead' with spanning 'fins' or 'flames' depending on one's interpretation, could likewise indicate speed (considering the spreading vector angles of the 'fins'), movement (colour silver for fluidity) and its high ambitions ('arrowhead' design) in its going global in the near future. The logo serves to create not just corporate visioning for its employees and current clients, but helps to attract the attention of future clients.

The corporate colour scheme of VCC, of shades of steel and blues was reflected consecutively for 2007 and 2008 in Geely's annual reports. This alignment was made more explicit in their corporate discourse in their 2007 report that echoed the values of VCC, who has an established brand of first and foremost, being a safe and environmental friendly car (Figure 1).

Figure 1. Caption theme reflected in Geely's 2007 annual report (p3:114), aligning their corporate theme with Volvo Car's overall branding. The words are also printed grey on blue that is reminiscent of Volvo Car Corporation colours, and values.

> Supplying the SAFEST, the MOST ENERGY EFFICIENT and
> the MOST ENVIRONMENTAL FRIENDLY vehicles.
> LET GEELY CARS REACH EVERYWHERE IN THE WORLD

In this data driven analysis of text in combination with visual images, the consistent message on all three metafunctional levels of meaning that came through from the data collected was how Geely's ambitions to constantly improve, expand and go global was iterated and reiterated, forming a semantic web of words often used in relation with Geely, whether in interviews with the organization's top management in their Hangzhou headquarters or in news articles being written about the organization.

It would be worth considering too in the process of doing a visual semiotics analysis on Geely's use of visuals in corporate communication, the highly pictographic and symbolic aspect of the written Chinese language in its characters. Each Chinese character would as much as possible convey a mental and visual image of what is meant. Like most other languages, the Chinese believe too that the values and qualities of the word/s would transfer onto the thereby object named. The word 'fire'or 火 (huŏ) is a pictographic representation of flames, and carries the additional connotations of heat, anger and rage. In similar vein, the name 'Geely' is the alliteration of the Chinese words 吉利 *Jílì* that translates to mean 'auspicious' in English. In 2007, Geely used a similar strategy of the precipitation of the ideal to material, through language use, in product naming in order to re-position itself into a higher-end market, moving from price-competitive cars to one focused on quality. By the end of 2007, it had launched three new sedans named "Geely Kingkong", "Free Cruiser" and "Vision" as part of their tri-pronged efforts in their "Transformation Strategy" in the areas of brand image, product quality and technology and innovation. These sedans subsequently accounted for 63% of the total sales volume for the year, an increase from the 40% of the previous year of 2006. These three products were a recurrent theme, highlighted and repeated many times over in 2007 and 2008 data on Geely. The product names in themselves is iterative of Geely's own aspirations as an organization, where expressed ideationally, it had goals and plans for its future, it had foresight and ambition (connotated in the word 'vision'), to become ambitiously large (connotated in the word 'Kingkong') and global (connotated in 'free', cross-border, also 'free' in the sense of the mind and its borderless creativity in human capital).

Geely had since its inception as an organization building refrigerators, had always been known as ambitious, some even described 'aggressive', which are the embodiment of Li Shu Fu's own values. Though as reflected in the data, aspirations and the possession of vision and foresight is not necessarily enough to lay the foundations for its success. What Geely needed was a tangible operational plan in order to actualize and make concrete its own aspirations.

4.2 Geely's Focused Strategic Direction

The operationalization of their aspirations and ambitions were embodied in Geely's 'Strategic Transformation' restructuring of the organization, not only in functional and divisional terms (Wang, 2011) but also in a paradigm shift in the ideology of top management and how Geely was managed, likewise, how it managed its acquisitions such as VCC from Ford. A fuller comparison between VCC and Geely can be found in Appendix A. The paragraphs below will focus on the metafunctional levels of analysis derived from the SFL framework.

Example 1 shows a typical example of text from the data collected, from the opening lines of Geely's Annual Report in 2007, an address from Geely's Chairman Li Shu Fu. That Geely is excelling in progress is expressed on the interpersonal level (highlighted in yellow in Example 1) by the constant emphasis of growth and expansion by acquisition. The participants that Geely attributes its success is expressed ideationally (highlighted in green in Example 1), that Geely functions as a Group with 'operating associates' working together on its "strategic transformation" is repeatedly stressed, where group work and team work are important features of its progress. And it is this concerted effort of working towards a change in strategy whether through acquisition or investing in its own R&D facilities is repeatedly stressed, that results in 'significant achievements' and 'improved profitability' in general. This positive attitude of Geely's towards their own progress, despite challenges faced by the financial crisis and market competition, continues through most annual reports.

Example 1: Financial Review, Geely Annual Report 2007:7

The Group's turnover amounted to HK$137 million for the year ended 31 December 2007, up 8% from the previous year. Profit attributable to the equity holders of the Company amounted to HK$315 million, representing an increase of 51% over 2006. The large increase in net profit was attributable to the strong growth in profit contributions from the Group's four operating associates – Zhejiang Geely Automobile Company Limited ("Zheijang Geely"), Shanghai Maple Guorun Automobile Company Limited ("Shanghai Maple"), Zhejiang Kingkong Automobile Company Limited ("Zhejiang Kingkong") and Zhejiang Ruhoo Automobile Company Limited ("Zhejiang Ruhoo") – (collectively referred as the "operating associates"). Their strong earnings growth, particularly in the second half of 2007, was mainly due to the initial success achieved by the operating associates' strategic transformation into higher value-added products, as evidenced by the strong performance of the three higher-end models launched over the last two years including the 2008 version of "Free Cruiser" economy sedans, the "Vision" mid-end sedans, and the "Geely Kingkong" family sedans. Significant achievements by the operating associates in improving customer satisfactions, and product reliability and quality also contributed to the improved profitability during the later part of the year.

In the past five years, Geely was not only going through a material transformation in terms of higher investment and growth in human capital through expanding its own R&D unit or via acquisition of expertise that led to technology and innovation breakthroughs of their own, but it was also experiencing a paradigm shift in management ideology that in turn, affected the manner in which the organization was managed based on their evolving management values that places significant emphasis among its employees. It has in place for example, a training programme that involves all levels of employees. Regular

Figure 2. Contents pages of Geely's Annual Reports 2007 (left) and 2008 (right) that demonstrates an ideological shift in management values

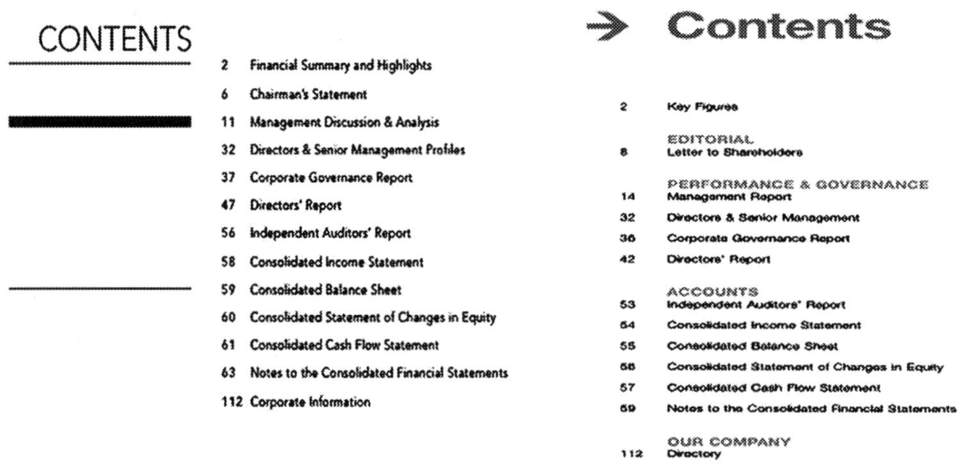
CONTENTS

Contents

lectures and educational sessions are conducted across its several education establishments that include the Beijing Geely University, the Sanya College of Hainan University and the Zhejiang Auto Engineering College that have in total, about 40,000 students in total. This shift in management values that puts the employee in focus, and attempts for management to be seen as more accessible was reflected already in their Annual Reports of 2007 and 2008, on the Contents page (Figure 2).

The key points of change noticeable would be the overall more structured approach to the management of the organization, with more divisions of specialty, one could say reflected metaphorically in the Contents page into "Editorial", "Performance and Governance", the various "Accounts" collected under the same heading and the presentation of the "Company". This information corresponds to the various Geely Groups that collectively form Geely Holding. "Performance and Governance" are emphasized and given their own section in the newly re-organized material, that also reveals a mindset of Geely focusing on its performance and manner of organization management. A 'flattening' out of hierarchy, though unusual for Chinese run and owned organizations, is nonetheless reflected in a change of tone from "Chairman's Statement" in 2007, to the use of a more egalitarian term "Editorial" and "Letter to Shareholders", without emphasizing the person behind this letter to the shareholders, even if it remains Geely's Chairman, Li Shu Fu.

Even though VCC had been managed by Ford, VCC as such still retained much of its Swedish management style that is known to be less hierarchical within the organization, more consensus seeking, more egalitarian in meetings and more decentralized in decision making powers. Thus Geely's beginnings of a more egalitarian approach towards their readers, shareholders and overall management style as reflected in their Annual Reports, can also be said to be a precursor alignment of values of Geely with the more egalitarian and environmentally conscious VCC. These values were iterated after the formal acquisition of VCC by Li, who in an unprecedented style of acquisition management, he said, "Volvo is Volvo and Geely is Geely. Volvo is premium, tasteful and low-profile, whereas Geely is a volume brand. We don't want to put the two together. We will give Volvo independence and autonomy. By setting it free, we will help Volvo return to its glories in the 1960s and 1970s." (The Economist 2010) This move effectively gave VCC autonomy to be run and managed by Swedish top executive management, where Geely had chosen to take the position of observer and learner, studying the more lateral organization structure of VCC with more decentralized decision making that empowers employees further out on the production line. This ideological shift from the vertical hierarchy of most Chinese organization management sets Geely apart as foremost in groundbreaking human resource management.

Apart from the two most prominent issues that were derived from the data, sections 3.3 and 3.4 outline the socio-political structures that shape Geely as an organization.

4.3 The Struggle with Mass Media

Perhaps the single overarching challenge that Geely faced initially in its globalising efforts was the distrust in western media that stemmed mostly from the lack of confidence in China made automobiles. Geely was also faced with industry's scepticism at Geely's ability to succeed on the international platform, being able to produce quality cars or manage more global brands, most notably VCC. As one article in China Daily reported by Liu and Zhang (2011) on Geely's marketing in the UK, the highlights in yellow showing the semantic network of words that express doubt, uncertainty and pensiveness towards Geely Automobile.

Example 2: Abstract from China Daily, 28 December 2011, *Geely seeks to prove quality to woo UK buyers.*

"As to the customers, the market is getting tougher and (the) latest reports I have seen suggest it's not just prices but also warranties which are influencing buying decisions," said Tim Williams, chief executive of the trade association Welsh Automotive Forum.

Williams said Geely will want to "focus on" quality and expressed uncertainty about the Chinese carmaker's prospects in the UK market. "We'll have to wait and see how well Geely does," he said.

"...being cheap is not good enough" according to Nikki Jones, director of the consulting company Calling Brands. Citing research, she said UK consumers have "lots of questions" about the safety and reliability of Chinese brands. "In the car industry, this is even more so the case. They (Geely) are trying to market themselves as good-value-for-money, but they need to make sure UK consumers understand what 'value' means," Jones said, referring to Geely vehicles' "poor performance" in crash tests.

A search and retrieve on the website autoblog.com with the keyword "Geely" will reveal headlines such as, "Geely set to reveal modified Rolls-Royce aping limousine in Beijing" (Bowman 2010a), "Geely to adopt (confusing) new multi-brand system" (Bowman 2010b) and "Beijing 2010: Geely's London Taxi-aping Englon TXN" (Bowman 2010c), all articles that help connotate Geely with a lack of creativity and innovation, but rather one of aping more renowned luxury brands.

Despite the negative press, there are however some indications that Geely's consistent effort towards quality, technological improvements, research and innovation are being recognized by western media. Norihiko Shirouzu (2009) of Wall Street Journal in particular, reported that since 2006 onwards Geely had managed not only to put together a talented management team with international experience that included at the time, product chief Frank Zhao who was a former Chrysler senior engineer in Detroit, and Peter Zhang who was a financial controller from BP PLC, but that Geely's tech center at Taizhou with its campus was indeed carrying out breakthrough research such as developing a "new car" fragrance for auto interiors.

A move that specifically caught the positive interest China's mass media was Geely's efforts in talent management and human capital upgrading and investment (described in more detail in section 4.4).

4.4 Alignment with China's Global Strategy

A point of success for Geely that comes across consistently in the data collected, is how Geely's strategic transformation, its focus on improving its technological and innovation platforms in the automobile industry is proving to be the turning point of the Chinese automobile industry in recent years. This means upgrading and developing the industry as such, so that Geely continues to receive the support of the Chinese government, as commented by Miao Yu, secretary of the Party Committee and vice minister in the State Ministry of Information and Industry, said: "Strategic decision-making determines the direction [that] Chinese automobile companies should take…Only by making wise strategic decisions can they keep an upper hand in development [where] the core or root of transformation rests in creativeness, brand-building and international cooperation." (Global Times, 2010)

Geely's efforts thus far have gained high appraisal from China's Party and State leaders, where President Hu Jintao also stated that he would support qualified companies like Geely and encourage the company to go global. The government also recognized Geely's efforts in technological innovations, where the Geely Technology System Innovation Programme won the National Grade II (Grade I remained vacant) Prize of Science and Technology Progress, which was the top prize among the category of programs of the state (Global Times 2010). This in turn had the ripple effect of improving the pool of talent and human capital. With its innovation policy, strategy and framework for introducing, training and putting in place, incentives to help retain talent within the organization, Geely stood at an advantaged position in the implementation of a national talent strategy to upgrade human capital. It was in this move that Geely got positive appraisal from China's mass media that included Xinhua News Agency, CCTV, Guangming Daily, Economic Daily, Workers Daily, Science and Technology Daily, china Education Daily and China Automotive News, where the main reports were that Geely's talent management was helping redefine China's automobile industry, where others could learn from Geely's practices, for both private and state owned enterprises.

5. CONCLUSION

Taking an Asian-founded multinational organisation in its globalising efforts, this chapter provides a novel perspective to the use of visual semiotics as both theory and framework of analysis in uncovering the supporting structures to corporate global ambitions. In particular, it takes the case of Geely's acquisition of VCC as an example of an emerging economy's efforts to bring its organizations global.

In summary, this chapter has illustrated that meaning and intent of a corporation is visually and linguistically coded in corporate communication. The data retrieved and the subsequent applied visual semiotics analysis revealed that Geely's globalising efforts began in the years prior to its 2010 acquisition of VCC. Pictures used in Geely's annual reports prior to its VCC acquisition indicated that as a growing enterprise, Geely was impassioned enough to envision itself as operating internationally, being seen on the global platform. It also had a strategic direction, encapsulated by its project of "strategic transformation" that targeted several organization functions and divisions that included, branding, technology, innovation and human capital investment. That Geely was made up of several teams or groups was made clear in their annual reports, interviews and subsequent news articles. Teamwork was important for the organization and this was much emphasized whether in informal talk or in formal press releases.

It is Geely's consistent effort at restructuring, seeking creativity, expanding in terms of new acquisitions, their very ambitions that have aligned their organization goals to that of China's state party, so that their efforts have been well recognized by the Chinese government, who continue to lend their support to the organization (Murphy & Lin 2014). To this extent, the conclusion is that Geely has thus far been successful at re-branding themselves from a relatively low cost market to one that focused on delivering quality automobiles to a higher end market. They have also thus far been successful at developing, training and retaining their human talent within the organization. And in an economy where the average turnover rate remains high, Geely could well be said to be pioneering in the field of talent management and retainment.

REFERENCES

Alvesson, M., & Karreman, D. (2000). Varieties of discourse: On the study of organizations through discourse analysis. *Human Relations*, *53*(9), 1125–1149. doi:10.1177/0018726700539002

Alvstam, C. G., & Ivarsson, I. (2014). The 'hybrid' emerging market multinational enterprise – the ownership transfer of VCC to China. In C. Alvstam, H. Dolles, & P. Ström (Eds.), *Asian Inward and Outward FDI: New Challenges in the Global Economy* (pp. 217–242). Palgrave Macmillan Asian Business Series. doi:10.1057/9781137312211.0017

Axelsson, A., & Bokedal, S. (2009). *Reward systems - motivating different generations. A case study of Volvo Car Corporation*. University of Gothenburg.

Barley, S. R. (1983). Semiotics and the study of occupational and organizational cultures. *Administrative Science Quarterly*, *28*(3), 393–413. doi:10.2307/2392249

Bessire, D., & Onnée, S. (2010). Assessing corporate social performance: Strategies of legitimation and conflicting ideologies. *Critical Perspectives on Accounting*, *21*(6), 445–467. doi:10.1016/j.cpa.2010.01.015

Bhatia, V. K. (2010). Interdiscursivity in professional communication. *Discourse & Communication*, *4*(1), 32–50. doi:10.1177/1750481309351208

Bogatyrev, P., & Lockwood, Y. (1976). Costume as a sign (the functional and structural concept of costumes in ethnography). In L. Matejka & I. R. Titunik (Eds.), *Semiotics of Art: Prague School Contributions* (pp. 13–19). Cambridge, MA: MIT.

Boltz, W. G. (1994). The origin and early development of the Chinese writing system. American American Oriental Society.

Bosnjak, S. B., & Lewandowski, S. (2010). *The extra cost of business process outsourcing: A study at volvo cars corporation*. University of Gothenburg.

Bowman, Z. (2010a). *Report: "Geely set to reveal modified Rolls-Royce aping limousine in Beijing" 13 April 2010*. Retrieved from http://www.autoblog.com/2010/04/13/geely-set-to-reveal-modified-rolls-royce-aping-limousine-in-beij/

Bowman, Z. (2010b). *Report: "Geely to adopt (confusing) new multi-brand system" 16 April 2010*. Retrieved from http://www.autoblog.com/2010/04/16/report-geely-to-adopt-confusing-new-multi-brand-system/

Bowman, Z. (2010c). *Beijing 2010: Geely's London Taxi-aping Englon TXN*. Retrieved from http://www.autoblog.com/2010/04/23/beijing-2010-geelys-london-taxi-aping-englon-txn/

Bradsher, K. (2010). Ford agrees to sell Volvo to a fast-rising Chinese company. *The New York Times: Global Business*. Retrieved from http://www.nytimes.com/2010/03/29/business/global/29auto.html

Brannen, M., Piekkari, R., & Tietze, S. (2014). The multifaceted role of language in international business: Unpacking the forms, functions and features of a critical challenge to MNC theory and performance. *Journal of International Business Studies*, *45*(5), 495–507. doi:10.1057/jibs.2014.24

Brannen, M. Y. (2004). When Mickey loses face: Recontextualization, semantic fit, and the semiotics of foreignness. *Academy of Management Review*, *29*(4), 593–616.

Broadfoot, K., Deetz, S., & Anderson, D. (2004). *Multi-levelled, multi-method approaches in organizational discourse. In The Sage Handbook of Organizational Discourse* (pp. 193–211). Sage Publications. doi:10.4135/9781848608122.n9

Bruks, F. (2008). *Object model for description of the logistical flow at Volvo Cars Corporation -A base for simulation containing logistical flows*. University of Gothenburg.

Caldas-Coulthard, C. R., & Coulthard, M. (Eds.). (1996). *Texts and Practices: Readings in Critical Discourse Analysis*. London: Routledge.

Candlin, C. N., & Maley, Y. (1997). Intertextuality and interdiscursivity in the discourse of alternative dispute resolution. In B. Gunnarsson, P. Linell, & B. Nordberg (Eds.), *The Construction of Professional Discourse* (pp. 201–222). London: Longman.

Chinese Champions. (2015). *Geely Profile*. Retrieved from http://www.chinese-champions.com/geely/

Cook-Greuter, S. R. (1995). *Comprehensive language awareness: A definition of the phenomenon and a review of its treatment in the postformal adult development literature*. Cambridge, MA: Harvard University.

Cordeiro-Nilsson, C. M. (2009). *Swedish Management in Singapore: A Discourse Analysis Study*. University of Gothenburg.

Czarniawska, B. (2007). Narrative inquiry in and about organizations. In D. Jean Clandinin (Ed.), *Handbook of Narrative Inquiry. Mapping a Methodology* (pp. 383–404). Newbury Park, CA: Sage. doi:10.4135/9781452226552.n15

Deng, Y. (2014). China: The post-responsible power. *The Washington Quarterly*, *37*(4), 117–132. doi:10.1080/0163660X.2014.1002159

Dicken, P. (2015). *Global shift: Mapping the changing contours of the world economy* (7th ed.). Sage Publications.

Fairclough, N. (2006). *Language and globalization*. New York: Routledge.

Fairclough, N. (2013). *Critical Discourse Analysis: The Critical Study of Language*. Abingdon, UK: Routledge.

Fairclough, N., & Thomas, P. (2004). The discourse of globalization and the globalization of discourse. In The Sage Handbook of Organizational Discourse, (pp. 379-396). Sage Publications. doi:10.4135/9781848608122.n18

Fairclough, N., & Wodak, R. (1997). Critical discourse analysis. In T. A. van Dijk (Ed.), *Discourse Studies: A Multidisciplinary Introduction* (Vol. 2, pp. 258–284). Beverly Hills, CA: Sage.

Gao, Z. (2015). The enterprise merger and acquisition effect on firm value - A discussion on Geely's acquisition of Volvo for example. *Modern Economy*, *6*(6), 717–726. doi:10.4236/me.2015.66068

Geely. (2009). *Annual Report 2009 – Geely*. Retrieved from http://www.geelyauto.com.hk/core/files/financial/en/2009-02.pdf

Geely. (2012). *Annual Report 2012 – Geely*. Retrieved from http://www.geelyauto.com.hk/core/files/financial/en/2012-02.pdf

Geely. (2015a). *Geely New Technology*. Retrieved from http://www.geely.com.sa/new-technology.html

Geely. (2015b). *Geely Company Brief*. Retrieved from http://www.geelyauto.com.hk/en/company_brief.html

Gertsen, M. C., & Søderberg, A. (2011). Intercultural collaboration stories: On narrative inquiry and analysis as tools for research in international business. *Journal of International Business Studies*, *42*(6), 787–804. doi:10.1057/jibs.2011.15

Global Times. (2010). *'Strategic transformation'-- one of the most profound innovations for Chinese automobile companies*. Retrieved from http://www.globaltimes.cn/autos/auto-china/industry/2011-01/603631.html

Grant, D. (2004). *The SAGE Handbook of Organizational Discourse*. London: SAGE.

Halliday, M. A. K. (1973). *Explorations in the Functions of Language*. London: Edward Arnold.

Halliday, M. A. K., & Matthiessen, C. M. I. M. (2004). *An Introduction to Functional Grammar* (3rd ed.). London: Arnold.

Heracleous, L. (2004). Interpretivist approaches to organizational discourse. In D. Grant, C. Hardy, C. Oswick, & L. Putnam (Eds.), *The Sage Handbook of Organizational Discourse* (pp. 175–192). Sage Publications. doi:10.4135/9781848608122.n8

Hill, A., & Brown, S. (2007). Strategic profiling: A visual representation of internal strategic fit in service organisations. *International Journal of Operations & Production Management*, *27*(12), 1333–1361. doi:10.1108/01443570710835642

Hodge, R., & Kress, G. (1988). *Social Semiotics*. Cambridge, MA: Polity.

Hodge, R., & Kress, G. R. (1993). *Language as Ideology*. London: Routledge.

Honzl, J., & Titunik, I. R. (1976). Dynamics of the sign in the theater. In L. Matejka & I. R. Titunik (Eds.), *Semiotics of Art: Prague School Contributions* (pp. 74–93). Cambridge, MA: MIT P.

Jakobson, R., & Sokol, E. (1976). Is the cinema in decline? In L. Matejka & I. R. Titunik (Eds.), *Semiotics of Art: Prague School Contributions* (pp. 145–152). Cambridge, MA: MIT.

Janssens, M., Lambert, J., & Steyaert, C. (2004). Developing language strategies for international companies: The contribution of translation studies. *Journal of World Business*, *39*(4), 414–430. doi:10.1016/j.jwb.2004.08.006

Jaworski, A., & Coupland, N. (Eds.). (1999). The Discourse Reader. London: Routledge.

Jönsson, S. A., & Wickelgren, M. (2011). *Volvo i våra hjärtan: Hur ska det gå?: En närdiskussion om "nationalklenoden" volvo*. Malmö: Liber.

Kress, G., & Van Leeuwen, T. (1992). Structures of visual representation. *Journal of Literary Semantics*, *21*(2), 91–117. doi:10.1515/jlse.1992.21.2.91

Kress, G. R., & Van Leeuwen, T. (2006). *Reading Images: The Grammar of Visual Design*. London: Routledge.

Lazonick, W., & O'Sullivan, M. (2000). Maximizing shareholder value: A new ideology for corporate governance. *Economy and Society*, *29*(1), 13–35. doi:10.1080/030851400360541

Leitch, S., & Palmer, I. (2010). Analysing texts in context: Current practices and new protocols for critical discourse analysis in organization studies. *Journal of Management Studies*, *47*(6), 1154. doi:10.1111/j.1467-6486.2009.00884.x

Li, F. (2013). Geely becomes China's top automobile export. *China Daily*. Retrieved from http://bit.ly/1XhXZiO

Li, W., & Wei, Y. (2012). Technology transfer, adaptation & assimilation and indigenous invention patent output: Evidence from Chinese high-tech industries. *Procedia Engineering*, *29*, 1392–1398. doi:10.1016/j.proeng.2012.01.146

Liu, C., & Zhang, H. (2011). Geely seeks to prove quality to woo UK buyers. *China Daily*. Retrieved from http://www.chinadaily.com.cn/bizchina/2011-12/28/content_14340471.htm

Louhiala-Salminenm, L. (2002). *Communication and language use in merged corporations: case Stora Enso and Nordea*. Working Paper no. 330. Helsinki School of Economics.

Lundbäck, M., & Hörte, S. (2005). Decision-making in conditions of constant change - a case within the automotive industry. *Management Decision*, *43*(2), 220–235. doi:10.1108/00251740510581939

Luo, Y., & Shenkar, O. (2006). The multinational corporation as a multilingual community: Language and organization in a global context. *Journal of International Business Studies*, *37*(3), 321–339. doi:10.1057/palgrave.jibs.8400197

Marschan, R., Welch, D. E., & Welch, L. S. (1997). Language: The forgotten factor in multinational management. *European Management Journal*, *15*(5), 591–598. doi:10.1016/S0263-2373(97)00038-8

Matejka, L., & Titunik, I. R. (1976). *Semiotics of art: Prague school contributions*. Cambridge, MA: MIT.

Milne, R. (2014). Li Shufu: an engineer with a mind for poetry and motion. *Financial Times*. Retrieved from http://on.ft.com/1T6wbr6

Mukarovsky, J. (1972). El arte como hecho semiolgico. *Casa De Las Amricas*, *12*(71), 51–54.

Mumby, D., & Clair, R. (1997). Organizational discourse. In T.A. Van Dijk (Ed.), Discourse as Structure and Process: Discourse Studies vol. 2 – a Multidisciplinary Introduction, (pp. 181-205). London: Sage.

Murphy, C., & Lin, L. (2014). China's Volvo Romance Rolls on, with Xi's backing. *Wall Street Journal, China Real Time, Economy & Business*. Retrieved from http://on.wsj.com/1Smj9FW

Ng, S. H., Ye, J., & Lee, C. (2011). Media discourse on globalization in China: A social—psychological analysis. *Journal of Language and Social Psychology*, *30*(2), 139–157. doi:10.1177/0261927X10397167

O'Brien, F., & Meadows, M. (2000). Corporate visioning: A survey of UK practice. *The Journal of the Operational Research Society*, *51*(1), 36–44. doi:10.1057/palgrave.jors.2600907

Parker, M. (1992). *Discourse Dynamics*. London: Routledge.

Philips, M., & Hardy, C. (2002). *Discourse Analysis: Investigating Processes of Social Construction*. Newbury Park, CA: Sage.

Piekkari, R., Vaara, E., Tienari, J., & Säntti, R. (2005). Integration or disintegration? Human Resource implications of the common corporate language decision in a cross-border merger. *Journal of Human Resource Management*, *16*(3), 333–347.

Potter, J., & Wetherell, M. (1987). *Discourse and Social Psychology*. London: Sage.

Randviir, A. (2007). On spatiality in Tartu–Moscow cultural semiotics: The semiotic subject. *Sign Systems Studies*, 137-159.

Schiffrin, D. (1994). *Approaches to Discourse*. Oxford, UK: Basil Blackwell.

Schweizer, R., & Lagerström, K. (2014). A business tale on marriage, divorce and remarriage in the corporate world: a conceptual framework of firms' disintegration process. In C. Alvstam, H. Dolles, & P. Ström (Eds.), *Asian Inward and Outward FDI: New Challenges in the Global Economy* (pp. 201–216). Palgrave Macmillan Asian Business Series. doi:10.1057/9781137312211.0016

Sebeok, T. A. (2001). *Global semiotics*. Bloomington, IN: Indiana Univ. Press.

Shirouzu, N. (2009). Is Geely capable of managing Volvo? *Wall Street Journal*. Retrieved from http://blogs.wsj.com/chinarealtime/2009/11/03/is-geely-capable-of-managing-volvo/

Stubbs, M. (1983). *Discourse analysis: The sociolinguistic analysis of natural language*. Oxford, UK: Basil Blackwell.

Tang, F. C., Gao, X. D., & Li, Q. (2008). Knowledge acquisition and learning: strategies in globalization of China's enterprises. In I. Alon & J. R. McIntyre (Eds.), *Globalization of Chinese Enterprises* (pp. 31–43). Basingstoke, UK: Palgrave Macmillan.

The Economist. (2010). *Face Value: Li Shufu. China's lucky man bags Volvo. Has the founder of Geely, an upstart carmaker, got what it takes to revive Volvo?*. Retrieved from http://www.economist.com/node/16750095

Tietze, S., Cohen, L., & Musson, G. (2003). *Understanding Organizations through Language*. London: Sage.

Van Dijk, T. A. (1998). *Ideology: A Multidisciplinary Approach*. London: Sage.

Van Dijk, T. A. 2008. *Discourse and Power*. Houndsmills, UK: Palgrave.

Waldmeir, P., & Reed, J. (2010). Man in the news: Li Shufu. *Financial Times*. Retrieved from http://on.ft.com/1T6PsbX

Wodak, R. (1997). *Gender and Discourse*. London: Sage.

Wu, C., Hu, M., & Mathews, J. A. (2014). Internal factors drive Chinese patent surge. *Nature, 509*(7501), 427.

Xia, Z., & Zhang, X. (2011). Strategic analysis of synergistic effect on M&A of Volvo Car Corporation by Geely automobile. *IBusiness, 3*(1), 5–15. doi:10.4236/ib.2011.31002

KEY TERMS AND DEFINITIONS

Automobile Industry/China/Sweden: The words "automobile" and "automobile industry" occur on pages 17, 18, 22, 25, 27 and 28 of the chapter contribution. One could say that the study of the internationalization efforts of an emerging market home-grown company, Geely, is set in the broader context of the emerging global automobile industry of China. China's Geely owns Swedish founded Volvo Car Corporation, the sales of which is also covered in the chapter. In that sense, Geely's internationalizing efforts can be said to have direct impact on the Swedish automobile industry scene. As such, this chapter is about the global automobile industry, in particular China's Geely and its ownership of Swedish founded Volvo Car Corporation.

Ideology: Ideology is defined in accordance to the Collins English Dictionary as "the body of doctrine or thought that guides an individual, social movement, institution, or group/ such a body forming a political or social program, along with the devices for putting it into operation."

Organization: The word 'organization' is defined in accordance to the Collins English Dictionary as "a business or administrative concern united and constructed for a particular end".

Systemic Functional Linguistics: Systemic functional linguistics (SFL) is an approach to linguistics that considers language as a social semiotic system.

Visual Semiotics: Visual semiotics is a sub-domain of semiotics within the field of linguistics that analyses the way visual images communicate a message.

APPENDIX

Table 1. A comparison between the corporate profiles of VCC and Geely Automobile, in illustration of their corporate visioning and ideology, 2007-2011.

Dimension	Volvo Car Corporation (VCC)	Geely
Products	• Total number of 11 models. • VCC operates in premium segment of cars with four versions: sedans (S40, S60 and S80), versatile estates (V40, V50, V70), cross country (XC60, XC70, XC90), coupes and convertible (C30, C70). • VCC cars have a distinct design, with cars from the 1970s to late 1990s having a square, boxy look. The shoulders were softened and rounded in later car designs that were in effort to steer from 'safe' to 'sexy'.	• More than 30 models from 8 main serials in their portfolio including Geely Free Cruise, Geely KINGKONG, Geely Vision, Shanghai Maple and Beauty Leopard, etc, • 8 main serials of engines including MR1.0L-1.8L, JL1.6L-1.8L and 4G1.0-1.8CVVT, etc • Early models were generally copies from other car brands. • No known or conscious current design strategy that says it is 'uniquely Geely' though they are known for candy coloured cars. • High financial investment in improving technology know-how, resulting in several successful products- Geely FC, Geely Panda, Emgrand series, etc.
Markets	• In 2009, Volvo recorded global sales of 334,808 cars, with ca. 2,300 local dealers from around 100 national sales companies worldwide. • The USA is VCC's largest market, followed by Sweden (12.5% global sales), Great Britain, Germany and China. • China sales is expected to increase considerably in the next ten years to come, possibly even overtaking Sweden as next largest market after USA. Total number of cars sold in China increased by 77.3% (22,405 cars in 2010 and 12,640 cars in 2009). • VCC considers itself a relatively small player in the global automobile market, where VCC had no such previous aggressive global sales strategy before being acquired by Geely, China.	• Approximately 200 cars in 1998 sold, but reached an annual sales volume of 20,099,388 in 2010, achieving an average annual increase of ca. 96%. • Average annual growth in 2010 was 22% which was seen as conservative, compared with its competitors such as Chery Automobile Co. Ltd and BYD company Ltd. • *"Geely is adjusting its strategic goal from 'rapid development' to 'steady development'," said Yang Jian, president of Geely.* (Source: Global Times. Published: January/10/2011 16:54) • 2011 sees the start of Geely's roll out five-year plan to sell 1 million units by 2015.
Branding and green technology	• Known from the beginning as safe, solid and reliable, VCC was the first company to produce cars with padded dashboards, with the first three-point seat belt for the middle of the rear seat and Side Impact Protection systems (SIPS). • Side airbags were introduced and installed as standard equipment in all models. City Safety was introduced to the cross-over XC60 where the car automatically stops at speeds below 31 km/h if obstruction is detected in front of it. Pedestrian Detection with auto brake was introduced in the new S60 • Environmentally conscious vehicles: ***Flexible- Fuel Vehicles*****:** Encompasses the entire life cycle of the car, from product development to production and recycling. ***Plug-In Hybrids*****:** Features both an electric motor and a conventional combustion engine. ***Battery Car*****:** Is based on a lithium battery that powers an electric engine. The battery can be charged through a normal electrical wall outlet. ***Gas-Turbine Hybrids*****:** Is a car fitted with both an electric motor and combustion engine and is self-charging.	In its brief history, Geely has suffered much from bad publicity due to its poor quality controls in its initial phases of producing cars. Geely continues to improve its brand image from low cost to high-end market both in and outside China. Geely does however have a few merits to its brand and amongst its numerous accomplishments are: ▪ In 2001, Geely's JI-6360 model was certified by the government making Geely the first private company qualified to produce automobiles in China. ▪ In 2005, Geely produced the first Chinese-designed automatic transmission, after the other state-owned car makers failed to develop such a transmission system. ▪ Geely's 4G18 engine, a self-developed automatic transmission with its own intelligent steering were introduced at the Chinese national innovation exhibition in 2005. ▪ In 2008, they participated in the North American International Auto Show in Detroit, winning the Special Contribution Grand Prize for Invention and Creation for their Blow-out Monitoring and Brake System ("BMBS"), a unique safety system independently developed by Geely in 2008. Following the lead of VCC in going green, five Geely research projects in 2006 were incorporated into a mixed fuel car "863" high-tech development programme. This research programme was supported by the Ministry of Science and Technology. 2 prototypes have been produced, using methyl as an alternative fuel. The prototypes were exhibited at international auto shows in Shanghai and Beijing. A five year energy efficiency and environmentally friendly auto development programme was also launched to develop new energy propelled cars. The company intends to develop five hybrid models over the coming years incorporating plug-in, stop-run, hybrid systems and electric only systems.

continued on following page

Table 1. Continued

Dimension	Volvo Car Corporation (VCC)	Geely
Branding and the Customer	**"Design Around you"** • Volvo is regarded as a safe and good quality car everywhere in the world and luxury car in certain parts like North America and China. • VCC is associated with the elegant Scandinavian design or the Swedish style. The safety record is also an assist for VCC, which is regarded as safer car in the world. • VCC can compete within the premium segment. Customer royalty can be kept only through the preserve of the brand value.	**"Multi-brand Strategy"** • Lacking a distinct iconic design, and resolving to dissolve "Geely" as a brand in itself by 2012, Geely's approach to the market is a stepped, multi-brand strategy that brings "World Quality" and "Chinese Wisdom" to high end market corners, hopefully into as many households as possible. • They plan to become one of the world's Top 500 enterprises through innovation and brand image building. • Management ideology has also shifted, to focus on safety and 'Quality', changing from 'rapid growth' to 'steady growth', transferring to 'brand line management' from 'product line management'. • Their branding aims to be comprehensive and as diverse as possible.
Global ambitions	In terms of ownership, VCC was Swedish owned until 1998 when AB Volvo wanted to divest its automobile business and fully concentrate on the commercial vehicle market. American Ford saw advantages in acquiring VCC that was a profitable prestigious mid-size European automobile manufacturer. This saw the beginnings of VCC's ownership outside of Swedish hands. In terms of production, VCC began producing several models of cars in Ghent, Belgium in 1965.	Geely's global ambitions for sales have been clear from all annual reports thus far, especially in their 2009 Annual Report that sees its Chinese calligraphic visuals draw Geely cars exiting China in all directions on the globe. Since 2002, Geely has established a dealership network with the more than 50 overseas distributors, reaching the total overseas sales of over 100,000 vehicles in total. Geely also has offices in its strategic markets in CIS, Middle East, Africa, Southeast Asia and Central and South America. In 2009, overseas assembly plants were established in Ukraine, Russia and Indonesia to produce vehicles in SKD/CKD. It has actively participated in international autoshows where in 2010, ca. 8% of its sales came from overseas, from mostly developing countries in SE-Asia, Africa, Russia, Peru and Uruguay. Its current ambition is to patiently but steadily conquer the European and American market. To help with their global ambitions, they have made a conscious effort in acquiring knowledge and expertise via global brands such as VCC from Ford and Drivetrain Systems International from Australia.

Chapter 13
Social Capital Management Challenges:
Thailand

Scott A. Hipsher
Naresuan University, Thailand

ABSTRACT

Social capital is an abstract concept, yet it is widely believed the core aspects of social capital, the quality and quantity of social relationships, are important factors in organizational and individual success. An examination of the use of bonding and bridging social capital within Thailand was made. It was found, in principle; the managing of social capital in Thailand is similar to managing social capital in other locations, although the specific practices should be aligned with the unique cultural values found in Thailand. It is suggested that creating and using both bridging and bonding social capital are important components of the business environments found in Thailand.

INTRODUCTION

Organizations and businesses are made up of people and the quality and quantity of personal relationships within an organization, as well as personal relationships connecting the organization to the wider environment, are important factors in organizational success. However, identifying and measuring the quality and quantity of these personal relationships, often called social capital, is problematic. Nevertheless, despite the difficulty in using, defining, and measuring social capital, it is generally agreed the quantity and quality of personal relationships are contributing factors to organizational and personal success.

In academia, the term social capital has evolved to be used to refer to the leveraging of personal relationships to create business or organizational competitive advantages. Yet, due to the abstract and contextual nature of personal relationships, there does not seem to be a consensus on the exact nature and definition of social capital nor on how it can be used to create competitive advantages (e.g. Bridge, 2014; Carpenter, Daniere, & Takahashi, 2004; Goulbourne & Solomos, 2003; Taylor,

DOI: 10.4018/978-1-5225-0276-0.ch013

2007; Wolfe, 2010). It has been speculated the extremely broad definition of the term as it is often used, covering almost all human relationships, can prevent the concept from being of practical use in conducting an objective analysis of actual practices within an organization (Dufhues, Buchenrieder, Quoc, & Munkung, 2011, p. 681).

The term social capital is often thought of as an abstract resource which alongside human, physical, and financial capital can be leveraged by an organization to create competitive advantages. It has been refer to as an "unquantifiable-but-appreciating resource" which helps produce innovation and increases knowledge flows (Wolfe, 2010, p. 214). Smedlund (2008) identified three uses of social capital by an organization, to create and transfer knowledge as well as in implementing decisions and policies. The author implied social capital can be controlled, managed, and utilized by an organization. On the other hand, Adler and Kwon (2002) claimed, "Social capital is the resource available to actors as a function of their location in the structure of their social relations" (p. 23), implying social capital is owned and used by individuals (actors) and not controlled by an impersonal organization.

Furthermore, social capital has also been thought of in less abstract terms and described as basically a relationship construct (Dufhues, et al., 2013). As a relationship construct, Bridge (2014) found social capital can be used to: (a) create trust, therefore there is less reliance on legal or regulatory enforcement; (b) create new linkages which can develop into new business partnerships; (c) provide advocacy and vouching for specific individuals; (d) assist mentoring; (e) become a source of new ideas; and (f) provide other assistance (e.g. financial loans or advice).

Adler and Kwon (2002) found there are two different views, or types, of relationship social capital. The first is bridging social capital which is focused on linking an individual to information and other resources controlled by other actors. A bridging focus on developing social capital would include creating connections with other actors both inside and outside the organization who control or have access to valuable resources including knowledge and information. The other type, or view, is of bonding social capital. This type of social capital is more concerned with relationships within groups and this view focuses on the development of more intangible benefits which are the products of close working relationships within an organization.

Furthermore, acquiring social capital has been connected with economic growth at the national level (Dinda, 2014; Inoguchi, 2000), entrepreneurial success (Nasrolahi, Mohammad, & Jalilvand, 2014), success in international business conducted by MNEs (Taylor, 2007) and improved leadership and organizational performance (Augusto, Couto, & Caiado, 2014). A cynic looking though the literature on social capital might be skeptical of all the claims about social capital and think it is being sold as a kind of magical cure-all for almost every problem an organization or society faces, yet few individuals disagree with the idea that having good relationships helps individuals, organizations, and society as a whole achieve a variety of objectives.

But from a practical standpoint, the desire to improve all human relationships might be too abstract and obvious of a goal to provide much direction for a leader of an organization. Instead, focusing on the benefits from bonding social capital on productivity and innovation, as well as the value of personal connections, bridging social capital, in gaining access to resources and information outside of the firm's boundaries, might help to provide practical and direct benefits to organizations and organizational leaders.

SOCIAL CAPITAL IN ASIA

Much of the research on social capital has been conducted in Western societies which, according to Hofstede's (1980, 1983) dimensions of culture, are more individualistic, have lower levels of uncertainty avoidance, and have lower power distances than is the norm in Asia and other parts of the world.

Adler and Kwon (2002) considered social capital as coming from relationships outside of the formal organizational structure and as fairly egalitarian in nature. Yet in Thailand, and in other parts of Asia, it has been found nearly are relationships are hierarchal in nature to some extent, based on age, social standing, rank, length of service to an organization, wealth, or other factors (Holmes, Tangtongtav, & Tomizawa, 1996). However one should not equate the hierarchal nature of nearly all personal relationships in Thailand, and many other countries with relatively higher power distance cultures, as being similar to formal and impersonal relationships found within a formal organizational structure. Instead these relationships can be similar to friendly and warm relationships found within a family (Hipsher, 2010a), such as between an older sibling and younger one, father and daughter, or uncle and nephew.

Using Hofstede's (1980, 1983) dimensions of culture, the concept of social capital in more individualistic societies (Western countries) might differ considerably from how the concept is used in more collectivist countries (the rest of the world). There have been many research findings showing business relationships in collectivist countries are significantly different from business relationships found in individualist societies (e.g. Bjerke 2000; Gallo, 2011; Shapiro, Gedaijlovis, & Erdener, 2003). As social capital increases when the quantity and quality of relationships increase (Taylor, 2007, p. 344), it would appear the acquiring and using of social capital will differ to some degree in different cultural environments and direct comparisons about use of social capital across cultures can be problematic (Dufhues, et al., 2011, p. 688).

Furthermore, it has been suggested social capital might play an even bigger role in organizational and individual success in Asia than in Western societies. Zhang and Fung (2006), when referring to the largest country and economy in Asia, believed, "China is a traditionally network-oriented economy, where social capital appears to be more important than in the other western economies, where individual orientation is emphasized" (p. 199). Additionally, Inoguchi (2000) reported, "Japanese society is often said to be one with a high premium on social capital" (p. 73).

In Chinese societies and in Chinese business networks, much has been written about a concept called *guanxi*, which has been labeled as a form of Asian social capital (Szeto, Wright, & Cheng, 2006). Zhang and Fung (2006) found *guanxi* as measured by donations and entertainment activity was associated with improved financial performance, although membership in trade organizations was not, as these memberships are seen in China as mostly symbolic and informal, while it is within formal networks, consisting of members working within a single value chain, that most business actually gets done.

Chang, Guo, Zolin, and Yang (2014) stressed the culturally specific aspects of *guanxi* and stated it is difficult for foreigners to use the networks of *guanxi* in China, according to their definition of the term. The authors claim that while *guanxi* is similar to the concept of social networks in Western environments; it is not exactly the same. While the authors felt *guanxi* was not the same as social capital, they did believe *guanxi* could be used to create social capital. Creating trust, or more specifically, reciprocal obligations, was considered to be the core nature of *guanxi*. While *guanxi* is usually thought of as strictly concerned with personal relationships, Li and Wright (2000) reported that the concept, as used by managers within China, included cultivating both person to person relationships as well as organization to organization relationships. It would appear *guanxi*, and similar concepts in other Asian societies, could fall within the broader definitions of social capital, yet also seem to include some specific applications that only apply within a specific cultural and legal environment.

Social capital plays a large role in relationship contracting, which is more common in Asia and developing countries than in Western societies. Relationship contracting refers to more emphasis on personal relationships and trust as opposed to impersonal formal contracts in arranging business exchanges between organizations. While the use of relationship contracting is often explained by looking at cultural differences, the impact of the legal systems would also appear to have a large impact on the effectiveness of relationship contracting. As managers operating in many developing economies such as Thailand have less confidence in the government's willingness and ability to impartially enforce private contracts, firms put emphasis on enforcing their own contract/agreements through the use of social capital and connections. Therefore the use of relationship contracting in Asia is more common than in Western societies, where more emphasis is placed on reliance on formal contracts and enforcement of the contracts by the legal system paid for and operated by the government (e.g. Hitt, Lee, & Yucel, 2002; Kim, Hoskisson, Tihanyi, & Hong, 2004; Nguyen, Weinstein, & Meyer, 2005; Peng & Zhou, 2005; Wu & Choi, 2004; Young, 2005).

It should not be assumed legal systems in which parties are expected to enforce their own contracts are inherently inferior to legal systems where the government enforces personal contracts and the written contract is consider always binding, as is the case in Western societies. The use of relationship contracting and informal contacts has the advantage of reducing the tax burden for everyone as the court system and regulatory agencies do not spend as much time and taxpayers' resources enforcing personal agreements. Also, instead of having to use considerable time and energy negotiating in order to create an acceptable agreement that tries to foresee all possible contingencies before any actual exchange takes place, relationship contracting can allow the negotiations to continue on after business relationships have begun. Therefore both parties have better information with which to negotiate at different points in the business relationship, which potentially can result in more equitable distribution of profits and more sustainable business partnerships (Van de Ven, 2004; Wu & Choi, 2004; Young, 2005).

THAILAND

Social Capital in Thailand

While strategic principles and operational practices and principles can often be transferred across cultural borders with limited need for adaptation to local environments, interpersonal business practices, where social capital is most likely to be used, usually need to conform to local cultural conditions (Hipsher, 2010b). So while firms around the world, using Porter's (1980) framework, effectively use low cost leadership or differentiation strategies, and the use of many global "best practices" is seen at the operational level across national borders, often driven by advances in technology, cultural differences have not been eliminated by globalization and therefore a convergence of business practices that involve interpersonal relationships where social capital is used has not happened.

The acquiring and use of social capital in Thailand has been studied and not surprisingly it has been reported there are both some similarities and some differences in acquiring and using social capital in Thailand compared to the acquiring and use of social capital in other different cultural environments. In comparisons with similar situations with low income individuals in Vietnam, Carpenter, et al. (2004),

Dufhues, et al. (2011), and Dufhues, Buchenrieder, and Munkung (2013) found bonding social capital was both preferred and more effective in Thailand while bridging capital, where individuals became more connected with people in power, was more effective in achieving objectives in Vietnam. Daniere, Takahashi, NaRanong, and Lan (2005), also in a comparison between Thailand and Vietnam, found poverty increased the difficulty of acquiring social capital to a greater extent in Thailand than in Vietnam, while increased social capital was associated with increased community participation in both locations.

Social capital has also been studied in relationship to migration from the countryside into the cities in Thailand. Curran, Garip, Chung, and Tangchonlatip (2005) found the amount of social capital and personal connections one already had with people living in the city, usually other immigrants from the same family or village, had an influence on the ability and desire of individuals from rural environments to migrate to the city, although the specific influence was found to be affected to some degree by one's gender. Once in the city, the distinction between migrant and those from the city is substantial, which results in most migrants developing more bonding and bridging social capital within their own migrant communities while having difficulties in acquiring bridging capital with the city natives who often controlled access to most of the resources such as jobs within the city (Gullette, 2014).

Hipsher (2010a) found the business practices in Thailand have been greatly influenced by operating in an environment where Theravada Buddhism is the religion of the vast majority of the people. For example, the fairly low locus of control found in many individuals is aligned with the teachings of *karma* and the focus on impermanent nature of the world. Also the hierarchical nature of society is often explained through the concept of *karma*, and Thailand is often "considered one of the most individualistic cultures in Southeast Asia" (Carpenter, et al., 2004, p. 549), which is consistent with Buddhist teachings on the individual nature of the path to *nirvana/nibbana*. Persons (2008) explained, "*Saksii* seems to be an independent, individualistic force with a Thai person that stands in contrast to the strong collectivist sanctions and pressures to conform" (p. 86).

Central features of Theravada Buddhism are the elimination of desire for material wealth and personal glory, to follow the middle path and avoid extremes in all actions; therefore outward displays of high levels of professional or personal ambition are generally frowned upon.

Four distinguishing features of Thai culture and work environments which might be especially influential in respect to managing social capital in Thailand are (a) the paternalistic nature of management, (b) the preference for personal as opposed to the bureaucratic control, (c) the need for flexibility, and (d) the concept of *sanuk* in the work place.

Paternal Style Management

Differences in national culture have been found to have a strong impact on differences in managerial values and practices (Ralston, Holt, Terpstra, & Cheng 1997; Ralston, 2008). Since Thai culture has been profoundly influenced by Theravada Buddhist teachings of *karma*, this has have resulted in most Thais being "reasonably comfortable with the notion that some individuals in society 'deserve' to have more power" (Holmes, et al., 1996, p. 62).

The paternalistic nature of management and leadership found in Southeast Asia is not necessarily the same as being authoritarian where the leader has all the power and the workers have no option but to follow the boss's orders. Rehbein (2007, p. 71) explained the leader-follower relationship in Southeast Asia "is not simple domination but something like an exchange of protection against loyalty." While workers have an expectation of loyalty to their bosses, much as children are expected to be loyal to their parents, the leaders also have expectations to protect the employers and to take their interests in considerations when making decisions, much as is expected of parents in relationships with their children. "Thais have grown to expect a leader to demonstrate a blend of authoritarianism and benevolence" (Holmes, et al., 1996, p. 62).

And this paternalistic nature of relationships in Thai society has been observed by outsiders for generations, as noted by Young (1900, p. 127) in his description of "slavery" during his visit to Thailand well over a hundred years ago:

There is nothing cruel or revolting in the treatment of the serfs, and many of them are sincerely attached to their masters, and have been known voluntarily to afford them any assistance they could when misfortunes have overtaken them. They are fed, clothed, and housed at the expense of their owners, and rarely experience in their dependent condition any real hardships. Away in the country the majority of the people prefer to live as the bondservants of some powerful person, who in return for their labour provides both them and their families with protection and support.

In more recent times, this paternalistic attitude towards authority has been associated with Thailand's difficulties in moving towards a more democratic political system (Chen, 2014; Lee, 2014; Hipsher 2010a).

Personal, not Bureaucratic

Loyalty in Thailand is normally thought of as a personal relationship as opposed to loyalty to abstract concepts such as an organization or country. Thais are generally more loyal to their bosses than to their company and loyalty to the King is generally stronger than loyalty to the state. On the job, Thais appear to mostly prefer organizing through personal relationship as opposed to using bureaucratic control. Personal relationships are flexible, contextual, arbitrary, and make extensive use of social capital. While bureaucratic control is consistent, inflexible, impersonal, and assists in creating business contracts between strangers while making use of much less social capital.

When dealing with individuals and firms from outside the organization, Thais generally prefer to rely on personal relationships as opposed to formal contracts. For example Johnsen (2007) noted in her study of the silk industry, "In Thailand, in particular, the contractual obligations of the relationships were seen to be less important than the goodwill between parties" (p. 142). While Petison and Johri (2008) reported in the automotive industry in Thailand, relationships between local suppliers and foreign manufacturers normally began as market-exchange types of relationships with a reliance on formal contracts. But as a personal relationship developed between parties the agreement became based more on trust and social capital and less emphasis was placed on the formal agreements. It was found the switch from a reliance on contracts to a reliance on the social capital of relationships was often beneficial to both parties as the local suppliers benefited from increased technical support from the foreign manufacturers while the foreign companies benefited by seeing less business intelligence leakage and increased understanding of local market conditions.

Flexibility

One of the main teachings of Theravada Buddhism is the impermanence of all material possessions and social relationships, therefore the need to be adaptable and flexible as change is an established part of life (e.g. Assavavirulhakarn, 2010; Davids, 1894; Jackson, 2003; King, 1964). Swierczek and Onishi (2003) reported on this preference for flexibility amongst Thai employees working for Japanese automakers:

Japanese management prefers specific company rules over flexible rules. Thai subordinates prefer flexibility. Thai employees feel that Japanese managers are too serious in decision making. Japanese managers feel very uncomfortable in the frequent decision changes of Thai subordinates who believe that a decision should be adjusted as the environment changes (p. 198).

Duong and Swierczek (2008) compared attitudes between Vietnamese and Thai managers and found Vietnamese managers were more long-term oriented while Thai managers appeared to be more comfortable with ambiguity and uncertainty. As opposed to a more rules based organization, the preference for more flexible organizations in Thailand requires more reliance on cooperation and trust, which are considered the prime components of social capital demonstrating the importance of social capital in Thailand.

Sanuk

In Thai, the same word *ngan,* can be used to refer to both work and a festival. It has been speculated this is because in the past in the village communities' work projects, or when individuals needed additional labor at harvest time, instead of using paid labor, the work event would be turned into a social event which included opportunities for feasting and socializing in exchange for one's labor. The distinction between work and play was intentionally lessened to create a form of payment for labor in these pre-cash Thai societies. While today Thais do distinguish between work and fun, in keeping with the traditions of the past, the separation between the two may not be as clearly marked in Thailand as in many other countries. The preference for a *sanuk* (fun) work environment in Thailand has been noted by many observers, for example:

For the Thais, good interpersonal relationships and a high level of fun are regarded as crucial factors for staying in a job. When these are missing, people will very likely seek alternative employment even if other extrinsic or intrinsic needs are fulfilled. What foreigners often view as a lack of "seriousness" in work attitudes are often an integral part of personal and group motivation and cohesion. Unlike in Western cultures, having fun is a legitimate and worthy aspect of work life. It is somewhat perplexing to the Western manager that having fun is a predominant feature of the Thai workplace (Kainzbauer 2009, p. 9).

Duong and Swierczek (2008), in a comparative analysis of Vietnamese and Thai managers, found Vietnamese managers were more performance oriented than were Thai managers. On the other hand, Thai managers expressed more job satisfaction and were more focused on developing good relationships at work than were their Vietnamese counterparts. Maintaining harmony and avoiding conflicts in the workplace have been found to often taken priority over operational efficiency in the Thai workplace, sometimes the more popular decision replaces the more profitable one (Holmes, et al., 1996).

While looking at this emphasis on *sanuk*, or fun, in the workplace one should not fall into believing a stereotype that Thais are not serious on the job, or are lazy. People in every culture prefer to work in a pleasant environment, and there is always a balance between the priority to enjoy one's work and being profitable and productive. Thais can work long and hard when it is required, but there is less of a belief in the value of work for work' sake. The difference between the attitudes of the Thais and those more commonly found in Western or East Asian cultures in regards to enjoying one's work is more of degree than of kind.

Chinese Influence

While culturally the majority of people in Thailand are "Thai," individuals in the top levels of most businesses and many of the wealthy and powerful individuals in Thailand come from ethnic Chinese families where individual values and work attitudes would seem to be the result of the mix of the East Asian/Confucian values passed down through the generations and Southeast Asia/Theravada Buddhist values picked up from the local environment. While most ethnic Chinese Thais (Sino-Thais), today, have Thai names, speak Thai as a first language, practice Theravada Buddhism and are outwardly very similar to the majority of the population, it would appear many business leaders and entrepreneurs in Thailand share some characteristics with individuals from East Asian cultures to a greater extent than does the average Thai person.

The domination of ethnic Chinese in the business environments in Thailand and the rest of Southeast Asia has been observed by writers throughout generations (e.g. Adams,1879; Evans, 2002; Hill, 2002; Naisbitt 1997; Young, 1900), while the development of networks built on trust and mutually beneficial cooperation within the ethnic Chinese business partners (bridging social capital) has been attributed with the domination of many industries by ethnic Chinese owned firms within Southeast Asia (e.g. Carney & Gedailovic 2003; Clarke 1998; Shapiro, et. al., 2003; Sim & Pandian, 2007; Suehiro & Wailerdsak 2004; Tsang 2001).

Chinese in Thailand were the prime movers in Thai economic development. They controlled modern banking and marketing systems throughout the country. This is because the Thais considered commerce ruthless and sinful acts for good Buddhists, and a lower class status job which the educated Thais are not attracted to (Chanthanom 1998, p. 272).

However it has been noted the management style of managers coming from the Peoples' Republic of China in Thailand are distinctly different from the management style of local Thai managers, whether ethnic Chinese or otherwise (Bunchapattanasakda & Wong, 2010).

Use of Social Capital in Thailand

An example of using bridging social capital can be seen within an interdependent network of independently owned businesses connected to the company, Star Tours (A pseudonym). Star Tours is a travel agency located in Bangkok and specializes in organizing tours for Thais to visit Siem Reap, Cambodia, the site of world famous historic temples and historical sites including Angkor Wat. Star Tours engages with a series of Thai-owned hotels, restaurants, and transportation companies in Siem Reap to provide a tour package for the customers. The restaurants are also linked with a network of Thai suppliers which provide the needed ingredients to make authentic Thai food for the tourists.

This network of firms operates on trust and constantly shifting agreements about how profits are to be divided as opposed to using more formal contracts. These arrangements provide Star Tours with the opportunity to provide a complete tour package to its customers while providing the Thai-owned companies in Siem Reap with a steady stream of customers. While the informal, personal, and flexible nature of the agreements can be attributed to Thai cultural factors, but there is also a practical aspect as getting a court to enforce a contract in either Cambodia or Thailand is too expensive, time-consuming, and uncertain to be practical. Therefore the development of trust and bridging social capital allows repeated transactions to be carried out in uncertain conditions with some confidence the other parties will not try to take advantage in any single situation. A loss of trust due to taking advantage of the other members of the network would exclude a company or individual from further business within the network, and therefore the risk of being excluded from future business activities works as a deterrent to opportunistic behavior.

Although this type of bridging social capital found throughout Asia and much of the economically developing economies of the world, works best between firms which are managed by their owners. Owners of companies who have almost unlimited arbitrary decision making powers can develop bridging social capital in a manner that is not possible for a hired manager. All the firms in the network connected with Star Tours are owner-managed.

An example of bonding social capital in Thailand is found within Siam Tailor and Laundry Shop (another pseudonym). This business consists of a tailoring, retail, and laundry business in Bangkok which specifically targets foreign tourists. The shop employs between 4 and 8 employees, depending on the time of year, and all employees are recruited from the same rural village and knew each other before coming to work in the city. Therefore, internally, the firm operates in many ways like a family business with a mix of social and professional interactions. Because of the personal bonds that are developed, employees are more likely to cover for each other when ill or when taken away by personal affairs, provide an already existing support network for new employees, and provide peer-pressure to maintain a level of output without the need for direct supervision.

The firm provides meals which the employees eat together, thereby strengthening the bonding social capital. Also many of the employees share rooms and often travel back and forth to the home village together. Siam Tailor and Laundry Shop is not just a job for these rural migrants to the city, but also in many ways a home away from home and the separation between personal and professional life is not always clearly defined.

DISCUSSION

It would appear creating bonding social capital is considered important in most Thai organization as it is common practice for larger Thai firms and organizations to frequently arrange trips or other social events so the employees can have fun while increasing the bonding social capital within the organization. A very common practice is to organize trips to Buddhist temples, once or twice a year, in order to allow employers and employees to share in "merit-making" while creating bonding opportunities during the shared travel experience and meals. While the creation of social events to create bonding social capital is nothing unique to Thai companies, these events seem to have significant importance to Thai employees and are often organized on a regular and frequent basis.

RECOMMENDATIONS

Human Resource Management

The goals of human resource (HR) management are to hire, retain, and improve the skills of quality employees. Therefore, it would appear managing social capital in any organization would begin with a company's HR policies and practices.

Despite globalization and the emergence of many operational global "best practices," effective HR management practices remain diverse and aligned with the specific cultural, legal, and competitive environment where they are used (e.g. Lamond & Zheng, 2010; Wang, Zhang, Lamond, & Ke, 2014; Zheng, 2013).

In recruitment and selection, it is often advocated to take a very systematic and objective approach in Western countries (e.g. Dessler, 2003; Simola, Taggar, & Smith, 2007) however in more collectivist cultures such as those found in Asia, recruitment and selection practices are often less formal and bureaucratic while being more arbitrary and personal (e.g. Hooi, 2008; Okpara & Wynn, 2008). Although these formal practices in many developed economies might be driven as much by need to prove compliance with equal opportunity laws as it does with organizational efficiency. In Thailand, Wu, Lawler, and Yi (2008) found formal job announcements were mostly used for professional positions while blue-collar positions were more likely to be filled through informal recruitment methods, often using the social capital of existing employee to recommend people for employment.

In Western societies, in recruitment and selection, the focus is almost entirely on finding the individual with the skills that best match the needs of the position and the organization. And while personality and ability to become part of the organizational team are considered, these are often of secondary importance. In collectivist and high power distance societies such as Thailand, often the ability to bond with the existing team members appears to increase in importance and the individual skills brought to the job might at times take a back-seat to the ability to fit smoothly into the existing social and hierarchical structures. An informal recruitment process where individuals moving into the organization already have established some social capital with existing employees might be helpful in having the new employee fit into the social structure more easily than if the individual came into the organization as a complete stranger with no social capital with the other members of the organization.

There appears to be more of a focus on informal and on-the job training as opposed to using formal training programs in many Thai firms, especially SMEs (Thassanabanjong, Miller, & Marchant, 2009). But this practice is most likely due to the smaller size and family ownership structures in most Thai companies and not due to any specific aspect of Thai culture as the use of formal training appears to realitvely common in larger firms and is sought after by Thai employees. Compensation is an important human resource issue in every organization, although it does not appear there are significant differences in issues to consider in selecting compensation approaches in Thailand as compared to other locations.

While there might not be major differences in approaches to training or compensation in organizations in Thailand in comparison to organizations in other locations, in managing social capital in Thailand, the structure and philosophy of the career development and performance management systems should most likely be given special consideration.

Formal performance appraisals where individuals are formally graded and ranked amongst their peers are both common and advocated in Western societies to encourage increased individual performance though competition (e.g. Endres & Mancheno-Smoak 2008; Longenecker, Fink, & Caldwell, 2014a,

2014b; Schmidt & Akdere, 2007). However, the use of these formal appraisal techniques is not common in Thailand, and one of the reasons often given to explain this is because a poor score on a performance appraisal can result in losing "face" (Persons, 2008) which makes it difficult or impossible to continue working in an environment where one has already lost face. Also Thais put a lot of emphasis on conflict avoidance (Onishi, & Bliss, 2006), while competition between employees generally increases the incidents of conflicts. Before implementing a formal performance appraisal system in Thailand, it is recommended to consider issues associated with social capital including both the problems arising from conflicts and loss of face a competitive type of performance appraisal system might bring in addition to any potential benefits.

Management/Leadership Style

Many Western management and leadership practices are based on assumptions employees share the individualistic and relatively low power distance and uncertainty avoidance cultural characteristics as their managers (Hofstede 1980). Yet there is extensive evidence that management and leadership practices are very contextual in nature and what works in one location does not automatically work in another (e.g. Pounder, 2001). For example, while "empowerment" is often advocated as a desirable management/ leadership practice in a Western context, it has been found to be less effective and accepted by employees in collectivist Asian contexts (Hui, Au, & Fock. 2004; Newburry & Yakova 2006). Kaweevisultrakul and Chan (2007) also reported on difficulties companies had in transferring some formal Western management practices to Thailand.

To create bonding social capital within an organization in Thailand, in addition to being flexible, realizing the preference for a paternalistic management style, and trying to create an enjoyable work environment, a manger should try to limit the amount of conflict created.

In Western cultures, conflict can be considered as being either productive or destructive, depending on the nature of the conflict. However to Thais, conflict is almost always considered to be negative and something to be avoided (Boonsathorn, 2007; Onishi, & Bliss, 2006; Sriussadaporn, 2006). The Western view is often one in which problems need to be confronted as soon as possible and a solution needs to be found. While Thais often believe if left alone, problems, especially personal issues between individuals, tend to take care of themselves and the damage to the social capital of the individual and the organization from directly addressing a conflict is not worth the possible gains made by tackling each and every personal issue as it arises.

Sriussadaporn (2006) reported many expatriate managers in Thailand have difficulty in getting real opinions from employees, instead it is felt employees often tell their managers what they think the boss wants to hear to avoid conflict. In addition foreign managers in Thailand often wish employees would have better time management skills and find orders, especially when issued harshly, are not always followed. Sriussadaporn gives the following advice to expatriate managers working in Thailand, "Thai employees expected their bosses to possess positive personal characters such as being friendly, generous, polite, and fair…"; "expatriates should never shout at or reprimand Thai employees in front of others with a loud and harsh tone of voice" and "expatriates should note that being nice and friendly is always a good strategy to gain Thai employees' acceptance" (p. 334). These management practices will most likely help a manger gain social capital with Thai employees and also are likely to increase the bonding social capital amongst the employees. Although this increased social capital might come at the cost of some organizational efficiency in the short term.

Also, it has generally been found that creating bridging social capital is necessary to create good relationships with suppliers and other members of a value chain within Thailand (Laosirihongthong, The, & Adebanjo, 2013). Doing business in Thailand without connections increases the challenges one faces.

Managing social capital in Thailand should not be thought of as being totally different from managing social capital in other locations, although there does seem to be some unique aspects in the creation and use of social capital in Thailand due to the cultural, historical, economic, and political environments. Furthermore, social capital is considered extremely important in organizations in Thailand and it is recommended managers in Thailand, both local and foreign, give significant attention to creating bonding and bridging social capital with individuals and organizations, as this capital can be very helpful in achieving organizational goals.

CONCLUSION

Cultural matters. Social capital is created through human interactions and human interactions are driven by cultural assumptions and values. Managers working in Thailand should realize the importance of social capital in the Kingdom as well as understanding the unique aspects of Thai culture, values, and approaches to social relationships which make up the foundation on which social capital is created and used in organizations within Thailand.

REFERENCES

Adams, W. H. D. (1879). *In the Far East: A narrative of exploration and adventure in Cochin-China, Cambodia, Laos and Siam*. London: Thomas Nelson and Sons.

Adler, P., & Kwon, S. (2002). Social capital: Prospects for a new concept. *Academy of Management Review*, *27*, 17–40.

Assavavirulhakarn, P. (2010). *The ascendancy of Theravada Buddhism in Southeast Asia*. Chiang Mai, Thailand: Silkworm.

Augusto, J., Couto, F. E., & Caiado, J. (2014). Human capital, social capital and organizational performance. *Management Decision*, *52*(2), 350–364. doi:10.1108/MD-04-2013-0260

Bjerke, B. V. (2000). A typified, culture-based, interpretation of management of SMEs in Southeast Asia. *Asia Pacific Journal of Management*, *17*(1), 103–132. doi:10.1023/A:1015441021413

Boonsathorn, W. (2007). Understanding conflict management styles of Thais and Americans in multinational corporations in Thailand. *The International Journal of Conflict Management*, *18*(3), 196–221. doi:10.1108/10444060710825972

Bridge, S. (2014). Exploring the nature of social capital to facilitate its inclusion in enterprise education. *Education + Training*, *56*(8/9), 839 – 851.

Bunchapattanasakda, C., & Wong, P. (2010). Management practices of Chinese managers in Chinese MNCs operating in Bangkok. *Cross Cultural Management: An International Journal*, *17*(3), 268–282. doi:10.1108/13527601011068360

Carney, M., & Gedailovic, E. (2003). Strategic innovation and the administrative heritage of East Asian family business groups. *Asia Pacific Journal of Management*, *20*(1), 5–26. doi:10.1023/A:1022062428231

Carpenter, J. P., Daniere, A. G., & Takahashi, L. M. (2004). Cooperation, trust, and social capital in Southeast Asian urban slums. *Journal of Economic Behavior & Organization*, *55*(4), 533–551. doi:10.1016/j.jebo.2003.11.007

Chang, A., Guo, C., Zolin, R., & Yang, X. (2014). Guanxi as a complex adaptive system: Definition, description and underlying principals. *Journal of Asia Business Studies*, *8*(2), 81–103. doi:10.1108/JABS-12-2012-0058

Chanthanom, S. (1998). *Globalization of the Golden Triangle: Cultural transformation in Burma, Laos and Thailand*. (Doctoral dissertation). University of Pittsburgh. UMI No. 9919264.

Chen, P. H. (2004). The vulnerability of Thai democracy: Coups d'etat and political changes in modern Thailand. In P. Liamputtong (Ed.), *Contemporary Socio-Cultural and Political Perspectives in Thailand* (pp. 185–207). Dordrecht, NL: Springer.

Clarke, L. D. (1998). *The role of overseas Chinese investment in the emerging countries of Southeast and East Asia: A Confucian model of the foreign direct investment decision-making process using factors unconsidered in the West* (Doctoral dissertation). Florida International University. UMI No. 9835704.

Curran, S. R., Garip, F., Chung, C. Y., & Tangchonlatip, K. (2005). Gendered migrant social capital: Evidence from Thailand. *Social Forces*, *84*(1), 225–255. doi:10.1353/sof.2005.0094

Daniere, A., Takahashi, L., NaRanong, A., & Lan, V. T. N. (2005). Social capital and urban environments in Southeast Asia: Lessons from settlements in Bangkok and Ho Chi Minh City. *International Development Planning Review*, *27*(1), 21–58. doi:10.3828/idpr.27.1.3

Davids, T. W. R. (1894). *Buddhism: A sketch of the life and teachings of Gautama, the Buddha*. London: Society for Promoting Christian Knowledge.

Dessler, G. (2003). *Human resource management* (9th ed.). Upper Saddle River, NJ: Prentice Hall.

Dinda, S. (2014). Inclusive growth through creation of human and social capital. *International Journal of Social Economics*, *41*(10), 878–895. doi:10.1108/IJSE-07-2013-0157

Dufhues, T., Buchenrieder, G., & Munkung, N. (2013). Social capital and market imperfections: Accessing formal credit in Thailand. *Oxford Development Studies*, *41*(1), 54–75. doi:10.1080/13600818.2012.753999

Dufhues, T., Buchenrieder, G., Quoc, H. D., & Munkung, N. (2011). Social capital and loan repayment performance in Southeast Asia. *Journal of Socio-Economics*, *40*(5), 679–691. doi:10.1016/j.socec.2011.05.007

Duong, C. M., & Swierczek, F. W. (2008). Corporate culture, leadership competencies, job satisfaction, job commitment, and job performance: A comparison of companies in Vietnam and Thailand. *Journal of American Academy of Business, Cambridge*, *13*(1), 159–165.

Endres, G. M., & Mancheno-Smoak, L. (2008). The human resource craze: Human performance improvements and employee engagement. *Organization Development Journal*, *26*(1), 69–78.

Evans, G. (2002). *A short history of Laos: A land in between*. Crows Nest, Australia: Allen and Unwin.

Gallo, F. T. (2011). *Business leadership in China: How to blend best Western practices with Chinese wisdom* (Revised ed.). Singapore: John Wiley & Sons.

Goulbourne, H., & Solomos, J. (2003). Families, ethnicity and social capital. *Social Policy and Society*, *2*(4), 329–338. doi:10.1017/S1474746403001362

Gullette, G. S. (2014). Rural–urban hierarchies, status boundaries, and labour mobilities in Thailand. *Journal of Ethnic and Migration Studies*, *40*(8), 1254–1274. doi:10.1080/1369183X.2013.836959

Hill, R. (2002). *Southeast Asia: People, land and economy*. Crows Nest, Australia: Allen & Unwin.

Hipsher, S. (2010a). *Business practices in Southeast Asia: An interdisciplinary analysis of Theravada Buddhist countries*. London: Routledge Publishing.

Hipsher, S. (2010b). Transfer or adapt: Evidence from the Theravada Buddhist countries of Southeast Asia. *Global Business and Organizational Excellence*, *39*(3), 35–43. doi:10.1002/joe.20317

Hitt, M. A., Lee, H., & Yucel, E. (2002). The importance of social capital to the management of multinational enterprises: Relational networks among Asian and Western firms. *Asia Pacific Journal of Management*, *19*(2/3), 353–372. doi:10.1023/A:1016247920461

Hofstede, G. (1980). Motivation, leadership, and organization: Do American theories apply abroad? *Organizational Dynamics*, *9*(1), 42–63. doi:10.1016/0090-2616(80)90013-3

Hofstede, G. (1983). The cultural relativity of organizational practices and theories. *Journal of International Business Studies*, *14*(1), 75–89.

Holmes, H., Tangtongtavy, S., & Tomizawa, R. (1996). *Working with the Thais: A guide to managing in Thailand* (3rd ed.). Bangkok: White Lotus.

Hooi, L. W. (2008). The adoption of Japanese recruitment practices in Malaysia. *International Journal of Manpower*, *29*(4), 362–378. doi:10.1108/01437720810884764

Hui, M. K., Au, K., & Fock, H. (2004). Empowerment effects across cultures. *Journal of International Business Studies*, *35*(1), 41–60. doi:10.1057/palgrave.jibs.8400067

Inoguchi, T. (2000). Social capital in Japan. *Japanese Journal of Political Science*, *1*(1), 73–112. doi:10.1017/S1468109900000141

Jackson, P. A. (2003). *Buddhadasa: Theravada Buddhism and the modernist reform in Thailand*. Chiang Mai: Silkworm.

Johnsen, R. E. (2007). The role of focal suppliers in strategic networks for internationalization: Perspectives from small and medium-sized Italian and Thai silk suppliers. *Journal of Fashion Marketing and Management, 11*(1), 135–147. doi:10.1108/13612020710734454

Kainzbauer, A. (2009). *Buddhism, 'sanuk' and intuition – making sense of Thai realities.* Paper presented at 1st Bangkok International Forum on Indigenous Management Practices, Kasetsart University, Bangkok, February 2–6, 2009.

Kaweevisultrakul, T., & Chan, P. (2007). Impact of cultural barriers on knowledge management implementation: Evidence from Thailand. *Journal of American Academy of Business, Cambridge, 11*, 303–308.

Kim, H., Hoskisson, R. E., Tihanyi, L., & Hong, J. (2004). The evolution and restructuring of diversified business groups in emerging markets: The lessons from *chaebols* in Korea. *Asia Pacific Journal of Management, 21*(1/2), 25–48. doi:10.1023/B:APJM.0000024076.86696.d5

King, W. L. (1964). *In the Hope of Nibbana*. LaSalle, IL: Open Court.

Lamond, D., & Zheng, C. (2010). HRM research in China: Looking back and looking forward. *Journal of Chinese Human Resources Management, 1*(1), 6–16. doi:10.1108/20408001011051179

Laosirihongthong, T., The, P. L., & Adebanjo, D. (2013). Revisiting quality management and performance. *Industrial Management & Data Systems, 113*(7), 990–1006. doi:10.1108/IMDS-02-2013-0058

Lee, A. (2014). For king and country? Thailand's political conflicts as dynamics of social closure. In P. Liamputtong (Ed.), Contemporary Socio-Cultural and Political Perspectives in Thailand (pp. 169-184). Springer.

Li, J., & Wright, P. C. (2000). Guanxi and the realities of career development: A Chinese perspective. *Career Development International, 5*(7), 369–378. doi:10.1108/13620430010379920

Longenecker, C. O., Fink, L. S., & Caldwell, S. (2014a). Current U.S. trends in formal performance appraisal: Practices and opportunities – Part One. *Industrial and Commercial Training, 46*(6), 321–326. doi:10.1108/ICT-03-2014-0018

Longenecker, C. O., Fink, L. S., & Caldwell, S. (2014b). Current US trends in formal performance appraisal: Practices and opportunities – Part II. *Industrial and Commercial Training, 46*(7), 393–399. doi:10.1108/ICT-03-2014-0019

Naisbitt, J. (1997). *Megatrends Asia: Eight Asian megatrends that are reshaping our world*. New York: Touchstone.

Nasrolahi, L., Mohammad, V., & Jalilvand, R. (2014). Examining the influence of social capital on rural women entrepreneurship. *World Journal of Entrepreneurship. Management and Sustainable Development, 10*(3), 209–227.

Newburry, W., & Yakova, N. (2006). Standardized preferences: A function of national culture, work interdependence and local embeddedness. *Journal of International Business Studies, 37*(1), 44–60. doi:10.1057/palgrave.jibs.8400179

Nguyen, T. V., Weinstein, M., & Meyer, A. D. (2005). Development of trust of interfirm relationships in Vietnam. *Asia Pacific Journal of Management*, *22*(3), 211–231. doi:10.1007/s10490-005-3567-4

Okpara, J. O., & Wynn, P. (2008). Human resource management practices in a transition economy. *Management Research News*, *31*(1), 57–76. doi:10.1108/01409170810845958

Onishi, J., & Bliss, R. E. (2006). In search of Asian ways of managing conflict. *The International Journal of Conflict Management*, *17*(3), 203–225. doi:10.1108/10444060610742326

Peng, M. W., & Zhou, J. Q. (2005). How network strategies and institutional transitions evolve in Asia. *Asia Pacific Journal of Management*, *22*(4), 321–336. doi:10.1007/s10490-005-4113-0

Persons, L. S. (2008). *Face dynamics, social power and virtue among Thai leaders: A cultural analysis* (Doctoral dissertation). Fuller Graduate Schools, School of Intercultural Studies.

Petison, P., & Johri, L. M. (2008). Dynamics of the manufacturer-supplier relationships in emerging markets: A case of Thailand. *Asia Pacific Journal of Marketing and Logistics*, *20*(1), 76–96. doi:10.1108/13555850810844887

Porter, M. E. (1980). *Competitive strategy*. New York: Free Press.

Pounder, J. S. (2001). 'New leadership' and university organisational effectiveness: Exploring the relationship. *Leadership and Organization Development Journal*, *22*(5/6), 281–290. doi:10.1108/EUM0000000005827

Ralston, D. A. (2008). The crossvergence perspective: Reflections and projections. *Journal of International Business Studies*, *39*(1), 27–40. doi:10.1057/palgrave.jibs.8400333

Ralston, D. A., Holt, D. H., Terpstra, R. H., & Cheng, Y. K. (1997). The impact of national culture and economic ideology on managerial work values: A study of the United States, Russia, Japan, and China. *Journal of International Business Studies*, *28*(2), 177–207. doi:10.1057/palgrave.jibs.8490097

Rehbein, B. (2007). Configurations of globalization in Laos and Cambodia. *Internationales Asienforum*, *38*(1/2), 67–85.

Schmidt, S. W., & Akdere, M. (2007). Measuring the effects of employee orientation training on employee perceptions of vision and leadership: Implications for human resources. *The Business Review, Cambridge*, *7*(1), 322–327.

Shapiro, D. M., Gedaijlovis, E., & Erdener, C. (2003). The Chinese family firm as a multinational enterprise. *The International Journal of Organizational Analysis*, *11*(2), 105–122. doi:10.1108/eb028965

Sim, A. B., & Pandian, J. R. (2007). An exploratory study of internationalization strategies of Malaysian and Taiwanese firms. *International Journal of Emerging Markets*, *2*(3), 252–273. doi:10.1108/17468800710758396

Simola, S. K., Taggar, S., & Smith, G. W. (2007). The employment selection interview: Disparity among research-based recommendations, current practices and what matters to human rights tribunals. *Canadian Journal of Administrative Sciences*, *24*(1), 30–44. doi:10.1002/cjas.4

Smedlund, A. (2008). The knowledge system of a firm: Social capital for explicit, tacit and potential knowledge. *Journal of Knowledge Management*, *12*(1), 63–77. doi:10.1108/13673270810852395

Sriussadaporn, R. (2006). Managing international business communication problems at work: A pilot study in foreign companies in Thailand. *Cross Cultural Management: An International Journal*, *13*(4), 330–344. doi:10.1108/13527600610713422

Suehiro, A., & Wailerdsak, N. (2004). Family business in Thailand: Its management, governance, and future challenges. *ASEAN Economic Bulletin*, *21*(1), 81–93. doi:10.1355/AE21-1E

Swierczek, F. W., & Onishi, J. (2003). Culture and conflict: Japanese managers and Thai subordinates. *Personnel Review*, *32*(1/2), 187–210. doi:10.1108/00483480310460216

Szeto, R., Wright, P. C., & Cheng, E. (2006). Business networking in the Chinese context. *Management Research News*, *29*(7), 425–438. doi:10.1108/01409170610690880

Taylor, S. (2007). Creating social capital in MNCs: The international human resource management challenge. *Human Resource Management Journal*, *17*(4), 336–354. doi:10.1111/j.1748-8583.2007.00049.x

Thassanabanjong, K., Miller, P., & Marchant, T. (2009). Training in Thai SMEs. *Journal of Small Business and Enterprise Development*, *16*(4), 678–693. doi:10.1108/14626000911000992

Tsang, E. (2001). Internationalizing the family firm: A case study of a Chinese family business. *Journal of Small Business Management*, *39*(2), 88–94. doi:10.1111/0447-2778.00008

Van de Ven, A. H. (2004). The context-specific nature of competence and corporate development. *Asia Pacific Journal of Management*, *21*(1/2), 123–147. doi:10.1023/B:APJM.0000024080.78798.59

Wang, G. C., Zhang, Y., Lamond, D., & Ke, J. (2014). Moving forward. *Journal of Chinese Human Resource Management*, *5*(1), 2–13. doi:10.1108/JCHRM-02-2014-0011

Wolfe, S. E. (2010). A social capital assessment of Canadian community's water management strategy. *Environmental Practice*, *12*(3), 214–226. doi:10.1017/S1466046610000220

Wu, C., Lawler, J. J., & Yi, X. (2008). Overt employment discrimination in MNC affiliates: Home-country cultural and institutional effects. *Journal of International Business Studies*, *39*(5), 772–792. doi:10.1057/palgrave.jibs.8400376

Wu, W. P., & Choi, W. L. (2004). Transaction cost, social capital and firms' synergy creation in Chinese business networks. *Asia Pacific Journal of Management*, *21*(3), 325–344. doi:10.1023/B:APJM.0000036466.90433.92

Young, C. S. (2005). Top management teams' social capital in Taiwan: The impact on firm value in an emerging economy. *Journal of Intellectual Capital*, *6*(2), 177–190. doi:10.1108/14691930510592780

Young, E. (1900). *The Kingdom of the Yellow Robe* (2nd ed.). Westminster, UK: Archibald Constable & Co.

Zhang, Q., & Fung, H. G. (2006). China's social capital and financial performance of private enterprises. *Journal of Small Business and Enterprise Development*, *13*(2), 198–207. doi:10.1108/14626000610665908

Zheng, C. (2013). Theoretical contexts of managing people in emerging Chinese multinational enterprises. *Journal of Chinese Human Resources Management*, *4*(1), 58–76. doi:10.1108/JCHRM-10-2012-0023

KEY TERMS AND DEFINITIONS

Bonding Social Capital: Social capital which is used to increased cohesiveness within a work group.

Bridging Social Capital: Social capital which connects individuals from one organization to individuals outside the organization.

Human Resource Management: Management functions designed to deal with the personnel issues of recruiting, selection, training, developing, and retaining an organization's workforce.

Relationship Contracting: Conducting business through agreements founded on mutual trust and personal relationships as opposed to the use of formal legal contracts.

***Sanuk*:** A Thai word which is commonly translated to as fun.

Sino-Thai: Of Thai nationality or located within Thailand, but having ancestry or origins in China.

Theravada Buddhism: The type of Buddhism widely practiced in Mainland Southeast Asia and Sri Lanka; as opposed to Mahayana Buddhism.

Chapter 14
Managing National Competitive Disadvantages:
Thailand

Scott A. Hipsher
Naresuan University, Thailand

ABSTRACT

There are a number of national competitive disadvantages multinational firms in Thailand face, but these disadvantages do not create insurmountable barriers. The national competitive disadvantages found in Thailand include a national brand which is not associated with advanced technology and a lack of an innovative national environment. At the strategic level, foreign multinationals can often overcome these disadvantages by using competitive advantages coming from their country of origin while local multinationals can select to operate in more mature industries or through positioning into segments where the national competitive disadvantages do not create significant barriers to success.

INTRODUCTION

Multinational Enterprises (MNEs) operating in developing economies, such as Thailand, operate in environments which are associated with having some national competitive disadvantages, yet we see many MNEs, some foreign and some local, which are able to work around these national competitive disadvantages while also taking advantage of some often overlooked national competitive advantages to achieve success.

This chapter will primarily focus on the strategic dimensions of selecting which industries and overall strategies to engage in and competitive positioning strategies within the environment found within Thailand.

DOI: 10.4018/978-1-5225-0276-0.ch014

NATIONAL COMPETITIVENESS

While it is companies, and not countries, which compete in the global marketplace, the connection between country of origin and the competitiveness of individual firms in specific industries has received a lot of attention. Torrisi and Uslu (2010) found firms within a specific industry could draw upon three different sources of national competitive advantage; basic requirements, efficiency enhancers, and innovation and sophistication factors. Basic requirements drive factor-driven economies, efficiency enhancers are important for cost advantages, and innovation and sophistication factors are used to create competitive advantage through differentiation. It would appear that in general, firms in developing economies have varying types and amounts of basic requirements and efficiency enhancers, but mostly lack the innovation and sophistication factors needed to gain an advantage in using differentiation strategies based on technology or national brand images of quality. The lack of innovation and sophistication factors will most likely limit the strategic options for firms originating from developing economies, but the availability of access to these factors can be used to advantage by foreign firms when operating in Thailand or other developing economies.

In 1990, Michael Porter introduced a framework which can be used to analysis the competitiveness of an industry within specific nations. This framework is often referred to as Porter's diamond and is made up of four categories The four categories are: (a) factor conditions, such as availability of raw materials and natural resources, skilled work force, etc…; (b) demand conditions, the higher and more sophisticated the demand the more likely an industry within a specific country is to develop world class producers; (c) related and supporting industries, the availability of suppliers and other supporting industries will increase the competitiveness of an industry; and (d) the strategies, structures, rivalries and management decisions of individual firms within the industry.

Using this framework, it would appear the more economically developed nations have advantages in many industries, especially those using high-end differentiation strategies and in the higher value-added segments of a supply chain. Industries and individual firms in developing economies face a number of obstacles in developing international competitiveness. These obstacles include controlled markets, lower levels of demand, less sophisticated local customers, lack of access to skilled workers and the lack of ability to effectively use existing knowledge which is available (Shenkar, 2009). As these obstacles can cross industries, the environmental limitations found in developing markets can have a knock-on effect as supporting industries are likely to be restrained by the same types of environmental conditions.

In existing measurements of national competitiveness, developed nations are almost always ranked above developing nations (Ju & Sohn, 2014). However, firms originating from developing economies often have some advantages over large multinationals originating from wealthy nations. These include the advantages of lower-priced labor costs, flexible ownership structures, and experience operating in unstable and informal environments. These factors often encourage the ability to be flexible and effectively react to environmental changes in a variety of developing market settings (Cuervo-Cazurra & Genc, 2008; Seshanna, 2009; Shenkar, 2009).

Additionally, companies from developing economies can often take advantage of some cost savings when compared to international MNEs, even when operating within the same country with access to the same labor market. One factor leading to cost advantages comes from companies originating from developed economies, even while operating in emerging markets, having tighter regulatory requirements as they are required to meet home country standards and are expected to respond to pressures from NGOs and the international media; while local firms normally operate in less stringent regulatory environments and are usually not targeted by NGOs and the international media for scrutiny over wages and working conditions (Globerman, 2014; Shenkar, 2009).

These additional costs might help explain the tendency of international MNEs to focus on the "top of the pyramid" of the markets in emerging and developing markets, which leaves most of the bottom and middle parts of the markets open to local firms, which may have cost advantages, to operate without significant direct international competition (London & Hart, 2004).

STRATEGIC APPROACHES

To overcome many of the identified national competitive disadvantages found in developing economies requires taking a strategic approach.

The term strategy as used in business refers to making long-term plans and the overall approach to gaining competitive advantages. There is no business strategy that can be universally applied in every situation which will lead to success. Business strategies require choices and tradeoffs; business strategy is not solely concerned with what a firm chooses to do, but also what a firm chooses not to do (Peng, 2002; Porter, 1996). Using Porter's (1980) framework of generic strategies, countless examples can be found of firms succeeding using low cost leadership, focused or many variations of differentiation strategies. While there are some universal best operational business practices that can be used across industrial and national borders, there are no best strategic practices that can be used successfully by all firms and strategies are often influenced by the level of economic development found in the specific environment (Hipsher, 2007, 2010a). The higher levels of wealth and income found in developed economies provide consumers and businesses more flexibility in purchasing decisions, which therefore allows companies to pursue a wider range of strategic options while attempting to capture the purchases of customers. As a result, more and more varied uses of differentiation strategies are found in more developed economies, while options for use of differentiation strategies in less developed economies appear to be relatively limited (Shah, 2012; Shenkar, 2009).

The external environment substantially influences the choice of strategies made by firms (e.g., Bach & Allen, 2010; Hagan & Amin, 1995; Kim, 2008). Furthermore, components of a firm's internal environmental, such as corporate culture, leadership and organizational structure also appear to have an impact on strategic choices (e.g. Epstein, Buhovac, & Yuthas, 2010; Franke, Mento, Prumo, & Edlund, 2007; Kipping & Cailluet, 2010).

Yet, the internal and external environments cannot be considered as being totally separate. Organizations are open, no closed, systems and the internal environmental is heavily influenced by the external environment. It appears organizational culture of an MNE is shaped to some extent by both the national culture of country of origin and national culture of the country of operation (Jung, Su, Baeza, & Hong 2008; Klein, Waxin, & Radnell, 2009; Prasnikar, Pahor, & Svetlik, 2008). National culture also has been shown to have an influence on choices of organizational structure (e.g. Li & Harrison, 2008; Walsh, 2004) and leadership styles (e.g. Chong & Thomas, 1997; Kanungo & Wright, 1983; Neelankavil, Mathur, & Zhang, 2000; Suutari, Raharjo, & Riikkila, 2002).

If we accept strategy is the linkage between a firm's internal and external environments as proposed by Ensign (2008); and accept that the internal and external environments of firms in emerging economies are generally different from the environments found in more developed economies (Shenkar, 2009); than it would be natural the strategies selected for use in firms in emerging economies will often be significantly different from those found in firms operating in the environments found in developed economies.

Strategies in Developing Economies

Academic theories about business strategy have mostly been developed by scholars examining business practices in the most developed economies around the world (Lau, 2006; Mathews, 2000). But, both the internal and external environments influencing the strategies of firms from developing economies can be often quite different from the environments influencing the firms that were explored when developing most strategic theories.

Strategic management theories generally make an assumption increasing competitiveness within a market and beating the competition are the primary purposes of strategic decision making. Much of the vocabulary and underlying assumptions found in the study of strategic management are competitive in nature and originate from studies of military strategy (e.g. Cummings, 2007; Grattan, 2005; Grattan, 2006; Tang, 2002). This focus on competition may work well as a foundation for formulating strategy in environments with relatively free markets and where the government's primary role in business is regulation. But in the environments found in many developing economies, where governments play a more direct role in business and often enforce regulations in a less consistent manner, it has been found building relationships and cooperation are often the primary strategic focuses of firms (e.g. Chattananon & Trimetsoontorn, 2009; Kim, 2008; Luk, et al., 2008). Instead of focusing solely on competition, often in emerging markets and developing economies the focus of strategy shifts away from competition and towards cooperation and the joining into existing business networks (e.g. Aribarg, 2005; Bjerke, 2000; Suehiro & Wailerdsak, 2004; Tsang, 2001).

Creating strategy involves long-term planning, and long term planning is more feasible in fairly stable environments. Developing countries are often associated with political and economic uncertainty, making strategic planning less effective; therefore firms in emerging markets and developing economies often take a more reactive, as opposed to proactive, approach to selecting strategic business practices (e.g. Bjerke, 2000; Ng & Dastmalchian, 2001; Shrestha & Gnyawali, 2013; Yu, 2001). It could be considered taking a flexible and reactive approach is as much of a strategic choice as is making specific large term plans. And the current political environment in Thailand creates a very unstable environment in which to plan and operate.

The primary factor separating a developing from a developed economy is the level of economic development. Firms originating from developed economies operate in environments where financial support, technology, and skilled labor are more abundant than what is normally found in developing countries (Zhang, Knight, & Tansuhaj, 2014). Strategic management theory often begins with the assumption firms have access to the resources necessary to engage in a variety of different strategies; however firms from developing countries usually have limited access to some vital resources such as technological innovation, financing, and skilled labor. Also, as there are fewer very large firms originating from developing countries, most firms coming from these markets lack the internal resources, traditions, and cultures which support formal strategic planning processes (Shrestha & Gnyawali, 2013; Singal & Jain, 2014). Therefore the strategic approaches used by MNEs originating from developing economies will often differ considerable from the approaches used by MNEs coming from more developed economies. These differences include use of less formal long-term planning processes, instead relying more on flexibility and being reactive to changes and opportunities as well as focusing on the middle and lower end of the markets, therefore not directly competing in the top of the pyramid markets with international MNEs.

Nation as a Brand

Despite the rhetoric about globalization of companies and products, brand names are usually associated in the minds of consumers with the country of origin of the MNE. Mercedes-Benz is thought of as a German company, Toyota as Japanese, Google as American, and Samsung as Korean. And the perceived country of origin has an influence on the preferences and buying patterns of products by retail consumers (Kan, Cliquet, & Gallo, 2014), as well as on financial investment decisions (Grimes, 2005; Kalamova & Konrad, 2010). Consumers often show preference for products associated with developed economies as these products usually have a better reputation for innovation and quality (Contractor, 2013; Herstein, Berger, & Jaffe, 2014). Also the county of origin of a firm will influence the external support it can expect. For example, Subrahmanya (2009) found despite similar internal environments, investors and other stakeholders generally were more likely to support the creating of technical innovation in firms from a developed country (Japan) than a developing country (India).

A nation's brand is shaped by a variety of factors, such as the economy, geography, culture, heritage, government, as well as perceived level of development in the fields of science and technology (Rojas-Méndez, 2013). Using Hofstede's (1980, 1983) dimensions of cultural, Overbaugh (2013) found relatively high scores in power distance and uncertainty avoidance, which are common in developing countries, have a negative impact on brand image in the minds of customers while there was not a significant correlation between brand image with the other dimensions. Ar and Kara (2014) discovered being from a developing economy (China) had a significant negative impact on a product's brand image and the consumer's trust and the perceived quality of a brand. Li, Wang, Jiang, Barnes, and Zhang (2014) found while there were some differences in preference for brands in different product categories, Chinese consumers consistently had more positive opinions of brands from developed economies than they had for local brands or products coming from other developing economies. Coming to a similar conclusion, Murtiasih, Sucherly, and Siringoringo (2014) reported Indonesian consumers had more favorable opinions of automobiles with European or American brand names, as these were associated with more advanced technology and higher quality, than with brand names associated with non-Western countries.

Both internationally and locally, products perceived as coming from developing economies appear to be at a disadvantage when competing using a differentiation strategy focusing on perceived quality, luxury, or advanced technology. National brand image, as well as other factors, will make it difficult for the foreseeable future for companies from developing markets to compete with companies from more developed economies in the luxury, top end, or high tech segments of the market.

Innovation

Innovation is often considered a necessary component in strategic competitiveness. However innovation might take on different characteristics in developing as opposed to developed economies. While, Pellicer, Yepes, and Rojas (2010) proclaimed every organization needs to invest in research and development (R & D) to remain competitive, it is questioned whether companies coming from developing or less developed economies such as Thailand can compete in markets relying on competitive advantages coming from developing new technology. Traditional R &D is often used to provide a company a first mover advantage (Poletti, Engelland, & Ling, 2011; Rahman & Bhattacharyya, 2003; Shao, 2011). But it has been suggested the majority of firms in developing economies do not have financial or human resources to effectively engage in R & D in order to create first mover advantages (De Valk, 2003; Hipsher, 2010a; Zhang, 2010). This does not imply that innovation in developing economies is not important, but the innovation needed is often in finding ways to adapt existing technology or ideas for use in a new environment.

Other barriers to creating technical or breakthrough innovation for firms in developing economies include the lack of spillover effects due to the limited number of interactions with other innovative organizations within the supply chain or as direct competitors (Lederman, 2010). Also, national cultures in most developing economies are collectivist in nature and have relatively higher power distance and uncertainty avoidance ranking, according to Hofstede's (1980, 1983) framework, and these cultural characteristics are seen to be barriers to creating some types of innovation (Ty, Walsh, & Anurit, 2010).

Li, Zhou, and Si (2010) broke down innovation into the categories of exploratory and exploitative. Exploratory innovation involves radical changes and is intended when pursuing entirely new opportunities. Exploitative innovation involves incremental changes intended to improve upon existing products or processes. The authors found the external environment had some impact on a firm's innovation strategy. In highly competitive environments, which are more likely found in developed economies, exploratory innovation has a higher payoff than exploitative innovation. The reverse is true in less competitive environment, such as found in many less developed and emerging economies, including Thailand, where exploitative innovation provides more competitive advantages.

Vernon (1966) proposed production of a particular product will move from developed to developing markets as the production of a product becomes more standardized, and competitive advantage moves from exploratory innovation to more incremental and exploitative innovation. While research on the product life cycle theory indicates that these days the factors driving the selection of location to manufacture any specific item is more nuanced than found in Vernon's research in the 1960s, many of the key principles of the framework appear to still be relevant. For example, the choice of suppliers for North American manufacturers becomes more motivated by price and less by innovation as a product category matures, resulting in shifting some production from developed to developing economies (Doha, Ajay, & Pagell, 2013). The creation of new product categories which require innovative and expensive research, such as often found in the technology or medical sectors, continues to be dominated by firms originating from developed economies, while firms from developing economies mostly compete in more mature industries or in using more focused strategies using advantages which are unique to the culture and require lower expenditures in research and development.

THAILAND

At the time of writing, Thailand us been experiencing very low economic growth in comparison to the rest of Asia, which has been mostly attributed to the continuation of political instability caused by the military's current political control over the country (Sangwongwanich, 2015). The nature, causes, and future of the political situation in Thailand are widely debated and appear to be quite complex, not easily understood and fairly unpredictable (e.g. Chen, 2014, Lee, 2014, Sinpeng, 2014). The GDP per capita of Thailand is roughly comparable to the GDP per capita of China, although if current economic growth forecasts are correct, China would be expected to surge ahead in the coming years. In Thailand, there is considerable disparity in income, both inter and intra-regionally with manufacturing, agriculture, and tourism being major drivers of the economy (Asian Development Bank, 2014). Increasing the competitive disadvantages faced by local firms comes from the fact the expenditures on research and development as measured as percentage of GDP in Thailand are far lower than the averages found in more developed economies (Post Reporters, 2015).

While economically Thailand is considered a developing or newly developed economy, depending on who is doing the categorization, culturally, along with Cambodia, Laos PDR, and Myanmar/Burma, it is part of the Theravada Buddhist region of Southeast Asia. Hipsher (2010b) found cultural factors associated with the country's religious heritage have influenced business practices in the country to some extent, for example a hierarchical/parental style of leader is often preferred, while an openness to change and a having a flexible approach are commonly seen management practices.

Thailand's National Competitive Advantages and Disadvantages

MNE's originating from developed economies operating in Thailand will approach using the country's national competitive advantages and disadvantages differently from how a local MNE will approach using Thailand's national competitive advantages and disadvantages. It is expected MNEs from developed economies will primarily use their national and company brand images to advantage in attracting customers to an international image of quality (e.g. McDonalds, Mercedes Benz, Heineken, Starbucks), and/or use their technological advantages to compete (e.g. Apple, Honda, Samsung).

While it is expected local MNEs would more likely focus on low-cost strategies (e.g. Chang Beer, MaMa (instant noodles), Ruang Khao (white spirits)), primarily aimed at local markets or other markets in developing economies. Another strategy seen is using unique aspects of the local culture and national image to create competitive advantages in specific niche markets (e.g. Thai boxing training centers, Amari Hotels and Spas, Puenthai (Jasmine Rice)).

Another option available is for MNEs from developed economies and MNEs from Thailand to work together within a value chain, where many of the global and higher value added activities, using global branding or technological advantages, are carried out by the MNEs from developed economies. While many of the lower value added activities are carried out by the MNEs from Thailand. We see examples of this strategy in Thailand in the retail, tourism and manufacturing industries.

EXAMPLES: TOYOTA

Toyota is a global company which has used its position as the world's largest automaker to gain economies of scale as a competitive advantage. Toyota was founded in 1933 in Japan and while its operations are global in nature, the company's headquarters are in Japan and its top leadership positions continue to be dominated by Japanese executives (Toyota, 2014)

Toyota Motors Thailand began in 1956 and one of its first major challenges was to convince Thai customers to buy a Japanese product (Petison & Johri, 2006), since at that time Japan was thought of as a developing economy producing low quality products as opposed to being a center of technological leadership. But the company was able to overcome the challenges and Toyota developed into the leading producer and seller of cars in Thailand, although sales have slumped in recent years due to increased competition and a poor performing local economy (Toyota, 2014).

Automobile manufacturing could be classified as in the mature stage of the product life cycle with relatively slow global sales growth and most innovations being of the incremental nature, although attempts to create radical innovation through alternative fuel sources or other breakthrough technology continues. The need for economies of scale and capital intensive investment would seem to be two factors contributing to the domination of the industry by companies originating from wealthier countries and having access to global markets. While automotive manufacturing plays a big part in the Thai economy, there are no indigenous automotive manufacturers selling cars using a Thai brand name operating in Thailand, although there are many local companies acting as suppliers to the foreign MNEs.

Toyota competes in Thailand mostly in the middle of the market with a focus on selling mid-priced cars in the urban areas and pick-up trucks in the rural regions. Over time, Toyota has increased the percentage of locally sourced components and valued-added activities in its Thai assembly plants and has worked to link the Toyota global brand name to the local environment (Nemoto, Hayashi, & Hashimoto, 2010; Petison & Johri, 2006).

Also, over the years, there has been slow process of delegating more responsibility to Thai managers (Petison & Johri, 2007) but the top level of management at Toyota in Thailand remains primarily Japanese.

Cost reduction and the use of lean manufacturing techniques have been found a central and critical component of strategies of companies in the automotive industry in Thailand, as well as globally (Hsu, Tan, & Laosirihongthong, 2014; Phongpetra & Johri, 2011; Rahman, Laosirihongthong, & Sohal, 2010). Therefore, aligned with Vernon's (1966) proposition, we are seeing, as the industry has matured, an increase in the amount of value added activities moving to developing countries including Thailand.

It was found consumer preferences as measured by willingness to pay for automobile brands in Thailand were closely tied to the country of origin. Thai consumers placed the highest value on German brands (Mercedes, BMW, Audi), next was American and Japanese brands while cars seen as coming from slightly lower-income countries (Korean and Malaysia) being the least preferred. Somewhat surprisingly, there was not much differentiation of perception of the quality of the different major Japanese auto manufacturers by Thai consumers (Thanasuta, Patoomsuwan, Chaimahawong, & Chiaravutthi, 2009). These results suggest the image coming from the country of origin can be even more important than the image of a particular brand in this industry in Thailand.

The automotive industry, and other industries which require large capital investment and the application of complex technologies, continue to be dominated by large MNEs which originated in more economically advanced economies. However, as the industry moves through the product life cycle, there are an increasing number of local firms using rather mature technology to supply many of the lower value-added components needed.

Within the automotive industry, transportation costs are significant and firms competing in the low to mid-price categories have found it more cost effective to assemble and source low value-added supplies closer to the point of sales than it is to globalize these processes and export from a single location. Therefore, while large MNEs in the automobile industries like Toyota can take advantage of global economies of scale in the higher value-added activities such as design, engine development, and branding, the company also is increasingly moving the assembly and lower value-added activities closer to the point of sale to further cost savings. This change has provided opportunities for local Thai companies to enter into global value channels, in much the same way as Japanese, Korean, and Taiwanese firms, which cooperated with MNEs from the US and other developed countries, had previously. However whether Thai firms will be able to use this opportunity to develop the skills needed to move up the value chain, as were firms in other Asian locations, is not yet clear.

EXAMPLE: CP GROUP

The CP Group, called Charoen Pokhpand in Thailand, is a large conglomerate involved in a series of unrelated diversification business activities which includes operating in agriculture, retail, real estate, phone service, manufacturing and many other sectors of the economy, although its primarily focus is on its vertically integrated (farm to fork) agricultural activities. Currently the company's agro-business and food business sector operates subsidiaries in China, Vietnam, Turkey, India, Malaysia, The United Kingdom, Laos, Russia, the Philippines, and Taiwan as well as being connected with an associated company in Cambodia (Charoen Pokhpand, 2014).

Unlike the automobile industry, agriculture is mostly associated with using multi-domestic rather than global strategies due to unique eating habits, climates, and cultural factors in different countries. The localized nature of the agricultural business prevents foreign MNEs from leveraging their technological advantages as the technology used in the home country often cannot be used in developing economies without significant adaptation to local conditions.

Therefore while we do not see any local Thai companies competing in the automobile sector, we do see indigenous Thai companies competing and even dominating locally in the agriculture sector of the economy.

The CP group can trace its origins to the founding of the Chia Tai Chung seed shop in Bangkok's Chinatown in 1921 by two brothers who were immigrants from China, Chia Ek Chor and Chia Seow Hui. Despite the years of political tensions between the family's country of origin, China, and their new home, Thailand, and being forced to take Thai names, the family has retained an interest in and attachment to its ancestral homeland. The company began expanding and internationalizing at a very early stage, due to connections with overseas Chinese business networks and later with support from the Thai government (Biers, Vatikiotis, Tasker, & Dairueng, 1999; Einhorn & Prasso, 1997; Pananond & Zeithaml, 1998). The firm remains primary an ethnic-Chinese family-owned operation with Chia Ek Chor's youngest son, Dhanin Chearavanont remaining as the head of the company even today, although Suphachai Chearavanon is expected to take over as head of the conglomerate when his father retires in 2015 (Fernquest, 2015).

The CP group has invested heavily in China ever since the Chinese communist government first cracked the door open to foreign investment; and CP was issued the Foreign Investor Certificate No. 001 for Shenzhen province (Vatikiotis, 2004).

Because of the breath of operations of the CP groups, attempts to generalize will naturally be imprecise. But we mostly see CP operating in more mature industries, such as one of the world's most mature industries, agriculture, which require less reliance on developing cutting edge new technologies and instead focuses more on incremental and adaptive innovation to create sustainable competitive advantages.

Throughout much of developing Asia, where the legal systems do not guarantee government or outside sources will enforce contracts, ethic Chinese firms have used various forms of relationship contracting as a competitive advantage (Carney & Gedailovic, 2003; Keller & Kronstedt, 2005; Shapiro, Gedaijlovis, & Erdener. 2003; Suehiro & Wailerdsak 2004; Yan & Sorenson 2004). The family-ownership structure can provide a competitive advantage as business owners negotiating with each other can develop trust and confidence in a manner that a CEO or other employee cannot, as decisions by employees of a corporation can be overturned by a board of directors or other higher authority. The leadership of CP has worked hard to develop personal relationships throughout the region with other ethnic Chinese business owners as well as with government leaders in the countries it operates in.

ANALYSIS AND RECOMMENDATIONS

Strategies for managing national competitiveness disadvantages in Thailand or other developing economies would appear to be shaped by the home of origin of the MNE. MNEs from more developed economies, such as Toyota, can often take advantage of their brand image, technology, and home country human capital to overcome many of the disadvantages of operating in a developing economy. However these advantages would appear to bring more benefits in industries where global economies of scale and/or high end differentiation strategies bring competitive advantage.

MNEs from developed economies can use their national brand image from the home country to create an image of high quality even if the product or service is mostly produced in a developing country which has a weaker national brand image in regards to quality or technology. For example, even if most of the production and value added activities done in producing a Toyota sold in Thailand are completed in Thailand, a Toyota is still thought of as a Japanese car by consumers and is considered of higher quality than would an automobile that is assumed to come from a developing economy, even within the country where it is manufactured. Much as Toyota has done, an international MNE operating in Thailand should try to balance its image as being somewhere between that of a locally responsive company and of a company using the technology from a more economically advanced nation.

On the other hand, we see many successful MNEs coming from Thailand, like the CP Group, and other developing economies, but competing in industries, or parts of a global value chain, where the national competitive disadvantages of being from a developing economy are of less importance.

As seen by the huge increase in manufacturing in China, companies from countries with lower incomes can use cost of labor and other cost advantages to compete in manufacturing in mature industries and in the lower value-added activities in global value chains. For example, many Thai companies have partnered with Toyota and other automakers to take over many of the lower-value added activities in the production of automobiles. Furthermore, as seen by the example of CP's success, low cost manufacturing is not the only strategy available to MNEs from developing economies. Firms from developing economies may not have the research or innovation capabilities to compete in industries where global economies of scale and technological innovation are highly rewarded, but can overcome these disadvantages by selecting strategies where they compete in developing economies in industries, or parts of a global value chain, where flexibility, local adaptation, or low costs provide competitive advantages.

Herstein, Berger, and Jaffe (2014) use Thailand, alongside a few other developing economies, as an example of a country with few national advantages to leverage as far as branding goes and recommended creating a regional brand or focus on the exotic image coming from the location of origin. While CP has followed this strategy at times, the CP name is used in some of the products from the group internationally; the company seems to use a variety of branding strategies to cope with the perceived disadvantages of coming from a developing economy. In China, the company mostly uses the Chia Tai corporate name which gives the impression of being a local Chinese company, as opposed to being of Thai origin. Other strategies the company uses is to gain the rights to use the brand names of successful international companies, such as it does with the thousands of 7-11 convenience stores it operates in Thailand, or within a partnership as it did previously with the retailer, Tesco-Lotus. Another strategy the company has used was to select the brand name "True," using an English term as opposed to a word or phrase in the Thai language, for its telecommunications operations. The selection of an English language brand name might help to create some ambiguity about the company's home of origin, which might be helpful in an industry associated with technology such as telecommunications.

CONCLUSION

There are a number of competitive disadvantages which come from operating a business in a developing economy such as Thailand. But there are also some advantages. To overcome the disadvantages and leverage advantages requires a strategic approach and it can be expected foreign firms will often take use a different strategy than will local firms.

Many MNEs, both foreign and domestic, have shown it is possible to operate successfully in Thailand, although each firm will often have to select industries, positioning strategies and choice of international business partnerships to compete in and develop strategies to overcome the national competitive disadvantages while leveraging each company's unique strengths and advantages.

REFERENCES

Ar, A. A., & Kara, A. (2014). Emerging market consumers' country of production image, trust and quality perceptions of global brands made-in China. *Journal of Product and Brand Management*, *23*(7), 491–503. doi:10.1108/JPBM-12-2013-0472

Aribarg, R. (2005). *Thai border town businessmen and the state: An examination of their influence on Thai foreign policy toward Burma*. (Doctoral Dissertation). Boston University, UMI No. 3157351.

Asian Development Bank. (2014). *Asian Development Outlook 2014: Fiscal policy for inclusive growth*. Mandaluyong City, Philippines: Asian Development Bank.

Bach, D., & Allen, D. B. (2010). What every CEO needs to know about nonmarket strategy. *MIT Sloan Management Review*, *51*(3), 41–48.

Biers, D., Vatikiotis, M., Tasker, R., & Dairueng, P. (1999). Back to school. *Far Eastern Economic Review*, *162*(14), 10–14.

Bjerke, B. V. (2000). A typified, culture-based, interpretation of management of SMEs in Southeast Asia. *Asia Pacific Journal of Management*, *17*(1), 103–132. doi:10.1023/A:1015441021413

Carney, M., & Gedailovic, E. (2003). Strategic innovation and the administrative heritage of East Asian family business groups. *Asia Pacific Journal of Management*, *20*(1), 5–26. doi:10.1023/A:1022062428231

Charoen Pokhpand. (2014). *2013 annual report for Charoen Pokhpand Foods Public Company Limited*. Retrieved from www.cpfworldwide.com/en/investor/financial-information/annual-report/

Chattananon, A., & Trimetsoontorn, J. (2009). Relationship marketing: A Thai case. *International Journal of Emerging Markets*, *4*(3), 252–274. doi:10.1108/17468800910968418

Chen, P. H. (2014). The vulnerability of Thai democracy: Coups d'etat and political changes in modern Thailand. In P. Liamputtong (Ed.), *Contemporary Socio-Cultural and Political Perspectives in Thailand* (pp. 185–207). Dordrecht, NL: Springer. doi:10.1007/978-94-007-7244-1_12

Chong, L. M., & Thomas, D. C. (1997). Leadership perceptions in cross-cultural context: Pakeha and Pacific Islanders in New Zealand. *The Leadership Quarterly*, *8*(3), 275–293. doi:10.1016/S1048-9843(97)90004-7

Contractor, F. J. (2013). Punching above their weight: The sources of competitive advantage for emerging market multinationals. *International Journal of Emerging Markets*, *8*(4), 304–328. doi:10.1108/IJoEM-06-2013-0102

Cuervo-Cazurra, A., & Genc, M. (2008). Transforming disadvantages into advantages: Developing-country MNEs in the least developed countries. *Journal of International Business Studies*, *30*(6), 957–979. doi:10.1057/palgrave.jibs.8400390

Cummings, S. (2007). Shifting foundations: Redrawing strategic management's military heritage. *Critical Perspectives on International Business*, *3*(1), 41–62. doi:10.1108/17422040710722551

De Valk, P. (2003). *How do firms learn? With case studies from Lao PDR.* Working Paper Series: Institute of Social Studies, The Hague, 385.

Doha, A., Ajay, D., & Pagell, M. (2013). The influence of product life cycle on the efficacy of purchasing practices. *International Journal of Operations & Production Management*, *33*(4), 470–498. doi:10.1108/01443571311307352

Einhorn, B., & Prasso, S. (1997, October 6). Anxious giant. *Business Week (Asian ed.)*.

Ensign, P. C. (2008). Small business strategy as a dynamic process: Concepts, controversies and implications. *Journal of Business and Entrepreneurship*, *20*(2), 25–43.

Epstein, M. J., Buhovac, A. R., & Yuthas, K. (2010). Implementing sustainability: The role of leadership and organizational culture. *Strategic Finance*, *91*(10), 41–48.

Fernquest, J. (2015, January 2). Thailand's biggest companies: Leadership change. *Bangkok Post*, p. B1.

Franke, R. H., Mento, A. J., Prumo, S. M., & Edlund, T. W. (2007). General Electric performance over a half century: Evaluation of effects of leadership and other strategic factors by quantitative case analysis. *International Journal of Business*, *12*(1), 137–151.

Globerman, S. (2014). Regulation and the international competitiveness of US-based companies. *Competitiveness Review*, *24*(5), 378–392. doi:10.1108/CR-11-2012-0026

Grattan, R. (2005). Strategy in the Battle of Britain and strategic management theory. *Management Decision*, *43*(10), 1432–1441. doi:10.1108/00251740510634967

Grattan, R. (2006). Robert McNamara's "11 lessons" in the context of theories of strategic management. *Journal of Management History*, *12*(4), 425–438. doi:10.1108/17511340610692770

Grimes, W. W. (2005). Japan as the "indispensible nation" in Asia: A financial brand for the 21st century. *Asia-Pacific Review*, *12*(1), 40–54. doi:10.1080/13439000500107937

Hagan, A. F., & Amin, S. G. (1995). Corporate executives and environmental scanning activities: An empirical investigation. *S.A.M. Advanced Management Journal*, *60*(2), 41–48.

Herstein, R., Berger, R., & Jaffe, E. D. (2014). How companies from developing and emerging countries can leverage their brand equity in terms of place branding. *Competitiveness Review*, *24*(4), 293–305. doi:10.1108/CR-04-2013-0046

Hipsher, S. (2007). Creating market size: Regional strategies for the world's least developed areas. In J. Stoner & C. Wankel (Eds.), Innovative Approaches to Reducing Global Poverty (pp. 153-174). Charlotte, NC: Information Age Publishing.

Hipsher, S. (2010a). Transfer or adapt: Evidence from the Theravada Buddhist countries of Southeast Asia. *Global Business and Organizational Excellence*, *39*(3), 35–43. doi:10.1002/joe.20317

Hipsher, S. (2010b). *Business practices in Southeast Asia: An interdisciplinary analysis of Theravada Buddhist countries*. London: Routledge Publishing.

Hofstede, G. (1980). Motivation, leadership, and organization: Do American theories apply abroad? *Organizational Dynamics*, *9*(1), 42–63. doi:10.1016/0090-2616(80)90013-3

Hofstede, G. (1983). The cultural relativity of organizational practices and theories. *Journal of International Business Studies*, *14*(1), 75–89.

Hsu, C. C., Tan, K. C., & Laosirihongthong, T. (2014). Antecedents of SCM practices in ASEAN automotive industry. *The International Journal of Logistics Management*, *25*(2), 334–357. doi:10.1108/IJLM-06-2012-0050

Ju, Y., & Sohn, S. Y. (2014). Development of a national competitiveness index based on a structural equation model. *Technology Analysis and Strategic Management*, *26*(5), 565–579. doi:10.1080/09537325.2014.896891

Jung, J., Su, X., Baeza, M., & Hong, S. (2008). The effect of organizational culture stemming from national culture towards quality management deployment. *TQM Journal*, *20*(6), 622–627. doi:10.1108/17542730810909374

Kalamova, M. M., & Konrad, K. A. (2010). Nation brands and foreign direct investment. *Kyklos*, *63*(3), 400–431. doi:10.1111/j.1467-6435.2010.00480.x

Kan, G., Cliquet, G., & Gallo, M. P. (2014). The effect of country image on hypermarket patronage intention. *International Journal of Retail & Distribution Management*, *42*(2), 106–130. doi:10.1108/IJRDM-09-2012-0080

Kanungo, R. N., & Wright, R. W. (1983). A cross-cultural comparative study of managerial job attitudes. *Journal of International Business Studies*, *14*(2), 115–129. doi:10.1057/palgrave.jibs.8490521

Keller, G. F., & Kronstedt, C. R. (2005). Connecting Confucianism, communism, and the Chinese culture of commerce. *The Journal of Language for International Business*, *16*(1), 60–75.

Kim, A. M. (2008). *Learning to be capitalists: Entrepreneurs in Vietnam's transition economy*. Oxford University Press. doi:10.1093/acprof:oso/9780195369397.001.0001

Kipping, M., & Cailluet, L. (2010). Mintzberg's emergent and deliberate strategies: Tracking Alcan's activities in Europe, 1928-2007. *Business History Review*, *84*(1), 79–95. doi:10.1017/S0007680500001252

Klein, A., Waxin, M. F., & Radnell, E. (2009). The impact of the Arab national culture on the perception of ideal organizational culture in the United Arab Emirates; An empirical study of 17 firms. *Education. Business and Society: Contemporary Middle Eastern Issues*, *2*(1), 44–56. doi:10.1108/17537980910938479

Lau, C. M. (2006). Achievements, challenges and research agendas for Asian management research studies. *Asian Business & Management*, *5*(1), 53–66. doi:10.1057/palgrave.abm.9200145

Lederman, D. (2010). An international multilevel analysis of product innovation. *Journal of International Business Studies*, *41*(4), 606–619. doi:10.1057/jibs.2009.30

Lee, A. (2014). "For king and country"? Thailand's political conflicts as dynamics of social closure. In P. Liamputtong (Ed.), *Contemporary Socio-Cultural and Political Perspectives in Thailand* (pp. 169–184). Dordrecht, NL: Springer. doi:10.1007/978-94-007-7244-1_11

Li, D., Wang, L. W., Jiang, Y., Barnes, B. R., & Zhang, H. (2014). The asymmetric influence of cognitive and affective country image on rational and experiential purchases. *European Journal of Marketing*, *48*(11/12), 2153–2175. doi:10.1108/EJM-09-2012-0505

Li, J., & Harrison, R. (2008). Corporate governance and national culture: A multi-country study. *Corporate Governance*, *8*(5), 607–621. doi:10.1108/14720700810913278

Li, Y., Zhou, N., & Si, Y. (2010). Exploratory innovation and exploitative innovation, and performance. *Nankai Business Review International*, *1*(3), 297–316. doi:10.1108/20408741011069223

London, T., & Hart, S. T. (2004). Perspective: Reinventing strategies for emerging markets: beyond the transnational model. *Journal of International Business Studies*, *35*(5), 350–370. doi:10.1057/palgrave.jibs.8400099

Luk, C., Yau, O., Sin, L., Tse, A., Chow, R., & Lee, J. (2008). The effects of social capital and organizational innovativeness in different institutional contexts. *Journal of International Business Studies*, *39*(4), 589–612. doi:10.1057/palgrave.jibs.8400373

Mathews, V. E. (2000). Management in a developing nation: And we thought American managers had it tough. *Multinational Business Review*, *8*(2), 10–15.

Murtiasih, S., Sucherly, S., & Siringoringo, H. (2014). Impact of country of origin and word of mouth on brand equity. *Marketing Intelligence & Planning*, *32*(5), 616–629. doi:10.1108/MIP-04-2013-0073

Neelankavil, J. P., Mathur, A. Y., & Zhang, Y. (2000). Determinants of managerial performance: A cross-cultural comparison of the perceptions of middle-level managers in four countries. *Journal of International Business Studies*, *31*(1), 121–140. doi:10.1057/palgrave.jibs.8490892

Nemoto, T., Hayashi, K., & Hashimoto, M. (2010). Milk-run logistics by Japanese automobile manufacturers in Thailand. *Procedia: Social and Behavioral Sciences*, *2*(3), 5980–5989. doi:10.1016/j.sbspro.2010.04.012

Ng, I., & Dastmalchian, A. (2001). Organizational flexibility in Western and Asian firms: An examination of control and safeguard rules in five countries. *Canadian Journal of Administrative Sciences*, *8*(1), 17–24.

Overbaugh, S. N. (2013). National culture, country-level competitiveness, and economic development. *International Journal of Business of Economics Perspectives*, *8*(1), 93–108.

Pananond, P., & Zeithaml, C. P. (1998). The international expansion process of MNEs from developing countries: A case study of Thailand's CP Group. *Asia Pacific Journal of Management*, *15*(2), 163–184. doi:10.1023/A:1015485413835

Pellicer, E., Yepes, V., & Rojas, R. J. (2010). Innovation and competitiveness in construction companies: A case study. *Journal of Management Research*, *10*(2), 103–115.

Peng, M. W. (2002). Towards an institution-based view of business strategy. *Asia Pacific Journal of Management*, *19*(2/3), 251–267. doi:10.1023/A:1016291702714

Petison, P., & Johri, L. M. (2006). Driving harmony: Philosophy of Toyota Motor Thailand. *Strategic Direction*, *22*(11), 3–5. doi:10.1108/02580540610708699

Petison, P., & Johri, L. M. (2007). Developing local talent in international subsidiaries: The importance of trust and respect in Toyota. *Development and Learning in Organizations: An International Journal*, *21*(3), 10–13. doi:10.1108/14777280710739061

Phongpetra, V., & Johri, L. M. (2011). Impact of business strategies of automobile manufacturers in Thailand. *International Journal of Emerging Markets*, *6*(1), 17–37. doi:10.1108/17468801111104359

Poletti, M. J., Engelland, B. T., & Ling, H. G. (2011). An empirical study of declining lead times: Potential ramifications on the performance of early market entrants. *Journal of Marketing Theory and Practice*, *19*(1), 27–38. doi:10.2753/MTP1069-6679190102

Porter, M. E. (1980). *Competitive strategy*. Free Press.

Porter, M. E. (1990). *The competitive advantage of nations*. Free Press. doi:10.1007/978-1-349-11336-1

Porter, M. E. (1996). What is strategy? *Harvard Business Review*, *74*(6), 61–78. PMID:10158474

Post Reporters (2015, January 30). FPO trims forecasts for GDP, exports. *Bangkok Post*, p. B2.

Prasnikar, J., Pahor, M., & Svetlik, J. V. (2008). Are national cultures still important in international business? Eussia, Serbia and Slovenia in comparison. *Journal of Contemporary Management Issues*, *13*(2), 1–26.

Rahman, S., Laosirihongthong, T., & Sohal, A. S. (2010). Impact of lean strategy on operational performance: A study of Thai manufacturing companies. *Journal of Manufacturing Technology Management*, *21*(7), 839–852. doi:10.1108/17410381011077946

Rahman, Z., & Bhattacharyya, S. K. (2003). Sources of first mover advantages in emerging market – an Indian perspective. *European Business Review*, *15*(6), 361–371. doi:10.1108/09555340310500541

Rojas-Méndez, J. I. (2013). The nation brand molecule. *Journal of Product and Brand Management*, *22*(7), 462–472. doi:10.1108/JPBM-09-2013-0385

Sangwongwanich, P. (2015, January 23). Bangkok rock bottom in 300-city economic survey. *Bangkok Post*, p. B1.

Seshanna, S. (2009). Globalization, income polarization and the rise of the "new challenger". In C. W. Mun & S. H. Ying (Eds.), *Singapore and Asia in a Globalized World, Contemporary Economic Issues and Politics* (pp. 155–172). Singapore: World Scientific.

Shah, A. M. (2012). Business strategies in the emerging markets. *Journal of Asia-Pacific Business*, *13*(1), 4–15. doi:10.1080/10599231.2011.616143

Shao, B. (2011). First mover advantages: Flexible or not? *Journal of Management and Marketing Research*, *7*(1), 1–13.

Shapiro, D. M., Gedaijlovis, E., & Erdener, C. (2003). The Chinese family firm as a multinational enterprise. *The International Journal of Organizational Analysis*, *11*(2), 105–122. doi:10.1108/eb028965

Shenkar, O. (2009). Becoming multinational: Challenges for Chinese firms. *Journal of Chinese Economic and Foreign Trade Studies*, *2*(3), 149–162. doi:10.1108/17544400910994733

Shrestha, B. K., & Gnyawali, D. R. (2013). Insights on strategic management practices in Nepal. *South Asian Journal of Global Business Research*, *2*(2), 191–210. doi:10.1108/SAJGBR-03-2012-0025

Singal, A. K., & Jain, A. K. (2014). Emerging market firms: Measuring their success with strategic positioning maps. *The Journal of Business Strategy*, *35*(1), 20–28. doi:10.1108/JBS-04-2013-0026

Sinpeng, A. (2014). Party-social movement coalition in Thailand's political conflict (2005-2011). In P. Liamputtong (Ed.), *Contemporary Socio-Cultural and Political Perspectives in Thailand* (pp. 157–168). Dordrecht, NL: Springer. doi:10.1007/978-94-007-7244-1_10

Subrahmanya, M. (2009). Case study: Nature and strategy of product innovations in SMEs: A case study-based comparative perspective of Japan and India. *Innovation: Management. Policy & Practice*, *11*(1), 104–113. doi:10.5172/impp.453.11.1.104

Suehiro, A., & Wailerdsak, N. (2004). Family business in Thailand: Its management, governance, and future challenges. *ASEAN Economic Bulletin*, *21*(1), 81–93. doi:10.1355/AE21-1E

Suutari, V., Raharjo, K., & Riikkila, T. (2002). The challenge of cross-cultural leadership interaction: Finnish expatriates in Indonesia. *Career Development International*, *7*(6/7), 415–429. doi:10.1108/13620430210449948

Tang, T. (2002). Powerhouse's management strategies for excellent business achievement. *Integrated Management Systems*, *13*(6), 366–374. doi:10.1108/09576060210436623

Thanasuta, K., Patoomsuwan, T., Chaimahawong, V., & Chiaravutthi, Y. (2009). Brand and country of origin valuations of automobiles. *Asia Pacific Journal of Marketing and Logistics*, *21*(3), 355–375. doi:10.1108/13555850910973847

Torrisi, C. R., & Uslu, G. (2010). Transitioning economics: A calculus of competitiveness. *Journal of Applied Business and Economics*, *11*(3), 39–54.

Toyota. (2014). *2014 annual report: Toyota Motor Company*. Retrieved from http://www.toyota-global.com/investors/ir_library/annual/pdf/2014/ar14_e.pdf

Tsang, E. (2001). Internationalizing the family firm: A case study of a Chinese family business. *Journal of Small Business Management*, *39*(2), 88–94. doi:10.1111/0447-2778.00008

Ty, M., Walsh, J., & Anurit, P. (2010). An empirical assessment of the relationship between national culture and learning capability in organizations in Cambodia. *International Business Research*, *3*(4), 81–90. doi:10.5539/ibr.v3n4p81

Vatikiotis, M. (2004). Optimism in the face of history. *Far Eastern Economic Review*, *167*(34), 26–29.

Vernon, R. (1966). International investment and international trade in the product cycle. *The Quarterly Journal of Economics*, *80*(2), 190–207. doi:10.2307/1880689

Walsh, K. (2004). Interpreting the impact of culture on structure: The role of change processes. *The Journal of Applied Behavioral Science*, *40*(3), 302–322. doi:10.1177/0021886304266845

Yan, J., & Sorenson, R. L. (2004). The Influence of Confucian ideology on conflict in Chinese family business. *International Journal of Cross Cultural Management*, *4*(1), 5–17. doi:10.1177/1470595804041521

Yu, T. (2001). The Chinese family business as a strategic system: An evolutionary perspective. *International Journal of Entrepreneurial Behaviour and Research*, *7*(1), 22–40. doi:10.1108/13552550110385736

Zhang, M., Knight, G., & Tansuhaj, P. (2014). International performance antecedents in emerging market SMEs: Evidence from China. *Journal of Global Marketing*, *27*(3), 161–177. doi:10.1080/08911762.2013.875242

Zhang, Y. (2010). The impact of free trade agreements on business activity: A survey of firms in the People's Republic of China. ADBI Working paper 251. Tokyo: Asian Development Bank Institution. Available at http:www.adbi.org/working-paper/2010/10/12/4088.impact.fta.business.activity.prc/

KEY TERMS AND DEFINITIONS

Developing Economy: A country where the average income is significantly lower than average incomes found in developed (wealthy) nations.

Exploitative Innovation: Incremental changes intended to improve upon existing products or processes.

Exploratory Innovation: Radical changes intended to create entirely new opportunities.

National Brand Image: The part of a company's brand image which is associated with the perception of stakeholders of the country associated with the company.

National Competitive Advantages: Competitive advantages for an organization that can be attributed to environmental factors found in the country of origin and country of operation.

National Competitive Disadvantages: Competitive disadvantages for an organization that can be attributed to environmental factors found in the country of origin and country of operation.

Strategic Management: Business decisions having a fundamental and long-term impact on an entire organization.

Chapter 15
International Business Diplomacy:
Lessons from Latin America

Francisco Javier Valderrey
Tecnológico de Monterrey, Campus Leon, Mexico

ABSTRACT

This chapter aims to analyze conflict resolution between Multinational Enterprises (MNEs) operating in Latin America and their host countries. The chapter focuses on the importance of establishing a policy for addressing local governments through permanent channels, as a strategy to solve disagreements with the authorities. The analysis includes different scenarios drawn from the experience of foreign firms in Argentina, Brazil, Chile, Colombia, Mexico, Peru and Venezuela. Thus, international managers may get a deeper view about the consequences of relying on formal diplomatic channels when conflict arises. Decision makers at MNEs need to evaluate separately each country outlook in order to assess the level of confidence that may be placed on diplomatic representation from the parent country and, consequently, the convenience of developing additional ties with local authorities through international business diplomacy.

INTRODUCTION

The environment for MNEs operating abroad has changed considerably over the last few decades, as globalization has reshaped the international business arena. The issues that require attention from international managers continue to grow in importance, while multiple new actors are making their debut into an increasingly sophisticated scenario. The spread of interested parties and the complexity of the MNE-host country relationships are urging to redefine the rules of engagement among all the stakeholders on a variety of situations. The negotiation table has enlarged to accommodate other guests beyond traditional delegates from the government and the external enterprise. Representatives from all corners of society, whether rightfully appointed or not, have now a saying in matters that no longer can be restricted to secretive negotiations. Conflicts, indeed, may arise from the array of demands and ex-

DOI: 10.4018/978-1-5225-0276-0.ch015

pectations of those who believe that are entitled to participate in decisions that affect the lives of many. Meanwhile, the number of MNEs is also increasing dramatically. In fact, by the end of last decade 82,000 already existed, accounting for roughly one third of international trade, and showing an expanding trend (Fienhold, 2014). In addition to global enterprises, there are nowadays numerous companies, certainly not as prominent, willing to protect their interests overseas. Hence, it becomes necessary to evaluate if traditional means for conflict solving can cope with an enlarged set of variables. Until recently, direct negotiations between the subsidiary and the government were adequate on minor disagreements between the parties. In the event of an escalation of the problem, the intervention of the diplomatic representatives from the parent country could suffice to prevent a clash. In fact, diplomacy was not confined to become an option of last resort: frequently both nations could maintain a positive relationship through established channels, fostering mutual collaboration.

In this chapter, we focus on conflict resolution between host country and MNEs. We analyze the collision of seven global corporations in the same number of countries. Although the cases presented refer specifically to Latin America, the lessons drawn may be useful to decision makers in other developing economies. Many of the problems described, such as differences in the response of society to certain topics, cross-cultural discrepancies, the role of government, corruption and bribery, taxation, social differences, ethics, among others, can be found in other continents, as well. The cases reflect the problems faced by an American firm in Mexico (Walmart) and four European organizations in Argentina, Brazil, Chile and Colombia (Repsol, Shell, Anglo American and Nestlé). The United States, Spain, the United Kingdom, Switzerland and The Netherlands are leading investors in Latin America, although presently there is a new breed of MNEs in the region. Accordingly, we included the adversities of a Chinese company in Peru (Shougang) and the hardships of a Mexican corporation in Venezuela (Cemex). This last case provides a clear example of the problems encountered by firms from less advance economies when they invest themselves in developing markets, as happens with the so-called "multilatinas" (Cuervo-Cazurra, 2010).

The Many Meanings of the Word Diplomacy

As previously stated, diplomacy has been of outmost importance for the solution of conflicts in international business. Diplomacy itself has been in existence since early times, probably since pre-recorded history, naturally following the path of civilization (Szykman, 1995). Over the centuries it has evolved, flourishing during the classical Greek world, the middle ages in Italy, the seventeen and eighteen centuries in Europe, and after World War II in the Unites States, when the study of diplomacy opened up to prepare foreign ministries to get closer attention to trade, economic and business concerns (Saner & Yiu, 2001). Diplomacy successfully established rules for negotiations, created protocols for carrying out conversations in order to maintain or save peace, and had a major impact in the advance of commercial and trade agreements. Even though, there are disagreements regarding the definition of diplomacy and the boundaries of its realm.

The view of diplomacy as a function performed exclusively by professional diplomats acting as representatives of sovereign states was widely accepted for a long time. As stated in the classical definition from the Satow's guide to diplomatic practice, diplomacy *is the application of intelligence and tact to the conduct of official relations between the governments of independent states* (Satow, 1979). New developments in advanced economies, though, have created a need for a comprehensive definition of diplomacy. Post-modern times are witnessing the proliferation of entities seeking representation for territories such as provinces, states or local entities; the opening of new forums, such as multilateral

Table 1. Different forms of diplomacy

Form of Diplomacy	Description
Traditional	Deals with matters of concern to sovereign states or international organizations, through official representatives coordinated by foreign ministries
Public	Addresses the public of other nations in order to change perceptions or influence people in those countries
Trade	Focuses on discussion of general agreements between nations on rules, standards and procedures for an orderly exchange of goods and services
Economic	Serves ideological purposes or a geo-economic interest by means of policies, strategies or actions taken to favor a national purpose
Commercial	Is *the work of state officials in diplomatic service who carry out activities that support international business**
Business	It *involves establishing and sustaining positive relationships with foreign government representatives and non-governmental stakeholders with the aim to build and sustain legitimacy in a foreign business environment***
Corporate	Is a process that helps building a corporation´s power and legitimacy, but not necessarily in other countries
Others forms of diplomacy	Includes a variety of forms in which diplomacy is used in specific fields, such as sports, religion or culture, among others

Own source, *definitions by Lee and Ruël (2012), **Wolters (2012).

institutions requiring highly specialized representatives; the emergence of diplomatic functions in transnational enterprises; and the flourishing of non-governmental organizations (NGOs) involved in public affairs (Saner & Yiu, 2001). New theories and models have been proposed, as well as new taxonomies that could encompass the different functions performed by diplomacy. With concepts such as "Track one-Track Two", "Track-one-and a Half" (Mapendere, 2000), and eventually "Multi-Track" diplomacy (Diamond & McDonald, 1996), scholars have attempted to bring forth a definition that could embrace all aspects of diplomacy, the main actors, as well as the diversity of roles played in the process of mediation by everyone possibly involved in international disputes. Many definitions have been proposed, as well, but no consensus has been reached.

In spite of the lack of acceptance of a universal interpretation of diplomacy, there is no disagreement about its relevance to the field of international business, particularly as related to MNEs and their interaction with local governments, NGOs or local communities (Suren, 2014). Diplomacy may possibly be classified as follows: traditional, public, trade, economic, commercial, business, corporate, and others forms of lesser importance to the field of business. Table 1 shows a concise definition for each of the main categories.

Traditional diplomacy, as circumscribed to matters of concern to sovereign states or international institutions, has routinely assisted MNEs, although striving to protect the general interest of the parent nation and its overseas investors, rather than the needs of individual firms. Through public diplomacy, an international actor addresses vast publics in other nations (Cull, 2007). Those activities could be of benefit to the country as a whole, but rarely help enterprises directly. Trade diplomacy focus on discussion of general agreements between nations on rules, standards and procedures for an orderly exchange of goods and services, while economic diplomacy serves ideological purposes or a geo-economic interest by means of policies, strategies or actions taken to favor a general purpose (Olier, 2011). Both trade and economic diplomacy indirectly benefits business by promoting the exchange of products and services, as well as direct investment. They bring the foreign ministry closer to the business community. Sometimes, though, companies have been prevented to pursue their own plans, as happens with boycotts or the so-called "voluntary export restrictions".

Commercial diplomacy has gone further to nurture firms established in external soil, as defined by Lee and Ruël, is *the work of state officials in diplomatic service who carry out activities that support international business*. Commercial diplomacy is also a common ground for international business and international relations (Lee & Ruël, 2012), and it has been present from ancient times, perhaps since the Phoenicians (Chamoun-Nicolas, 2008). Its efficiency has been evaluated with promising results, especially in developing markets (Ruël & Zuidema, 2012). There is an assortment of activities performed by commercial diplomats, grouped as: *intelligence, communication, referral, advocacy, coordination and logistics* (Naray, 2008). The range of tools is rather large, as indicates an alternative classification that includes network activities, intelligence, image and business support targeting specifically the interest of enterprises: buyer-seller meetings, market research, promotions of products, negotiations or coordination of legal actions and many others (Lee & Ruël, 2012). Nonetheless, there is still a client-provider gap in the following areas: "partner search, market information search, investment facilitation, trade fairs, contract negotiation and problem-solving and trade disputes". Companies demand rapid response in those areas, a deeper analysis, a proactive attitude and a stronger commitment from the supporting authorities, among other actions (Kostecki, & Naray, 2007). Commercial diplomacy is essential for corporations acting overseas but, unfortunately, is not tailor made for MNEs and its scope is perhaps too broad.

Undoubtedly, business diplomacy gets closer to the reality of MNEs established away from home, helping in the solution of immediate struggles with foreign actors, while serving different purposes in the long run. Business diplomacy may be viewed in many ways, but a recent definition by Wolters adds to those widely accepted the elements of legitimacy and complexity of operations (Fienhold, 2014).

Business diplomacy involves establishing and sustaining positive relationships (by top executives or their representatives) with foreign government representatives and non-governmental stakeholders (economic and non-economic) with the aim to build and sustain legitimacy (safeguard corporate image and reputation) in a foreign business environment. (Wolters, 2012).

This type of diplomacy is supposedly inherent to the activities of all employees of an organization that work abroad, as well as those whose decisions may affect relationships across borders. Nevertheless, major responsibility resides with senior executives, whose leadership positions entitle them to mediate in conflicts beyond the interest of their corporation (Abbas, 2009). International managers in those positions should be actively scanning the environment for threats and opportunities and, ideally, they should receive proper training through development of competencies in addition to those generally acquired at business schools (Saner, Yiu, & Sondergaard, 2000).

The concept of business diplomacy contains four different areas: Intra-Firm; Inter-Firm; Home Country Government; and International Business. The first area of business diplomacy is conducted within the organization in order to gain internal efficiencies; the second one refers to relationships with other organizations; the third one deals with the authorities where the MNE operates, while the last one addresses issues with multiple stakeholders in international ground. The area of diplomacy targeting international business covers relations with local governments, NGOs, and local communities with is multiple actors. As opposed to commercial diplomacy, a subject of interest to scholars for a longer time, there is no clear classification of the ample set of tools available for this particular function. Anyhow, a study suggests positive effects from the use of international business diplomacy to the reputation of the company, its image and other non-financial indicators (Suren, 2014). Most probably, the benefits go far beyond those proved by incipient research.

Finally, corporate diplomacy is often considered as an equivalent term to business diplomacy, in the sense that is a process that helps building a corporation´s power and legitimacy (Ordeix-Rigo & Duarte, 2009). Corporate diplomacy is also viewed as part of public relations and related to the firm´s efforts to interact with a wider range of stakeholders (Macnamara, 2012). Enterprises make use of the extensive tools available from corporate diplomacy, but not necessarily to solve conflicts with foreign parties. Thus, the concept of *business diplomacy* prevails when looking at conflict resolution between MNEs with host countries or other relevant agents acting locally there, especially if the world *international* is used to strengthen such expression.

LATIN AMERICA: A FERTILE GROUND FOR CONFLICT

Conflicts indeed exist where foreign enterprises interfere with local interest. The matter has been the subject of scholarly analysis, although many questions remain unanswered. A study conducted back in 1980 showed surprising results over the nature of those conflicts. In fact, Negandhi and Baliga asserted that national origin of the MNE, differences in expectations from both sides and market conditions had an impact on the intensity of the conflict, whereas technology, company size and many internal attributes were not significant to the conflicts analyzed (Negandhi & Baliga, 1980). Although research has continued to enlighten the phenomenon, MNEs have evolved, the role of government has changed and new actors have become a part of those negotiations. The implications are many for firms operating in developing nations where the institutional, economic and legal framework, along with the cultural barriers and a way of conducting business too different from the parent country, force international decision makers to be on constant alert. Therefore, it is imperative to take a closer look at exemplary situations where foreign and local interests clash.

Latin America is a formidable laboratory for such purpose. It is a geographical area of the Americas that comprises countries where Spanish and Portuguese language are spoken, from the southern border of the United States to the southernmost part of South America, including also the Caribbean islands. Although countries are bound by historical heritage, common languages and similar stages of economic development, the region resembles a kaleidoscope where a never ending display of collisions at all levels of society show a wide range of results, and business is no exception. Latin America has hosted external companies for centuries and most of the times obtaining very little as compared to the wealth of mineral or human resources offered in exchange. MNEs have been often perceived as predators, either called upon by necessity or self-invited, in most cases. MNEs, at times, have been fundamental to the economic development of backward countries, but too often the relationship has turned sour. Presently, direct investment is welcome, although MNEs are under siege in some countries where governments have strong ideological commitments. Those enterprises established in this territory face barriers, oppressive regulatory agencies (Montoya & Trillas, 2009), limitations or uncertainties that are not present in developed markets. This has happened for a long time and will most probably continue in the foreseeable future.

The markets that are more attractive to investors are: Argentina, Brazil, Chile, Mexico, Colombia, Peru, and Venezuela. Due to the traditional lack of political consistency, economic stability, and the many variables to compare, it is an impossible task to present an irrefutable ranking of Latin American countries by importance. Accordingly, the selected markets are those generally kept under watch by international corporations and by consultancy firms or economic research centers focused on this part of the planet. We include in Table 2 a comparison among those countries, using a number of variables

Table 2. Comparison of seven countries in Latin America

Country	Area Km2	Population Millions (Rounded)	GDP US$ Billions	External Debt US$ Billions	Business Climate*	P.P.P. US$	Country Risk**
Argentina	2,780,400	43	$484.6	$111.5	61	$18,600	7
Brazil	8,514,877	203	$2,190	$475.9	60	$18,600	3
Chile	756,102	17	$281.7	$119	86	$19,100	n/a
Colombia	1,138,910	46	$369.2	$85.83	119	$11,100	4
Mexico	1,964,375	120	$1,327	$354.9	95	$15,600	3
Peru	1,285,216	30	$210.3	$50.15	123	$11,100	3
Venezuela	912,050	29	$367.5	$74.87	20	$13,600	7

With data from The World Factbook (CIA), *According to the Business Climate Index (BCI) driven by Getulio Vargas Foundation (FGV) and the University of Munich. (2015), where a higher score indicates easiness of doing business, ** According to - Country Risk Classifications of the Participants to the Arrangement on Officially Supported Export Credits (OECD 2015). A higher value indicates a higher risk.

that illustrate major differences in geography, demography, macroeconomic data, country risk, and other variables that could be most appealing to MNEs. Some are drawn from international statistics, while others are obtained from qualitative assessment.

There are important differences among the selected countries beyond those shown in Table 2. The language is the cultural divide, with Brazil being the only non-Spanish speaking country. Brazil is also the most successful developing its own technology, such as in aerospace, bioenergy or deep-water oil drilling, although Mexico is catching up, mainly due to the spillover effect from MNEs. In fact, Mexico is capitalizing on the vicinity to the US market, widening the industrial base, while diminishing the dependency of petroleum exports. Venezuela is moving in the completely opposite direction, with oil export dependency as never seen before. Argentina has become also fully dependent upon the export of commodities, while Colombia, Peru and Chile show a relatively balanced economy. Commodities, nevertheless, dictate the fate of Latin America prosperity, in a never-ending cycle of dependency from sales of raw materials and limited value-added operations.

DOING BUSINESS WHERE REALITY OVERCOMES FICTION

The following cases bring forth some issues to the discussion about MNE performance in developing nations, such as: corruption, the power of trade unions, questionable governance, the importance of ethnical minorities or industrial elites, and, overall, the role of government in the economy and society. Those topics are important in other evolving markets, but add some special flavor to the Latin American context, with each country using its own seasoning. Cases will be presented separately, using a common structure: a) description of the conflict and b) stakeholder´s involvement. The first part, after a brief introduction of the company involved, provides background information about the conflict. The second part describes, succinctly, the actions taken from the different actors involved: host governments, MNEs, parent countries and other stakeholders[1].

Case 1: Mexico – Walmart and the Teotihuacan Pyramids

Since 1962, Walmart has been "saving people money so they can live better". From a humble beginning, the gigantic American corporation has become the undisputed worldwide leader in retailing, with direct presence in 27 countries. Well over 2 million employees operate 11,000 retail units with additional sales through e-commerce, reaching annual revenues of approximately US$473 billion (Walmart). Undoubtedly, Walmart has reshaped business and shaken markets around the globe, as described by the so-called "Walmart effect", with all the positive and negative connotations (unparalleled competition for local retailers, reduced wages, additional disposable income for consumers, reduced inflation, etc.).

Conflicting Situation

Mexican people are proud of their heritage, proclaiming to be descendants of ancient cultures capable of building cities and monuments, many centuries before Columbus. The Teotihuacan Pyramids, for instance, rival those built in ancient Egypt. The pyramids are well preserved and in the proximity of the capital, Mexico City. Few kilometers away from the historical site, Walmart built in 2004 a new supermarket unit; the project made perfect sense if only taking into account financial figures, but it started a controversy that jeopardized its corporate image, in both Mexico and the US. After meticulous research, the company chose a plot of land near the archeological area, which was lacking proper building permits.

The project raised public attention due to the proximity of the historical site and the unusual promptness of construction. Suspiciously, documents vanished, maps were altered to fit the location into authorized building areas and higher local representatives granted doubtful permits to accommodate the desires of the foreign corporation. The store eventually opened up to the public, in spite of concerns for bribery and wrongdoing from a number of local bureaucrats. A year later, though, a former senior officer at Walmart acted as a whistleblower, denouncing a meticulous strategy to make illegal payments to the authorities in charge of the building permits of the Teotihuacan Pyramids unit and many others. The former executive confessed only to senior directors, who reduced the investigation to a mild internal inquiry (Gustin, 2012). Few years later, the New York Times published an article describing in detail the corruption scheme. Only then, Walmart contacted the Securities and Exchange Commission and the Department of Justice. Presently, Walmart has publicly declared its intention to cooperate with prosecutors, but no final settlement has been reached as yet (Barstow & Xanic von Bertrab, 2012). Yet, new accusations of bribery surfaced in Mexico, such as in case of the San Pedro store in Nuevo León (Cedillo, 2012).

Stakeholder's Involvement

At first, only local authorities were involved, mainly those responsible for issuing the permits. Later on, the controversy went up to the Mexican Congress, although legal actions were not taken, neither against the American company nor against the corrupted officers. Walmart´s top executives in Mexico tried to avoid or perhaps cover up the whole situation, while those at the headquarters chose to keep a low profile until the media forced them to admit the wrongdoing. American authorities were not actively involved during the initial stage of the conflict. Later on, their intervention was of paramount importance, taking the matter to its own jurisdiction, under the Foreign Corrupt Practices Act and the Sarbanes-Oxley Act. Surprisingly enough, few stakeholders intervened in this case. The press and the community raised some complaints, but newspapers in other countries made little noise. The numerous NGOs critical to the largest retailer in the world did not take advantage of the many illegal actions involved.

Case 2: Argentina – Fighting over a Dead Cow

Spain is well known for historical or cultural reasons, but it is difficult to relate the country to the energy industry, especially since less than one percent of the oil consumed nationally comes from the local territory. Yet, Repsol is a Spanish integrated energy corporation with direct presence in 39 countries and 24,000 employees worldwide. It was founded in 1987 after bringing together several companies covering a broad range of activities, from exploration to distribution of oil related products. Two years later Repsol was privatized and ever since has grown through mergers and acquisitions into a world-class organization and a major investor in the region (Repsol).

Conflicting Situation

In 2011, the leading energy enterprise in Argentina made a striking announcement: the discovery of one of the largest shale gas and oil deposits in the planet at *Vaca Muerta,* which literally means death cow in Spanish, located in the Neuquén Province. Suddenly, the nation had the chance to become a global player in the energy industry and overcome the many obstacles that hindered economic growth for decades. There was an obstacle, though: the finder of the deposits, Repsol-YPF S.A. (YPF), was under the control of Repsol, the Spanish energy corporation, holding the majority of shares. Until that moment, the foreign investor and local officials maintained a friendly relationship, especially since YPF was the largest taxpayer and the second private employer in Argentina (Bermejo & Garciandía, 2012).

Unfortunately, the Vaca Muerta reservoir soon turned the relationship sour, when a year later Cristina Kirchner, the charismatic president of the South American state, announced the expropriation of 51% of the shares owned by Repsol, under allegations of insufficient investments and production from the parent company. The decision was clearly discriminatory, since expropriation only targeted one among the different shareholders at YPF. The Spanish firm was also to receive economic compensation as determined by Argentinian tribunals. The MNE immediately demanded compensation of approximately US$10 billion, taking its allegations to the International Centre for Settlement of Investment Disputes and pursuing legal action in Argentina, Spain and the United States. Furthermore, the Spanish government clearly backed Repsol and brought forth the controversy to the European Union. Litigation only stopped in 2014 after the MNE accepted the sale of its Argentinean assets in exchange for future payments in excess than $6 billion and a mutual agreement to stop any possible legal action.

Stakeholder's Involvement

The government was of paramount importance in this case. President Cristina Kirchner`s attempts to take full control of the economy led to an international dispute, unseen in Argentina since the Falkland Islands (or Islas Malvinas) war. The consequences were not as dramatic as those seen after the UK military response, but economic damage was substantial and the nation suffered from a lack of credibility in international markets. The use of legal action for ideological purposes was contrary to international law as well as ineffective: the president used the full power of the state against a MNE, but her actions caused major turmoil. Repsol did not waste a minute before protesting the expropriation decision, while trying to reach a consensual agreement with the government. The company also asked for protection from the parent country, while searching for informal negotiation channels (The Economist, 2012).

Ultimately, Repsol could obtain fair compensation, which demonstrates the importance of using international and commercial diplomacy. Spain acted decisively to favor its national interest: almost immediately after the expropriation announcement, the foreign secretary Margallo stated his opposition, making the conflict a national priority and using all soft and hard power within his reach. Public opinion was majorly supportive of President Cristina Kirchner, although many were skeptical about the way she proceeded and the consequences to international credibility. Surprisingly, the most active among other shareholders was Pemex, the Mexican oil company that owned close to 10% of Repsol. Pemex acted as intermediary in the conflict, but probably after secretive conversations with YPF for possible exploitation of *Vaca Muerta* reservoir. Nonetheless, was not the only interested party, as Chevron reached publicly an agreement with Argentina to replace Repsol at *Vaca Muerta*.

Case 3: Brazil – Raizen, the "Sugar Blues"

Shell Oil is one of the largest and better-known energy and petrochemical corporations. It is a global firm headquartered in the Netherlands, although the parent company is incorporated in the United Kingdom. It has a direct investment in seventy countries, with a workforce of 92,000 employees, producing over 3 million barrels of oil per day and operating more than 30 refineries and petrochemical plants (Shell). Its annual revenues are equally impressive, 451 billion dollars approximately, more than the GDP of the vast majority of sovereign nations. Shell had an early start in 1833 and is one of the so-called "seven sisters", the petroleum companies that dominated the international market for several decades.

Conflicting Situation

Brazil is well known for its soccer frenzy, tropical beaches or carnival, but not that many people are aware of its achievements in biofuel technology. Millions of vehicles throughout the country use ethanol and therefore sugar cane plantations are of vital importance. In 2010, Shell founded a joint venture with the Brazilian enterprise Cosan, the largest national ethanol producer, to meet demand from internal and export markets. A US$2 billion deal created Raizen, a new firm with a 50% participation from Shell and Cosan. From the very start, Raizen became a leading ethanol producer, as well as the largest fuel distributor in the home market.

Brazil´s unquenchable thirst for ethanol has created a pressing need for more sugar cane plantations, but the lack of availability of suitable land has pushed growers into the Amazonian rain forest. For decades, farmers have evicted different tribes with the assistance of ruthless private security guards and too often with the consent of the authorities. Local growers, in turn, were selling their crops to intermediaries and large volume buyers such as Cosan, uninterested in the consistent pattern of human right violations committed against native tribes. The Guarani, one of those ancestral tribes with close to 70,000 members in Brazil and many thousands more in Paraguay, Bolivia and Argentina, was able to draw public attention and confronted Raizen as the main responsible for their deteriorating conditions and the damage to the environment. They appealed to federal authorities, who uphold their constitutional rights to the land they historically occupied. The Ministry of Justice confirmed the usufruct of their territory by the Guarani and Raizen pledged not to source sugar cane from protected territories. Shell image was severely damaged. Although the MNE committed no violations against the tribe, it showed permissiveness towards its partner.

Stakeholder's Involvement

Brazilian authorities disregarded at first the many reports of human right violations, clearly favoring economic development and the expansion of growers into indigenous territories. Society is divided in the subject of native population´s rights to the use of land, with a lot of criticism from those who see that tribes are granted vast territories that could easily accommodate the growing population from megacities, such as Sao Paulo. Justice prevailed at last and the authorities agreed to enforce the law. Shell clearly neglected its due diligence while reviewing the partnership with Cosan and afterwards, when the issue gained public recognition. The response from the headquarters was probably weak, forwarding complains to the subsidiary, in spite of the own codes of conduct and publicly stated corporate values. The Dutch government stayed out of the conflict.

The Netherlands use commercial diplomacy with exemplary effectiveness with smaller firms. Corporations of this size many times follow their own procedures, without involvement of the established diplomatic channels. ONGs from different countries supported the demands of Guarani people. Probably, without their intervention the conflict will still be unsolved. SOMO (Centre for Research of Multinational Corporations), for instance, joined the Dutch Association of Investors for Sustainable Development, questioning Shell at their own headquarters in the Netherlands. The press also draws global attention to the situation.

Case 4: Chile – A Diamond Is Forever, Copper Is Not

Anglo American PLC is a global and diversified organization, with headquarters in London, mining activities in South Africa, Latin America and Australia, and offices spread all throughout the planet (Anglo American). Today, it is a leading producer of iron ore, coal, copper, nickel, niobium, phosphates, platinum and diamonds, with annual revenues of approximately US$31 billion and 151,200 employees. Sir Ernest Oppenheimer founded Anglo American in 1917, after raising capital in the United States and Britain to start a mining venture in South Africa. In 1926, the company became the largest single shareholder of The Beers, the company that coined the slogan "a diamond is forever", expanded operations in Canada in 1961, Chile in 1980, and Australia in the year 2,000.

Conflicting Situation

During the last few decades, Chile has diversified its economy, trading partners and exports. Nowadays is frequent to see Chilean wines, salmon and a number of products displayed in American and European shelves. Nevertheless, the country is still dependent upon its commodity exports, especially copper, a mineral abundant in Chile. Copper deposits lured Anglo American PLC to establish a subsidiary that eventually acquired some of the richest mines, such as Los Bronces, El Soldado, Mantos Blancos, Sur Andes or Mantoverde, along with companies in different stages of the mining process. However, as the old adagio says, the devil is in the details. Indeed, the sale contract for those assets contained an option for the seller to buy back up to 49% of the shares at specified times during the following 50 years.

The option sounded bizarre at the time, especially for a company leaving the industry, but it was also transferable. Later on, the state-controlled mining enterprise, Codelco, acquired the option. Because of souring commodity prices in international markets, the new value of copper mines multiplied, which tempted Codelco to exercise the option. Representatives of both firms met at Davos in 2011 and the Chilean director confirmed to Anglo American CFO the intention to acquire those shares. The offer was agreeable to both sides and the experts started to define the right price to close the deal: the final price was set at US$6 billion for almost half of the total ownership. Anglo American, unsatisfied with the figures, sold a 24.5% of the property to Mitsubishi Trading for a similar amount of money. The sale was announced and immediately afterwards the Chilean company accused the British company of breaching its contract. Anglo American counterattacked with lawsuits that created a "no man´s land". Finally, in 2012 both companies recognized the mutual benefit of leaving litigation aside and signed a new contract. Codelco and Mitsubishi created a joint venture with nominal participation of Anglo American, which in turn received satisfying compensation, while retaining some ownership of the mines.

Stakeholder's Involvement

The authorities fully supported the state owned enterprise in different ways. Apparently, local courts were protective versus Codelco and the authorities threatened to intervene, suggesting the possibility of nationalization of the mines. Ultimately, the authorities had to back up as they witnessed a deterioration of the relationship with the United Kingdom. Anglo American PLC made costly mistakes, by failure to understand the implications of the fine print, such as the buy-back option. Apparently, their leaders acted with manifest disregard of the law and failed to ask for the support of the parent country.

The United Kingdom, indeed, had more than a saying with a nation traditionally regarded as a close friend and important investor. British diplomats were not called into the action. Presumably, their intervention could have been useful, although not as strong as to jeopardize the good relations between both countries. Too many parties had a saying in this dispute: Codelco workers, unions, competitors in Chile and abroad, political parties taking a stand to entice voters and governments interested on the stability of the copper market.

Case 5: Colombia – A Widow Defying a Multinational Corporation

Nestlé, the Swiss iconic group, has been "providing safe, quality nutrition, for more than 140 years". The company has a direct presence in 86 countries, employing 330,000 people, marketing more than 2,000 brands and annual worldwide sales close to US$100 billion. Undoubtedly, Nestlé is a symbol of quality for baby foods, bottled water, cereals, chocolate, coffee, frozen foods, dairy and many other products (Nestlé). Although the company is a leader in several categories, the company has also faced criticism, such as in the notorious case of its infant formula sold in Africa, Asia and Latin America.

Conflicting Situation

On March 2012, a Colombian widow disrupted the harmony of the placid canton of Vaud, when she filed a suit against almighty Nestlé. Truly enough, the widow was defying the MNE and charging the company for its indirect responsibility in a murder of a union leader, although fellow co-nationals in her homeland perpetrated the crime. The woman, though, was not standing on her own. In fact, she had the support of her trade union and got legal assistance from the European Center for Constitutional and Human Rights, an NGO based in Berlin (ECCHR). She presented the legal case to the Swiss authorities because of the alleged responsibility from Nestlé, the parent company, as well as from upper management in Switzerland and Colombia.

Back in 2005, trade union leader Luciano Romero was tortured and killed by paramilitary groups, financially supported by local business people, landlords and probably with the consent of the police and the armed forces. At the time of the killing, Mr. Romero had long been separated from the company. Nonetheless, he had represented workers at Cicolac for a number of years, during which he was falsely labeled as a guerrilla fighter by company directors. By disseminating such information in a civil-war torn nation, as the widow stated, the MNE put a death sentence to Luciano Romero. The Swiss tribunals closed the case against Nestlé on formal grounds, referring that the statute of limitations of seven years had been exceeded. The widow, under the advice of ECCHR appealed to the Swiss Supreme Court of Justice, which in turn reaffirmed the previous verdict. Finally, a complaint was submitted to the European Court of Human Rights against Switzerland.

Stakeholder's Involvement

Colombian authorities had little involvement in this case. Although a local judge made some recommendations against Cicolac, nothing appears to have been done. The perpetrators of the murder, though, were put in jail. From the very beginning Nestlé denied all charges and avoided the issue altogether, making no moves toward reaching an amicable settlement. Headquarters announced a fierce legal battle, stating no involvement or responsibility (OIDHACO, 2012).

As expected, Swiss authorities were officially neutral, although some criticism arose arguing that local courts gave favorable treatment to the iconic company. Some NGOs supported the widow´s appeal: the trade union and, above all, ECCHR. This organization provided meaningful assistance to Mrs. Romero and, ultimately, pursued legal action against the MNE and Switzerland.

Case 6: Peru – New "Conquistadores" Are Not Welcome

Shougan Hierro Perú, SAA is the Peruvian subsidiary of the Shougang Group, a giant steel company based in the People´s Republic of China (Shougang). The industrial group was founded in 1919, but the expansion landmark came after Mao Tse Tung´s revolution. Ever since, Shougang Group established itself as one of the leading iron producers in China, covering also many segments of the mining process. After the economic awakening of the Asian colossus, the MNE expanded into foreign markets, mainly Australia and Peru, through acquisitions of companies and large mineral deposits. Currently is a state-controlled enterprise with approximately 70,000 employees, revenues in excess of US$34 billion and is ranked as number 348 among the Fortune Global 500 companies (Fortune, 2014).

Conflicting Situation

When the "conquistadores" arrived from Spain to the Andes in the sixteen century, they were astonished at the sight of the wealth accumulated by the Inca civilization. In fact, they were sitting on top of one of the richest gold deposits in the planet. Spain continued mineral extraction and so did the newborn Peruvian nation after independence. Mineral deposits are continuously being replaced by new discoveries and, as in the past, the richness of Peru keeps attracting foreigners, whether from Europe, Asia or North America. Apparently is China's turn to tab those resources, much needed to keep its industries running.

In 1993 the Chinese enterprise Shougang, formalized the acquisition of Hierro Perú, the legal owner of the largest iron ore deposit in the country. The US$120 million deal included lifetime extraction rights, infrastructure and seaport facilities, under the promise of further investments. Those investments came much later, only after many years when the company declared massive losses, avoiding therefore tax payments, performance bonus to employees and the promised modernization of facilities. During those years, also, there were mounting complains of environmental damage and infringement of employment laws. Labor unrest increased after near half of the workers were replaced by Chinese nationals with reduced wages and deprived of social benefits (Martinez, 2012). Shougan was also fined for environmental damages, failure to meet tax payments and health violations. The list also included allegations of excessive use of force against demonstrators. Finally, trade unions initiated a large-scale strike.

Stakeholder's Involvement

The authorities had been accused of wrongdoing from the very beginning in this particular case. Allegations of a fraudulent arrangement for the sale of Hierro Perú were commonplace, especially after experts attempted to dig into the original sales contract. The set price appeared to be unrealistic and other clauses were considered frivolous. Once the Chinese took charge of the company, the government avoided all interference with the MNE, even after significant violations of the law. At first Shougan denied every controversial subject, ignoring complains from workers and the community as a whole. Eventually, the company saw a need for a change of course, especially after prolonged strikes eroded the profitability of the operation.

The firm´s reputation was severely damaged, which in turn poisoned the relationship with workers and authorities. The long lasting strike was the turning point towards a responsible involvement. China always stood for the protection of home companies, even at the cost of damaging relationships with host countries. Shougan used hard bargaining power during most stages of the negotiations, but eventually realized that the use of soft power could lead to better results. Nowadays China is the largest investors in the Peruvian mining industry. The power of the yuan has a facilitating effect for market penetration in Peru, and elsewhere in the area (Ellis, 2014). Few other stakeholders played a significant role in the conflict, perhaps with the exemption of ONGs trying to protect workers from clear violations of their labor rights (Kotschwar, Moran, & Muir, 2011).

Case 7: Venezuela – We Need Your Cement to Build Our Revolution

Cemex is a Mexican building materials company and one of the leading cement manufacturers in the world. It started in Northern Mexico in 1906 and ever since has been an icon of the Monterrey area industrial might. In 1992, after dominance of the local cement market, Cemex acquired two companies in Spain and started a rapid expansion into external markets. Approximately 43,000 employees work at Cemex, a firm with annual sales of US$15 billion and direct presence in 50 countries (Cemex). It has been described as the most global among the multilatinas (El Economista, 2014).

Conflicting Situation

It came as no surprise the announcement made in 2008 by Hugo Chavez promulgating the nationalization of the cement industry in Venezuela. In fact, five years before the government imposed substantial price controls and, thereafter, MNEs suffered continuous harassments from the authorities. Cement is important for construction, but it becomes vital to a government pledging to provide housing for millions of followers. The Venezuelan president claimed that three foreign cement makers, Cemex from Mexico, Holcim from Switzerland and Lafarge from France, were obstructing the so called "Bolivarian revolution".

Election Day was getting closer and so those enterprises were expropriated at once. Holcim and Lafarge rapidly came to terms with the authorities, securing a minority ownership in the new ventures. Cemex, on the contrary, fully opposed the expropriation of its subsidiary, fearing insufficient compensation. At the time, the Mexican company had a 52% market share in the cement industry, three plants, and employed more than 3,000 people in Venezuela. Cemex received immediate assistance from the parent country, with unquestionable support from diplomats and officials at the highest level. Corporate lawyers took the issue to the World Bank, demanding immediate stoppage to the government intervention and compensation of US 1,300 million. After a confrontation that severely damaged the relationship between the two countries, the company and Venezuela signed a final agreement ending all possible legal fights: Cemex was to receive US$600 million plus cancellation of US$154 million in debt.

Stakeholder's Involvement

President Chavez followed a careful plan before taking over the MNEs. A critical campaign against those companies was orchestrated and there was a clear warning after the MNEs failed to align to the official plans for internal growth. His moves were clearly conceived, executed and communicated. Expropriation might be questionable, but was not a capricious act. Surely compensation was unfair, although within reasonable numbers. Cemex should probably have taken action long before the announcement, but it didn´t waste a minute afterwards. Corporate lawyers started a legal battle and management pulled some strings at the highest level of government to support its claims. They also orchestrated a campaign to make the quarrel known at international forums (García, Martínez, Torres & Pacheco, 2012).

The Mexican government was quick to react, first out of pride and later under the pressure of one of the most powerful leaders in Mexico, Don Lorenzo Zambrano, who was the CEO of Cemex for many years, growing the company into a multinational corporation. Consequently, nationalization of Cemex became one of the most important issues of Mexican foreign policy at that time. In this case, few were the actors moved by purely economic interest. Society approved confiscation of a foreign enterprise and raised no further questions. On the political side, though, many stakeholders were opposing Hugo Chavez, in addition to those who think that expropriation is a word to be kept out of dictionaries of modern economics.

FINDINGS

The information used in the cases comes from the review of news in local media of each of the seven countries during the past ten years, from 2004 to 2014. For educational purposes, the cases were chosen to be recent, with notoriety, backed by sufficient information for analysis and illustrative for international

Table 3. Use of international business diplomacy in selected cases

Country/Firm	Role of Government	MNE Reaction	Parent Country	Stakeholder's Actions
Mexico/ Walmart	Weak	Strong	Weak	Moderate
Argentina/ Repsol	Strong	Strong	Strong	Strong
Brazil/ Shell	Moderate	Moderate	Weak	Strong
Chile/ Anglo American	Strong	Strong	Weak	Strong
Colombia/ Nestlé	Weak	Weak	Weak	Strong
Peru/ Shougan	Strong	Strong	Strong	Strong
Venezuela/ Cemex	Strong	Strong	Strong	Strong

Own source.

managers. It is evident the much reduced sample of MNEs, which goes along the lines of the limited number of studies focusing on the use of business diplomacy. All of the companies are prominent on the industries and markets considered. The selection of MNEs attempted to include major investing countries in Latin America, such as the United States, Spain, The Netherlands, United Kingdom and Switzerland, some of the leading investors in the region. Companies from China are also gaining importance and, consequently an example was included, although the lessons drawn are not easily applicable for managerial decisions in western corporations. Finally, the case of one of the best-known multilatinas was also analyzed. This example is illustrative of the difficulties faced by MNEs from emerging countries investing in similar economies, something that surely deserves further research.

The analysis was based on four variables: role of host-country, management of conflict by MNE, intervention of parent country and other stakeholder´s actions[2]. Following is a summary of the results and Table 3 shows a comparison for all the cases.

In the Walmart case, the financial and legal consequences are not known yet, but the damage to corporate image is immense, in both Mexico and the US. On the positive side, the company has changed internal policies and procedures, which most probably will help guiding Walmart to societal acceptance. The Repsol case is exemplary about the perils of nationalization and expropriation in unstable markets. Constant evaluation of country risk is necessary for those firms established in developing economies where surprises may have costly consequences. In the absence of solid legal frameworks international managers need to be on alert for political change and use all the tools available from diplomacy, whether through official channels or from their own corporate initiative. The Shell case refers to human right violations, which are almost unheard of in developed economies. Many international managers are hesitant to take sides on those conflicts since those actions involve the host government directly. Thus, international business people face a dual interest: they need to abide to international and corporate rules that prohibit such violations, but they are pressured as well to make the operation profitable. Shell was successful in Brazil, but its image afterwards has suffered the "sugar blues".

Anglo America, in Chile, learnt the veracity behind the proverb: "a bad agreement is better than a good lawsuit". The saying proves the value of using all means of diplomacy at the disposal of the MNE that is confronting the host country, even when the local governments act disguised as state owned companies or angry citizens. In the end, Anglo American learned the lesson: copper is not forever, as happens to many other assets in countries with a tortuous legal system. The Nestlé case deals with the issue of corporate legal responsibility, raising a question: should international corporations and their head officers be held responsible when the subsidiary fails to prevent crimes, agrees to unethical practices or gets involved with individuals, officers or companies that are violating the law? The question remains unanswered. Shougan, finally had to embrace the community, after doing business carelessly for many years. This is now an expected behavior from many Chinese corporations in Latin America. In the years to come, international business people from China should learn more about their new counterparts, and this works both ways for the operation to be profitable in the long run. Globalization calls for fairness in business, new *conquistadores* are not welcome. Finally, the case of Cemex in Venezuela touches again the issue of nationalization of MNEs operating in unstable markets, especially if targeting strategic industries. The experience of the Mexican company teaches that international managers need to be on constant alert if they move in shaky grounds. This particular case had a happy ending: in fact, Cemex received a relatively fair compensation at times of financial hardship and hefty debts.

Variables were defined as follows:

1. **Role of Government:** It describes the magnitude of its intervention.
2. **MNE Reaction:** It values the management of the conflict by the MNE.
3. **Parent Country:** It reflects the support obtained through official diplomatic means.
4. **Stakeholder's Actions:** Those are the actions undertaken by actors, local or foreign, assuming an active participation in the conflict.

Categories were evaluated as weak, moderate and strong, according to the perception after reviewing available information. Lastly, a final evaluation was derived from the observed use of commercial and business diplomacy and the outcome for MNEs. There is no sufficient information as to establish logical relationships. Anyhow, Table 4 presents a subjective evaluation about the impact of the conflict and the outcome for the companies involved. It is presented for illustrative purposes.

For the comparison presented on Table 4 categories were defined as follows:

1. **Use of CD:** It shows the use of commercial (or formal diplomacy).
2. **Use of BD:** It accounts for the use of business diplomacy.
3. **Impact of Crisis:** It values the degree of importance of conflict for the MNE.
4. **Outcome for MNE:** It reflects whether the final output should be considered as negative, neutral or positive.

Table 4. Use of business diplomacy and outcome of conflicts

Country/Firm	Use of CD	Use of BD	Impact of Crisis	Outcome for MNE
Mexico/Walmart	Weak	Strong	Strong	Negative
Argentina/Repsol	Strong	Strong	Strong	Positive
Brazil/Shell	Weak	Weak	Strong	Negative
Chile/Anglo American	Weak	Strong	Moderate	Negative
Colombia/Nestlé	Weak	Weak	Weak	Neutral
Peru/Shougan	Strong	Strong	Moderate	Negative
Venezuela/Cemex	Strong	Strong	Strong	Positive

Own source.

Categories were evaluated as weak, moderate and strong as related to the use of commercial or business diplomacy, and the impact of conflict to the MNE, according to available information. Finally, we included an appraisal of the perceived outcome to the enterprise.

FINAL THOUGHTS

In order to use international business diplomacy effectively managers should possess several key abilities and talents, such as knowledge of international relations and diplomacy, multicultural mind-set, political and communication skills, analytic competencies, role versatility and tolerance for ambiguity (Saner, Yiu & Sondergaard, 2000). Above all, those in charge of international business diplomacy should have the capability of finding solutions to unexpected problems, as well as the authority to represent a corporation, may be a country, on a multiple stakeholders setting. When conflict arises, international experience may be also a great ally to business diplomats.

Those recommendations are probably universal, but as found in the cases analysed, managers require additional competencies for solving conflicts in the Latin American context. Perhaps the very start of the training for those who desire to perform business diplomacy in developing nations might be found at the OECD Guidelines for MNEs. The very existence of such a document proves the importance of the issue of corporate responsibility when conducting business overseas. As defended by Fienhold, external guidelines such as those of OECD, have greater impact that internally created codes of conduct and could be of value when facing the complexity of international business conflicts and its many consequences for MNEs (Fienhold, L., 2014). Concepts as global governance, ethics in business or corporate responsibility acquire a different dimension in foreign countries.

International business diplomacy is gaining recognition among MNEs (Ruël, 2013), not so much among small-medium enterprises. Further studies are needed in order to analyze the percentage of large companies established abroad that adhere to general guidelines for using business diplomacy and whether those protocols are internal or externally proposed, as well as the consequences to the betterment of the organization. In spite of the benefits of international business diplomacy research, this topic is relatively new. There is a clear need for additional field research, which might be conducted by future international managers, current practitioners, or scholars. Hopefully, they will be the readers of this book.

REFERENCES

Abbas, A. (2009). Managers and diplomacy. *International Journal of Commerce and Management*, *19*(4).

Anglo American. (n.d.). *At a glance – Anglo American*. Retrieved from http://angloamerican.com/about-us/at-a-glance

Ayub, M., Avila, F., & Chisholm, D. (2011). *The Basics of International Negotiation: A Student Handbook*. VDM Verlag Müller.

Barstow, D., & Xanic von Bertrab, A. (2012, December 17). The bribery aisle: How Wal-Mart got its way in Mexico. *The New York Times*. Retrieved from http://www.nytimes.com/2012/12/18/business/walmart-bribes-teotihuacan.html?pagewanted=all&_r=1

Bermejo García, R., & Garciandía Garmendia, R. (2012, December). La expropiación de YPF (Repsol) a la luz del derecho internacional. *Revista Electrónica de Estudios Internacionales*, (24). Retrieved from http://www.reei.org/index.php/revista/num24/articulos/expropiacion-ypf-repsol-luz-derecho-internacional

Cedillo, J. A. (2012, May 3). El congreso de Nuevo León señala corrupción de una tienda de Walmart. *CNN Mexico*. Retrieved from: http://mexico.cnn.com/nacional/2012/05/03/el-congreso-de-nuevo-leon-senala-corrupcion-de-una-tienda-walmart

CEMEX. (n.d.). *About Us | CEMEX*. Retrieved from http://www.cemex.com/AboutUs.aspx

Centre for Research on Multinational Corporations. (2012). *Shell: Two unresolved CSR issues in 2011*. Amsterdam, Netherlands: SOMO.

Chamoun-Nicolas, H. (2008). *Negotiate like a Phoenician: Discover Tradeables*. Keynegotiations, Llc.

Cuervo-Cazurra, A. (2010). Multilatinas. *Universia Business Review*, *25*, 138–154.

Cull, N. J. (2007). Public Diplomacy: Lessons from the Past. A report for the Public Diplomacy Group of the Foreign and Commonwealth Office, London.

Diamond, L., & McDonald, J. (1996). *Multi-Track Diplomacy: A Systems Approach to Peace*. Kumarian Press.

Economista, E. (2014, September 16). Cemex, la empresa más global de América Latina. *El Economista*. Retrieved from http://eleconomista.com.mx/industrias/2014/09/16/cemex-empresa-mas-global-americaeconomia

Ellis, R. E. (2014). *China on the ground in Latin America: Challenges for the Chinese and impacts on the region*. New York, NY: Palgrave Macmillan. doi:10.1057/9781137439772

Fienhold, L. (2014) *Risks of MNCs involved in international business diplomacy: the OECD Guidelines for Multinational Enterprises as a facilitator?* Retrieved from http://purl.utwente.nl/essays/65304

Fortune. (2014). *Shougang Group - Global 500 2014*. Retrieved from http://fortune.com/global500/shougang-group-348/

García Soto, C. A., Martínez Cerda, J. L., Torres Durán, N. I., & Pacheco Buelna, D. (2012). Estrategias financieras como generadoras de valor: El caso reciente de Cemex. *ITSON*. Retrieved from http://www.itson.mx/publicaciones/pacioli/Documents/no56/estrategiasfinancieras.pdf

Gustin, S. (2012, April 23). How big a deal is Walmart's Mexico bribery scandal? *Time*. Retrieved from http://business.time.com/2012/04/23/how-big-a-deal-is-wal-marts-mexico-bribery-scandal/

Kostecki, M., & Naray, O. (2007). Commercial diplomacy and international business. The Hague: Netherlands Institute of International Relations 'Clingendael'.

Kotschwar, B., Moran, T., & Muir, J. (2011). Do Chinese mining companies exploit more? *Americas Quarterly*. Retrieved from http://www.americasquarterly.org/do-chinese-mining-companies-exploit-more

Lee, D., & Ruël, H. (2012). Introduction: Commercial Diplomacy and International Business: Merging International Business and International Relations. In Commercial Diplomacy and International Business: A Conceptual and Empirical Exploration (9th ed.; pp. 13-19). Emerald Group Publishing Limited.

Macnamara, J. (2012). Corporate and organisational diplomacy: An alternative paradigm to PR. *Journal of Communication Management*, *16*(3), 312–325. doi:10.1108/13632541211245794

Mapendere, J. (2000). *Defining Track One-and-a-Half Diplomacy: Its Complementarity and the Analysis of Factors that Facilitate its Success*. Ottawa, Canada: Royal Roads University.

Martinez Carlevarino, P. (2012). *The Peruvian mining sector: An overview*. Retrieved from PWC website: http://www.pwc.com/ca/en/events/publications/pwc-mining-in-peru-2-2012-01-en.pdf

Montoya, M. A., & Trillas, F. (2009). The measurement of regulator independence in practice: Latin America and the Caribbean. *International Journal of Public Policy*, *4*(1/2), 113–134. doi:10.1504/IJPP.2009.021550

Naray, O. (2008). *Commercial Diplomacy: A Conceptual Overview*. 7th World Conference of TPOs. Lecture, The Hague, The Netherlands.

Negandhi, A. R., & Baliga, B. R. (1980). Multinational corporations and host governments' relationships: Comparative study of conflict and conflicting issues. *Human Relations*, *33*(8), 517–541. doi:10.1177/001872678003300801

Nestlé. (n.d.). *About us | Nestlé global*. Retrieved from http://www.nestle.com/aboutus

OIDHACO. (2012). *Violence against trade unionists in Colombia*. Retrieved from European Center for Constitutional and Human Rights website: http://www.oidhaco.org/uploaded/content/article/1969946869.pdf

Olier, E. (2011). *Geoeconomía: las claves de la economía global*. Madrid: Prentice Hall.

Ordeix-Rigo, E., & Duarte, J. (2009). From Public Diplomacy to Corporate Diplomacy: Increasing Corporation's Legitimacy and Influence. *The American Behavioral Scientist*, *53*(4), 549–564. doi:10.1177/0002764209347630

Repsol. (n.d.). *Repsol North America | Integrated oil and gas company - repsol.com*. Retrieved from http://www.repsol.com/us_en/usa/about-repsol-north-america/about-us/default.aspx

Ruël, H. (2013). *Diplomacy means business*. Retrieved from Windesheimreeks kennis en onderzoek website: http://www.windesheim.nl

Ruël, H., & Zuidema, L. (2012). *The effectiveness of commercial diplomacy; a survey among Dutch embassies and consulates*. Discussion papers in diplomacy.

Saner, R., & Yiu, L. (2001). *International economic diplomacy: mutations in post-modern times*. Retrieved from: http://clingendael.info/publications/2003/20030100_cli_paper_dip_issue84.pdf

Saner, R., Yiu, L., & Sondergaard, M. (2000). Business diplomacy management: A core competency for global companies. *The Academy of Management Perspectives*, *14*(1), 80–92. doi:10.5465/AME.2000.2909841

Satow, E. M., In Gore-Booth, P. H., & In Pakenham, D. (1979). *Satow's Guide to diplomatic practice* (5th ed.). London: Longman.

Shell. (n.d.). *The Shell global homepage - Shell Global*. Retrieved from http://www.shell.com

Shougang Group. (n.d.). *China Shougang Group | Company profile*. Retrieved from http://www.shougang.com.cn/shougang_cn_web/gsjj/index.htm

Suren, L. (2014). *International Business Diplomacy: A strategy for increasing MNC's performance? A systematic review on the basis of five European MNC's*. Retrieved from http://purl.utwente.nl/essays/65296

Szykman, S. (1995). *Diplomacy: An Historical Perspective*. Retrieved from http://www.diplom.org/Zine/S1995R/Szykman/History.html

The Economist. (2013, July 27). Flogging a dead cow. *The Economist*. Retrieved from http://www.economist.com/news/americas/21582304-recently-nationalised-oil-company-agrees-big-foreign-investment-flogging-dead-cow

The World Factbook. (2013). Washington, DC: Central Intelligence Agency. Retrieved from https://www.cia.gov/library/publications/the-world-factbook/index.html

Walmart. (n.d.). *Walmart Corporate: Our Story*. Retrieved from http://corporate.walmart.com/our-story/

Wolters, T. (2012). *Business diplomacy in multinational corporations: An exploratory qualitative study* (Master's thesis, University of Twente, Enschede, Netherlands). Retrieved from http://purl.utwente.nl/essays/62485

KEY TERMS AND DEFINITIONS

Commercial Diplomacy: The activities conducted by representatives of the diplomatic service of a given country in order to support business activities of their citizens, companies and official entities, with the purpose of fostering international trade and commerce.

Conflict Resolution: The set of strategies and tactics aimed at resolving conflicts between different parties with adversarial interests.

Diplomacy: The art of conducting official relations with sovereign nations, international institutions and organizations through negotiation, agreements and communication.

Emerging Markets: Nations making rapid progress to become developed economies. Typically are economies with high rates of growth, positive macroeconomic indicators and a promising outlook, although lagging behind advanced economies.

Foreign Direct Investment: The investment made by foreign entities in a different country, with the purpose of maintaining a long term business presence in such nation.

International Relations: The field of political science dealing with a broad range of actors relevant to the foreign affairs of a nation.

Negotiation: The process among different entities or persons by which every part involved looks to maximize its own benefit or agree to the common solution of a problem.

Stakeholders: People or entities with an interest in an organization, business venture or an issue of concern to themselves.

ENDNOTES

1. The information used to describe the seven cases was collected from abundant newspapers articles, blogs or general media coverage of the different situations, in addition to data and opinions from official reports from the companies involved. Documents were cited only if a relevant contribution was obtained from the source.
2. Laura Fienhold (2014) primarily bases the methodology for this study on previous research. Her investigation served a different purpose and the fundamentals of her methodology were more solid.

Chapter 16
Institutional Leadership and Governance:
The African Perspective

Muritala Olakitan Awodun
Kwara State University, Nigeria

ABSTRACT

This chapter, which is about institutional leadership and governance, examines leadership from the institutional perspective, but, in the African context. Context is virtually important because it shapes the opportunity structure of any time (Mayo & Nohria, 2005). The peculiarity of the African continent would require that the chapter examines leadership and governance as most of the economies of Africa are still practically dominated by government activities in so many dimensions where governance is poor. Neglecting governance therefore would mean not doing justice to the leadership context. Since leadership in context is not leadership that emerges solely from the qualities of the human character, but leadership that springs forth from an appreciation and understanding of one's situation in the world, and the situation, in this respect includes; economic, social and political conditions that change over time, and these changes require distinct leadership styles and approaches for success, the tripod of institution, leadership and governance are therefore critical for success.

1. INTRODUCTION

...Africa's most valuable resources is not its oil, it's not its diamond, it is the talent and creativity of its people. The true wealth of Africa is its more than 900 million consumers, and its countless entrepreneurs and business leaders who are already demonstrating the wealth of the continent by building successful enterprises... Mahajan, 2009

The concern of this chapter is not only about leadership but also about governance. The peculiarity of the African continent gives credence to the fact that we examine not only leadership but governance as most of the economies of Africa are still practically dominated by government activities in so many

DOI: 10.4018/978-1-5225-0276-0.ch016

dimensions and governance in the public sector has been at a significant distance from what obtains in the private sector. Neglecting governance therefore would mean not doing justice to the leadership context as should be the case (Adair, 2010).

Leadership in context is not leadership that emerges solely from the qualities of the human character, but leadership that springs forth from an appreciation and understanding of one's situation in the world. What really is this situation? It means and includes; economic, social and political conditions that change over time, and these changes require distinct leadership styles and approaches for success (Mayo & Nohria, 2005). Governance, on the other hand, is all about the exercise of power within the limits placed on leadership. In other words, governance is the exercise of the power of leadership with the sole purpose of meeting the expectations of the constituents that entrusted the leader with the responsibility of leadership.

It is therefore important to note from the onset that the concept of role is key to our understanding of leadership. We may want to begin to wonder that by origin, a role is a part taken by an actor in a play. However, and in the wider perspective that we have used the concept, it means a person's characteristic or expected function (Adair, 2010). It is from this perspective that the phrase, 'role model' emerged as a person who is regarded by others as an outstanding good example of a particular role. Thus the role of the individual is sometimes synonymous to the activities by which the leadership performance of the individual is adjudged.

Every man has the potentials of leadership. While some actualise the potentials, some others do not. At one time or another in our lives, we face the challenges of leadership and the need to tap into those potentials to address them. It is established that in the today's world, there are no limits to the opportunities that one may face or encounter. The challenges seem to be increasing, but through our various responses, and the manner of those responses, the extent of change and impact we exert on the world in which we live and work is determined (Kouzes & Posner, 2002).

This chapter in addition to the above introduction includes a theoretical framework conceptualizing institutional leadership and governance. This is followed by a background on African Leadership and Governance, and Contextualizing African Leadership as Leader of Ship or Leader of Sheep? The concept of 'Leadership Presence' is the subject of the section that follows with emergence of the concept of 'Leadership Absence' in Africa. The concluding part of this chapter is on Successful Leadership Measures and the Recipe for Africa.

2. THE THEORETICAL FRAMEWORK

The concept of leadership has changed over time. In the past, we have been told that leaders are born. This began with the premise that there was a trait that marked a leader, and originally that trait was heredity. In the African setting, this was a very prominent basis for leadership. Based on this premise, the firstborn son of a reigning king was automatically considered a leader in waiting or leadership material (Lundy, 1986; Lippit, 2002). However, history has revealed the problems with depending on bloodlines for leadership determination that it is now clear that leadership does not necessarily have to be hereditary.

As a result of the problems of relying solely on heredity to determine leadership, studies shifted from heredity trait to charisma as a basic determinant of leadership. This was also very prominent in the early days of the independent nations of Africa. Charismatic personalities emerged as the leaders of the various African states, but their performances revealed that the basis of their selection (charisma) was indeed a wrong premise of thrusting leadership on them. The charismatic leadership proposition therefore also failed the test of reality as we found situations where less charismatic leaders succeeded where charismatic individuals failed (Lippit, 1998). The charismatic theory of leadership has therefore faced its own challenges that have made it an inappropriate and unacceptable theory of leadership.

Then came, the 'invincible-hero' school of leadership which have produced case studies, biographies, and autobiographies describing how successful leaders accomplished their outstanding results. What this school proposes is that leadership lessons could be leanrnt through the study of the cases of successful leaders. However, relying on how someone has led as a basis for someone else is somehow limiting and as such cannot be relied upon in its entirety. Moreso, when there is no certainty that the study of an invincible hero could be patterned perfectly by a prospective leader. Since this approach obviously could not say who will succeed or fail until after the 'fact', its limitations in the determination of leadership also became obvious. The above limitation of the invincible hero leadership theory resulted in the emergence of the more promising method of prediction in the study of leadership, which is, the study of personal style.

The focus of leadership on personal style provided insights into how to interact and how to present information to others. This concept of personal style is significant in the sense that leaders are expected to know how to work with followers. Even when possessing a style by a leader could be helpful, however, it is not a sufficient guide. It has since been discovered that many leaders who have the same style end up with varying levels of results, hence the conclusion that style is not enough. It is one thing to know how to work with your followers, but it is another thing to actually get them to follow the style in working with them. What makes for success therefore goes beyond style, meaning style is not enough.

With the above limitation of style, the leadership theory shifted its focus to skills, knowledge and competencies as the critical components of leadership. The assumption upon which the skills and competencies theory was based is that weak results are caused by weak skills and competencies. However, under the assumption that knowledge which is a core component of this theory, could lead to the generation of a list of essential skills for developmental plans, leaders therefore started developing plans. This resulted in some improvements in leadership performances, but not uniformly. The underlying submission arising from the above therefore is that skills and competencies are helpful, but they present an incomplete picture because successful leaders never had the same key skills and competencies. Obviously too, knowledge alone does not equate leadership, hence rendering the skills and competencies approach also inadequate (Daft & Lengel, 1998; Lippit, 2002).

The limitations of the skill and competencies approach made researchers turn to innovation as the answer to the leadership question. Since organizations crave to be innovative to survive, succeed and lead, the search for a leader that can drive innovative organizations by leading innovation therefore becomes a preferred option. In the words of Hill, Brandeau, Truelove and Lineback (2011):

Innovation is a team sport where individual efforts of members of the organization are combined as separate slices of genius into a single work of collective genius.

Thus an innovative leader is regarded as one who understands the nature of innovation and how it works, and so can appreciate that alone they cannot force it to happen or make it happen. Leadership is about "setting the stage" – that is, creating a place where people are willing and able to innovate time and again, and the leader not performing on it but rather allowing his followers to perform after having identified them but providing direction and keeping the identified followers focused on the vision.

In other words, instead of trying to come up with a vision and make innovation happen, a leader of innovation creates a place – a context, an environment – where people are willing and able to do the hard work that innovative problem solving requires. This seems to be the leadership context that appears most acceptable and most successful in this age and time where competition is global and stiff, and no organization or nation can ignore another as we all compete in the global environment.

It is safe to conclude therefore that leadership is not a trait or a matter of intelligence. Leadership is the ability to set a realistic direction, develop effective plans, get others to implement the plans, and measure results. Too frequently leadership is equated to vision, but we know that vision without implementation is hallucination. Therefore vision does not equal leadership as words do not equal accomplishment. Leadership is therefore all about creating a way for people to contribute to making something extraordinary happen, and this would be our adopted position of leadership as it captures our focus on institutional leadership and governance appropriately.

Leaders need an explicit framework to broaden their mind-set, encourage examination of options, and produce results. Leaders are usually bombarded with concerns, problems and demands, and they want solutions, preferably quickly and cheaply. Wishing for a simple answer, however, will not make a leader appear or make it work if it appears. Solutions are part of a complicated environment, and they are never simple. Leaders must focus on results to achieve them, hence this chapter will draw from the results-driven Leadership Spectrum Framework of Awodun & Ajia (2012).

3. THE LEADERSHIP SPECTRUM FRAMEWORK

A spectrum is visible when electromagnetic waves pass through a prism revealing colours. As light is spread out, the colours become visible. The array has no gaps or missing shades, otherwise reality will be distorted (Lippit, 2002). A prism, however, cannot disperse light into anything less than the full spectrum. Likewise a leader must consider the full spectrum or the entire range of priorities before setting goals. The Leadership Spectrum Framework properly targets attention and direction. Letting one priority go unnoticed means losing talent, ignoring quality, losing market share, or burning through venture capital too rapidly. The Leadership Spectrum Framework is therefore results oriented as it is a model that pays attention to the entire organization for results. The results-driven Leadership Spectrum Framework must therefore include each of the following seven priorities:

1. **Inventor:** Developing new products or services.
2. **Catalyst:** Winning, serving and retaining customers.
3. **Developer:** Developing supportive infrastructure & system.
4. **Performer:** Focusing on processes, efficiencies and quality.
5. **Protector:** Building work culture and developing people.
6. **Challenger:** Scanning the future and seizing opportunities.
7. **Innovator:** Creating a work environment that elicits, combines and converts the individual capacities into collective genius.

None of the above seven priorities can be neglected by any leader that intends to succeed and it is from this point of view that this chapter will examine leadership and governance in Africa. How often do leaders in Africa, whether in private or government institutions develop new products or services, in the course of their leadership that may qualify such leader to be classified as an inventor?

Also the ability of the leadership of the African institutions (private or public) to serve and retain their customers that may qualify such leadership to be categorized as a catalyst is considered along with the efforts to develop supportive infrastructure and systems that qualifies the leadership as a developer. The concern of the leadership on processes, efficiencies and quality for which they may be termed performer would be examined. Of concern also is the ability to build skills, work culture and develop people that make them a protector would be discussed.

The scanning ability of the future and emerging opportunities requiring strategic decisions that may be the basis that will qualify the leadership of any institution to be seen as a challenger; i.e. possessing the capacity to face unprecedented challenges that may result in a vicious cycle of stress and sacrifices, with little or no recovery time built in (Boyatzis & McKee, 2005). On a final note is the ability to create an innovative work environment that would bring the collective genius of the organization to play on the stage set by the leadership is what qualifies a leader to be classified as an innovator.

4. BACKGROUND ON AFRICAN LEADERSHIP AND GOVERNANCE

Africa Leaders have recognized that the public image of Africa has not kept up with the optimism and expectations of the entire world on the continent. This position is rightly reflected in the following quotation of the South African President:

We should do the branding properly to tell this very, very positive story. (Thabo Mbeki, World Economic Forum on Africa, Cape Town, 2006)

What could possibly be responsible for this position? We need not be told that most African countries are, from the neutral stuff perspective, the wealthiest countries in the world with their rich natural and mineral resources supported with good climate and soil conditions that are more than adequate for agriculture. In addition, some of these countries are equally rich in intellectual capital but most of their best brains are evidently scattered all around the world due to lack of infrastructure within their various countries that could optimally utilize their various potentials. The irony of the above natural wealth is that these African countries are heavily underdeveloped and their standard of living is relatively low. Hence they are ranked amongst the poorest nations of the world. There is abject poverty as most of the population of Africa live on less than $2 a day. Corruption is flagrantly celebrated and development is relatively slow as the nations of Africa suffer from political instability all as a result of poor leadership and bad governance.

Africa and its nations are therefore in need of leaders that can lift the nations out of the rubbles of poverty, underdevelopment, political instability, among others. The African nations need leaders who are credible, selfless, visionary, skilful, compassionate, and determined to turn the huge potentials existing in the 'so called' problems of Africa into possibilities. Such leadership is required both in the private (business) and public (government) sectors of the economies of the nations of African. However, it is not as if there are no leaders with these qualities in Africa, but there are not enough of them, particularly in the public (government) sector where the resources of Africa are entrusted in the hands of people who are lacking in the required qualities of leadership, hence the under-performance seen all over the length and breadth of African nations. There are however exceptional situations that are worthy of being singled out as presented below, particularly people in private enterprises.

In Africa, entrepreneurship has been the driving force for growth as is generally the case in countries around the world. The ability of entrepreneurs to see opportunities, where others only see problems, has helped transform communities and economies all over the world, Africa inclusive. As rightly pointed out by Richard Branson in his foreword to the book; *Africa's Greatest Entrepreneurs*,

One of the most exciting places where this entrepreneurial spirit is very alive is across Africa. I've had the great privilege to be involved in several new businesses in Africa and I'm constantly amazed by the incredible energy, determination and innovation coming from entrepreneurs across the continent. (Makura, 2008)

This position confirms that the continent is not lacking in leadership in the business circle but lacking more in leadership and governance in the public circle.

As has been earlier established, leadership is about organizing a group of people to achieve a common goal. It is about guiding others into a new and better experience. It comes with a responsibility to deliver in line with the expectations of the people. This responsibility is saddled on the leader who can be likened to the pilot of an airplane (or captain of a ship), given the responsibility to skilfully fly a plane (or sail a ship) full of people using the laws of aerodynamics to overcome the laws of gravity. Without the leader, who in this case is the pilot (or captain), and the plane (or ship) which we can liken to the organization, the people are purely subjected to the law of gravity (low level living). However, with a leader in the true sense to chart the course and steer the plane, the laws of aerodynamics (high flying) is put into motion, making it possible for both the leader and the led to climb higher and operate at an altitude where only eagles operate (Fola-Alade, 2012).

Also established is the fact that leadership is an identifiable set of skills and practices available to all of us and not just a set of people. This is because the traits (characteristics) of leadership, as will be enumerated later in this chapter, are present (though in diverse quantities) in each of us. Moreover, these characteristics could be worked on to improve on them by anyone that so desire. This therefore confirms the fact that leadership is not lacking in Africa or in Africans. Leadership is a relationship between those who aspire to lead and those who choose to follow. Success in leadership, business or life remains a function of how well people work, live and play together. Successful leadership depends wholly on the capacity to build and sustain those human relationships that enable people to get extra-ordinary things done on a regular basis.

From the above position, it is appropriate to conclude that leadership is not about personality but about practice. In this regard, Kouzes & Posner (2002) looking into the dynamic process of leadership uncovered five practices common to what they termed 'personal-best leadership experience'. For a leader to succeed, he/she is therefore expected to:

- **Model the Way:** Through exemplary behaviours, find your voice, voice your values and act your values.
- **Inspire a Shared Vision:** By envisioning the future and enlisting others in shared vision.
- **Challenge the Process:** Seeking for opportunities, innovating change, experimenting and taking risks.
- **Enable Others to Act:** Fostering collaboration, teamwork and building trust.
- **Encourage the Heart:** Encourage, appreciate, and celebrate by linking reward with performance.

Having defined leadership as a reciprocal process between those who aspire to lead and those who choose to follow, it could therefore be examined within the precept of the five practices above. It is obvious that leadership requires modelling the way to go through exemplary behaviours, envisioning the future and enlisting followers inspired by a shared vision. It involves challenging the process through innovation, experimentation and risk taking, building trust and fostering collaboration through teamwork, and linking reward to performance.

The above five practices are further expressed in the form of ten commitments of leadership presented as the behavioural skills set of leadership, and these are subsequently regarded as the essentials of leadership which leaders that aspire to be successful must possess, and if lacking, endeavour to acquire.

However, those to be led (the constituents) also have their sets of expectations that balance the relationship already established. These expectations are captured in a set of twenty characteristics of admired leaders which represents what people look for and admire in their leaders. The constituents' expected characteristics from their leaders are; honesty, forward-looking, competence, inspiration, intelligence, fair-minded, broad-minded, supportive, straightforwardness, dependable, cooperative, determined, imaginative, ambitious, courageous, caring, maturity, loyalty, self-control, and independent-minded.

The foundational characteristics upon which leadership expectations are built, from the constituents' perspective, is credibility and this is based on the first four of the above listed twenty characteristics:

- Honesty.
- Forward-looking.
- Competence.
- Inspiration.

These foundational characteristics are what, based on assumption seem to be very low in the context of Leadership in Africa when compared to other parts of the world.

5. CONTEXTUALIZING AFRICAN LEADERSHIP: LEADER OF SHIP OR LEADER OF SHEEP?

The principles of leadership, in the African context, are not significantly different from what it is across the world and in all other continents. However, leadership perspective or the societal perspective of leadership when examined may appear quite different from the norm. What has predominated in the African societies in the past could be seen as quite diverse from the western context hence my poser thus in a public presentation: 'leader of ship or leader of sheep?' (Awodun, 2014) While the former may appropriately describe the known concept of leadership, the latter describes otherwise. It is in the context of the latter that institutional leadership and governance in Africa is viewed in this chapter.

As we have rightly established, leadership is a relationship between the leader and the led. This relationship requires some practices from the leader which are in form of commitments earlier identified. At the same time the led are full of expectations from the leader and these expectations have been contextualized in the form of the twenty characteristics also earlier identified. It is based on this relational process that the leadership context in Africa is examined.

We also have established that for the above relationship to be possibly seen accomplished, there must exist an organization where the leader and the led both belong, a stage of performance. However the organization which provides the platform for leadership could be in form of a ship with the captain sailing the entire people in the ship to their agreed destination. The people in the ship however are sailing along with the captain based on some agreed purpose, set goals and objectives with the expectation that the captain has the credibility, knowledge, skills and competencies to sail them successfully to their agreed destination.

However, there is also the scenario of a shepherd who in his own right is a leader of sheep. However, in this case, the sheep are not consciously involved in determining or setting the purpose, goals and objectives and therefore merely accepts and follows the shepherd to the destination that the shepherd so decides. Since there is no involvement of the sheep in determining the end in the first instance, the sheep only accepts whatever is the decision of the shepherd without any ability to complain since there is no expected end from the led in the first instance.

What is witnessed in most African nations, particularly in the public sector is similar to the shepherd and the sheep. The pattern of relationship is such that the populace have little or nothing to say as per the determination of their expectations from their leaders, and as such only accept whatever level of performance without subjecting them to any form of performance assessment afterwards. The situation in the public sector of most African nations is therefore that of the shepherd and the sheep with the leader more of that of sheep than that of a ship.

Otherwise, how do you explain the case of a public servant entrusted with the responsibility of leading a government institution and mis-applying the institution's funds without any form of challenge whatsoever from either within the institution or from outside. The public expectations from the leadership in African nations are dismally low, and the ability to ask for or conduct a performance assessment of leaders for proper accountability of the responsibility accorded the leadership is practically absent. It is this structural defect that makes it inappropriate to see the situation in most African nations not as that of leader-ship but leader-sheep.

If governance is about the exercise of power within the limits placed on leadership, then good governance is therefore identified with the presence of strong institutions and processes as a result of the responsible use of the power of governance. The society where good governance predominates delivers beneficial outcomes to its constituents, meaning therefore that societies where such institutions, processes and systems are weak is a function of weak/poor leadership and governance. The impact of the absence of good leadership and governance in African nations cannot be better revealed than in a country like Nigeria where the institutions are deliberately weakened and flagrant failures to establish the rule of law and order in most cases. Despite the huge natural and mineral resources of the country, there is obvious institutional failure as most infrastructure are in very bad state unable to support business and commercial activities capable of promoting growth and development.

The African Leader-sheep situation is glaringly displayed as institutional structures are either absent or where they are present, not operational or ineffective. The constituents accept whatever level of performance moving on as if nothing is wrong, hence from leader to leader, the situation gets worse. The peculiarity of the African Leader-sheep is therefore something that is worthy of special attention for us to understand why this peculiarity and what can be done to correct it.

6. 'LEADERSHIP PRESENCE' AND 'LEADERSHIP ABSENCE' IN AFRICA

In the book *Leadership Presence*, Halpern and Lubar (2003), co-founders of the Ariel Group wrote:

Great actors have it. Great political leaders have it too, as do great business executives... But it's not limited to people in mighty positions. Your local pizza guy may have it. Your doctor may have it. Your daughter's piano teacher may have it too. All these people -well known or not- are compelling individuals who attract your attention almost effortlessly. They have something, a magnetism that pulls others to them. When they enter the room, the energy level rises. You perk up, stop what you're doing, and focus on them. You expect something interesting to happen. It's as though a spotlight shines on them. What is it they have? They have presence. (p. 1)

Halpern & Lubar (2003) thought of presence in a different and deeper way than what is expressed above. They saw presence as the ability to connect authentically with the thoughts and feelings of others. Most people think you are born with presence, or without it, or that circumstances lead you, if you're lucky, to develop it at an early age. And if the right circumstances never quite align? Well, too bad. But we were made to realize that presence is the result of certain ongoing choices you make, the results of actions you take or fail to take. Presence was presented by them as a set of skills, both internal and external, that virtually anyone can develop and improve.

Presence in leadership is the dramatic techniques to reach out, motivate and inspire others. It is the ability to effectively connect with the aspirations and expectations of the constituents. The leaders without presence is completely disconnect from the led and cannot therefore deliver to the satisfaction of the people. Leadership presence reveals what great leaders have always known: that the secret to having a commanding presence is not about personal power, but about empowering others. What is obvious is that leaders with presence would have set agenda, goals and objectives in line with the expectations of the people because of his established relationship with the people through his presence.

On the other hand, a leader without presence would be setting goals and objectives completely different from the expectations of the people because of his or her disconnect from the people, or lack of presence. It is therefore appropriate to refer to the situation where the leader is not connected to the led as a state of 'leadership absence', and this is what predominates in most of the African nations.

Looking at the African leadership situation and performance of most African leaders of the public sector, what is obviously seen is leadership absence as the various leaders are completely not connected to the constituents. This is because most of the leaders pursue goals that are of personal interests as against the people's interest. These goals are set in the first instance, because of the obvious disconnect between the leaders and the led.

The case of the North Africa crisis started by the so-called Jasmine Revolution initially ignited by public outrage over the self immolation of a street vendor, Mohammed Mouazizi, on December 17, 2010 would be just appropriate at this point. Even when the President, Zine El Abidine Ben Ali a month after, specifically on January 14, 2011 stepped down, his decision was far from abating the revolutionary fervor against the rule of privileged elites in Tunisia. The crisis got stronger and eventually spread to the most of the Middle East. This revolutionary fire engulfed Hosni Mubarak, who also had ruled Egypt with a tight grip for almost thirty years as he was ousted on February 11, 2011 with the crisis spreading to Libya, Syria, and Yemen.

What is obvious about the crisis is the complete disconnect from the people by the leaders of these nations, the fruit of which is the abject poverty of the people as a result of the poor leadership and governance in these countries as the leaders fail to govern to meet the expectations of the people. Taking the case of Egypt in particular, an average Egyptian has an income level of about 12 percent of the average citizen of the United States of America. Life expectancy in Egypt is about ten years less than that of United States of America as 20 percent of the Egyptian population is in dire poverty. Why is Egypt poor or poorer than some other developed countries? The answer to this question is directly linked to the leadership question as some of the Egyptians themselves said about their problems as presented by Acemoghu & Robinson (2012):

We are suffering from corruption, oppression and bad education. We are living amid a corrupt system which has to change. I hope that by the end of this year we will have an elected government and that universal freedoms are applied and that we put an end to the corruption that has taken over this country.

The protesters all spoke in one voice against corruption of the government and inability of public officers to deliver public services, as well as lack of equality of opportunity. These protests are the extreme state of leadership disconnect evidenced by lack of leadership presence which we have come to term 'leadership absence'. The leaders have failed repeatedly to align with the goals and aspirations of the constituents and after several oppression and suppression of the people's wish, the bubble eventually burst and the leadership fell apart.

What lessons are there for us as Africans? The leaders of Africa must connect appropriately with the people. Leadership presence must be adopted as leaders must govern to ensure that the people's expectations are met. Failure to do so will sooner than later result in leadership failure once the institutional failure is established. The predominant pursuit of leadership absence by our leaders for their selfish interests should be dropped for leadership presence in the interest of all and the good of the continent.

It is in the light of the above that we can look forward to that situation when, both in the private and the public sectors of Africa, the leadership context would require, as presented above, the five legged leadership characteristics while the followership expectations of leadership will exhibit the twenty leadership characteristics. The basis of leadership in Africa could therefore be established as would be put across in the next section of this chapter.

7. SUCCESSFUL LEADERSHIP MEASURES AND RECIPE FOR AFRICA

Strong leadership may be the most important factor in an organization's success, because what happens at the top (of the company, group, team, or squad) has an impact on everything else. If the leader's attitude is poor, the team's attitude will follow. Be it a Fortune 500 company, a small business, a nonprofit, an infantry platoon, a school, a community, a family, or any other group that has a common purpose, leadership matters (Crandall, 2007).

Are you successful as a leader? Before you answer, consider this scenario painted by Eric G. Kail (2007):

I am looking for a master carpenter to produce a handcrafted wooden desk for you as a token of appreciation for all you have done for the organization. This is not just any desk, but a great desk that reflects the strength and integrity of both giver and recipient. I have selected a master carpenter based on the quality of the products of his labor. By selecting this carpenter to build your desk, I passed up other carpenters with more impressive woodworking power tools and state-of-the-art showrooms. I also ignored some carpenters who have created thousands of production-line desks in their manufacturing plants. These others are very efficient, but to them, your desk was just another dollar figure in their profit margins. The bottom line is that I judged each carpenter by evaluating the wood on which they labored, not the carpenters themselves or their tools. (pp. 4-5)

That brings us back to the original question. Are you a successful leader developer? Along with managing resources and setting direction for your group or unit, you have a responsibility to develop your subordinate leaders (Kail, 2007).

As leaders, we often place heavy emphasis on the bottom line and our personal accomplishments. But think ahead to your retirement dinner or ceremony: Would you prefer a slide show and handouts detailing all the deals you made, complete with statistics and charts demonstrating your prowess at leading within the organization, or do you want to share one last evening with those whose lives your leadership changed? These are the people who will carry on in your place primarily because of your investment in their lives. One of the most important things you can do as a leader is to develop other leaders. Those leaders will affect hundreds, if not thousands, of other people.

African leaders must realize that leadership is a relationship between the leader and the led, and this relationship can be established with leadership presence. In doing so, African leaders must recognize the fact that the constituents have expectations and their performance would be measured in terms of the constituents' expectations. The impact of leadership must be felt through their presence as the present situation of leadership pursuit of personal interests and agenda at the expense of national interests and agenda which we have termed as leadership absence should stop as the continent consciously develop leaders that would see the transformation of the huge potentials of the continent as their uppermost priority for the benefit of all.

The leadership challenge for Africa is a responsibility of each and every African as Africa is in desperate need of leadership that will model the way, inspire the shared vision, challenge the process, enable others to act, encourage the heart and be present, and not absent. This is our collective responsibility as we take up the challenge to lead in every endeavor of life to make Africa great. We all therefore have roles to play in the leadership challenge that is facing the continent today, and it is by each and every one of us playing our roles in line with the stated principles and practices presented in this chapter that the expected development of our nations could be realized.

All the world's a stage,
And all the men and women merely players.
They have their exits and their entrances;
And one man in his time plays many parts....
(William Shakespeare, As You Like It)

REFERENCES

Acemoglu, D., & Robinson, J. (2012). *Why Nations Fail: The Origins of Power, Prosperity and Poverty*. New York: Crown Business.

Adair, J. (2010). *The Leadership of Muhammad*. London: Kogan Page.

Awodun, M. O. (2014). *Leader of Ship or Leader of Sheep*. Paper presented at a Youth Forum in Ilorin, Kwara State, Nigeria.

Awodun, M. O., & Ajia, A. (2012). Leaders are Born and Made. In M. O. Awodun (Ed.), *Statecraft: Laying the Foundation for Modern Development*. Kwara State, Nigeria: Kwara State University Press.

Boyatzis, R. E., & McKee, A. (2005). *Resonant Leadership*. Boston: Harvard Business School Press.

Crandall, D. (Ed.). (2007). *Leadership Lessons from West Point*. John Willey & Sons.

Daft, R. L., & Lengel, R. H. (1998). *Fusion Leadership: Unlocking the Subtle Forces that Change People and Organizations*. San Francisco, CA: Berrett Koehler Publishers.

Fola-Alade, S. (2012). *How to Become a Leader in Your Field: The Keys to Your Next Level Influence*. Empowerment Initiative Limited.

Halpern, B. L., & Lubar, K. (2003). *Leadership Presence*. Gotham Books.

Hill, L. A., Brandeau, G., Truelove, E., & Lineback, K. (2011). *Collective Genius: The Art and Practice of Leading Innovation*. Boston: Harvard Business Review Press.

Hill, L. A., & Lineback, K. (2011). *Being the Boss: The 3 Imperatives for Becoming a Great Leader*. Harvard Business Review Press.

Kail, E. G. (2007). Becoming a Leader Developer. In Leadership Lessons from West Point. John Wiley & Sons.

Kouzes, J. M., & Posner, B. Z. (2002). *The Leadership Challenge*. John Wiley & Sons.

Lippit, M. B. (1998). *The Leadership Spectrum Profile: Targeting Enterprise Priorities*. Potomac, MD: Enterprise Management.

Lippit, M. B. (2002). *The Leadership Spectrum*. Davies-Black Publishing.

Lundy, J. L. (1986). *Lead, Follow, or Get Out of the Way: Leadership Strategies for the Thoroughly Modern Manager*. San Diego, CA: Slawson Communications.

Mahajan, V. (2009). *Africa Rising: How 900 Million African Consumers offer more than you think*. Pearson Education.

Makura, M. (2008). *Africa's Greatest Entrepreneurs*. Penguin Books.

Mayo, A. J., & Nohria, N. (2005). *Their Times: The Greatest Business Leaders of the Twentieth Century*. Harvard Business School Press.

Sachs, J. D. (2008). *Common Wealth: Economics for a Crowded Planet*. The Penguin Press.

KEY TERMS AND DEFINITIONS

Governance: The exercise of power within the limits placed on leadership. In other words, governance is the exercise of the power of leadership with the sole purpose of meeting the expectations of the constituents that entrusted the leader with the responsibility of leadership.

Institutional Leadership: Is about organizing a group of people, within a set up, to achieve a common goal. It is about guiding others into a new and better experience and it comes with a responsibility to deliver in line with the expectations of the people.

Leadership: A relationship between those who aspire to lead and those who choose to follow. It is therefore a reciprocal process between the leader and the led (follower).

Leadership Absence: On the other hand, is the case of a leader setting goals and objectives that are completely different from the expectations of the people, because of his or her disconnect from the people, or what is called lack of presence.

Leadership Presence: Refers to the dramatic techniques to reach out, motivate and inspire others by a person saddled with the responsibility to lead. It is the ability to effectively connect with the aspirations and expectations of the constituents by a leader.

Role Model: A person who is regarded by others as an outstanding good example of a particular role.

Roles: Refer to a person's characteristic or expected function within a particular setting.

Chapter 17
Operational Structure of Multinational Enterprises in Africa

Edet E. Okon
University of Uyo, Nigeria

ABSTRACT

The operational structures of Multinational Enterprises (MNEs) in Africa, a developing and emerging economy do not necessarily differ from those of the developed or even Less Developed Economies (LDEs) except in few areas such as size and capital outlay. Meanwhile, both MNEs of African origin and those which originate from outside Africa do have salient attributes: they have many foreign affiliates or subsidiaries in foreign countries; they operate in a wide variety of countries around the globe; the proportion of assets, revenues, or profits is high; their employees, stockholders, owners, and managers are from many different countries; and they are involved in much more than merely establishing sales office, but incorporate a full range of manufacturing, research and development activities. This chapter examined operational structures of MNEs with focus on meaning, attributes, financing, exchange rate risk and international financial investment, strategies for improved financing and outlay of MNEs in selected African countries.

INTRODUCTION

African countries continue to experience growth in multinational enterprises which has equally been observed to play a major role in the development of Africa's economy. Multinational Enterprises in Africa dates back to the nineteenth century during the European domination of African territories, where the author is of the opinion that the colonial powers were out for their business exploit mainly to secure materials for their manufacturing industries. This prompted the establishment of foreign branches of MNEs, the headquarters, which already exist in their home countries in Europe or elsewhere in the world. Other factors played as 'raison d'etre' for establishing MNEs in Africa. These include market expansion and technological advancement. Currently, many MNEs indigenous to Africa have sprang-up

DOI: 10.4018/978-1-5225-0276-0.ch017

as a result of globalization with its competitiveness in businesses that are internationally-oriented. The existence of MNEs in Africa, be it of African origin or foreign-based and the spate at which MNEs is expanding in this region largely contribute to the development of Africa's economy; which, at best in global ranking is described as developing.

In order to give more attention to the growth and development of African economy, African countries have come together to form African Multinational Enterprises (AMNEs) at the level of public, private or mixed sectors. AMNEs refer basically to enterprises owned and controlled by more than one African country. The motive behind the formation of AMNEs is for analysis of economic development in Africa with an assessment of regional cooperation and industrial organization. Thus, the pattern of growth – macro and structural – of the African economy; present sub-regional arrangements; potential sources of financing are deciphered in addition to an overview of MNEs and Africa's economy; operational meaning and importance of MNEs and expansion of African economy are the major focus of this chapter.

BACKGROUND

The world of business is changing and we are now witnessing the beginning of the end of old economic order which has for decades been dominated by the triad economies (US, Europe and Japan). The new economic order is a multi-polar world characterized by multiple centres of economic power and activity (Accenture, 2007). What is most important change about this new order is the remarkable rise of emerging market multinationals (EMMs) while the share and influence of multinational companies from developed countries is declining. Fan (2008) asserts that the market intelligence has become more globalized than ever and this is a major challenge to most multinational organizations around the world. It is also important to note that market development can be viewed from the perspective of multinationals from developed countries and those from emerging markets. Fan (2008) argues that emerging markets multinational firms are more aggressive and ambitious in their operations and are likely to take western multinationals by storm just as Japanese companies did in the late 1970s. These emerging market multinationals are largely from Latin America, Asia Pacific and South Africa.

Mthombeni (2006) described a Multinational enterprises (MNEs), also known as Multinational corporation/company (MNC), Transnational corporation, and by many other names as a "firm that owns or controls income-generating assets in more than one country." The author further posited that a transnational corporation would probably be achieved by linking the firm or company to the form of trade it engages in. Hence, MNE is a company that has established an international presence by engaging in foreign direct investment (FDI). This differs from general trade because FDI represents the physical extension of operations and the investment of equity funds and stock in several countries.

The degree of multi-nationality of firms, Spero and Hart (2003) highlighted as:

1. They have many foreign affiliates or subsidiaries in foreign countries;
2. They operate in a wide variety of countries around the globe;
3. The proportion of assets, revenues, or profits is high;
4. Their employees, stockholders, owners, and managers are from many different countries; and
5. They are involved in much more than merely establishing sales office, but incorporate a full range of manufacturing, research and development activities.

Grunberg (2001) described MNEs as economic firm that have their head offices in their country of origin (their home country) and produce or distribute products or services in foreign countries (the host country) where they establish a branch or affiliate. According to Nickels, McHUGH and McHUGH (2002), a multinational corporation (either multinational enterprise) is an organization that manufactures and markets products in many different countries and has multinational stock ownership and multinational management. Akpan (2003) defined a multinational company (MNC), also known as multinational enterprise (MNE) as a company that does business and has assets in two or more countries. In the words of Rugman and Hodgetts (2003), a multinational enterprise (MNE) is a company that is headquartered in one country but has operations in one or more other countries. The author noted that multinationals often downplay the fact that they are foreign-held as their names may not necessarily indicate where they originate. This also portrays that many large MNEs have world holdings far beyond that which is known to the casual observer, yet these companies have dramatic impact on the quality of the goods and services being produced around the world.

The motivation to invest capital in a foreign country is to provide a return in excess of that obtained domestically. Expansion into foreign markets is the reason for most investment abroad. Other reasons include securing the necessary raw materials, generating foreign exchange, lowering operating costs. Pugel (2007) viewed MNE as a firm that owns and controls operations in more than one country. The parent firm in the MNE is the headquarters or base firm, located in the home country of MNE. The parent firm has one or more affiliates (subsidiaries or branches) located in one or more host countries. Pinelo (1973) described a multinational corporation as one that does most of its business across national boundaries.

Multinational Enterprises have economic power, especially when comparing the annual sales of multinational companies with the Gross Domestic Products (GDP) of some nations. In most cases, the annual sales of MNEs can be larger than the GDP of some nations. This is clear evidence that MNEs offer careers for global businesses. In other words, MNEs are typically extremely large corporations; but not all large firms involved in global businesses are multinationals. For instance, a business could literally be exporting everything it produces, thus delivering 100 per cent of its sales and profits globally, and still not be a multinational corporation. Only firms that have manufacturing capacity or some other physical presence in different nations can truly be called multinational. Needham and Drainsfield (2000) noted that MNEs are mainly Public Limited Companies (PLCs). A multinational is a company with its headquarters in one country but with operations in other countries. Needham and Drainsfield reported

Figure 1. The triad 'bloc' of MNEs
Source: Modified from Needham, D. & Drainsfield, R (2000)

Table 1. The world's largest 500 multinational enterprises, 2000

Country	No. of MNEs
United States	185
European Union	141
Japan	104
Canada	15
China	12
Switzerland	11
South Korea	11
Autralia	7
Brazil	3
Rusia	2
Norway	2
Mexico	2
Venezuela	1
South Africa	1
Singapore	1
Malaysia	1
India	1
TOTAL	500

Source: Rugman and Hodgetts (2003), adapted from Fortune, the Future Global 500, 2001.

that there are over 12,000 MNEs, the largest 500 which account for over 80 per cent of the world's foreign direct investment. Again, some 434 of the world's top 500 MNEs are from what is referred to as the triad blocs of the European Union, Japan and the USA as illustrated in Figure 1.

Similarly, Rugman and Hodgetts (2003) reported that over 60,000 MNEs with largest 500 account for 80 per cent of all worlds' foreign direct investment. Unfortunately, of this number Africa has only one, represented by South Africa. Although the number may change between the year 2000 and 2015, it is observed that there is still an imbalance in the spread of MNEs across the world, with Africa still at the bottom line. A breakdown of these 500 largest multinationals is given on Table 1.

A multinational enterprise has two major areas of concern, namely the home country of its headquarters and host countries which it operates. A multinational enterprise is able to draw on a common pool of resources, including assets, patents, trademarks, information and people. Salient features of MNEs include the fact that the affiliates must be responsive to important environmental factors. These include competitors, customers, suppliers, financial institutions and government. Environmental factors can affect both the home and host country environments. MNEs can use the same suppliers overseas that they employ domestically and it is common to find home country-based suppliers following their MNE customers to other geographic locals in order to provide the same types of services worldwide.

MNEs can draw on a common pool of resources, including assets, patents, trademarks, information, and human resources. The affiliates are parts of the same company, hence, will have access to assets that are often not available to outsiders. In this case, different companies can compete vigorously in the same environment. For instance, both Ford and General Motors compete vigorously in Europe and many of the design and styling changes developed for their European cars have now been introduced in US models.

MNEs can link together the affiliates and business partners with a common strategic vision. In this case, the firms with whom the MNE works fit into the company's overall plan of what it wants to do and how it intends to go about implementing the strategy. Companies, therefore, strife to become MNEs for a number of reasons: one of the reasons being to diversify themselves against the risks and uncertainties of the domestic business cycle. By setting up operations in another country, MNEs can often diminish the negative effects of economic swings in the home country. This is a form of diversification. Companies also strive to become MNEs in order to tap the growing world market for goods and services. This is part of the process of growth in an integrated world market, sometimes called "globalization" (the rapid growth of similar goods and services produced and distributed by MNEs on a worldwide scale).

Further, firms can strive to become MNEs in response to increased foreign competition and a desire to protect their home market share. Most MNEs establish operations in the home countries of their major competitors. This strategy serves a dual purpose – it takes away business from their competitors by offering customers other choices, and it lets the competitors know that if they attack the MNEs' home market, they will face a similar response.

Companies also become MNEs in order to reduce costs. Such costs include transportation; overheads that would have warranted through the middlemen, among others. The operation of businesses as MNEs help to tap local resources, make rapid and adequate response to customers' needs and take advantage of local resources through a process known as "internationalization" of control within the MNE, thus, there is cost reduction.

Multinational enterprises also have the ability to overcome tariff and non-tariff barriers by serving a foreign market from within. This is most likely to be when MNE operate within the same region. Within Africa for instance, MNEs of the continent's origin and operating within the region can promote free movement of factors of production without paying tariff.

MNE IN SELECTED COUNTRIES IN AFRICA

South African MNCs

According to Taal (2014), South African companies continue to be expanding into the African continent and are experiencing better growth prospects. South Africa's economy is seen as slow to stagnant in comparison to some countries to the north and much like MNCs from abroad, South African MNCs have noticed a growing urbanized population looking for convenience and accessibility. Those companies that are succeeding are those that recognize not just the new wealth of Africa, but the workers, lower income earners who also consider themselves urban consumers. A report in respect of the retail industry showed that in 2010, 25.7 percent of South Africa's overall merchandise export basket was destined for other African markets. By the first half of 2014, this ratio had increased to 30 percent. Therefore, for many South African retailers the future looks to be firmly to the north. In some cases the companies are only hosted in one country outside of South Africa on the African continent. In most cases the bulk of those companies foreign affiliates are offshore – such as is the case with Sappi with a strong presence in North America and Europe, and Network Healthcare Holdings, that has many operations in the United Kingdom. These off-continent operations are not yet tracked. Perhaps, in coming years it would be prudent to do so. Standard Bank Group is present in its various forms in the most countries, nineteen with Shoprite, the pioneer in African expansion, still in sixteen countries. Evidently Mauritius is no longer a favored

Table 2. Egyptian TNCs

Company	Sector
Abu Qir Fertilizers and Chemical Industries	Chemical and chemical products
Al Chark Insurance C0.	Insurance
Alexandria Minerals Oils Co.	Food products, beverages, and tobacco
Alexandria National Iron and Steel co.	Iron and steel
Aluminum Co. Of Egypt	Iron and steel
American Group for Food	Diversified group
ASEC Cement Co.	Building materials
Delta Industrial Company	Engineering
Eastern Co.	Diversified group
Egypt Air	Air transport
Egyptian Aluminum Products Co.	Aluminum
Egyptian cement Co.	Building materials

(Afribiz, 2010)

destination for investment having dropped from three to one company operation. Kenya has also disappeared from the list of South African Multinational destinations, the local companies, it seems proving dominant in their own markets are Swaziland, Zambia Botswana, Lesotho, Ghana, Mozambique, Namibia, Tanzania, Malawi, Nigeria, Uganda, Zimbabwe, Mauritius, Angola, DRC, Guinea, Mali. Host to two companies include: Congo, Kenya, Madagascar, and South Sudan. Host to one company include: Benin, Cameroon, Côte d'Ivoire, Guinea-Bissau, Ivory Coast, Liberia, Mauritania, Rwanda, Sénégal, Sierra Leone, and Sudan. Although the assets will remain, they will be wholly foreign-owned and controlled.

Transnational Corporations in Egypt

Transnational corporations (TNC), which originate in Egypt, are listed below (see Table 2).

Nigeria

Nigeria has been a focus for international business investment because of its potential for market expansion as the most populated nation on the African continent. As a result, many advanced nations and other African countries aim to establish their investment in Nigeria. On the other hand, the nation's staggering progress for development, at least, to be at par with her contemporaries decades ago; but which have assumed development status far beyond the line of Nigeria is course for concern. Consequently, government policies in recent times are formulated to attract foreign investment. This has opened the avenue for new comers into the Nigerian Markets to compete with the old entrants. Among the new entrants are China, Japan, South Korea, South Africa, Egypt, among others. Until recently, Nigeria's major investors basically, have been America and Europe. According to Companies and Allied Matters Act (CAMA) 2004 and Investment and Securities Act 2004 (2011 ed.), foreign companies intending to carry on business in Nigeria would have to satisfy the following legal requirements (Table 3):

Table 3. MNEs in Nigeria

Name	Industry
Shell Petroleum Development Company (SPDC)	Oil & Gas
Chevron	Oil & Gas
Mobil	Oil & Gas
NNPC	Oil & Gas
MTN	Telecommunication
Nestlé Nigeria	FMCG
Total	Oil & Gas
Dangote	FMCG
Nigeria Breweries	FMCG
Glo	Telecommunication
NLNG	Oil & Gas
Unilever	FMCG
Guinness	FMCG
Etisalat	Telecommunication
First Bank of Nigeria	Banking
Julius Berger	Construction
Cadbury	FMCG
Eni (Saipem) formerly AGIP	Oil & Gas

1. Subject to sections 56 to 59 of the Companies and Allied Matters Act (CAMA), every foreign company which before or after the commencement of this Act was incorporated outside Nigeria, and having the intention of carrying on business in Nigeria shall take all steps necessary to obtain incorporation as a separate entity in Nigeria for that purpose, but until so incorporated, the foreign company shall not carry on business in Nigeria or exercise any of the powers of a registered company and shall not have a place of business or an address for service of documents or processes in Nigeria for any purpose other than the receipt of notices and other documents, as matters preliminary to incorporation under the CAMA.
2. Any act of the company in contravention of subsection (1) of this section shall be void.
3. Nothing in this section shall affect the status of:
    a. Any foreign company which before the commencement of this Act was granted exemption from compliance with part x of the companies Act 1968.
    b. Any foreign companies exempted under any treaty to which Nigeria is a party.

FINANCING OF MULTINATIONAL ENTERPRISES

Grunberg (2001) explained that MNEs finance some portion of their overseas operations by transferring funds from the parent firm in the home country to the branch or affiliate in the home country. This transfer of funds is what is called foreign direct investment (FDI) because it involves engagement in directly productive activities overseas with the purpose of owning or controlling overseas assets. In essence, FDI is a vital ingredient and key feature of MNEs. It involves the establishment of foreign production facilities or the purchase of an existing foreign business and of acquiring ownership control of such a domestic firm. The control over operations immediately suggests that more than mere flows of financial capital is often accompanied by, inter alia, technological knowledge and increased leverage and management of foreign markets. This further implies that FDI serves as the "backbone of the MNE." The transferring of capital, technology and know-how, mobilizing untapped and under-utilized resources, MNEs can increase productivity, foster growth through its financing power.

Multinational enterprises use flow of foreign direct investment to establish or finance its foreign affiliates. Pugel (2007) pointed out that in two different ways; a multinational enterprise is more than just the flow of foreign direct investment. First, foreign affiliates usually receive only part, and often a rather small part, of their total financing from the direct investment flows. Second, the multinational enterprise transfers many other things to its foreign affiliates in addition to the direct investment financing. The MNE typically provides its affiliates with a variety of intangible assets for the affiliates to use. These intangible assets can include proprietary technology, brand names, marketing capabilities, trade secrets, and managerial practices.

Pugel maintained that a foreign affiliate can obtain financing either from its parent (or other parts of the MNE) or from outside lenders and investors (for instance banks or the buyers of bonds that the affiliate issues). The former is foreign direct investment, whereas, the latter is not. For instance, Pugel reported that in year 2000, for all MNEs in the world, foreign affiliates had $21 trillion of financing in place, in $6 trillion of that financing was provided by foreign direct investment by the multinational enterprises. According to evidence from US – based multinationals borrowing in the host countries provides more than half of the outside financing. The reason for foreign direct investment (FDI) providing so little of the affiliates' total funding as highlighted by Pugel include the need by parent firm to reduce the risks to which its foreign activities are exposed. One of these risks is unexpected changes in exchange rates, which can alter the value of its direct investments. Risk – reducing strategy can be applied whereby a parent company that has foreign – currency assets in its affiliates can take on foreign – currency liabilities as well, by borrowing in foreign currencies that are used to finance the affiliate. This process involves exchange rate risk which includes hedging.

Akpan (2003) opined that for most companies wishing to establish a foreign subsidiary, there are three methods of financing. These are highlighted as follows:

1. Exporting funds (capital). When looking at MNEs of African origin, then export of capital from Africa uses foreign currency, which needs to be bought with African currencies in operation.
2. Raising the funds in the country in which the subsidiary is to be located.
3. Raising funds in one of the international finance markets where interest rates are lowest.

In comparing the alternative sources, Akpan (2003: 98) said, "It should be remembered that the objectives are twofold. Firstly, the company will want to pay the lowest interest possible but secondly, it will wish to minimize exchange rate risk. When assets and liabilities used to finance them are dominated in different currencies, a change in the relative values of the currencies will result in the company incurring exchange rate losses or making exchange rate profits. However, in making international financing decisions, it is desirable to minimize the possibility of such gains or losses. Exporting funds directly from Africa will have the advantage of being relatively simple. There is the further advantage that the company is presumably known to investors in its domestic economy. A company of African origin with a good track record can easily raise loan within the continent than as would be obtained outside the continent. The loan being raised in home currency can be used to buy the relevant foreign currency for investment abroad. The problem with this approach to financing is that the company is completely exposed to exchange rate risk. Furthermore, as many countries have fairly stringent exchange control regulations, there may be problems in repatriating funds.

Raising the required finance in the country in which the subsidiary is to be located, is obviously attractive. Having the assets and liabilities denominated in the same currency eliminates exchange rate risk. However, it will rarely be possible to raise all the required finance in a country where the company is not known. Firstly, the parent company will inevitably be required to put up some equity in the new venture. Secondly, capital markets in some countries are not highly developed and it is unlikely that sufficient funds could be raised.

In some cases, direct foreign investment in a subsidiary is initially financed by foreign currency, borrowing from Eurobank or the issue of Eurobond. Eurobank is a bank that participates in Eurocurrency market by accepting deposits and providing loans in foreign currencies. Eurocurrency market is the international money market in currencies of nations outside the locality. Eurocurrency (Eurofunds, Euromoney) is a currency that is circulating outside the nation where it was issued, example, Eurodollars. Eurodollar is a U.S dollar deposited in a foreign bank and used in European money market. Eurobond is an international bond issued in a country other than the one in whose currency the bond is denominated. Eurobond can be issued in any currency but the requirements for ease of conversion and stability have made the U.S. dollar, the Deutschemark, etc the most popular. Euro is the official currency of 11 countries in the European Union. On January 1, 1999, the euro became the single currency of the 11 participating countries – Austria, Belgium, Finland, France, Germany, Ireland, Italy, Luxembourg, Netherlands, Portugal, and Spain. The major disadvantage of overseas borrowing is that the loan has to be repaid in the currency of issue. The borrower thus runs the risk of an exchange loss (or the possibility of gain) should either of the currencies be revalued between the time of borrowing and the time of repayment.

Exchange Rate Risk and International Financial Investment

Activities of multinational enterprises involve exchange of money. Again, payments or receipt of money are done at future dates with antecedent of uncertainty in knowing the exchange rate that will be practicable as at the future date to translate a country's currency into another. This means that exchange rate changes over time. Pugel (2007) explained that in a floating rate system, spot exchange rates change from minute to minute because supply and demand is constantly at influx. Floating rate sometimes change quickly by large amounts as a result of large shifts in supply and demand. In a fixed – rate system, spot exchange rates can equally change from minute to minute, but the range of the rate is typically limited to a small band around the par value as long as the fixed rate is defended successfully by the government authorities. This does not mean that in a fixed rate system large change cannot occur; but this is often so when the currency is devalued or revalued by the authorities. Of course, some portion of the change in spot exchange rates in either system can be predicted by participants in the foreign exchange market, another part – often a large part – of exchange rate change cannot be predicted.

Therefore, a person or an enterprise such as MNE is exposed to exchange rate risk if the value of income or net worth changes when exchange rates change unpredictably in the future. The fact that exchange rates can change over time calls for two types of responses. Enterprises may try to avoid gambling on what exchange rates would be in the future, can acquire exposures to exchange rate risk in the course of their regular activities but seek to reduce (or eliminate) their risk exposure by 'hedging'. Hedging, a position exposed to rate risk, is the act of reducing or eliminating a net asset or net liability position in the foreign market. On the other hand, enterprises having a fair knowledge of exchange rate may anticipate a rise or fall in exchange rate with expectation to gamble when this occurs in future. In this case, such enterprise is willing to take on hold positions that are exposed to exchange rate risk, and likes to bet that exchange rate will move in their favor so that they make a profit. This process is known as speculation. Put shortly therefore, speculating is the act of taking a net asset position ("long") or a net liability position ("short") in some asset class in a foreign currency.

SPECIFIC WAYS FOR IMPROVING FINANCIAL BASE FOR THE DEVELOPMENT OF MNEs IN AFRICA

Africa can develop and expand her MNEs through a number of regimes including strengthening her economic institutions such as export – import bank, known as African Export – Import Bank (AFREXIM); African Development Bank (ADB), among others. These institutions can issue bonds, partner with foreign global partners and give loans. African Export-Import Bank, also referred to as Afreximbank, is an International financial institution, headquartered in Cairo, Egypt, whose primary objective is to promote and finance trade within the African continent and trade between Africa and other continents. The headquarters of Afreximbank are located at 72 (B) El Maahad El Eshteraky Street, in the Heliopolis neighbourhood in the city of Cairo, the capital and largest city in Egypt. The bank maintains a second branch at 2 Gnassingbe Eyadema Street, Asokoro, Abuja, the capital city of Nigeria. The bank's third branch is located at Eastgate Building, Third Floor, North Wing, Gold Bridge, in Harare, the capital and largest city in Zimbabwe.

African Export-Import Bank ("Afreximbank or the "Bank") is an international partnership of African States, international organizations, public and private institutions and investors which was set up in 1993 to facilitate additional flow of resources in support of African Foreign Trade. We exist to finance, promote, and expand intra-Africa and extra-African trade. To serve our members we employ three principal delivery channels; extend direct credit to eligible African exporters providing pre- and post-shipment finance; extend direct and indirect credit to the African business community through local African intermediaries comprised by Banks and other African Institutions; promote and finance intra- African trade and support the development of trade finance in all African member states (www.afreximbank.com, accessed 2015).

Structures of the Bank

The Bank has full juridical personality under the laws of the State Parties to the Bank Establishment Agreement and is endowed with immunities, privileges and concessions pursuant to it. The constitution of the Board and Management reflects its broad constituency, ownership and mandate. The Bank's Board of Directors is comprised by four Directors elected by Class 'A' Shareholders, including one member appointed by the African Development Bank; four Directors elected by Class `B' Shareholders; and two elected by Class C' Shareholders. Members of the Board of Directors are elected for a term of three years and may be re-elected. The Board meets once every three months or as often as the business of the Bank may require. The President is an ex-officio member and Chairman of the Board of Directors. News Letter We facilitates the flow of resources in support of African Foreign Trade.

Increased confidence is being shown in the Bank through increased investments by existing shareholders. Issues of Joining the Bank and Accessing Afrexim Bank Facilities: The Bank welcomes partnerships and, applications for membership and applications for credit facilities from eligible entities and individuals who are engaged in the promotion, development and business of trade Finance in Africa as well as those individuals and institutions that either trade with Africa or are interesting in developing trade Finance in Africa. The overarching goal is to harness synergies to finance and develop intra-Africa trade and enhance the region's access to critical imports and exports for sustainable economic development for our region that have a genuine interest in developing trade finance in Africa or ascribe to similar objectives. Therefore, all Independent African States and Institutions; all African Public and private sector Institutions; International Financial Institutions and Economic Organizations that can be able to subscribe for a minimum for each class.

Strategic Partnerships

Export-Import Bank of China Grants US$100 million Line of Credit to Afreximbank as part of its drive to promote access to essential capital equipment and export, generating imports, the Bank, has intensified efforts to diversify its sources of funding by aggressively mobilizing funds under its ECA Loans Facilitation Program. Under this program, the Bank selectively works with other ECAs to promote the acquisition of essential goods, especially capital goods and/or services by African counterparties. On May 13, 2009 the Bank signed a US$ 100 million Trade and Project Financing Facility with Exim Bank of China. Under the Facility, US$20 million will be used by Afreximbank to fund short-term trade finance activities and US$80 million will be channeled into medium term project finance on-lending to its clients in support of acquisition of a variety of Chinese goods and services from a broad range of sectors including, industry and agro-industry, telecommunications, energy and environmental protection, transportation, water supply and sanitation.

The African Export – Import Bank (AFREXIM) continues to partner with trading giants globally to expand its horizon in investments. Bloomberg (2015) reported that AFREXIM is to generate over $1 Billion in bonds and loans in Renminbi, the Chinese currency, as trade with China rises. Bloomberg, who quoted Jean-Louisa Ekra, President of the Cairo-based lender, as saying a Eurobond of between $400 Million and $600 Million might in turn be sold in the Month (June 2015), spoke in Abidjan, Ivory Coast where the bank opened its third regional office after Harere in Zimbabwe and Abuja. According to Bloomberg, the firm will seek the loan from 35 banks later in the year.

Meanwhile, the reason to raise fund in Chinese currency may not be unconnected with the increasing volume of trade between Africa and China in recent years. This assertion is confirmed by Bloomberg who posited thus: "AFREXIM is considering borrowing in Chinese renminbi to take advantage of rising trade in Africa with China, which is the top trading partner of Africa's five-largest economies, including South Africa, Nigeria and Angola", P.26.

AFREXIM Bank Responds to the Economic Crisis

The negative consequences of the global economic crisis on African trade and trade finance are currently being seriously felt on the African continent. Afreximbank understands the ramifications of the current global financial crisis on African trade and trade finance, given its history and raison d'etre. The Bank was established in 1993 to deal with a similar credit crunch that Africa was facing. To assist its member countries satisfy essential import needs given the drastic cut in credit lines, the Bank is actively: deepening existing business relationships with core OECD partner banks to ensure that credit lines from those banks are maintained; and intensifying its program of expanding partnership arrangements with Pan-African entities, including African Development Bank (AfDB), Africa Finance Corporation (AFC), ECOWAS Bank for investment and Development (EBID), African Trade Insurance Agency (ATI), Shelter Afrique and the Eastern and Southern African Trade and Development Bank (PTA Bank), for the purpose of pooling technical and financial resources as well as sharing risks in the funding of viable trade and project ventures. Discussions are also ongoing with major multilateral institutions to ensure that the Bank can support the increased demand for its services. Afreximbank understands the current global financial crisis. Hence, the Bank is also championing the creation of an Alliance of African International Financial Institutions (AAIFI), made up of African multilateral financial institutions and multinational banks. The move will assist Bank members to share business risks, financial resources, and expertise in such a way as to allow member institutions achieve their mandate efficiently in the collective interest of the Continent.

African Development Bank

African Development Bank Group (AfDB) is a multilateral development finance institution established to contribute to the economic development and social progress of African countries. The AfDB was founded in 1964 and comprises three entities: The African Development Bank, the African Development Fund and the Nigeria Trust Fund. The AfDB's mission is to fight poverty and improve living conditions on the continent through promoting the investment of public and private capital in projects and programs that are likely to contribute to the economic and social development of the region· The AfDB is a financial provider to African governments and private companies investing in the regional member countries (RMC). While it was originally headquartered in Abidjan, Côte d'Ivoire, the bank's headquarters moved to Tunis, Tunisia in 2003, due to the Ivorian civil war; before returning in September 2014.

The historical birth of the bank could be traced to the end of the colonial period in Africa, where there was a growing desire for more unity within the continent which led to the establishment of two draft charters, one for the establishment of the Organization of African Unity (established in 1963, later replaced by the African Union), and for a regional development bank. A draft accord was therefore submitted to top African officials, then to African Ministers, before being cosigned by twenty-three African governments on August 4, 1963, in the form of an agreement establishing the African Development Bank. The agreement came into force on 10 September 1964. Although established officially under the auspices of the Economic Commission for Africa, the AfDB began operation in 1966. Originally, only African countries were able to join the bank. However, since 1982 it has allowed the entry of non-African countries as well. During its forty years of operations, AfDB has financed 2,885 operations, for a total of $47.5 billion. In 2003, it received an AAA rating from the major financial rating agencies and had a capital of $32.043 billion. The African Development Bank Group has two other entities: the African Development Fund (ADF) and the Nigeria Trust Fund (NTF).

African Development Fund

This was established in 1972. The African Development Fund started operations in 1974. It provides development finance on concessional terms to low-income RMCs which are unable to borrow on the non-concessional terms of the AfDB.

In harmony with its lending strategy, poverty reduction is the main aim of ADF activities. Twenty-four non-African countries along with the AfDB constitute its current membership. The largest ADF shareholder is the United Kingdom, with approximately 14% of the total working shares followed by United States with approximately 6.5 percent of the total voting shares, followed by Japan with approximately 5.4 percent. The Federal Reserve Bank of New York was designated as the depositor bank for the fund according to telegraphs sent from the U.S. Embassy in Abidjan in 1976. The ADF's general operations are decided by a Board of Directors, six of which are appointed by the non-African member states and six designated by the AfDB from among the bank's regional Executive Directors. The ADF's sources are mainly contributions and periodic replacements by non-African member states. The fund is usually replenished every three years, unless member states decide otherwise. The total donations, at the end of 1996, amounted to $12.58 billion. The ADF lends at no interest rate, with an annual service charge of 0.75%, a commitment fee of 0.5%, and a 50-year repayment period including a 10-year grace period. The tenth United Kingdom replenishment of the ADF was in 2006.

Nigeria Trust Fund

The Nigeria Trust Fund (NTF) was established in 1976 by the Nigerian government with an initial capital of $80 million. The NTF is aimed at assisting in the development efforts of the poorest AfDB members. The NTF uses its resources to provide financing for projects of national or regional importance which further the economic and social development of the low-income RMCs whose economic and social conditions require financing on non-conventional terms. In 1996, the NTF had a total resource base of $432 million. It lends at a 4% interest rate with a 25-year repayment period, including a five-year grace period.

Management and Control

In terms of management and control, the AfDB is controlled by a Board of Executive Directors, made up of representatives of its member countries. The voting power on the Board is split according to the size of each member's share, currently 60%-40% between African (and "regional") countries and "non-regional" member countries ("donors"). The largest African Development Bank shareholder is Nigeria with nearly 9 percent of the vote. All member countries of the AfDB are represented on the AfDB Board of Executive Directors. Mr. Donald Kaberuka is the 7th elected President of the African Development Bank Group, having taken the oath of office on September 1, 2005. However, the baton will be changed in August 2015, following the election on May 2015 which saw the emergence of Nigeria's outgoing Minister of Agriculture and Rural Development, Akinwumi Adesina. Adesina on assumption of office on August 2015 will be 8th President of the African Development Bank (AfDB). Mr. Adesina, 55, will succeed incumbent president, Donald Kaberuka, at the end of his second term as President of the Bank in August 2015. He chairs the Boards of both the African Development Bank and the African Development Fund. Mr. Kaberuka is a former finance minister of Rwanda.

Member governments are officially represented at the AfDB by their Minister of Finance, Planning or Cooperation who sits on the AfDB Board of Governors. The AfDB Governors meet once a year (at the Annual Meetings of the AfDB each May) to take major decisions about the institution's leadership, strategic directions and governing bodies. The Governors typically appoint a representative from their country to serve in the offices of the AfDB's Board of Executive Directors. Day-to-day decisions about which loans and grants should be approved and what policies should guide the AfDB's work are taken by the Board of Executive Directors. Each member country is represented on the Board, but their voting power and influence differs depending on the amount of money they contribute to the AfDB. The African Development Bank is using a Unit of Account which is registered as XUA as ISO 4217 standard currency code. It is not exchanged directly by individuals; it is used for accounting between state members.

The primary function of AfDB is making loans and equity investments for the socio-economic advancement of the RMC. Second, the bank provides technical assistance for development projects and programs. Third, it promotes investment of public and private capital for development. Fourth, the bank assists in organizing the development policies of RMCs. The AfDB is also required to give special attention to national and multinational projects which are needed to promote regional integration.

The AfDB promotes economic development and social progress of its RMCs in Africa and the bank commits approximately 3 billion dollars annually to African countries. It's relatively small lending and tendency to follow in the footsteps of more prominent public institutions like the World Bank, implies that the African Development Bank has been receiving little interest from civil society organizations as well as academia. AfDB emphasizes the role of women along with education reforms, and lent its support to key initiatives such as debt alleviation for Heavily Indebted Poor Countries and the New Partnership for Africa's Development (NEPAD). The Bank is currently based in Tunis, Tunisia after relocating from its headquarters in Abidjan, Côte d'Ivoire because of instability there. It employs approximately 1,020 employees as of 2007, and has 78 members: 53 countries in Africa and 25 American, European, and Asian countries.

One of emerging views, repeatedly cited by the AfDB's Board of Directors and management, is that the AfDB should be more "selective" and "country-focused" in its operations. Though this policy has still to be clearly defined, it appears to be driving certain lending priorities. The infrastructure sector, including power supply, water and sanitation, transport and communications, has traditionally received the largest share of AfDB lending. This focus was re-affirmed in the AFDB's 2003-2007 Strategic Plan, which identified infrastructure as a priority area for AfDB lending. In 2005, the AfDB approved 23 infrastructure projects for approximately $982 million, which totaled 40 percent of AfDB approvals that year. Given the increased attention to infrastructure development in Africa from donors and borrowers, it is likely that AfDB's infrastructure lending will increase significantly in the coming years. In 2007, infrastructure operations accounted for approximately 60 percent of the bank's portfolio. Regional integration infrastructure projects will be a key part of the AfDB's future business. According to the AfDB's *2005 Annual Report*, regional economic blocs will make Africa "more competitive in the global market", while transport and power interconnections between smaller African economies will help create larger markets in the continent. The AfDB's member countries claim that AFDB, as a multilateral institution, is particularly suited to support regional integration projects.

The AfDB has been designated the lead agency to facilitate "NEPAD infrastructure initiatives", which are regional integration projects led by African Regional Economic Communities (RECs). Additionally, the AfDB hosts the Infrastructure Consortium for Africa (ICA). The ICA was established by G8 countries to coordinate and encourage infrastructure development in Africa, focusing on regional infrastructure development in particular. The AfDB helps to prepare projects so they may obtain financing from others sources through an initiative called the Infrastructure Project Preparation Facility (IPPF). So even if the AfDB is not directly involved in financing a particular infrastructure project, it may have helped to make it possible.

Energy projects are likely to become a more important area of the AFDB's infrastructure work, given the lack of access to energy services across Africa and continued high oil prices affecting oil-importing countries. It is not clear if the AFDB's role in the energy sector will prioritize energy projects for domestic consumption or for export, although the AfDB has supported both in the past. The AFDB is currently drafting an energy policy and developing its contribution to the G8-mandated Clean Energy Investment Framework. Although there is no official statement or consensus to this effect, AFDB lending for agriculture, (non-infrastructure) rural development and social sectors, such as health and education, is reportedly likely to decrease over the coming years.

The AfDB's financial standing has been restored from the near collapse of 1995, but its operational credibility remains a work-in-progress. A working group convened by the Center for Global Development, an independent Washington think tank, released a report in September 2006 that offered six recommendations for Bank's president and board of directors on broad principles to guide the Bank's renewal. The report contains six recommendations for management and shareholders as they address the urgent task of reforming Africa's development bank. Prominent among the recommendations is a strong focus on infrastructure. AfDB is still a relatively small source of development finance for Africa. According to the most recent figures, the AfDB provides only 6 percent of total development assistance to the continent. Through its International Development Association (IDA), the World Bank annually approves about four times more in low-interest loans and grants to Africa than the AfDB does. The AfDB lacks the financial resources, the staff capacity and the range of staff skills and experience of the World Bank. For example, at the World Bank there is more than four times the number of staff working on any given project than at the AfDB. A number of the AfDB's projects, especially its policy loans, are financed jointly with the World Bank and other donors. The AfDB also relies extensively on World Bank research and analysis. As a larger institution and often the lead financier on joint projects, the World Bank attracts more attention than the AFDB.

While the AfDB's lending had not expanded significantly in recent years, 2006 figures indicate that things may be changing. Between 2005 and 2006, the AfDB's lending activities increased by more than 30 percent to $3.4 billion. Over the same period, private sector operations doubled in value. The AfDB has specific mandates from the New Partnership for Africa's Development (NEPAD) and other international organizations to take the lead amongst financial and development institutions in areas such as infrastructure, regional integration, and banking and financial standards in Africa. These mandates have also increased the AfDB's profile in the media. The increased international emphasis on Africa's development needs in recent years (for example, surrounding the 2005 Gleneagles G8 Summit), and on the importance of infrastructure investment in Africa, has highlighted the role of the AfDB.

Some research have indicated that a high percentage of respondents in African countries have marked preference for additional aid from the African Development Bank, despite its relatively low rating against most of the aid effectiveness criteria found to be important by donor recipients. This suggests that donor recipients in Africa views on the 'multilateral donor of choice' are informed by additional aid effectiveness criteria that are not commonly identified or reported against, though exactly what those criteria have not been discussed.

In general, whereas there have been progress at all levels with regard to democracy, growth and restoring the macro-economic balances in Africa over the past fifteen years, half of sub-Saharan Africa lives on under one dollar a day, and AIDS is threatening the social fabric of the continent. The studies conducted by various organizations (including the African Development Bank and the World Bank) show that, with the exception of northern and southern Africa, the United Nations Millennium Development Goals (reducing by half the number of persons living in poverty and without access to potable water by 2015) will in most cases not be attained. Nevertheless, these same studies indicate that the majority of the African countries can make notable progress to these ends.

CHALLENGES FACING MNEs IN AFRICA

According to Khan (2014), globalization may be a fact of life, but it remains highly fragile. Embedding global market forces in shared values and institutionalized practices, and bridging the gaps in global governance structures are among the most important challenges faced by policymakers and corporate leaders alike. According to Khan, MNEs face other equally important challenges such as ability to adapt to the cultural differences, standards and practices. Again, the author stated that the challenge of political instability is traditionally associated with developing or emerging countries for MNEs coming from developed nations where MNEs from developing countries consider economic risk such as exchange rate risk as a greater challenge. Also, appropriate market segmentation, relating to the low spending power of the major part of the market and developing effective marketing strategies to apply in different sections of the transforming society are other major issues facing MNEs in emerging markets, the author further stressed. Other challenges highlighted by Khan include: balancing the price and quality; understanding the influence of institutions such as judicial system, political system, education system and mixes of traditional local culture and modern global culture; industrial infrastructure is inefficient, lack of intellectual property right protection, high tariffs, expensive bureaucracy, ambiguous rules and regulations, monopolistic practices, control of distribution systems, unreliable and low quality suppliers; high price sensitivity, local needs and limited purchasing power are the characteristics of emerging markets; absence of specialized intermediaries, regulatory system and contract-enforcing mechanisms are other critical issues in the emerging markets. Other risks for MNES are: transactional risks, income risks from operation, income risks from financing, and accounting risks due to fluctuations in the rate of exchange of the local currency; political risks, inflation risks, bank instability, and legal risks (Khan, 2014). Further, the author noted that corporate social responsibility is growing challenge for the MNEs operating in emerging countries. MNEs are expected to balance their role in economic development with social responsibilities toward the country in which they operate.

It is a fact that MNE has global outlook, hence, is prone to competitive abilities. It is therefore important for multinationals from developing countries such as those in Africa, among others to carefully assess the impact of MNEs in the advanced nations if they have to succeed in their market development strategies. Failure to do this will immensely harm their market development initiatives (Fan, 2008). Another market development challenge for multinationals in Africa is how to create new competitive advantages in the market. The establishment of MNE in Africa should therefore characterize with pre and post establishment learning about organizational behavior. This is crucial for them to fulfill a successful catch up strategy, and this learning process is likely to be long and expensive, especially where the technology continues to advance rapidly and competition from the incumbent firms remains fierce. African Multinationals must be serious in acquiring and accumulating business skills, new knowledge and expertise to be able to operate with cost-based competencies and location-based advantages and have ownership or firm specific advantages. Multinational Companies in Africa is equally challenged by cultural distance in their efforts to develop new markets. Each African country has her cultural milieu and Multinational firms have a country of origin that has got a culture different from other countries. Since cultures differ across national boundaries, it may be difficult to agree in business terms where such agreement is in conflict due to cultural barriers of the countries involved. In view of the forgoing, the management team of a multinational who intend to develop a new market need to understand the culture of the host country of their new market if sound and acceptable decisions must be taken for market development. In other cases, the challenge of skill gap in managerial ability among African countries and between Africa and the outside world is posing threat to market development and expansion. The managerial competences and practices found in African countries tend to differ from those of the advanced economies, making African MNEs to continue in hiring the services of foreign experts. African multinational firms entering new markets are facing stiff competition globally. This can result in MNEs in African quitting the market. This may be compounded when considering the cost implication. When the costs involved is so high, it may affect returns, especially where there is external financing resulting in very high liability ratio. Other challenges affecting African MNEs include low level of business technology, poor market information and limited research output; product and packaging modifications; logistics; ineffective distribution networks due to inadequate transportation infrastructure and trade restrictions.

THE ORGANIZATIONAL STRUCTURE OF A MULTINATIONAL COMPANY

According to Bert Markgraf, Demand Media, Multinational companies, especially smaller ones, face more organizational challenges than companies operating in only one national market. They have to maintain functional organizational units, but they have to fulfill these functions in different ways, depending on where the business in operating. The essential challenge is to create differentiated organizational units responsible for the foreign markets while coordinating operations across the whole company.

Functional

A functionally organized multinational company uses corporate functions as the basis for its organizational structure. Production, human resources, design and customer service are typical functional units. If a functionally organized company has a centralized structure, all operations are based in the home country and individual employees have responsibilities for different national markets. This type of organization is efficient and effective for companies that are too small to have overseas subsidiaries. Larger companies can have this type of organization, but in a decentralized form, where foreign employees carry out some of the work in their own countries. In this case, companies have to pay special attention to coordinating activities.

Geographic

A common form of organizational structure for larger companies and businesses that require a presence in the foreign markets is one that is based in geography. In addition to the home office or headquarters, semi-independent operations are established in the countries where the company is active. For larger corporations, these can take the form of subsidiaries, while smaller companies can have something as simple as an agent or a small office. This structure affords flexibility; the head office can transfer responsibilities abroad if required by local conditions and if the foreign operation is competent, but it can also take over local operations if needed.

International Division

One way multinational companies can accommodate foreign operations without disrupting the organization in their home market is to create an international division. This structure is suited to larger corporations, but it is also effective for smaller companies that have an established home market and a rapidly growing international business. It leaves the company free to maintain the focus on its home market in its main organization while leaving the international division free to adapt to the foreign markets in which it is active.

Matrix

A matrix organizational structure combines the efficiency of the functionally organized company with the flexibility of extensive local operations. Foreign workers report to local managers for questions about their work, while they report to the head office for all other functions. The home organization retains control of disciplinary matters, pay and promotions, while the employees carry out the work according to local requirements. This is a suitable organizational form for smaller companies active in only one or two foreign markets, but it is mainly used by larger corporations who have extensive foreign operations.

Nigerian National Petroleum Corporation (NNPC) is the state oil corporation through which the federal government of Nigeria regulates and participates in the country's petroleum industry. NNPC was established on April 1, 1977 as a merger of the Nigerian National Oil Corporation and the Federal Ministry of Mines and Steel. NNPC by law manages the joint venture between the Nigerian federal government and a number of foreign multinational corporations, which include Royal Dutch Shell, Agip, ExxonMobil, Chevron, and Texaco (now merged with Chevron). Through collaboration with these companies, the Nigerian government conducts petroleum exploration and production. In 2007, the head of the Nigerian wing of Transparency International said salaries for NNPC workers were too low to prevent graft. The NNPC Towers in Abuja is the headquarters of NNPC. Consisting of four identical towers, the complex is located on Herbert Macaulay Way, Central Business District Abuja. NNPC also has zonal offices in Lagos, Kaduna, Port Harcourt and Warri. It has an international office located in London, United Kingdom.

FINAL THOUGHTS

African countries are increasing committed to the development of Multinational Enterprises (MNEs) in this 21st Century. In view of this, these countries are strengthening their integration ability to overcome the consequences of financial risks, limited market and low competitiveness ability. Among African countries, therefore, indigenous Multinational Enterprises are springing up with potentials for global competitiveness. For instance MTN group, a MNE with origin in South Africa is cutting across continents with very large market. On the other hand, Multinational Enterprises originating from advanced countries of Europe and America with affiliates in Africa are providing strong competition to Africa's MNEs. Institutions such as African Development Bank (AfDB), New Partnership for African Development (NEPAD) are strategic enough to provide the financial and specialized know-how for the sustenance of existing African-based MNEs and provide platforms for establishing more.

Promoting MNEs through Africa's (Regional) Economic Integration

One of the most recent and vibrant economic grouping that has dynamics to create an atmosphere for expanding business horizon that can in turn promotes the development of MNEs with origin in Africa is the New Partnership on African Development (NEPAD). According to Akanbi (2006), the NEPAD was established as a child of necessity in 2003. It was conceived by African leaders, midwifed through consultations with global partners, and delivered within the continent in order to address the myriads of contemporary socio-economic and political challenges facing Africa at the dawn of the 21st Century. These challenges, the author highlighted to include extreme poverty. Akanbi noted that NEPAD is set against clearly identified objectives to:

1. Make Africa attractive to both domestic and foreign investors;
2. Tap the vast economic potentials of the continent;
3. Achieve and sustain an average GDP growth rate of over 7 per cent per annum by 2015;
4. Ensure that the continent achieves the agreed International Development Goals (MDGs);
5. Increase investment in human resources development
6. Promote sub-regional and continental economic growth, among others.

In a view to implementing the objectives of NEPAD, certain strategies have been put in place by NEPAD. These strategies include:

1. Capital Flows Initiative (CFI), including debt relief, private capital flows and Foreign Direct Investment (FDI);
2. Market Access Initiative (MAI), including export diversification, barrier removal and value addition, Manufacturing, Mining, Services and Tourism;
3. Bridging the Infrastructure Gap, in energy, transport, education, health, water and sanitation;
4. Bridging the Digital divide through investment in Information and communications Technology (ICT);
5. Human Resource Development Initiative, including reversing the Brain Drain Syndrome; among others.

The objectives of NEPAD and strategies mapped out for implementing these objectives highlighted above point to the endearing nature of Africa's environment for MNEs to thrive.

CONCLUSION

Based on the facts enunciated in this chapter, it is concluded; among others that Multinational Enterprises in Africa have functional, geographical, international division and matrix organizational structures. Africa's multinational enterprises use corporate functions as the basis for its organizational structure. These include production, human resources, and design and customer service units. Consequently, all operations are not based in the home country. Also, Africa's MNEs in addition to the home office or headquarters have semi-independent operations established in the countries where the company is active with few countries outside Africa. Multinational companies in Africa also create international division by leaving the company free to maintain the focus on its home market in its main organization while leaving the international division free to adapt to the foreign markets in which it is active. It is also concluded that MNEs in Africa combines the efficiency of the functionally organized company with the flexibility of extensive local operations. Foreign workers report to local managers for questions about their work, while they report to the head office for all other functions. The home organization retains control of disciplinary matters, pay and promotions, while the employees carry out the work according to local requirements.

Given the spate at which MNEs are flourishing in Africa as an alternative market in the emerging economy's context, the operational structures of these MNEs are becoming more fascinating and dynamic. This holds more productive ability in the near future.

Recommendations

In view of the conclusions drawn the following recommendations are made:

1. The relatively bigger countries in Africa should invest in the relatively smaller countries through the establishment of MNEs in those countries.
2. Multinational Enterprises in Africa should pay attention to products which Africa has absolute advantage.
3. MNEs operation in Africa should focus on production of finished goods to add value to products.
4. Africa should encourage the development of indigenous MNEs through tax rebate and low tariff.
5. There should be a concerted effort by African countries to encourage the use of e-business to eliminate geographical divide in business operations within and outside Africa.

REFERENCES

Accenture. (2007). *The rise of the multi-polar world*. Available at http://www.accenture.com

Afribiz. (2010). *Multinational Corporations Originating in Egypt*. Available at http://www.afribiz.info/content/2010/transnational-corporations-originating-in-egypt

Akanbi, G. O. (2006). Nigeria and Promotion of NEPAD Objectives (M. Daura, Ed.). Academic Press.

Akpan, A. U. (2003). *Fundamentals of International Accounting*. Calabar – Nigeria: Index *Educational Foundations*.

Bloomberg. (2015, June 3). AFREXIM Mulls $1 Billion Loan. *The Nation*, p. 26.

Companies Proceeding Rule Fan, . (2008). The Rise of Emerging Market Multinationals And its Impact on Marketing. *Marketing Intelligence & Planning*, *26*, 4.

Grunberg, L. (2001). The IPE of Multinational Corporations. In D. N. Balaam & M. Veseth (Eds.), *Introduction to International Political Economy* (2nd ed.). Upper Saddle River, NJ: Prentice-Hall.

Khan, M. A. (2014). *Challenges for MNEs Operating in Emerging Markets.* Retrieved from www.aabri.com/LV14045.pdf

Mthombeni, M. S. (2006). *The Role of Multinational Corporations in South Africa: a Political Economic Perspective.* (Unpublished Dissertation). Department of Political Science, Faculty of Humanities, University of the Free State, Bloemfontein.

Needham, D., & Dransfield, R. (2000). *Advanced Business.* Heinemann.

Nickels, W. G., McHUgh, J. M., & McHugh, S. M. (2012). *Understanding Business.* New York: McGraw Hill Irwin.

Nigeria's Technical Aid Corps: Issues and Perspective. (2006). Ibadan: Dokun Publishing House.

Pinelo, A. J. (1973). *The Multinational Corporation as a Force in Latin American Politics.* New York: Praeger Publishers.

Pugel, T. A. (2007). *International Economics* (13th ed.). New York: McGraw-Hill Irwin.

Report by Labour Research Service. (n.d.). Available at http://www.fes-southafrica.org/media/MNC%20Trend%20Report%20%20FES%20draft%202014.pdf

Rugman, A. M., & Hodgets, R. M. (2003). *International Business* (3rd ed.). PearsonEducation Ltd.

Spero, J. E., & Hart, J. A. (2003). *The Politics of International Economic Relations* (6th ed.). Belmont: Wadsworth/Thomson.

Taal, M. (2014). *South African Multinationals in Africa – Trends in 2013/2014.* Academic Press.

KEY TERMS AND DEFINITIONS

Economy: Describes the productive and consumption ability of a country, region, continent and even the entire globe and the monetary inflow and outflow resulting in these economic activities.

Exchange Rate: Ratio in which a country's currency translate with the currency of other countries in the international (exchange) market.

Exchange Rate Risk: Loss associated with currency exchange due to disparity in value.

Multinational Enterprises in Africa: These are those MNEs which have either parent or subsidiaries for business operation within African continent.

Operational Structures: Are issues and components, which facilitate the performance of an organization. In this context, they are issues and components which facilitate the performance of MNEs in Africa.

Parent Company: The operational headquarter of a Multinational Enterprise.

Strategic Partnership: Union of corporate bodies or countries for the integration of ideologies and economic prospects where they have diverse advantage for improvement in the economy.

Subsidiary: An affiliate or branch office of a Multinational Enterprise usually located across countries globally.

Chapter 18
Multinational Enterprises and African Economy

Edet E. Okon
University of Uyo, Nigeria

ABSTRACT

Africa's economy, an emerging economy is gradually being re-positioned in the global economy as a focus of investment. Multinational Enterprises (MNEs) have helped to shape the economy of Africa. An overview of Africa's economy was examined; top 20 Africa's largest economies were highlighted; major sectors perceived as paths to growth of Africa's economy were examined – Agriculture, Banking, Consumer goods, infrastructure, mining, oil and gas, and telecommunications. The chapter also enunciated the concept, 'diversified economy' in relation to oil exporters, the transition economies and the pre-transition economies. It is therefore concluded that Multinational Enterprises will continue to contribute to the growth of Africa's economy, especially as more indigenous enterprises are being launched by African countries. It is therefore recommended that African countries should continue to diversify her economy to take advantage of large labor potential and natural resources endowment.

INTRODUCTION

The realization by African countries of the pace at which her development effort can be accelerated through activities of MNEs is being heightened as African countries are showing greater involvement in the establishment of MNEs beyond the shores of African continent. African economy is largely described as "a developing economy". This concept (of a developing) will further be understood with description of associated terms such as development, growth, and economy, among others. Kelleher and Klein (2006) viewed development as an economic process which enables an increasing number of people to produce enough wealth to support an acceptable quality of life. The interpretation of this view is that development is measured in qualitative terms based on human living and lifestyle or quality of live. In other perspective, development could be measured in terms of a society achieving a modern technology-based lifestyle – how many people in a given society can afford to use what?

DOI: 10.4018/978-1-5225-0276-0.ch018

Is the level of development in a given society capable of answering the question of poverty? These questions capture the situation in Africa where the level of technological development is acclaimed as low; incidence of poverty largely ascribed as high and general quality of life among the masses perceived as low. The case of Africa thus portrays a vicious cycle where a network of four interrelated; mutually reinforcing factors severely inhibit improvement in economic growth and development. This being the case in Africa, except a few countries, the role of MNEs in the development of African economy can better be embraced.

Chukwuemeka, Anazodo and Nzewi (2011) said that it is open secret that after several years of independence of countries like, Nigeria, Ghana, Ethiopia, Sierra Leone, South Africa etc., only very little improvement has been recorded in just few sectors of the economy of these countries. Some of these economies still operated on monocultures and vertically integrated with the parent industries of the neo-colonials themselves (Izunwa, 2005). It is against this background that the following thought provoking questions and assertions bug the mind. Can African nations be truly independent when the activities of multinational enterprises have partially destroyed local entrepreneurship drive, which have an important effect on development? Does the presence of global firms raise the cost of capital and makes insufficient fund available to local firms? This counters the development posture of leaders of the third world nations, agreeing with this point, Bernal (2005), stated that “it is frequently contended that the international firm sups up local capital either by borrowing locally or by receipt of investment incentives”. Multinational enterprises do not encourage improvement of balance of payment of host countries. Multinational enterprises have been used as a foreign policy instrument of their home governments, to the disadvantage of host country’s economic development (Ugwu, 2010). Multinational enterprises are accused of not transferring technology since they fail to impart specialized technical know-how to host country nationals.

It is generally recognized that the African nations, apart from being the cradle of the human race, compared to the rest of the world, is the best endowed with the richest natural resources the world has ever seen. She has landmass several times the size of Europe. She is rich in oil deposits, gold, diamond, iron or copper, various types of wood etc (Aja, 2009). And for centuries Africa and Africans built an economy able to produce its own food and its own tools including weapons. The Europeans who came to Africa in the 15th and 16th centuries were interested mainly in goods like gold and other natural products like pepper, spices and ivory for which there was a great demand in Europe. Politically, most of the third world nations have been free for a long time.

But economically, an enormous position of the continent remains in chains. Basic economic realities remain unchanged from the colonial period. To fully appreciate the role of the multinational enterprises in the exploitation of the third world nations, it is necessary to understand the character of the new states, its level of development, and basic thrust of their foreign policy. For many years after independence of many third world nations and up till now, they continued by and large with policies which at the international level ensured close collaboration with the metropolis emphasizing the special relationship between them and their colonizers (Ake, 1981). The industrial sector was dominated by low technology and the pattern of relationship between her and multi-nationals being based primarily on joint ventures did not encourage the development of an auto centric industrial base. New states lacked the capacity to exploit local raw materials, work intermediate industries and produce capital goods, which along could provide the basis for production and reproduction required for national development.

An Overview of Africa's Economy

Africa's economy is largely described as developing with dotted number of countries described as Less Developed or simply underdeveloped. It will really be a long literature trying to describe why Africa's economy is developing, less developed or underdeveloped. However, this is summarized under a Vicious Cycle with key factors which continue to impede development. These four broad factors are dual economy, low productivity, insufficient capital and low human services. A dual economy is used here to describe an economy where a few elitist groups have the power to live in luxury while the vast majority of the populace lives in abject poverty. The elitist group (occupying a negligible percentage of the populace) may be real estate owners, top government functionaries (especially the political class), importers and those in the financial sectors and a few professionals. There may also exist, a sizeable proportion of the populace who are in the middle class. In this type of economy, there is a sharp contrast in the style of living between the rural and urban dwellers. In Africa, agricultural practices are almost left into the hands of rural dwellers who still apply crude means of production with very low productivity for the immediate family needs. They know very little in the use of modern technology and machinery and even when they are aware, it is far from their usage since the means to acquire such modern technique is just and illusion.

The second factor, low productivity culminates from the first and other adjoining factors. Productivity simply means output of goods and services in relation to the time directed for the production of such goods and services. Low productivity continues to pervade development of African economy because of its continued attachment to subsistence economy. Kelleher and Klein (2006) maintained that low productivity limits not only future growth but also the wages workers can earn, contributing in part to what the economists call the poverty trap.

Insufficient capital is yet another component of the vicious cycle because it springs out from low productivity which equally results in low per capita income. Capital in this case includes physical capital, financial capital. Kelleher and Klein observed that an economy with large subsistence sectors and low productivity have little capital. The authors described physical capital, often called infrastructures to include such things as factories, farms, roads, railroads, telephones, banks, and machinery, financial capital includes bank deposits, earnings from international trade, and money. The authors clarified that goods an economy produces for immediate consumption, such as food, cars, and clothes, are not capital. Therefore, capital refers to the finances plus the facilities needed to produce wealth.

Generally, dual economy, productivity, and capital are closely related factors. These factors combine to make an economy remain a subsistence economy. A subsistence economy with low productivity and little capital thus experiences great difficulty in generating enough growth to attain a self-sustained development and thus struggle with the cycle of underdevelopment as indicated in the arrow closing the vicious cycle in Figure 1.

Human capital is needed in for a successful development process. This is why the educational sector in Africa should be re-positioned for the task of manpower development with functional skills to drive the business opportunities for economic development.

Top 20 Largest Economies in Africa

A highlight of top largest economies in Africa 2015 is necessary. Meanwhile, with an area of about 30.2 million square kilometers, Africa is world's second largest continent. Africa has a total population of 1.111 billion people based on 2013 figure (www.africaranking.com/largest-economies-inafrica, accessed

Figure 1. Vicious cycle of underdevelopment
Source: Kelleher and Klein (2006)

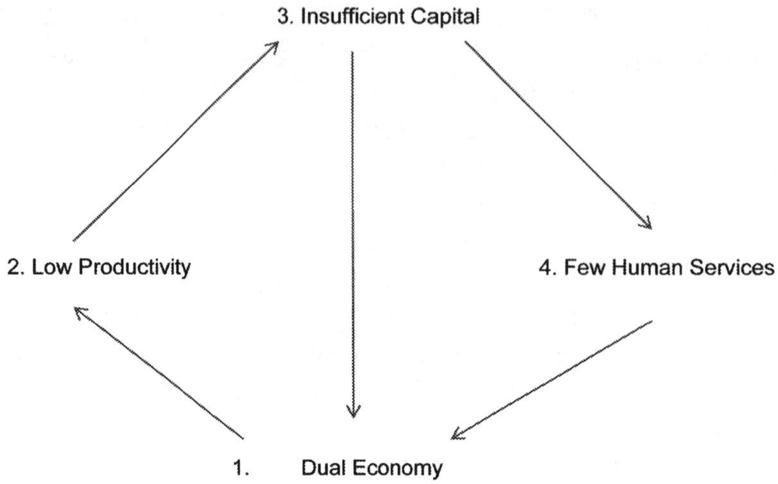

2015. Algeria is the largest country (by area) in Africa and Nigeria is the largest country by population. In 2014, Nigeria surpassed South Africa as Africa's largest economy. Top 20 largest economies in Africa is given as follows:

1. **Nigeria – GDP:** *$594.257 Billion.* Nigeria is classified as a mixed economy emerging market. Its stock exchange is the second largest in Africa. This federal constitutional republic rebased its GDP from 1990 to 2010. This resulted in an 89 per cent increase in the estimated size of the economy. Based on this, Nigeria is the largest economy in Africa.
2. **South Africa – GDP:** *$341.216 Billion.* The slow pace of global economic growth continued to impact on South Africa's development negatively. With around 25 per cent of the population without work, unemployment is the nation's biggest social challenge. The growth reached 1.9 per cent in 2013 compared to 2.5 per cent in 2012.
3. **Egypt – GDP:** *$275.748 Billion.* Officially, the Arab Republic of Egypt, this transcontinental country entered political uncertainty after the ouster of President Mohamed Morsi in July 2013. Economic growth has been just above the 2 per cent mark in the fiscal years 2011/2012 and 2012/2013. Egypt's economy is one of the largest and most diversified in the Middle East. Tourism, agriculture, services and industry contribute to GDP growth significantly.
4. **Algeria – GDP:** *$219.453 Billion.* Officially, the People's Democratic Republic of Algeria, this nation is the tenth largest country in the world and the largest country in Africa and the Mediterranean. Its economy performed well in 2013, growing by 3 per cent. This is due to political stability. The GDP growth was driven by investment by public enterprises and private demand. Unemployment fell slightly in 2013. Currently, it stands at 9.8 per cent.
5. **Angola – GDP:** *$129.785 Billion.* Officially the Republic of Angola, this country is a member state of the African Union. It is Africa's second largest oil producer. Its economy grew by 5.1 per cent in 2013, below the estimate of 7.1 per cent. Growth was driven by agriculture, non-oil energy, fisheries, and construction and manufacturing sectors.

6. **Morocco – GDP:** *$114.7 Billion.* Morocco's GDP grew by 4.7 per cent in 2013, much better than the growth rate of 2.7 in 2012. This is due to the country's vibrant agricultural sector.
7. **Libya – GDP:** *$67.622 Billion.* Officially the State of Libya, this country had the highest HDI in Africa in 2009. The Civil War and NATO led Military intervention in 2011 affected the economy negatively. According to the Libyan Ministry of Economy, GDP declined sharply in 2013 due to oil blockades. It is expected to rebound during the 2014/2015. The nation's economy depends upon revenue from the oil sector, which accounts for 80 per cent of GDP.
8. **Sudan – GDP:** *$63 Billion.* The nation's real GDP grew by 3.6 per cent in 2013. The growth was driven by mining and agriculture and the inflows from oil transit fees and the transitional financial arrangement (TFA) with South Sudan.
9. **Kenya – GDP:** *$56.3 Billion.* Kenya's growth in the first three quarters of 2013 (5.2 per cent, 4.3 per cent and 4.6 per cent) was driven by tourism, financial intermediation, agriculture and construction. The nation is recovering from the showdown it went through in 2011.
10. **Ethiopia – GDP:** *$51 Billion.* Ethiopia's economy grew by 9.7 per cent in 2012/2013. Growth has been robust during the last decade.
11. **Ghana – GDP:** *$50 Billion.* Ghana had maintained an average growth of around 6 per cent over the past Six years. However, it decelerated to 4.4 per cent in 2013, much lower than 7.9 per cent in 2012.
12. **Tunisia – GDP:** *$45.611 Billion.* The nation's growth of 2.6 per cent in 2013 was below the forecast of 4.5 per cent. The growth rate was 3.7 per cent in 2012. This showdown is due to political deadlock, fragile social context and stagnation in the Euro zone.
13. **Tanzania – GDP:** *$36.6 Billion.* The GDP growth of around 7 per cent is driven by Communications, financial intermediary, transport, agriculture, construction and manufacturing. Investments in infrastructure will definitely support growth.
14. **Democratic Republic of Congo – GDP:** *$30.8 Billion.* Mining, trade, agriculture and construction contributed to GDP growth of 8.1 per cent in 2013. It was 7.2 per cent in 2012. DRC's economy remained robust in 2013. Mining has been the main driver of growth.
15. **Ivory Coast – GDP:** *$32 Billion.* Ivory Coast grew by 8.8 per cent in 2013. This is largely due to major public works projects. The growth rate is estimated to be around 9 per cent in the next two years. Prospects of the nation are bright.
16. **Cameroun – GDP:** *$30 Billion.* Cameroun has to use growth to reduce poverty. However, it has remained stable in a region that is affected by political and security crises. Growth in 2013 was driven by the tertiary sector, which accounted for 47.8 per cent of GDP.
17. **Uganda – GDP:** *$23.053 Billion.* Absolute poverty continued to drop, from 24.5 per cent in 2009/2010 to 22.2 per cent in 2012/2013. The nation is on track to achieve its Millennium Development Goals (Goals) for poverty reduction by 2015. The nation's GDP grew by 5.2 per cent in 2013.
18. **Zambia – GDP:** *$22.416 Billion.* Zambia's growth in real terms decreased to 6.5 per cent in 2013. This was mainly due to a reduction in agricultural output. Copper contributes about 70 per cent to the nation's export earnings.
19. **Gabon – GDP:** *$20.644 Billion.* Vigorous public investment, revenue from forestry, rising oil prices, revenue from mining, membership of Franc zone and private investment have contributed to Gabon's macroeconomic stability. The country's GDP grew by 5.5 per cent in 2013.
20. **Equatorial Guinea – GDP:** *$15.396 Billion.* Oil and Gas contribute significantly to Equatorial Guinea's economy. The economy of Equatorial Guinea was affected by recession in 2013. It was

due to fall in revenue from oil and lower oil and gas output. It experienced negative GDP growth of -1.4 per cent after positive 5.3 per cent growth in 2012. Experts estimate negative growth in 2014 (-1.8 per cent) and 2015 (-8.5 per cent).

MAJOR SECTORS PERCEIVED AS PATHS TO GROWTH OF AFRICA'S ECONOMY

Africa's growth prospects are bright and differ not only country by country but also sector by sector. The following seven major areas are considered here - agriculture, banking, consumer goods, infrastructure, mining, oil and gas, and telecommunications. It is expected that about 200 million Africans are entering the consumer goods market this 2015. Banking and telecommunications are growing rapidly too, and infrastructure expenditures are rising significantly faster in Africa than in the world as a whole. The continent has more than one-quarter of the world's arable land. Eleven of its countries rank among the top ten sources for at least one major mineral. Africa seems to produce 13 percent of global oil in recent times up from 9 percent in 1998. For many companies, this is a future worth investing in (http://www.mckinsey.com/insights/economic_studies/africas_path_to_growth_sector_by_sector, accessed 2015). Of course, no meaningful development can thrive in an economy without a sound and functional education system. Therefore, the education sector also forms a major path to the growth of African economy. In 2008, Africans spent $860 billion on goods and services—35% more than Indians spent (Chironga, Leke, Wamelen & Lund, 2011). As Africa's economies progress, opportunities are opening in sectors such as retailing, telecommunications, banking, infrastructure-related industries, resource-related businesses, and all along the agricultural value chain. Consider that telecom companies in Africa have added 316 million subscribers—more than the entire U.S. population—since 2000. According to UN data, Africa offers a higher return on investment than any other emerging market. For several reasons: Competition is less intense and few foreign companies have a presence there, and pent-up consumer demand is strong. Companies that desire revenues and profits can no longer ignore Africa. Smart multinational companies are busy planting their stakes in the ground. Nokia and Coca-Cola have distribution networks in nearly every African country; Unilever has a presence in 20 African nations, Nestlé in 19, Standard Chartered Bank in 14, Barclays in 12, and Société Générale in 15. Homegrown giants are expanding: Ecobank and South African Breweries each operate in over 30 African countries, while MTN and Shoprite are in 16 African countries each. Companies that enter Africa now, we believe, can shape industry structures, segment markets, and establish brands (https://hbr.org/2011/05/the-globe-cracking-the-next-growth-market-africa, accessed 2015).

Agriculture

According to Jayaram, Riese and Sanghvi (2010), http://www.mckinsey.com/insights/economic_studies/africas_path_to_growth_sector_by_sector, accessed 2015; agriculture is Africa's largest economic sector, representing 15 percent of the continent's total GDP, or more than $100 billion annually. It is highly concentrated, with Egypt and Nigeria alone accounting for one-third of total agricultural output and the top ten countries generating 75 percent.

Africa's agro-ecological potential is massively larger than its current output, however—and so are its food requirements. While more than one-quarter of the world's arable land lies in this continent, it generates only 10 percent of global agricultural output. So there is huge potential for growth in a sector now expanding only moderately, at a rate of 2 to 5 percent a year. Jayaram, Riese and Sanghvi highlighted four main challenges inhibit the faster growth of agricultural output in Africa.

- **Fragmentation:** With 85 percent of Africa's farms occupying less than two hectares, production is highly fragmented. In Brazil, Germany, and the United States, for example, only 11 percent or less of farms operate on this scale. Therefore, new industry models that allow small farms to gain some of the benefits of scale are required.
- **Interdependence and Complexity:** A successful agricultural system requires reliable access to financing, as well as high-quality seeds, fertilizer, and water. Other essentials include access to robust markets that could absorb the higher level of agricultural output, a solid postharvest value chain for the output of farmers, and programs to train them in best practices so that they can raise productivity. Africa has diverse agro-ecological conditions, so countries need to adopt many different farming models to create an African green revolution.
- **Underinvestment:** To make the agricultural system work better, experts estimate, sub-Saharan Africa alone requires additional annual investments of as much as $50 billion. African agriculture therefore needs business models that can significantly increase the level of investment from the private and public sectors, as well as donors.
- **Enabling Conditions:** A successful agricultural transformation requires some basics to be in place—transportation and other kinds of infrastructure, stable business and economic conditions, and trained business and scientific talent. Many African countries are making great strides in laying the groundwork, but others are lagging behind.

In addition to these four, there is the problem of mono-economy. Most African countries concentrate on one product instead of a diversified economy. Consequently, any structural defect in production or price fluctuation can distort the economy.

Over the past few years, as a way of solving the food crisis which engulfed the entire world over there have been reenergizing of efforts to improve African agriculture, since Africa is known for its fertile land. African countries have committed themselves to increasing agriculture's share of their budgets to 10 percent, donors are making significantly increased commitments, and private-sector players and investment funds are pouring serious money into the area. These increased investments flow toward three general opportunities. The first is developing technological breakthroughs, such as drought-tolerant maize, that would have high returns on investment and could sustainably raise small farmers from poverty. Second, new value chain approaches aim to improve access to markets and help groups of farmers raise their productivity. The third opportunity is the development of selected large tracts of high-potential agricultural land.

New models for large-scale change led by the public or private sectors also have a lot of potential. They include plans rolled out under the Comprehensive Africa Agriculture Development Program, an initiative to help African countries increase their economic growth through agriculture-led expansion. In our work in Africa, several approaches have seemed promising. One is a new kind of industry structure—nucleus farms—to accelerate the productivity of small-holders. These 50-hectare farms are operated by sophisticated farmers who also help small farmers in their areas to become more productive and to market through the nucleus farm. Other approaches include warehouse aggregators (entrepreneurs who own warehouses used to distribute fertilizer and seed and to store crops) and more efficiently run farming cooperatives. Similarly, our work with food manufacturers and retailers shows that end-to-end supply chains that can effectively source produce from African farmers have great potential. Fifty years after the start of the Asian green revolution, Africa too is poised for one. This will be a complex and difficult undertaking, but the continent seems to be on the right path.

Banking

Grandis, Pinshaw, Sanghvi (2010) said that Africa's banking sector has grown rapidly in the last decade. Sub-Saharan Africa has become a substantial player in emerging-market banking, with total 2008 assets of $669 billion, while North Africa's asset base has grown substantially, to $497 billion. Africa's banking assets thus compare favorably with those in other emerging markets, such as Russia (with $995 billion). Almost 50 percent of the growth at Africa's largest banks came from portfolio momentum—the market's natural increase—compared with only about 17 percent from inorganic (or M&A-driven) sources. Underpinning this portfolio momentum is strong overall market expansion: the financial sector is outgrowing GDP in most of the continent's main markets. Between 2000 and 2008, for example, Kenya's GDP grew by 4.4 percent annually, its financial sector by 8.5 percent. The only significant exception is Egypt, where regulatory restrictions have limited the sector's growth to only 2.3 percent annually, compared with 4.8 percent for GDP, (Grandis, Pinshaw, Sanghvi added).

Financial reforms have largely enabled this growth. Nigerian banking reform promoted a swift consolidation (from 89 to 25 banks between 2004 and 2006) that unlocked the sector's potential—bigger banks with better capabilities could drive down their costs, allowing them to penetrate a larger portion of the unbanked population and to ride on the back of rapid economic growth. As a result, total banking assets grew by more than 59 percent annually from 2004 to 2008. In August 2009, the newly appointed central-bank governor initiated reforms to increase accountability and transparency. M&A activity has also improved productivity, as smaller, less-efficient institutions are being acquired by larger ones. From 2004 to 2009, some 430 M&A deals involved financial institutions in Africa, and about 40 percent were cross-border, with the acquirer originating elsewhere in Africa or outside it. Banks in South Africa are especially active in gaining footholds outside their home market. Further market consolidation is taking place within countries. New entrants are also gaining share in countries where governments are allowing private banks to enter. Algeria, for example, has been opening up to private players since 1990. From 1990 to 2006, 12 new private-sector banks entered this market. Although lower growth is expected in the African banking sector in the next few years, attractive opportunities remain—expanding current product offerings, increasing product penetration, bringing the unbanked into the financial system, and capitalizing on the rise of a new consumer class by developing innovative service and channel offerings. Banks have employed several strategies to capture this growth. Sub-Saharan Africa has become a substantial player in emerging-market banking.

- **Geographic Expansion:** The pan-African Ecobank Transnational has more than 11,000 employees in more than 750 branches in 30 African countries. The key to the success of this strategy is the interconnection between the independent subsidiaries, which can tailor offerings to the local market and still benefit from regional connections, such as shared financial and personnel resources.

- **Entering New Segments:** South Africa's Capitec Bank leverages a technology-driven, low-cost banking model attractive to formerly unbanked customers. Its business model has four pillars: affordability, accessibility, simplicity, and personal service.
- **Product Innovation:** African Bank, a niche South African institution, emerged in the early 2000s to fill the gap between traditional banks and micro lenders. It offers innovative credit and savings products to salaried low- and middle-income customers. Loan applications are assessed in minutes thanks to sophisticated credit-scoring engines and a simplified application process that employs the latest technology, such as biometric scanners.
- **Improved Penetration:** As the financial sophistication of existing customers increases, African banks are selling additional products to meet their clients' evolving needs. In addition to basic transactional products, for example, many banks now offer a credit card or overdraft facility.
- **Channel Innovation:** New entrants without established branch networks can adopt a game-changing strategy: using only electronic channels. The mobile-payment service of Kenya's M-Pesa, for example, has helped formerly unbanked customers by filling a gap in the market.
- **Expanding along the Value Chain:** Nigerian banks are expanding and building in-house capabilities in areas that were traditionally the preserve of foreign players. In doing so, the Nigerian institutions have exploited synergies across their business units. In addition to these banks, the Pan African Bank – United Bank for Africa (UBA), First Bank, among others are fast expanding in business operations, thus improving the funding of MNEs.

Consumer Goods

Russo and Fiorini (2010) maintained that resources are not Africa's only driver of growth. Underlying it, the African consumer is on the rise. From 2005 to 2008, consumer spending across the continent increased at a compound annual rate of 16 percent, more than twice the GDP growth rate. GDP per capita rose in all but two countries. Many consumers have moved from the destitute level of income (less than $1,000 a year) to the basic-needs ($1,000 to $5,000) or middle-income (up to $25,000) levels. In Nigeria, for example, the collective buying power of households earning $1,000 to $5,000 a year doubled from 2000 to 2007, reaching $20 billion. Nearly seven million additional households have enough discretionary income to take their place as consumers. This evolution is critically important to consumer-facing businesses, from fast-moving consumer goods manufacturers to banks to telecommunications companies: when people begin earning money at the basic-needs level, they start buying and consuming goods and services. Additionally, we have observed that most consumer categories exhibit an *S*-curve growth pattern: in other words, when a country achieves a basic level of income, growth rates accelerate three- to fourfold. While the exact inflection point differs among categories, many of them are just entering this phase of accelerated growth. The enormous expansion of mobile telephony in Africa provides clear evidence of this phenomenon. Despite the recent slowdown in economic expansion, GDP per capita should continue on its positive trajectory of a 4.5 percent compound annual growth rate (CAGR) until 2015. That would mean a more than 35 percent increase in spending power. Combined with strong population growth (2 percent) and continued urbanization (3 percent), this increase leads us to estimate that 221 million basic-needs consumers will enter the market by 2015. As a result, the number of attractive or highly attractive national markets—with more than ten million consumers and gross national income exceeding $10 billion a year—will increase to 26 in 2014, from 19 in 2008. By 2015, 221 million additional basic-needs consumers will enter the market in Africa.

Many local and multinational consumer companies are already thriving in Africa and delivering handsome returns to their shareholders. To succeed, consumer companies must address five major challenges, some familiar to businesses operating in other emerging markets.

- **Heterogeneous Market Structure:** Africa has more than 50 countries, with large differences in spending power and consumer behavior, so a one-size-fits-all approach will not work. One consumer goods company approached this problem by segmenting African markets into four tiers, according to market potential and competitive dynamics. In tier-three markets, for example, consumers have low spending power and the infrastructure is poor, so this company simplified production by minimizing the number of SKUs, built strong distribution partnerships, concentrated marketing expenditures at the point of sale, and used smaller pack sizes to increase trial purchases and volumes. In tier-one markets, the company takes a totally different approach: in these relatively wealthy areas, consumers are easier to reach, so it uses direct distribution and sales, offers a full suite of SKUs, and focuses marketing on building the brand through a broad range of advertising approaches.
- **Low Affordability Levels:** Ninety-five percent of the population and 71 percent of the income remain at the base of the pyramid. Companies thus will not be able to build sizable businesses through premium goods alone; they will have to reinvent their business models to deliver the right products at the right price point. To meet these consumers' needs effectively, companies must tailor the way they design products and create product portfolios. Additionally, they must learn to compete against local players that have fundamentally different cost structures.
- **Underdeveloped Distribution and Route to Market:** Modern trade is still nascent in most of Africa. The traditional mom-and-pop shops, open markets, umbrella vendors, and the like dominate the retail scene, making up more than 85 percent of the trade volumes. Poor roads and infrastructure can make delivering products to consumers a daunting task, so companies must build strong sales and distribution networks by leveraging a mix of third-party, wholesale, and direct-distribution models.
- **Nascent Categories:** In Africa, many categories still are not fully developed; for example, usage per capita of toothpaste is lower there than it is in comparable Asian countries. Data about consumers' needs and behavior are scarce, making it harder to develop specific consumer insights. In addition, the state of the communications media and education levels make it challenging to reach consumers with specific product messages. Competing in Africa therefore is not a share game. Rather, companies need to bring a market-development mind-set, investing in consumer education and nontraditional marketing techniques.
- **Talent Shortages:** Despite the abundant work opportunities, talent remains scarce across Africa. Truly competing and winning in the long term, however, will require local know-how and talent. At first, companies will need to bridge the gap by using a mix of local and international employees. In parallel, investments in developing and retaining local talent are required. Local capability-building programs, attractive career paths, and apprenticeship opportunities will be critical to achieving long-term success.

Infrastructure

Cloete, Faulhaber and Zils (2001) reported that between 1998 and 2007, spending on African infrastructure rose at a compound annual rate of 17 percent—up from $3 billion in 1998 to $12 billion in 2008, significantly outstripping the growth of global infrastructure investment.[1] Africa accounted for 11 percent of total global private-sector and foreign-funded investment from 1999 to 2001 and for 17 percent from 2005 to 2007. This growth has been driven largely by increased funding from non-OECD[2] governments—particularly China's, which provided 77 percent of it in 2007. The private sector is still the largest single source of funds (45 percent in 2007). Rapid growth has attracted many multinational companies within and outside Africa. While this growth has been substantial, the size of the investment gap that must be closed if the continent is to realize the United Nations' Millennium Development Goals is more than $180 billion for sub-Saharan Africa alone (2007–14). Governments and the private sector must therefore substantially increase their infrastructure spending. For Nigeria, which aims to be among the world's top 20 economies by 2020, reaching the same infrastructure levels that Brazil has today would require investments in excess of $190 billion—60 percent of today's GDP—or an additional 3 percent of GDP for the next 20 years. So the growth trend in African infrastructure is far from over, and several countries have already announced significant additional spending. South Africa, for example, will invest $44 billion in transport, fuel, water, and energy infrastructure from 2009 to 2011—a 73 percent increase in annual spending from the levels of 2007 to 2008. Since infrastructure investments also offer a high stimulus multiple in times of economic slowdown, Angola, Kenya, Mozambique, Nigeria, and Senegal have announced essentially similar programs, though on a much smaller scale. Examined at a more granular level, this remarkable growth has clearly occurred in a limited set of countries and sectors. Algeria, Kenya, Morocco, Nigeria, South Africa, and Tunisia were responsible for 75 percent of the investment from 1997 to 2007. Infrastructure spending, fueled by an oil boom, is also growing rapidly in Angola. There is however, infrastructure partnerships of which the private sector, though well placed to lead or support most types of infrastructure development and operation, often needs some government participation.

Lying behind this unevenness are big variations in the size of African economies, economic volatility, political stability, and the quality of logistics, health care, and skills. Almost three-quarters of these countries do not have GDPs large enough to sustain projects of more than $100 million (a comparatively small budget for, say, a port, an airport, a major road, or a power project).[3] Similarly, the quality of roads and the density of populations vary considerably. Fifteen African countries are landlocked, and African transport costs are up to four times higher than those in the developed world, complicating the importation of equipment and materials. Infrastructure investment has been similarly concentrated in specific sectors. Mobile telephony accounted for more than 30 percent of it from 1997 to 2007 because this market was very attractive and the required infrastructure had a relatively short payback period. Electricity generation, distribution, and transmission accounted for 23 percent of investment as countries across the continent developed large-scale projects (for example, the Bujagali hydroelectric power plant, in Uganda). Infrastructure for natural-gas transmission made up a further 10 percent. Investments in rail, largely in South Africa, took 11 percent of the total. Those in other transportation assets, such as roads, ports, and airports, were limited by poor business cases and long payback periods. Likewise, investments in water and waste made up only 1 percent of the total, given the poor business case for private players. Yet investment in African infrastructure can be very profitable, with returns "up to twice as high as we get elsewhere," according to one expert. We have identified five keys to success.

- **Arrive Early and Take a Long-Term View:** If a company is to offset short-term currency risks and create the sustained relationships critical to success in Africa, a long-term view is essential. The construction company Julius Berger Nigeria, for example, has more than 100 years' experience in Nigeria, and the industrial conglomerate Mota-Engil first entered Angola in 1946. Both are now benefiting from the infrastructure booms in these two countries.
- **Build Relationships:** The reality of Africa is relationships in quasi-monopolistic markets, as its most important asset classes require special and hence scarce skills, and the operators and project sponsors are typically state-owned monopoly players (for instance, rail roads, airport companies, or road agencies). Finding the right local company to partner with gives multinational companies immediate access to excellent political and business relationships, as well as expertise in managing local labor and regulations. Both APM Terminals and DP World, for example, operate most of their African ports with local partners. In many countries, partnering with local companies is required (and where not required, usually favored) in the tender process.
- **Be Vigilant:** While risk management is important in all infrastructure projects, it is especially so in Africa, where the range of potential issues is wide and often unpredictable. Equipment problems at Mombasa port, in Kenya, for example, have caused significant, unexpected delays in the delivery of equipment for infrastructure projects in Burundi, Rwanda, southern Sudan, and Uganda.
- **Manage Actively:** Because Africa's business environment is so volatile, active management through the entire project life cycle is essential. One company developing a power plant in the Congo, for instance, discovered through active risk management that significant absenteeism in the workforce could be traced to the local traditional leader's dislike of the company's agreement with him. It had to resolve the dispute quickly to prevent a shutdown.
- **Diversify Your Project Portfolio:** No company can avoid all the risks associated with infrastructure in Africa. Successful companies therefore maintain a wide portfolio of projects. One approach is to diversify by geography: for example, APM Terminals operates ports in seven African countries. The other is diversification by sector: GE provides equipment for both power plants and railways; Julius Berger, construction services for transportation, commercial and residential property, ports, and the oil and gas industries in Nigeria. Fast-growing companies have used different strategies to combine these sources of success. Some go deep into one country and then proliferate across its business environment, especially if relationships and local understanding are critical. This approach is most important for construction companies and funders, since asset-specific expertise is not the most essential value driver for them. The engineering, construction, and petrochemical company Odebrecht, for example, entered Angola to develop the Capanda hydroelectric dam and has since expanded into residential and commercial construction, mining projects, and a partnership in a diamond exploration venture.

Other companies do business in a broad range of geographies, but in a specific class of assets (for example, ports and airports). This approach makes sense, especially for operators. If there are network effects beyond an individual country's borders, it is best to operate assets in a highly standardized way at a global level. DP World, for example, entered Africa through the Doraleh Container Terminal, located at the port of Djibouti, in 2000 and has since expanded to six terminals across Africa.

Mining

Bardouille, Hamblin, and Pley (2010) asserted that Africa's mining sector presents a paradox: although the continent is strongly endowed with mineral resources, mining has not been the consistent engine of economic development that people in many countries have hoped for. Nor, to date, has Africa attracted a share of global mining investment commensurate with its share of global resources. Unlike the output of most economic sectors (though like oil and gas), most minerals are globally traded. Global demand is therefore driven primarily by the needs of developed nations and the pace of growth in a few large developing countries. What's more, mining areas in Africa compete with that elsewhere for development funding. From a growth perspective, the question facing the sector is thus whether and how Africa can make its full potential contribution to satisfying the world's ever-growing need for mineral resources and capture wider socioeconomic benefits from their development. Many parts of Africa have long been known to be rich in mineral resources. Eleven of its countries, especially in southern and western Africa, rank among the top ten sources for at least one major mineral. The continent has a majority of the world's known resources of platinum, chromium, and diamonds, as well as a large share of the world's bauxite, cobalt, gold, phosphate, and uranium deposits. The development of these resources has faced more significant challenges, however, when compared with the experience of more developed mineral-rich countries, such as Australia or Chile. Even outside well-publicized conflict zones, many African countries have been thought to pose high political and economic risks for investors. Furthermore, infrastructure problems often hinder development: many bulk mineral deposits require multibillion-dollar investments in rail and port facilities to allow ore or semi processed minerals to reach their markets. Such investment decisions are not taken lightly, especially for less stable countries where the rule of law and security of tenure are not necessarily guaranteed.

Largely as a result, Africa's pattern of mining investment differs from that in other regions of the world. Of the five largest global diversified mining companies, only one has a major share of its production in Africa. With the diversified majors relatively quiet, junior mining companies and major ones focused on diamonds and precious metals have played a significant role in developing the continent's resources. In recent years, newer players, such as Chinese and Indian companies, have entered the scene, but few projects have been developed to the point of production. The recent financial and economic crisis has hit the global mining industry hard—and Africa at least as severely as other regions. Commodity prices slumped by 60 to 70 percent in late 2008, although they have since recovered considerably. There is now less appetite for the relatively high risk that usually comes with mining in many African countries. Despite the recent market turbulence, most observers expect demand for major mined commodities to grow strongly in the next 10 to 20 years, to support increased urbanization and infrastructure build-out in China and the emergence of India's middle class. Africa, given its share of global resources, will surely play a significant part in meeting that demand. Africa is rich in resources, with about 11 African countries among the top ten global resource countries in at least one major mineral.

For mining companies and investors, the economic crisis has taken the froth out of the market. But it hasn't fundamentally changed many of the factors that will shape long-term investment decisions, including political and economic stability, taxation regimes, and the availability of infrastructure. Nor, of course, has it changed the underlying geology. Lower commodity prices and stock market valuations have shifted the "build or buy" balance between in-house exploration and development, on the one hand, and mergers and acquisitions, on the other. If valuations continue to recover, this window of opportunity may be short-lived. Over the longer term, international companies considering investments in Africa will need to spend time and energy to gain a deeper understanding of the unique challenges of every African country. They should learn from the success stories of other players, assess risk comprehensively, and determine the role each country will play in their portfolios. Mining projects will need to include the broader socioeconomic-development programs that have been commonplace in petroleum for many years. In many cases, these programs will be achieved through partnerships between mining companies and other parties, which will provide financing and infrastructure development.

Africa's governments will play a major role in shaping the future environment. In recent years, governments have expressed frustration about the way the continent's resource endowment hasn't translated into economic development. The African Union and the UN Economic Commission for Africa (UNECA) have developed the African Mining Vision 2050, which sets out a number of ideas for increasing the resource wealth flowing to the nations that host mining operations. Some of these ideas would transfer wealth from mining companies to governments—for example, by making the auctioning of exploration rights more effective and linking taxation to commodity prices more closely. Others, such as the better management of resource income and the active development of the supply and infrastructure sectors, aim to create a more favorable environment for economic development.

Oil and Gas

Roelofsen and Sheng (2010) deciphered that African oil and gas have become important components of the world's hydrocarbon supply–demand balance. By 2015, 13 percent of global oil production will take place in Africa, compared with 9 percent in 1998—a 5 percent compound annual growth rate (CAGR). African oil projects have attracted substantial investment thanks to their cost competitiveness versus those in other regions. What's more, the oil and gas sector is a foundational element of economic growth for the continent, as 19 African countries are significant producers. It accounts for a significant part of the state's revenues there and represents a prime mover for employment, domestic power development, and, in many cases, infrastructure development (for instance, schools, hospitals, and roads). The sources of growth in oil and gas are evolving. In the past decade, production increases came primarily from deep water oil in Angola and Nigeria, along with new sources in countries such as Chad and Sudan, as well as offshore gas in Egypt. Production of deep water oil will continue to grow (in the Gulf of Guinea, for example), while onshore gas and new-resource development in emerging East African hydrocarbon producers (such as Uganda) are expected to become the other main engines for growth.

International oil companies as a group have fared well in Africa, as the licensing of acreage and M&A gave them access to valuable properties. These companies have also moved expeditiously into the new, technically complex frontiers of liquid natural gas, deep water oil, and underdeveloped countries (Chad, for example). Superior operating capabilities and financial muscle continue to give the internationals a competitive advantage in Africa; however, sustained growth has eluded those that acquired little and mainly operated more mature fields or had operations in countries with geopolitical and security risks. Large and growing companies are impacting positively in Africa. Roelofsen and Sheng said that in recent years, oil production has grown more rapidly in Africa than in any other region, while the production of gas has increased more rapidly in Africa than anywhere but the Middle East.

Indigenous national oil companies have set ambitious goals to become stand-alone, commercially viable domestic (and in some cases international) operating organizations. The inefficiencies of working in bureaucratic environments where these companies must strive to meet economic and sociopolitical missions have stifled their development, however. National oil companies have been further constrained by the challenge of developing local technical, commercial, and managerial capabilities. These companies must transform them fundamentally and create systems, a performance culture, and governance models along the lines of those found in commercially driven enterprises. Also, in recent years, new kinds of competitors have entered and grown in Africa, once the domain of the large international oil companies. Smaller independent oil companies (such as Addax, Heritage Oil, and Tullow Oil) have made successful finds in emerging basins. National oil companies from outside Africa, including China (CNPC, CNOOC, and Sinopec), Malaysia (Petronas), and Russia (Gazprom) have also aggressively invested in the continent, linking broader infrastructure investments and government-to-government relationships with access to resources. The challenge for these competitors in the years ahead will be to build sustainable enterprises and local capabilities beyond the scope of an individual project or investment. As for the countries that host oil and gas operations, they should continue to offer international and national oil companies alike an attractive investment environment, which ought to foster competition for natural resources, greater efficiency in the oil and gas sector, and the building of sustainable capabilities. Governments must also focus on new ways to leverage their resource sectors to capture the economic multiplier of broader GDP growth—for example, by using oil and gas as the catalyst for downstream energy (such as power stations, refineries, and retail outlets) and related industrial development (petrochemicals and basic materials).

Telecommunications

Gaibi, Maske, and Moraje (2010) averred that Telecommunications has been an important driver of Africa's economic growth in the last five years. The market is increasingly competitive, and world-class local enterprises are emerging in voice and data services. Telecom revenues have increased at a compound annual growth rate (CAGR) of 40 percent, and the number of subscribers rapidly exceeded 400 million. To meet the increased demand, investment in telecom infrastructure—about $15 billion a year—has also grown massively, with a 33 percent CAGR from 2003 to 2008. But annual growth will slow down to the low double digits—still quite enviable by Western standards—as the traditional urban markets become saturated; penetration in major cities such as Abidjan (Côte d'Ivoire), Lusaka (Zambia), and Libreville (Gabon) is 70 percent or more. Still up for grabs are two key pockets of growth, data and rural voice, with an additional revenue pool of $12 billion to $15 billion by 2012.

About 50 percent of the growth in voice will come from rural areas. To capture this opportunity, however, operators and regulators must forge new industry practices. The industry structure should be rationalized, for example, because many markets, even smaller ones, have four or more players. Also needed are new operating models, which might be created by slashing the cost of deploying base stations by 50 percent or more, innovating in distribution and recharging practices, and seeking more individualized pricing models, ideally delivered directly to customers rather than through advertising. Data services are the other large growth pocket, of about $5 billion, and that's not all. Experience in other countries suggests that a 10 percent increase in broadband penetration translates into additional GDP growth of some 0.5 to 1.5 percent. Social welfare improves as well; many small-boat fishermen in Senegal, for example, now use mobile-data services to select the best ports for unloading their catch each morning, increasing sales by 30 percent. Applications such as mobile health care will also provide significant benefits, helping governments to stretch thin resources further. McKinsey's experience in developing markets indicates that 80 percent of health care issues can be resolved by mobile phone, at a cost per capita that is 90 percent lower than that of traditional health care models. On the other hand,

Chironga, Leke, Wamelen Lund, (2011) categorized African economies under the following groups: the diversified economy; the oil exporters; transition economies and pre-transition economies.

The Diversified Economies

According to the authors, Africa's four most advanced economies—Egypt, Morocco, South Africa, and Tunisia—have well-developed manufacturing and service industries. They have relatively high per capita incomes and more stable GDP growth than most of the other economies, despite the political risks that have come to the fore in North Africa. Services, such as banking, telecom, and retailing, have accounted for more than 70% of GDP growth in these countries over the past decade. These countries are also Africa's largest consumer markets; 90% of households there have some discretionary income. That makes them ideal places for consumer-facing businesses to anchor their operations. Walmart, for example, recently struck a $2.4 billion deal to pick up a 51% stake in one of South Africa's largest retailers, Massmart, which has stores in 13 other African countries. However, these economies have higher labor costs than China or India and struggle to compete even in low-value manufacturing industries. They need to expand exports, improve education to create a skilled workforce, and build infrastructure.

The Oil Exporters

Africa's oil and gas exporters have the continent's highest per capita incomes but are the least diversified economies. Three of the largest—Algeria, Angola, and Nigeria—have already attracted the world's petroleum majors and have rapidly growing consumer markets. In Angola, for instance, retail banking is expected to grow by 6.8% a year through 2020, telecommunication services by 5.2% a year, and nonfood consumer goods by 4.4% a year. Because of their income levels, the oil exporters are attractive markets for high-end goods and services. Africa's oil exporters face the same challenges as many resource-rich nations: maintaining political stability; resisting the temptation to overinvest, which would make them vulnerable if commodity prices decline; and creating a diversified economy. Nigeria has already begun the transition to a diversified economy. While resources have accounted for 35% of the country's GDP growth since 2000, services have accounted for 37%. The number of telecommunications subscribers there increased from practically zero in 2000 to 63 million by 2008, and banking assets grew fivefold.

The Transition Economies

Africa's transition economies—such as Ghana, Kenya, Uganda, and Senegal—have lower per capita incomes than the countries in the first two groups but are growing rapidly. Though their agriculture and resource sectors together account for as much as 35% of GDP, and two-thirds of exports, these countries increasingly export manufactured goods to other African countries. The penetration of banking, telecom, and modern retailing is much lower than it is in the diversified economies, but that offers attractive opportunities. Companies targeting these markets must tailor products to poorer customers. Still, early entrants will find less competition here, and the rapid growth is expected to continue. Several transition economies are likely to increase their commodity exports in the coming years, which could facilitate growth. In Ghana and Uganda, for instance, recent oil discoveries will boost tax revenues, making it easier for them to diversify their economies.

The Pre-Transition Economies

These economies are poor, with annual per capita GDP of just $353 on average. But some of them are expanding rapidly. The three largest—the Democratic Republic of the Congo, Ethiopia, and Mali—have grown, on average, 7% a year since 2000. However, their growth has been erratic in the past. The economies of the Democratic Republic of the Congo, Ethiopia, and Mali have grown 7% a year since 2000. These pre-transition economies differ greatly, but all of them lack the basics, such as stable governments, strong public institutions, and sustainable agricultural development. Multinational companies must track these economies, but only those that can handle the risks should enter them.

ROLE OF MULTINATIONAL ENTERPRISES ON AFRICA'S ECONOMY

In the author's opinion, MNEs and its key feature FDI tends to originate more from developed economies than developing economies such as Africa. Grunberg (2001) noted that the very poorest countries many of them in Africa, are essentially bystanders in the global activity, attracting less than one per cent of all FDI flows. Africa has remained the focus of multinationals in recent times, most of the investments coming from European nations, Asian tigers, and the United States of America. It is a fact that the competitive global market has prompted countries at all levels of development to find new ways to channel FDI to their countries for purposes of development. Apart from its potential to pool the largest source of external finance for developing countries, FDI has elastic potential to generate employment, raise productivity, transfer skills and technology, enhances exports and contribute to the long-term economic development of developing countries of Africa.

A study from the Initiative for Global Development reveals that while revenues from the biggest American firms consistently dropped between 2006 and 2009, the top 30 MNCs based in sub-Saharan Africa grew at an astonishing 30% per year during the same period (Ruxin, 2011). Ruxin further explained that MNCs based in some of the poorest countries are in fact among the fastest growing in the world, and tremendously profitable opportunities are rooted right here in Africa's emerging economics. The private sector of sub-Saharan Africa is becoming a force for job creation, new products, and economic stability. The MNCs highlighted in the study span industries from agribusiness and banking to petroleum and tourism. These are large-scale operations that create jobs, build income, and help the countries modernize infrastructure; they can mark the difference between weak economic development and sustainable poverty alleviation in the developing world.

What makes homegrown African MNCs different from the rest? In answering the question, Ruxin noted that MNCs based in sub-Saharan Africa have long prioritized local capacity building. An aluminum smelter manufacturer in Mozambique sponsored training programs for workers, building the skills of the local workforce. SEACOM, a privately owned cable company, installed thousands of miles undersea fiberoptic cable across Africa, increasing broadband capacity and affecting a 5000 percent increase in internet use in Kenya alone.

There is therefore the need to ensure the continued growth of Africa's MNCs. First and foremost, good governance is essential. Corruption must be kept at bay, and non-competitive, antiquated tariffs need to be dismantled. Strong physical infrastructure is also critical, since no company can thrive without dependable electricity, access to good roads, and efficient and fast telecommunication networks.

With strong foundations, Africa will be ideal for local and foreign investment. In Rwanda, the leading cell phone and internet carrier of South Africa has made massive investments in infrastructure. A gourmet coffee shop, Bourbon Coffee, originated in Kigali and has since opened cafes in Washington D.C., Manhattan, and soon in Boston – making it Rwanda's first multinational chain. Can African MNCs ever become major world players in the same way that companies from Asia and the US are today? Based on the current trajectory, that once unimaginable scenario seems – for the first time – possible.

The benefits of multinational corporations to the economy of Africa are enormous. African countries would have been more developed than most countries that are now among economic giants; including those that were at par or even behind some African countries like Nigeria, Egypt, among others, but for lack of economic diversification which hindered the development of MNEs. Nigeria in particular would have been ahead of Malaysia, Indonesia and even Brazil if not for policy reversals and inconsistencies, which least favored the development of MNEs.

Osuagwu and Ezie (2013) averred that multinational corporations transfer technologies, capital and the culture of entrepreneurship. They increase investment levels and income in the host countries; they promote improvement in their immediate environment; create access to high quality managerial skills; improve the balance of payment of host countries by increasing exports and decreasing imports; help to equalize the costs of factors of production. They stimulate domestic production and enhance efficiency and effectiveness in the production process; they stimulate positive responses from local operators. Most Nigerian entrepreneurs, who are now excelling in MNEs started by working for the multinational corporations, where they acquired relevant skills and knowledge that gave them the impetus to launch out. Multinational corporations also acquire raw materials with ease from any overseas source at competitive prices and can easily export components and finished goods for assembly or distribution in foreign markets. They create several other opportunities in the host country that create employment and improve living standards of the host communities. Looking at the fortune of about 500 companies Nigeria, only very few play big in the Nigerian economy, although their products are sufficiently visible. Nigeria is a big consumer of the products and services of multinational and transnational corporations and deserves to host a good number of them at this stage of our development.

Schneidman (2007) noted that corporations are committing themselves to looking beyond public relations to genuine social and economic needs in host countries. The challenge for African governments and donor agencies, however, is to more clearly understand how Corporate Social Responsibilities (CSR) program contribute to the development process. In particular, an effort should be made to quantify in a more systematic and transparent way how CSR programs promote growth and development. Companies also need to be more involved in the development dialogue that takes place among host governments, bilateral donors, and the international financial institutions (IFIs). Some worry that as corporations become involved in education, community development, or environmental programs in host countries, they are taking on functions that African governments ought to be performing. In that way, corporations might be contributing to the phenomenon of "weak states" that are regarded as an impediment to development in Africa.

The simple fact is, however, that many African governments do not have the capacity to implement broad-based development programs. If they did, the bilateral donors and the IFIs would not be involved either. Nevertheless, companies should ensure that their CSR programs become self-sustaining and that there is a significant capacity building component to what they do. Given the current commodity boom, international companies will be making increasingly large investments in Africa, especially in the extractive sectors. Not only will this generate significant revenues for the companies and host governments, but it will raise expectations among host governments and civil society organizations that the companies will take a more active and visible, role in giving back to the communities in which they are active.

With an estimated 800 Chinese companies actively operating in Africa, they too need to be part of this dialogue. There are important environmental and health concerns surrounding Chinese corporate involvement in such areas as mining and hydroelectric dam construction in Africa, as well as worries over Chinese corporate conduct in dealing with African officials. Consequently, it is essential both for Africa and for China's reputation as a responsible actor in world affairs that Chinese companies take steps to demonstrate that they are constructive corporate citizens.

Evidence abound that Chinese companies on the continent are becoming aware of this need. There is no question that multinational companies investing in Africa have the resources, and the responsibility, to contribute to Africa's development. At the same time, international companies need to enhance their understanding of the development process in order to integrate with national development strategies to maximize the results of their social investments. Some companies have already hired development specialists to oversee CSR programs and others will likely follow suit. It is an immediate challenge, as noted above, for companies to organize their input so that their CSR efforts are coordinated with other donor programs. Given the increasing resources that companies are investing in Africa, the World Bank and donor agencies need to reach out on a more systematic basis to bring the companies into the development process to ensure that all parties coordinate the design and implementation of their development efforts.

Chironga, Leke, Wamelen Lund, (2011) observed that Africa is benefitting from the increases in commodity prices. Oil prices have shot up since 1999, when they were less than $20 a barrel, reaching more than $145 a barrel in 2008, and prices for minerals, grains, and other raw materials have also soared. Yet that trend explains only part of the African story. Natural resources directly accounted for just about a quarter (24%) of GDP growth from 2000 through 2008. Other industries, such as wholesale and retail trade, transportation, telecommunications, and manufacturing, contributed the rest. In fact, countries that export commodities grew just a tad faster, at 5.4% a year, than non-exporters, which on average grew 4.6% from 2000 through 2008.

Three factors are responsible. One, several African countries, such as Angola and Mozambique, halted deadly hostilities, creating the political stability necessary for growth. The number of serious conflicts in Africa—those in which deaths exceed 1,000 people a year—declined from an average of 4.8 a year in the 1990s to 2.6 in the 2000s. Two, economies became healthier as governments shrank budget deficits, trimmed foreign debt, and brought down inflation. Since 2000, African countries have cut their combined foreign debt from 82% of GDP to 59% and reduced budget deficits from 4.6% of GDP to 1.8%, which sent inflation rates tumbling from 22% to 8%. Africa will continue to profit from the rising global demand for oil, natural gas, minerals, food, and other natural resources. The continent has abundance of riches; including 10% of the world's oil reserves, 40% of its gold ore, and 80% to 90% of its deposits of chromium and platinum group metals. To exploit them, African governments are forging new types of partnerships in which buyers from countries such as China and India provide up-front payments, invest in infrastructure, and share management skills and technology.

Long-term growth will get a boost from Africa's demographic and social trends. The population is young, growing, and migrating to the metropolitan centers. In 1980, 28% of Africans lived in cities; today 40% do—a proportion close to China's and larger than India's. Workers in cities earn higher pay than those in rural areas and can afford to buy products and services beyond the necessities of food and shelter. That expands demand, which leads to a virtuous cycle of growth and job creation.

Many people picture Africans as subsistence farmers, but there's a sizable middle class on the continent. By 2008, 16 million African households had incomes above $20,000 a year—a level that enabled them to buy houses, cars, appliances, and branded products. Another 27 million households earned $10,000 to $20,000. In addition, 41 million households reported incomes of $5,000 to $10,000—the level at which families starts spending more than half their income on nonfood items. By 2020 the total number of households in all three segments will reach 128 million, which should make Africa one of the fastest-growing consumer markets of this decade.

Rugraff and Hansen (2011) used the theory of multinational corporation-local firm relations to reflect the impact of MNEs and noted that the theory of MNC-local firm relations is mainly informed by three economic traditions, namely trade economics, industrial organization and international business. These are summarized by the author in relation to African economies thus:

Trade Economy

Multinational Enterprises can improve the economy of African countries by allowing for capital flows between capital-rich and capital-poor countries. A comparative approach can be developed, aiming to enhance the distribution of the gain for a capital-scarce country of additional investments coming from a capital-abundant country between countries with strong and weak currencies. The additional foreign capital could enhance welfare by increasing production and improving the allocation of scarce resources. This can also allow for the possibility of economies-of-scale and product differentiation. Rugraff and Hansen (2011) postulated the New Trade Economic theory which features two main frameworks, the vertical multinational and the horizontal-multinational framework. The vertical multinational separates the stages of production geographically and localizes labor-intensive activities in developing countries to take advantage of relatively abundant unskilled labor, whereas the horizontal multinationals duplicate the same product or service in different locations. In terms of MNC effects, New Trade Economics predicted that MNCs produce both crowding-in effects and crowding-out effects. The authors further explained that a special advantage which Foreign Multinationals have over the indigenous host-country rivals could be in the area of use of superior technology or lower costs due to economies of scale, they may initially produce crowding-out of local investment. On the other hand, they may in the longer run 'crowd in' due to high transportation costs that force the MNCs to source locally, thereby creating a catalyst impact on local firms in the intermediate goods industry. The catalyst effect results from MNCs' demand for a larger variety of intermediate goods and a rise in the quantities supplied which stimulates economies-of-scale. The equilibrium that will emerge depends on the impact of both opposed effects. While New Trade Economic models abandoned the strict assumptions of the original neoclassical theory thus empirically producing more robust predictions, they still belong to the neoclassical body, which may be effective in tackling problems of resource allocation and equilibrium thanks to prize- and/or quantity-based adjustment mechanisms, but is inadequate in conceptualizing the variations and complexity in MNC strategy and effects.

Industrial Organization

The Industrial Organization literature on MNCs aimed to study the consequences of 'the entry into a national industry of a firm established in a foreign market'. Markets are full of imperfections of the structural type – proprietary technology, privileged access to inputs, economies of scale, control of distribution systems and product differentiation – that can be used by firms to increase their monopoly power and to internationalize. The main idea of this school of thought is that the characteristics of the industry fundamentally affect the strategy and performance of firms, and indeed, the effects that MNCs may have on host countries. Thus, industry characteristics may impact whether or not MNCs crowd in or crowd out local firms; whether they transfer technology and knowledge from parents to affiliates; whether they foster linkages to local firms; and whether they suppress or foster competition in the host country.

International Business

From the mid-1970s, microeconomic literature on MNCs emerged, literature that later would provide one of the main pillars of International Business. Early International Business literature, in line with the Industrial Organization 'Structure-Conduct-Performance paradigm', argued that multinationals possess special assets in comparison to local firms that allow them to overcome the disadvantage of foreignness. The firm-specific know-how, its knowledge-capital and its technology assets appear to be key ownership advantages. Internationalization per se reinforces the multinational's advantages by providing opportunities to divide marketing risks, by slicing up the value chain on the base of the territories' comparative advantages, and by providing access to new resources and assets. The multinationals' ownership advantage is often reinforced by the ability they have to access finance, internationally and in the host economy, compared to local firms which are most of the time financially constrained. There is also the advantage of MNEs which relates to the ability to organize cross-border transactions in the face of market imperfections; the ability to leverage resources across borders; and the advantage related to coordinating knowledge diffusion and development across borders. Moreover, host countries would have great problems matching the bargaining power of MNCs and would tend to strike unfavorable deals with the MNCs. MNCs were expressions of efficiency and therefore welfare enhancing. Similarly, more recent resource-based perspectives and knowledge-based perspectives look at MNCs as superior vehicles for cross-border knowledge and resource transfer and thereby as potentially benefiting host countries. But it can be inferred from the market-power view that if MNCs are about extending market power to foreign locations, local firms may be harmed. And if MNCs are about the effective transfer of superior knowledge and technology to subsidiaries, they may have a high potential for producing demonstration and competition effects. Moreover, as recognized by modern International Business theory, as MNC boundaries are becoming increasingly fuzzy, and as MNCs are increasingly locating the development and exploitation of their ownership-specific advantages in business networks and strategic alliances, new opportunities for acquiring technology, knowledge and market access for local firms in emerging economies are provided.

SPECIFIC ROLES OF MNEs IN THE GROWTH AND DEVELOPMENT OF AFRICAN ECONOMIES

Specific roles of MNEs in the growth and development of African economies include the following:

1. Capital and investment expansion;
2. Employment and production;
3. Skills and technological development;

4. Integration into global economy;
5. Expansion of international trade;
6. Promotes international integration;
7. Effective utilization of resources.
8. Introduces better and cheaper products and sharpen competition.

Capital and Investment Expansion

Multinational Enterprises have large capital and equally have the potential for investment expansion given the large pool of capital. It is however observed in Chapter 10 that African MNEs are not among the top 500 MNEs in global ranking. Nonetheless, the growth in business activities across the region holds brighter prospects for Africa's MNEs to compete at global level. For instance MTN group, a South African MNE is fast expanding with subsidiaries across continents.

Employment and Production

The role of MNEs in the world economy will likely continue to grow, as governments everywhere compete hard to attract foreign investment to their country. Foreign direct investment, which is a good measure of the growing internationalization of production, is worth about a quarter of world GDP. Foreign affiliates of MNEs account for about a third of world exports. These MNEs are likely to bring in more jobs, better pay, better conditions and better practices to host countries, especially developing countries. MNEs' seem to have superior technical know-how and modern management practices, which provide them with the wherewithal to pay high wages, compared to what may apply to local workers in local firms. This issue could better be examined by comparing labor practices between local and foreign firms.

Hijzen and Swaim (2008) reported that foreign multinationals pay 40% higher in average wages than local firms, and the differential is higher in low-income countries. They may offer higher pay than their local counterparts because this helps to minimize worker turnover and reduce monitoring costs. Besides paying higher wages, multinationals differ from local firms in many other ways, such as being much larger and more productive. This raises the possibility that MNEs pay higher wages only because they prefer to invest in capital-intensive sectors and rely on highly skilled employees. But the pattern would not imply that they offer better rewards to equally qualified workers performing similar work in other firms. The authors argue that more precise comparisons are required to detect whether MNEs pay higher wages and offer better working conditions. For this purpose, they examine how conditions change if a local firm is taken over by a foreign one, as well as the experiences of workers that move from a local to a foreign firm.

Salary Structure of Selected MNEs in Nigeria

How much do MNEs in Africa really pay their workers? Although not everyone considers pay package as the first thing for picking up a particular job, but there is no denying that pay packages determine a whole lot of things when it comes to picking up jobs. It does seem like many corporate organisations are waking up to the reality that if they must engage and keep the best hands, paying encouraging salaries, rather than stipends is the right thing. It is the author's opinion that with attractive pay package, workers will raise productivity, hence; contributing positively to the overall economic development of the society in which the MNEs operate. This therefore raises concerns on the attractiveness of Africa-based MNEs in terms of their pay package. It is imperative therefore to look at a few of them and the industries they represent. It is also important to note that within same industry, there are disparities in salary scale depending on company policies, department and of course the level of the staff in the company – entry, middle or management. A few MNEs based in Nigeria with their salary structure are highlighted below using the home currency (Naira). For instance, MTN (Telecoms) pays her entry level staff up to N2.5million per annum, while Nestle Nigeria Plc pays about N1million to N2.5million in annual salaries.

Taal (2014) explained that the influence both of the highly paid mining sector companies and the salary of Shoprite Checkers CEO, James Basson who took home at 2013 salary of R49 656 000, a 22% increase on that of R40 620 000 paid in 2012. In the past six years CEOs have, on average, doubled their salaries. Workers in their annual report, companies are often very proud about saying how many jobs they have created. Yet very little detail is disclosed on what those jobs are, where they are, who has them, what type of employment, as if a job, any job, is sufficient contribution to a society where unemployment is rampant.

Workers and other stakeholders though, would say that the ability to create good jobs is a key performance indicator for a company and as such should be addressed in detail in the annual report. In 2013 the MNCs included in the study reported a total of 592 168 workers across operations. This is an increase of 11 441 workers, or 2% on the previous year's total. It is however difficult to analyze as so little detail is given on who these workers are and their forms of employment. Median wages for low wage work in South Africa progress from about R1300 in 1997 to just over R3300 per month in 2013. These figures show us just how little percentage increases mean when we are talking about the difference between CEOs earning almost R1million per month and workers on less than R5 000 per month.

It is however important to consider the salary and wages of workers in terms of real wage. Real wages simply means wages after price increases are taken into account and is meant to provide an assessment of purchasing power. After all, it hardly matters if a worker earns more than he/she used to, if the earnings cannot buy anything more than it used to. Available statistics indicate that real median pay for minimum or low wage work in South Africa has remained stagnant over the last twenty years. Real median low pay increased by only 2.95% between 1997 and 2013. What this means is that there has been no increase in the minimum wage, although minimum wages are not routinely increased on an annual basis. Where there have been increases these are not in general substantial.

Skills and Technological Development

One of the most important roles of MNEs in Africa is the development of skills and technology. Multinational Enterprises are known for operating with highly skilled professionals and the use of modern technologies. These skills and technologies are often transferred form the parent companies to their subsidiaries. Therefore, MNEs originating from the advanced countries with high level skilled manpower with sophisticated technologies help to develop the skills and integrate their technologies to their host countries. Many countries that are less endowed with skills and technologies have developed through this avenue. Africa in particular are enjoying skills development and integration of technologies resulting from the growth of Multinationals from America, Western Europe, and recently, the Asian tigers.

Integration into Global Economy

MNEs enterprises promote global economy. African economy is increasingly becoming globalized with the influx of MNEs from other continents. On the other hand, the growth of African MNEs with presence within and beyond African countries is increasingly giving Africa a position in the global scene.

Expansion of International Trade

Multinational Enterprises help in the expansion of international trade between Africa and the rest of the world. The continent is not only endowed with resources which attract the operation of MNEs, the economy is emerging with stable democratic governments in recent time across the region. Its policies have been redirected to favor business investment.

Promotes International Integration

MNEs promote international integration as countries sharing business environment find it easier to harmonize their business philosophies, political ideologies and business ethics. This has been the reason for Africa's hitherto and seemingly political forum, organization of African Unity (OAU) being metamorphosed into a veritable economic integration known as New Partnership for African Development (NEPAD).

Effective Utilization of Resources

Multinational Enterprises have facilitated the utilization of the resources endowment of Africa, therefore attention is increasingly being diverted from being exporters of raw materials to manufacturing giants and operators of service industries, among others. Resources which were untapped are now being scrambled for by Asian tigers, which are giving the old investors stiff competition.

STRATEGIES TO BE ADOPTED TO ENCOURAGE THE DEVELOPMENT OF MNEs

Development of Superior-Based Business Production and Services

African countries need the production of superior-based products to break the market competitiveness. Fill and Fill (2005) considered that business products contribute to customers' perception and evaluation. These will in no a small way influences patronage. Products here mean more than just the pure physical form and utility they outwardly present. The two main types of attributes a product represent are tangible and intangible attributes. The tangible attributes provide marks which separate, distinguish and differentiate the basic product from competitive offerings. Intangible attributes are technical service and support, financial service, warranties to embellish products and assist differentiation.

Analyze the Business Environment

There is need to analyze the business environment. The environment here includes its customers, suppliers, competitors, as well as the social and economic influences in its operations.

Chironga, Leke, Wamelen Lund, (2011), suggested that corporations must start developing their strategies by recognizing that Africa is not one economy. Africa is home to 50-plus nations, each with its own policies and attitudes toward multinational companies, as well as its own languages, currency, and traditions. Successful companies use filters to decide which countries to enter and tailor their entry strategies to specific sectors. They focus their efforts on key markets, but those that think broadly benefit from greater scale and diversified risks. Economists usually group countries by income level or geography. It can also be organized according to their economic diversification and level of exports. As economies develop, agriculture and natural resources account for a smaller and smaller share of GDP, while the share of manufacturing and services grows. That boosts per capita income, with a 15% increase in manufacturing and services as a share of GDP usually resulting in a doubling of per capita income. Exports are the means by which emerging economies earn hard currency to pay for imports of capital goods. In most African countries, capital goods imports account for roughly half of investment, making exports a critical enabler of growth. Africa's growth accelerated rapidly after 2000 and continued even during the global recession.

Since the year 2000, the continent has been the world's third-fastest growing region, outpacing Eastern Europe and Latin America. Classified by these two parameters, which together provide a snapshot of how developed markets are, African countries fall into four broad clusters. Africa's 50-plus nations are at different stages of development, as their widely varying levels of exports and economic diversification reveal. They fall into four main categories: oil exporters, diversified economies, transition economies, and pre-transition economies.

Chironga, Leke, Wamelen Lund, (2011) suggested that winning in Africa requires executives to understand the business environment in each country they enter and to tailor their plans accordingly. It demands innovation; the winners are often companies that tackle complex challenges creatively. In our work, we have found four other elements critical to success in Africa.

Pick the Right Entry Strategy

Once a company has identified the countries and industries in which it would like to have a presence, it must choose an approach. Should it start from scratch and grow on its own? Should it build a presence by acquiring small local players? Should it take a stake in a Pan-African player? The answer will depend on the industry. In relatively well developed sectors such as retail banking and telecom, it's probably too late to deploy only an organic strategy using traditional business models. African banks, such as Ecobank and Standard Bank, as well as foreign banks like Standard Chartered and Barclays, have already spent decades establishing operations in many countries. More recently, some have grown their footprints by buying up local banks. New entrants will increasingly have to use M&A as an entry strategy. One option is to knit together a Pan-African operation by acquiring regional players. Another is to buy a stake in a big African company. That's what China's ICBC did, purchasing 20% of Standard Bank in 2008. The alliance gave ICBC immediate access to the 17 African countries in which Standard Bank operates and enabled it to finance the activities of Chinese companies all over Africa.

Organic growth strategies are possible in sectors such as retailing. Formal retailing is limited in most African countries, and that allows global players to move in. Zara, the Spanish retailer, has opened 12 stores across North Africa in the past five years. Shoprite had just one store outside its home country of South Africa in 1995 but has since become the continent's largest food retailer, opening 71 stores in other African nations. Organic growth is also possible in industries where disruptive technologies create new products and services. Consider Safaricom's mobile-phone-based money-transfer service, M-Pesa, which enables customers to deposit and withdraw money from a network of agents. Launched in Kenya in 2007, M-Pesa captured 6.5 million customers in just two years' time, and it has since been launched in Tanzania and South Africa as well.

Get–and Get to–Customers

Consumer preferences vary enormously across Africa, so companies must invest in market intelligence. Brand-conscious consumers will save up to buy premium items, but most people have low incomes and lack access to credit. Using imaginative strategies—selling products in small quantities; offering credit, hire purchase, and layaway plans; and educating consumers—is essential. Developing innovative, low-priced consumer products and services is often critical. For example, Nokia focuses on phone models priced from $20 to $50 and adjusts profit targets to reflect the lower prices instead of adopting a global benchmark. By 2020, more than half of Africa's 244 million households will have annual incomes of more than $5,000, suggesting that they will enjoy discretionary spending power. Reaching customers is arguably as tough as understanding their needs. Africa's infrastructure is poor, and more sales occur through informal channels, such as vendors and family-run businesses, than through stores and malls. Companies can overcome these challenges only by being flexible. Some foreign companies have a single national distributor; others over half a dozen. But all find they need more people to manage distributors in Africa than they do elsewhere. In Nigeria, P&G appointed exclusive distributors for seven geographic areas and hired employees to support each one, which it doesn't do in any other country. You must be patient—building a logistics network in Africa takes time. P&G spent 10 years building its Nigerian network.

Multinationals can hasten the expansion of formal retailing channels by co-investing in mall development or selling through multi-brand stores. One successful European retailer has become a mall developer in Africa, which ensures strategic locations for its stores as well as anchor tenants for its malls. Shoprite is taking a similar tack as it expands across the continent. In many African countries, informal retail channels account for more than 80% of retail sales. Companies must find innovative ways to work with them. Coke has created a network of micro distribution centers to reach informal retailers in both rural and urban areas. It comprises 2,800 small businesses that use bicycles and manual pushcarts to deliver products over unpaved roads. Infrastructure gaps demand creative solutions from service providers, too. For example, to ensure that it has continuous electrical power, Africa's largest cellular services operator, MTN, has built generators into each of its 5,000-plus towers in Nigeria. It uses a fleet of trucks to feed them diesel. By providing better service, MTN has acquired 31 million subscribers and built a $4.5 billion business in the country. Despite the added costs, its profit margins in Nigeria are routinely above 50%.

Fill the Skills Gap

High-skilled workers in Africa are similar to those in other emerging economies. The best-educated attend top universities, often overseas. Each year 200,000 students from sub-Saharan Africa study abroad. At the other end of the spectrum, there's also little difference between Africans and workers from other developing economies. One study found that factory workers in Kenya are as productive as those in China and India, but the overall production costs in Kenya are higher because of poor regulation and infrastructure—problems that are likely to go away. What's missing is a cadre of midlevel managers—a shortage that reflects the weaknesses in Africa's secondary and tertiary education systems. To fill the gaps as their operations grow, multinational companies use several strategies:

Bringing in Midlevel Expatriates

Particularly in the early years, foreign companies import managers to start operations and groom local talent. Successful organizations create clear expectations about talent development; draw up targets; and monitor progress. One multinational company has reinforced its middle management in Nigeria with expatriate managers from other emerging markets, such as India, who have the skills and experience needed to deal with the Nigerian environment.

Setting Up Extensive Training Programs

Multinationals usually find that employees at all levels in Africa need training. Some invest in the local education system to develop people with the skills they require. Such programs may also help them win support from governments; companies can leverage them to obtain permits to enter markets, get tax credits, or gain access to land and other resources. A major oil company in Angola has created a program to train 14- to 16-year-olds as upstream specialists. It also works with a local university to increase the number of engineers and scientists graduating every year and funds a law program in oil and gas that produced its first class, of 28 graduates, in 2008.

Insisting on Global Rotations

Other corporations rotate senior executives and emerging leaders recruited in Africa through positions abroad so that they can bring home an array of skills to share. A case in point is the financial services firm Old Mutual, which maintains a constant flow of talent between its offices in Africa and those overseas.

Buying Talent

Entry strategies that rely on M&A have one key advantage: the talent that comes with acquisitions. Mobile Telecommunications Company, for example, inherited a slew of senior and midlevel executives when it bought Celtel, then Africa's leading mobile player, six years ago.

Manage Risks

Political instability is one of the two biggest risks foreign companies face on the continent, as the world is witnessing in North Africa. The other is adverse actions by governments, such as reneging on contracts or passing legislation that hampers operations—which some resource companies have experienced in West Africa. Abrupt changes in import tariffs and quotas can also affect operations.

Diversifying across geographic markets mitigates these risks: In addition, companies can create coalitions of stakeholders that help them detect potential problems early so that they can head them off or draw up contingency plans. Companies can do this in three ways:

Building Partnerships

Local business people and politicians usually know the political landscape and learn of changes long before they hit the news. Such partners can help foreign companies navigate bureaucracies and foster relationships with official and unofficial powers.

Wooing the Influential

Smart companies identify key influencers, such as congressional representatives, regulators, and mayors, in each country. They take the time to figure out, say, who among the top 50 influencers are their strong supporters; who's indifferent but can be turned into a supporter; and who'll never support them. They actively cultivate the first two groups.

Putting Key Stakeholders on Their Boards

Inviting key public and private sector stakeholders to join a country board aligns their incentives with the company's. It gives the locals a stake in the company's success. In many ways Africa holds the same potential that China did 20 years ago. A large rural population is moving to the cities, landing jobs with higher incomes, and starting to enjoy discretionary spending. Demand is growing, and foreign direct investment has soared: from $9.4 billion in 2000 to $46.4 billion in 2009. Just as investing in China embodies some political risk, so too does doing business in Africa. Companies must think carefully about the approaches they adopt, but it will be worthwhile. Above all, first movers will have the opportunity to forge strong local partnerships and capture market share before everyone wakes up to the buzz around the Bright Continent.

Final Thought

This chapter paid attention and discussed MNEs and African economy, paying particular attention on the overview of Africa's economy, Top 20 largest economies in Africa, major sectors perceived as paths to growth of Africa's economy, diversified economies and specific roles of MNEs in the development of Africa's economy. It is clear that given the rate at which MNEs are expanding Africa's market, the economy will continue to grow, become more diversified and more dynamic. In diversifying Africa's economy therefore, more attention should be directed towards the industrial, financial and educational sector, especially at tertiary level of education. To achieve these however, the infrastructures have to be improved. A concerted effort, given medium and long term economic planning through integration will give Africa's economy a boost.

CONCLUSION

Given the present growth rate of indigenous MNEs, in Africa, economic development is expected to accelerate for a dynamic and strong economy with stronger competitive ability in the global economy. Also, it is concluded that African economies are still weak at the global scene; indigenous MNEs are still facing stiff competition with foreign MNEs, indigenous MNEs in Africa, except in few cases are still limited in terms of the number of subsidiaries outside African countries. It is therefore concluded that Multinational Enterprises will continue to contribute to the growth of Africa's economy, especially as more indigenous enterprises are being launched by African countries. Other conclusions arrived at in line with the concepts deciphered in this chapter include the following: African economies are still weak at the global scene; indigenous MNEs are still facing stiff competition with foreign MNEs, indigenous MNEs in Africa, except in few cases are still limited in terms of the number of subsidiaries outside African countries. However, it is also concluded that MNEs in Africa contribute a reasonable percentage of her Gross Domestic Products (GDP).

Recommendations

The recommendations made are based on the conclusions earlier drawn and include the following, among others: Africa's economy should be diversified further; joint ownership of MNEs among African countries will be a boost to economic dynamism in the face of global competitiveness. This can be achieved through the strengthening of economic integration such as New Partnership on African Development (NEPAD). It is further recommended that African countries should continue to diversify her economy to take advantage of large labor potential and natural resources endowment.

REFERENCES

Aja, E. (2009). The evil consequences of trans-national corporations. *International Journal of Politics*, *4*(4), 45–50.

Ake, C. (1981). *African Political Economy*. Essex, UK: Longman Group.

Bardouille, P., Hamblin, A., & Pley, H. (2010). *Mining: Unearthing Africa's Potential*. Academic Press.

Bernel, R. (1990). Foreign investment and development in Jamaica. *American Economic Affairs*, *38*(2), 40–50.

Chironga, M., Leke, A., Wamelen, A. V., & Lund, S. (2011). The Globe: Cracking the Next Growth Market – Africa. *Harvard Business Review*. Retrieved from https://hbr.org/2011/05/the-globe-cracking-the-next-growth-market-africa

Chukwuemeka, E., Anazodo, R., & Nzewi, H. N. (2011). Underdevelopment and the Multinationals – A Political Commentary. *Journal of Sustainable Development*. Retrieved from www.ccsenet.org/journal/index.php/jsd/article/viewfile/11603/8237

Cloete, R., Faulhaber, F., & Zils, M. (2010). Infrastructure: A long Road ahead. In Africa's Path to Growth: Sector by Sector. McKinsey & Co.

Fill, C., & Fill, K. E. (2005). *Business to Business Marketing: Philosophies, Systems and Communication*. Prentice Hall.

Gaib, Z., Maske, A., & Moraje, S. (2010). Telecommunications: From Voice to Data. In Africa's Path to Growth: Sector by Sector. McKinsey & Co.

Grandis, H. D., & Pinshaw, G. (2010). Banking: Building on Success. In Africa's Path to Growth: Sector by Sector. McKinsey & Co.

Grunberg, L. (2001). The IPE of Multinational Corporations. In D. N. Balaam & M. Veseth (Eds.), *Introduction to International Political Economy* (2nd ed.). Upper Saddle River, NJ: Prentice-Hall.

Hijzen, A., & Swain, P. (2008). Do Multinationals promote better pay working conditions? *OECD Observer*, 269. Available at http://www.oecdobserver.org

Izunwa, M.E. (2005). African Development: From history to future possibilities. *Journal of Africa in a New World Order*, *2*(1), 141-147.

Jayaram, K., Riese, J., & Sanghvi, S. (2010). Agriculture: Abundant opportunities. In Africa's Path to Growth: Sector by Sector. McKinsey & Co.

Kelleher, A., & Klein, L. (2006). *Global Perspective: A Handbook for Understanding Global Issues*. Pearson Prentice Hall.

McKinsey & Company Insights and Publications. (2010). *Africa's Path to Growth: Sector by Sector.* Author.

Osuagwu, G. O., & Ezie, O. (2013). Multinational Corporation and the Nigerian Economy. *International Journal of Academic Research in Business and Social Sciences*, *3*(4), 359–369. Retrieved from www.hrmars.com/admin/pics/1786.pdf

Roelofsen, O., & Sheng, P. (2010). Oil and Gas: New Sources of Growth. In Africa's Path to Growth: Sector by Sector. McKinsey & Co.

Rugraff, E., & Hansen, M. W. (Eds.). (2011). Multinational Corporations and Local Firms in Emerging Economies. Amsterdam: Amsterdam University Press.

Russo, B., & Fiorini, R. (2010). Consumer Goods: Two Hundred Million New Comers. In Africa's Path to Growth: Sector by Sector. McKinsey & Co.

Ruxin, J. (2011). African Multinational Corporations are catching up. *Forbes Investing Digest*. Retrieved from www.forbes.com/sites/joshuaruxin/2011/06/09/african-multinational-corporations-are-catching-up/

Schneidman, W. W. (2007). *Multinational Corporations and Economic Development in Africa*. Retrieved from Csis.org/publication/multinational-corporations-andeconomic-development-africa

Taal, M. (2014). *South African Multinationals in Africa – Trends in 2013/2014*. A Report by Labour Research Service. Available at, http://www.fes-southafrica.org/media/MNC%20Trend%20Report%20%20FES%20draft%202014.pdf

Ugwu, M. (2011). *Fundamentals of International Politics*. Onitsha: BTC.

KEY TERMS AND DEFINITIONS

Africa's Economy: Describes the productive and consumption ability and the monetary inflow and outflow resulting in these economic activities in Africa.

Diversified Economy: A situation where productive activities are carried out in different aspects for increased output and economic development.

Economy: Describes the productive and consumption ability of a country, region, continent and even the entire globe and the monetary inflow and outflow resulting in these economic activities.

Economic Growth: An experience in an economy that characterize increased Gross Domestic Product (GDP).

Pre-Transition Economy: Describes a situation of economic activities which hold little or no prospects for development.

Skilled Gap: Disparity in level of competencies in task performance which exist between workers in different countries based on the quality of education obtained in those countries.

Transition Economy: A state of productive activities emerging out of underdevelopment that hold prospects for high level of development from underutilization of resources to the utilization of resources in full capacity to attain the status of a developed, wealthy and rich economy; a fast developing economy.

Chapter 19
Standards Certifications and Exports Performance:
Evidence from the Processed Food Industry in Colombia

Cristina Robledo-Ardila
Universidad EAFIT, Colombia

Sara Aguilar-Barrientos
Universidad EAFIT, Colombia

Kelly Gonzalez-Tapias
Universidad EAFIT, Colombia

Ana María Gomez-Trujillo
Universidad EAFIT, Colombia

Camila Uribe-Villa
Universidad EAFIT, Colombia

ABSTRACT

The integration of the world economy and the internationalization of companies have resulted in consumers' demand for high quality goods. Standards have emerged as a way of reducing the information asymmetries that consumers face when purchasing a product, and have gained importance in the processed food industry as they allow them to assess the quality of goods and may influence the export performance of certified firms (An & Maskus, 2009). Certifications may act as promoters of international trade, but they can also constitute a barrier when the costs associated with the certification process exceed the potential benefits (Jarasueiya et al., 2006). The present study aims to compare the export performance of certified vs. non-certified firms in the Colombian processed food industry. A Mann-Whitney Test was used to analyze the difference of exports value for the selected companies, and then, non-structured interviews to the quality managers of these companies were conducted to gain greater understanding about the impact of standards certifications on their export performance.

DOI: 10.4018/978-1-5225-0276-0.ch019

INTRODUCTION

The study of the effects of standard certifications in the food industry has drawn great attention from academics and policy makers through the last decade. Especially, considering that the internationalization of the economy and fast pace of technological change has contributed to the emergence of consumers who demand more sophisticated products (Trienekens & Zuurbier, 2007).

In the case of the processed food industry, consumers now demand higher quality goods (Vieira & Traill, 2007). Scandals around the world regarding health and social issues (use of pesticides and environmental pollution, bad conditions of farmers, etc.) have caused a rising awareness about environmental and social concerns, and have modified consumers' preferences for sustainable and traceable products, an also for high quality goods with a positive impact on society (Chemnitz, 2011).

For the specific case of emerging markets, previous studies show contrasting views on the positive or negative effects of standards certifications at the market, firm or consumer levels. From one perspective, standards emerged as a mean to control quality and to guarantee welfare to consumers, producers and society, and became an essential aspect for the well-functioning of the industry (Reardon et al, 2005). But, at the same time, they created challenges for developing countries' producers when trying to reach developed countries' markets (Jongwanich, 2009). Nevertheless, empirical analysis at the company level in emerging markets is still lacking, particularly relating to the effects on export performance.

The aim of this study is to compare the export performance of certified vs. non-certified firms to determine if certified exports do perform better than non-certified ones. Through a Mann-Whitney Test, the average value of exports of the two groups will be analyzed for the case of companies holding the ISO-9001, HACCP and GMP certifications. Non-structured interviews to quality managers of the studied companies enabled gaining further insight into the perceived impact of such certifications.

The chapter is structured as follows: the first section offers a literature review offering the contrasting views of the effects of standards certifications, with a special focus on the food industry; then, a combination of quantitative and qualitative approaches were used to examine the data to find that standards certifications do contribute to improved export performance.

LITERATURE REVIEW

Globalization has led to multiple changes in business practices. Through the last few decades competitiveness has augmented, resulting in an increased requirement for companies to adapt to the conditions of global markets (Masakure, Henson, & Cranfield, 2008). Supply chains have been modified, international trade has grown, and aspects such as quality and environmental issues have gained importance in international scenarios (Vieira & Traill, 2007).

In order to compete in such context, firms need to transform themselves to effectively face multiple challenges, which may pose additional barriers to organizations from emerging markets (Humphrey, Schmitz, 2004). In such context, governmental institutions and states play a key role in setting the institutional and legal framework for international trade, through measures and regional or multilateral efforts to liberalize trade and reduce barriers (UNCTAD, 2012). In 1995, The World Trade Organization (WTO) was created as a multilateral effort towards the liberalization of international trade in order to promote the free movement of goods and services, to enhance development and reduce poverty levels (Salles, 2006). Since then, significant attention has been paid to the decrease of tariff measures, as the most common barrier to trade; more recently, and despite the advances in such front, technical barriers have been a key subject of international debate (Chen, Wilson & Otsuki, 2008), being standards one of the topics considered and discussed on this area.

As defined by the International Standard Organization (ISO), a standard is a "document that provides requirements, specifications, guidelines or characteristics that can be used consistently to ensure that materials, products, processes and services are fit for their purpose" (ISO, 2013). It differs from a regulation since the requirements established to obtain it are voluntary and not mandatory by law, as it is the case for regulations (Swann, 2010). Nevertheless, several studies argue that standards are not voluntary in practice because, even though they are not imposed by legal authorities, they have become commercial requirements (Chemitz, 2011; Fulponi, 2007; Henson & Jaffee, 2004; Henson and Reardon, 2005; Swann, 2010 among others).

In the case of producers from developing countries, the effects of standards certifications over export performance and access to developed markets has been subject of academic, social and political debate. Especially, considering that these companies face challenges associated with meeting the requirements of certifying institutions which result in increased production costs, difficult access to technology to improve their processes (Jayasuriya et al, 2006), the implementation of long testing procedures and inspections, and high investments. As a consequence, exports from developing markets have been significantly reduced (Chen, Wilson & Otsuki, 2008).

Contrasting this perspective of standards certifications as technical barriers to trade (An & Maskus, 2009; Castagnino et al, 2010; Czubala et al, 2009; Humphrey & Schmitz, 2004; Jayasuriya et al 2006; Masakure et al, 2008; Vieira & Traill, 2007), several studies assert that standard certifications act as promoters of International trade (Chemitz, 2011; Chen, Otsuki & Wilson, 2006; Czubala et al, 2009; Maskus, 2009). Both perspectives are detailed in the following lines.

Standards as Technical Barriers to Trade

The increasing liberalization of trade remains as a topic of study to economists, and a key point of the agenda of international organizations. The WTO was created to encourage the free movement of products and services across frontiers, and has shown progress in reducing significantly trade barriers in the form of tariffs and quotas (Salles, 2006). However, sanitary and environmental measures have emerged as restrictions to international trade topics when talking about internationalization (Salles, 2006). The use of standards seeking for the compliance of strict requirements in order to enter a given market, is becoming an obstacle for some companies trying to reach international markets (Jarasuriya, MacLaren, & Mehta 2006). Although, these requirements are often not enforced or mandatory, they restrict the free trade by imposing companies the adoption of certain characteristics in order to be accepted by consumers in a determined market (Chemitz, 2011).

The United Nations Conference on Trade and Development (UNCTAD) has conducted several studies in which evidence is clear regarding the restrictive effects of standards in the reduction of developing countries' exports (Chen, Otsuki and Wilson, 2006). Such decrease on exports can be explained by the fact that standards and certification procedures do not increase consumer demand (Chen et al, 2008); they result in higher costs for producers (Czubala et al, 2009; Maskus, 2009); and they require improved equipment, managerial and production processes and providing training of personnel (Jarasueiya et al, 2006). Therefore, companies are not motivated to expand internationally (Chen et al, 2008; Czubala et al, 2009; Maskus, 2009) and prefer to remain in the domestic market or other scenarios where consumers do not demand high quality standards (Czubala et al, 2009; Maskus, 2009).

Standards as Promoters of Trade

On a contrasting view, several studies have shown that certifications are useful when penetrating international markets (Fulponi, 2006; Chemitz, 2011; Sharma et al, 2010; Valkila, & Nigren, 2010; Vieira & Traill, 2007).

Globalization has caused consumers around the world to be aware of international markets' trends through the spread use of information technologies, resulting in increased demand for high quality products with a positive impact over the health and welfare of buyers and producers. This makes it necessary for producers to count with relevant information to determine the quality of a product (Potosky & Prakash, 2009), and to comply with it. And for consumers, to make informed decisions when acquiring a good or service (Cao & Prakash, 2010).

When considering international trade, information asymmetries may arise from the existing gap of information between sellers and buyers in the international marketplace, due to barriers such as distance, language and culture. This makes it difficult to disseminate such information, and as a consequence, the need for international standards is reinforced in order to reduce such asymmetries by decreasing buyers' uncertainty when assessing the quality of a product (Potosky & Prakash, 2009). This way, standards certifications enable buyers to assess the quality of products, thus enhancing international trade through an increase in exports of certified firms which are able to provide what the market requests (Cao & Prakash, 2010).

Further on, standards certifications have a positive effect over foreign direct investment and trade (Clougherty, 2008); and they enhance the probability of a company to undertake exports and improve the quality of products in order to increase the number of exporting markets (Chen et al, 2008). Although the benefits of standards seem to be centered in the improvement of a product, it is important to highlight that processes are also modified when trying to comply with a standard. Regarding this, it has been identified that in most cases, companies need to redefine their processes if they want to obtain a certification, which results in higher productivity and improved competitiveness, generating therefore enhanced opportunities in foreign markets (Vieira & Traill, 2007).

In general terms, several studies at the country and firm level show, through statistical models, how throughout the history companies have increased their exports based on the acquisitions of standards, due to improved processes and quality that result in higher consumer satisfaction. Empirical studies conducted in India, Argentina, Brazil, and Pakistan provide evidence of the positive effect of standards in the promotion of international trade (Fulponi, 2006; Chemitz, 2011; Sharma et al, 2010; Valkila, & Nigren, 2010; Vieira & Traill, 2007).

In light of evidence to support both perspectives: one that highlights the potential benefits of the adoption of international standards to international trade, and one that addresses the potential negative effects that derive from them; it is important to balance benefits and costs and to determine if the benefits obtained by adopting a certification equal or exceed the costs necessary to implement them. Therefore, standards should be adopted just if benefits are higher (An & Maskus, 2009).

Table 1. Most common standards in the food industry

Standard	Brief Description
Good Agricultural Practices (GAPs)	It sets rules for agricultural practices relating to minimum requirements for storage and production. It is granted by GLOBAL GAP, a non-governmental organization supported by more than 142 certifying entities around the world (GLOBAL GAP, 2013).
Hazard Analysis of Critical Control Points (HACCPs)	It is a system aiming to the identification, evaluation and control of the processes that are precarious to human health and safety (Trieneken et al, 2007).
Good Manufacturing Practices (GMP)	It assures the quality of products (Trieneken et al, 2007).
ISO9000	It is a standard which focuses on quality management (Trieneken et al, 2007) and is granted by the International Organization for Standardization supported by certified institutions around the world (ISO, 2013).
British Retail Consortium BRC	It assures the supervision of quality, safety and operational criteria of suppliers of food products and is granted by BRC Global standards an organization which seeks consumer protection (BRC Global, 2013).
Safe Quality Food (SQF)	It is a standard that examines the quality across the supply chain and is granted by the Safe Quality Food institute (Trieneken et al, 2007).

Source: Own elaboration

Standards in the Processed Food Industry

The existing literature relating to the role of international standards in the processed food industry focuses on describing the certifications adopted by this sector and how they impact firms from developing countries when trying to conquer developed markets. This phenomenon can be explained by: 1) the growing trend of exports of agricultural and food products from developing to developed markets, and 2) the requirements that developed markets are imposing to the entrance of these kind of products into their boundaries (Chemnitz, 2011).

At the international level, the Food and Agricultural Organization (FAO), and The World Health Organization (WHO) deal with the assurance of high quality food products and make efforts to preserve consumer's health and the welfare of society. To fulfill this goal the Codex Alimentarius was created, which is a collection of "international food standards, guidelines and codes of practice that contribute to the safety, quality and fairness of the international food trade" (Codexalimentarius, 2013). This initiative that aims at protecting human health has been adopted by 171 countries, accounting for 99% of the total world population (Codexalimentarius, 2013). Other organizations, such as the ISO, have also developed different standards that pursued various objectives. Table 1, provides a summary of some important standards in the food industry.

On a favorable perspective, it could be argued that standards certifications allow certified producers of food products to gain competitiveness through requirements to improve the quality of products and processes, thus increasing exports due to the preference of consumers for certified food products. On an opposite view, it could be affirmed that standards in the food industry generally constitute a barrier for the development of the international trade involving food products, since developing countries companies face difficulties when trying to meet the necessary criteria to acquire a certification (Chen, Otsuki and Wilson, 2006). In this regard, the improvement in a process, which usually involves changes in the equipment, training of labor, and automation of certain aspects in the production chain, brings

Table 2. Standards as barriers to trade vs. Standards as promoters of trade

	Arguments	Authors
Standards as barrier to trade	Enterprises in developing countries usually face challenges when meeting the conditions imposed by standards, due basically to an increase in production costs and the lack of the required technology to improve their processes; thus reducing their exports.	An and Maskus (2009) Castagnino et al (2010) Chen, Otsuki and Wilson (2006) Czubala et al (2009) Humphrey and Schmitz (2004) Jayasuriya et al (2006) Jongwanich (2009) Masakure et al (2008) Maskus (2009) Otsuki et al (2001)
	Standards and certification procedures do not increase consumer demand; consequently companies are not motivated to expand internationally.	
	Standards certification impose new challenges to firms, such as the improvement of equipment, and managerial and production processes, resulting in costly investments that may cause firms from developing countries to prefer the local market and therefore decreasing their exports.	
Standards as promoters of trade	Standards reduce international information asymmetries enabling buyers to differentiate quality products in different markets, thus enhancing international trade.	Cao and Prakash (2010) Chemitz (2011) Clugherty and Grajek (2008) Fulponi (2006) Potosky and Prakash (2009) Sharma et al (2010) Vakila, and Nigren (2010) Vieira and Traill (2007)
	Standards contribute to the satisfaction of demanding consumers who require high quality products; therefore certified companies can access a greater number to foreign markets.	
	Standards improve products and processes increasing companies' competitiveness. A competitive company can gain enhanced access to international markets.	

Source: Own elaboration

alongside related costs which in most of the cases are hardly covered by these enterprises (Fulponi, 2006; Jayasuriya et al, 2006).

Also, the rapid proliferation of international standards is pressing companies to adopt them in order to improve their ability to compete in global markets (Henson & Spencer, 2005; Fulponi, 2006), causing a decrease in exports from continents like Africa (Otsuki et al, 2001), and in general from developing countries, which find problems when meeting standards' requirements (Jongwanich, 2009). A summary of these perspectives is provided in Table 2.

Processed Food Industry in Colombia

The processed food industry in Colombia is composed by those products that undergo through three basic steps in their production process: First, the reception and control of raw materials, second the production process, and third, packing and storage of the final product (BPR Benchmark, 2013). Therefore, the processed food industry is formed by products with added value, which are the result of a combination of labor, technology and materials to create a final good. The industry includes the production of oils, cocoa and other processed food products (BPR Benchmark, 2013). Currently, consumers in this country are going along with global trends relating to healthy food products, forcing organizations to offer products in accordance with the new trendy demands by adopting international standards that certify high quality and fair practices inside the companies (Euromonitor, 2013).

This industry is highly important for the Colombian economy. According to BPR Benchmark (2013), it ranks 7th out of a total of 83 industries, based on 6 different financial indicators: Operational margin, net margin, debt level, sales growth, account receivables turnover and inventory turnover. It also accounts for 18% of the industrial production of the country, generating added value for more than two million dollars (accounting for 13% in the industrial added value) and creating more than 78.000 direct employments (SENA, 2007).

In the year 2012 this industry represented a 0.53% of the national GDP and a 4.38% of the industrial GDP (BPR Benchmark, 2013). Total sales have also shown growth of 8.1% in 2011, and 3.9% in 2012, The difference in sale's growth between 2011 and 2012 can be explained by the lower rates in consumption and the moderate expectations of Colombian economic growth during 2012 (BPR Benchmark, 2013). This industry is highly concentrated in 34 enterprises, out of a total of 416, which account for 80% of total sales (BPR Benchmark, 2013)..

Regarding International trade, it is important to highlight that the processed food industry in Colombia accounts for 13% of the non-traditional exports (SENA, 2006), with total exports of USD1.949 million in 2012 (BPR Benchmark, 2013). The main destination markets for Colombian processed foods are Venezuela, United States, Peru, Africa, Ecuador, and the rest of Latin-American nations (BPR Benchmark, 2013).

METHODOLOGY

In order to compare the export performance of certified vs. non-certified firms in the processed food sector in Colombia, a Mann-Whitney test was conducted. In 2013, the industry was formed by 545 companies out of which 74 organizations exported in a regular basis (BPR Benchmarking, 2013). For this first stage, data about exports values in USD was collected using BPR Benchmark and the corporate websites of the selected companies, as well as newspaper articles and press releases. Then, non-structured interviews to the quality managers of 28 companies were conducted in order to assess their perception of the impact of standards certifications over the export operations of the companies.

The collected data was analyzed using content analysis. This second stage allowed, not only to gather missing information about certifications, but also to gain deeper understanding about the relationship between standards and export performance. Through the interviews the managers were asked the following questions:

- Is this company certified? If the answer is yes, please provide the name of the certifications and the date when you acquired them. If the answer is no, please let us know why you are not certified.
- Do you think standards have an impact on exports? If the answer is yes, which one?
- Is there any other impact derived from standards certifications that you would like to address?

In summary, complete data was collected for 54 exporters, out of which 42 have acquired at least one standard and 12 do not hold any certification. Companies with no data available were excluded from the analysis. Although a variety of standards were found in the companies of the analyzed sample (ISO 14001, HACCP, ISO 22000, BRC FOOD, GMP, ISO9001, BASC, OSHAS, EFSIS, KOSHER, JALAL), most of them were only related to one or two enterprises, therefore, the analysis was made for the ISO9001 (31 certified companies), HACCP (17 certified companies) and GMP (13 certified companies), due to three particular reasons: 1) those standards are the most common certifications in the processed food industry in Colombia; 2) they stand for high quality in products and processes (Trieneken et al, 2007); and 3) quality managers perceive them as important elements inside the firms' processes.

Table 3. Descriptive statistics

Variable	Obs	Mean	Std. Dev.	Min.	Max
Exports 2012	74	8.831.619	2.11e+07	100	1.40e+08

Figure 1. Exports 2012 (US dollars): Own construction based on BPR benchmark
Source: Own elaboration

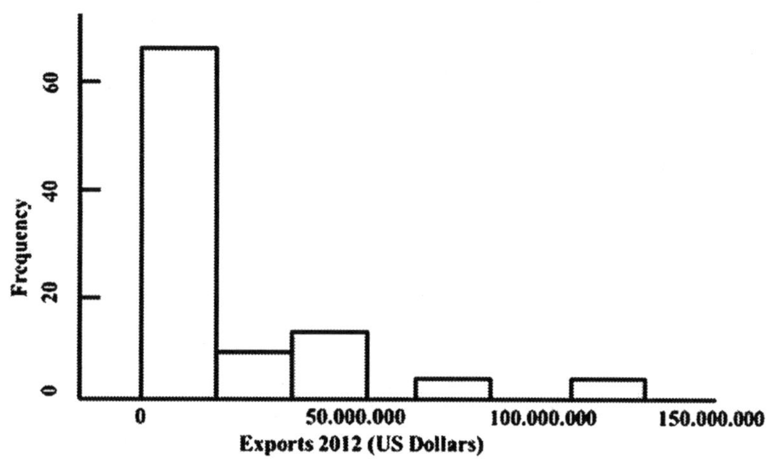

For this cross sectional study the total value of exports (USD) of the year 2012 was used in order to compare the performance of certified vs. non-certified firms. The year 2012 was selected as it provided the most recent and complete available data for this industry.

Exports Performance of Certified vs. Non-Certified Firms

In Table 3, descriptive statistics of the exports from the 74 enterprises of the processed food industry in Colombia in 2012 is provided (details can be found in Appendix Table 8). The data (exports) oscillated between 100 and 140 millions of US dollars. The mean and standard deviation are of 8.831.619 and 211.000.000 respectively. The fact that the second value (standard deviation) is significantly higher than the first one (mean) implies high variations in the exports value of the companies.

The data does not present a normal distribution, which can be observed in the histogram and the results of Figure 1, which makes it necessary to use special methods for the treatment and analysis thereof. Besides, it is possible to see a concentration of more than 80% in the left side of the graph, which means these companies have the lowest level of exports, and that 20% of the companies account for most of the industry's exports.

Analysis of Results of Mann-Whitney Test for Certified vs. Non-Certified Firms

In order to compare the impact of standards on exports of certified and non-certified firms, a Mann-Whitney test was conducted. The analysis that was considered the most appropriate for the data is the

Table 4. ISO-9001 certified vs. non-certified companies

Ranksum Exports_2012 by (ISO 9001) Porder			
Two - Sample Wilcoxon Rank - Sum (Mann-Whitney) Test			
ISO9001	**obs**	**Rank sum**	**Expected**
0	41	1195	1537.5
1	33	1580	1237.5
Combined	74	2775	2775
	unadjusted variance	8456.25	
	adjusted for ties	0.00	
	adjusted variance	8456.25	
Ho:exp~2012(iso9001==0) = exp~2012(iso9001==1)			
z = -3.725			
Prob > |z|= 0.0002			
P{exp~2012(iso9001==0) > exp~2012(9001==1)} = 0.247			

Source: Calculations of the authors

identification of changes between exports of firms that are certified with ISO-9001, HACCP and GMP and those that are not. The method used for these purposes is a statistical hypothesis test in which the null hypothesis is that the parameters of centralization of the two populations are equal and the test statistic is the Mann-Whitney test.

The Mann-Whitney test is a non-parametric test for independent random samples that is valid under a wide range of distributions different from the normal one (Newbold, 1998). Exhibit 1, contains information about kurtosis and skewness, and shows that the closeness of those is not to 3 and 0 respectively. It also contains a formal proof which asserts the non-normality of the distribution, thus concluding the statistical relevance of the Mann-Whitney test under randomness and independence of the samples as an alternative to the two-sample t test (Walpole et al, 2007).

When testing the similarity of midrange for firms with and without ISO-9001 (Table 4.) using the Mann-Whitney statistic test, we reject the hypothesis with a level equal to 98% of confidence. In addition it can be inferred that only 24.7% of companies without ISO-9001 exported more than those certified firms, which shows that the percentage of companies holding the certification export more than non-certified ones.

In the case of companies with HACCP the same result was obtained. That is, companies with this certification do not export a similar amount than companies without the same standard. Even, we can say that 70.5% of HACCP certified companies exported more than the contrast group (Table 5).

In the case of GMP, results are rather different from other certifications. Certified companies did not show a significantly higher export performance when compared to their counterparts; then, it can be inferred that firms with this kind of certification, trade an amount approximately equal to the exporting companies that do not hold the GMP certification, and that 49.5% of the latter group exports more than the first group (Table 6). Thus, this leads not to accept the null hypothesis for this GMP certification.

In general terms, the Mann-Whitney test allows inferring that in the case of ISO9001 and HACCP Standards, certified companies export more than non-certified firms. However, the same cannot be said

Table 5. HACCP certified vs. non-certified companies

Ranksum Exports_2012, by(HACCP) Porter			
Two-Sample Wilcoxon Rank-Sum (Mann - Whitney) Test			
HACCP	**obs**	**Rank Sum**	**Expected**
0	56	1893	2100
1	18	882	675
Combined	74	2775	2775
	unadjusted variance	6300.00	
	adjusted for ties	0.00	
	adjusted variance	6300.00	
Ho:exp~2012(hccp==0) = exp~2012(haccp==1)			
z = -2.608			
Prob > lzl= 0.0091			
P{exp~2012(haccp==0) > exp~2012(haccp==1)} = 0.295			

Source: Calculations of the authors

for the case of GMP certified companies, since the results evidenced that their exports are not significantly higher for those non GMP certified enterprises.

The Impact of Standards Certifications Over Export Performance

On a second stage, and in order to give robustness to the study, non-structured interviews to the quality managers of 28 firms were conducted. Through these interviews it was possible to validate the results

Table 6. GMP certified vs. non-certified companies

Ranksum Exports_2012, by(GMP) Porter			
Two-Sample Wilcoxon Rank-Sum (Mann - Whitney) Test			
Gmp	**Obs**	**Rank Sum**	**Expected**
0	60	2242	2250
1	14	533	525
Combined	74	2775	2775
	Unadjusted variance	5250.00	
	Adjusted for ties	0.00	
	Adjusted variance	5250.00	
Ho:exp~2012(gmp==0) = exp~2012(gmp==1)			
Z = -0.110			
Prob > lzl= 0.9121			
P{exp~2012(gmp==0) > exp~2012(gmp==1)} = 0.490			

Source: Calculations of the authors

obtained in the Mann-Whitney test, and to gain deeper understanding about the manager's perceptions of the influence of standards certifications over the export performance of the selected companies.

The interviews with the quality managers of the analyzed companies are consistent with the findings of the Mann-Whitney test findings. 89% of a total of 28 interviewed managers expressed that certifications have helped the companies to increase their exports (82%) by: obtaining more customers (68%), influencing the number of export markets (67.9%), updating technology (21.4%), and improving the quality of their products (82.1%).

A total of 25 out of 28 (89.3%) of the interviewed quality managers agreed on the importance of quality standards for their products and said that since the acquisition of the standards, the companies had increased the productivity levels and competitiveness, which allowed them to satisfy better customers' requirements. In this sense, a quality manager of a medium size company said:

Certifications are useful for this company. When we engaged in the process of acquiring the standards we currently have, the whole company started to transform to comply with the requirements. It was hard because it takes a lot of money and work; however after the years it is impressive to see how people are committed to quality and work easily under high quality standards.

Another interviewed quality manager when asked if he considered that standards had increased the exports of the company, answered:

I am sure exports have increased since we are certified. We can see here in the production facility how the work we do grows every day for external markets. We also started to export to more countries, and now we are not only in Latin America but also in the United States, I guess Americans demand more when talking about quality.

Although most of the managers coincided in the importance of standards and its impact on exports regarding the volume and number of markets, three (3) of them said that certifications are not needed to increase exports, and that they lack of importance in the sector. In this sense, one of the quality managers expressed that:

Standards are like a university degree that people only use to guarantee some knowledge, but that is not necessary to actually know a lot. Certifications are not needed by this company, we exported before we had them because we already knew how to do it and after we got them, we continue exporting to the same customers we used to do before. Of course the numbers of markets have increased and so have exports; however, it is due to a sales work rather than to the acquisition of standards.

Other managers referred to the priority to access only particular certifications:

The only standard that is actually important is the FDA one. If you have that standard you can go to the United States and if you are in that market everyone is going to buy your products, therefore we do not need to obtain other certifications to increase our exports.

Nevertheless, these divergent positions show the opinion of just 10% of the interviewed quality managers, which shows how their perceptions confirm the statistical findings.

Table 7 provides a summary of the information collected through the interviews and detailed information of the content analysis of the quality managers, perceptions about the impact of standards certifications can be found in Appendix 2. According to Table 7, 89.3% of the managers expressed that standards influence exports positively, and only 11% of them affirmed that certifications have a neutral effect over

Table 7. Impact of standards certifications

Company	Certifications				Impact of Certifications				
	ISO9001	GMP	HACCP	None	Neutral Impact	Number of Markets	Volume of Exports	Technology Update	Improved Quality
A	x	x				x	x	x	x
B	x					x	x		x
C	x				x				
D	x					x			x
E	x					x	x		x
F	x					x	x		x
G	x					x	x		x
H	x						x		x
I	x					x	x		x
J				x			x		x
K				x			x		x
L	x					x	x		x
M	x		x			x	x	x	x
N		x				x	x	x	
O				x			x		
P	x		x			x	x	x	x
Q						x	x	x	x
R				x			x		x
S					x				
T	x					x	x		x
U				x		x	x		x
V	x					x	x		x
W				x		x	x		x
X				x		x			x
Y		x				x	x	x	x
Z	x					x	x		x
AA				x	x				
BB				x			x		x
Total	15	3	2	9	3	19	23	6	23
%	53.6%	10.7%	7.1%	32.1%	10.7%	67.9%	82.1%	21.4%	82.1%

Source: Own elaboration

export performance. In relation with quality, 82% of the managers stated explicitly an improvement as a consequence of certification processes, and 21% experienced optimization in the production process. It is important to highlight that in every case, managers addressed positive or neutral effects of standard certifications over export performance, and in none of the cases negative results were mentioned.

DISCUSSION

Through this study it is possible to infer that companies and buyers have a higher preference for certified products as they are becoming more aware of the environmental and quality issues. This can be observed in the findings which suggest that the firms having ISO9001 and HACCP certifications export more than their counterparts; and that these certifications influence companies positively through the improvement in the quality products and processes, and the increase of international markets. For these reasons, it is viable to argue that these certifications enable organizations to gain competitiveness in the international scenario (Fulponi, 2006).

This chapter supports the theoretical framework that enhances the benefits of certification in firms' exports (An & Maskus, 2009; Castagnino et al, 2010; Czubala et al, 2009; Humphrey & Schmitz, 2004; Jayasuriya et al 2006; Masakure et al, 2008; Vieira & Traill, 2007). Although it does not measure the increase in exports, it shows that certified companies have greater exports than non-certified firms, confirming previous research such as the one by Mangelsdorf, Portugal and Wilson (2012) that studied the influence of standards in China, and found that the exports performance of the food industry in this country increased as the number of standards did on the period from 1992-2008. Also, this study confirms the one of Martincus et al (2010) which showed how ISO9001 helped Argentinian firms positively by increasing its exports.

This empirical study shows the influence of standards in Colombian companies' exports performance; therefore, it encompasses important evidence regarding the benefits that certifications bring to international trade. The study provides an insight of the processed food industry behavior and the most important certifications that frame the industry, showing the importance of quality matters inside its companies, and reaffirming the existing theory in regards to the positive influence of standards in exports increase.

As the first empirical study on the field within the Colombian context, this paper addresses the influence of standards certification in the case of exporters in the processed food industry. The results of the Mann-Whitney test offer evidence about the existent difference in terms of export performance of certified vs. non-certified firms on ISO9001, HACCP and GMP. In the case of ISO9001 and HACCP, evidence shows that certified firms do export more, as measured in terms of USD value, than non-certified ones. But in the particular case of GMP, it was found that the certified company's exports are not significantly higher than those of non-certified firms. However, the reason of this relation is not explained, so it is not possible to infer causality between the acquisition of certifications and exports performance, just association.

The findings suggest that there is a positive relation between standards certifications and higher export performance, supporting the theory of uncertainty reduction for buyers when acquiring certified products and services. This encourages international trade (Potosky and Prakash, 2009) and increases certified companies' exports. Nevertheless, due to its exploratory nature, this study cannot determine the nature of the relationship between the variables of export performance and standards certifications, considering the endogenous relation between them.

As a result of the content analysis of the data collected through the interviews to quality managers of the firms, it is possible to infer a causal relation between standards certifications and export performance in the case of the Colombian processed food industry through the increase in the number of exports markets and the total value of exports. Also, it has been found that 32% of the studied companies are not certified, basically because of the high costs and internal changes associated with the acquisition of standards. Nevertheless, such firms are considering to become certified in the future in order to access the potential benefits derived from the adoption of the standards and the certification process.

Other findings suggest that some companies consider that some standards can be substituted by others that fulfill similar objectives, and therefore it is only necessary to have a broad certification that holds the required demands of external markets, as it was stated by 3 companies. Company I, for instance, argued that ISO9001 was a complete standard and therefore they did not need to obtain another one. Meanwhile, Company N highlighted the importance of GMP as an enclosing certification; and Company S, only gave importance to the requirements of the FDA by cataloguing these as "standards".

It is also important to highlight that the interviews with the quality managers of the analyzed companies found that 89% of a total of 28 interviewed managers think that certifications have helped the companies to increase its exports (82%) by obtaining more customers (68%), guaranteeing the permanence on some markets, and increasing productivity and quality on their products (82%). 25 out of 28 quality managers agreed on the importance of quality standards for their products and said that, since the acquisition of the standards, the company had increased the productivity levels and competitiveness. These findings confirm the results obtained in the test.

CONCLUSION

The findings of this exploratory study contribute to the existent literature in the field by supporting the perspective of standards certifications as promoters of international trade (Fulponi, 2006; Chemitz, 2011; Sharma et al, 2010; Valkila, & Nigren, 2010; Vieira & Traill, 2007). In the particular case of the Colombian processed food industry, the exports performance of 51 firms was analyzed through a Mann-Whitney test resulting in evidence about higher performance of certified firms, for the case of ISO9001 and HACCP, when compared to non-certified ones. All this due to the fact that the certification processes require for them to assure the quality of the products and processes.

Then, the content analysis of the interviews to quality managers provides their perception regarding the influence of standards on exports performance. 89.3% of the interviewed managers affirmed that certifications influenced exports positively by increasing the volume of international sales and the number of penetrated markets. This particular fact (the numbers of markets) is important because increasing the number of destination markets means diversifying the exports of the companies, which contributes to decreasing market risk and improving the international presence of the companies (Denis et al, 1985). It also contributes to the acquisition of international knowledge and the improvement of distribution channels (Al-Marhubi, 2000).

As a conclusion, it is possible to say that ISO9001 and HACCP standards do not only contribute to the improvement of Colombian food industry companies in relation to the quality of their products, but also act as drivers for the penetration of international markets by leading these companies to have more exports than those that are not certified. As for the GMP standard, it is not possible to affirm the same since the Mann-Whitney test results do not support such affirmation; these results seem to be inconsistent with the managers' perceptions.

LIMITATIONS OF THE STUDY AND IMPLICATIONS FOR FURTHER RESEARCH

Hypothesis tests are one of the statistical techniques used in empirical research because of its simplicity and the countless real life situations that have contrasting alternative hypotheses (Walpole et al, 2007). However, one must be careful accepting and rejecting hypotheses and making generalizations from them. In this particular case, the main limitation is the small size of the sample according Walpole et al (2007), which will make the test less efficient than its corresponding parametric procedure (when both methods are applicable) not using all the information provided by the sample. Also, according to Newbold (1998), this can lead to the non-rejection of a false null hypothesis.

It is to also important to highlight the conditions that led to a preference for a non-parametric test rather than one that compares means. The first is appropriate under a range of assumptions about the population distribution, and the second one, the one that contrasts means, is highly sensitive to outliers. However, non-parametric methods have more complications when extending the problem to the construction of more complex models (Newbold, 1998).

Another limitation for this research is that exports were measured using the total value in USD, which may affect the study results since important phenomena such as inflation and exchange rates volatility are not being taken into consideration (MacCarthy, 2000).

Although this research allowed showing that certified companies have higher exports than those companies that do not hold the studied certification, further research is recommended in order to measure the actual influence that certifications exert over export performance.

Future research should focus on more robust models that allow deeper inferences about how important the trade certifications are. However, a cross sectional model that has as endogenous variable the net exports of a company on one year, and as exogenous variable a categorical variable that contains information about certified vs. non-certified companies in the year of study, along with a group of control variables for size and other characteristics of the company and the industry, may affect the estimate.

In order to correct the presence of theoretical endogenousness, it is necessary to seek for an instrumental variable in order to correct this issue and to create an equations system to obtain the parameters.

It will be also important to conduct a longitudinal research aiming to determine how certifications affect exports performance through the years, which could show an insight of the impact of standards in exports over time. Other variables, such as numbers of international penetrated markets and exported volumes, can be used to enrich the knowledge in this field.

REFERENCES

Al-Marhubi, F. (2000). Export diversification and growth: An empirical investigation. *Applied Economics Letters*, *7*(9), 559–562. doi:10.1080/13504850050059005

Almeida, J. S. (2006). *Una década de funcionamiento del sistema de solución de diferencias comerciales de la OMC: Avances y desafíos* (Vol. 65). United Nations Publications.

An, G., & Maskus, K. E. (2009). The Impacts of Alignment with Global Product Standards on Exports of Firms in Developing Countries. *World Economy*, *32*(4), 552–574. doi:10.1111/j.1467-9701.2008.01150.x

BACEX. (2013). *Banco de datos de Comercio exterior y servicio de procesamiento de información de importaciones y exportaciones*. Retrieved from: https://www.mincomercio.gov.co/publicaciones.php?id=10235

Cao, X., & Prakash, A. (2011). Growing exports by signaling product quality: Trade competition and the cross-national diffusion of ISO 9000 quality standards. *Journal of Policy Analysis and Management*, *30*(1), 111–135. doi:10.1002/pam.20546

Chen, M. X., Otsuki, T., & Wilson, J. S. (2006). *Do standards matter for export success?* (Vol. 3809). World Bank Publications.

Chen, M. X., Wilson, J. S., & Otsuki, T. (2008). Standards and export decisions: Firm-level evidence from developing countries. *The Journal of International Trade & Economic Development*, *17*(4), 501–523. doi:10.1080/09638190802250027

Clougherty, J. A., & Grajek, M. (2008). The impact of ISO 9000 diffusion on trade and FDI: A new institutional analysis. *Journal of International Business Studies*, *39*(4), 613–633. doi:10.1057/palgrave.jibs.8400368

Czubala, W., Shepherd, B., & Wilson, J. S. (2009). Help or Hindrance? The Impact of Harmonized Standards on African Exports. *Journal of African Economies*, *18*(5), 711–744. doi:10.1093/jae/ejp003

Denis, J. E., & Depelteau, D. (1985). Market knowledge, diversification and export expansion. *Journal of International Business Studies*, *16*(3), 77–89. doi:10.1057/palgrave.jibs.8490460

Jayasuriya, S., MacLaren, D., & Mehta, R. (2006). *Meeting food safety standards in export markets: issues and challenges facing firms exporting from developing countries*. In *IATRC Summer Symposium, Food Regulation and Trade: Institutional Framework, Concepts of Analysis and Empirical Evidence*, Bonn, Germany.

Mann, H., & Whitney, D. (1947). On the test whether one of two random variables is stochastically larger than the other. *Annals of Mathematical Statistics*, 18.

Martincus, C. V., Castresana, S., & Castagnino, T. (2010). ISO Standards: A Certificate to Expand Exports? Firm-Level Evidence from Argentina. *Review of International Economics*, *18*(5), 896–912. doi:10.1111/j.1467-9396.2010.00915.x

Masakure, O., Henson, S., & Cranfield, J. (2009). Standards and export performance in developing countries: Evidence from Pakistan. *The Journal of International Trade & Economic Development*, *18*(3), 395–419. doi:10.1080/09638190902986538

Newbold, P. (1998). *Estadística para los Negocios y la Economía*. Madrid: Prentice Hall.

Potoski, M., & Prakash, A. (2009). Information asymmetries as trade barriers: ISO 9000 increases international commerce. *Journal of Policy Analysis and Management*, *28*(2), 221–238. doi:10.1002/pam.20424

Servicio Nacional de Aprendizaje SENA. (2007). *Caracterización ocupacional de la industria de procesamiento de alimentos*. Mapa industrial del procesamiento de alimentos.

Swann, G. P. (2010), *International Standards and Trade: A Review of the Empirical Literature*. OECD Trade Policy Working Papers, No. 97. OECD Publishing. doi: 10.1787/5kmdbg9xktwg-en

Valkila, J., & Nygren, A. (2010). Impacts of Fair Trade certification on coffee farmers, cooperatives, and laborers in Nicaragua. *Agriculture and Human Values*, *27*(3), 321–333. doi:10.1007/s10460-009-9208-7

Vieira, L. M., & Traill, W. B. (2007). The role of food standards in international trade: Evidence from Brazilian beef exports to the EU market. *Journal of International Development*, *19*(6), 755–764. doi:10.1002/jid.1405

Walpole, R., Myers, R., Myers, S., & Ye, K. (2007). *Probabilidad y Estadística para ingeniería y ciencias*. Pearson Educación.

KEY TERMS AND DEFINITIONS

Certification: Guarantee granted by an official institution stating the compliance of quality standards of an organization.

Emerging Markets: Developing countries, in which investment would be expected to achieve higher returns but be accompanied by greater risk. These economies are still considered underdeveloped from a regulatory point of view.

Exports Performance: Exports behavior in terms of quantity, and measured in USD.

International Trade: Foreign operations such as imports and exports.

Processed Food Industry: The industry in which processed food goods are produced. It includes three basic steps in the production process: the reception and control of raw materials, the production process, and packing and storage of the final product.

Quality: Essential or distinctive characteristic of a process which make it outstanding.

Standards: Parameters set for general compliance in terms of quality in organizational processes.

APPENDIX 1

Table 8. Kurtosis and Skewness

sum exports_2012, detail					
exports_2012					
	Percentiles	**Smallest**	**Obs**	74	
1%	100	100	**Sum of Wgt**	74	
50%	2612	1530			
10%	7049	1719	**Mean**	8831619	
25%	99554	2612	**Std. Dev**	2,11E+07	
50%	426837				
		Largest	**Variance**	4,44E+14	
75%	6397312	2,25E+07	**Skewness**	4,133783	
90%	3,23E+07	2,50E+07	**Kurtosis**	23,42663	
95%	4,25E+07	8,08E+07			
99%	1,40E+08	1,40E+08			
***1. Normality tests: Ho: Data are normally distributed**					
****1.1 exports_2012**					
swilk exports_2012					
Shapiro-wilk W test for normal data					
Variable	**obs**	**w**	**v**	**z**	**Prob>z**
exporta~2012	74	0.46988	34.139	7.702	0.00000

Source: Calculations of the authors

APPENDIX 2

Table 9. Content analysis of the quality manager's perception about the impact of standards certifications

Companies	Quality Manager' Perceptions (Quotes)	No Impact	Number of Markets	Volume of Exports	Technology Update	Improved Quality
A	Certifications are useful for this company. When we engaged in the process of acquiring the standards we have, the whole company started to transform to comply with the requirements. It was hard because it needs a lot of money and work; however after the years it is impressive to see how people are committed to quality and work easily under high quality standards. After we acquired certifications we began to export to more countries which increased the products exported.		x	x	x	x
B	"I am sure exports have increased since we are certified. We can see here in the production facility how the work we do grows every day for external markets. We also started to export to more countries, and now we are not only in Latin America but also in the United States, I guess Americans demand more when talking about quality. The whole company is now committed to quality"		x	x		x
C	Standards are like a university degree that people only use to guarantee some knowledge, but that is not necessary to actually know a lot. Certifications are not needed by this company, we exported before we had them because we already knew how to do it and after we got them, we continue exporting to the same customers we used to do before. Of course, the numbers of markets have increased and so have exports; however, it is due to a sales work rather than to the acquisition of standards.	x				
D	Since we became certified all the employees started to appreciate quality and work towards it. We also started to export to other countries.		x			x
E	Getting ISO9001 has been a great step for this company. People are working hard to have quality, not only in the production process, but in other areas of the enterprise. Exports have increased in volume and we also opened new markets.		x	x		x
F	Standards have impacted in a good way this company. Since we are certified our main goal is quality and our exports have increased. We export now to other countries where we weren't before.		x	x		x
G	Of course standards affect exports in a positive way. They allow working with quality and they increase exports.		x	x		x
H	ISO9001 Has helped us to improve our quality, and it has also increased our number of exports.			x		x
I	ISO9001 is a good certification; it involves aspects of HACCP and GMP. It contributes to our quality and of course to increase our exports and countries where we sell. We do not need another certification.		x	x		x
J	Although we are not certified, we know that standards improve the quality of the company and also help to increase exports. Therefore, we are working hard to obtain standards.			x		x
K	We are not still certified, but we are doing everything to get first ISO9001, then we will move to other certifications. We are almost there. We want to get this standard because it helps to improve quality and to increase exports.			x		x
L	Standards are good not only for quality but also for increasing exports and to open new markets. It has worked with us.		x	x		x

continued on following page

Table 9. Continued

Companies	Quality Manager' Perceptions (Quotes)	No Impact	Number of Markets	Volume of Exports	Technology Update	Improved Quality
M	Standards are definitely good. HACCP, for instance, has helped us to improve some processes in the production plant. ISO9001 has contributed to improve quality in a lot of areas of the company. These standards have resulted in the increase of our exports and the countries we export to.		x	x	x	x
N	GMP is the best standard because it covers other aspects of ISO9001 or HACCP. This certification has helped us to improve our production plant and to increase our exports. After we got it, we opened new markets.		x	x	x	
O	We are going to get standards because we know they can increase our exports.			x		
P	Standards have been good for us. Since we are certified we have better products, our production plant has changed to be more complex, and we have started to export more and to more countries.		x	x	x	x
Q	Standards have impacted our exports. We now export more and we have new markets. We also improved our quality and our production process.		x	x	x	x
R	We have to get standards because we know they help companies to export more and of course impact positively the quality of the enterprises.			x		x
S	The only standard that is actually important is the FDA one. If you have that standard you can go to the United States and if you are in that market everyone is going to buy your products, therefore we do not need to obtain other certifications to increase our exports.	x				
T	Since we have these standards we export more. We also started to export to more countries. Standards have increased the quality of the company.		x	x		x
U	We are working to get standards. We are aware that they help us to increase our exports, the number of markets, and they affect in a good way our quality.		x	x		x
V	ISO9001 increased our exports; our products are now in more countries. People are working committed with quality.		x	x		x
W	We are not certified, but we are aware of the importance of getting standards. We know that if we get a certification we will be able to go to more countries, and to sale more in external markets. We are working in order to improve our quality and get a standard.		x	x		x
X	Standards are good for improving quality, and if your quality is better you can start thinking in export. That's why we are trying to get ISO9001.		x			x
Y	GMP has not only affected positively exports and markets, but also our production plant which is now more complete, and the quality of the whole company		x	x	x	x
Z	ISO9001 contributed positively to increase our exports and quality; however we are working to get GMP because with this standard we could go to different countries.		x	x		x
AA	We are fine the way we are. We don't export a lot, we focus on the internal market, and therefore we don't need standards. Customers we have outside Colombia buy our products despite we are not certified.	x				
BB	We understand that standards are good to increase the exports and also to improve our quality, therefore we are working to be certified.			x		x
	Total	3	19	23	6	23
	%	10.7%	67.9%	82.1%	21.4%	82.1%

Source: Own elaboration

Chapter 20
Social Capital Management Challenges in Malaysia

Shankar Chelliah
Universiti Sains Malaysia, Malaysia

Ming Huoy Lee
Universiti Sains Malaysia, Malaysia

ABSTRACT

The main objective in this chapter is to understand the challenges of Social Capital Management in Malaysia. In the same time will also explore how social capital able affect Malaysian firms to be successful in international business with the global market's environment, there is full of uncertainty impact that may affect the entrepreneur's international performance. At the end of this chapter able to have an idea how to handle social capital and outcome all challenges. Not just so, in the chapter enable managers to discover more about Malaysian culture, value and firm behavior. Social capital might not a common term that can be found in business area. In this chapter we will discuss further more in the term of social capital.

INTRODUCTION: WHAT IS SOCIAL CAPITAL

The main objective in this chapter emphasizing the challenges of Social Capital Management in Malaysia. In the same time will also explore how social capital able affect Malaysian firms to be successful in international business with the global market's environment, there is full of uncertainty impact that may affect the entrepreneur's international performance, with comparing with example from other country. At the end of this chapter able to have clear idea how to handle social capital and outcome all challenges. The chapter enable manager and student to discover more about Malaysian culture, value and firm behaviour. Social capital might not a common term that can be found in business area. In this chapter will further discuss more into the term of social capital. As Social capital is becoming an important concept for multinational firms. Malaysia is a fast-paced developing country (Burt, 1997). As country getting develop the connection within foreign nation will be relatively increased as well. Malaysian firms getting involve in global markers operation and foreign investment or trade. Malaysian

DOI: 10.4018/978-1-5225-0276-0.ch020

firms operating in global markets might face adequate resources to compete effectively; therefore access and connection is a significant material for them to be successful and competitive. Access of networking needed resources through formal and informal relationships with other firms. This is where social capital start up in business field. Malaysia is also a member of Asian countries, Malaysian cultures also emphasized a lot on relationships.

Social capital became relatively popular in recently year. However we might not be realize the term has been presence for almost a century. "Social capital" firstly appeared in a book published in 1916 in the United States that discussed how neighbors could work together to oversee schools, the Author of the book Lyda Hanifan referred to social capital as "those tangible assets count for most in the daily lives of people: namely goodwill, fellowship, sympathy, and social intercourse among the individuals and families who make up a social unit".

After the publication of Lyda's book giving researcher the fundamental idea and theory to research and explore the meaning of social capital. Until today still hard to develop or define a united definition of social capital. The term of "social capital" come with the combination of social and capital, meaning a social community and capital which include some relation of money or value, how can link both of words? In simple we can conclude that a group of community that connecting each other with a trust to shared values and understandings and work together to build a concrete and stronger capital (Roudini & Osman, 2012).

China, one of the most resourceful and opportunities among Asian countries with emphasizing the value of relationship, whereas United States might not be emphasizing strong relationship as compare with Asian countries. Most Asian countries emphasizing on relation capital, based on theory of GuanXi (China), KanKei (Japan) and Inmak (Korea), provides the framework for business dealings in many Asian countries. To expand business toward global, firms have to confront with countless challenges and trouble in building their strong relationship and connection. Understanding each country and region culture are required a strong knowledge and capabilities. Business owners or firms may not be capable enough to have knowledge that able to encounter a strong social capital management. Some business owner need to hirer or outsource employees or agency that able to help them to provide the social capital management.

Social capital is giving global firms a potential competitive advantage in global markets. To be success and survive in global market, Malaysian firms must develop social capital and learn to manage relational networks to gain and sustain a competitive advantage in global markets. To establish a well-developed strong social capital firms need learn how to develop and manage social capital. Technical knowledge need to be transfer from human to human, this bring that social capital structure mainly come from human, building human capital or social capital always involve time (Bourdieu, 1986).

Social capital will bring advantages is firm able to management in good way. Without a good manage of social capital can cause disadvantages. Some firms limit by their networks and thus experience opportunity costs and path dependence. Asian countries often have strong network ties in their domestic markets, including Malaysian firms. For Malaysian firms to explore new networking outside nation, in parallel they also need develop more ties in global market to operate effectively. As a result, the development and management of social capital become more critical importance for competitive advantage in global markets, challenges always come across in the path build workable social capital management. (Chelliah, Mohamed, & Yusliza, 2010)

In some research point out that the term of social capital is similar with social networking. True, social networking share a much similar meaning with social capital, but social capital involve more higher of integration or cooperation between firms in business market field.

In United Kingdom, researcher define potential benefits of social capital can be seen by looking at social bonds. Friends and families can help in the path of building a strong networking – emotionally, socially and economically (Alder, 1991). OECD defined Social Capital as "networks together with shared norms, values and understandings that facilitate co-operation within or among groups".

When mention about networks, commonly will related with friends, family networks, networks of former colleagues, and social networking. Networking and social capital is not able to present with a word. Social capital involve higher level of shared norms, values, understandings and trust in social networks. Sociologists sometimes speak of norms as society's unspoken and largely unquestioned rules. Norms and understandings may not become apparent until they're broken. In panic situation, human might do something that breach the norms to protect themselves or other from harm.

For SMEs and born global firms in Malaysia, social capital that build from their friend and family and even former colleagues are relatively important. A SME named CAPE Tech Sdn Bhd in Malaysia, start-up with a new invention of rub-clean technology, which not familiar by most of the manufacturing company and once facing bankruptcy. As the strong social capital management done by founder, enable they get their very first business from founder's former employment company.

BACKGROUND: SOCIAL CAPITAL MANAGEMENT

Social Capital is one of the key element that contribute success business or entrepreneur. Innovation, knowledge transfer and skill development will happen by an important mechanism, which is social capital that give individual access to variety of sources (Coleman, 1988) and also involve human capital as well. Whereas social capital management is the knowledge of manage and establish a sustainable social capital relationship within two or more firms. Social capital management involve much more complexity of knowledge and understanding.

Definition

Before the further understand of Social Capital management challenges in Malaysia, firstly need to understand the definition of Social Capital. In simple social networking can be defined as a connection or a relationship within a party or more in a socialize environment that involve value shared. In the past, Social capital defined as the sum of the actual and potential resources embedded within, available through and derived from the network of relationships possessed by an individual or social unit (Nahapiet & Ghoshal, 1998).

The completed definition that united by recently researchers as:

The image of atomistic actors competing for profits against each other in an impersonal marketplace is increasingly inadequate in a world in which firms are imbedded in networks of social, professional and exchange relationships with other organizational actors... Such networks encompass a firm's set of relationships, both horizontal and vertical, with other organizations—be they suppliers, customers, competitors, or other entities—including relationships across industries and countries (Gulati, Nohria, & Zaheer, 2000).

In the definition of social capital has strong connection or relationship between two or more parties able to gain profit and bring a valid value on it, extend more from benefits it also matching of people to economic opportunities, mutual aid and insurance, which may change individual behavior, as well as effective collective action (Pierre-Richard Agénor & Dinhb, 2015).

Throughout Social capital will help SMEs Malaysia forming a fair, ethical, transparent, and honesty business structure (Bueno, Salmador, & Rosriguez, 2004; De Castro & Saez, 2008; Subramaniam & Youndt, 2005).

In this chapter, Social Capital is a social relationship within two or more parties to connect or combine together to build a mutual profit and goal, by fully utilize the social capital element. The element of social capital

1. Knowledge of foreign market opportunities;
2. Advice and experiential learning; and
3. Referral trust and solidarity by a third party.

How Does Social Capital Work in the World?

Social capital involve wide variety of values and benefits come across with the trust, reciprocity, information and cooperation within the society and networking. Social capital is not a socialize activities to only expand or explore new connection, but yet is a socialize activities that able to bring benefits and values for both parties. Both parties will build a strong and firm relationship where trust will come across. Knowledge transfer and cooperation enable each party received the best from the other party and fulfil each other's weakness (Andersson & Evangelista, 2006; Pierre-Richard Agénor & Dinhb, 2015; Senik, Isa, Scott-Labb, & Entrekin, 2010).

How social capital works in the true world is different from social networking. As we mention early of the chapter, we rise up example how important social capital to SMEs and MNCs, eventually social capital not only limit to business firms but also in daily. Example, each individual might not a have knowledge in all area, therefore many company set-up program office to develop a project, where program office function to gather all stakeholder or member from different department work together to complete the project. Throughout the project, knowledge transfer and exchange happen, and also where social capital happen, each individual and cooperate able to receive benefits, value and along the project.

The findings of (Roudini & Osman, 2012) study in Pakistan SMEs shows special care must be taken by SMEs managers in highlighting certain investment which related to human capital in Pakistani context, as human capital is related to social capital. Furthermore researcher also shows there are positive relationship within customer capital, structural capital, social capital, technological capital, spiritual capital and the organizational performance for electrical and electronics manufacturing SMEs in Pakistan. Having good human capital management able to create concrete social capital management, as throughout the chain human is the core element (see Figure 1).

The important of social capital in economic growth and development has attracted the interest to researchers and policymakers. As defined by Putnam (1993), social capital consists of "those features of social organization, such as networks of individuals or households, and the associated norms and values that create externalities for the community as a whole." There are economists questioned the classification of social networking that can create capital, but at least we can understand that social capital shares involve also physical and human capital and able to generate external effects and future benefits. These

Figure 1. Conceptual framework of positive influence of social capital on the organisation performance in SMEs
(Roudini & Osman, 2012)

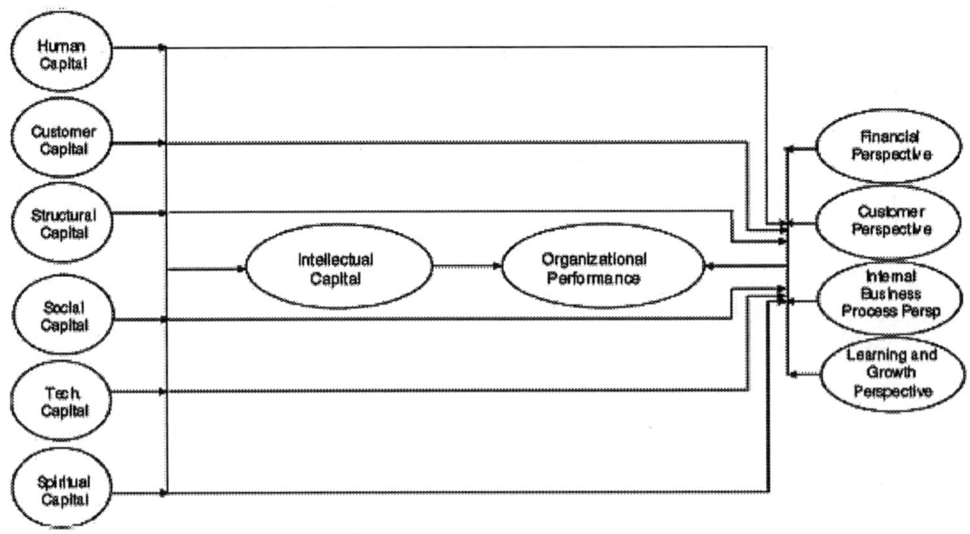

externalities and benefits include information sharing among individuals and firms, and the matching of people to economic opportunities, mutual aid and insurance, which may affect expectations and individual behavior, as well as effective collective action.

Social capital also benefits certain agents to cope with market imperfections. Social capital able to effect globally as it help to the creation and development of social capital and connecting firms to link together as partner to expand bigger market, work together a build strong financial status that can reduce uncertainties, therefore social capital helps to smooth economic shocks. But argument in some researchers have shown that strong social capital may cause corruption in the country and increase the degree of income inequality and civic norms became stronger in countries than formal protect contracts and property rights. Not just some argument point that social capital may directly by reducing costs and increasing efficiency, but will cost impact to human capital and access (Chou, 2006; Pierre-Richard Agénor & Dinhb, 2015; Ponzetto & Troiano, 2014; Routledge & Von Amsberg, 2003). In total, social capital is able to bring a lot of benefit to the business world. Social capital is able to cause a reduction in spending on education and promote growth. Therefore government and company spending money to build a better social capital management, however the negative site by be increase in spending on social capital and cut in spending on infrastructure or other spending.

Social Capital Works through Multiple Channels

- Knowledge transfer or information flows: Exchanging ideas and knowledge among each individual.
- Norms of reciprocity which rely on social networks: Bonding networks that connect individual that are similar sustain particularized reciprocity. A network or social capital relationship that connects individuals that capable to sustain generalized reciprocity.
- Collective action depends upon social networks.

- Broader identities and solidarity are encouraged by social networks that help gather individual to become a body to complete a goal.

Example of Social Capital in Our Daily Life

Do you ever informally helping your neighbor to look after their house? If yes, then you are already taking part in social capital networking. Do you come across facing difficulty on finishing your assignment? And few of you will gather together to figure out how to complete the assignment or come together as a team to finish up the assignment? If yes, you are also taking part in social capital activities. Eventually social capital can happen any way or any time in your daily life. Even a simple action take we done every day might be a participation of social capital activity. Some social capital activities may happen on to receive the actual value or money, but as a care or support, just like an exchange of experience cancer survivor to cancer patient is also consider as kind of social capital, where members able receive courage and support from the group. Social capital mostly from friendship networks, neighborhoods, schools, clubs, bars and anywhere.

SOCIAL CAPITAL MANAGEMENT IN MALAYSIA

As example and definition of Social capital already shows, now will discuss social capital activities that happened in Malaysia. How Malaysian firms manage social capital activities in their organisation. When come to Social Capital Management, manager and firms need to be caution and patient when come to social capital management, because social capital might happen easily but there are many factors that influencing social capital especially in Malaysia (Senik et al., 2010). Market trend in Malaysia and Malaysian entrepreneur behaviour is also very important factor for us to understand more of the challenge of Social Capital Management in Malaysia. To set a scope for our chapter, in this chapter the target character is Malaysia's SMEs (Lin & Chaney, 2007).

Malaysian SMEs hold 80% of Malaysia's total business firms. They are important contributor toward the growth of Malaysia economics. Enable firm to be competitive in international market. Knowledge, skills, capabilities and networking are key factors for Malaysian SMEs to be global firm or born global firm. Entrepreneurs and entrepreneurship has recently undergone a metamorphosis as the assumptions underlying the theory of entrepreneurship being challenged in the wake of economic meltdown globally. Foreign investor coming into Malaysia and number of Malaysians have the chance to study in foreign country or work abroad, and started to build on connection within foreigner. New knowledge received from foreign country is a gain for local to transfer and adopt it to enhance Malaysia technology. As a result, significant growth in the number of Malaysian born global firms, Malaysian also became more competitive in global. As stepped into the new era of world, internationalize became increasingly common and knowledge transfer dramatically important to keep advance, whereas social capital help to faster this process.

Social Capital Management is relatively important element no matter for multinational firms and SME firms to operating or competes in global markets. Firm that operates business in global market, rarely have solid resource to compete effectively or sustainable in the market. As we know Asian country emphasizes on relationship, where social capital take place strongly. Malaysia as a part of Asian Country, Malaysia do share the similar culture and the culture inside Malaysia is much more complex, to have a better understand about Malaysia, the best way will be looking into Malaysian' culture via Hofstede culture dimension. Malaysia can be considered as a masculine country, these individuals are taught to appreciate strong and independent heroes who personify superiority. Malaysia is a low uncertainty avoidance country, where Malaysia takes serious on trust when it came to business, and able make decisions in situation of limited information, which is very different from western culture. Hofstede study shown national or local culture can actually influence the entrepreneur business strategy in certain country. Although a solid conclusion cannot be made on the standard value that can be found in Malaysian culture, but we can have a preliminary idea on the behaviour of a Malaysian entrepreneur.

Keep in mind, Malaysia is a diversify country that contain many races, languages and religion. Foreigner can understand culture of Malaysia in basic, but for step into Malaysia must be conscious on the background of the person they deal with and the area they would like to invest. In Malaysia the three main races are Malay, Chinese and India, follow by minority that have special background, culture, religion, language and races. Each culture and norm inside different races are different. Even languages in Malaysia can be categorise into many type, including dialect that locally use are different. It is difficult to define a country culture, believe or behave as a whole, because there are different languages or dialects, culture, norms, believe and behaviour that shares within the country. Different races with different religion and culture in Malaysia cause difficulty for foreigner to understand the real colour of Malaysia and took years to learn and understand. To completely understand different culture that exist in own country may take years.

Much of the impetus has derived from the growing acceptance of notion that entrepreneurs are able to rejuvenate organizations, spurs the expansion of business, creates new employment potential and fuels economic growth of a nation. Inspired by phenomena such as the explosion of growth in Asian countries, such as Vietnam, China, India, Singapore and Malaysia, and the attendant innovativeness in the areas of product development, information technology, and modern agriculture, entrepreneurship is now a vital field of inquiry among these nations.

Existing literature in entrepreneurship largely stems from the work of Max Weber who believes in Calvinist ethic influencing entrepreneurial traits and behaviour and American management theories which emphasis on culture of individualism. These views have dominated the world view of entrepreneurship. As the international interest in this phenomenon increases especially when Asian countries becomes forefront in the economic growth of the world, the relevance and applicability of a special set of entrepreneurial attributes across cultural and national context becomes an important line of inquiry.

In Malaysia, more and more SMEs are moving towards global market. The statistics of global firms in Malaysia are growing and active in global market. Skill and high technology have in a country can show how well the country works on innovation. Now, Malaysia's companies slowly been well-know all around the world, the reason of increasing number of born global firms.

The Uppsala Model by (Johanson & Wiedersheim, 1975) has been shows two patterns firms going international. First pattern, firms will go from no regular export activities, then later on firms will exporting their product via independent representatives, then moving into sales subsidiaries, before firms start to manufacture in foreign country. Firms will start their entry a market by using a low risk and low commitment strategy, such as with direct exporting, if successful their will only continue to increasing to high risk and high commitment strategy via manufacturing subsidiaries and foreign sales. Second pattern, firms will choose to enter a new market by going into third countries with less education, business practices, culture, and industrial development differences (see Figure 2).

Figure 2. Production structure and key channels
(Source: From Social capital, product imitation and growth with learning externalities, Pierre-Richard Agénor & Dinhb, 2015)

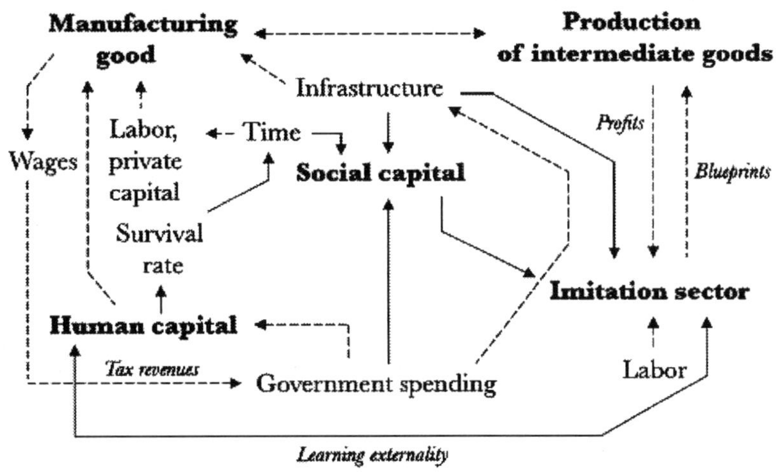

From the figure above shows how social capital works in market. Positive relationship between human capital and production, time devoted to market work, the stock of imitated goods, and public capital. Time became one of the important element in the chart, time allocation because relatively important on the human capital stock. Sharing useful knowledge among firms affect time, and cost. Indeed that human capital can cause effective social capital. Just an example, to explore a new technology or theory might cause years to be happen and need to undergo countless experiment and failure, but if the knowledge can be pass to us, we can learn in within few days or few months (Pierre-Richard Agénor & Dinhb, 2015; Putnam, 1993).

Among the traits and characteristics studied about demographics, such as family background, age, education, gender, and experience; Researcher also reach on psychological variables, such the need for achievement, power, control, as well as attitudes towards ambiguity and risk-taking; and behavioural variables, such as initiative, energy, drive and self-confidence. Personal demographics and psychological characteristics can used to determine likely or not a person to start a business argued that no personal factors can proof that can be used to determine or predict who will seek out an entrepreneurial career. According to Hofer and Sandberg, behavioural skills was the important factor for a new firm success to recognizing needs associated with environmental changes, motivated to act on an individual perceptions, taking effective actions based on perceptions, and motivating others to act in concert.

The behaviour can be influence of national values by have pointed out that cultural value has a significant effect on entrepreneurial behaviour, following the stream of thought mentioned earlier in this work. There are certain cultures will generate more entrepreneurial behaviour than others. Researchers have investigate that individualistic cultures will actually born individual as individual entrepreneur, individual entrepreneur usually show high levels of personal confidence, initiative and courage, but in the same time promoting lower level of social capital management. Hence, collectivist societies seem more suited to promoting corporate entrepreneurship. Malaysia is collectivist societies, usually Malaysian firms are collective economic activity predominates; the bad thing for this collectivist societies is there may be fewer opportunities for individuals to develop the capabilities and skills needed to create new firms.

In some company they started to aware of the importance of social capital, and change started to make form their human capital, company try to recruit more diversify CEO or director or top management, as they how that social capital and knowledge exchange will be happen and enabling the company to be much more resource in the term of knowledge and can be outstanding and capable in the global market. Research proofs a positive influence towards firm performance from a greater diversity in human and social capital of the directors or top management. The reason is the greater diversity of human and social capital able to link to a wider range of knowledge and information, directly helping the company to solve complicated problems (Chan Aun Ooi, Hooy, & Som, 2015; Pitcher & Smith, 2001; Schneider & Angelmar, 1993)

CHALLENGES OF SOCIAL CAPITAL MANAGEMENT IN MALAYSIA

Diversify Culture in Malaysia

There are few challenges for Malaysian firms in managing Social Capital. As Malaysia have diversity culture, races and value that bring out a complex mixture. Different languages, races, religions and believes in Malaysia. Social Capital Management became one of most challenging task in Malaysia. Hence, the growth of Malaysian SME in global market, social capital is one of the element that can be lack of and attention need to pay as an important part. Working with a different background counterpart or a foreigner, more flexible and adaptable behaviour need to be made to merger their culture, norms and value. Unable to merger and adapt on the culture, there may cause loss in trust and cause even more challenge in social capital management. Example; Asian culture focus more on value on relationship (Kuanxi & Kansen) as compare with western country that value more on profit and result orientation.

Diversify of cultures, religions and races, may involve element of helping "own" individual. With the mind-set of helping only their "own" group will be barrier and key challenge for social capital management. Eventually each individual has their own speciality and skill, if each individual able to connecting to each other, and together will generate a powerful knowledge and skill hub that can be overcome a lot of problem and change create a gain of knowledge, skill and ability.

Social capital relationships take place between individuals and how they form networks influences the formation of organizational networks but with the essential of value. These network ties are therefore socially embedded. Defined as 'a set of actors connected by a set of ties', networks may provide actors with the opportunity to establish a set of ties through which they have access to and share information and resources. 'Actors' in the literature on social networks can be broadly classified into two categories: firms and individuals. Building a strong social capital relationship within the country might seem to be difficult and not easy, how about building it oversea where there is a foreign land for Malaysian firms.

Knowledge Sharing Is Not Practice

Most of the firms in Malaysia did not practice to make any documentation of each work process or experience. The practice traditionally used to pass down work process mainly from one person to another. Pass down and knowledge transfer involve human and social capital, where social capital management became strictly important, if the pass down and knowledge transfer did not able to completely move to another person will cost difficult for company to produce high quality and knowledgeable employees.

Just take an example; Alex, a Logistics Manager for ten years in Company A. Recently Alex received a better offer from other company and he made the decision to resign, the notice period is three months, after two week Alex resign, Company successfully hired John as the new Logistics Manager and John will join Company A one month later, Alex has only two month left to pass down all knowledge and task to the John. In this example, like us think how much knowledge can John received from Alex? In ten years Alex has already come across numbers of issue and solution, which is useful for John and Company but Alex not able to giving all this back to the company and will bring away the knowledge together with him. John as a new manager might face the similar issue that Alex face but he need to explore the solution himself again, which is a waste of time for John and company. There are also individual that has the mind-set of not willing to share, and this eventually creating a big challenges on Social capital management. Knowledge of the first person may not be 100% transferring the content to the following person. Even two business partners work together they may not exchange any valuable knowledge to each other, due the mind-set of not willing to share. If company able implement knowledge management documentation inside the organisation therefore is plus for the company to save time and cost to solve problem and train new hirer, in the same time reduce the challenge of social capital management (Adler & Kwon, 2002).

In Malaysia, some firms are conglomerate business or known as family business. They are willing to share the knowledge within their own family members or few numbers of members that classified as their close relatives or friends. This culture creates knowledge sharing within their own connection and circle, the knowledge sharing will not happen outside of their group or network.

Conservative mind-set among family business or most of the small business in Malaysia causing knowledge sharing unable to reach the ultimate level, eventually exchange of knowledge with people outside of the range might not be a bad or negative practice, where we can build a social capital relationship that exchange the knowledge two or more parties have any reach the mutual benefit, where each of them able to use the knowledge they gain from others and use to enhance or improve the quality of product, management skill or design in process. Conservative mind-set that believe sharing knowledge to other may let other overcome themselves should not be exist, sharing knowledge within other or even your competitor might a way to let yourself to explore more benefits. However conservative mind-set is always the main challenges for social capital management in Malaysia.

The Era of Internet of Everything

Firms today not just able to purchase any raw materials from nearby physical suppliers but firms can also buy material via internet. In the same time, firms can even able to set up factories or manufacturing plant that close to their headquarters without the concern of to be near with their suppliers. The moment firms starting their business, they can actually start to build connection by using the power of internet. The firms actually will seek for the planet's best manufacturing locations because political and economic barriers have fallen and vast quantities of information at their fingertips by using internet. They also find for talent across the globe, firms also will follow the investor wherever they are, and learn to manage their overseas operations from home country. Example can see from the case of Bento Koike, who set up Tecsis to manufacture wind turbine blades in 1995. The company imports raw materials and customer from North America and Europe. Yet Koike created his globe-girding start-up near São Paulo in his native Brazil because a sophisticated aerospace industry had emerged there, which enabled him to develop innovative blade designs and manufacturing know-how. Tecsis has become one of the world's market leaders, having installed 12,000 blades in 10 countries in the past decade and racked up revenues of $350 million in 2007 (Hasliza Abdul Halim, Noor Hazlina Ahmad, Seyedeh Khadijeh Taghizadeh, T. Ramayah, & Mohamad, 2015).

With the convenient of internet, we almost can have everything by using internet. But trust within each other became relatively low. Low tier of relationship cause new challenge for Social Capital management, how can firms build the extreme trust within each other with a virtual relationship? This may be the new evolution of social capital.

The importance of internet in this new era cannot be denied. Social Capital management may come across facing challenges not only in human behaviour but also toward technology. Technology in the world is getting advance, in the same time crime not only happen in physical world but also in the virtual world. This is one of the caution must be include in social capital management.

Since the existing of social networking services and application, the communication style has dramatically changes. Numbers of option in choosing communication channel. In corporate, employee usually will use email, instant messages and calls to communication with internal and external counterpart. For MNCs, knowledge sharing across boarder will happen via networking system. But the challenge in social capital management is communication breakdown. Malaysian united from races and stay together in country and same time languages as well. Translation from the original text may be different from the actual content. Both parties if decide to choose the communication way they must ensure both parties having the same understanding and get the benefits from the communication. As the same concern to SMEs in Malaysia, when they work with foreign counterpart, they must understand communication style well, bear in mind the same word might not mean the same for each individual.

Firms' Behaviour

Firms' behaviour is a characterized that cause significant networking capabilities. Because firms look to expand into lead markets from an early stage, they are often required to find partners in these lead markets who are able to complement their own competencies. These networks are useful in providing the firm with access to knowledge, and this knowledge applied can lower the levels of risk and uncertainty inherent in international markets. To be innovative and advance, many SMEs are starting to use internet to expand their networking and businesses. Finally, Malaysian SMEs are also characterized with two further traits. It is argued that they have a strong marketing capability in that they often have a customized product that is targeted specifically at the needs of their customers. In addition, as some Malaysian born global firms have been shown to be leaders in certain product market or capability niche, they often develop highly innovative products to create markets (see Figure 3 and Table 1).

Refer to Figure 3 and Table 1 shows, in networking perspective the relationships of network or social capital will lead to SMEs internationalization their business. There still have other perspective that explained network will bring SME internationalization, just like the network approach. The term of network relates to a collection of 'actors' including people, departments, or business, and their strategic links such as family, community, finance, or business alliances with each other. Social Networking of a company also link with governments, agencies and other firms to assist the process. Somehow networking will influence strategic decisions and will involve the exchange of resources among different members, occurs that in SME internationalization process, SME's networking is view as most relevant reason, especially for the small firm. This is because it is convenient for explaining 'why' and 'how' firms internationalize.

Figure 3. The framework of firm behaviour over international performance through social capital and adaptive capabilities

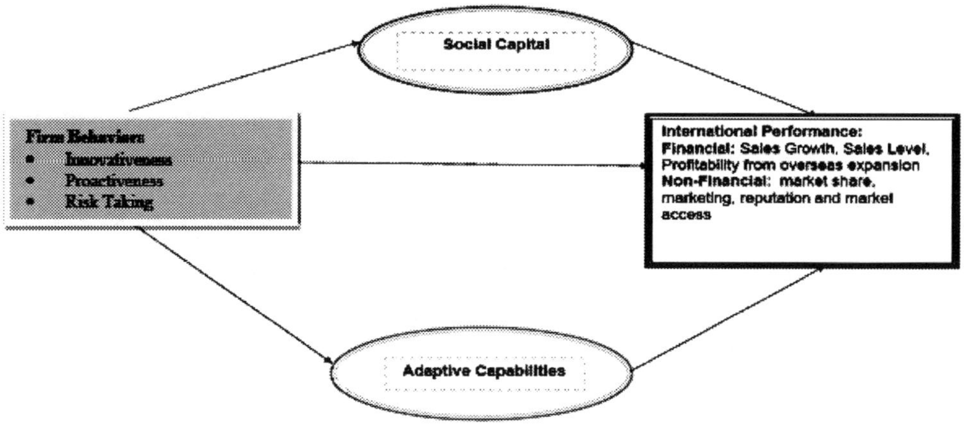

Table 1. Summary of the mediator analysis

	Dependent Variable = Firm's Performance		Conclusion
	Without Mediator	With Mediator	
Firm behaviour	0. 257**	0.023	Partial Mediation
Social Capital		0.417***	
Adaptive Capability		0.426***	

(Source: from Author: The Effects of Mediating Factors: Social Network and Adaptive Capabilities to the Relationship between Malaysian Born Global Entrepreneur's Behaviours on International Performance, 2013)

From all stated shows network is very important for SME to walk further to global market. The relationship among member will get stronger, later on making the firms getting easier to enter a certain market and can easily get the knowledge of the market, by having the knowledge of the market, the firm can easily know how create the needs for the customer and understand the different of the needs of the customer in certain country.

According to, a distinctive characteristic of an entrepreneurial firm is its flexibility in adapting to a rapidly changing environment. Adaptive capability comes in many forms, such as putting new ideas into action, modifying existing product attributes to meet changes in customer demand, amending existing products to explore new markets, or upgrading products rapidly. Adaptive capability is essential to the achievement of superior performance by internationalizing entrepreneurial firms because such firms must often tailor their products to meet the different cultural and technological standards of the markets they enter

Uncertainty in Market Economics

There are a lot of uncertainty may happen in the market economics. In a transitioning environment, prospector strategies enable entrepreneurial firms to foresee these changes ahead of their competitors and make them actively seek or create methods to cope with these changes, no matter whether these changes are related to their present line of operations or not compared with other firms, Born Global firm need to be more adaptive, they need to changes whenever they need, they can't just stay at the same area and the same technology for too long, the market is highly competitive. Example, China entrepreneur, when China economic develop so fast toward global, China' entrepreneur must able to change and adapted new environment.

Uncertainty of market economics may affect the relationship of firm networking, this is also a challenges for social capital management. Any changes in the country, example of currency rate, political issue and other issue, will generate a break up of their relationship. It is difficult for firm to made arrangement on this. However, transaction specificity makes entrepreneurial firms vulnerable, particularly true for entrepreneurial firms in emerging economies, which have limited resources to fund reactions to such changes. Therefore, in contrast to large multinational enterprises, which have slack resources reacting slow to similar changes in the environment.

Flexibility is refers to the capacity of a firm's strategic plan to change as environmental opportunities or threats emerge. The term of flexibility is to investigate how environmental and firm characteristics affect the design of strategic planning systems. Kukalis theory told us that firm in complex condition settings can actually maximize performance by adopting flexible planning systems. By having a flexible planning system it actually allowing firms to adjust their strategic plans quickly to pursue opportunities and keep up with environmental change. (Kukalis, 1989)theorized that firms in highly complex environments need flexible planning systems because of the frequency of change in their business environments. International entrepreneur also will facing dilemma on their business decision. Entrepreneur need to make ethical decision as well.

There are three major perspectives that will show the adaptive capabilities of entrepreneur. The first international entrepreneurship perspective underscores brokering, value creation, resource stretching or leveraging, and seeking the opportunity through a risk seeking behaviour, proactive and combination of innovative capability (McDougall & Oviatt, 2000). Second perspective is about opportunities, the effects from opportunities to create future services and goods that are discovered then evaluated (Shane & Venkataraman, 2000). Third perspective is about process of enactment and discovery. From these three major perspectives, we can conclude that there have provided a base to conceptualize the capability of international entrepreneurship (Baker, Gedajlovic, & Lubatkin, 2005).

Social Capital Mediates the Positive Effect of Firm's Behaviour on Its International Performance

To extend the current discussion and research efforts in the area of Malaysian firms to embrace this broader perspective, going beyond exports, and embracing the whole variety of different functions that firms can own in an international setting. There are getting more and more Global firms in Malaysia. Regarding the finding, we found that the numbers of male born global firms are almost the majority from the result, but the numbers of female born global firms seem like getting higher than expected. This is a good result that been found, meaning the develop of economics not just successful bring up more and more born global firms but also attract more and more female entrepreneur involve in Malaysia economics market.

Entrepreneur has risk-taker behaviour, innovation and proactive is very important for the entrepreneur made decision toward global market. In international market there are full of uncertainty and ambiguity as compare to local market, whereas foreign market are not familiar with us. Cross-border risk, culture risk, country risk and many other risks we need to deal with in the foreign market. Without a behaviour that can accept this challenge, the firms will not able to make sustainable business in the international market. However from the result that I get from my research found that, actually behaviour of an entrepreneur will not bring very great effect on their international performance. This may because of certain behaviour has on you somehow never guarantee that you are successful in the future. Same as a business, the founder has the Born Global behaviour but not guarantee that he or she will successful in the future as well, because entering global market behaviour is not key to successful, behaviour just a start-up factor or a foundation for a business.

Social capital is a factor that can influence the firm's international performance. Without a good and variety connection of the network, we may not easily expand our business to international market. By having proactive and outgoing behaviour we will build a better social network compare to non-proactive person, able to get trust and expand network connect to other, personal behaviour is very important. When we enter a foreign market, many rule and regulation we may not understand, customer needs, supplier chain and other factor. By having a good connection with the foreign market we can operate the business in their country much more easy. Example doing business in China, GuanXi is a very important issue and factor when doing business in China. Good social network also can easy found a new opportunity in a recent country. The observation from the result, Malaysian firms feel that relationship and connection is very important, because by having other support, business can move more easily. This is not hard understood because Malaysian culture consider as collectivism culture. Hence, from the research we also found that most of the respondents agree upon that social network can influence or affecting the international performance and above is the reason why most of them choose agree for the question under the title of social networking.

Adaptive capabilities are actually slight same as pro-activeness of the entrepreneur. There are a lot of change and uncertainty in the international market. Malaysia was a country that is low uncertainty avoidance cultures, meaning Malaysian's firms will prefer more interested in exploring new ways of doing things, although this will necessarily imply some level of uncertainty. Competition on the economics market development and invention of new product will never stop to an end. As a firm that doing business in the global market, flexibility and able to adapt and change in the any economic or market environment is a must for the entrepreneur. Hence, when the business is going global and going expand, dilemma when making decision will happen. When doing business over sea, ethical decision must also take in count, we no longer see our business as a self-interest business; profit is also not always view as the most important factor when doing decision. So to get a good performance in the international market, we not just need to keep on competing, develop and invent, but we must also keep on dealing with dilemma and ethical issues. Without dealing the ethical issues in a wise decision, may bring a bad consequences to our business.

Combination of good social network, behaviour and adaptive capabilities, will bring out great outcome for the international performance. Step upon international, firms can generate better profit on their sales; because their products or services are selling throughout worldwide, no more struggling targeting the sales in the local market. Low labour cost, low material cost, better supply resource and more customers can be found throughout the world. Example if the firm build factory in India and manufacture the product there, the production cost can be reduce, because of the low labour cost. Firm also can sell the production in India as well, because of huge population in India.

Another way that we can access a strong connection on networking is from working area, many of the respondents have working experience before their start-up the business. From working area, we can

Table 2. Malaysian SMEs

In Malaysia, the criteria used to define SME contributed by government agencies and prominent researchers in the areas of SMEs in Malaysia. According to the definition, a small-scale firm is a company with less than 50 full-time employees and with an annual turnover of not more than RM10 million, where, a medium-scale enterprise is a company with 51 to 150 employees and with an annual turnover of between RM10 million and RM25 million.

meet a lot of subordinate and co-workers; expert and future investor or employee, all of them may help up us when we start-up the business or expand the business. But first we also need to build good reputation when we are working in the company, so that other will trust on you and will help you up and also likely to join your business or invest on the business.

However, we also need to understand why from the research found that firm's behaviour can affect the firm's international performance and with a significant value, but is not a very highly significant level compare to other variable. What I can conclude is that the Born Global behaviour is the foundation for social networking and adaptive capabilities. Proactive, innovative and risk-taking is the characteristic for Born Global. Proactive, meaning a person willing took the first step to communicate with other and work before is been told and proactive is perfectly reflected on social networking and adaptive capabilities (see Table 2).

HOW TO OVERCOME THE CHALLENGES OF SOCIAL CAPITAL MANAGEMENT IN MALAYSIA?

After discover the challenges of social capital in Malaysia, now we will discuss on the way to overcome the challenges of social capital in Malaysia.

Implement Sharing and Caring Culture in Malaysia

Malaysia firms should encourage employee to have a positive attitude on sharing and exchanging knowledge within each other. Conservative mind-set should be taken away. How can we change the mind-set of the other? Success business story that is the outcome from social capital should be promoted in the media. Government have to act as the middle man to gather all firms together and build the workshop to let them able to exchange their skill and knowledge.

Implement Knowledge Management Documentation

Malaysian firms also need to implement their employee to document all their work procedure. This will able to let firms to save a lot of time to train new hirer and able to ensure all knowledge that prior employee have able to be pass down to the successor.

Depth Understand of Culture and Languages

Malaysia firms not only need understand the culture of foreign country but also need to have a depth understand on the culture and languages of local. Without a good understand of the counterpart it will not be a successful social capital. This is because social capital requires trust and strong relationship. To build a strong relationship and trust, huge effort need to putted in the process. Respect and understand also need to come along. Without a close understanding of counterpart culture and languages we might able to mix into their society and not became a member that they trust and willing to exchange all the valuable knowledge.

CONCLUSION

Malaysia is a developing country and most of Malaysian firms hope to be internationalization. To reach the dream, firms have long been regarded as an incremental process and increase commitment to international markets in a gradual, stepwise manner through a series of evolutionary 'stages'. But there are many ambiguous and challenges in the journey of success. Social capital management might not be difficult to understand, but is difficult to fully implement the management on social capital. Social capital management incur knowledge, understanding, capable and precise. To having a successful social capital management, the manager need to be very precise when they made any decision and able to influences stakeholder to be collaborative and able to work together.

Typically, these are smaller entrepreneurial firms that internationalize from inception or begin shortly thereafter. Their main source of competitive advantage is often related to a more sophisticated knowledge base that they use to exploit the dynamics of an increasingly global market environment. Social capital able to bring huge contribution and there is growing evidence, the same contribution also goes to the emergence of 'born-again' global firms. These are firms that have been well established in their domestic markets, with apparently no great motivation to internationalize, but which have suddenly embraced rapid and dedicated internationalization due to they have built social capital relationship with foreign firm. The mediator factors such as social network and adaptive capabilities leading to such a strategy are explored, in another word social network plus adaptive capabilities generate the good social capital. Social capital activities within and outside of the SMEs network will enhances firm's performance. Therefore, there is still limited information on SMEs firm's behaviour from developing countries in particular, Malaysian SMEs to overseas. Thus, this study aims to see some evidence of the international performance of the SMEs behaviour for emerging countries to another emerging country with a diverse culture.

Therefore, this study provides related information regarding the business environment phenomenon that makes the born global SMEs in Malaysia to go international with the instant success. It also provides the firm's behavioural factors that will help SMEs, especially from Malaysia to go abroad. As we know, the SMEs become more competitive, where executives will need to ensure that their organizations develop, produce, sell, market, and distribute goods to customers as effectively and efficiently as possible. Therefore, SMEs in developing and emerging countries can used this information to focus on implementing top global processes in their organizations by adapting them as locally as needed, and linking them globally. Finally, the study examines how SMEs should utilize on the strength of their firm resources, in an attempt to maximize the benefits of international investment.

REFERENCES

Adler, P. S., & Kwon, S. W. (2002). Social Capital Prospect for a New Concept. *Academy of Management Review*, *27*(1), 17–40.

Agénor, & Dinhb. (2015). Social capital, product imitation and growth with learning externalities. *Journal of Development Economics*, *114*, 45–54.

Alder, N. (1991). International Dimenstions of Organizational Behavior (2nd ed.). Academic Press.

Andersson, S., & Evangelista, F. (2006). The Entrepreneur in the Born Global firm in Australis and Sweden. *Journal of Small Business and Enterprise Development*, *13*(4), 642–659. doi:10.1108/14626000610705796

Baker, T., Gedajlovic, E., & Lubatkin, M. (2005). A Framework for Comparing Entrepreneurship Processes across Nations. *Journal of International Business Studies*, *36*(5), 492–504. doi:10.1057/palgrave.jibs.8400153

Bourdieu, P. (1986). *The forms of capital. Handbook of Theory and Research for The Sociology of Education*. Greenwood New York.

Bueno, E., Salmador, M. P., & Rosriguez, O. (2004). The Role of Social Capital in Today's Economy: Empirical Evidence of New Model of Intellectual Capital. *European Management Journal*, *17*(4), 556–574.

Burt, R. S. (1997). The Contingent Value of Social Capital. *Administrative Science Quarterly*, *43*(2), 339. doi:10.2307/2393923

Chelliah, S., Mohamed, S., & Yusliza, M. Y. (2010). Internationalization and Performance: Small and Medium Enterprises (SMEs) in Malaysia. *International Journal of Business and Management*, *5*(6), 27–37. doi:10.5539/ijbm.v5n6p27

Chou, Y. K. (2006). Three simple models of social capital and economic growth. *Journal of Socio-Economics*, *35*(5), 889–912. doi:10.1016/j.socec.2005.11.053

Coleman, J. S. (1988). Social Capital in The Creation of Human Capital. *American Journal of Sociology*, *96*, 95–120. doi:10.1086/228943

De Castro, G. M., & Saez, P. L. (2008). Intellectual Capital in High-Tech Firms the Case of Spain. *Journal of Intellectual Capital*, *9*(1), 25–36. doi:10.1108/14691930810845786

Gulati, R., Nohria, N., & Zaheer, A. (2000). Strategic Networka. *Strategic Management Journal*, *21*(3), 203–215. doi:10.1002/(SICI)1097-0266(200003)21:3<203::AID-SMJ102>3.0.CO;2-K

Halim, Ahmad, Taghizadeh, Ramayah, & Mohamad. (2015). Promoting Innovative Performance through Social Embeddedness: An Analysis on Innovative Human Capital among SMEs. International Journal of Innovation. *Management and Technology*, *6*(2), 81–87.

Johanson, J., & Wiedersheim, P. F. (1975). The Internationalization of Firm-four Swedish Cases. In P. J. G. Buckley (Ed.), *The Internationalization of the Firm: International Thomson Publication*. doi:10.1111/j.1467-6486.1975.tb00514.x

Kukalis, S. (1989). The Relationship among from Characteristics and Design of Strategic Planning Systems in Large Organizations. *Journal of Management*, *15*(4), 565–579. doi:10.1177/014920638901500406

Lin, K. H., & Chaney, I. (2007). The Influence of Domestic Interfirm Networks on the Internationalization Process of Taiwanese SMEs. *Asia Pacific Business Review*, *13*(4), 565–583. doi:10.1080/13602380701345499

McDougall, P. P., & Oviatt, B. M. (2000). International Entrepreneurship: The Intersection of Two Research Paths. *Academy of Management Journal*, *43*(5), 902–906. doi:10.2307/1556418

Nahapiet, J., & Ghoshal, S. (1998). Social Capital, Intellectual Capital, and The Organisation Advantage. *Academy of Management Review*, *23*(2), 242–266.

Ooi, C. A., Hooy, C. W., & Som, A. P. M. (2015). Diversity in human and social capital: Empirical evidence from Asian Tourism firms in corporate board composition. Elsevier. *Tourism Management*, 139–153.

Pitcher, P., & Smith, A. D. (2001). Top Management Team Heterogeneity: Personality, Power, and Proxies. *Organization Science*, *12*(1), 1–18. doi:10.1287/orsc.12.1.1.10120

Ponzetto, G. A., & Troiano, U. (2014). *Social Capital, Government Expenditures and Growth*. Centre for Economic Policy Research, Discussion Paper No. 9891.

Putnam, R. (1993). *Making Democracy Work*. Princeton, NJ: Princeton University Press.

Roudini, A., & Osman, M. H. M. (2012). *The Role of International Entrepreneurship Capability on International Performance in Born Global Firm*. Academic Press.

Routledge, B. R., & Von Amsberg, J. (2003). Social Capital and Growth. *Journal of Monetary Economics*, *50*(1), 167–194. doi:10.1016/S0304-3932(02)00210-6

Schneider, S. C., & Angelmar, R. (1993). Cognition in Organzational Analysis: Who's Minding the Store? *Organization Studies*, *14*(3), 347–374. doi:10.1177/017084069301400302

Senik, Z. C., Isa, R. M., Scott-Labb, B., & Entrekin, L. (2010). *Influential Factors for SME Internationalization: Evidence from Malaysia*. Academic Press.

Shane, S., & Venkataraman, S. (2000). The Promise of Entrepreneurship as a Field of Research. *Academy of Management Review*, *25*(1), 217–226.

Subramaniam, M., & Youndt, M. A. (2005). The Influence of Intellectual Capital on The Type of Innovation Capilities. *Academy of Management Journal*, *48*(3), 450–463. doi:10.5465/AMJ.2005.17407911

KEY WORDS AND DEFINITIONS

Challenges: Take part in overcome or complete the difficulty that hardly to be completely solve.

Connection: A network connectivity within individual or firms by building a strong relationship and trust.

Networking Management: A professional management technic that help to manage networking within individual or firms, by providing solution to individual or firm that able to enhance networking ability and overcome all kind of challenges in building a strong and effective networking.

Social Capital: Those tangible assets count for most in the daily lives of people: namely goodwill, fellowship, sympathy, and social intercourse among the individuals and families who make up a social unit.

Social Capital Management: A professional management technique to manage social capital within company, by providing an effective plan and suggestion to top management level to refers to the connections between individuals and entities that can be economically valuable. The connections of relationship can be individual and firms that can lead to a mutual benefits or creating powerful value.

Compilation of References

Aaker, D. A., & Jacobson, R. (1994). The financial information content of perceived quality. *JMR, Journal of Marketing Research, 31*(May), 191–201. doi:10.2307/3152193

Aaker, D. A., & Jacobson, R. (2001). The value relevance of brand attitudes in high-technology markets. *JMR, Journal of Marketing Research, 38*(November), 485–493. doi:10.1509/jmkr.38.4.485.18905

Abbas, A. (2009). Managers and diplomacy. *International Journal of Commerce and Management, 19*(4).

Accenture. (2007). *The rise of the multi-polar world.* Available at http://www.accenture.com

Acemoglu, D., Johnson, S., & Robinson, J. A. (2002). Reversal of fortune: Geography and institutions in the making of the modern world income distribution. *The Quarterly Journal of Economics, 117*(4), 1231–1294.

Acemoglu, D., & Robinson, J. (2012). *Why Nations Fail: The Origins of Power, Prosperity and Poverty.* New York: Crown Business.

Adair, J. (2010). *The Leadership of Muhammad.* London: Kogan Page.

Adams, W. H. D. (1879). *In the Far East: A narrative of exploration and adventure in Cochin-China, Cambodia, Laos and Siam.* London: Thomas Nelson and Sons.

Adler, P. S., & Kwon, S. W. (2002). Social Capital Prospect for a New Concept. *Academy of Management Review, 27*(1), 17–40.

Adler, P., & Kwon, S. (2002). Social capital: Prospects for a new concept. *Academy of Management Review, 27*, 17–40.

Afribiz. (2010). *Multinational Corporations Originating in Egypt.* Available at http://www.afribiz.info/content/2010/transnational-corporations-originating-in-egypt

Agénor, & Dinhb. (2015). Social capital, product imitation and growth with learning externalities. *Journal of Development Economics, 114*, 45–54.

Aghina, W., De Smet, A., & Heywood, S. (2014, September). *The past and future of global organizations.* Retrieved from: http://www.mckinsey.com/insights/organization/the_past_and_future_of_global_organizations

Aghion, P., Algan, Y., Cahuc, P., & Shleifer, A. (2010). Regulation and Distrust. *The Quarterly Journal of Economics, MIT Press, 125*(3), 1015–1049. doi:10.1162/qjec.2010.125.3.1015

Agosin, M., & Machado, R. (2005). Foreign investment in developing countries: Does it crowd in domestic investment? *Oxford Development Studies, 33*(2), 149–162. doi:10.1080/13600810500137749

Aharoni, Y., & Hirsch, S. (1997). Enhancing competitive advantages in technological intensive industries. In J. H. Dunning & K. A. Hamdani (Eds.), *The New Globalism and Developing Countries* (pp. 260–302). Tokyo: United Nations University Press.

Aidt, T. S. (2003). Economic analysis of corruption: A survey. *The Economic Journal, 113*(491), 632–652. doi:10.1046/j.0013-0133.2003.00171.x

Aitken, B. J., & Harrison, A. E. (1999). Do domestic firms benefit from direct foreign investment? Evidence from Venezuela. *The American Economic Review, 89*(3), 605–618.

Aizenman, J., & Marion, N. (2004). The merits of horizontal versus vertical FDI in the presence of uncertainty. *Journal of International Economics, 62*(1), 125–148. doi:10.1016/j.jinteco.2003.08.003

Aja, E. (2009). The evil consequences of trans-national corporations. *International Journal of Politics, 4*(4), 45–50.

Akanbi, G. O. (2006). Nigeria and Promotion of NEPAD Objectives (M. Daura, Ed.). Academic Press.

Akçomak, I. S., & Ter Weel, B. (2009). Social capital, innovation and growth: Evidence from Europe. *European Economic Review, 53*(5), 544–567. doi:10.1016/j.euroecorev.2008.10.001

Ake, C. (1981). *African Political Economy*. Essex, UK: Longman Group.

Akpan, A. U. (2003). *Fundamentals of International Accounting*. Calabar – Nigeria: Index *Educational Foundations*.

Aksoy, L., Cooil, B., Groening, C., Keiningham, T. L., & Yalçın, A. (2008). The long-term stock market valuation of customer satisfaction. *Journal of Marketing, 72*(July), 105–122. doi:10.1509/jmkg.72.4.105

Albuquerque, E. (2003). *Immature systems of innovation: Introductory notes about a comparison between South Africa, India, Mexico and Brazil based on science and technology statistics*. Available at: http://www.cedeplar.ufmg.br/pesquisas/td/TD%20221.pdf

Alder, N. (1991). International Dimenstions of Organizational Behavior (2nd ed.). Academic Press.

Alexeev, M., & Pyle, W. (2003). A note on measuring the unofficial economy in the former Soviet Republics. *Economics of Transition, 11*(1), 153–175. doi:10.1111/1468-0351.00143

Al-Marhubi, F. (2000). Export diversification and growth: An empirical investigation. *Applied Economics Letters, 7*(9), 559–562. doi:10.1080/13504850050059005

Almeida, J. S. (2006). *Una década de funcionamiento del sistema de solución de diferencias comerciales de la OMC: Avances y desafíos* (Vol. 65). United Nations Publications.

Almeida, P., & Phene, A. (2004). Subsidiaries and Knowledge creation: The influence of the MNC and host country on innovation. *Strategic Management Journal, 25*(89), 847–864. doi:10.1002/smj.388

Alper, A., & Sassard, S. (2013, August). America Movil makes $9.6 billion bid for rest of KPN. *Reuters*. Retrieved from http://www.reuters.com/article/2013/08/09/us-mexico-americamovil-idUSBRE97807T20130809?feedType=RSS&feedName=businessNews&rpc=408

Alsea. (n.d.). *Investor Relations*. Accessed 2015, Jun 17: http://www.alsea.net/relacion-con-inversionistas/unidades-alsea/unidades-alsea/en/es/es/es/

Alter, S. (2013, February). Work System Theory: Overview of Core Concepts, Extensions, and Challenges for the Future. *Journal of the Association for Information Systems, 14*(2), 72-121. Retrieved from: http://www.stevenalter.com/work-system-basics-2/

Alvarez, I., & Magaña, G. (2007). Technological development in middle income countries. In J. A. Alonso (Ed.), *Co-operation with Middle-income Countries*. Madrid: Ed. Complutense.

Alvarez, I., & Marin, R. (2013, March). FDI and Technology as Levering Factors of Competitiveness in Developing Countries. *Journal of International Management*, *19*(3), 232–246. doi:10.1016/j.intman.2013.02.005

Alvarez, I., Marín, R., & Fonfría, A. (2009). The role of networking in the competitiveness of firms. *Technological Forecasting and Social Change*, *76*(3), 410–421. doi:10.1016/j.techfore.2008.10.002

Alvesson, M., & Karreman, D. (2000a). Varieties of discourse: On the chapter of organizations through discourse analysis. *Human Relations*, *53*(9), 1125–1149. doi:10.1177/0018726700539002

Alvesson, M., & Karreman, D. (2000b). Taking the linguistic turn in organizational research: Challenges, responses, consequences. *The Journal of Applied Behavioral Science*, *36*(2), 136–158. doi:10.1177/0021886300362002

Alvstam, C. G., & Ivarsson, I. (2014). The 'hybrid' emerging market multinational enterprise – the ownership transfer of VCC to China. In C. Alvstam, H. Dolles, & P. Ström (Eds.), *Asian Inward and Outward FDI: New Challenges in the Global Economy* (pp. 217–242). Palgrave Macmillan Asian Business Series. doi:10.1057/9781137312211.0017

AMX. (2005). *Informe Anual 2005: Una Gran Historia. América Móvil. ....(2010) Informe Anual 2010: Entrando a una Nueva Dimensión*. América Móvil.

Ancori, B., Bureth, A., & Cohendet, P. (2000). The Economics of Knowledge: The Debate about Codification and Tacit Knowledge. *Industrial and Corporate Change*, *9*(2), 255–287. doi:10.1093/icc/9.2.255

Andersen, O. (1993). On the Internationalization Process of Firms: A Critical Analysis. *Journal of International Business Studies*, *24*(2), 209–231. doi:10.1057/palgrave.jibs.8490230

Anderson, C. (2007). *The Long Tail*. Random House Business Books.

Anderson, C. J., & Tverdova, Y. V. (2003). Corruption, political allegiances, and attitudes toward government in contemporary democracies. *American Journal of Political Science*, *47*(1), 91–109. doi:10.1111/1540-5907.00007

Andersson, S., & Evangelista, F. (2006). The Entrepreneur in the Born Global firm in Australis and Sweden. *Journal of Small Business and Enterprise Development*, *13*(4), 642–659. doi:10.1108/14626000610705796

An, G., & Maskus, K. E. (2009). The Impacts of Alignment with Global Product Standards on Exports of Firms in Developing Countries. *World Economy*, *32*(4), 552–574. doi:10.1111/j.1467-9701.2008.01150.x

Anglo American. (n.d.). *At a glance – Anglo American*. Retrieved from http://angloamerican.com/about-us/at-a-glance

Anokhin, S., & Schulze, W. S. (2009). Entrepreneurship, innovation, and corruption. *Journal of Business Venturing*, *24*(5), 465–476. doi:10.1016/j.jbusvent.2008.06.001

Anselin, L., Cohen, J., Cook, D., Gorr, W., & Tita, G. (2000). Spatial analyses of crime. Measurement and analysis of crime and justice. In D. Duffee (Ed.), *Criminal Justice* (pp. 213–262). Washington, DC: National Institute of Justice.

Anshen, M. (1960). The Manager and the Black Box. *Harvard Business Review*.

Anwar, S. T. (2011). Cultural misunderstanding: The Danone-Wahaha joint venture in China. In H. Deresky (Ed.), *International Management: Managing Across Borders and Cultures* (7th ed.; pp. 157–158). Upper Saddle River, NJ: Pearson.

Ar, A. A., & Kara, A. (2014). Emerging market consumers' country of production image, trust and quality perceptions of global brands made-in China. *Journal of Product and Brand Management*, *23*(7), 491–503. doi:10.1108/JPBM-12-2013-0472

Aribarg, R. (2005). *Thai border town businessmen and the state: An examination of their influence on Thai foreign policy toward Burma*. (Doctoral Dissertation). Boston University, UMI No. 3157351.

Arnold, D. J., & Quelch, J. A. (1998). New Strategies in Emerging Markets. *Sloan Management Review*. Retrieved from http://sloanreview.mit.edu/article/new-strategies-in-emerging-markets/

Arnold, U. (1989). Global Sourcing: An Indispensable Element Worldwide Competition. *International Management Review*, *29*(4), 14–28.

Asian Development Bank. (2014). *Asian Development Outlook 2014: Fiscal policy for inclusive growth*. Mandaluyong City, Philippines: Asian Development Bank.

Asmussen, C. G. (2009). Local, Regional, or Global? Quantifying MNE Geographic Scope. *Journal of International Business Studies*, *40*(9), 1192–1205. doi:10.1057/jibs.2008.85

Aspe-Armella, P. (1993). *Economic Transformation, The Mexican Way*. The MIT Press.

Assavavirulhakarn, P. (2010). *The ascendancy of Theravada Buddhism in Southeast Asia*. Chiang Mai, Thailand: Silkworm.

Association of National Advertisers (2004). *The state of marketing accountability study*. New York: ANA.

Association of National Advertisers. (2005). *The path to marketing accountability study*. New York: ANA.

Association of National Advertisers. (2007a). *Brand deterioration: how to identify, measure, and respond*. New York: ANA.

Association of National Advertisers. (2007b). *Marketing accountability study*. New York: ANA.

Association of National Advertisers. (2007c). *Survey of finance managers*. New York: ANA.

Association of National Advertisers. (2008). *Marketing accountability study*. New York: ANA.

Atkinson, J., & Heritage, J. (Eds.). (1984). *Structures of Social Action: Studies in Conversation Analysis*. Cambridge, UK: Cambridge University Press.

Augusto, J., Couto, F. E., & Caiado, J. (2014). Human capital, social capital and organizational performance. *Management Decision*, *52*(2), 350–364. doi:10.1108/MD-04-2013-0260

Austin, J. E. (1990). *Managing in Developing Countries: Strategic Analysis and Operating Techniques*. New York: The Free Press.

Austin, J. L. (1962). *How to Do Things with Words*. Oxford, UK: Oxford University Press.

Awodun, M. O. (2014). *Leader of Ship or Leader of Sheep*. Paper presented at a Youth Forum in Ilorin, Kwara State, Nigeria.

Awodun, M. O., & Ajia, A. (2012). Leaders are Born and Made. In M. O. Awodun (Ed.), *Statecraft: Laying the Foundation for Modern Development*. Kwara State, Nigeria: Kwara State University Press.

Axelsson, A., & Bokedal, S. (2009). *Reward systems - motivating different generations. A case study of Volvo Car Corporation*. University of Gothenburg.

Aydın, T. O. (2012).. . *International Review of Management and Marketing*, *2*(2), 106–111. Available at www.managementjournal.info/

Ayub, M., Avila, F., & Chisholm, D. (2011). *The Basics of International Negotiation: A Student Handbook*. VDM Verlag Müller.

BACEX. (2013). *Banco de datos de Comercio exterior y servicio de procesamiento de información de importaciones y exportaciones*. Retrieved from: https://www.mincomercio.gov.co/publicaciones.php?id=10235

Bach, D., & Allen, D. B. (2010). What every CEO needs to know about nonmarket strategy. *MIT Sloan Management Review*, *51*(3), 41–48.

Bahktin, M. (1986). *Speech Gnres and Other Late Essays* (C. Emerson & M. Holquist, Eds.). Austin, TX: University of Texas Press.

Bain, J. S. (1956). *Barriers to New Competition: Their Character and Consequences in Manufacturing Industries*. Cambridge, MA: Harvard University Press. doi:10.4159/harvard.9780674188037

Baker, K. A. (2002). *Organizational Culture* [Online]. Retrieved from www.au.af.mil/au/awc/awcgate/doe/benchmark/ch11.pdf/

Baker, T., Gedajlovic, E., & Lubatkin, M. (2005). A Framework for Comparing Entrepreneurship Processes across Nations. *Journal of International Business Studies*, *36*(5), 492–504. doi:10.1057/palgrave.jibs.8400153

Bala, Y. (2011). *The new human resources management in the 21st century: a strategic view*. Annual Conference on Innovations in Business & Management, London, UK. Retrieved from http://www.cibmp.org/Papers/Paper519.pdf

Baporikar, N., & Deshpande, M. (2013). Excellence Strategies of Pune Auto Component SMEs in the Borderless World. In Strategic Initiatives for Competitive Advantage in the Knowledge Society (pp. 144-154), Bloomsbury Publishing India Pvt Limited.

Baporikar, N. (2014a). Information Strategy as Enabler of Competitive Advantage. *International Journal of Strategic Information Technology and Applications*, *5*(1), 30–41. doi:10.4018/ijsita.2014010103

Baporikar, N. (2014b). Knowledge Management Initiatives in Indian Public Sector. In Y. Al-Bastaki & A. Shajera (Eds.), *Building a Competitive Public Sector with Knowledge Management Strategy* (pp. 53–89). Hershey, PA: Business Science Reference. doi:10.4018/978-1-4666-4434-2.ch002

Baporikar, N. (2015a). Drivers of Innovation. In P. Ordoñez de Pablos, L. Turró, R. Tennyson, & J. Zhao (Eds.), *Knowledge Management for Competitive Advantage During Economic Crisis* (pp. 250–270). Hershey, PA: Business Science Reference.

Baporikar, N. (2015b). Effect of National Culture on Development of International Business in the Sultanate of Oman. In B. Christiansen (Ed.), *Handbook of Research on Global Business Opportunities* (pp. 268–288). Hershey, PA: Business Science Reference.

Barboza, D. (2009). Danone exits China venture after years of legal dispute. *New York Times*. Accessed Jun 15, 2015: http://www.nytimes.com/2009/10/01/business/global/01danone.html?_r=0

Bardouille, P., Hamblin, A., & Pley, H. (2010). *Mining: Unearthing Africa's Potential*. Academic Press.

Barkema, H. G., & Vermeulen, F. (1998). International expansion through start-up or acquisition: A learning perspective. *Academy of Management Journal*, *41*(1), 7–26. doi:10.2307/256894

Barlett, C. A., & Ghosal, S. (1987a). Managing Across Borders: New Organizational Responses. *International Executive*, *29*(3), 10–13.

Barlett, C. A., & Ghosal, S. (1987b). Managing across Borders: New Strategic Requirements. *Sloan Management Review*, *28*(4), 7–17.

Barlett, C. A., & Ghosal, S. (1988). Organizing for Worldwide Effectiveness: The Transnational Solution. *California Management Review*, *31*(1), 54–74. doi:10.2307/41166538

Barlett, C. A., & Ghosal, S. (1992). What Is a Global Manager? *Harvard Business Review*, *70*(5), 124–132.

Barlett, C. A., & Ghosal, S. (2000). Going Global. *Harvard Business Review*, *78*(2), 132–142.

Barley, S. R. (1983). Semiotics and the study of occupational and organizational cultures. *Administrative Science Quarterly*, *28*(3), 393–413. doi:10.2307/2392249

Barney, J. (2004). Introduction: William Ouchi's Theory Z: How American business can meet the Japanese Challenge. *The Academy of Management Executive*, *18*(4), 106–107. doi:10.5465/AME.2004.15268703

Barney, J. B. (1991). Firm resources and sustained competitive advantage. *Journal of Management*, *17*(1), 99–120. doi:10.1177/014920639101700108

Barstow, D. (2012). Vast Mexico Bribery Case Hushed Up by Wal-Mart After Top-Level Struggle. *The New York Times*. Retrieved from http://www.nytimes.com/2012/04/22/business/at-wal-mart-in-mexico-a-bribe-inquiry-silenced.html?pagewanted=all&_r=0

Barstow, D., & Xanic von Bertrab, A. (2012, December 17). The bribery aisle: How Wal-Mart got its way in Mexico. *The New York Times*. Retrieved from http://www.nytimes.com/2012/12/18/business/walmart-bribes-teotihuacan.html?pagewanted=all&_r=1

Barth, M. E., Clement, M. B., & Kaznik, R. (1998, March). Brand value and capital market valuation. *Journal of Accounting Studies*, 41-68.

Bartlett, C. A., & Beamish, P. W. (2011). *Transnational management: Text, cases and readings in cross border management* (6th ed.). Burr Ridge, IL: McGraw-Hill/Irwin.

Bartlett, C. A., & Ghoshal, S. (2002). *Managing Across Borders: The Transnational Solution*. Harvard Business Press.

Bartlett, C. A., Ghoshal, S., & Beamish, P. W. (2008). *Expanding abroad: Motivations, means, and mentalities in Transnational Management: Text, Cases, and Readings in Cross-Border Management* (5th ed.). New York: McGraw-Hill/Irwin.

Bartlett, C., & Ghoshal, S. (1989). *Managing across borders*. Cambridge, MA: Harvard Business School Press.

Bartlett, C., & Ghoshal, S. (1998). *Managing across Borders: The Transnational Solution* (2nd ed.). London: Random House.

Battilana, J., Leca, B., & Boxenbaum, E. (2009). How actors change institutions: Towards a theory of institutional entrepreneurship. *The Academy of Management Annals*, *3*(1), 65–107. doi:10.1080/19416520903053598

Baum, C. F., Schaffer, M. E., & Stillman, S. (2003). Instrumental variables and GMM: Estimation and testing. *The Stata Journal*, *3*(1), 1–31.

Baumgartner, T., Hatami, H., & Vander Ark, J. (2012). *Sales Growth: Five proven strategies from the world's sales Leaders*. Hoboken, NJ: Wiley & Sons Inc.

Baumol, W. J. (1996). Entrepreneurship: Productive, unproductive, and destructive. *Journal of Business Venturing*, *11*(1), 3–22. doi:10.1016/0883-9026(94)00014-X

Beaman, K., Guy, G. R., & Sexton, D. E. (2008). *Managing and measuring return on marketing investment, Research Report 1435-08-RR*. New York: The Conference Board.

Beauchamp, T., Bowie, N., & Arnold, D. (2008). *Ethical Theory and Business* (8th ed.). Upper Saddle River, NJ: Prentice Hall.

Behan, K., & Holms, D. (1999). *Introducing to information technology* (1st ed.). (M. Azaraksh & J. Mehrdad, Trans.). Tehran: Samt Pub.

Bek, M. A., Bek, N. N., Sheresheva, M. Y., & Johnston, W. J. (2013). Perspectives of SME innovation clusters development in Russia. *Journal of Business and Industrial Marketing*, *28*(3), 240–259. doi:10.1108/08858621311302895

Belderbos, R., & Sleuwaegen, L. (2005). Competitive drivers and international plant configuration strategies: A product-level test. *Strategic Management Journal*, *26*(6), 577–593. doi:10.1002/smj.466

Bennet, J. (2002). Multinational corporations, social responsibility and conflict. *Journal of International Affairs*, 393. Retrieved from http://0proquest.umi.com.millenium.itesm.mx/

Bergdahl, M. (2004). *What I Learned from Sam Walton: How to Compete and Thrive in a Wal-Mart World*. John Wiley & Sons Inc.

Berkeley University. (2005). *The Theory of economic growth*. Retrieved from http://eml.berkeley.edu/~webfac/trehan/e100b_sp05/chap4.pdf

Bermejo García, R., & Garciandía Garmendia, R. (2012, December). La expropiación de YPF (Repsol) a la luz del derecho internacional. *Revista Electrónica de Estudios Internacionales*, (24). Retrieved from http://www.reei.org/index.php/revista/num24/articulos/expropiacion-ypf-repsol-luz-derecho-internacional

Bernel, R. (1990). Foreign investment and development in Jamaica. *American Economic Affairs*, *38*(2), 40–50.

Bessire, D., & Onnée, S. (2010). Assessing corporate social performance: Strategies of legitimation and conflicting ideologies. *Critical Perspectives on Accounting*, *21*(6), 445–467. doi:10.1016/j.cpa.2010.01.015

Beugelsdijk, S. (2006). A note on the theory and measurement of trust in explaining differences in economic growth. *Cambridge Journal of Economics*, *30*(3), 371–387. doi:10.1093/cje/bei064

Beyene, T., Hinds, P. J., & Crampton, C. D. (2009). *Walking through jelly: language proficiency, emotions and disrupted collborationin global work*. Harvard Business School Working Paper 09-13. Retrieved from http://bit.ly/1zFix3r

Bhatia, V. K. (2010). Interdiscursivity in professional communication. *Discourse & Communication*, *4*(1), 32–50. doi:10.1177/1750481309351208

Bidgoli, H. (1999). *Handbook for Management Information System*. Harcourt Brace & Company.

Biers, D., Vatikiotis, M., Tasker, R., & Dairueng, P. (1999). Back to school. *Far Eastern Economic Review*, *162*(14), 10–14.

Bilkey, W., & Tesar, G. (1977). The Export Behavior of Smaller Wisconsin Manufacturinf Firms. *Journal of International Business Studies*, *9*(1), 93–98. doi:10.1057/palgrave.jibs.8490783

Birkinshaw, J. (2002). The art of Swedish management. *Business Strategy Review*, *13*(2), 11–19. doi:10.1111/1467-8616.00205

Bjerke, B. V. (2000). A typified, culture-based, interpretation of management of SMEs in Southeast Asia. *Asia Pacific Journal of Management*, *17*(1), 103–132. doi:10.1023/A:1015441021413

Bjørnskov, C. (2003). *Corruption and social capital*. Aarhus School of Business, Department of Economics.

Bjørnskov, C. (2006). The multiple facets of social capital. *European Journal of Political Economy*, *22*(1), 22–40. doi:10.1016/j.ejpoleco.2005.05.006

Bjørnskov, C. (2011). Combating corruption: On the interplay between institutional quality and social trust. *The Journal of Law & Economics*, *54*(1), 135–159. doi:10.1086/652421

Blomkvist, K., Kappen, P., & Zander, I. (2014). Win, Place, or Show? How Foreign Investment Strategies Contribute to the Technological Growth of the Multinational Corporation. *Long Range Planning*, *47*(1-2), 16–31. doi:10.1016/j.lrp.2013.10.001

Blomström, M., & Kokko, A. (1997). *How Foreign Investment Affects Host Countries*. Policy Research Working Paper Series, 2-44.

Blomström, M., & Kokko, A. (1998). Multinational corporations and spillovers. *Journal of Economic Surveys*, *12*(3), 247–277. doi:10.1111/1467-6419.00056

Bloom, N., Garicano, L., Sadun, R., & Reenen, J. V. (2010). *The Distinct Effects of Information Technology and Communication Technology on Firm Organization*. Harvard Business School Working Paper Series, 11-023.

Bloomberg. (2015, June 3). AFREXIM Mulls $1 Billion Loan. *The Nation*, p. 26.

Bloomfield, B., & Coombs, R. (1992). Information technology, control and power: The centralization and decentralization debate revisited. *Journal of Management Studies*, *29*(4), 459–484. doi:10.1111/j.1467-6486.1992.tb00674.x

Bloor, T., & Bloor, M. (1995). *The Functional Analysis of English: A Hallidayan Approach*. London: Arnold.

Boatright, J. (2003). *Ethics and the Conduct of Business* (4th ed.). Upper Saddle River, NJ: Prentice Hall.

Bock, W., Field, D., Zwilenberg, P., & Rogers, K. (2015, February). *The Growth of the Global Mobile Internet Economy*. Retrieve from https://www.bcgperspectives.com/content/articles/telecommunications_connected_world_growth_global_mobile_internet_economy/

Boets, I. (2008). *Managing Risk in Emerging Markets: An overview of common risk factors in emerging markets and lessons learned from organizations that have ventured into this arena*. Retrieved from http://www.cga-canada.org/en-ca/AboutCGACanada/CGAMagazine/2008/Nov-Dec/Pages/ca_2008_11-12_bsin_feature.aspx

Bogatyrev, P., & Lockwood, Y. (1976). Costume as a sign (the functional and structural concept of costumes in ethnography). In L. Matejka & I. R. Titunik (Eds.), *Semiotics of Art: Prague School Contributions* (pp. 13–19). Cambridge, MA: MIT.

Boltz, W. G. (1994). The origin and early development of the Chinese writing system. American American Oriental Society.

Boonsathorn, W. (2007). Understanding conflict management styles of Thais and Americans in multinational corporations in Thailand. *The International Journal of Conflict Management*, *18*(3), 196–221. doi:10.1108/10444060710825972

Bosnjak, S. B., & Lewandowski, S. (2010). *The extra cost of business process outsourcing: A study at volvo cars corporation*. University of Gothenburg.

Boston Consulting Group. (2013). *Multinational Companies Target High Growth in Emerging Markets Despite Challenges, A BCG Survey Reveals That Execution Holds Back the High Ambitions of Global Companies*. Retrieved from http://www.marketwired.com/press-release/multinational-companies-target-high-growth-in-emerging-markets-despite-challenges-1830340.htm

Boulding, K. (1967). *Human values and Economic Policy*. New York: New York University Press.

Bourdieu, P. (1986). *The forms of capital. Handbook of Theory and Research for The Sociology of Education*. Greenwood New York.

Boussebaa, M., Sinha, S., & Gabriel, Y. (2014). Englishization in offshore call centers: A postcolonial perspective. *Journal of International Business Studies*, *45*(9), 1152–1169. doi:10.1057/jibs.2014.25

Bowersox, D. J., & Calantone, R. J. (1998). Executive Insights: Global Logistics. *Journal of International Marketing*, *6*(4), 83–93.

Bowman, Z. (2010a). *Report: "Geely set to reveal modified Rolls-Royce aping limousine in Beijing" 13 April 2010*. Retrieved from http://www.autoblog.com/2010/04/13/geely-set-to-reveal-modified-rolls-royce-aping-limousine-in-beij/

Bowman, Z. (2010b). *Report: "Geely to adopt (confusing) new multi-brand system" 16 April 2010*. Retrieved from http://www.autoblog.com/2010/04/16/report-geely-to-adopt-confusing-new-multi-brand-system/

Bowman, Z. (2010c). *Beijing 2010: Geely's London Taxi-aping Englon TXN*. Retrieved from http://www.autoblog.com/2010/04/23/beijing-2010-geelys-london-taxi-aping-englon-txn/

Boyatzis, R. E., & McKee, A. (2005). *Resonant Leadership*. Boston: Harvard Business School Press.

Brache, A. P. (2002). *How organizations work*. New York, NY: John Wiley & Sons, Inc.

Bradsher, K. (2010). Ford agrees to sell Volvo to a fast-rising Chinese company. *The New York Times: Global Business*. Retrieved from http://www.nytimes.com/2010/03/29/business/global/29auto.html

Brannen, M. Y. (2004). When Mickey loses face: Recontextualization, semantic fit and the semiotics of foreignness. *Academy of Management Review*, *29*(4), 593–616.

Brannen, M. Y. (2004). When Mickey loses face: Recontextualization, semantic fit, and the semiotics of foreignness. *Academy of Management Review*, *29*(4), 593–616.

Brannen, M. Y., & Doz, Y. L. (2012). Corporate languages and strategic agility: Trapped in your jargon or lost in translation? *California Management Review*, *54*(3), 77–97. doi:10.1525/cmr.2012.54.3.77

Brannen, M. Y., Piekkari, R., & Tietze, S. (2014). The multifaceted role of language in international business: Unpacking the forms, functions and features of a critical challenge to MNC theory and performance. *Journal of International Business Studies*, *45*(5), 495–507. doi:10.1057/jibs.2014.24

Brannen, M. Y., & Salk, J. E. (2000). Partnering across borders: Negotiating organizational culture in a German-Japanese joint venture. *Human Relations*, *53*(4), 451–487. doi:10.1177/0018726700534001

Breemen, D. (2014). *Five reasons why foreign MNC's fail in China*. Retrieved from https://www.linkedin.com/today/post/article/20140415073136-109792243-five-reasons-why-foreign-mnc-s-fail-in-china/

Bridge, S. (2014). Exploring the nature of social capital to facilitate its inclusion in enterprise education. *Education + Training, 56*(8/9), 839 – 851.

Broadfoot, K., Deetz, S., & Anderson, D. (2004). *Multi-levelled, multi-method approaches in organizational discourse. In The Sage Handbook of Organizational Discourse* (pp. 193–211). Sage Publications. doi:10.4135/9781848608122.n9

Brockbank, W. (1999). If HR were really strategically proactive: Present and future directions in HR's contribution to competitive advantage. *Human Resource Management*, *38*(4), 337–352. doi:10.1002/(SICI)1099-050X(199924)38:4<337::AID-HRM8>3.0.CO;2-5

Brouthers, L. E., O'Donnell, E., & Hadjimarcou, J. (2005). Generic product strategies for emerging market exports into triad nation markets: A mimetic isomorphism approach. *Journal of Management Studies*, *42*(1), 207–225. doi:10.1111/j.1467-6486.2005.00495.x

Brozik, D. (1994). The second dimensions for successful management. *Manage*, *45*(4), 4–8.

Bruks, F. (2008). *Object model for description of the logistical flow at Volvo Cars Corporation -A base for simulation containing logistical flows*. University of Gothenburg.

Buckley, P. J., & Casson, C. C. (1998). Analyzing Foreign Market Entry Strategies: Extending the Internalization Approach. *Journal of International Business Studies*, *29*(3).

Buckley, P. J., & Casson, M. (1976). *The Future of Multinational Enterprise*. London: Holmes & Meier. doi:10.1007/978-1-349-02899-3

Buckley, P. J., & Casson, M. C. (1998). Analyzing foreign market entry strategies: Extending the internalization approach. *Journal of International Business Studies*, *29*(3), 539–561. doi:10.1057/palgrave.jibs.8490006

Buckley, P. J., Clegg, J., & Tan, H. (2006). Cultural awareness in knowledge transfer to China-the role of guanxi and mianzi. *Journal of World Business*, *41*(3), 275–288. doi:10.1016/j.jwb.2006.01.008

Buckley, P. J., Pass, C. L., & Prescott, K. (1988). Measure of International Competitiveness: A Critical Survey. *Journal of Marketing Management*, *4*(2), 175–200. doi:10.1080/0267257X.1988.9964068

Buckley, P. J., Pass, C. L., & Prescott, K. (1990a). Measure of International Competitiveness: Empirical Findings from British Manufacturing Companies. *Journal of Marketing Management*, *6*(1), 1–13. doi:10.1080/0267257X.1990.9964112

Buckley, P. J., Pass, C. L., & Prescott, K. (1990b). The Implementation of an International Market Servicing Strategy in UK Manufacturing Firms. *British Journal of Management*, *1*(3), 127–136. doi:10.1111/j.1467-8551.1990.tb00001.x

Buckley, P., & Ghauri, P. (2004). Globalisation, Economic Geography and the Strategy of the Multinational Enterprises. *Journal of International Business Studies*, *35*(2), 81–98. doi:10.1057/palgrave.jibs.8400076

Bueno, E., Salmador, M. P., & Rosriguez, O. (2004). The Role of Social Capital in Today's Economy: Empirical Evidence of New Model of Intellectual Capital. *European Management Journal*, *17*(4), 556–574.

Bunchapattanasakda, C., & Wong, P. (2010). Management practices of Chinese managers in Chinese MNCs operating in Bangkok. *Cross Cultural Management: An International Journal*, *17*(3), 268–282. doi:10.1108/13527601011068360

Burke, E. (2002). *Digital Government; the next step to reengineering the Federal government* [Online]. Retrieved from http://pionline.org

Burlingame, J. F. (1961). Information Technology and decentralization. *Harvard Business Review*. Retrieved from http://study.com/academy/lesson/bureaucratic-organizations-mechanic-organic-bureacracies.html

Bursik, R. J., & Grasmick, H. G. (1993). *Neighborhoods and crime: The dimensions of effective community control*. Lexington Books.

Burt, R. S. (1997). The Contingent Value of Social Capital. *Administrative Science Quarterly*, *43*(2), 339. doi:10.2307/2393923

Busenitz, L. W., Gomez, C., & Spencer, J. W. (2000). Country institutional profiles: Unlocking entrepreneurial phenomena. *Academy of Management Journal*, *43*(5), 994–1003. doi:10.2307/1556423

Business Wire. (2011, Jul 1). *General Mills completes Yoplait acquisition*. Accessed 2015, Jun 15: http://www.businesswire.com/news/home/20110701005199/en/General-Mills-Completes-Yoplait-Acquisition#.VX80IEYm968

Bustillo, M. (2012). Wal-Mart Faces Risk in Mexican Bribe Probe. *The Wall Street Journal*. Retrieved from http://www.wsj.com/articles/SB10001424052702303978104577360283629622556

Buzzell, R. D. (1968). Can you standardize multinational marketing? *Harvard Business Review*, *46*(November/December), 102–113.

Buzzell, R. D., & Gale, B. T. (1987). *The PIMS* principles*. New York: Free Press.

Cainelli, G., Mancinelli, S., & Mazzanti, M. (2007). Social capital and innovation dynamics in district-based local systems. *Journal of Socio-Economics*, *36*(6), 932–948. doi:10.1016/j.socec.2007.01.023

Cäker, M., Andersson, T., & Wickelgren, M. (2011). Formal incentive systems in organizations with a swedish management style: Conflict or interaction? *Conference: The Actor-Reality Perspective*. Retrieved from http://bit.ly/1xjBUi7

Caldas-Coulthard, C. R., & Coulthard, M. (Eds.). (1996). *Texts and Practices: Readings in Critical Discourse Analysis*. London: Routledge.

Candlin, C. N., & Maley, Y. (1997). Intertextuality and interdiscursivity in the discourse of alternative dispute resolution. In B. Gunnarsson, P. Linell, & B. Nordberg (Eds.), *The Construction of Professional Discourse* (pp. 201–222). London: Longman.

Cantwell, J. (1989). *Technological Innovation and Multinational Corporations*. Oxford, UK: Basil Blackwell.

Cantwell, J. (1995). The globalization of technology: What remains of the product cycle model? *Cambridge Journal of Economics*, *19*(1), 155–174.

Cantwell, J. (2005). Innovation and competitiveness. In J. Fagerberg, D. Mowery, & R. Nelson (Eds.), *The Oxford Handbook of Innovation*. Oxford, UK: Oxford University Press.

Cao, X., & Prakash, A. (2011). Growing exports by signaling product quality: Trade competition and the cross-national diffusion of ISO 9000 quality standards. *Journal of Policy Analysis and Management*, *30*(1), 111–135. doi:10.1002/pam.20546

Carmona-Lavado, A., Cuevas-Rodríguez, G., & Cabello-Medina, C. (2010). Social and organisational capital: Building the context for innovation. *Industrial Marketing Management*, *39*(4), 681–690. doi:10.1016/j.indmarman.2009.09.003

Carneiro, J., Rocha, A., & Silva, J. F. (2008). Challenging the uppsala internationalization model: A contingent approach to the internationalization of services. *BAR. Brazilian Administration Review*, *5*(2), 85–103. doi:10.1590/S1807-76922008000200002

Carney, M., & Gedailovic, E. (2003). Strategic innovation and the administrative heritage of East Asian family business groups. *Asia Pacific Journal of Management*, *20*(1), 5–26. doi:10.1023/A:1022062428231

Carney, M., Gedajlovic, E., & Yang, X. (2009). Varieties of Asian capitalism: Toward an institutional theory of Asian enterprise. *Asia Pacific Journal of Management*, *26*(3), 361–380. doi:10.1007/s10490-009-9139-2

Carpenter, J. P., Daniere, A. G., & Takahashi, L. M. (2004). Cooperation, trust, and social capital in Southeast Asian urban slums. *Journal of Economic Behavior & Organization*, *55*(4), 533–551. doi:10.1016/j.jebo.2003.11.007

Castañer, X., & Genç, M. E. (2011). Expanding to institutionally different countries. In T. Das (Ed.), *Strategic alliances in a globalizing world* (pp. 1–25). Charlotte, N.C.: Information Age Pub.

Castellacci, F. (2008). Technology clubs, technology gaps and growth trajectories. *Structural Change and Economic Dynamics*, *19*(4), 301–314. doi:10.1016/j.strueco.2008.07.002

Caux Round Table. (2015). Retrieved from http://www.cauxroundtable.org/

Caves, R. E. (1971). International corporations: The industrial economics of foreign investment. *Economica*, *38*(149), 1–27. doi:10.2307/2551748

Cavusgil, S. T., Ghauri, P. N., & Akcal, A. A. (2013). *Doing business in emerging markets* (2nd ed.). San Francisco, CA: Sage.

Cedillo, J. A. (2012, May 3). El congreso de Nuevo León señala corrupción de una tienda de Walmart. *CNN Mexico*. Retrieved from: http://mexico.cnn.com/nacional/2012/05/03/el-congreso-de-nuevo-leon-senala-corrupcion-de-una-tienda-walmart

CEMEX. (2015). *CEMEX Group*. Retrieved from http://www.cemex.com/AboutUs/History.aspx, on June 11, 2015.

CEMEX. (n.d.). *About Us | CEMEX*. Retrieved from http://www.cemex.com/AboutUs.aspx

Centre for Research on Multinational Corporations. (2012). *Shell: Two unresolved CSR issues in 2011*. Amsterdam, Netherlands: SOMO.

Chamoun-Nicolas, H. (2008). *Negotiate like a Phoenician: Discover Tradeables*. Keynegotiations, Llc.

Chan, A. K. (1990). Localization in international branding. *International Journal of Advertising*, *9*(1), 81–91.

Chandler, A. D. (2003). *Strategy and Structure: Chapters in the History of the American Industrial Enterprise*. Washington, DC: Beard Books.

Chang, A., Guo, C., Zolin, R., & Yang, X. (2014). Guanxi as a complex adaptive system: Definition, description and underlying principals. *Journal of Asia Business Studies*, *8*(2), 81–103. doi:10.1108/JABS-12-2012-0058

Chang, E. C., & Chu, Y. (2006). Corruption and trust: Exceptionalism in Asian democracies? *The Journal of Politics*, *68*(02), 259–271. doi:10.1111/j.1468-2508.2006.00404.x

Chanthanom, S. (1998). *Globalization of the Golden Triangle: Cultural transformation in Burma, Laos and Thailand*. (Doctoral dissertation). University of Pittsburgh. UMI No. 9919264.

Charoen Pokhpand. (2014). *2013 annual report for Charoen Pokhpand Foods Public Company Limited*. Retrieved from www.cpfworldwide.com/en/investor/financial-information/annual-report/

Chattananon, A., & Trimetsoontorn, J. (2009). Relationship marketing: A Thai case. *International Journal of Emerging Markets*, *4*(3), 252–274. doi:10.1108/17468800910968418

Chelliah, S., Mohamed, S., & Yusliza, M. Y. (2010). Internationalization and Performance: Small and Medium Enterprises (SMEs) in Malaysia. *International Journal of Business and Management*, *5*(6), 27–37. doi:10.5539/ijbm.v5n6p27

Chen, M. X., Otsuki, T., & Wilson, J. S. (2006). *Do standards matter for export success?* (Vol. 3809). World Bank Publications.

Chen, M. X., Wilson, J. S., & Otsuki, T. (2008). Standards and export decisions: Firm-level evidence from developing countries. *The Journal of International Trade & Economic Development*, *17*(4), 501–523. doi:10.1080/09638190802250027

Chen, P. H. (2004). The vulnerability of Thai democracy: Coups d'etat and political changes in modern Thailand. In P. Liamputtong (Ed.), *Contemporary Socio-Cultural and Political Perspectives in Thailand* (pp. 185–207). Dordrecht, NL: Springer.

Child, J., Rodrigues, S. B., & Tse, K. K.-T. (2012). The Dynamics of influence in corporate co-evolution. *Journal of Management Studies*, *49*(7), 1246–1273. doi:10.1111/j.1467-6486.2012.01057.x

Childs, M. L., & Jin, B. (2014). Is Uppsala Model valid to fashion retailers?: An analysis from internationalisation patterns of fast fashion retailers. *Journal of Fashion Marketing and Management*, *18*(1), 36–51. doi:10.1108/JFMM-10-2012-0061

Chiles, T. H., Bluedorn, A. C., & Gupta, V. K. (2007). Beyond creating distraction and entrepreneurial discover: A radical Austrian approach to entrepreneurship. *Organization Studies*, *28*(4), 467–493. doi:10.1177/0170840606067996

Chinese Champions. (2015). *Geely Profile.* Retrieved from http://www.chinese-champions.com/geely/

Chironga, M., Leke, A., Wamelen, A. V., & Lund, S. (2011). The Globe: Cracking the Next Growth Market – Africa. *Harvard Business Review*. Retrieved from https://hbr.org/2011/05/the-globe-cracking-the-next-growth-market-africa

Chong, L. M., & Thomas, D. C. (1997). Leadership perceptions in cross-cultural context: Pakeha and Pacific Islanders in New Zealand. *The Leadership Quarterly*, *8*(3), 275–293. doi:10.1016/S1048-9843(97)90004-7

Chouliaraki, L. (1998). Regulation in "progressivist" pedagogic discourse: Individualized teacher–pupil talk. *Discourse & Society*, *9*(1), 5–32. doi:10.1177/0957926598009001001

Chou, Y. K. (2006). Three simple models of social capital and economic growth. *Journal of Socio-Economics*, *35*(5), 889–912. doi:10.1016/j.socec.2005.11.053

Chudnovsky, D., & Lopez, A. (2003). Diffusion of environmentally friendly technologies by multinational corporations in developing countries. *Journal of Technology Management & Sustainable Development*, *2*(1), 5–18. doi:10.1386/ijtm.2.1.5/0

Chukwuemeka, E., Anazodo, R., & Nzewi, H. N. (2011). Underdevelopment and the Multinationals – A Political Commentary. *Journal of Sustainable Development*. Retrieved from www.ccsenet.org/journal/index.php/jsd/article/viewfile/11603/8237

Cisco. (2014). *2014 Connected world Technology final report*. Retrieved from http://www.cisco.com/c/dam/en/us/solutions/collateral/enterprise/connected-world-technology-report/cisco-2014-connected-world-technology-report.pdf

Clarke, L. D. (1998). *The role of overseas Chinese investment in the emerging countries of Southeast and East Asia: A Confucian model of the foreign direct investment decision-making process using factors unconsidered in the West* (Doctoral dissertation). Florida International University. UMI No. 9835704.

Cleary, M. R., & Stokes, S. C. (2006). *Democracy and the culture of skepticism: Political trust in Argentina and Mexico.* New York, NY: Russell Sage.

Cloete, R., Faulhaber, F., & Zils, M. (2010). Infrastructure: A long Road ahead. In Africa's Path to Growth: Sector by Sector. McKinsey & Co.

Clougherty, J. A., & Grajek, M. (2008). The impact of ISO 9000 diffusion on trade and FDI: A new institutional analysis. *Journal of International Business Studies*, *39*(4), 613–633. doi:10.1057/palgrave.jibs.8400368

CNNExpansión. (2012, Oct 2). *Sigma renueva acuerdo con Yoplait* [Sigma renews agreement with Yoplait]. Accessed 2015, Jun 15: http://www.cnnexpansion.com/negocios/2012/10/02/sigma-renueva-acuerdo-por-yoplait

Coe, N. M., Dicken, P., & Hess, M. (2008). Global production networks: Realizing the potential. *Journal of Economic Geography*, *8*(3), 271–295. doi:10.1093/jeg/lbn002

Coleman, J. S. (1988). Social Capital in The Creation of Human Capital. *American Journal of Sociology*, *96*, 95–120. doi:10.1086/228943

Coleman, J. S., & Coleman, J. S. (1994). *Foundations of social theory*. Harvard University Press.

Colley, R. (1961). *Defined advertising goals for measured advertising results*. New York: Association of National Advertisers.

Collis, D. (2014). *International Strategy: Context, Concepts and Implications*. John Wiley & Sons, Inc.

Colton, T. (1995). *Moscow: Governing the socialist metropolis*. Cambridge: Belknap Press. doi:10.4159/harvard.9780674283725

Companies Proceeding Rule Fan, . (2008). The Rise of Emerging Market Multinationals And its Impact on Marketing. *Marketing Intelligence & Planning*, *26*, 4.

Contractor, F. J. (2013). Punching above their weight: The sources of competitive advantage for emerging market multinationals. *International Journal of Emerging Markets*, *8*(4), 304–328. doi:10.1108/IJoEM-06-2013-0102

Cook-Greuter, S. R. (1995). *Comprehensive language awareness: A definition of the phenomenon and a review of its treatment in the postformal adult development literature*. Cambridge, MA: Harvard University.

Cordeiro-Nilsson, C. M. (2009). *Swedish Management in Singapore: A Discourse Analysis Chapter.* (Doctoral Dissertation). Department of Philosophy, Linguistics and Theory of Science, University of Gothenburg, Gothenburg, Sweden.

Cordeiro-Nilsson, C. M. (2009). *Swedish Management in Singapore: A Discourse Analysis Study*. University of Gothenburg.

Cordeiro-Nilsson, C. M. (2010). A discourse analysis chapter of assimilation and integration of management style: The case of Swedish managers in Singapore. *The New English Teacher*, *4*(1), 13–53.

Cordeiro-Nilsson, C. M., & Hawamdeh, S. (2011). Leveraging socio-culturally situated tacit knowledge. *Journal of Knowledge Management*, *15*(1), 88–103. doi:10.1108/13673271111108710

Coulter, M. (2005). *Strategic Management in Action* (3rd ed.). Prentice Hall.

Coviello, N. E., Ghauri, P. N., & Martin, K. (1998). International Competitiveness: Empirical Findings from SME Service Firms. *Journal of Marketing Management*, *6*(2), 8–27.

Cowden, B. J., & Alhorr, H. S. (2013). Disruptive innovation in multinational enterprises. *The Multinational Business Review*, *21*(4), 358–371. doi:10.1108/MBR-05-2013-0027

Craig, C. S., & Douglas, S. P. (2000). Configural advantage in global markets. *Journal of International Marketing*, *8*(1), 6–25. doi:10.1509/jimk.8.1.6.19564

Crandall, D. (Ed.). (2007). *Leadership Lessons from West Point*. John Willey & Sons.

Crawford, D., & Esterl, M. (2007, Nov 16). Siemens ruling details bribery across the globe. *Wall Street Journal*.

Crick, D. (1999). An investigation into SMEs' use of languages in their export operations. *International Journal of Entrepreneurial Behaviour and Research*, *5*(1), 19–31. doi:10.1108/13552559910259810

Čudanov, M., Jaško, O., & Jevtić, M. (2009). Influence of Information and Communication Technologies on Decentralization of Organizational Structure. *ComSIS*, *6*(1), 93–109. doi:10.2298/CSIS0901093C

Cuervo-Cazurra, A. (2007). Sequence of value-added activities in the multinationalization of developing country firms. *Journal of International Management*, *13*(3), 258–277. doi:10.1016/j.intman.2007.05.009

Cuervo-Cazurra, A. (2010). Multilatinas. *Universia Business Review*, *25*, 138–154.

Cuervo-Cazurra, A., & Genc, M. (2008). Transforming disadvantages into advantages: Developing-country MNEs in the least developed countries. *Journal of International Business Studies*, *30*(6), 957–979. doi:10.1057/palgrave.jibs.8400390

Cuervo-Cazurra, A., & Genc, M. E. (2011). Obligating, pressuring, and supporting dimensions of the environment and the non-market advantages of developing country multinational companies. *Journal of Management Studies*, *48*(2), 441–455.

Cull, N. J. (2007). Public Diplomacy: Lessons from the Past. A report for the Public Diplomacy Group of the Foreign and Commonwealth Office, London.

Culpan, R., & Kucukemiroglu, O. (1993). A Comparison of U.S. and Japanese Management Styles and Unit Effectiveness. *Management International Review*, *33*(1), 27–42.

Cummings, S. (2007). Shifting foundations: Redrawing strategic management's military heritage. *Critical Perspectives on International Business*, *3*(1), 41–62. doi:10.1108/17422040710722551

Curran, S. R., Garip, F., Chung, C. Y., & Tangchonlatip, K. (2005). Gendered migrant social capital: Evidence from Thailand. *Social Forces*, *84*(1), 225–255. doi:10.1353/sof.2005.0094

Cutler, A. (2012). *Native Listening: Language Experience and the Recognition of Spoken Words*. Cambridge, MA: MIT Press.

Czarniawska, B. (2007). Narrative inquiry in and about organizations. In D. Jean Clandinin (Ed.), *Handbook of Narrative Inquiry. Mapping a Methodology* (pp. 383–404). Newbury Park, CA: Sage. doi:10.4135/9781452226552.n15

Czarnitzki, D., & Kraft, K. (2011). Spillovers of Innovation Activities and Their Profitability. *Oxford Economic Papers*, gpr020.

Czinkota, M. R. (1982). *Export Development Strategies: US Promotion Policies*. New York: Praeger Publishers.

Czinkota, M. R., & Ronkainen, I. A. (2010). *International marketing*. Mason, OH: South-Western.

Czubala, W., Shepherd, B., & Wilson, J. S. (2009). Help or Hindrance? The Impact of Harmonized Standards on African Exports. *Journal of African Economies*, *18*(5), 711–744. doi:10.1093/jae/ejp003

D'Iribarne, P. (2007). Growing together in Mexico. In *Successful companies in the developing world: Managing in synergy with cultures* (pp. 37–64). Paris: Agence Française de Développement.

Daft, R. (2004). *Administración*. Editorial Trillas.

Daft, R. L., & Lengel, R. H. (1998). *Fusion Leadership: Unlocking the Subtle Forces that Change People and Organizations*. San Francisco, CA: Berrett Koehler Publishers.

Dahles, H. (2008). Entrepreneurship and the legacies of a development state: Singapore enterprises venturing across boarders. *Journal of Developmental Entrepreneurship*, *13*(4), 485–508. doi:10.1142/S1084946708001095

Dai, L., Eden, L., & Beamish, P. W. (2013). Place, space, and geographical exposure: Foreign subsidiary survival in conflict zones. *Journal of International Business Studies*, *44*(6), 554–578. doi:10.1057/jibs.2013.12

Dakhli, M., & De Clercq, D. (2004). Human capital, social capital, and innovation: A multi-country study. *Entrepreneurship and Regional Development*, *16*(2), 107–128. doi:10.1080/08985620410001677835

Daniere, A., Takahashi, L., NaRanong, A., & Lan, V. T. N. (2005). Social capital and urban environments in Southeast Asia: Lessons from settlements in Bangkok and Ho Chi Minh City. *International Development Planning Review*, *27*(1), 21–58. doi:10.3828/idpr.27.1.3

Das, T. K., & Teng, B.-S. (1999). Managing risks in strategic alliances. *The Academy of Management Executive*, *13*(4), 50–62.

Davidson, W., & de la Torre. (1989). *Managing the global corporation*. New York: McGraw-Hill.

Davids, T. W. R. (1894). *Buddhism: A sketch of the life and teachings of Gautama, the Buddha*. London: Society for Promoting Christian Knowledge.

De Castro, G. M., & Saez, P. L. (2008). Intellectual Capital in High-Tech Firms the Case of Spain. *Journal of Intellectual Capital*, *9*(1), 25–36. doi:10.1108/14691930810845786

De Dominicis, L., Florax, R. J., & De Groot, H. L. (2013). Regional clusters of innovative activity in Europe: Are social capital and geographical proximity key determinants? *Applied Economics*, *45*(17), 2325–2335. doi:10.1080/00036846.2012.663474

De la Torre, A., Didier, T., & Pinat, M. (2014). *Can Latin America Tap the Globalization Upside?* Policy Research Working Paper Series.

De Valk, P. (2003). *How do firms learn? With case studies from Lao PDR*. Working Paper Series: Institute of Social Studies, The Hague, 385.

Dearmon, J., & Grier, K. (2009). Trust and development. *Journal of Economic Behavior & Organization*, *71*(2), 210–220. doi:10.1016/j.jebo.2009.02.011

Deetz, S. (2003). Reclaiming the legacy of the linguistic turn. *Organization*, *10*(3), 421–429. doi:10.1177/13505084030103002

DeForrest, M. E. (1994). Thinking of a Plant in Mexico? *The Academy of Management Executive*, *8*(1), 33–40.

DeGeorge, R. T. (1993). *Competing with Integrity in International Business*. New York: Oxford University Press.

Del Sol, P., & Kogan, J. (2007). Regional competitive advantage based on pioneering economic reforms: The case of Chilean FDI. *Journal of International Business Studies*, *38*(6), 901–927. doi:10.1057/palgrave.jibs.8400299

Deng, Y. (2014). China: The post-responsible power. *The Washington Quarterly*, *37*(4), 117–132. doi:10.1080/0163660X.2014.1002159

Denis, J. E., & Depelteau, D. (1985). Market knowledge, diversification and export expansion. *Journal of International Business Studies*, *16*(3), 77–89. doi:10.1057/palgrave.jibs.8490460

Denk, N., Kaufmann, L., & Roesch, J.-F. (2012). Liabilities of foreignness revisited: A review of contemporary studies and recommendations for future research. *Journal of International Management*, *18*(4), 322–334. doi:10.1016/j.intman.2012.07.001

Deshpande, M., & Baporikar, N. (2014). Excellence in a Borderless World: Evidence from Pune Auto-Components SMEs. *Journal of Shinawatra University*, *1*(2), 182–196.

DesJardins, J. (2009). *An Introduction to Business Ethics* (3rd ed.). New York, NY: McGraw-Hill Higher Education.

Dessler, G. (2003). *Human resource management* (9th ed.). Upper Saddle River, NJ: Prentice Hall.

Dhanaraj, C., Lyles, M. A., Steensma, H. K., & Tihanyi, L. (2004). Managing tacit and explicit knowledge transfer in IJVs: The role of relational embeddedness and the impact on performance. *Journal of International Business Studies*, *35*(5), 428–442. doi:10.1057/palgrave.jibs.8400098

Diaconu, L., & Cuza, A. L. (2008). *The multinational companies and the emerging markets*. Retrieved from http://steconomice.uoradea.ro/anale/volume/2008/v1-international-business-and-european-integration/018.pdf/

Diamond, L., & McDonald, J. (1996). *Multi-Track Diplomacy: A Systems Approach to Peace*. Kumarian Press.

Dibrell, C. C., & Miller, T. (2002). Organization Design: The continuing influence of information technology. *Management Design Journal*, *40*(6). doi:10.1108/00251740210434016

Dicken, P. (2015). *Global shift: Mapping the changing contours of the world economy* (7th ed.). Sage Publications.

DiMaggio, P. J., & Powell, W. W. (1983). The iron cage revisited: Institutional isomorphism and collective rationality in organisational fields. *American Sociological Review*, *48*(2), 147–160. doi:10.2307/2095101

Dinda, S. (2014). Inclusive growth through creation of human and social capital. *International Journal of Social Economics*, *41*(10), 878–895. doi:10.1108/IJSE-07-2013-0157

Dixit, A. (2009). Governance institutions and economic activity. *The American Economic Review*, 3–24.

Doha, A., Ajay, D., & Pagell, M. (2013). The influence of product life cycle on the efficacy of purchasing practices. *International Journal of Operations & Production Management*, *33*(4), 470–498. doi:10.1108/01443571311307352

Doh, P. J., Rodriguez, P., Uhlenbruck, K., Collins, J., & Eden, L. (2003). Coping with corruption in foreign markets. *The Academy of Management Executive*, *17*(3), 114–127. doi:10.5465/AME.2003.10954775

Doh, S., & Acs, Z. J. (2010). Innovation and social capital: A cross-country investigation. *Industry and Innovation*, *17*(3), 241–262. doi:10.1080/13662711003790569

Doloreux, D., & Parto, S. (2005). Regional innovation systems: Current discourse and unresolved issues. *Technology in Society*, *27*(2), 133–153. doi:10.1016/j.techsoc.2005.01.002

Dominion CSR. (n.d.). Retrieved from http://www.dominioncsr.com/business/risk_management.php

Donaldson, T., Werhane, P., & Cording, M. (2002). *Ethical issues in business: a philosophical approach*. Upper Saddle River, NJ: Prentice Hall.

Douglas, S. P., & Craig, C. S. (1989). Evolution of global marketing strategy: Scale, scope, and synergy. *The Columbia Journal of World Business*, *24*(3), 47–58.

Dreischmeier, R., Close, K., & Trichet, P. (2015, March). *bcg perspectives*. Retrieve from https://www.bcgperspectives.com/content/articles/digital_economy_technology_strategy_digital_imperative/

Driffield, N., & Love, J. H. (2007). Linking FDI motivation and host economy productivity effects: Conceptual and empirical analysis. *Journal of International Business Studies*, *38*(3), 460–473. doi:10.1057/palgrave.jibs.8400268

Driffield, N., Love, J. H., & Menghinello, S. (2010). The Multinational Enterprise as a Source of International Knowledge Flows: Direct Evidence from Italy. *Journal of International Business Studies*, *41*(2), 350–359. doi:10.1057/jibs.2009.57

Driffield, N., Love, J., & Yong, Y. (2014, January). Technology Sourcing and Reverse Productivity Spillovers in the Multinational Enterprise: Global or Regional Phenomenon? *British Journal of Management*, *25*, 24–41. doi:10.1111/1467-8551.12009

Duan, Y., & Kong, Y. (2008). *The role of R&D offshoring in explaining the patent growth of China and India at USPTO*. Management of Innovation and Technology, 2008. ICMIT 2008. 4th IEEE International Conference on 2008.

Du-Babcock, B. (2006). An analysis of top management strategies and the turn-taking behaviour in the Hong Kong bilingual environment: The impact of cultural and language use. *Journal of Business Communication*, *43*(1), 21–42. doi:10.1177/0021943605282373

Dubrow, A. (2011, June). *A decade of discover*. The University of Texas at Austin. Retrieved from http://www.utexas.edu/know/2011/06/21/tacc_anniversary/

Duce, M. (2003). *Definitions of Foreign Direct Investment (FDI): a methodological note*. Banco de España.

Dufhues, T., Buchenrieder, G., & Munkung, N. (2013). Social capital and market imperfections: Accessing formal credit in Thailand. *Oxford Development Studies*, *41*(1), 54–75. doi:10.1080/13600818.2012.753999

Dufhues, T., Buchenrieder, G., Quoc, H. D., & Munkung, N. (2011). Social capital and loan repayment performance in Southeast Asia. *Journal of Socio-Economics*, *40*(5), 679–691. doi:10.1016/j.socec.2011.05.007

Du, J., Lu, Y., & Tao, Z. (2008). Economic institutions and FDI location choice: Evidence from US multinationals in China. *Journal of Comparative Economics*, *36*(3), 412–429. doi:10.1016/j.jce.2008.04.004

Dunning, J. H. (2006). Towards a new paradigm of development: implications for the determinants of international business. *Transnational Corporations, 5*(1), 173-227.

Dunning, J. (1973). The determinants of international production. *Oxford Economic Papers*, *25*, 289–335.

Dunning, J. (1989). The Study of International Business: A Plea for a More Interdisciplinary Approach. *Journal of International Business Studies*, *20*(3), 411–436. doi:10.1057/palgrave.jibs.8490371

Dunning, J. (2009). Location and the Multinational Enterprise: A Neglected Factor? *Journal of International Business Studies*, *40*(1), 5–19. doi:10.1057/jibs.2008.74

Dunning, J. H. (1979). Explaining Changing Patterns of the International Production: In Defence of the Eclectic Theory. *Oxford Bulletin of Economics and Statistics*, *41*(4), 269–295. doi:10.1111/j.1468-0084.1979.mp41004003.x

Dunning, J. H. (1988). The Eclectic Paradigm of International Production: A Restatement and Some Possible Extensions. *Journal of International Business Studies*, *19*(1), 1–31. doi:10.1057/palgrave.jibs.8490372

Dunning, J. H. (1993). *Multinational Enterprises and the Global Economy*. New York: Addison Wesley Pub. Co.

Dunning, J. H. (2002). *Global capitalism, FDI and competitiveness*. Edward Elgar Publishing. doi:10.4337/9781843767060

Dunning, J. H., Fujita, M., & Yakova, N. (2007). Some macro-data on the regionalisation/globalisation debate: A comment on the Rugman/Verbeke analysis. *Journal of International Business Studies*, *38*(1), 177–199. doi:10.1057/palgrave.jibs.8400241

Duong, C. M., & Swierczek, F. W. (2008). Corporate culture, leadership competencies, job satisfaction, job commitment, and job performance: A comparison of companies in Vietnam and Thailand. *Journal of American Academy of Business, Cambridge*, *13*(1), 159–165.

Duranti, A. (1997). *Linguistic anthropology*. Cambridge, UK: Cambridge University Press. doi:10.1017/CBO9780511810190

Durlauf, S. N., & Johnson, P. A. (1995). Multiple regimes and cross-country growth behaviour. *Journal of Applied Econometrics*, *10*(4), 365–384. doi:10.1002/jae.3950100404

Durlauf, S., & Aghion, P. (2005). *Handbook of economic growth*. Elsevier.

Dutta, S., Lanvin, B., & Wunsch-Vincent, S. (2014). *The Global Innovation Index 2014. The Human Factor in Innovation*. Cornell University, INSEAD, and WIPO.

Duval, E. (2004). Learning Technology Standardization: Making Sense of it All. *ComSIS*, *1*(1), 33–43. doi:10.2298/CSIS0401033D

Economista, E. (2014, September 16). Cemex, la empresa más global de América Latina. *El Economista*. Retrieved from http://eleconomista.com.mx/industrias/2014/09/16/cemex-empresa-mas-global-americaeconomia

Edmonton. (n.d.). Retrieved from http://www.edmonton.ca/city_government/documents/ERM_CBRP_Model_Sept_05.pdf

Edward, J. (1999). *Electronic commerce change organizational structure*. Department of Management Science, School of Business Public Management.

Einhorn, B., & Prasso, S. (1997, October 6). Anxious giant. *Business Week (Asian ed.)*.

Ellis, P. (2000). Social Ties and Foreign Market Entry. *Journal of International Business Studies*, *31*(3), 443–469. doi:10.1057/palgrave.jibs.8490916

Ellis, R. E. (2014). *China on the ground in Latin America: Challenges for the Chinese and impacts on the region*. New York, NY: Palgrave Macmillan. doi:10.1057/9781137439772

Emis. (2015, July 27). *Companies*. EMIS Professional Database. Retrieved from http://ebiblio.cetys.mx:2083/php/companies?pc=MX&cmpy=2408922

Endres, G. M., & Mancheno-Smoak, L. (2008). The human resource craze: Human performance improvements and employee engagement. *Organization Development Journal*, *26*(1), 69–78.

Ensign, P. C. (2008). Small business strategy as a dynamic process: Concepts, controversies and implications. *Journal of Business and Entrepreneurship*, *20*(2), 25–43.

Epstein, M. J., Buhovac, A. R., & Yuthas, K. (2010). Implementing sustainability: The role of leadership and organizational culture. *Strategic Finance*, *91*(10), 41–48.

Erramilli, M. K., Agarwal, S., & Kim, S.-S. (1997). Are Firm-Specific Advantages Location-Specific Too? *Journal of International Business Studies*, *28*(4), 735–757. doi:10.1057/palgrave.jibs.8490117

Euler Hermes Group. (2015). *Euler Hermes country risk ratings: June 2015 review*. Accessed 2015, Jul 7: www.eulerhermes.com/mediacenter/Lists/mediacenter-documents/Country-Risk-Ratings-Q2-2015.pdf

Evans, G. (2002). *A short history of Laos: A land in between*. Crows Nest, Australia: Allen and Unwin.

Eyring, M. J., Johnson, M. W., & Nair, H. (2011). *New Business Models in Emerging Markets*. Retrieved from http://hbr.org/2011/01/new-business-models-in-emerging-markets

Fagerberg, J., & Srholec, M. (2008). *Technology and development: unpacking the relationship(s)*. TIK Working Papers on Innovation Studies No. 20080623. Centre for Technology, Innovation and Culture, University of Oslo, Oslo.

Fagerberg, J. (1996). Technology and competitiveness. *Oxford Review of Economic Policy*, *12*(3), 39–51. doi:10.1093/oxrep/12.3.39

Fagerberg, J., & Srholec, M. (2007). National innovation systems, capabilities and economic development. *Research Policy*, *37*(9), 1417–1435. doi:10.1016/j.respol.2008.06.003

Fagerberg, J., & Srholec, M. (2009). Innovation systems, technology and development: Unpacking the relationships. In B. A. Lundvall, K. J. Joseph, C. Chaminade, & J. Vang (Eds.), *Handbook of Innovation Systems and Developing Countries: Building Domestic Capabilities in a Global Setting* (pp. 83–115). Cheltenham, UK: Edward Elgar Publishing. doi:10.4337/9781849803427.00010

Fairclough, N., & Thomas, P. (2004). The discourse of globalization and the globalization of discourse. In The Sage Handbook of Organizational Discourse, (pp. 379-396). Sage Publications. doi:10.4135/9781848608122.n18

Fairclough, N. (1992). *Discourse and Social Change*. Cambridge, MA: Polity Press.

Fairclough, N. (1993). Critical discourse analysis and the marketization of public discourse: The universities. *Discourse & Society*, *4*(2), 133–168. doi:10.1177/0957926593004002002

Fairclough, N. (1995). *Media Discourse*. London: Edward Arnold.

Fairclough, N. (2005). Discourse analysis in organization studies: The case for critical realism. *Peripheral Vision*, *26*(6), 915–939.

Fairclough, N. (2006). *Language and globalization*. New York: Routledge.

Fairclough, N. (2013). *Critical Discourse Analysis: The Critical Study of Language*. Abingdon, UK: Routledge.

Fairclough, N., & Wodak, R. (1997). Critical discourse analysis. In T. van Dijk (Ed.), *Discourse as Social Interaction: Discourse Studies: A Multidisciplinary Introduction* (Vol. 2). London: Sage.

Fairclough, N., & Wodak, R. (1997). Critical discourse analysis. In T. A. van Dijk (Ed.), *Discourse Studies: A Multidisciplinary Introduction* (Vol. 2, pp. 258–284). Beverly Hills, CA: Sage.

Fan, Y. (2008). The rise of emerging market multinationals and its impact on marketing. *Marketing Intelligence & Planning*, *26*(4), 353–358. doi:10.1108/02634500810879269

Feltz, A., & Cokely, E. T. (2008). The Fragmented Folk: More Evidence of Stable Individual Differences in Moral Judgments and Folk Intuitions, In B.C. Love, K. McRae, & V.M. Sloutsky (Eds.), *Proceedings of the 30th Annual Conference of the Cognitive Science Society*. Austin, TX: Cognitive Science Society, 1771–76.

Ferguson, C. R., & Dickenson, R. (1982). *Critical success factors for directors in the eighties. Business Horizons*.

Fernquest, J. (2015, January 2). Thailand's biggest companies: Leadership change. *Bangkok Post*, p. B1.

Fidrmuc, J., & Gërxhani, K. (2008). Mind the gap! Social capital, East and West. *Journal of Comparative Economics*, *36*(2), 264–286. doi:10.1016/j.jce.2008.03.002

Fienhold, L. (2014) *Risks of MNCs involved in international business diplomacy: the OECD Guidelines for Multinational Enterprises as a facilitator?* Retrieved from http://purl.utwente.nl/essays/65304

Figueira-de-Lemos, F., Johanson, J., & Vahlne, J. (2011). Risk management in the internationalization process of the firm: A note on the Uppsala model. *Journal of World Business*, *46*(2), 143–153. doi:10.1016/j.jwb.2010.05.008

Fill, C., & Fill, K. E. (2005). *Business to Business Marketing: Philosophies, Systems and Communication*. Prentice Hall.

Financial Times. (2016, December). *FT Lexicon*. Retrieved from http://lexicon.ft.com/Term?term=foreign-direct-investment

Flores, R. G., & Aguilera, R. V. (2007). Globalization and location choice: an analysis of US multinational firms in 1980 and 2000. *Journal of International Studies*, 1-2. Retrieved from www.jibs.net

Flores, R. G., & Aguilera, R. V. (2007). Globalization and locational choice: An analysis of US multinational firms in 1980 and 2000. *Journal of International Business Studies*, *38*(7), 1187–1210. doi:10.1057/palgrave.jibs.8400307

Florida, R. (2002). The rise of the creative class. *The Washington Monthly*, *34*(5), 15–25.

Fola-Alade, S. (2012). *How to Become a Leader in Your Field: The Keys to Your Next Level Influence*. Empowerment Initiative Limited.

Forsgren, M., & Hagström, P. (2007). Ignorant and impatient internationalization?: The Uppsala Model and internationalization patterns for internet-related firms. *Critical Perspectives on International Business*, *3*(4), 291–305. doi:10.1108/17422040710832559

Fortune. (2014). *Shougang Group - Global 500 2014*. Retrieved from http://fortune.com/global500/shougang-group-348/

Fosu, A., Bates, R., & Hoeffler, A. (2006). Institutions, governance and economic development in Africa: An overview. *Journal of African Economies*, *15*(1Supplement 1), 1–9. doi:10.1093/jae/ejk004

Fowler, R., Hodge, B., Kress, G., & Trew, T. (1979). *Language and Control*. London: Routledge & Kegan Paul.

Franke, R. H., Mento, A. J., Prumo, S. M., & Edlund, T. W. (2007). General Electric performance over a half century: Evaluation of effects of leadership and other strategic factors by quantitative case analysis. *International Journal of Business*, *12*(1), 137–151.

Fredriksson, R., Barner-Rasmussen, W., & Piekkari, R. (2006). The multinational corporation as a multilingual organization: The notion of a common corporate language. *Corporate Communications: An International Journal*, *11*(4), 406–423. doi:10.1108/13563280610713879

Friedland, R., & Alford, R. R. (1991). Bringing society back in: Symbols, practices and institutional contradictions. In W. W. Powel & P. J. DiMaggio (Eds.), *The New Institutionalism in Organisational Analysis* (pp. 232–267). Chicago: University of Chicago Press.

Frost, T. (2001). The geographic sources of foreign subsidiaries' innovations. *Strategic Management Journal*, *22*(2), 101–123. doi:10.1002/1097-0266(200101)22:2<101::AID-SMJ155>3.0.CO;2-G

Fukuyama, F. (2001). Social capital, civil society and development. *Third World Quarterly*, *22*(1), 7–20. doi:10.1080/713701144

Fukuyama, F. (2003). *Social capital and civil society. Foundations of social capital*. Cheltenham, UK: Edward Elgar Publishing.

Gaber, Sexton, Sen, & Lin (2009, October). Customer input: incorporate perceived value into marketing strategy. *Business Digest*, 3-9.

Gaddy, C., & Ickes, B. W. (1999). An accounting model of the virtual economy. *Post-Soviet Geography and Economics*, *40*(2), 79–97.

Gaib, Z., Maske, A., & Moraje, S. (2010). Telecommunications: From Voice to Data. In Africa's Path to Growth: Sector by Sector. McKinsey & Co.

Gallo, F. T. (2011). *Business leadership in China: How to blend best Western practices with Chinese wisdom* (Revised ed.). Singapore: John Wiley & Sons.

Gammelgaard, J., & Dörrenbächer, C. (Eds.). (2013). *The global brewery industry: Markets, strategies, and rivalries*. Cheltenham, UK: Edward Elgar. doi:10.4337/9781781006351

Gammeloft, P., Barnard, E., & Madhok, A. (2010). Emerging multinationals, emerging theory: Macro and micro-level perspectives. *Journal of International Management*, *16*(2), 95–101. doi:10.1016/j.intman.2010.03.001

Gao, Z. (2015). The enterprise merger and acquisition effect on firm value - A discussion on Geely's acquisition of Volvo for example. *Modern Economy*, *6*(6), 717–726. doi:10.4236/me.2015.66068

García Soto, C. A., Martínez Cerda, J. L., Torres Durán, N. I., & Pacheco Buelna, D. (2012). Estrategias financieras como generadoras de valor: El caso reciente de Cemex. *ITSON*. Retrieved from http://www.itson.mx/publicaciones/pacioli/Documents/no56/estrategiasfinancieras.pdf

Gatignon, H., & Anderson, E. (1988). The multinational corporations' degree of control over foreign subsidiaries: An empirical test of a transaction cost explanation. *Journal of Law Economics and Organization*, *4*(2), 305–336.

Geely. (2009). *Annual Report 2009 – Geely*. Retrieved from http://www.geelyauto.com.hk/core/files/financial/en/2009-02.pdf

Geely. (2012). *Annual Report 2012 – Geely*. Retrieved from http://www.geelyauto.com.hk/core/files/financial/en/2012-02.pdf

Geely. (2015a). *Geely New Technology*. Retrieved from http://www.geely.com.sa/new-technology.html

Geely. (2015b). *Geely Company Brief*. Retrieved from http://www.geelyauto.com.hk/en/company_brief.html

Gehani, R. (2013). Innovative Strategic Leader Transforming From a Low-Cost Strategy to Product Differentiation Strategy. *Journal of Technology Management & Innovation*, *8*(2), 144–155.

Geppert, M. (2005). Global, National and Local Practices in Multinational Corporations – Towards a Socio-political Framework. *International Journal of Human Resource Management*.

Gerschenkron, A. (1962). *Economic Backwardness in Historical Perspective*. Cambridge, MA: Berlknap Press.

Gertsen, M. C., & Søderberg, A. (2011). Intercultural collaboration stories: On narrative inquiry and analysis as tools for research in international business. *Journal of International Business Studies*, *42*(6), 787–804. doi:10.1057/jibs.2011.15

Ghafurian, A. (2003). The effects from applying IT in organizations. *Economy of World Journal*.

Ghemawat, P. (1986). Sustainable advantage. *Harvard Business Review*, *64*, 53–58.

Ghemawat, P. (2001). Distance still matters: The hard reality of global expansion. *Harvard Business Review*, *79*(8), 137–147. PMID:11550630

Ghemawat, P. (2003). Semiglobalization and international business strategy. *Journal of International Business Strategy*, *34*(2), 138–152. doi:10.1057/palgrave.jibs.8400013

Ghemawat, P., & Hout, T. (2008). Tomorrow's Global Giants. Not the Usual Suspects. *Harvard Business Review*, *86*(11), 80–88.

Ghosal, S., & Barlett, C. A. (1990). The multinational corporation as an interorganizational network. *Academy of Management Review*, *15*(4), 603–625.

Ghoshal, S., & Nohria, N. (1993). Horses for Courses: Organizational Forms for Multinational Corporations. *MIT Sloan Management Review*, *34*(2), 23–35.

Ghura, D., & Goodwin, B. (2000). Determinants of private investment: A cross-regional empirical investigation. *Applied Economics*, *32*(14), 1819–1829. doi:10.1080/000368400425044

Gillen, D. (2001). *Benchmarking and performance measurement: the role in quality management. Amsterdam*. Retrieved from School of Business & Economics - Wilfrid Laurier University website: https://www.wlu.ca/documents/4293/Benchmarking.pdf

Glass, A., & Kamal, S. (1999). Multinational Firms and Technology Transfer. *The Scandinavian Journal of Economics*, 495–513.

Global Financial Integrity. (2013). *Report*. Available at: http://www.gfintegrity.org/wp-content/uploads/2014/12/Illicit-Financial-Flows-from-Developing-Countries-2003-2012.pdf

Global Times. (2010). *'Strategic transformation'-- one of the most profound innovations for Chinese automobile companies*. Retrieved from http://www.globaltimes.cn/autos/auto-china/industry/2011-01/603631.html

Globerman, S. (2014). Regulation and the international competitiveness of US-based companies. *Competitiveness Review*, *24*(5), 378–392. doi:10.1108/CR-11-2012-0026

Gokhberg, L. (Ed.). (2007). *Science, technology and innovation in Russia and OECD countries*. Moscow: State University, High School of Economics.

Goldberg, P. K., & Pavcnik, N. (2007). Distributional effects of globalisation in developing countries. *Journal of Economic Literature*, *45*(1), 39–82. doi:10.1257/jel.45.1.39

Goodale, J. (1973). Effects of Personal Background and Training on Work Values of the hard-core unemployed. *The Journal of Applied Psychology*, *57*(1), 1–9. doi:10.1037/h0034190

Goodwin, G. P., & Darley, J. M. (2008). The Psychology of Meta-ethics: Exploring Objectivism. *Cognition*, *106*(3), 1339–1366. doi:10.1016/j.cognition.2007.06.007 PMID:17692306

Gordon, G., & Williams, T. (2001). How do you Spell Success in Mexico? CALICA. *Business Horizons*, *44*(1), 11–18. doi:10.1016/S0007-6813(01)80003-3

Goulbourne, H., & Solomos, J. (2003). Families, ethnicity and social capital. *Social Policy and Society*, *2*(4), 329–338. doi:10.1017/S1474746403001362

Gowans, C. (2004). *Moral Relativism*. Stanford Encyclopedia of Philosophy. Retrieved from http://plato.stanford.edu/entries/moral-relativism/

Grandis, H. D., & Pinshaw, G. (2010). Banking: Building on Success. In Africa's Path to Growth: Sector by Sector. McKinsey & Co.

Grant, D. (2004). *The SAGE Handbook of Organizational Discourse*. London: SAGE.

Grattan, R. (2005). Strategy in the Battle of Britain and strategic management theory. *Management Decision*, *43*(10), 1432–1441. doi:10.1108/00251740510634967

Grattan, R. (2006). Robert McNamara's "11 lessons" in the context of theories of strategic management. *Journal of Management History*, *12*(4), 425–438. doi:10.1108/17511340610692770

Greer, S. K., & Stephens, C. (1996). Employee issues for companies in Mexico. *California Management Review*, *38*(3), 121–145. doi:10.2307/41165846

Gregory, J. R. (2003). *The best of branding*. New York: McGraw-Hill.

Gregory, J. R. (2005). *Driving brand equity*. New York: ANA. Hamel, Gary & Prahalad, C. K.(1985), Do you really have a global strategy? *Harvard Business Review*, *63*(July/August), 139–148.

Greiner, L. E. (1998). Evolution and revolution as organizations grow. *Harvard Business Review*, *76*(3), 55–68. PMID:10179654

Griliches, Z. (1979). Issues in assessing the contribution of research and development to productivity growth. *The Bell Journal of Economics*, *10*(1), 92–116. doi:10.2307/3003321

Grimes, W. W. (2005). Japan as the "indispensible nation" in Asia: A financial brand for the 21st century. *Asia-Pacific Review*, *12*(1), 40–54. doi:10.1080/13439000500107937

GRUMA. (2015). *GRUMA Group*. Retrieved from http://www.gruma-en.com/ on July 3, 2015.

Grünberg, A. (2014). Saying and doing: Speech actions, speech acts and related events. *European Journal of Philosophy*, *22*(2), 173–199. doi:10.1111/j.1468-0378.2011.00481.x

Grunberg, L. (2001). The IPE of Multinational Corporations. In D. N. Balaam & M. Veseth (Eds.), *Introduction to International Political Economy* (2nd ed.). Upper Saddle River, NJ: Prentice-Hall.

Guarino, P. (2010). *Emerging Markets: Growth, Opportunities and Challenges.* Retrieved from http://www.elementi-consulting.com/insights/emerging-markets-growth-opportunities-and-challenges/

Guillén, M., & García-Canal, E. (2011). The Rise of Emerging Market Multinationals. *IESE Insight,* (10), 13-19.

Guillen, M., & Garcia-Canal, E. (2013). *Emerging Markets Rule: Growth Strategies of the New Global Giants.* McGraw-Hill. Retrieved from http://knowledge.wharton.upenn.edu/article/emerging-market-multinationals-new-giants-on-the-block/

Gulati, R., Nohria, N., & Zaheer, A. (2000). Strategic Networka. *Strategic Management Journal, 21*(3), 203–215. doi:10.1002/(SICI)1097-0266(200003)21:3<203::AID-SMJ102>3.0.CO;2-K

Gullette, G. S. (2014). Rural–urban hierarchies, status boundaries, and labour mobilities in Thailand. *Journal of Ethnic and Migration Studies, 40*(8), 1254–1274. doi:10.1080/1369183X.2013.836959

Gupta, D. (Ed.). (1991). *Social stratification.* New Delhi: Oxford University Press.

Gustin, S. (2012, April 23). How big a deal is Walmart's Mexico bribery scandal? *Time.* Retrieved from http://business.time.com/2012/04/23/how-big-a-deal-is-wal-marts-mexico-bribery-scandal/

Gutierrez, B., Spencer, S. M., & Zhu, G. (2012). Thinking globally, leading locally:Chinese, Indian, and Western leadership. *Cross Cultural Management, 19*(1), 67–86. doi:10.1108/13527601211195637

Hagan, A. F., & Amin, S. G. (1995). Corporate executives and environmental scanning activities: An empirical investigation. *S.A.M. Advanced Management Journal, 60*(2), 41–48.

Halim, Ahmad, Taghizadeh, Ramayah, & Mohamad. (2015). Promoting Innovative Performance through Social Embeddedness: An Analysis on Innovative Human Capital among SMEs. International Journal of Innovation. *Management and Technology, 6*(2), 81–87.

Hall, E. T., & Hall, R. M. (1987). *Hidden Differences. Doing Business with the Japanese.* New York: Anchor Press Doubleday.

Halliday, M. A. K. (1993). Quantitative studies and probabilities in grammar. In M. Hoey (Ed.), Data, Description, Discourse: Papers on the English Language in Honour of John McH Sinclair. London: HarperCollins.

Halliday, M. A. K. (1973). *Explorations in the Functions of Language.* London: Edward Arnold.

Halliday, M. A. K. (1975). *Learning How to Mean: Explorations in the Development of Language.* London: Edward Arnold. doi:10.1016/B978-0-12-443701-2.50025-1

Halliday, M. A. K. (1985). *An Introduction to Functional Grammar.* London: Edward Arnold.

Hallin, C., & Holmström Lind, C. (2012). Revisiting the external impact of MNCs: An empirical study of the mechanisms behind knowledge spillovers from MNC. *International Business Review, 21*(2), 167–179. doi:10.1016/j.ibusrev.2010.12.003

Halmos, K. (2011). The Effect of FDI, exports and GDP on income inequality in 15 Eastern European Countries. *Acta Polytechnica Hungarica, 8*(1), 123–136.

Halpern, B. L., & Lubar, K. (2003). *Leadership Presence.* Gotham Books.

Hansen, G. S., & Wernerfelt, B. (1989). Determinants of Firm Performance: The Relative Importance of Economic and Organizational Factors. *Strategic Management Journal, 10*(05), 399–411. doi:10.1002/smj.4250100502

Hardy, C., & Maguire, S. (2008). Institutional entrepreneurship. In R. Greenwood, C. Oliver, R. Suddaby, & K. Sahlin-Andersson (Eds.), The Handbook of Organisational Institutionalism. Sage.

Hartman, L., & DesJardins, J. (2008). *Business Ethics: Decision-making for Personal Integrity and Social Responsibility* (2nd ed.). Boston: McGraw-Hill/Irwin.

Hartzell, S. (2003). *Types of Contemporary Organizational Designs: Matrix, Team & Network Designs*. Retrieved from http://study.com/academy/lesson/types-of-contemporary-organizational-designs-matrix-team-network-designs.html

Harzing, A. W. (2000). 'An Empirical Analysis and Extension of the Bartlett and Ghosal Typology of Multinational Companies.'. *Journal of International Business Studies*, *31*(1), 101–119. doi:10.1057/palgrave.jibs.8490891

Hashim, M., & Hameed, F. (2012). Human Resource Management in 21st Century: Issues & Challenges & Possible Solutions to Attain Competitiveness. *International Journal of Academic Research in Business and Social Sciences*, *2*(9). Retrieved from http://www.hrmars.com/admin/pics/1090.pdf

Hassel, A., Höpner, M., Kurdelbusch, A., Rehder, B., & Zugehöret, R. (2003). Two Dimensions of the Internationalization of Firms. *Journal of Management Studies*, *40*(3), 705–723. doi:10.1111/1467-6486.00357

Heckelman, J. C., & Powell, B. (2010). Corruption and the institutional environment for growth. *Comparative Economic Studies*, *52*(3), 351–378. doi:10.1057/ces.2010.14

Heller, F. A., & Yukl, G. (1969). Participation, managerial decision-making and situational variables. *Organizational Behavior and Human Performance*, *4*(3), 227–241. doi:10.1016/0030-5073(69)90007-5

Hellman, J. S., Jones, G., & Kaufmann, D. (2003). Seize the state, seize the day: State capture and influence in transition economies. *Journal of Comparative Economics*, *31*(4), 751–773. doi:10.1016/j.jce.2003.09.006

Hennart, J. F. (2009). Down with MNE-Centric Theories! Market Entry and Expansion as the Bundling of MNE and Local Assets. *Journal of International Business Studies*, *40*(9), 1432–1454. doi:10.1057/jibs.2009.42

Henry, L. C. (1992). *IT for Management* (6th ed.). Mcgraw Hill.

Heracleous, L. (2004). Interpretivist approaches to organizational discourse. In D. Grant, C. Hardy, C. Oswick, & L. Putnam (Eds.), *The Sage Handbook of Organizational Discourse* (pp. 175–192). Sage Publications. doi:10.4135/9781848608122.n8

Herstein, R., Berger, R., & Jaffe, E. D. (2014). How companies from developing and emerging countries can leverage their brand equity in terms of place branding. *Competitiveness Review*, *24*(4), 293–305. doi:10.1108/CR-04-2013-0046

Heston, A., & Kumar, V. (2008). Institutional flaws and corruption incentives in India. *The Journal of Development Studies*, *44*(9), 1243–1261. doi:10.1080/00220380802264960

Hewett, K., Roth, M. S., & Roth, K. (2003). Conditions influencing headquarters and foreign subsidiary roles in marketing activities and their effects on performance. *Journal of International Business Studies*, *34*(6), 567–585. doi:10.1057/palgrave.jibs.8400054

He, Z. (2000). Corruption and anti-corruption in reform China. *Communist and Post-Communist Studies*, *33*(2), 243–270. doi:10.1016/S0967-067X(00)00006-4

Hijzen, A., & Swain, P. (2008). Do Multinationals promote better pay working conditions? *OECD Observer*, 269. Available at http://www.oecdobserver.org

Hill, A., & Brown, S. (2007). Strategic profiling: A visual representation of internal strategic fit in service organisations. *International Journal of Operations & Production Management*, *27*(12), 1333–1361. doi:10.1108/01443570710835642

Hill, J. S., & Still, R. R. (1984). Adapting products to ldc tastes. *Harvard Business Review*, *62*(March/April), 92–101.

Hill, L. A., Brandeau, G., Truelove, E., & Lineback, K. (2011). *Collective Genius: The Art and Practice of Leading Innovation*. Boston: Harvard Business Review Press.

Hill, L. A., & Lineback, K. (2011). *Being the Boss: The 3 Imperatives for Becoming a Great Leader*. Harvard Business Review Press.

Hill, R. (2002). *Southeast Asia: People, land and economy*. Crows Nest, Australia: Allen & Unwin.

Hippert, C. (2002). Multinational corporations, the politics of the world economy, and their effects on women's health in the developing world: A review. *Health Care for Women International*, *23*(8), 861–869. doi:10.1080/07399330290107476 PMID:12487701

Hipsher, S. (2007). Creating market size: Regional strategies for the world's least developed areas. In J. Stoner & C. Wankel (Eds.), Innovative Approaches to Reducing Global Poverty (pp. 153-174). Charlotte, NC: Information Age Publishing.

Hipsher, S. (2010a). *Business practices in Southeast Asia: An interdisciplinary analysis of Theravada Buddhist countries*. London: Routledge Publishing.

Hipsher, S. (2010b). Transfer or adapt: Evidence from the Theravada Buddhist countries of Southeast Asia. *Global Business and Organizational Excellence*, *39*(3), 35–43. doi:10.1002/joe.20317

Hirschi, T. (2002). *Causes of delinquency*. Transaction Publishers.

Hitt, M. A., Lee, H.-U., & Yucel, E. (2002). The importance of social capital to the management of multinational enterprises: Relational networks among Asian and western firms. *Asia Pacific Journal of Management*, *19*(2-3), 353–372. doi:10.1023/A:1016247920461

Hjøllund, L., Paldam, M., & Svendsen, G. T. (2001). Social capital in Russia and Denmark: A comparative study. Department of Economics, Faculty of Business Administration, Aarhus School of Business.

Hodge, R., & Kress, G. (1988). *Social Semiotics*. Cambridge, MA: Polity.

Hodge, R., & Kress, G. R. (1993). *Language as ideology* (2nd ed.). London: Routledge.

Hodge, R., & Kress, G. R. (1993). *Language as Ideology*. London: Routledge.

Hofstede, G. (1980). Motivation, leadership, and organization: Do American theories apply abroad? *Organizational Dynamics*, *9*(1), 42–63. doi:10.1016/0090-2616(80)90013-3

Hofstede, G. (1983). The cultural relativity of organizational practices and theories. *Journal of International Business Studies*, *14*(1), 75–89.

Hofstede, G. (1984). *Culture's consequences: International differences in work-related values*. London: Sage.

Hofstede, G. (1993). Cultural constraints in management theories. *The Executive*, *7*(1), 81–95.

Hofstede, G. (1997). *Cultures and organizations: software of the mind*. London: Mc Graw Hill.

Hofstede, G. (2001). *Culture's consequences, comparing values, behaviours, institutions and organizations across nations*. Thousand Oaks, CA: Sage.

Hofstede, G. H. (1980). *Culture Consequences: International Differences in Work-related Values*. Beverly Hills, CA: Sage Publications.

Hofstede, G., & Bond, M. H. (1988). The Confucius connection: From cultural roots to economic Growth. *Organizational Dynamics*, *16*(4), 4–21. doi:10.1016/0090-2616(88)90009-5

Holm, U., & Pedersen, T. (Eds.). (2000). The Emergence and the Impact of MNC Centres of Excellence. London: MacMillan.

Holmes, H., Tangtongtavy, S., & Tomizawa, R. (1996). *Working with the Thais: A guide to managing in Thailand* (3rd ed.). Bangkok: White Lotus.

Honzl, J., & Titunik, I. R. (1976). Dynamics of the sign in the theater. In L. Matejka & I. R. Titunik (Eds.), *Semiotics of Art: Prague School Contributions* (pp. 74–93). Cambridge, MA: MIT P.

Hood, N., & Young, S. (1979). *The Economics of Multinational Enterprise*. London: Longman.

Hooi, L. W. (2008). The adoption of Japanese recruitment practices in Malaysia. *International Journal of Manpower*, *29*(4), 362–378. doi:10.1108/01437720810884764

Horwath, J., & Morrison, T. (2000). Identifying and implementing pathways for organizational change- using The Framework for the Assessment of Children in Need and their Families as a case example'. *Child & Family Social Work*, *5*(3), 245–255. doi:10.1046/j.1365-2206.2000.00171.x

Hoskisson, R. E., Eden, L., Ming Lau, C., & Wright, M. (2000). Strategy in Emerging economies. *Academy of Management Journal*, *43*(3), 249–267. doi:10.2307/1556394

House, R. J., Hanges, P. J., Havidan, M., Dorfman, P. W., & Gupta, V. (2004). Culture, leadership and organizations: the GLOBE chapter of 62 societies. Thousand Oaks, CA: Sage.

Hsieh, M., & Tsai, K. (2007). Technological capability, social capital and the launch strategy for innovative products. *Industrial Marketing Management*, *36*(4), 493–502. doi:10.1016/j.indmarman.2006.01.002

Hsu, C. C., Tan, K. C., & Laosirihongthong, T. (2014). Antecedents of SCM practices in ASEAN automotive industry. *The International Journal of Logistics Management*, *25*(2), 334–357. doi:10.1108/IJLM-06-2012-0050

Hui, M. K., Au, K., & Fock, H. (2004). Empowerment effects across cultures. *Journal of International Business Studies*, *35*(1), 41–60. doi:10.1057/palgrave.jibs.8400067

Hult, T. G. (2012). A focus on international competitiveness. *Academy of Marketing Science. Journal*, *40*(2), 195-201.

Hutzschenreuter, T., & Grone, F. (2009). Changing Vertical Integration Strategies under Pressure from Foreign Competition: The Case of US and German Multinationals. *Journal of Management Studies*, *46*(2), 269–307. doi:10.1111/j.1467-6486.2008.00811.x

Hymer, S. H. (1976). *The international operations of national firms: A study of direct foreign investment* (Vol. 14). Cambridge, MA: MIT Press.

Hymer, S. H. (1976). *The International Operations of National Firms: A Study of Direct Foreign Investment*. Cambridge, MA: MIT Press.

Ichii, S., Hattori, S., & Michael, D. (2012). How to Win in Emerging Markets: Lessons from Japan. *Harvard Business Review*, 126-130.

Indicators of Innovation. (2008). *Data book*. Moscow: State University, High School of Economics.

Inoguchi, T. (2000). Social capital in Japan. *Japanese Journal of Political Science*, *1*(1), 73–112. doi:10.1017/S1468109900000141

International Chamber of Commerce. (2015). Retrieved from http://www.iccwbo.org/

International Labour Organization. (2015a). *ILO Declaration on Fundamental Principles and Rights at Work*. Retrieved from http://www.ilo.org/declaration/lang--en/index.htm

International Labour Organization. (2015b). Retrieved from http://www.ilo.org/global/lang--en/index.htm

International Telecommunication Union. (2015). *The world in 2015 ICT Facts and Figures*. Retrieved from: https://www.itu.int/en/ITU-D/Statistics/facts/ICTFactsFigures2015.pdf

Introduction. (1997). Invan Dijk, T. (Ed.), *Discourse as Structure and Process: A Multidisciplinary Introduction* (Vol. 1). London: Sage.

Iwasaki, I., & Tokunaga, M. (2014). Macroeconomic impacts of FDI in transition economies: A meta-analysis. *World Development*, *61*, 53–69. doi:10.1016/j.worlddev.2014.03.022

Izunwa, M.E. (2005). African Development: From history to future possibilities. *Journal of Africa in a New World Order*, *2*(1), 141-147.

Jackson, G., & Deeg, R. (2008). Comparing capitalism: Understanding institutional diversity and its implications for international business. *Journal of International Business Studies*, *39*(4), 540–561. doi:10.1057/palgrave.jibs.8400375

Jackson, P. A. (2003). *Buddhadasa: Theravada Buddhism and the modernist reform in Thailand*. Chiang Mai: Silkworm.

Jacobs, F. R., & Chase, R. B. (2011). *Operations and Suply Chain Managemet* (13th ed.). Singapore: McGraw-Hill Education.

Jacobs, S. (1989). Speech acts and arguments. *Argumentation*, *3*(4), 345–365. doi:10.1007/BF00182603

Jaguli, A. R., Malek, M. M., & Palil, M. R. (2014). Do MNCS' high quality and standard requirements matter? A channel for vertical spillovers. *International Journal of Business & Society*, *15*(1), 127-150.

Jain, R., Gorti, V., Sen, K., & Sexton, D. E. (2015). *Brand equity & optimal pricing*. Paper presented at ReThink Conference, ARF, New York, NY.

Jain, A. K. (2001). Corruption: A review. *Journal of Economic Surveys*, *15*(1), 71–121. doi:10.1111/1467-6419.00133

Jain, S. C. (1989). Standardization of international marketing strategy: Some research hypotheses. *Journal of Marketing*, *53*(January), 70–79. doi:10.2307/1251525

Jakobson, R., & Sokol, E. (1976). Is the cinema in decline? In L. Matejka & I. R. Titunik (Eds.), *Semiotics of Art: Prague School Contributions* (pp. 145–152). Cambridge, MA: MIT.

Janssens, M., Lambert, J., & Steyaert, C. (2004). Developing language strategies for international companies: The contribution of translation studies. *Journal of World Business*, *39*(4), 414–430. doi:10.1016/j.jwb.2004.08.006

Javorcik, B. S. (2008). Can survey evidence shed light on spillovers from foreign direct investment? *The World Bank Research Observer*, *23*(2), 139–159. doi:10.1093/wbro/lkn006

Jaworski, A., & Coupland, N. (Eds.). (1999). The Discourse Reader. London: Routledge.

Jayaram, K., Riese, J., & Sanghvi, S. (2010). Agriculture: Abundant opportunities. In Africa's Path to Growth: Sector by Sector. McKinsey & Co.

Jayasuriya, S., MacLaren, D., & Mehta, R. (2006). *Meeting food safety standards in export markets: issues and challenges facing firms exporting from developing countries*. In *IATRC Summer Symposium, Food Regulation and Trade: Institutional Framework, Concepts of Analysis and Empirical Evidence*, Bonn, Germany.

Johanson, J., & Vahlne, J. (1977). The internationalization process of the firm--A model of knowledge development and increasing foreign market commitments. *Journal of International Business Studies*, *8*(1), 23.

Johanson, J., & Vahlne, J. (2009). The Uppsala internationalization process model revisited: From liability of foreignness to liability of outsidership. *Journal of International Business Studies*, *40*(9), 1411–1431. doi:10.1057/jibs.2009.24

Johanson, J., & Vahlne, J. E. (1977). The internationalization process of the firm: A model of knowledge development and increasing foreign market commitments. *Journal of International Business Studies*, *8*(1), 23–32. doi:10.1057/palgrave.jibs.8490676

Johanson, J., & Wiedersheim-Paul, F. (1975). The Interantionalization of the Firm: Four Swedish Cases. *Journal of Management Studies*, *12*(3), 305–322. doi:10.1111/j.1467-6486.1975.tb00514.x

Johnsen, R. E. (2007). The role of focal suppliers in strategic networks for internationalization: Perspectives from small and medium-sized Italian and Thai silk suppliers. *Journal of Fashion Marketing and Management*, *11*(1), 135–147. doi:10.1108/13612020710734454

Johnson, G., & Scholes, K. (2007). *Exploring Corporate Strategy* (8th ed.). Financial Times/Prentice Hall.

Johnson, G., & Scholes, K. (2007). *Exploring Corporate Strategy*. Financial Times/Prentice Hall.

Johnson, S., Mcmillan, J., & Woodruff, C. (2002). Courts and relational contracts. *Journal of Law Economics and Organization*, *18*(1), 221–277. doi:10.1093/jleo/18.1.221

Jönsson, S. (1995). *Goda Utsikter: Svenskt Management*. Gothenburg: BAS.

Jönsson, S. A., & Wickelgren, M. (2011). *Volvo i våra hjärtan: Hur ska det gå?: En närdiskussion om "nationalklenoden" volvo*. Malmö: Liber.

Jung, J., Su, X., Baeza, M., & Hong, S. (2008). The effect of organizational culture stemming from national culture towards quality management deployment. *TQM Journal*, *20*(6), 622–627. doi:10.1108/17542730810909374

Ju, Y., & Sohn, S. Y. (2014). Development of a national competitiveness index based on a structural equation model. *Technology Analysis and Strategic Management*, *26*(5), 565–579. doi:10.1080/09537325.2014.896891

Kaasa, A. (2009). Effects of different dimensions of social capital on innovative activity: Evidence from Europe at the regional level. *Technovation*, *29*(3), 218–233. doi:10.1016/j.technovation.2008.01.003

Kail, E. G. (2007). Becoming a Leader Developer. In Leadership Lessons from West Point. John Wiley & Sons.

Kainzbauer, A. (2009). *Buddhism, 'sanuk' and intuition – making sense of Thai realities*. Paper presented at 1st Bangkok International Forum on Indigenous Management Practices, Kasetsart University, Bangkok, February 2–6, 2009.

Kalamova, M. M., & Konrad, K. A. (2010). Nation brands and foreign direct investment. *Kyklos*, *63*(3), 400–431. doi:10.1111/j.1467-6435.2010.00480.x

Källström, A. (1997). The Swedish leadership style. *Ledelse Og Erhvervsøkonomi*, *61*(1), 67–73.

Kan, G., Cliquet, G., & Gallo, M. P. (2014). The effect of country image on hypermarket patronage intention. *International Journal of Retail & Distribution Management*, *42*(2), 106–130. doi:10.1108/IJRDM-09-2012-0080

Kanungo, R. N., & Wright, R. W. (1983). A cross-cultural comparative study of managerial job attitudes. *Journal of International Business Studies*, *14*(2), 115–129. doi:10.1057/palgrave.jibs.8490521

Kaplan, R. S., & Norton, D. P. (2005). The Balanced Scorecard: Measures That Drive Performance. *Harvard Business Review*. Retrieved from https://hbr.org/2005/07/the-balanced-scorecard-measures-that-drive-performance

Kaplan, R. S., & Norton, D. (1992). The Balanced Scorecard: Measures that Drive Performance. *Harvard Business Review*, *70*(1), 71–79. PMID:10119714

Kaplinsky, R. (2000). Spreading the gains from globalisation: What can be learned from value chain analysis? *The Journal of Development Studies*, *37*(2), 117–146. doi:10.1080/713600071

Kashani, K. (1989). Beware the pitfalls of global marketing. *Harvard Business Review*, *67*(September/October), 91–98.

Kawachi, I., Kennedy, B. P., & Wilkinson, R. G. (1999). Crime: Social disorganisation and relative deprivation. *Social Science & Medicine*, *48*(6), 719–731. doi:10.1016/S0277-9536(98)00400-6 PMID:10190635

Kaweevisultrakul, T., & Chan, P. (2007). Impact of cultural barriers on knowledge management implementation: Evidence from Thailand. *Journal of American Academy of Business, Cambridge*, *11*, 303–308.

Kelleher, A., & Klein, L. (2006). *Global Perspective: A Handbook for Understanding Global Issues*. Pearson Prentice Hall.

Keller, G. F., & Kronstedt, C. R. (2005). Connecting Confucianism, communism, and the Chinese culture of commerce. *The Journal of Language for International Business*, *16*(1), 60–75.

Keller, K. (2002). *Branding and Brand Equity*. Cambridge: Marketing Science Institute. doi:10.4135/9781848608283.n8

Kennedy, B. P., Kawachi, I., Prothrow-Stith, D., Lochner, K., & Gupta, V. (1998). Social capital, income inequality and firearm violent crime. *Social Science & Medicine*, *47*(1), 7–17. doi:10.1016/S0277-9536(98)00097-5 PMID:9683374

Khan, M. A. (2014). *Challenges for MNEs Operating in Emerging Markets*. Retrieved from www.aabri.com/LV14045.pdf

Khanna, T., Palepu, K. G., & Sinha, J. (2005). Strategies That Fit Emerging Markets. *Harvard Business Review*. Retrieved from http://hbr.org/2005/06/strategies-that-fit-emerging-markets/ar/1

Khanna, T. (2014). Contextual intelligence. *Harvard Business Review*, *92*(9), 58–68. PMID:25509576

Khanna, T. (2014, September). Contextual Intelligence. *Harvard Business Review*, *92*(9), 58–68. PMID:25509576

Khanna, T., & Palepu, K. G. (2010). *Winning in emerging markets*. Boston, MA: Harvard Business Press.

Kim, A. M. (2008). *Learning to be capitalists: Entrepreneurs in Vietnam's transition economy*. Oxford University Press. doi:10.1093/acprof:oso/9780195369397.001.0001

Kim, H., Hoskisson, R. E., Tihanyi, L., & Hong, J. (2004). The evolution and restructuring of diversified business groups in emerging markets: The lessons from *chaebols* in Korea. *Asia Pacific Journal of Management*, *21*(1/2), 25–48. doi:10.1023/B:APJM.0000024076.86696.d5

Kim, L. (1997). *Imitation to Innovation: The Dynamics of Korea's Technological Learning*. Boston: Harvard Business School Press.

King, W. L. (1964). *In the Hope of Nibbana*. LaSalle, IL: Open Court.

Kipping, M., & Cailluet, L. (2010). Mintzberg's emergent and deliberate strategies: Tracking Alcan's activities in Europe, 1928-2007. *Business History Review*, *84*(1), 79–95. doi:10.1017/S0007680500001252

Kitching, J., Hart, M., & Wilson, N. (2015). Burden or benefit? Regulation as a dynamic influence on small business performance. *International Small Business Journal*, *33*(2), 130–147. doi:10.1177/0266242613493454

Kjiroski, I. (2014). *Human resource management –new challenges in the modern era*. Retrieved from http://www.eapm.org/wp-content/uploads/2014/05/Macedonia-HRM-challenges-of-the-modern-era.pdf

Klein, A., Waxin, M. F., & Radnell, E. (2009). The impact of the Arab national culture on the perception of ideal organizational culture in the United Arab Emirates; An empirical study of 17 firms. *Education. Business and Society: Contemporary Middle Eastern Issues*, *2*(1), 44–56. doi:10.1108/17537980910938479

Knack, S., & Keefer, P. (1997). Does social capital have an economic payoff? A cross-country investigation. *The Quarterly Journal of Economics*, *112*(4), 1251–1288. doi:10.1162/003355300555475

Knight, G. A., & Cavusgil, S. T. (2004). Innovation, organizational capabilities, and the born-global firm. *Journal of International Business Studies*, *35*(2), 124–141. doi:10.1057/palgrave.jibs.8400071

Kogut, B. (1985). Designing global strategies: Comparative and competitive value-added chains. *Sloan Management Review*, (Fall): 27–38.

Kogut, B. (1985). Designing global strategies: Comparative and competitive value-added chains. *Sloan Management Review*, (Summer): 15–27.

Kogut, B., & Kulatilaka, N. (1994). Operating flexibility, global manufacturing, and the option value of a multinational network. *Management Science*, *40*(1), 123–139. doi:10.1287/mnsc.40.1.123

Kogut, B., & Zander, U. (2003, November). Knowledge of the Firm and the Evolutionary Theory of the Multinational Corporation. *Journal of International Business Studies*, *34*(6), 516–529. doi:10.1057/palgrave.jibs.8400058

Komives, S. R., Lucas, N., & McMahon, T. R. (2013). *Exploring Leadership: For College Students Who Want to Make a Difference* (3rd ed.). Jossey-Bass.

Kostecki, M., & Naray, O. (2007). Commercial diplomacy and international business. The Hague: Netherlands Institute of International Relations 'Clingendael'.

Kostova, T., & Zaheer, S. (1999). Organisational legitimacy under conditions of complexity: The case of the multinational enterprise. *Academy of Management Review*, *24*, 64–81.

Kotler, P., Jatusripitak, S., & Maesincee, S. (1997). *The marketing of nations*. New York: The Free Press.

Kotschwar, B., Moran, T., & Muir, J. (2011). Do Chinese mining companies exploit more? *Americas Quarterly*. Retrieved from http://www.americasquarterly.org/do-chinese-mining-companies-exploit-more

Kourdi, J. (2009). *Business Strategy: A Guide to Taking Your Business Forward*. John Wiley & Sons.

Kouzes, J. M., & Posner, B. Z. (2002). *The Leadership Challenge*. John Wiley & Sons.

Kozlowski, S. W. J., Chao, G. T., Grand, J. A., Baun, M. T., & Kuljanin, G. (2013). Advancing multilevel research design: Capturing the dynamics of emergence. *Organizational Research Methods*, *16*(4), 581–615. doi:10.1177/1094428113493119

Krechowicz, D., & Hiranya, F. (2009). *Emerging Risks: Impacts of Key Environmental Trends in Emerging Asia*. Retrieved from http://www.wri.org/publication/emerging-risks/

Kress, G. R., & Van Leeuwen, T. (2006). *Reading Images: The Grammar of Visual Design*. London: Routledge.

Kress, G., & Van Leeuwen, T. (1992). Structures of visual representation. *Journal of Literary Semantics*, *21*(2), 91–117. doi:10.1515/jlse.1992.21.2.91

Krugman, P. (1994). Competitiveness: A dangerous obsession. *Foreign Affairs*, *73*(2), 28–44. doi:10.2307/20045917

Kukalis, S. (1989). The Relationship among from Characteristics and Design of Strategic Planning Systems in Large Organizations. *Journal of Management*, *15*(4), 565–579. doi:10.1177/014920638901500406

Kumar, N. (1996). Foreign direct investments and technology transfers in development: a perspective on recent literature. United Nations University, Institute of Technologies.

Kumaraswamy, A., Mudambi, R., Saranga, H., & Tripathy, A. (2012). Catch-up strategies in the Indian auto components industry: Domestic firms' responses to market liberalization. *Journal of International Business Studies*, *43*(4), 368–395. doi:10.1057/jibs.2012.4

Kvint, V. (2015). *Strategy for the Global Market: Theory and Practical Applications*. Academic Press.

Kwok, C. Y., & Tadesse, S. (2006). The MNC as an agent of change for host-country institutions: FDI and corruption. *Journal of International Business Studies*, *37*(6), 767–785. doi:10.1057/palgrave.jibs.8400228

La Porta, R., Lopez-de-Silanes, F., Shleifer, A., & Vishny, R. W. (1997). Legal determinants of external finance. *The Journal of Finance*, *52*(3), 1131–1150. doi:10.1111/j.1540-6261.1997.tb02727.x

Lall, S. (1996). *Learning from the Asian Tigers*. London: Macmillan. doi:10.1057/9780230389892

Lall, S. (1997). Investment, technology and international competitiveness. In J. H. Dunning & K. A. Hamdani (Eds.), *The New Globalism and Developing Countries* (pp. 239–259). Tokyo: United Nations University Press.

Lall, S. (2000). Technological change and industrialization in the Asian newly industrializing economies: achievements and challenges. In L. Kim & R. Nelson (Eds.), *Technology, Learning & Innovation Experiences of Newly Industrializing Economies* (pp. 13–68). Cambridge, UK: Cambridge University Press.

Lall, S. (2001). What competitiveness is and why it is important. In S. Lall (Ed.), *Competitiveness, Technology and Skills* (pp. 1–30). Cheltenham, UK: Edward Elgar. doi:10.4337/9781781950555.00008

Lall, S. (2004). The employment impact of globalisation in developing countries. In E. Lee & M. Vivarelli (Eds.), *Understanding Globalisation, Employment and Poverty Reduction* (pp. 73–101). New York: Palgrave Macmillan.

Lall, S., & Teubal, M. (1998). Market-stimulating technology policies in developing countries: A framework with examples from East Asia. *World Development*, *26*(8), 1369–1385. doi:10.1016/S0305-750X(98)00071-0

Lam, A., & Lundvall, B. (2007). *The learning organisation and national systems of competence building and innovation.* MPRA Paper No. 12320, 1-28. Available at: http://mpra.ub.uni-muenchen.de/12320/

Lambert-Mogiliansky, A., Majumdar, M., & Radner, R. (2007). Strategic analysis of petty corruption: Entrepreneurs and bureaucrats. *Journal of Development Economics*, *83*(2), 351–367. doi:10.1016/j.jdeveco.2006.06.002

Lamond, D., & Zheng, C. (2010). HRM research in China: Looking back and looking forward. *Journal of Chinese Human Resources Management*, *1*(1), 6–16. doi:10.1108/20408001011051179

Langhoff, T. (1997). The influence of culture differences on internationalisation processes of firms: an introduction to a semiotic and intercultural perspective. In I. Bjorkman & M. Forsgren (Eds.), *The nature of the international firm.* Copenhagen: Handelshojskolens Forlag.

Laosirihongthong, T., The, P. L., & Adebanjo, D. (2013). Revisiting quality management and performance. *Industrial Management & Data Systems*, *113*(7), 990–1006. doi:10.1108/IMDS-02-2013-0058

Laroche, M., Kirpalani, V. H., Pons, F., & Zhou, L. (2001). A model of advertising standardization in multinational corporations. *Journal of International Business Studies*, *32*(2), 249–266. doi:10.1057/palgrave.jibs.8490951

Larsson, T. (2006). Reform, corruption, and growth: Why corruption is more devastating in Russia than in China. *Communist and Post-Communist Studies*, *39*(2), 265–281. doi:10.1016/j.postcomstud.2006.03.005

Lasserre, P. (2007). Global Strategic Management (2nd ed.). Palgrave Macmillan.

Latus, A. (2001). Moral relativism and objectivism. *Introduction to Philosophy*. Retrieved from http://www.ucs.mun.ca/~alatus/phil1200/RelativismObjectivism.html

Lau, C. M. (2006). Achievements, challenges and research agendas for Asian management research studies. *Asian Business & Management*, *5*(1), 53–66. doi:10.1057/palgrave.abm.9200145

Lauden, C. K. (2000). Management Information Systems. *Higher Education Studies, 1*(1).

Laurent, A. (1983). The cultural diversity of Western conceptions of management. *International Studies of Management & Organization*, *13*(1-2), 75–96. doi:10.1080/00208825.1983.11656359

Lavidge, R., & Steiner, G. (1961). A model for predictive measurements of advertising effectiveness. *Journal of Marketing*, *25*(October), 137–169.

Lazonick, W., & O'Sullivan, M. (2000). Maximizing shareholder value: A new ideology for corporate governance. *Economy and Society*, *29*(1), 13–35. doi:10.1080/030851400360541

Leavitt, H. J., & Whisler, T. L. (1958). Management in the 1980's. Carnegie Instit Ute Of Technology.

Leavitt, H. J., & Whisler, T. L. (1958). Management in the 1980's. *Harvard Business Review*, (November-December): 1858.

Ledeneva, A. (1998). *Russia's economy of favours: Blat, networking, and informal exchange*. Cambridge, UK: Cambridge University Press.

Lederman, D. (2010). An international multilevel analysis of product innovation. *Journal of International Business Studies*, *41*(4), 606–619. doi:10.1057/jibs.2009.30

Lederman, D., Loayza, N., & Menendez, A. M. (2002). Violent crime: Does social capital matter? *Economic Development and Cultural Change*, *50*(3), 509–539. doi:10.1086/342422

Lee, A. (2014). For king and country? Thailand's political conflicts as dynamics of social closure. In P. Liamputtong (Ed.), Contemporary Socio-Cultural and Political Perspectives in Thailand (pp. 169-184). Springer.

Lee, D., & Ruël, H. (2012). Introduction: Commercial Diplomacy and International Business: Merging International Business and International Relations. In Commercial Diplomacy and International Business: A Conceptual and Empirical Exploration (9th ed.; pp. 13-19). Emerald Group Publishing Limited.

Lee, A. (2014). "For king and country"? Thailand's political conflicts as dynamics of social closure. In P. Liamputtong (Ed.), *Contemporary Socio-Cultural and Political Perspectives in Thailand* (pp. 169–184). Dordrecht, NL: Springer. doi:10.1007/978-94-007-7244-1_11

Lee, E., & Vivarelli, M. (2006). The social impact of globaliSation in the developing countries. *International Labour Review*, *145*(3), 167–184. doi:10.1111/j.1564-913X.2006.tb00016.x

Leff, N. H. (1964). Economic development through bureaucratic corruption. *The American Behavioral Scientist*, *8*(3), 8–14. doi:10.1177/000276426400800303

Lehnert, K., Benmamoun, M., & Zhao, H. (2013). FDI inflow and human development: Analysis of FDI's impact on host countries' social welfare and infrastructure. *Thunderbird International Business Review*, *55*(3), 285–298. doi:10.1002/tie.21544

Leitch, S., & Palmer, I. (2009). Analysing texts in contexts: Current practices and new protocols for Critical Discourse Analysis in Organization Studies. *Journal of Management Studies*, *47*(6), 1194–1212. doi:10.1111/j.1467-6486.2009.00884.x

Lenartowicz, T., & Johnson, J. P. (2007). Staffing managerial positions in emerging markets: A cultural perspective. *International Journal of Emerging Markets*, *2*(3), 207–214. doi:10.1108/17468800710758369

Lessard, D. R., & Reavis, C. (2009). *CEMEX: Globalization "The CEMEX Way". A Study Case*. The MIT Sloan School of Management.

Leszczyńska, D., & Pruchnicki, E. (2003). The evolution of knowledge transfer and the location of a multinational corporation: Theory and mathematical model. *Multinational Business Review*, *23*(2), 111–129. doi:10.1108/MBR-06-2014-0031

Levi Strauss & Co. (2015). *People - Levi Strauss*. Retrieved from http://www.levistrauss.com/sustainability/people/#employee-community-involvement

Levin, M., & Satarov, G. (2000). Corruption and institutions in Russia. *European Journal of Political Economy*, *16*(1), 113–132. doi:10.1016/S0176-2680(99)00050-6

Levitt, T. (1983). The globalization of markets. *Harvard Business Review*, *61*(May/June), 92–102.

Li, F. (2013). Geely becomes China's top automobile export. *China Daily*. Retrieved from http://bit.ly/1XhXZiO

Licht, A. N., & Siegel, J. I. (2006). The social dimensions of entrepreneurship. In M. Casson & B. Yeung (Eds.), *Oxford Handbook of Entrepreneurhip*. Oxford University Press.

Li, D., Wang, L. W., Jiang, Y., Barnes, B. R., & Zhang, H. (2014). The asymmetric influence of cognitive and affective country image on rational and experiential purchases. *European Journal of Marketing*, *48*(11/12), 2153–2175. doi:10.1108/EJM-09-2012-0505

Light, I., & Isralowitz, R. E. (1997). *Immigrant entrepreneurs and immigrant absorption in the United States and Israel*. Aldershot, UK: Ashgate England.

Li, J., & Harrison, R. (2008). Corporate governance and national culture: A multi-country study. *Corporate Governance*, *8*(5), 607–621. doi:10.1108/14720700810913278

Li, J., & Wright, P. C. (2000). Guanxi and the realities of career development: A Chinese perspective. *Career Development International*, *5*(7), 369–378. doi:10.1108/13620430010379920

Lilie, M., Patrick, R., & Lindblom, S. (2012). *International Finance Corporation Risk Taking: A Corporate Governance Perspective*. Retrieved from http://www.ifc.org/wps/wcm/connect/9ff11a804c40464698dddaf12db12449/RiskGov-July2012.pdf

Lilly, M. (2005). *Organizational Structure and Designs with Case Study: QUALCOMM*. Retrieved from http://www.emaytrix.com/mgmt307/section3.php/

Lindell, M., & Arvonen, J. (1996). The Nordic management style – an investigation. In S. Jönsson (Ed.), *Perspectives of Scandinavian Management* (pp. 11–36). Gothenburg Research Institute.

Lin, K. H., & Chaney, I. (2007). The Influence of Domestic Interfirm Networks on the Internationalization Process of Taiwanese SMEs. *Asia Pacific Business Review*, *13*(4), 565–583. doi:10.1080/13602380701345499

Lippit, M. B. (1998). *The Leadership Spectrum Profile: Targeting Enterprise Priorities*. Potomac, MD: Enterprise Management.

Lippit, M. B. (2002). *The Leadership Spectrum*. Davies-Black Publishing.

Lipsey, R. E. (2002). *Home and Host Country Effects of FDI*. NBER Working Paper No. 9293. JEL No. F21, F23, O01, O03, O04.

Lipsey, R. E., & Sjöholm, F. (2005). Host country impacts of inward FDI: Why such different answers? In M. Blomström, E. Graham, & T. Moran (Eds.), *The Impact of Foreign Direct Investment on Development: New Measurements, New Outcomes, New Policy Approaches* (pp. 23–43). Washington, DC: Institute for International Economics.

Liu, C., & Zhang, H. (2011). Geely seeks to prove quality to woo UK buyers. *China Daily*. Retrieved from http://www.chinadaily.com.cn/bizchina/2011-12/28/content_14340471.htm

Li, W., & Wei, Y. (2012). Technology transfer, adaptation & assimilation and indigenous invention patent output: Evidence from Chinese high-tech industries. *Procedia Engineering*, *29*, 1392–1398. doi:10.1016/j.proeng.2012.01.146

Li, X., & Pai, Y. (2010). The changing geography of innovation activities: What do patent indicators imply? In X. Fu & L. Soete (Eds.), *The Rise of Technological Power in the South*. Basingstoke, UK: Palgrave MacMillan.

Li, Y., Ye, F., & Sheu, C. (2014). Social capital, information sharing and performance. *International Journal of Operations & Production Management*, *34*(11), 1440–1462. doi:10.1108/IJOPM-03-2013-0132

Li, Y., Zhou, N., & Si, Y. (2010). Exploratory innovation and exploitative innovation, and performance. *Nankai Business Review International*, *1*(3), 297–316. doi:10.1108/20408741011069223

Lohmann, J. (2011). Do language barriers affect trade? *Economics Letters*, *110*(2), 159–162. doi:10.1016/j.econlet.2010.10.023

London, T., & Hart, S. T. (2004). Perspective: Reinventing strategies for emerging markets: beyond the transnational model. *Journal of International Business Studies*, *35*(5), 350–370. doi:10.1057/palgrave.jibs.8400099

Longenecker, C. O., Fink, L. S., & Caldwell, S. (2014a). Current U.S. trends in formal performance appraisal: Practices and opportunities – Part One. *Industrial and Commercial Training*, *46*(6), 321–326. doi:10.1108/ICT-03-2014-0018

Longenecker, C. O., Fink, L. S., & Caldwell, S. (2014b). Current US trends in formal performance appraisal: Practices and opportunities – Part II. *Industrial and Commercial Training*, *46*(7), 393–399. doi:10.1108/ICT-03-2014-0019

Lopez-Cordova, E. (2003). NAFTA and Manufacturing Productivity in Mexico. *Journal of the Latin American and Caribbean Economic Association*, *3*, 55.

Louhiala-Salminenm, L. (2002). *Communication and language use in merged corporations: case Stora Enso and Nordea*. Working Paper no. 330. Helsinki School of Economics.

Lowenberg, A. D. (1992). A post-apartheid constitution for South Africa: Lessons from public choice. *The Cato Journal*, *12*(2), 297–319.

Lu, J. W., & Beamish, P. W. (2004). International diversification and firm performance: The S-Curve Hypothesis. *Academy of Management Journal*, *47*(4), 598–609. doi:10.2307/20159604

Luk, C., Yau, O., Sin, L., Tse, A., Chow, R., & Lee, J. (2008). The effects of social capital and organizational innovativeness in different institutional contexts. *Journal of International Business Studies*, *39*(4), 589–612. doi:10.1057/palgrave.jibs.8400373

Lundbäck, M., & Hörte, S. (2005). Decision-making in conditions of constant change - a case within the automotive industry. *Management Decision*, *43*(2), 220–235. doi:10.1108/00251740510581939

Lundvall, B. (2007). National innovation systems-analytical concept and development tool. *Industry and Innovation*, *14*(1), 95–119. doi:10.1080/13662710601130863

Lundvall, B. A., Johnson, B., Andersen, E. S., & Dalum, B. (2002). National systems of production, innovation and competence building. *Research Policy*, *31*(2), 213–231. doi:10.1016/S0048-7333(01)00137-8

Lundy, J. L. (1986). *Lead, Follow, or Get Out of the Way: Leadership Strategies for the Thoroughly Modern Manager*. San Diego, CA: Slawson Communications.

Luo, X., Zhou, L., & Liu, S. S. (2005). Entrepreneurial firms in the context of China's transition economy: An integrative framework and empirical examination. *Journal of Business Research*, *58*(3), 277–284. doi:10.1016/S0148-2963(03)00159-0

Luo, Y., & Shenkar, O. (2006). The multinational corporation as a multilingual community: Language and organization in a global context. *Journal of International Business Studies*, *37*(3), 321–339. doi:10.1057/palgrave.jibs.8400197

Luo, Y., Shenkar, O., & Nyaw, M. (2002). Mitigating liabilities of foreignness: Defensive versus offensive approaches. *Journal of International Management*, *8*(3), 283–300. doi:10.1016/S1075-4253(02)00073-X

Luo, Y., Sun, J., & Wang, S. L. (2011). Comparative strategic management: An emergent field in international management. *Journal of International Management*, *17*(3), 190–200. doi:10.1016/j.intman.2011.05.002

Luo, Y., & Wang, S. L. (2012). Foreign direct investment strategies by developing country multinationals: A diagnostic model for home country effects. *Global Strategy Journal*, *2*(3), 244–261. doi:10.1111/j.2042-5805.2012.01036.x

Ly, A., Esperanca, J. P., Pereira, I. N., & Amaral-Baptista, M. A. (2013). The ten most influential global languages: exploring their effect on international trade. *Academy of Management Proceedings 2013*. Retrieved from http://bit.ly/1I3I1vC

Macnamara, J. (2012). Corporate and organisational diplomacy: An alternative paradigm to PR. *Journal of Communication Management*, *16*(3), 312–325. doi:10.1108/13632541211245794

Magee, S. P. (1981, November). The Appropriability Theory of the Multinational Corporation. *The Annals of the American Academy of Political and Social Science*, *458*(1), 123–135. doi:10.1177/000271628145800110

Ma, H. (2000). Of Competitive Advantage: Kinetic and Positional. *Business Horizons*, *43*(1), 53–64. doi:10.1016/S0007-6813(00)87388-7

Mahajan, N. (2014, February 11). *CKGSB Knowledge*. Retrieved from http://knowledge.ckgsb.edu.cn/2014/02/11/china-business-strategy/venkatesh-shankar-interview-new-lands-innovation/

Mahajan, V. (2009). *Africa Rising: How 900 Million African Consumers offer more than you think*. Pearson Education.

Makela, K., Kalla, H. K., & Piekkari, R. (2007). Interpersonal similarity as a driver for knowledge sharing within multinational corporations. *International Business Review*, *16*(1), 1–22. doi:10.1016/j.ibusrev.2006.11.002

Makura, M. (2008). *Africa's Greatest Entrepreneurs*. Penguin Books.

Malchow-Moller, N., Markusen, J. R., & Schjerning, B. (2007). *An analysis Foreign firms, domestic wages*. Working Paper 13001. Retrieved from http://www.nber.org/papers/w13001

Manakkalathil, J., & Rudolf, E. (2005). Corporate Social Responsibility in International Development: An Overview and critique. *Journal of Advanced Management*. Retrieved from http://0-proquest.umi.com.millenium.itesm.mx/

Mani, S. (2004). Institutional support for investment in domestic technologies: An analysis of the role of government in India. *Technological Forecasting and Social Change*, *71*(8), 855–863. doi:10.1016/j.techfore.2004.01.011

Mann, H., & Whitney, D. (1947). On the test whether one of two random variables is stochastically larger than the other. *Annals of Mathematical Statistics*, 18.

Manolopoulos, D., Dimitratos, P., Young, S., & Lioukas, S. (2009). Technology Sourcing and Performance of Foreign Subsidiaries in Greece: The Impact of MNE and Local Environmental Contexts. *Management International Review*, *49*(1), 43–60. doi:10.1007/s11575-008-0124-7

Manolova, T. S., Eunni, R. V., & Gyoshev, B. S. (2008). Intuitional environments for entrepreneurship: Evidence from emerging economies in Eastern Europe. *Entrepreneurship Theory and Practice*, *32*(1), 203–218. doi:10.1111/j.1540-6520.2007.00222.x

Mapendere, J. (2000). *Defining Track One-and-a-Half Diplomacy: Its Complementarity and the Analysis of Factors that Facilitate its Success*. Ottawa, Canada: Royal Roads University.

Marschan-Piekkari, R., Welch, D. E., & Welch, L. S. (1999a). In the shadow: The impact of language on structure, power and communication in the multinational. *International Business Review*, *8*(4), 421–440. doi:10.1016/S0969-5931(99)00015-3

Marschan-Piekkari, R., Welch, D. E., & Welch, L. S. (1999b). Adopting a common corporate language: IHRM implications. *International Journal of Human Resource Management*, *10*(3), 377–390. doi:10.1080/095851999340387

Marschan, R., Welch, D., & Welch, L. (1997). Language: The forgotten factor in multinational management. *European Management Journal*, *15*(5), 591–598. doi:10.1016/S0263-2373(97)00038-8

Marshall, J. (2008). *Finance: friend or foe?* Paper presented at the 2008 ANA Marketing Conference.

Marsh, C. (2000). Social capital and democracy in Russia. *Communist and Post-Communist Studies*, *33*(2), 183–199. doi:10.1016/S0967-067X(00)00003-9

Martincus, C. V., Castresana, S., & Castagnino, T. (2010). ISO Standards: A Certificate to Expand Exports? Firm-Level Evidence from Argentina. *Review of International Economics*, *18*(5), 896–912. doi:10.1111/j.1467-9396.2010.00915.x

Martinez Carlevarino, P. (2012). *The Peruvian mining sector: An overview*. Retrieved from PWC website: http://www.pwc.com/ca/en/events/publications/pwc-mining-in-peru-2-2012-01-en.pdf

Masakure, O., Henson, S., & Cranfield, J. (2009). Standards and export performance in developing countries: Evidence from Pakistan. *The Journal of International Trade & Economic Development*, *18*(3), 395–419. doi:10.1080/09638190902986538

Maskell, P. (2001). Towards a knowledge-based theory of the geographical cluster. *Industrial and Corporate Change*, *10*(4), 921–943. doi:10.1093/icc/10.4.921

Mason, E. S. (1939). Price and Production Policies of Large-Scale Enterprises. *The American Economic Review*, *29*(3), 61–74.

Matejka, L., & Titunik, I. R. (1976). *Semiotics of art: Prague school contributions*. Cambridge, MA: MIT.

Mathews, J. A., & Hu, M. (2007). Enhancing the role of universities in building national innovative capacity in Asia: The case of Taiwan. *World Development*, *35*(6), 1005–1020. doi:10.1016/j.worlddev.2006.05.012

Mathews, V. E. (2000). Management in a developing nation: And we thought American managers had it tough. *Multinational Business Review*, *8*(2), 10–15.

Mauro, P. (1995). Corruption and growth. *The Quarterly Journal of Economics*, *110*(3), 681–712. doi:10.2307/2946696

Maxton, G. P., & Wormald, J. (2004). *Time for a model change: Re-engineering the global automotive industry*. Cambridge, UK: Cambridge University Press. doi:10.1017/CBO9780511488535

May, K. E. (2014). *Work in the 21st Century: The Changing Role of Human Resources*. Terranova Consulting Group Society for Industrial and Organizational Psychology. Retrieved from http://www.siop.org/tip/backissues/tipjan98/may.aspx

Mayo, A. J., & Nohria, N. (2005). *Their Times: The Greatest Business Leaders of the Twentieth Century*. Harvard Business School Press.

McCann, P., Mudambi, R., (2005). Analytical differences in the economics of geography: the case of the multinational firm. *Environment and Planning*, *37*, 1857–1876.

McCarthy, D. J., Puffer, S. M., Graham, L. R., & Satinsky, D. M. (2014). Emerging innovation in emerging economies: Can institutional reforms help Russia break through its historical barriers? *Thunderbird International Business Review*, *56*(3), 243–260. doi:10.1002/tie.21619

Mcclure, D. I. (2001). *Electronic government: Challenges must be addressed with effective leadership and management*. Available: http://www.govgovnow.ir/em/do 1959.pdt/

McDougall, P. P., & Oviatt, B. M. (2000). International Entrepreneurship: The Intersection of Two Research Paths. *Academy of Management Journal*, *43*(5), 902–906. doi:10.2307/1556418

McGregor, D. (1960). *The human side of enterprise*. New York: McGraw-Hill.

McGregor, D. (1960). *The Human Side of Enterprise*. New York: McGraw-Hill.

McKinsey & Company Insights and Publications. (2010). *Africa's Path to Growth: Sector by Sector.* Author.

McKinsey Global Institute. (2014). *Global flows in a digital age: How trade, finance, people, and data connect the world economy*. McKinsey Global Institute.

Mead, R. (1998). *International management* (2nd ed.). Cambridge, MA: Blackwell Publishers.

Medina Nuñez, I. (1995). Telefonos de Mexico: Modernizacion, Privatizacion y Nuevas Relaciones Laborales. Espiral: *Estudios sobre Estado y Sociedad*, *3*(May-Aug), 133-153.

Mehri, N. S. (2004). Applying IT in organizations. *Political Economical Information Journal*, 181-182.

Messner, S. F., Baumer, E. P., & Rosenfeld, R. (2004). Dimensions of social capital and rates of criminal homicide. *American Sociological Review*, *69*(12), 882–903. doi:10.1177/000312240406900607

Meyer, K. E., & Thu Tran, Y. T. (2004). *Entry and growth strategies for emerging economies*. Retrieved from http://r4d.dfid.gov.uk/PDF/Outputs/CNEM/dp38.pdf

Meyer, K. E. (2004). Perspectives on multinational enterprises in emerging economies. *Journal of International Business Studies*, *35*(4), 259–276. doi:10.1057/palgrave.jibs.8400084

Meyer, K. E., & Estrin, S. (2001). Brownfield entry in emerging markets. *Journal of International Business Studies*, *32*(3), 575–584. doi:10.1057/palgrave.jibs.8490985

Meyer, K. E., Mudambi, R., & Narula, R. (2011). Multinational enterprises and local contexts: The opportunities and challenges of multiple embeddedness. *Journal of Management Studies*, *48*(2), 235–252.

Meyer, K. E., & Peng, M. W. (2005). Probing theoretically into Central and Eastern Europe: Transactions, resources, institutions. *Journal of International Business Studies*, *36*(6), 600–621. doi:10.1057/palgrave.jibs.8400167

Michael, B. (2005). *Corporate social responsibility in International Development: an overview and critique*. ABI/INFORM Global.

Milne, R. (2014). Li Shufu: an engineer with a mind for poetry and motion. *Financial Times*. Retrieved from http://on.ft.com/1T6wbr6

Mintzberg, H. (1984). Power and Organization Life Cycles. *Academy of Management Review*, *9*(2), 207–224.

Mintzberg, H. (1990). The Design School: Reconsidering The Basic Premises Of Strategic Management. *Strategic Management Journal*, *11*(3), 171–195. doi:10.1002/smj.4250110302

Misztal, B. (1996). *Trust in modern societies*. Cambridge, MA: Polity Press.

Mizik, N., & Jacobson, R. (2008). The financial value impact of perceptual brand attributes. *JMR, Journal of Marketing Research*, *45*(February), 15–32. doi:10.1509/jmkr.45.1.15

Moffett, M. H., Stonehill, A. I., & Editeman, D. (2003). *Fundamentals of Multinational Finance*. Pearson Education, Inc.

Monczka, R. M., & Trent, R. J. (1991). Global Sourcing: A Development Approach. *International Journal of Purchasing and Materials Management*, *27*(2), 2–8.

Montoya, M. A., & Trillas, F. (2009). The measurement of regulator independence in practice: Latin America and the Caribbean. *International Journal of Public Policy*, *4*(1/2), 113–134. doi:10.1504/IJPP.2009.021550

Morris, R. J., & Lawrence, A. T. (2001). Nike's dispute with the University of Oregon. *Case Research Journal*, *21*(3), 129–146.

Mowery, D. C., & Oxley, E. (1995). Inward technology transfer and competitiveness: The role of national innovation systems. *Cambridge Journal of Economics*, *19*(1), 67–93.

Mthombeni, M. S. (2006). *The Role of Multinational Corporations in South Africa: a Political Economic Perspective*. (Unpublished Dissertation). Department of Political Science, Faculty of Humanities, University of the Free State, Bloemfontein.

Mudambi, R. (2008). Location, control and innovation in knowledge-intensive industries. *Journal of Economic Geography*, *8*(5), 699–725. doi:10.1093/jeg/lbn024

Mukarovsky, J. (1972). El arte como hecho semiolgico. *Casa De Las Amricas*, *12*(71), 51–54.

Mumby, D., & Clair, R. (1997). Organizational discourse. In T.A. Van Dijk (Ed.), Discourse as Structure and Process: Discourse Studies vol. 2 – a Multidisciplinary Introduction, (pp. 181-205). London: Sage.

Mumby, D., & Clair, R. (1997). Organisational discourse. In T. van Dijk (Ed.), *Discourse as Social Interaction. Discourse Studies. A Multidisciplinary Introduction* (Vol. 2). London: Sage.

Murphy, C., & Lin, L. (2014). China's Volvo Romance Rolls on, with Xi's backing. *Wall Street Journal, China Real Time, Economy & Business*. Retrieved from http://on.wsj.com/1Smj9FW

Murphy, J. T. (2002). Networks, trust, and innovation in Tanzania's manufacturing sector. *World Development*, *30*(4), 91–619. doi:10.1016/S0305-750X(01)00131-0

Murphy, K. M., Shleifer, A., & Vishny, R. W. (1993). Why is rent-seeking so costly to growth? *The American Economic Review*, 409–414.

Murtiasih, S., Sucherly, S., & Siringoringo, H. (2014). Impact of country of origin and word of mouth on brand equity. *Marketing Intelligence & Planning*, *32*(5), 616–629. doi:10.1108/MIP-04-2013-0073

Nahapiet, J., & Ghoshal, S. (1998). Social Capital, Intellectual Capital, and The Organisation Advantage. *Academy of Management Review*, *23*(2), 242–266.

Naisbitt, J. (1997). *Megatrends Asia: Eight Asian megatrends that are reshaping our world*. New York: Touchstone.

Naray, O. (2008). *Commercial Diplomacy: A Conceptual Overview*. 7th World Conference of TPOs. Lecture, The Hague, The Netherlands.

Narula, R., & Wakelin, K. (1995). *Technological competitiveness, trade and foreign direct investment*. Research Memorandum, 2/95—019. MERIT, Maastricht.

Nasrolahi, L., Mohammad, V., & Jalilvand, R. (2014). Examining the influence of social capital on rural women entrepreneurship. *World Journal of Entrepreneurship. Management and Sustainable Development*, *10*(3), 209–227.

National Bureau of Statistics. (2006). *China statistics yearbook on high-tech technology industry*. Beijing: Chinese Statistical Press.

Needham, D., & Dransfield, R. (2000). *Advanced Business*. Heinemann.

Neelankavil, J. P., Mathur, A. Y., & Zhang, Y. (2000). Determinants of managerial performance: A cross-cultural comparison of the perceptions of middle-level managers in four countries. *Journal of International Business Studies*, *31*(1), 121–140. doi:10.1057/palgrave.jibs.8490892

Nee, V. (1996). The emergence of a market society: Changing mechanisms of stratification in China, *101*(4). *American Journal of Sociology*, *101*(4), 908–949. doi:10.1086/230784

Negandhi, A. R., & Baliga, B. R. (1980). Multinational corporations and host governments' relationships: Comparative study of conflict and conflicting issues. *Human Relations*, *33*(8), 517–541. doi:10.1177/001872678003300801

Nelson, R. (1993). *National Innovation Systems: A Comparative Analysis*. Oxford, UK: Oxford University Press.

Nelson, R. R., & Nelson, K. (2002). Technology, institutions and innovation systems. *Research Policy*, *31*(2), 265–272. doi:10.1016/S0048-7333(01)00140-8

Nemoto, T., Hayashi, K., & Hashimoto, M. (2010). Milk-run logistics by Japanese automobile manufacturers in Thailand. *Procedia: Social and Behavioral Sciences*, *2*(3), 5980–5989. doi:10.1016/j.sbspro.2010.04.012

Nestlé. (n.d.). *About us | Nestlé global*. Retrieved from http://www.nestle.com/aboutus

Newbold, P. (1998). *Estadística para los Negocios y la Economía*. Madrid: Prentice Hall.

Newburry, W., & Yakova, N. (2006). Standardized preferences: A function of national culture, work interdependence and local embeddedness. *Journal of International Business Studies*, *37*(1), 44–60. doi:10.1057/palgrave.jibs.8400179

Newman, L. K., & Nollen, D. S. (1996). Culture and Congruence: The Fit Between Management Practice and National Culture. *Journal of International Business Studies. Fourth Quarter*, *27*(4), 753–779. doi:10.1057/palgrave.jibs.8490152

Ng, I., & Dastmalchian, A. (2001). Organizational flexibility in Western and Asian firms: An examination of control and safeguard rules in five countries. *Canadian Journal of Administrative Sciences*, *8*(1), 17–24.

Ng, S. H., Ye, J., & Lee, C. (2011). Media discourse on globalization in China: A social—psychological analysis. *Journal of Language and Social Psychology*, *30*(2), 139–157. doi:10.1177/0261927X10397167

Nguyen, T. V., Weinstein, M., & Meyer, A. D. (2005). Development of trust of interfirm relationships in Vietnam. *Asia Pacific Journal of Management*, *22*(3), 211–231. doi:10.1007/s10490-005-3567-4

Nickels, W. G., McHUgh, J. M., & McHugh, S. M. (2012). *Understanding Business*. New York: McGraw Hill Irwin.

Nie, N. H., Powell, G. B., & Prewitt, K. (1969). Social structure and political participation: Developmental relationships, Part I. *The American Political Science Review*, *63*(2), 361–378. doi:10.2307/1954694

Nigeria's Technical Aid Corps: Issues and Perspective. (2006). Ibadan: Dokun Publishing House.

Niskanen, W. A. (1975). Bureaucrats and politicians. *The Journal of Law & Economics*, *18*(3), 617–643. doi:10.1086/466829

Nivre, J., Allwood, J., Grönqvit, L., Gunnarsson, M., Ahlsén, E., Vappula, H., & Ottesjö, C. et al. (2004). *Gothenburg Transcription Standard 6.4*. Department of Linguistics. Gothenburg University.

Nonaka, I. (1994). A dynamic theory of organizational knowledge creation. *Organization Science*, *5*(1), 14–37. doi:10.1287/orsc.5.1.14

Noorani, H. (2001). *Foreign Investment in Emerging Economies*. Retrieved from http://www.powerfulmethods.com/FIEE.pdf

North, D. C. (1989). Institutions and economic growth: A historical introduction. *World Development*, *17*(9), 1319–1332. doi:10.1016/0305-750X(89)90075-2

North, D. C. (1990). *Institutions, institutional change and economic performance*. Cambridge University Press. doi:10.1017/CBO9780511808678

North, D. C. (2005). Institutions and the process of economic change. *Management International*, *9*(3), 1–7.

Nottebohm, O., Manyika, J., Bughin, J., Chui, M., Syed, A.-R., & Ledezma, O. (2012). *En linea y en crecimiento: el impacto de internet en los países aspirantes*. McKinsey & Company.

O'Brien, F., & Meadows, M. (2000). Corporate visioning: A survey of UK practice. *The Journal of the Operational Research Society*, *51*(1), 36–44. doi:10.1057/palgrave.jors.2600907

OECD Investment Division. (n.d.). Retrieved from www.oecd.org/investment/gfi-8/

OECD. (2009). *OECD patent statistics manual*. Available at: http://browse.oecdbookshop.org/oecd/pdfs/free/9209021E.PDF

OECD. (2011). *OECD Science, Technology and Industry Scoreboard 2011*. Retrieved from OECD iLibrary: http://www.oecd-ilibrary.org/sites/sti_scoreboard-2011-en/03/10/index.html?contentType=&itemId=%2Fcontent%2Fchapter%2Fsti_scoreboard-2011-31-en&mimeType=text%2Fhtml&containerItemId=%2Fcontent%2Fserial%2F20725345&accessItemIds=

OECD. (2013). *OECD Factbook 2013: Economic, Environmental and Social Statistics*. Retrieved from OECD iLibrary: http://www.oecd-ilibrary.org/sites/factbook-2013-en/04/02/01/index.html?itemId=/content/chapter/factbook-2013-34-en

OECD. (2013). *Russia. Modernising the economy*. Available at: http://www.oecd.org/russia/Russia-Modernising-the-Economy-EN.pdf

O'Grady, S., & Lane, H. W. (1996). The Psychic Distance Paradox. *Journal of International Business Studies*, *27*(2), 309–333. doi:10.1057/palgrave.jibs.8490137

Ohmae, K. (2006). Growing in a Global Garden. *Leadership Excellence*, *23*(9), 14–15.

OIDHACO. (2012). *Violence against trade unionists in Colombia*. Retrieved from European Center for Constitutional and Human Rights website: http://www.oidhaco.org/uploaded/content/article/1969946869.pdf

Okpara, J. O., & Wynn, P. (2008). Human resource management practices in a transition economy. *Management Research News*, *31*(1), 57–76. doi:10.1108/01409170810845958

Olier, E. (2011). *Geoeconomía: las claves de la economía global*. Madrid: Prentice Hall.

Onishi, J., & Bliss, R. E. (2006). In search of Asian ways of managing conflict. *The International Journal of Conflict Management*, *17*(3), 203–225. doi:10.1108/10444060610742326

Ooi, C. A., Hooy, C. W., & Som, A. P. M. (2015). Diversity in human and social capital: Empirical evidence from Asian Tourism firms in corporate board composition. Elsevier. *Tourism Management*, 139–153.

Ordeix-Rigo, E., & Duarte, J. (2009). From Public Diplomacy to Corporate Diplomacy: Increasing Corporation's Legitimacy and Influence. *The American Behavioral Scientist*, *53*(4), 549–564. doi:10.1177/0002764209347630

Osuagwu, G. O., & Ezie, O. (2013). Multinational Corporation and the Nigerian Economy. *International Journal of Academic Research in Business and Social Sciences*, *3*(4), 359–369. Retrieved from www.hrmars.com/admin/pics/1786.pdf

Ouchi, W. G. (1981). *Theory Z: How can American business meet the Japanese challenge*. Reading, MA: Addison-Wesley.

Ouchi, W. G. (1981). *Theory Z: How can American business meet the Japanese challenge*. Reading, MA: Addison-Wesley. doi:10.1016/0007-6813(81)90031-8

Overbaugh, S. N. (2013). National culture, country-level competitiveness, and economic development. *International Journal of Business of Economics Perspectives*, *8*(1), 93–108.

Oviatt, B. M., & McDougall, P. P. (1994). Toward a theory of international new ventures. *Journal of International Business Studies*, *25*(1), 45–64. doi:10.1057/palgrave.jibs.8490193

Oxley, J. E. (1999). Institutional environment and the mechanisms of governance: The impact of intellectual property protection on the structure of inter-firm alliances. *Journal of Economic Behavior & Organization*, *38*(3), 283–309. doi:10.1016/S0167-2681(99)00011-6

Ozawa, T. (2011). The (Japan-born) 'flying-geese' theory of economic development revisited – and reformulated from a structuralist perspective. *Global Policy*, *2*(3), 272–285. doi:10.1111/j.1758-5899.2011.00093.x

Palmer, D. (2008). *Does the Center Hold?* Boston: McGraw-Hill.

Pananond, P., & Zeithaml, C. P. (1998). The international expansion process of MNEs from developing countries: A case study of Thailand's CP Group. *Asia Pacific Journal of Management*, *15*(2), 163–184. doi:10.1023/A:1015485413835

Parker, M. (1992). *Discourse Dynamics*. London: Routledge.

Park, S. H., & Luo, Y. (2001). Guanxi and organisational dynamics: Organisational networking in Chinese firms. *Strategic Management Journal*, *22*(5), 455–477. doi:10.1002/smj.167

Paus, E., & Robinson, M. D. (1999). Real wage performance under greater trade openness: Lessons from Latin America and Asia. *Journal of Developing Areas*, *33*(2), 269–288.

Pellicer, E., Yepes, V., & Rojas, R. J. (2010). Innovation and competitiveness in construction companies: A case study. *Journal of Management Research*, *10*(2), 103–115.

Peng, M. W. (2002). Towards an institution-based view of business strategy. *Asia Pacific Journal of Management*, *19*(2/3), 251–267. doi:10.1023/A:1016291702714

Peng, M. W. (2006). Making M&A fly in China. *Harvard Business Review*, *84*(3), 26–27.

Peng, M. W., & Zhou, J. Q. (2005). How network strategies and institutional transitions evolve in Asia. *Asia Pacific Journal of Management*, *22*(4), 321–336. doi:10.1007/s10490-005-4113-0

Perlmutter, H. V. (1969). The Tourtous Evolution of the Multinational Corporation. Columbia Journal of World Business, 4(1), 9-18.

Persons, L. S. (2008). *Face dynamics, social power and virtue among Thai leaders: A cultural analysis* (Doctoral dissertation). Fuller Graduate Schools, School of Intercultural Studies.

Peteraf, M. A. (1993). The cornerstones of competitive advantage: A resource-based view. *Strategic Management Journal*, *14*(3), 179–191. doi:10.1002/smj.4250140303

Peters, T. (1979, September). *Beyond the matrix organization*. McKinsey & Company. Retrieved from http://www.mckinsey.com/insights/organization/beyond_the_matrix_organization

Peters, T. (2014). Tom Peters on leading the 21st-century organization. *McKinsey Quarterly*. Retrieved from http://www.mckinsey.com/insights/organization/tom_peters_on_leading_the_21st_century_organization

Petison, P., & Johri, L. M. (2006). Driving harmony: Philosophy of Toyota Motor Thailand. *Strategic Direction*, *22*(11), 3–5. doi:10.1108/02580540610708699

Petison, P., & Johri, L. M. (2007). Developing local talent in international subsidiaries: The importance of trust and respect in Toyota. *Development and Learning in Organizations: An International Journal*, *21*(3), 10–13. doi:10.1108/14777280710739061

Petison, P., & Johri, L. M. (2008). Dynamics of the manufacturer-supplier relationships in emerging markets: A case of Thailand. *Asia Pacific Journal of Marketing and Logistics*, *20*(1), 76–96. doi:10.1108/13555850810844887

Petro, N. (1995). *The rebirth of Russian democracy: An interpretation of political culture*. Cambridge, MA: Harvard University Press.

Petrović-Ranđelović, M. (2012). Foreign direct investment as a mechanism for achieving social progress in the host country. *New Challenges in Changing Labour Markets,* 337.

Peyman, Y., Mohsen, A. S., Hassan, G., Aboulghassim, F., & Zaman, A. (2011). The Analysis of the Relationship between Organizational Structure and Information Technology (IT): And the Barriers to Its Establishment at the University of Isfahan from the Faculty Member's Viewpoints. *Higher Education Studies, 1*(1). Retrieved from www.ccsenet.org/hes/

Phene, A., & Almeida, P. (2008). Innovation in multinational subsidiaries: The role of knowledge assimilation and subsidiary capabilities. *Journal of International Business Studies*, *39*(5), 901–919. doi:10.1057/palgrave.jibs.8400383

Pheng, L. S., & Yuquan, S. (2002). An exploratory study of Hofstede's cross-cultural dimensions in construction projects. *Management Decision*, *40*(1), 7–16. doi:10.1108/00251740210423036

Philips, M., & Hardy, C. (2002). *Discourse Analysis: Investigating Processes of Social Construction*. Newbury Park, CA: Sage.

Phongpetra, V., & Johri, L. M. (2011). Impact of business strategies of automobile manufacturers in Thailand. *International Journal of Emerging Markets*, *6*(1), 17–37. doi:10.1108/17468801111104359

Piekkari, R. (2008). Languages and careers in multinational corporations. In S. Tietze (Ed.), *International management and language* (pp. 128–137). London: Routledge.

Piekkari, R., Vaara, E., Tienari, J., & Säntti, R. (2005). Integration or disintegration? Human Resource implications of the common corporate language decision in a cross-border merger. *Journal of Human Resource Management*, *16*(3), 333–347.

Pinelo, A. J. (1973). *The Multinational Corporation as a Force in Latin American Politics*. New York: Praeger Publishers.

Piscitello, L. (2004). Corporate diversification, coherence and economic performance. *Industrial and Corporate Change*, *13*(5), 757–787. doi:10.1093/icc/dth030

Pitcher, P., & Smith, A. D. (2001). Top Management Team Heterogeneity: Personality, Power, and Proxies. *Organization Science*, *12*(1), 1–18. doi:10.1287/orsc.12.1.1.10120

Platteau, J. (1994). Behind the market stage where real societies exist: The role of public and private order institutions. *The Journal of Development Studies*, *30*(3), 533–577. doi:10.1080/00220389408422328

Poletti, M. J., Engelland, B. T., & Ling, H. G. (2011). An empirical study of declining lead times: Potential ramifications on the performance of early market entrants. *Journal of Marketing Theory and Practice*, *19*(1), 27–38. doi:10.2753/MTP1069-6679190102

Ponzetto, G. A., & Troiano, U. (2014). *Social Capital, Government Expenditures and Growth*. Centre for Economic Policy Research, Discussion Paper No. 9891.

Popov, V. (2001). Reform strategies and economic performance of Russia's regions. *World Development*, *29*(5), 865–886. doi:10.1016/S0305-750X(01)00006-7

Porter, M. E., Delgado, M., Ketels, C., & Stern, S. (2008). Moving to a new global competitiveness index. In *The Global Competitiveness Report 2008–2009*. World Economic Forum.

Porter, M.E. (2001). *Strategy and the Internet*. Academic Press.

Porter, M. (1990). The Competitive Advantage of Firms in Global Industries. In *The Competitive Advantage of Nations*. New York, NY: Free Press. doi:10.1007/978-1-349-11336-1_2

Porter, M. (1990). *The Competitive Advantage of Nations*. New York: The Free Press. doi:10.1007/978-1-349-11336-1

Porter, M. E. (1980). *Competitive strategy*. New York: Free Press.

Porter, M. E. (1980). *Competitive Strategy*. New York: Free Press.

Porter, M. E. (1980). *Competitive Strategy: Techniques for Analyzing Industries and Competitors*. New York: Free Press.

Porter, M. E. (1985). *Competitive Advantage: Creating and Sustaining Superior Performance*. New York: The Free Press.

Porter, M. E. (1996). What is strategy? *Harvard Business Review*, *74*(6), 61–78. PMID:10158474

Porter, M. E., & Kramer, M. R. (2006). The link between competitive advantage and corporate social responsibility. *Harvard Business Review*, *84*(12), 78–92. PMID:17183795

Post Reporters (2015, January 30). FPO trims forecasts for GDP, exports. *Bangkok Post*, p. B2.

Pothukuchi, V., Damanpour, F., Choi, J., Chao, C., & Seung, H. P. (2002). National and organizational culture differences and international joint venture performance. *Journal of International Business Studies*, *33*(2), 243–266. doi:10.1057/palgrave.jibs.8491015

Potoski, M., & Prakash, A. (2009). Information asymmetries as trade barriers: ISO 9000 increases international commerce. *Journal of Policy Analysis and Management*, *28*(2), 221–238. doi:10.1002/pam.20424

Potter, J. (1997). Discourse analysis as a way of analysing naturally occurring talk. In D. Silverman (Ed.), *Qualitative Research: Theory, Methods and Practice*. London: Sage.

Potter, J., & Wetherell, M. (1987). *Discourse and Social Psychology*. London: Sage.

Pounder, J. S. (2001). 'New leadership' and university organisational effectiveness: Exploring the relationship. *Leadership and Organization Development Journal*, *22*(5/6), 281–290. doi:10.1108/EUM0000000005827

Prahalad, C. K., & Doz, Y. (1987). *The Multinational Mission: Balancing Local Demands and Global Vision*. New York: The Free Press.

Prasnikar, J., Pahor, M., & Svetlik, J. V. (2008). Are national cultures still important in international business? Eussia, Serbia and Slovenia in comparison. *Journal of Contemporary Management Issues*, *13*(2), 1–26.

Pugel, T. A. (2007). *International Economics* (13th ed.). New York: McGraw-Hill Irwin.

Putnam, R. (1993). *Making Democracy Work*. Princeton, NJ: Princeton University Press.

Putnam, R. D. (1995). Bowling alone: America's declining social capital. *Journal of Democracy*, *6*(1), 65–78. doi:10.1353/jod.1995.0002

Putnam, R. D., Leonardi, R., & Nanetti, R. Y. (1994). *Making democracy work: Civic traditions in modern Italy*. Princeton University Press.

Qian, Y., & Xu, C. (1998). Innovation and bureaucracy under soft and hard budget constraints. *The Review of Economic Studies*, *65*(1), 151–164. doi:10.1111/1467-937X.00039

Quelch, J. A., & Hoff, E. J. (1986). Customizing global marketing. *Harvard Business Review*, *64*(May/June), 59–68.

Rafsanjani, H. K., Zeinolabedini, M., Mir, M., & Far, I. M. (2014). Studying the effect of education, trade, and FDI on income inequality in Iran. *Management and Administrative Sciences Review*, *3*(4), 733–745.

Rahman, S., Laosirihongthong, T., & Sohal, A. S. (2010). Impact of lean strategy on operational performance: A study of Thai manufacturing companies. *Journal of Manufacturing Technology Management*, *21*(7), 839–852. doi:10.1108/17410381011077946

Rahman, Z., & Bhattacharyya, S. K. (2003). Sources of first mover advantages in emerging market – an Indian perspective. *European Business Review*, *15*(6), 361–371. doi:10.1108/09555340310500541

Rajaram, V. R., & Lance, B. L. (2010). How Emerging Market Firms Compete in Global Markets. *Journal of Emerging Knowledge on Emerging Markets*, 2. Retrieved from http://digitalcommons.kennesaw.edu/cgi/viewcontent.cgi?article=1017&context=jekem/

Ralston, D. A. (2008). The crossvergence perspective: Reflections and projections. *Journal of International Business Studies*, *39*(1), 27–40. doi:10.1057/palgrave.jibs.8400333

Ralston, D. A., Holt, D. H., Terpstra, R. H., & Cheng, Y. K. (1997). The impact of national culture and economic ideology on managerial work values: A study of the United States, Russia, Japan, and China. *Journal of International Business Studies*, *28*(2), 177–207. doi:10.1057/palgrave.jibs.8490097

Ramienski, D. (2008). *Looking For a Holistic Approach*. Available: http://www.federalnewsradio.com/?nid=169&sid=1377323

Randviir, A. (2007). On spatiality in Tartu–Moscow cultural semiotics: The semiotic subject. *Sign Systems Studies*, 137-159.

Rau, P. R., & Preble, J. F. (1987). Standardization of marketing strategy by multinationals. *International Marketing Review*, *4*(3), 18–28. doi:10.1108/eb008333

Reed, M. (2000). The limits of discourse analysis. *Organization*, *7*(3), 524–530. doi:10.1177/135050840073011

Rehbein, B. (2007). Configurations of globalization in Laos and Cambodia. *Internationales Asienforum*, *38*(1/2), 67–85.

Reichel, J. (1988). The Internationalization of Importing Companies. *European Journal of Marketing*, *22*(10), 31–40. doi:10.1108/EUM0000000005302

Reid, S. D. (1981). The Decision-Maker and Export Entry and Expansion. *Journal of International Business Studies*, *12*(2), 101–102. doi:10.1057/palgrave.jibs.8490581

Reif, W. E. (1968). Computer technology and management organization. Bureau of Business and Economic Research, College of Business Administration, University of Iowa.

Report by Labour Research Service. (n.d.). Available at http://www.fes-southafrica.org/media/MNC%20Trend%20Report%20%20FES%20draft%202014.pdf

Repsol. (n.d.). *Repsol North America | Integrated oil and gas company - repsol.com*. Retrieved from http://www.repsol.com/us_en/usa/about-repsol-north-america/about-us/default.aspx

Reuters. (2014, July). America Movil to Own Just Over Half of Telekom Austria. *New York Times*. Retrieved from http://www.nytimes.com/reuters/2014/07/14/business/14reuters-mexico-americamovil.html

Rexha, N., & Miyamoto, T. (2000). International Sourcing: An Australian Perspective. *Journal of Supply Chain Management*, *31*(1), 27–34. doi:10.1111/j.1745-493X.2000.tb00067.x

Riaz, S. (2009). The global financial crisis: An institutional theory. *Critical Perspectives on International Business*, *5*(1), 26–35.

Richardson, K. (1998). Signs and wonders: interpreting the economy through television. In A. Bell & P. Garrett (Eds.), *Approaches to Media Discourse*. Oxford, UK: Blackwell.

Rigby, D. K. (2013). *Management tools 2013 - An executives guide*. Boston: Bain & Company, Inc.

Roaf, J. (2000). *Corruption in Russia*. IMF Conference on Post-Election Strategy.

Robbins, S. F., & Judge, T. A. (2007). *Organizational Behaviour* (12th ed.). Pearson Education Inc.

Robertson, C. J., & Watson, A. (2004). Corruption and change: The impact of foreign direct investment. *Strategic Management Journal*, *25*(4), 385–396. doi:10.1002/smj.382

Rodrik, D. (1996). Coordination failures and government policy: A model with applications to East Asia and Eastern Europe. *Journal of International Economics*, *40*(1-2), 1–22. doi:10.1016/0022-1996(95)01386-5

Rodrik, D. (1999). *The New Global Economy and Developing Countries: Making Openness Work. Policy Essay no. 24*. Washington, DC: Overseas Development Council.

Roelofsen, O., & Sheng, P. (2010). Oil and Gas: New Sources of Growth. In Africa's Path to Growth: Sector by Sector. McKinsey & Co.

Roessner, J. D., Porter, A. L., Newman, N., & Cauffiel, D. (1996). Anticipating the future high-tech competitiveness of nations: Indicators for twenty-eight countries. *Technological Forecasting and Social Change*, *51*(2), 133–149. doi:10.1016/0040-1625(95)00195-6

Rogers, E. M. (1962). *Diffusion of Innovation*. New York: Free Press.

Rojas-Méndez, J. I. (2013). The nation brand molecule. *Journal of Product and Brand Management*, *22*(7), 462–472. doi:10.1108/JPBM-09-2013-0385

Rondinelli, D. (2002). Transnational corporations: International citizens or new soveriegns? *Business and Society Review*, *107*(4), 391–413. doi:10.1111/1467-8594.00143

Root, F. (1994). *Entry Strategies for International markets*. Routledge.

Rose-Ackerman, S. (1999). *Corruption and government: Causes, consequences, and reform*. Cambridge University Press. doi:10.1017/CBO9781139175098

Rosenfeld, R., Baumer, E. P., & Messner, S. F. (2001). Social capital and homicide. *Social Forces*, *80*(1), 283–310. doi:10.1353/sof.2001.0086

Rose, R. (2000). How much does social capital add to individual health? *Social Science & Medicine*, *51*(9), 1421–1435. doi:10.1016/S0277-9536(00)00106-4 PMID:11037227

Rostow, W. W. (1960). *The Stages of Economic Growth: A Non-Communist Manifesto*. Cambridge, UK: Cambridge University Press.

Roth, K., Schweiger, D. M., & Morrison, A. J. (1992). Global Strategy Implementation at the Business Unit Level: Operational Capabilities and Administrative Mechanisms. *Journal of International Business Studies*, *22*(3), 369–402. doi:10.1057/palgrave.jibs.8490307

Roudini, A., & Osman, M. H. M. (2012). *The Role of International Entrepreneurship Capability on International Performance in Born Global Firm*. Academic Press.

Routledge, B. R., & Von Amsberg, J. (2003). Social Capital and Growth. *Journal of Monetary Economics*, *50*(1), 167–194. doi:10.1016/S0304-3932(02)00210-6

Rudolph, Alice (1985). Standardization not standard for global marketers. *Marketing News*, 3-4.

Ruël, H. (2013). *Diplomacy means business*. Retrieved from Windesheimreeks kennis en onderzoek website: http://www.windesheim.nl

Ruël, H., & Zuidema, L. (2012). *The effectiveness of commercial diplomacy; a survey among Dutch embassies and consulates*. Discussion papers in diplomacy.

Rugman, A. (2005). *The Regional Multinationals*. Cambridge, UK: Cambridge University Press. doi:10.1017/CBO9780511614071

Rugman, A. M. (1981). *Inside the Multinationals: The Economics of Internal Markets*. New York: Columbia University Press.

Rugman, A. M. (1982). Internationalization and Non-equity Forms of International Involvement. In A. M. Rugman (Ed.), *New Theories of the Multinational Enterprise* (pp. 9–23). London: Croom Helm.

Rugman, A. M. (2003). Regional strategy and the demise of globalization. *Journal of International Management*, *9*(4), 409–417. doi:10.1016/j.intman.2003.08.004

Rugman, A. M., & Doh, J. P. (2008). *Multinationals and Development*. New Haven, CT: Yale University Press. doi:10.12987/yale/9780300115611.001.0001

Rugman, A. M., & Hodgets, R. M. (2003). *International Business* (3rd ed.). PearsonEducation Ltd.

Rugman, A. M., & Verbeke, A. (2001). Location, competitiveness and the multinational enterprise. In A. M. Rugman & T. L. Brewer (Eds.), *The Oxford Handbook of International Business* (pp. 150–179). Oxford, UK: Oxford University Press. doi:10.1093/0199241821.003.0006

Rugman, A. M., & Verbeke, A. (2001). Subsidiary-specific advantages in multinational enterprises. *Strategic Management Journal*, *22*(3), 237–250. doi:10.1002/smj.153

Rugman, A. M., & Verbeke, A. (2004). A perspective on regional and global strategies of multinational enterprises. *Journal of International Business Studies*, *35*(1), 3–18. doi:10.1057/palgrave.jibs.8400073

Rugraff, E., & Hansen, M. W. (Eds.). (2011). Multinational Corporations and Local Firms in Emerging Economies. Amsterdam: Amsterdam University Press.

Russo, B., & Fiorini, R. (2010). Consumer Goods: Two Hundred Million New Comers. In Africa's Path to Growth: Sector by Sector. McKinsey & Co.

Ruxin, J. (2011). African Multinational Corporations are catching up. *Forbes Investing Digest*. Retrieved from www.forbes.com/sites/joshuaruxin/2011/06/09/african-multinational-corporations-are- catching-up/

Saadatmandi, H. (2004). *Studying the relation between the IT and organization structure and the barroirs against launching it in Iran national steel company*. (Ms Thesis). Teharan University, Management School.

Sachs, J. D. (2008). *Common Wealth: Economics for a Crowded Planet*. The Penguin Press.

Sala-I-Martin, X., Blanke, J., Drzeniek, M., Geiger, T., Mia, I., & Paua, F. (2008). The global competitiveness index: prioritizing the economic policy agenda. In *The Global Competitiveness Report 2008–2009*. World Economic Forum.

Saldanha, J. P., Mello, J. E., Knemeyer, M. A., & Vijayaraghavan, T. (2015, January). Implementing Supply Chain technologies in Emerging markets: An institutional theory Perspective. *Journal of Supply Chain Management*, *51*(1), 5–26. doi:10.1111/jscm.12065

Sampson, R. J., Morenoff, J. D., & Earls, F. (1999). Beyond social capital: Spatial dynamics of collective efficacy for children. *American Sociological Review*, *64*(5), 633–660. doi:10.2307/2657367

SanAntonio, P. M. (1987). Social mobility and language use in an American company in Japan. *Journal of Language and Social Psychology*, *6*(3–4), 191–200. doi:10.1177/0261927X8763003

Sanders, N. R. (2008, May). Pattern of information technology use: The impact on buyer–suppler coordination and performance. *Journal of Operations Management*, *26*(3), 349–367. doi:10.1016/j.jom.2007.07.003

Saner, R., & Yiu, L. (2001). *International economic diplomacy: mutations in post-modern times*. Retrieved from: http://clingendael.info/publications/2003/20030100_cli_paper_dip_issue84.pdf

Saner, R., Yiu, L., & Sondergaard, M. (2000). Business diplomacy management: A core competency for global companies. *The Academy of Management Perspectives*, *14*(1), 80–92. doi:10.5465/AME.2000.2909841

Sangwongwanich, P. (2015, January 23). Bangkok rock bottom in 300-city economic survey. *Bangkok Post*, p. B1.

Santiso, J. (2007). *The emergence of Latin multinationals*. OECD Emerging Markets Network Working Paper. Retrieved from: http://www.oecd.org/dev/40512615.pdf

Satow, E. M., In Gore-Booth, P. H., & In Pakenham, D. (1979). *Satow's Guide to diplomatic practice* (5th ed.). London: Longman.

Sauvant, P. K., Maschek, W. A., & McAllister. (2009). *Foreign direct investment by emerging market multinational enterprises, the impact of the financial crisis and recession and challenges ahead.* OECD Global Forum on International Investment.

Schegloff, E. (1997). Whose text? Whose context? *Discourse & Society*, *8*(2), 165–183. doi:10.1177/0957926597008002002

Schein, E. H. (1985). *Organizational Culture and Leadership*. San Francisco, CA: Jossey-Bass.

Schiffrin, D. (1994). *Approaches to Discourse*. Oxford, UK: Basil Blackwell.

Schiffrin, D., Tannen, D., & Hamilton, H. E. (2001). *The Handbook of Discourse Analysis*. Oxford, UK: Blackwell.

Schleh, E. C. (1977). A matter of management style. *Management Review*, *66*(8), 8–14.

Schmidt, S. W., & Akdere, M. (2007). Measuring the effects of employee orientation training on employee perceptions of vision and leadership: Implications for human resources. *The Business Review, Cambridge*, *7*(1), 322–327.

Schneider, S. C., & Angelmar, R. (1993). Cognition in Organzational Analysis: Who's Minding the Store? *Organization Studies*, *14*(3), 347–374. doi:10.1177/017084069301400302

Schneidman, W. W. (2007). *Multinational Corporations and Economic Development in Africa*. Retrieved from Csis.org/publication/multinational-corporations-andeconomic-development-africa

Schoors, K., & Bartoldus, V. (2001). *The productivity effect of foreign ownership on domestic firms in Hungary*. In *EAE Conference, Philadelphia*, PA.

Schweizer, R., & Lagerström, K. (2014). A business tale on marriage, divorce and remarriage in the corporate world: a conceptual framework of firms' disintegration process. In C. Alvstam, H. Dolles, & P. Ström (Eds.), *Asian Inward and Outward FDI: New Challenges in the Global Economy* (pp. 201–216). Palgrave Macmillan Asian Business Series. doi:10.1057/9781137312211.0016

Scott, W. R. (1995). *Institutions and organisations.* Sage.

Scott, W. R. (2008). Institutions and organisations: Ideas and interests. *Sage (Atlanta, Ga.)*.

Searle, J. R. (1969). *Speech Acts: An Essay in the Philosophy of Language*. Cambridge, UK: Cambridge University Press. doi:10.1017/CBO9781139173438

Sebeok, T. A. (2001). *Global semiotics*. Bloomington, IN: Indiana Univ. Press.

See, E. (2008). *What marketing thinks*. Association of National Advertisers.

Segal-Horn & Faulkner. (1999). *The Dynamics of International Strategy.* Thomson.

Seligman, S. D. (1999). *Chinese business etiquette: A guide to protocol, manners, and culture in the People's Republic of China*. New York: Warner Books.

Sen, K. (2015). *Why pv models are necessary for complete understanding*. Working paper.

Senge, P. (1997). The Fifth Discipline: The Art and Practice of The Learning Organization. London: Random House.

Senik, Z. C., Isa, R. M., Scott-Labb, B., & Entrekin, L. (2010). *Influential Factors for SME Internationalization: Evidence from Malaysia*. Academic Press.

Servicio Nacional de Aprendizaje SENA. (2007). *Caracterización ocupacional de la industria de procesamiento de alimentos*. Mapa industrial del procesamiento de alimentos.

Seshanna, S. (2009). Globalization, income polarization and the rise of the "new challenger". In C. W. Mun & S. H. Ying (Eds.), *Singapore and Asia in a Globalized World, Contemporary Economic Issues and Politics* (pp. 155–172). Singapore: World Scientific.

Sexton, D. E. (1997). Building global brands. *The Advertiser.*

Sexton, D. E. (1999). Global marketing: balancing global thoughts and local actions. *The Advertiser*, 12-18.

Sexton, D. E. (2004a). Managing brand equity over time. *Quarterly Review of Canada China Business Council*, 9-11.

Sexton, D. E. (2004b). Should your brand be global*? Chazen Web Journal of International Business*, 1-13.

Sexton, D. E. (2005). Building the brand scorecard. *The Advertiser*, 54-58.

Sexton, D. E. (2006a). Implementing your global strategy in country markets. *Effective Executive,* 16-20.

Sexton, D. E. (2006b). Pricing, perceived value, and communications. *The Advertiser*, 56-58.

Sexton, D. E. (2007a). Coordinating brands globally. *Global CEO*, 9-13.

Sexton, D. E. (2007b). The keys to strategic success. *Effective Executive*, 32-34.

Sexton, D. E. (2008). Think markets not countries. *Effective Executive,* 28-30.

Sexton, D. E. (2009a). Achieving marketing nirvana. *Advertiser*, 18.

Sexton, D. E. (2009c). *Value Above Cost: How CVA® Drives Financial Performance, the Most Important Metric You've Never Used.* Upper Saddle River, NJ: FT Press (Wharton School Publishing).

Sexton, D. E. (2010). Competing with customer value added. *Effective Executive*, 44-47.

Sexton, D. E. (2014a). Implementing marketing metrics in organizations: opportunities and challenges. In The Handbook of Customer Equity (pp. 431-447). Northampton, MA: Elgar Publishing.

Sexton, D. E. (2015b). International marketing strategy – does country nationality matter? *Journal of Marketing Trends*, 47-54.

Sexton, D. E., & Association of National Advertisers. (2013). *Global brand equity survey results.* New York: ANA.

Sexton, D. E., & Charney, C. (2015a). *Emerging markets attractiveness study*. New York: AMA.

Sexton, D. E., & Rogers, D. (2012). *Marketing roi in the era of big data.* New York: BRITE.

Sexton, D. E. (2009b). *Marketing 101* (2nd ed.). Hoboken, NJ: John Wiley & Sons, Inc.

Sexton, D. E. (2014b). Using metrics to achieve 'steering control' of your marketing actions. *Effective Executive*, *17*(1), 7–19.

Shah, A. M. (2012). Business strategies in the emerging markets. *Journal of Asia-Pacific Business*, *13*(1), 4–15. doi:10.1080/10599231.2011.616143

Shane, S., & Venkataraman, S. (2000). The Promise of Entrepreneurship as a Field of Research. *Academy of Management Review*, *25*(1), 217–226.

Shane, S., Venkataraman, S., & Macmillan, I. (1995). Cultural differences in innovation championing strategies. *Journal of Management*, *21*(5), 931–952. doi:10.1177/014920639502100507

Shao, B. (2011). First mover advantages: Flexible or not? *Journal of Management and Marketing Research*, *7*(1), 1–13.

Shapiro, D. M., Gedaijlovis, E., & Erdener, C. (2003). The Chinese family firm as a multinational enterprise. *The International Journal of Organizational Analysis*, *11*(2), 105–122. doi:10.1108/eb028965

Sharma, K. (2000). *Rediscovering dharavi: Stories from Asia's largest slum*. New Delhi: Penguin Books.

Shaw, W., & Barry, V. (2007). *Moral Issues in Business* (10th ed.). Belmont: Thomson Wadsworth.

Shell. (n.d.). *The Shell global homepage - Shell Global*. Retrieved from http://www.shell.com

Shenkar, O. (2009). Becoming multinational: Challenges for Chinese firms. *Journal of Chinese Economic and Foreign Trade Studies*, *2*(3), 149–162. doi:10.1108/17544400910994733

Shirouzu, N. (2009). Is Geely capable of managing Volvo? *Wall Street Journal*. Retrieved from http://blogs.wsj.com/chinarealtime/2009/11/03/is-geely-capable-of-managing-volvo/

Shougang Group. (n.d.). *China Shougang Group | Company profile*. Retrieved from http://www.shougang.com.cn/shougang_cn_web/gsjj/index.htm

Shrestha, B. K., & Gnyawali, D. R. (2013). Insights on strategic management practices in Nepal. *South Asian Journal of Global Business Research*, *2*(2), 191–210. doi:10.1108/SAJGBR-03-2012-0025

Sim, A. B., & Pandian, J. R. (2007). An exploratory study of internationalization strategies of Malaysian and Taiwanese firms. *International Journal of Emerging Markets*, *2*(3), 252–273. doi:10.1108/17468800710758396

Simola, S. K., Taggar, S., & Smith, G. W. (2007). The employment selection interview: Disparity among research-based recommendations, current practices and what matters to human rights tribunals. *Canadian Journal of Administrative Sciences*, *24*(1), 30–44. doi:10.1002/cjas.4

Sinani, E., & Meyer, K. E. (2004). Spillovers of technology transfer from FDI: The case of Estonia. *Journal of Comparative Economics*, *32*(3), 445–466. doi:10.1016/j.jce.2004.03.002

Singal, A. K., & Jain, A. K. (2014). Emerging market firms: Measuring their success with strategic positioning maps. *The Journal of Business Strategy*, *35*(1), 20–28. doi:10.1108/JBS-04-2013-0026

Singh, J. (2007). Asymmetry of knowledge spillovers between MNCs and host country firms. *Journal of International Business Studies*, *38*(5), 764–786. doi:10.1057/palgrave.jibs.8400289

Sinha, A. (2005). *The regional roots of development politics in India: A divided Leviathan*. Bloomington, IN: Indian University Press.

Sinpeng, A. (2014). Party-social movement coalition in Thailand's political conflict (2005-2011). In P. Liamputtong (Ed.), *Contemporary Socio-Cultural and Political Perspectives in Thailand* (pp. 157–168). Dordrecht, NL: Springer. doi:10.1007/978-94-007-7244-1_10

Sjöholm, F. (1999). Technology gap, competition and spillovers from direct foreign investment: Evidence from establishment data. *The Journal of Development Studies*, *36*(1), 53–73. doi:10.1080/00220389908422611

Slim Helú, C. (2015, July 27) *Business Activity*. Retrieved from: http://www.carlosslim.com/act_empresarial_ing.html

Smedlund, A. (2008). The knowledge system of a firm: Social capital for explicit, tacit and potential knowledge. *Journal of Knowledge Management*, *12*(1), 63–77. doi:10.1108/13673270810852395

Smith, N., & Thomas, E. (2014a). Innovation in emerging economies: The spillover effects of foreign direct investment and institutions in Russia. In S. Marinova (Ed.), Institutional Impacts on Firm Internalisation. Palgrave McMillan.

Smith, N., Thomas, E., & Antoniou, C. (2014). Multi-national firms, corruption and innovation in Russia. In A. Verbeke, R.V. Tulder, & S. Lundan (Eds.), Multinational Enterprises, Markets and Institutional Diversity. Emerald Group Publishing Limited.

Smith, N., Thomas, E., & Antoniou, C. (2014b). Multi-national firms, corruption and innovation in Russia. In A. Verbeke, R.V. Tulder, & S. Lundan (Eds.), Multinational Enterprises, Markets and Institutional Diversity. Emerald Group Publishing Limited.

Smith, A. (1812). *An Inquiry into the nature and causes of the wealth of nations* (Vol. 3). London: J.M- Dent & Sond LTD.

Smith, N., & Thomas, E. (2015a). The role of foreign direct investment and state capture in shaping innovation outcome in Russia. *Europe-Asia Studies*, *67*(5), 777–808. doi:10.1080/09668136.2015.1042430

Smith, N., & Thomas, E. (2015b). Socio-institutional environment and innovation in Russia. *Journal of East-West Business*, *21*(3), 182–204. doi:10.1080/10669868.2015.1021066

Sondhi, S. (2000). Combating corruption in India.*Paper for the XVIII World Congress of International Political Science Association*, Quebec City, Canada.

Spar, D. (1999). Foreign investment and human rights international. *Challenge*, 1–2.

Spero, J. E., & Hart, J. A. (2003). *The Politics of International Economic Relations* (6th ed.). Belmont: Wadsworth/Thomson.

Srinivas, M. N. (Ed.). (1996). *Caste: Its twentieth century avatar*. New Delhi: Penguin Books.

Sriussadaporn, R. (2006). Managing international business communication problems at work: A pilot study in foreign companies in Thailand. *Cross Cultural Management: An International Journal*, *13*(4), 330–344. doi:10.1108/13527600610713422

Stark. (n.d.). Inverting Donaldson's Framework: A Managerial Approach To International Conflicts Of Cultural And Economic Norms. *Business Ethics Quarterly*. doi:.10.1017/bcq.2015.30

Starosta de Waldemar, F. (2012). New products and corruption: Evidence from Indian firms. *The Developing Economies*, *50*(3), 268–285. doi:10.1111/j.1746-1049.2012.00171.x

Steer, L., & Sen, K. (2010). Formal and informal institutions in a transition economy: The case of Vietnam. *World Development*, *38*(11), 1603–1615. doi:10.1016/j.worlddev.2010.03.006

Steyaert, C., Ostendorp, A., & Gaibrois, C. (2011). Multilingual organizations as "linguascapes": Negotiating the position of English through discursive practices. *Journal of World Business*, *46*(3), 270–278. doi:10.1016/j.jwb.2010.07.003

Stopford, J. M., & Wells, L. T. (1972). *Managing the multinational enterprise: Organization of the firm and ownership of the subsidiaries*. New York: Basic Books.

Stopford, J. M., & Wells, L. T. (1972). *Managing the Multinational Enterprise: Organization of the Firm and Ownership of the Subsidiary* (French ed.). Basic Books.

Stubbs, M. (1983). *Discourse analysis: The sociolinguistic analysis of natural language*. Oxford, UK: Basil Blackwell.

Subrahmanya, M. (2009). Case study: Nature and strategy of product innovations in SMEs: A case study-based comparative perspective of Japan and India. *Innovation: Management. Policy & Practice*, *11*(1), 104–113. doi:10.5172/impp.453.11.1.104

Subramaniam, M., & Hewett, K. (2004). Balancing standardization and adaptation for product performance in international markets: testing the influence of headquarters-subsidiary contact and cooperation. *Management International Review*, *44*, 171-194.

Subramaniam, M., & Youndt, M. A. (2005). The Influence of Intellectual Capital on The Type of Innovation Capilities. *Academy of Management Journal*, *48*(3), 450–463. doi:10.5465/AMJ.2005.17407911

Suehiro, A., & Wailerdsak, N. (2004). Family business in Thailand: Its management, governance, and future challenges. *ASEAN Economic Bulletin*, *21*(1), 81–93. doi:10.1355/AE21-1E

Sullivan, D. (1994). Measuring the Degree of Internationalization of a Firm. *Journal of International Business Studies*, *25*(2), 325–342. doi:10.1057/palgrave.jibs.8490203

Suren, L. (2014). *International Business Diplomacy: A strategy for increasing MNC's performance? A systematic review on the basis of five European MNC's*. Retrieved from http://purl.utwente.nl/essays/65296

Suutari, V., Raharjo, K., & Riikkila, T. (2002). The challenge of cross-cultural leadership interaction: Finnish expatriates in Indonesia. *Career Development International*, *7*(6/7), 415–429. doi:10.1108/13620430210449948

Swann, G. P. (2010), *International Standards and Trade: A Review of the Empirical Literature*. OECD Trade Policy Working Papers, No. 97. OECD Publishing. doi: 10.1787/5kmdbg9xktwg-en

Sweeney, E. P. & Hardaker, G. (1994). The importance of organizational and national culture. *European Business Review, 94*(5),3.

Sweeney, P. D., & McFarlin, D. B. (2002). *Organizational Behavior: Solutions for Management*. New York, NY: McGraw-Hill.

Swierczek, F. W., & Onishi, J. (2003). Culture and conflict: Japanese managers and Thai subordinates. *Personnel Review*, *32*(1/2), 187–210. doi:10.1108/00483480310460216

Szeto, R., Wright, P. C., & Cheng, E. (2006). Business networking in the Chinese context. *Management Research News*, *29*(7), 425–438. doi:10.1108/01409170610690880

Szykman, S. (1995). *Diplomacy: An Historical Perspective*. Retrieved from http://www.diplom.org/Zine/S1995R/Szykman/History.html

Szymanski, D. M., Bharadwaj, S. G., & Varadarajan, P. R. (1993). Standardization versus adaptation of international marketing strategy: An empirical investigation. *Journal of Marketing*, *57*(October), 1–17.

Taal, M. (2014). *South African Multinationals in Africa – Trends in 2013/2014*. A Report by Labour Research Service. Available at, http://www.fes-southafrica.org/media/MNC%20Trend%20Report%20%20FES%20draft%202014.pdf

Taal, M. (2014). *South African Multinationals in Africa – Trends in 2013/2014*. Academic Press.

Tabellini, G. (2008). Presidential address institutions and culture. *Journal of the European Economic Association*, *6*(2-3), 55–294.

Tang, F. C., Gao, X. D., & Li, Q. (2008). Knowledge acquisition and learning: strategies in globalization of China's enterprises. In I. Alon & J. R. McIntyre (Eds.), *Globalization of Chinese Enterprises* (pp. 31–43). Basingstoke, UK: Palgrave Macmillan.

Tang, T. (2002). Powerhouse's management strategies for excellent business achievement. *Integrated Management Systems*, *13*(6), 366–374. doi:10.1108/09576060210436623

Tan, J. (2009). Multinational Corporations and Social Responsibility in Emerging Markets: Opportunities and Challenges for Research and Practice. *Journal of Business Ethics*, *1*(32), 55–75.

Taylor, R. B., Gottfredson, S. D., & Brower, S. (1984). Block crime and fear: Defensible space, local social ties, and territorial functioning. *Journal of Research in Crime and Delinquency*, *21*(4), 303–331. doi:10.1177/0022427884021004003

Taylor, S. (2007). Creating social capital in MNCs: The international human resource management challenge. *Human Resource Management Journal*, *17*(4), 336–354. doi:10.1111/j.1748-8583.2007.00049.x

Teece, D. (1977). Technology transfer by multinational firms: The resource cost of transferring technological know-how. *The Economic Journal*, *87*(346), 242–262. doi:10.2307/2232084

Teece, D. J. (1980). Economies of scope and the scope of the enterprise. *Journal of Economic Behavior & Organization*, *1*(3), 223–247. doi:10.1016/0167-2681(80)90002-5

Telekom. (2015, July) Home Page. *Telekom Austria Group*. Retrieved from: http://www.telekomaustria.com

Tenzer, H., Pudelko, M., & Harzing, A. W. (2014). The impact of language barriers on trust formation in multinational teams. *Journal of International Business Studies*, *45*(5), 508–535. doi:10.1057/jibs.2013.64

Terjesen, S., Tenzer, H., Hinger, J., & Harzing, A. W. (2014). *Language in international business: a review and agenda for future research*. Paper presented at the 40th Annual Conference of the European International Business Academy (EIBA), Uppsala, Sweden.

Thanasuta, K., Patoomsuwan, T., Chaimahawong, V., & Chiaravutthi, Y. (2009). Brand and country of origin valuations of automobiles. *Asia Pacific Journal of Marketing and Logistics*, *21*(3), 355–375. doi:10.1108/13555850910973847

Thassanabanjong, K., Miller, P., & Marchant, T. (2009). Training in Thai SMEs. *Journal of Small Business and Enterprise Development*, *16*(4), 678–693. doi:10.1108/14626000911000992

The Economist. (2010). *Face Value: Li Shufu. China's lucky man bags Volvo. Has the founder of Geely, an upstart carmaker, got what it takes to revive Volvo?*. Retrieved from http://www.economist.com/node/16750095

The Economist. (2011, Dec 3). *The hopeful continent: Africa rising*. Accessed June 8, 2013: http://www.economist.com/node/21541015

The Economist. (2013). *Multinationals in emerging markets, Must try harder. The ambitions of Western firms in emerging markets far exceed their efforts*. Retrieved from http://www.economist.com/news/business/21586320-ambitions-western-firms-emerging-markets-far-exceed-their-efforts-must-try-harder

The Economist. (2013, July 27). Flogging a dead cow. *The Economist*. Retrieved from http://www.economist.com/news/americas/21582304-recently-nationalised-oil-company-agrees-big-foreign-investment-flogging-dead-cow

The Guardian. (2015). *Child labour on Nestlé farms: Chocolate giant's problems continue*. Retrieved from http://www.theguardian.com/global-development-professionals-network/2015/sep/02/child-labour-on-nestle-farms-chocolate-giants-problems-continue

The Millennium Project. (2010). *Some Elements of the Next Global Economic System: How Might These New Elements Affect the Human Condition over the Next 20 Years?*. Retrieved from http://www.millennium-project.org/millennium/RTD-Econ.html

The United States Department of Justice. (2015). *Foreign Corrupt Practices Act*. Retrieved from http://www.justice.gov/criminal/fraud/fcpa/

The World Factbook. (2013). Washington, DC: Central Intelligence Agency. Retrieved from https://www.cia.gov/library/publications/the-world-factbook/index.html

Theingi, P. S., & Phungphol, Y. (2008). Social capital in Southeast Asian business relationships. *Industrial Marketing Management*, *37*(5), 523–530. doi:10.1016/j.indmarman.2007.09.014

Thibodeau, P. (2012, Nov 29). In a symbolic shift, IBM's India workforce likely exceeds U.S. *Computerworld*. Accessed June 4, 2015: http://www.computerworld.com/article/2493565/it-careers/in-a-symbolic-shift--ibm-s-india-workforce-likely-exceeds-u-s-.html

Tietze, S., Cohen, L., & Musson, G. (2003). *Understanding Organizations through Language*. London: Sage.

Tietze, S., & Dick, P. (2013). The victorious English language: Hegemonic practices in the management academy. *Journal of Management Inquiry*, *22*(1), 122–134. doi:10.1177/1056492612444316

Titiev, M. (1958). *Introduction to Cultural Anthropology*. New York: Henry Holt and Co.

Torrisi, C. R., & Uslu, G. (2010). Transitioning economics: A calculus of competitiveness. *Journal of Applied Business and Economics*, *11*(3), 39–54.

Toyota. (2014). *2014 annual report: Toyota Motor Company*. Retrieved from http://www.toyota-global.com/investors/ir_library/annual/pdf/2014/ar14_e.pdf

Tran, Q., & Tian, Y. (2013). Organizational Structure: Influencing Factors and Impact on a Firm. *American Journal of Industrial and Business Management*, *3*(02), 229–236. doi:10.4236/ajibm.2013.32028

Transparency International. (2015). *Corruption Perceptions Index*. Accessed Jun 8, 2015: http://www.transparency.org/research/cpi

Tsai-Ju, L. (2015). Clusters, technological knowledge spillovers, and performance: The moderating roles of local ownership ties and a local market orientation. *Management Decision*, *53*(2), 469–490. doi:10.1108/MD-09-2014-0560

Tsang, E. (2001). Internationalizing the family firm: A case study of a Chinese family business. *Journal of Small Business Management*, *39*(2), 88–94. doi:10.1111/0447-2778.00008

Twigg, J. L., & Schecter, K. (2003). Social capital and social cohesion in post-soviet Russia. Armong: ME Sharpe, United States.

Ty, M., Walsh, J., & Anurit, P. (2010). An empirical assessment of the relationship between national culture and learning capability in organizations in Cambodia. *International Business Research*, *3*(4), 81–90. doi:10.5539/ibr.v3n4p81

Uchida, Y., & Cook, P. (2005). The transformation of competitive advantage in East Asia: An analysis of technological and trade specialization. *World Development*, *33*(5), 701–728. doi:10.1016/j.worlddev.2005.01.005

Ugwu, M. (2011). *Fundamentals of International Politics*. Onitsha: BTC.

UNCTAD. (2005). *World Investment Report Transnational Corporations and the Internationalization of R&D*. New York: United Nations.

UNCTAD. (2007). *World Investment Report Transnational Corporations, Extractive Industries and Development*. New York: United Nations.

UNCTAD. (2014). *World investment report 2014*. New York: United Nations.

UNCTAD. (2015). *OECD patent statistics manual*, available at: http://browse.oecdbookshop.org/oecd/pdfs/free/9209021E.PDF

UNCTAD. (2015, May 18). *Global investment trends monitor no. 19*. Accessed June 5, 2015: http://unctad.org/en/pages/publications/Global-Investment-Trends-Monitor-%28Series%29.aspx

United Nations Global Compact. (2010). Communication on Progress. Retrieved from https://www.unglobalcompact.org/system/commitment_letters/5943/original/UN_Global_Compact_2010.pdf?1281012742

United Nations Global Compact. (2015a). *BASF SE*. Retrieved from https://www.unglobalcompact.org/what-is-gc/participants/1194-BASF-SE

United Nations Global Compact. (2015b). *Our Participants*. Retrieved from https://www.unglobalcompact.org/what-is-gc/participants/search?utf8=%E2%9C%93&search[keywords]=&search[initiatives][]=19&search[per_page]=50&search[sort_field]=sector&search[sort_direction]=asc

United Nations Global Compact. (2015c). Retrieved from https://www.unglobalcompact.org/

United Nations Global Compact. (2015d). *UN Global Compact Expels 657 Companies in 2014*. Retrieved from https://www.unglobalcompact.org/news/1621-01-14-2015

United Nations Global Compact. (2015e). *The Universal Declaration of Human Rights*. Retrieved from http://www.un.org/en/documents/udhr/

United Nations Office of Drugs and Crime. (2004). *United Nations Convention Against Corruption*. Retrieved from https://www.unodc.org/documents/treaties/UNCAC/Publications/Convention/08-50026_E.pdf

United Nations. (2015). *Report of the United Nations Conference on Environment and Development*. Retrieved from http://www.un.org/documents/ga/conf151/aconf15126-1annex1.htm

Universe. (2015, July) *Telefonos de Mexico S.A. de C.V.* Retrieved from: http://www.fundinguniverse.com/company-histories/telefonos-de-mexico-s-a-de-c-v-history/

Uslaner, E.M. (2004). Trust and corruption. *The New Institutional Economics of Corruption*, 76.

Uzzi, B. (1997). Social structure and competition in inter-firm networks: The paradox of embeddedness. *Administrative Science Quarterly*, *42*(1), 35–67. doi:10.2307/2393808

Vahlne, J.-E., Ivarsson, I., & Johanson, J. (2011). The tortuous road to globalization of Volvo's heavy truck business - Extending the scope of the Uppsala model. *International Business Review*, *20*(1), 1–14. doi:10.1016/j.ibusrev.2010.05.003

Vahlne, J., & Ivarsson, I. (2014). The globalization of swedish MNEs: Empirical evidence and theoretical explanations. *Journal of International Business Studies*, *45*(3), 227–247. doi:10.1057/jibs.2013.60

Vahlne, J., & Johanson, J. (2013). The Uppsala Model on evolution of the multinational business enterprise: From internalization to coordination of networks. *International Marketing Review*, *30*(3), 189–210. doi:10.1108/02651331311321963

Vakratsas, D., & Ambler, T. (1999). Advertising effects. *Journal of Marketing*, *63*(January), 26–43. doi:10.2307/1251999

Valkila, J., & Nygren, A. (2010). Impacts of Fair Trade certification on coffee farmers, cooperatives, and laborers in Nicaragua. *Agriculture and Human Values*, *27*(3), 321–333. doi:10.1007/s10460-009-9208-7

Van de Kuil, A. (2008). *Strategies of multinational corporations in the emerging markets China and India*. GRIN Publishing GmbH. Retrieved from http://www.grin.com/en/e-book/117743/strategies-of-multinational-corporations-in-the-emerging-markets-china/

Van de Ven, A. H. (2004). The context-specific nature of competence and corporate development. *Asia Pacific Journal of Management*, *21*(1/2), 123–147. doi:10.1023/B:APJM.0000024080.78798.59

Van Dijk, T. A. 2008. *Discourse and Power.* Houndsmills, UK: Palgrave.

Van Dijk, T. A. (1998). *Ideology: A Multidisciplinary Approach.* London: Sage.

van Dijk, T. A. (2001). Discourse, ideology and context. *Folia Linguistica*, *35*(1-2), 11–40. doi:10.1515/flin.2001.35.1-2.11

Van Heel, B., Lukic, V., & Leeuwis, E. (2014, September). *Cross-Border E-Commerce Makes the World Flatter.* Retrieved from https://www.bcgperspectives.com/content/articles/transportation_travel_tourism_retail_cross_border_ecommerce_makes_world_flatter/

van Leeuwen, T. (1993). Genre and field in critical discourse analysis: A synopsis. *Discourse & Society*, *4*(2), 193–223. doi:10.1177/0957926593004002004

Vatikiotis, M. (2004). Optimism in the face of history. *Far Eastern Economic Review*, *167*(34), 26–29.

Vaughn, R. (1980). How advertising works. *Journal of Advertising Research*, *30*(1), 57–66.

Veliyath, R. & Brouthers, L. (2010). How Emerging Market Firms Compete in Global Markets. *Journal of Emerging Knowledge on Emerging Markets*, *2*(3).

Vernon, R. (1966). International investment and international trade in the product cycle. *The Quarterly Journal of Economics*, *80*(2), 190–207. doi:10.2307/1880689

Vieira, L. M., & Traill, W. B. (2007). The role of food standards in international trade: Evidence from Brazilian beef exports to the EU market. *Journal of International Development*, *19*(6), 755–764. doi:10.1002/jid.1405

Waldmeir, P., & Reed, J. (2010). Man in the news: Li Shufu. *Financial Times*. Retrieved from http://on.ft.com/1T6PsbX

Wal-Mart. (2015). *Global Statement of Ethics*. Retrieved from https://walmartethics.com/uploadedFiles/Content/U.S.%20-%20English.pdf

Walmart. (n.d.). *Walmart Corporate: Our Story*. Retrieved from http://corporate.walmart.com/our-story/

Walpole, R., Myers, R., Myers, S., & Ye, K. (2007). *Probabilidad y Estadística para ingeniería y ciencias*. Pearson Educación.

Walsh, K. (2004). Interpreting the impact of culture on structure: The role of change processes. *The Journal of Applied Behavioral Science*, *40*(3), 302–322. doi:10.1177/0021886304266845

Walton, R. E. (1982). Social Choice in the Development of Advanced Information Technology. *Technology in Society.*, *4*(1), 41–49. doi:10.1016/0160-791X(82)90013-6

Wang, G. C., Zhang, Y., Lamond, D., & Ke, J. (2014). Moving forward. *Journal of Chinese Human Resource Management*, *5*(1), 2–13. doi:10.1108/JCHRM-02-2014-0011

Wang, J., & Blomström, M. (1992). Foreign investment and technology transfer: A simple model. *European Economic Review*, *36*(1), 137–155. doi:10.1016/0014-2921(92)90021-N

Waterman, R. H. Jr, Peters, T. J., & Phillips, J. R. (1980, June). Structure is not organization. *Business Horizons*, *23*(3), 14–26. doi:10.1016/0007-6813(80)90027-0

Watson, R. (1997). Ethnomethodology and textual analysis. In D. Silverman (Ed.), *Qualitative Research: Theory, Method and Practice*. London: Sage.

Wedeman, A. (2004). The intensification of corruption in China. *The China Quarterly*, *180*, 895–921. doi:10.1017/S0305741004000670

Weihrich, H. (1999). Analyzing the competitive advantages and disadvantages of Germany with the tows matrix—an alternative to porter's model. *European Business Review*, *99*(1), 9–22. doi:10.1108/09555349910251822

Welch, D. E., & Welch, L. S. (2008). The importance of language in international knowledge transfer. *Management International Review*, *48*(3), 339–360. doi:10.1007/s11575-008-0019-7

Welch, D. E., Welch, L. S., & Piekkari, R. (2005). Speaking in tongues: The importance of language in international management processes. *International Studies of Management & Organization*, *35*(1), 10–27.

Welch, L., & Luostarinen, R. (1988). Internationalization: Evolution of a Concept. *Journal of General Management*, *14*(2), 34–55.

Wells, L. (1983). *Third World Multinationals*. The MIT Press.

Wells, L. (2009). *Third World Multinationals: A look back*. Cambridge University Press.

Welter, F., & Smallbone, D. (2003). Entrepreneurship and enterprise strategies in transition economies: An institutional perspective. In D. Kirby & A. Watson (Eds.), *Small Firms and Economic Development in Developed and Transition Economies*. Burlington, VA: Ashgate Publishing.

Wernerfelt, B. (1984). A resource-based view of the firm. *Strategic Management Journal*, *5*(2), 171–180. doi:10.1002/smj.4250050207

Wheelen, T. L., & Hunger, D. J. (2002). *Strategic Management & Business Policy*. Pearson Education Inc.

Whisler, T. L. (1970b). *Information Technology and Organizational Change*. Wadsworth.

Wight, J. (1976). Speech acts: Thought acts. *Educational Review*, *28*(3), 168–179. doi:10.1080/0013191760280302

Wikipedia Contributors. (2015). *Spillover effect*. Retrieved from Wikipedia: https://en.wikipedia.org/w/index.php?title=Spillover_effect&oldid=691313422

Wilber, K. (2006). *Integral Spirituality: A startling new role for religion in the modern and postmodern world*. Boston: Integral Books.

Williams, J., & Sickles, R. C. (2002). An analysis of the crime as work model: Evidence from the 1958 Philadelphia birth cohort study. *The Journal of Human Resources*, *37*(3), 479–509. doi:10.2307/3069679

Williamson, C. R. (2009). Informal institutions rule: Institutional arrangements and economic performance. *Public Choice*, *139*(3/4), 371–387. doi:10.1007/s11127-009-9399-x

Williamson, O. (2000). The new institutional economics: Taking stock, looking ahead. *Journal of Economic Literature*, *38*(3), 595–613. doi:10.1257/jel.38.3.595

Winston, M. (2011). Multinational Corporations. In D. K. Chatterjee (Ed.), Encyclopedia of Global Justice (pp. 730-733). Springer Netherlands. doi:10.1007/978-1-4020-9160-5_544

Wiseman, J. (1990). Principles of political economy: An outline proposal, illustrated by application to fiscal federalism. *Constitutional Political Economy*, *1*(1), 101–124. doi:10.1007/BF02393035

Wodak, R. (1997). *Gender and Discourse*. London: Sage.

Wodak, R., de Cillia, R., Reisigl, M., & Liebhart, K. (1999). *The Discursive Construction of National Identity*. Edinburgh, UK: Edinburgh University Press.

Wolfe, S. E. (2010). A social capital assessment of Canadian community's water management strategy. *Environmental Practice*, *12*(3), 214–226. doi:10.1017/S1466046610000220

Wolters, T. (2012). *Business diplomacy in multinational corporations: An exploratory qualitative study* (Master's thesis, University of Twente, Enschede, Netherlands). Retrieved from http://purl.utwente.nl/essays/62485

Wooffitt, R. (2001). Researching psychic practitioners: conversation analysis. In M. Wetherell, S. Taylor, & S. Yates (Eds.), *Discourse as Data: A Guide for analysis*. London: Sage Publications.

World Economic Forum. (2015). *The Global Competitiveness Report 2014-2015*. Retrieved from http://www.weforum.org/reports/global-competitiveness-report-2014-2015

Wright, A. L., & Zammuto, R. F. (2013). Creating opportunities for institutional entrepreneurship. *Journal of Business Venturing*, *28*(1), 51–68. doi:10.1016/j.jbusvent.2011.11.005

Wu, C., Hu, M., & Mathews, J. A. (2014). Internal factors drive Chinese patent surge. *Nature, 509*(7501), 427.

Wu, C., Lawler, J. J., & Yi, X. (2008). Overt employment discrimination in MNC affiliates: Home-country cultural and institutional effects. *Journal of International Business Studies*, *39*(5), 772–792. doi:10.1057/palgrave.jibs.8400376

Wu, W. P., & Choi, W. L. (2004). Transaction cost, social capital and firms' synergy creation in Chinese business networks. *Asia Pacific Journal of Management*, *21*(3), 325–344. doi:10.1023/B:APJM.0000036466.90433.92

Wu, Y. (2013). Business English as a lingua franca (BELF). *International Education Studies*, *6*(10), 130–138. doi:10.5539/ies.v6n10p130

Xia, Z., & Zhang, X. (2011). Strategic analysis of synergistic effect on M&A of Volvo Car Corporation by Geely automobile. *IBusiness*, *3*(1), 5–15. doi:10.4236/ib.2011.31002

Yang, Q., Mudambi, R., & Meyer, K. E. (2008). Conventional and reverse knowledge flows in multinational corporations. *Journal of Management*, *34*(5), 882–902. doi:10.1177/0149206308321546

Yan, J., & Sorenson, R. L. (2004). The Influence of Confucian ideology on conflict in Chinese family business. *International Journal of Cross Cultural Management*, *4*(1), 5–17. doi:10.1177/1470595804041521

Yeung, H. W. C. (1994). Third world multinationals revisited: A research critique and future agenda. *Third World Quarterly*, *15*(2), 297–317. doi:10.1080/01436599408420381

Yip, G. S. (1989). Global Strategy a World of Nations? *Sloan Management Review*, *31*(1), 29–41.

Yip, G. S. (1991a). A Performance Comparison of Continental and National Businesses in Europe. *International Marketing Review*, *8*(2), 31. doi:10.1108/02651339110137774

Yip, G. S. (1991b). Strategies in Global Industries: How U.S. Businesses Compete. *Journal of International Business Studies*, *22*(4), 749–753. doi:10.1057/jibs.1991.56

Yip, G. S. (1994). Industry Drivers of Global Strategy and Organization. *International Executive*, *36*(5), 529–556. doi:10.1002/tie.5060360503

Yip, G. S. (1996). Global Strategy as a Factor in Japanese Success. *International Executive*, *38*(1), 145–167. doi:10.1002/tie.5060380111

Yip, G. S. et al.. (1988). How to Take Your Company to the Global Market. *The Columbia Journal of World Business*, *23*(4), 37–48.

Yip, G. S., Biscarri, J. G., & Monti, J. A. (2000). The Role of the Internationalization Process in the Performance of Newly Internationalizing Firms. *Journal of International Marketing*, *8*(3), 10–35. doi:10.1509/jimk.8.3.10.19635

Yip, G. S., Joansson, J. K., & Johan, R. (1997). Effects of Nationality on Global Strategy.[MIR]. *Management International Review*, *37*(4), 365–385.

Yip, G. S., & Madsen, T. L. (1996). Global account management: The new frontier in relationship marketing. *International Marketing Review*, *13*(3), 24–42. doi:10.1108/02651339610122982

Young, C. S. (2005). Top management teams' social capital in Taiwan: The impact on firm value in an emerging economy. *Journal of Intellectual Capital*, *6*(2), 177–190. doi:10.1108/14691930510592780

Young, E. (1900). *The Kingdom of the Yellow Robe* (2nd ed.). Westminster, UK: Archibald Constable & Co.

Yu, T. (2001). The Chinese family business as a strategic system: An evolutionary perspective. *International Journal of Entrepreneurial Behaviour and Research*, *7*(1), 22–40. doi:10.1108/13552550110385736

Zak, P. J., & Knack, S. (2001). Trust and growth. *The Economic Journal*, *111*(470), 295–321. doi:10.1111/1468-0297.00609

Zhang, F. (2008). *Corporate Social Responsibility in Emerging Markets: The Role of Multinational Corporations*. An Initial Paper for the Launch of the Foreign Policy Centre Project on "Corporate Responsibility in Emerging Markets" in association with Coca-Cola Great Britain.

Zhang, Y. (2010). The impact of free trade agreements on business activity: A survey of firms in the People's Republic of China. ADBI Working paper 251. Tokyo: Asian Development Bank Institution. Available at http:www.adbi.org/working-paper/2010/10/12/4088.impact.fta.business.activity.prc/

Zhang, M., Knight, G., & Tansuhaj, P. (2014). International performance antecedents in emerging market SMEs: Evidence from China. *Journal of Global Marketing*, *27*(3), 161–177. doi:10.1080/08911762.2013.875242

Zhang, Q., & Fung, H.-G. (2006). China's social capital and financial performance of private enterprises. *Journal of Small Business and Enterprise Development*, *13*(2), 198–207. doi:10.1108/14626000610665908

Zheng, C. (2013). Theoretical contexts of managing people in emerging Chinese multinational enterprises. *Journal of Chinese Human Resources Management*, *4*(1), 58–76. doi:10.1108/JCHRM-10-2012-0023

Zhou, M., & Patrick, B. (2012). *Innovation Management Se*. Retrieved from http://www.innovationmanagement.se/2012/05/17/7-key-steps-to-successful-open-innovation-in-china/

Ziadi, J., & Kuofie, M. (2006). Impact of ICT on organizations in Tunisia. *The Electronic Journal on Information Systems in Developing Countries*, *28*(4), 1–8.

About the Contributors

Mohammad Ayub Khan is Full-Professor and Director of the Marketing and International Business Department and has remained Director of the International Business Department, Director of the University Honors Program; National Coordinator of International Business Academy and Divisional Coordinator of Internationalization of the Business Faculty, at Tecnológico de Monterrey, campus Monterrey, México. His research interests are cross cultural management, international negotiation and business management education. He has co-authored books titled "The Basics of International Negotiation" and "Diverse Contemporary Issues facing the Business Management Education in Developing Countries".

* * *

Sara Aguilar-Barrientos holds a Master's in Science degree in Management from Universidad EAFIT and is a current doctoral student at Centrum Business School. She is the Academic Coordinator of the Undergraduate program in International Business and assistant professor at the International Business Department in Universidad EAFIT (Medellin, Colombia) since 2012. She is a member of the International Studies Research Group and her research interests include intercultural studies, negotiation and firm internationalization. She has served as a lecturer for the undergraduate, MBA and Master in Human Development programs.

Muritala Awodun is the Dean of the School of Business and Governance (SBG), Kwara State University, Malete. He was the (founding) Director of KWASU Centre for Entrepreneurship, a position he held from inception of the Centre in 2009 till June 2014. He holds a Bachelor of Science (Honours) Degree in Economics, Master of Science Degree in Economics, and Doctor of Philosophy (Ph. D) in International Business. Dr Awodun is an alumnus of the prestigious Harvard Business School Executive Education Program (Leading with Impact) June – July, 2014, and the Massachusetts Institute of Technology (MIT) Global Start-Up Workshop (GSW) African Scholar in Entrepreneurship Education for 2013. He has published seven books, edited some other books and contributed chapters to several others. He also has published several business/industry case studies and referred research papers in various peer reviewed journals. He is on the Editorial Board of Lagos Organization Review, Public Sector Review, Management Discoveries, Community Entrepreneurship Review, Unillorin Journal of Management, and Financial Standard Newspaper. Dr Awodun also reviews for the Academy of International Business. Awodun is a member of the on-going European Commission sponsored 'Transnational Diaspora Entrepreneurship Research' made up of 27 universities and research institutions spread over Europe, United States, Latin America, Asia, Australia and Africa. He is also a member of the University Fellows

International Research Consortium conducting 'Survey on Communication in the Workplace' in 29 countries. He was a member of the Ford Foundation/Nigerian Copyright Commission Research Team that conducted the Survey of Copyright Piracy in Nigeria between 2005 and 2007 (published in 2008). Dr Awodun also served as the National Researcher for the World Intellectual Property Organization (WIPO) in the conduct of research on the 'Economic Impact of Copyright-Based Industries in Nigeria' in 2008. He is a Fellow of the Institute of Entrepreneurs, Nigeria, and the Institute of Direct Marketing of Nigeria. Awodun is also a Member of the Chartered Institute of Administration (Nigeria), Nigerian Institute of Management (Chartered), Academy of Management and Academy of International Business. Dr Awodun received the ENACTUS Nigeria Leadership Award in March 2014 for his excellent leadership of Kwara State University (KWASU) Centre for Entrepreneurship. Under his directorship, KWASU Centre for Entrepreneurship won the Country Prize of Saville Foundation Pan-African Entrepreneurship Education Award for 2013 organized by 'Teach-A-Man-To-Fish' a United Kingdom non-profit organization in April 2014. Dr. Awodun is also the winner of the 2014 African Entrepreneurship Education Award of Excellence received in Ghana in November 2014 from African Development Magazine, and the African Leader of Integrity Merit Award in April 2015 received at Lome, Togo. He is an Associate Professor of International Business and Entrepreneurship (since 2012) with teaching and research interests in Business Economics, Business Strategy, Enterprise Creation, Entrepreneurship Education and International Business.

Neeta Baporikar is currently Director/Professor (Business Management) at Harold Pupkewitz Graduate School of Business (HP-GSB), Namibia. Prior to this she was Head-Scientific Research, with Ministry of Higher Education CAS-Salalah, Sultanate of Oman, Professor (Strategic Management and Entrepreneurship) at IIIT Pune and BITS India. With more than a decade of experience in industry, consultancy and training, she made a lateral switch to research and academics in 1995. Dr. Baporikar holds D.Sc. (Management Studies) USA, PhD in Management, University of Pune INDIA with MBA (Distinction) and Law (Hons.) degrees. Apart from this, she is also an External Reviewer, Oman Academic Accreditation Authority, Accredited Management Teacher, Qualified Trainer, Doctoral Guide and Board Member of Academics and Advisory Committee in accredited B-Schools. Reviewer for international journals, she has to her credit 5 conferred doctorates, several refereed research papers, and authored books in the area of Entrepreneurship, Strategy, Management and Higher Education.

Shankar Chelliah currently affiliates with Universiti Sains Malaysia (USM), based in Penang, Malaysia. Prior becoming academician, he has fifteen years of corporate experiences by holding various positions in blue chip companies such as Motorola and Intel. Currently positioned in the section of International Business and teaching subjects such as international new venture, international trade law, and international business management. Apart from supervising students at postgraduate level, he is actively involved in consultancy services and social responsibility initiatives to key clients from the industry. His current research interests include: (a) internationalization – medical tourism, strategies in international trade, born global firms, SMEs etc, (b) green management as competitive capabilities in organizations and (c) strategic management in education – internationalization of education, holistic approach to education, and understanding the future challenges of education. Dr.Shankar Chelliah has published more than 60 publications in monographs, chapter in books, international peer-reviewed journals and both international and local conference proceedings in the above areas. He also actively writes in the media mass on the areas relates to his research topics to outreach the community.

Cheryl Marie Cordeiro is a Research Fellow at the Centre for International Business Studies (CIBS), School of Business, Economics and Law at the University of Gothenburg, Sweden. Her research interests can be found at the intersections of culture, language, management & organisation, in the broader field of International Business. She has a PhD in general linguistics, focusing on Swedish management in Singapore.

Francisco Alfonso Espinoza Francisco A. Espinoza is professor of the Marketing and International Business Department at ITESM, Monterrey Campus. He is co-author (L. Hartmann, J. Des Jardins) of the book Business Ethics: Decision Making for Personal Integrity & Social Responsibility (Spanish). He created a business ethics course at under-graduated level, as well as its online version. On undergraduate level he has taught Business Ethics and International Services Development; on graduate level, he has taught Business Ethics at Universidad Autónoma de Tamaulipas. He has lectured conferences in the United States, South America, and Mexico. Dr. Espinoza received a degree of Industrial and Systems Engineering from ITESM, Monterrey Campus; a MBA and a Service Administration Certificate from EGADE Business School, México. Furthermore, he received a Master of Arts in Philosophy, a Business Ethics Certificate, and a PHD from Loyola University Chicago.

Ana Maria Gomez-Trujillo is an international business magister at Universidad EAFIT, Colombia, with experience in research about internationalization of companies and interested in culture studies.

Kelly J. Gonzalez-Tapia is an international negotiator affiliated with the Universidad EAFIT, Colombia.

Andreas M. Hartmann has been an associate professor at Tecnológico de Monterrey in Monterrey, Mexico since 2006, where he teaches in the fields of strategic management, cross-cultural management, and international negotiation. His research focuses on multinational companies, knowledge-based firms, and cross-cultural aspects of management. A native German, he is fluent in English, Spanish, and French. Prior to his current position, he worked as a language teacher and as a free-lance translator and conference interpreter in Europe and Mexico. Andreas M. Hartmann holds a PhD in International Business and an MBA from the Tecnológico de Monterrey as well as a double Master's degree in Translation and Conference Interpreting from the University of Heidelberg.

Scott Hipsher has worked in academia, private sector firms, NGOs, US military and as a self-employed horse racing trainer. He is currently working at Narasuan University. Dr. Hipsher has worked in Canada, Vietnam, Japan, Thailand, China and his native country of the USA. He is the author of the books: Private Sector's Role in Poverty Reduction in Asia, Business Practices in Southeast Asia: An Interdisciplinary Analysis of Theravada Buddhist Countries, and Expatriates in Asia: Breaking Free from the Colonial Paradigm, and The Nature of Asian Firms: An Evolutionary Perspective. In addition, Dr. Hipsher is the author of numerous academic journal articles, book chapters, magazine and newspaper articles and academic conference papers.

Ming Huoy Lee graduated from Universiti Sains Malaysia (USM) in 2014. Majoring in International Business and minoring in Japanese Language. Experience working in Human Resource department, sales and marketing department and supply chain department.

Edet E. Okon, born 40 years ago hails from IBIADIM OKU USUK royal house in EKI CENTRAL, EKI, EFIK EBURUTU dynasty, Cross River State of Nigeria. The author is an educationist, specializing in Vocational Business Education (Accounting). Edet Okon obtained the Nigeria Certificate in Education (NCE) in Business Education (Double Major) in 1997; Bachelor of Science Degree in Business Education (B.Sc.Ed.) in 2004; Master of Science Degree in Business Education (M.Sc.Ed.) in 2011; and is expected to bag the Degree of Doctor of Philosophy (Ph.D) in Business Education, having successfully defended his Thesis, entitled, "Influence of Returns on Investment (ROI) in Business Education on Undergraduates Skill Development" on December 16, 2015.As an educationist of high professional standing, the author is poised at impacting positively in the development of Business Education at global level through the development of Business Education Models (BEM) with consideration to emerging market's global economy; quality assurance and international bench mark minimum academic standards (IBMAS) and best practices. The quest for the development of Business Education at the global and university level motivated the author to join the Nigeria's Technical Aid Corps (TAC) Scheme in 2013/2014 as a Lecturer, following his excellent performance at interviews twice - in Abeokuta (February 2013) and Abuja (December 2013). He has attended the orientation and induction exercise twice in Abuja (July 2013) and Akure (February 2014). However, he is yet to be posted to any of Africa, Caribbean and Pacific (ACP) country in line with the scheme's objectives. Edet Okon has published over 15 scholarly Articles in reputable international journals. He has co-authored a book, "Diverse Contemporary Issues facing Business Management Education," with IGI Global Publishers, USA. This book, "Challenges facing MNEs Operating in Emerging Markets" is the author's second (co-authored) book. The author enjoys a blissful family life.

Ekaterina Panarina is an Associate Professor in Business Administration and Marketing at Perm National Research Polytechnic University. She teaches courses in Business Management and Marketing with a focus on innovation and business competitiveness. Dr. Panarina received her PhD in Management from Chelyabinsk State University in 2005 and her MA in Education from the University of Missouri - St. Louis in 2007. From 2009 until 2013, Dr. Panarina taught Marketing and Entrepreneurship courses at the Moscow International Higher School of Business as an Associate Professor. She has published extensively on the subjects of Business Management, Marketing and implementing Growth Strategies. Dr. Panarina worked with Dr. Andrew Hardin, Associate Professor and Director of the Center for Entrepreneurship at the University of Nevada – Las Vegas, to develop business and innovation program strategies for Russian institutions of higher education.

Jorge Ramirez holds a PhD in Business Administration from the ITESM CCM - University of Arizona and has professional certifications in digital telecommunications and Information Technology Management (ITIL). He is currently Director of the MBA and he is teaching in EGADE Business School CEM. He was IT director and Networks and telecommunications Director at ITESM Campus Toluca. Also he was director of Engineering Department at Radio and Mexican Television. He has extensive experience as a leader in the design and implementation of projects of Technology and several research papers in various national and international conferences. He is a member of the research group in Social Media at ITESM Campus Estado de Mexico and a contributing editor - reviewer of the digital magazine RECAI. He was the Mexican leader in the EU project FORESTA (Information Technology political dialogue) under the framework of the FP7. His areas of interest are Business Intelligence, Management information technologies, Business Analytics and Virtual Worlds.

Cristina Robledo-Ardila holds a Master's degree in International Business from Grenoble Graduate School of Business in France. She has been an assistant professor and a full time faculty member at the International Business Department in Universidad EAFIT (Medellín, Colombia) since January 2010. She is a member of the International Studies Research Group and her research interests include Firm Internationalization Strategies and Processes, as well as Intercultural Communication. She has served as a professor for the undergraduate, MBA and MIB programs.

Donald E. Sexton is Professor of Marketing and Decisions, Risk, and Operations, Columbia University. PhD. and MBA, University of Chicago, economics and statistics; BA, Wesleyan University, mathematics and economics. Professor Sexton has been teaching for more than forty-five years at Columbia, has served as the chair of the International Business Division, and is a recipient of the Business School's Distinguished Teaching Award. Don has taught at several institutions including the University of California-Berkeley, INSEAD, China Europe International Business School, Australian School of Business, Moscow School of Management, Indian School of Business, and at several other institutions around the world. . His numerous articles have appeared in journals such as the Harvard Business Review, Journal of Marketing Research, and Management Science. His best-selling books, Marketing 101 and Branding 101, have been translated into several languages including Chinese, Russian, Turkish, Polish, Vietnamese, and Indonesian. Don's book, Value Above Cost: Driving Superior Financial Performance with CVA®, the Most Important Metric You've Never Used. (Wharton), explains how marketing determines financial performance and is available in Chinese. Don is often quoted in media such as the New York Times, Business Week, Ad Age, WCBS, Beijing's China Economic Daily, and the Xinhua News Agency. He received the 2011 Marketing Trends Award for his work on marketing and branding strategy and is President of the New York American Marketing Association. Don is the founder and president of The Arrow Group, Ltd.® an organization that has provided consulting and training services in the areas of marketing and branding to many leading companies such as GE, Pfizer, IBM, Citibank, Unilever, Volkswagen, MetLife, Sony, Verizon, PepsiCo, and DuPont.

Natalya Smith is a freelance researcher and a visiting scholar at University of Essex (UK). She holds BSc in Economics from Moscow State University (Russia); MSc in International Business and a Ph.D in Management from Aston University (UK). She worked at Aston, Liverpool and Leicester Universities (UK). Her research is in international business (political) economics and innovation with a focus on institutions. She has worked on various economic issues in Russia. She is an author and a co-author of publications in books and academic journals (including Europe-Asia Studies and the Journal of East-West Business) and has presented in AIB and AIB-UKI conferences.

Ekaterina Thomas holds MSc in International Business and PhD in Management from Aston University, UK. Her research interests include international aspects of innovation with a particular focus on Russia's economy. Furthermore, Ekaterina is interested in technological learning and innovation; industrial development and catching-up of developing and emerging markets; evolution of innovation systems; political economy of science and foreign investment in modern Russia.

Camila Uribe-Villa is last semester Economics undergraduate program student at EAFIT University. She has worked as a research assistant at the Center for Economic and Finance Research.

Francisco Javier Valderrey Villar completed a Bachelor of Business Administration at the University of Houston, Texas, with a major in economics. Later on, he earned a master´s degree in International Management from Thunderbird, Arizona and a Ph.D. in Administration and Marketing from Universitat de Valencia, Spain. His doctoral research focused on strategy in the tourism industry. Francisco Valderrey occupied several positions at multinational enterprises and was a co-founder of a technology company in California. Afterwards, he joined Tecnológico de Monterrey, first as a professor and eventually as a degree program director for international business. Presently he is a full time and research professor at Campus León. He has also been teaching international business courses at universities in China, Italy and Spain. He has co-authored two books, Mercadotecnia: conceptos y estrategias (ISBN: 9789706640352, ISBN. 9706640355), published in 2003 in Spain, and Fundamentos de Mercadotecnia (ISBN: 9786074386639), published in Mexico in 2013. His research focus primarily on marketing in China, as a part of the Cátedra Asia Pacífico, with different publications. Most recently, he started a research group dedicated to the issue of technology and global business and he was also appointed as a member of the Editorial Board of the Chinese Business Review journal (ISSN: 1537-1506). He also represents the city of León, Mexico, as a member of the board of the Sister Cities program.

Jorge Alberto Wise-Lozano is professor of marketing and international business. PhD from EGADE Business School. Worked for ITESM (Monterrey Tech) from 1988 to 2013 in Campus Monterrey, Cuernavaca, Puebla, and Hermosillo. Now works at CETYS Universidad since 2014 in Campus Mexicali, Tijuana and Ensenada in charge of the Center of Excellence for Business Competitiveness (CECE). Regular visiting professor at de IESEG Business School, Lille, France; Universidad Cristobal Colon, Campus Calasanz, Veracruz, Mexico; Université Montpellier 1, Montpelier, France; and Porzheim University, Germany. Also, has lectured at Jacobs University, Bremen in Germany; ITESO, Guadalajara, Mexico; European School of Management, Campus ESCP-EAP, Madrid, Spain; Copenhagen Business School, Denmark; Monterey Institute of International Studies, California, USA; EADA Business School, Barcelona, Spain; UNITEC, Tegucigalpa, Honduras; and Universidad de Monterrey, México. Has professional experience working for Mexican and international firms. Also consulting and training for companies such as FEMSA, Uniblock, CEMEX, Nol-Mex, Nassar Electronics, among others. Had made professional and research presentations. Authored research presented in different forums. Awarded as Best Professor (2010), Best Reviewer by Academy of Management (2005) and by International Business Information Management Association (2007). Regular reviewer for conferences and journals such as Journal of Transnational Business Institution Management; International Journal of Business Competition and Growth; Portuguese Journal of Management Studies; Negocios: Revista Académica del Tecnológico de Monterrey; Eastern Academy of Management, European Marketing Academy; Society for Consumer Psychology; Journal of Business Research, Association for Consumer Research, Academy of International Business, Academy of Management.

Osmar Hazael Zavaleta-Vazquez is currently National Director of Energy Management Programs and full-time professor of the department of Finance and Economics of EGADE Business School, where he teaches Financial Econometrics, Time Series, Valuation of Financial Derivatives, Investment Management, Statistical Methods, among other courses. Osmar Zavaleta holds a Ph.D. in Finance from A.B. Freeman School of Business of Tulane University (2006). Furthermore, he has a Master in Finance from Tulane University (2003), a Master in Applied Statistics from Tecnológico de Monterrey, Monterrey Campus (1997), and a Master in Industrial Engineering, also from Tecnológico de Monterrey, Monterrey

Campus (1993). His BS is in Industrial Physics Engineering at Tecnológico de Monterrey, Monterrey Campus (1991). Dr. Zavaleta was the Dean of the College of Business Administration at Tecnológico de Monterrey, Monterrey Campus (2007-2011). He was Associate Dean of the College of Business Administration (2003-2007) and the Academic Director of the BA in International Commerce (1998-2003), also at Tecnológico de Monterey, Monterrey Campus. Furthermore, from 1994 to the present, he has been professor of the areas of Financial Econometrics, Statistics, Finance, and Management Sciences at Monterrey Campus and at EGADE Business School of Tecnologico de Monterrey.

Index

N

O

P

Q

R

S

T

U

V

Printed in the United States
By Bookmasters